Henry Hart Milman D. D

The History of Christianity

from the Birth of Christ to the Abolition of Paganism in the Roman Empire by

Henry Hart Milman "The history of Christianity" 3

Henry Hart Milman D. D

The History of Christianity
from the Birth of Christ to the Abolition of Paganism in the Roman Empire by Henry Hart Milman "The history of Christianity" 3

ISBN/EAN: 9783741177163

Manufactured in Europe, USA, Canada, Australia, Japa

Cover: Foto ©Andreas Hilbeck / pixelio.de

Manufactured and distributed by brebook publishing software (www.brebook.com)

Henry Hart Milman D. D

The History of Christianity

THE

HISTORY OF CHRISTIANITY,

FROM THE BIRTH OF CHRIST TO THE ABOLITION OF
PAGANISM IN THE ROMAN EMPIRE.

BY HENRY HART MILMAN, D.D.,
DEAN OF ST. PAUL'S

IN THREE VOLUMES.—Vol. III.

A NEW AND REVISED EDITION

LONDON:
JOHN MURRAY, ALBEMARLE STREET.
1867.

The right of Translation is reserved.

LONDON: PRINTED BY WILLIAM CLOWES AND SONS, STAMFORD STREET
AND CHARING CROSS.

CONTENTS OF VOL. III.

BOOK III.—*continued.*

CHAPTER VI.—*continued.*

Julian .. .. Page 1

CHAPTER VII.

Valentinian and Valens 30

CHAPTER VIII.

Theodosius — Abolition of Paganism 50

CHAPTER IX.

Theodosius — Triumph of Trinitarianism — The great Prelates of the East 100

CHAPTER X.

The great Prelates of the West.. 150

CHAPTER XI.

Jerome — The Monastic System 190

BOOK IV.

CHAPTER I.

The Roman Empire under Christianity .. .. Page 238

CHAPTER II.

Public Spectacles 300

CHAPTER III.

Christian Literature 349

CHAPTER IV.

Christianity and the Fine Arts 371

CHAPTER V.

Conclusion 406

Index 427

HISTORY OF CHRISTIANITY.

BOOK III.—*continued.*

CHAPTER VI.—*continued.*

Julian.

INSTEAD of the Christian hierarchy, Julian hastened to environ himself with the most distinguished of the Heathen philosophers. Most of these, indeed, pretended to be a kind of priesthood. Intercessors between the deities and the world of man, they wrought miracles, foresaw future events; they possessed the art of purifying the soul, so that it should be reunited to the Primal Spirit: the Divinity dwelt within them.

The obscurity of the names which Julian thus set up to rival in popular estimation an Athanasius or a Gregory of Nazianzum, is not altogether to be ascribed to the final success of Christianity. The impartial verdict of posterity can scarcely award to these men a higher appellation than that of sophists and rhetoricians. The subtlety and ingenuity of these more imaginative, perhaps, but far less profound, *schoolmen* of Paganism, were wasted on idle reveries, on solemn trifling, and questions which it was alike useless to agitate and impossible to solve. The hand of death was alike upon the religion, the philosophy, the eloquence, of Greece; and the temporary movement which Julian excited was but a feeble quivering, a last impotent struggle, preparatory to total dissolution. Maximus appears, in his own time, to have been the most eminent of his class. The writings of Libanius and of Iamblichus alone survive, to any extent, the general wreck of the later Grecian literature. The genius and the language of Plato were alike wanting in his degenerate disciples. Julian himself is, perhaps, the best, because the plainest and most perspicuous, writer of his time: and the "Cæsars" may rank as no unsuccessful attempt at satiric irony.

Maximus was the most famous of the school. He had been among the early instructors of Julian. The Emperor had scarcely assumed the throne, when he wrote to Maximus in the most urgent and flattering terms: life was not life without him.[a] Maximus obeyed the summons. On his journey through Asia Minor, the cities vied with each other in doing honour to the champion of Paganism. When the Emperor heard of his arrival in Constantinople, though engaged in an important public ceremonial, he broke it off at once and hastened to welcome his philosophic guest. The roads to the metropolis were crowded with sophists, hurrying to bask in the sunshine of imperial favour.[b] The privilege of travelling at the public cost by the posting establishment of the empire, so much abused by Constantius in favour of the bishops, was now conceded to some of the philosophers. Chry-

[a] Epist. xv. The nameless person to whom the first epistle is addressed is declared superior to Pythagoras or Plato. Epist. l. p. 878.
[b] The severe and grave Priscus despised the youths who embraced philosophy as a fashion. Κορυβαντιώντας δεῖ σοφίᾳ μειρακίων, Vit. Prisc. apud Eunap., Ed. Boissm. p. 67.

santhius, another sophist of great reputation, was more modest and more prudent; he declined the dazzling honour, and preferred the philosophic quiet of his native town. Julian appointed him, with his wife, to the high-priesthood of Lydia; and Chrysanthius, with the prophetic discernment of worldly wisdom, kept on amicable terms with the Christians. Of Libanius, Julian writes in rapturous admiration. Iamblichus had united all that was excellent in the ancient philosophy and poetry; Pindar, Democritus, and Orpheus, were blended in his perfect and harmonious syncretism.[e] The wisdom of Iamblichus so much dazzled and overawed the Emperor that he dared not intrude too much of his correspondence on the awful sage. "One of his letters surpassed in value all the gold of Lydia." The influence of men over their own age may in general be estimated by the language of contemporary writers. The admiration they excite is the test of their power, at least with their own party. The idolatry of the philosophers is confined to the few initiate; and even with their own party, the philosophers disappointed the high expectations which they had excited of their dignified superiority to the baser interests and weaknesses of mankind. They were by no means proof against the intoxication of court favour; they betrayed their vanity, their love of pleasure. Maximus himself is accused of assuming the pomp and insolence of a favourite; the discarded eunuchs had been replaced, it was feared by a new, not less intriguing or more disinterested, race of courtiers.

To the Christians, Julian assumed the language of the most liberal toleration. His favourite orator thus

[e] Epist. xv.

described his policy. "He thought that neither fire nor sword could change the faith of mankind; the heart disowns the hand which is compelled by terror to sacrifice. Persecutions only make hypocrites, who are unbelievers throughout life, or martyrs honoured after death.[d] He strictly prohibited the putting to death the Galileans (his favourite appellation of the Christians), as worthy rather of compassion than of hatred.[e] "Leave them to punish themselves, poor, blind, and misguided beings, who abandon the most glorious privilege of mankind, the adoration of the immortal gods, to worship the mouldering remains and bones of the dead."[f] He did not perceive that it was now too late to reassume the old Roman contempt for the obscure and foreign religion. Christianity had sate on the throne; and disdain now sounded like mortified pride. And the language, even the edicts, of the Emperor, under the smooth mask of gentleness and pity, betrayed the bitterness of hostility. His conduct was a perpetual sarcasm. It was the interest of Paganism to inflame, rather than to allay, the internal feuds of Christianity. Julian revoked the sentence of banishment pronounced against Arians, Apollinarians, and Donatists. He determined, it is said, to expose them to a sort of public exhibition of intellectual gladiatorship. He summoned the advocates of the several sects to dispute in his presence, and presided with mock solemnity over their debates. His own voice was drowned in the clamour, till at length, as

---

[d] Liban. Orat. Parent. v. l. p. 562.
[e] He asserts, in his 7th epistle, that he is willing neither to put to death, nor to injure the Christians in any manner; but the worshippers of the gods were on all occasions to be preferred— προτιμᾶσθαι. Compare Epist. lii.
[f] His usual phrase was, "worshippers of the dead, and of the bones of men."

though to contrast them, to their disadvantage, with the wild barbarian warriors with whom he had been engaged,—"Hear me," exclaimed the Emperor; "the Franks and the Alemanni have heard me." "No wild beasts," he said, "are so savage and intractable as Christian sectaries." He even endured personal insult. The statue of the "Fortune of Constantinople," bearing a cross in its hand, had been set up by Constantine. Julian took away the cross, and removed the Deity into a splendid temple. While he was employed in sacrifice, he was interrupted by the remonstrances of Maris, the Arian bishop of Chalcedon, to whom age and blindness had added courage. "Peace," said the Emperor, "blind old man, thy Galilean God will not restore thine eyesight." "I thank my God," answered Maris, "for my blindness, which spares me the pain of beholding an apostate like thee." Julian calmly proceeded in his sacrifice.[a]

The sagacity of Julian perceived the advantage to be obtained by contrasting the wealth, the power, and the lofty tone of the existing priesthood with the humility of the primitive Christians. On the occasion of a dispute between the Arian and orthodox party in Edessa, he confiscated their wealth, in order, as he said, to reduce them to their becoming and boasted poverty. "Wealth, according to their admirable law," he ironically says, "prevents them from attaining the kingdom of heaven."[b] *Taunts their profession of poverty.*

But his hostility was not confined to these indirect and invidious measures, or to quiet or insulting scorn. He began by abrogating all the exclusive privileges of the clergy; their immunity from *Privileges withdrawn.*

---

[a] Socrates, iii. 12.   [b] Socrat. iii. 13.

taxation, and exemptions from public duties. He would not allow Christians to be prefects, as their law prohibited their adjudging capital punishments. He resumed all the grants made on the revenues of the municipalities, and the supplies of corn for their maintenance. It was an act of more unwarrantable yet politic tyranny to exclude them altogether from the public education. By a familiarity with the great models of antiquity, the Christian had risen at least to the level of the most correct and elegant of the Heathen writers of the day. Though something of Oriental expression, from the continual adoption of language or of imagery from the Sacred Writings, adhered to their style, yet even that gives a kind of raciness and originality to their language, which, however foreign to the purity of Attic Greek, is more animating and attractive than the prolix and languid periods of Libanius, or the vague metaphysics of Iamblichus. Julian perceived the danger, and resented this usurpation, as it were, of the arms of Paganism, and their employment against their legitimate parent. It is not, indeed, quite clear how far, or in what manner, the prohibition of Julian affected the Christians. A general system of education, for the free and superior classes, had gradually spread through the empire.[1] Each city maintained a certain number of professors, according to its size and population, who taught grammar, rhetoric, and philosophy. They were appointed by the magistracy, and partly paid from the municipal funds. Vespasian first assigned stipends to professors in Rome, the Antonines

---

[1] There is an essay on the professors / Monsieur Naudet, Mém. de l'Institut, and general system of education, by / vol. x. p. 399.

extended the establishment to the other cities of the empire. They received two kinds of emoluments; the salary from the city, and a small fixed gratuity from their scholars. They enjoyed considerable immunities, exemption from military and civil service, and from all ordinary taxation. There can be no doubt that this education, as originally designed, was more or less intimately allied with the ancient religion. The grammarians, the poets,[h] the orators, the philosophers of Greece and Rome, were the writers whose works were explained and instilled into the youthful mind. "The vital principle, Julian asserted, in the writings of Homer, Hesiod, Demosthenes, Herodotus, Thucydides, Isocrates, Lysias, was the worship of the gods. Some of these writers had dedicated themselves to Mercury, some to the Muses. Mercury and the Muses were the tutelar deities of the Pagan schools." The Christians had glided imperceptibly into some of these offices, and perhaps some of the professors had embraced Christianity. But Julian declared that the Christians must be shameful hypocrites, or the most sordid of men, who, for a few drachms, would teach what they did not believe.[m] The Emperor might, with some plausibility, have insisted that the ministers of public instruction paid by the state, or from public funds, should at least not be hostile to the religion of the state. If the prohibition extended no farther than their exclusion from the public professorships, the measure might have worn some

[h] Homer, then considered, if not the parent, the great authority for the Pagan mythology, was the elementary school-book.

[m] When Christianity resumed the ascendancy, this act of intolerance was adduced in justification of the severities of Theodosius against Paganism. Petunt etiam, ut illis privilegia deferas, qui loquendi et docendi nostris communem usum Juliani lege proxima denegarunt. Ambros. Epist. Resp. ad Symmach.

appearance of equity; but it was the avowed policy of Julian to exclude them, if possible, from all advantages derived from the liberal study of Greek letters. The original edict disclaimed the intention of compelling the Christians to attend the Pagan schools; but it contemptuously asserted the right of the government to control men so completely out of their senses, and, at the same time, affected condescension to their weakness and obstinacy.[a] But if the Emperor did not compel them to learn, he forbade them to teach. The interdict, no doubt, extended to their own private and separate schools for Hellenic learning. They were not to instruct in Greek letters without the sanction of the municipal magistracy. He added insult to this narrow prohibition: he taunted them with their former avowed contempt for human learning; he would not permit them to lay their profane hands on Homer and Plato. "Let them be content to explain Matthew and Luke in the churches of the Galileans."[o] Some of the Christian professors obeyed the imperial edict.[p] Proæresius, who taught rhetoric with great success at Rome, calmly declined the overtures of the Emperor, and retired into a private station. Musonius, a rival of the great Proæresius, was silenced. But they resorted to an expedient which shows that they had full freedom of Christian instruction. A Christian Homer, a Christian Pindar, and other works were composed in which Christian sentiments and opinions were interwoven into the lan-

---

[a] Julian. Epist. xlii. p. 420. Socrates, v. 18. Theodoret, iii. 8. Sozomen, v. 18. Greg. Naz. Or. iii. p. 51, 96, 97.
[o] Julian. Epist. xlv.
[p] The more liberal Heathens were disgusted and ashamed at this measure of Julian. "Illud autem erat inclemens obruendum perenni silentio, quod arcebat docere magistros, rhetoricos, et grammaticos, ritû Christiani cultores." Amm. Marcell. xx. c. 10.

CHAP. VI.   ARTS OF JULIAN.

guage of the original poets. The piety of the age greatly admired these Christian parodies, which, however, do not seem to have maintained their ground even in the Christian schools.[q]

Julian is charged with employing unworthy or insidious arts to extort an involuntary assent to Paganism. Heathen symbols everywhere replaced those of Christianity. The medals display a great variety of deities, with their attributes. Jupiter is crowning the Emperor, Mars and Mercury inspire him with military skill and eloquence. The monogram of Christ disappeared from the Labarum, and on the standards were represented the gods of Paganism. As the troops defiled before the Emperor, each man was ordered to throw a few grains of frankincense upon an altar which stood before him. The Christians were horror-stricken, when they found that, instead of an act of legitimate respect to the Emperor, they had been betrayed into paying homage to idols. Some bitterly lamented their involuntary sacrilege, and indignantly threw down their arms; some of them are said to have surrounded the palace, and loudly avowing that they were Christians, reproached the Emperor with his treachery, and cast down the largess that they had received. For this breach of discipline and insult to the Emperor, they were led out to military execution. They vied with each other, it is said, for the honours of martyrdom.[r] But the bloody scene was interrupted

Arts of Julian to undermine Christianity.

---

[q] After the death of Julian, they were contemptuously thrown aside by the Christians themselves. Τῶν δὲ οἴ πίνω ἐν τῷ ἴσῳ μὴ γραφῆναι λογίζεται. Socrates, E. H. iii. 16.

[r] Jovian, Valentinian, and Valens, the future Emperors, are said to have been among those who refused to serve in the army. Julian, however, declined to accept the resignation of the former.

by a messenger from the Emperor, who contented himself with expelling them from the army, and sending them into banishment.

Actual persecutions, though unauthorised by the imperial edicts, would take place in some parts from the collision of the two parties. The Pagans, now invested in authority, would not always be disposed to use that authority with discretion, and the Pagan populace would seize the opportunity of revenging the violation of their temples, or the interruption of their rites, by the more zealous Christians. No doubt the language of an address delivered to Constantius and Constans had expressed the sentiments of a large party among the Christians. "Destroy without fear, destroy ye, most religious Emperors, the ornaments of the temples. Coin the idols into money, or melt them into useful metal. Confiscate all their endowments for the advantage of the Emperor and of the government. God has sanctioned, by your recent victories, your hostility to the temples." The writer proceeds to thunder out the passages of the Mosaic law, which enforce the duty of the extirpation of idolaters.* No doubt, in many places, the eager fanaticism of the Christians had outstripped the tardy movements of imperial zeal. In many cases it would now be thought an act of religion to reject—in others, it would be impossible to satisfy—the demands for restitution. The best authenticated acts of direct persecution relate to these disputes. Nor can Julian himself be exculpated from the guilt, if not of conniving at, of faintly rebuking these tumultuous acts of revenge or of wanton outrage. In some of the Syrian towns, Gaza, Hierapolis, and Cæsarea, the Pagans

---

* Julius Firmicus Maternus, de Errore Profanorum Religionum, c. 29.

had perpetrated cruelties too horrible to detail. Not content with massacring the Christians, with every kind of indignity, they had treated their lifeless remains with unprecedented outrage. They sprinkled the entrails of their victims with barley, that the fowls might be tempted to devour them. At Heliopolis, their cannibal fury did not shrink from tasting the blood and the inward parts of murdered priests and virgins. Julian calmly expresses his regret that the restorers of the temples of the gods have in some instances exceeded his expressed intentions; which, however, seem to have authorised the destruction of the Christian churches, or at least some of their sacred places.[1]

Restoration of temples.

Julian made an inauspicious choice in the battle-field on which he attempted to decide his conflict with Christianity. Christianity predominated to a greater extent in Constantinople and in Antioch than in any other cities of the empire. In Rome he might have appealed to the antiquity of Heathenism, and its eternal association with the glories of the republic. In Athens, he would have combined in more amicable confederacy the philosophy and the religion. In Athens his accession had given a considerable impulse to Paganism; the temples with the rest of the public buildings, had renewed their youth.[a]

Julian contends on ill-chosen ground.

---

[1] Greg. Nazianz. Socrates, iii. 14. Sozomen, v. 9. Compare Gibbon, vol. iv. p. 116, who has referred the following passage in the Misopogon to these scenes.

Ὅτι τὰ μὲν τῶν θεῶν ἀνέστησαν αὐτίκα τεμένη· τοὺς τάφους δὲ τῶν ἀθέων ἀνέτρεψαν πάντας ὑπὸ τοῦ συνθήματος, ὃ δὴ δέδοται παρ' ἐμοῦ πρώην, οὕτως ἐνήρθησαν τὸν νοῦν, καὶ μετέωροι γενόμενοι τὴν διανοίαν, ὅτι καὶ πλέον ἐπεξελθεῖν τοῖς εἰς τοὺς θεοὺς πλημμελοῦσιν ἢ βούλωμαι μοι ἦν. Misopogon, p. 361.

Did he mean by the τάφοι chapels, like those built over the remains of St. Babylas, in the Daphne, at Antioch, or the churches in general?

[a] Mamertinus, probably, highly paints the ruin, that he may exalt the

Eleusis, which had fallen into ruin, now reassumed its splendour, and might have been wisely made the centre of his new system. But in Constantinople all was modern and Christian. Piety to the imperial founder was closely connected with devotion to his religion. Julian could only restore the fanes of the tutelary gods of old Byzantium; he could strip the Fortune of the city of her Christian attributes; but he could not give a Pagan character to a city which had grown up under Christian auspices. Constantinople remained contumaciously and uniformly Christian. Antioch had been a chief seat of that mingled Oriental and Grecian worship of the Sun which had grown up in all the Hellenised parts of Asia; the name of Daphne given to the sacred grove, implied that the fictions of Greece had been domiciliated in Syria.

Constantinople.
Antioch.

Antioch was now divided by two incongruous, but equally dominant passions—devotion to Christianity, and attachment to the games, the theatre, and every kind of public amusement. The bitter sarcasms of Julian on the latter subject are justified and confirmed by the grave and serious admonitions of Chrysostom. By a singular coincidence, Antioch came into collision with the strongest prejudices of Julian. His very virtues were fatal to his success in the re-establishment of Paganism; its connexion with the amusements of the people Julian repudiated with philosophic disdain. Instead of attempting to purify the degenerate taste, he had all the austerity of a Pagan monk. Public exhibitions were interdicted to his reformed priesthood;

---

restorer. "Ipsæ illæ bonarum artium magistræ et inventrices Athenæ omnem cultum publicâ privatimque perdide- | runt. In miserandam ruinam conciderat Eleusinia." Mamert. Orat. Actio. ix. p. 147.

JULIAN AT ANTIOCH.

once, at the beginning of the year, the Emperor entered the theatre, remained in undisguised weariness, and withdrew in disgust. He was equally impatient of wasting his time as a spectator of the chariot race; he attended occasionally, out of respect to the presiding deity of the games; saw five or six courses, and retired.[x] Yet Paganism might appear to welcome Julian to Antioch. It had still many followers, who clung with fond attachment to its pomps and gay processions. The whole city poured forth to receive him; by some he was hailed as a deity. It happened to be the festival of Adonis; and the loud shouts of welcome to the Emperor were mingled with the wild and shrill cries of the women, wailing that Syrian symbol of the universal deity, the Sun. It might seem an awful omen that the rites which mourned the departure of the genial deity should welcome his ardent worshipper.[y] The outward appearance of religion must have affected Julian with alternate hope and disappointment. From all quarters, diviners, augurs, magicians, enchanters, the priests of Cybele and of the other Eastern religions, flocked to Antioch. His palace was crowded with men, whom Chrysostom describes as branded with every crime, as infamous for poisonings and witchcrafts. "Men who had grown old in prisons and in the mines, and who maintained their wretched existence by the most disgraceful trades, were suddenly advanced to places of dignity, and invested with the priesthood and sacrificial functions.[z] The severe Julian, as he passed through the city, "was encircled by the profligate of every age,

Julian at Antioch.

---

[x] Misopogon, p. 339, 340. Amm. xxii. 9.
[y] "Evenerat iisdem diebus annuo currru completo Adonica ritu veteri celebrari." Amm. Marc. xxii. 9.
[z] Chrysostom contra Gent.

and by prostitutes with their wanton laughter and shameless language. Among the former, the ardent, youthful, and ascetic preacher probably included all the Theurgists of the philosophic school; the latter sentence describes the festal processions, which no doubt retained much of their old voluptuous character. Julian ascended the lofty top of Mount Casius, to solemnise, under the broad and all-embracing cope of heaven, the rites of Jupiter Philius.[a] But in the luxurious groves of Daphne, he was doomed to a melancholy disappointment. The grove remained with all its beautiful scenery, its shady recesses, its cool and transparent streams, in which the Heathen inhabitants of Antioch had mingled their religious rites with their private enjoyments. But a serious gloom, a solemn quiet, pervaded the whole place. The temple of Apollo, the magnificent edifice in which the devotion of former ages had sacrificed hecatombs, where the clouds of incense had soared above the grove, and in which the pomp of Oriental worship had assembled half Syria, was silent and deserted. He expected (in his own words[b]) a magnificent procession, victims, libations, dances, incense, boys with white and graceful vests and with minds as pure and unspotted, dedicated to the service of the god. He entered the temple; he found a solitary priest, with a single goose for sacrifice. The indignant Emperor poured out his resentment in the bitterest language; he reproached the impiety, the shameful parsimony of the inhabitants, who enjoyed the large estates attached to the temple,

---

[a] The Jupiter Philius, or Casius. This god was the tutelary deity of Antioch, and appears on the medals of the city. St. Martin, note to Le Beau, iii. 6.
[b] Misopogon, 362.

and thus neglected its services; who at the same time permitted their wives to lavish their treasures on the infamous Galileans, and on their scandalous banquets, called the Maiuma.

Julian determined to restore the majesty of the temple and worship of Apollo. But it was first necessary to dispossess the Christian usurper of the sacred place. The remains of Babylas, the martyred Bishop of Antioch, who had suffered, probably in the Decian persecution, had been removed eleven years before to Daphne; and the Christians crowded to pay their devotions near his tomb. The Christians assert, that the baffled Apollo confessed himself abashed in the presence of the saint; his oracle dared not break silence.[*] At all events, Julian determined to purify the grove from the contamination of this worship. The remains of Babylas were ordered to be transported back to Antioch. They were met by a solemn procession of a great part of the inhabitants. The relics were raised on a chariot, and conducted in triumph, with the excited multitude dancing before it, and thundering out the maledictory psalm:—"Confounded be all they that worship carved images, and delight in vain idols." Julian attempted to punish this outburst of popular feeling. But the firmness of the first victim who endured the torture, and the remonstrances of the Prefect Sallust, brought him back to his better temper of mind. The restoration of the temple was urged on with zealous haste. A splendid peristyle arose around it; when at midnight Julian received the intelligence that the temple was on fire. The roof and all the ornaments were entirely consumed, and the statue

[*] Chrysostom, Orat. in S. Babylam.

of the god himself, of gilded wood, yet of such astonishing workmanship that it is said to have enforced the homage of the conquering Sapor, was burned to ashes. The Christians beheld the manifest wrath of Heaven, and asserted that the lightning had come down and smitten the idolatrous edifice. Julian ascribed the conflagration to the malice of the Christians. The most probable account is, that a devout worshipper had lighted a number of torches before an image of the Queen of Heaven, which had set fire to some part of the building. Julian exacted, as it were, reprisals on Christianity; he ordered the cathedral of Antioch to be closed. His orders were executed with insult to the sacred place, and the spoliation of the sacred vessels.[d]

Julian, in the mean time, was not regardless of the advancement of the Pagan interest in other parts of the empire. Alexandria could not be at peace while any kind of religious excitement inflamed the minds of men. The character of George, the Arian bishop of Alexandria, is loaded by Heathen as well as by Christian writers with every kind of obloquy. His low birth; the base and sordid occupations of his youth; his servile and intriguing meanness in manhood; his tyranny in power, trace, as it were, his whole life with increasing odiousness. Yet, extraordinary as it may seem, the Arian party could find no man of better reputation to fill this important post; and George, the impartial tyrant of all parties, perished at last, the victim of his zealous hostility to Paganism. A chief cause of the unpopularity of George was the assertion of the imperial right over the fee-simple of the land on which

Alexandria.

George, Arian Bishop of Alexandria.

---

[d] Amm. Marc. xxii. 13. Theodor. iii. 11. Sozomen, v. 20.

Alexandria was built. This right was gravely deduced from Alexander the Great. During the reign of Constantius, George had seized every opportunity of depressing and insulting Paganism; he had interdicted the festivals and the sacrifices of the Heathen; he had pillaged the gifts, the statues, and ornaments of their temple; he had been heard, as he passed the temple either of Serapis himself, or of the Fortune of the city, to utter the contemptuous expression, "How long will this sepulchre be permitted to stand?"* He had discovered a cave where the Mithriac mysteries were said to have been carried on with a horrible sacrifice of human life. The heads of a number of youths were exposed (probably disinterred from some old cemetery near which these rites had been established), as of the victims of this sanguinary idolatry. The insults and outrages rankled in the hearts of the Pagans. The fate of Artemius, the Duke of Egypt, the friend and abettor of George in all his tyrannical proceedings, prepared the way for that of George. Artemius was suspected of being concerned in the death of Gallus. He was charged with enormous delinquencies by the people of Alexandria. Whether as a retribution for the former offence against the brother of Julian, or as the penalty for his abuse of his authority in his government, Artemius was condemned to death. The intelligence of his execution was the signal for a general insurrection of the Pagans in Alexandria. The palace of George was invested by a frantic mob. In an instant he was dragged forth, murdered, trampled under foot, _{His death.} dragged along the streets, and at length torn limb from limb. With him perished two officers of

---

* Amm. Marcell. xxii. 11. Socrates, iii. 2.

the empire, Dracontius, master of the mint, and the Count Diodorus; the one accused of having destroyed an altar of Serapis, the other of having built a church. The mangled remains of these miserable men were paraded through the streets on the back of a camel, and at length, lest they should be enshrined and worshipped as the relics of martyrs, cast into the sea. The Christians, however, of all parties, appear to have looked with unconcern on the fate of this episcopal tryant,' whom, the general hatred, if it did not excite them to assist in his massacre, prevented them from attempting to defend. Julian addressed a letter to the people of Alexandria. While he admitted, in the strongest terms, the guilt of George, he severely rebuked their violence and presumption in thus taking the law into their own hands, and the horrible inhumanity of tearing like dogs the bodies of men in pieces, and then presuming to lift up their blood-stained hands to the gods. He admitted that their indignation for their outraged temples and insulted gods might naturally madden them to just resentment; but they should have awaited the calm and deliberate course of justice, which would have exacted due punishment from the offender. Julian secured to himself part of the spoils of the murdered prelate. George had a splendid library, rich not merely in the writings of the Galileans, but, what Julian esteemed as infinitely more precious, the works of the Greek orators and philosophers. The first he would willingly have destroyed, the latter he commanded to be carefully reserved for his own use.⁸

---

¹ "Poterantque miserandi homines | odio omnes indiscreté flagrabant."
ad crudele supplicium devoti, Christia- | Amm. Marcell. xxii. 11.
norum adjumento defendi, si Georgii | ⁸ Julian. Epist. ix. & x.

In the place of George arose a more powerful adversary. Julian knew and dreaded the character of Athanasius, who, during these tumults, had quietly resumed his authority over the orthodox Christians of Alexandria. The general edict of Julian for the recall of all exiles contained no exception; and Athanasius availed himself of its protecting authority.[b] Under his auspices, the church, even in these disastrous times, resumed its vigour. The Arians, terrified perhaps by the hostility of the Pagans, hastened to reunite themselves to the church; and Julian heard, with bitter indignation, that some Pagan females had received baptism from Athanasius. Julian expressed his astonishment, not that Athanasius had returned from exile, but that he had dared to resume his see. He ordered him into instant banishment. He appealed, in a letter to the prefect, to the mighty Serapis, that if Athanasius, the enemy of the gods, was not expelled from the city before the calends of December, he should impose a heavy fine. "By his influence the gods were brought into contempt; it would be better, therefore, that 'this most wicked Athanasius' were altogether banished from Egypt." To a supplication from the Christian inhabitants of the city in favour of Athanasius, he returned a sarcastic and contemptuous reply, reminding the people of Alexandria of their descent from Pagan ancestors, and of the greatness of the gods they worshipped, and expressing his astonishment that they should prefer the worship of Jesus, the Word of God, to that of the Sun, the glorious and visible and eternal emblem of the Deity.[i]

---

[b] Julian. Epist. xxvi. p. 398.   [i] Julian. Epist. xl. p. 378.

In other parts, justified perhaps in their former excesses, or encouraged to future acts of violence, by the impunity of the Alexandrians, Paganism awoke, if not to make reprisals by conversion, at least to take a bloody revenge on its Christian adversaries.[l] The atrocious persecutions of the fanatic populace, in some of the cities of Syria, have already been noticed. The aged Mark of Arethusa was, if not the most blameless, at least the victim of these cruelties whose life ought to have been sanctified even by the rumour which ascribed the preservation of Julian, when an infant, to the pious bishop. Mark was accused of having destroyed a temple; he was summoned to rebuild it at his own expense. But Mark, with the virtues, inherited the primitive poverty of the Apostles; and, even if he had had the power, no doubt, would have resisted this demand.[k] But the furious populace, (according to Sozomen, men, women, and schoolboys), seized on the old man, and inflicted every torment which their inventive barbarity could suggest. The patience and calm temperament of the old man resisted and survived the cruelties.[m] Julian is said to have expressed no indignation, and ordered no punishment. The prefect Sallust reminded him of the disgrace to which Paganism was exposed, by being thus put to shame by a feeble old man.

The policy of Julian induced him to seek out every alliance which could strengthen the cause of Paganism against Christianity. Polytheism courted an unnatural

<small>Death of Mark of Arethusa.</small>

---

l Julian. Epist. x. p. 377.

k According to Theodoret, 'Ο δὲ, ἕως εἰς Ἀρεθοίας ἔφη, τὸ ἔβολὸν τοὺς ἵνα δοῦναι, τῷ πάντα δοῦναι. E. E., II. iii. 7.

m Sozomen gives the most detailed account of this cruel scene, clearly a popular tumult, which the authorities in no way interfered to repress. E. H., v. 10.

union with Judaism; their bond of connection was their common hatred to Christianity. It is not clear whether Julian was sufficiently acquainted with the writings of the Christians, distinctly to apprehend that they considered the final destruction of the Jewish temple to be one of the great prophecies on which their religion rested. The rebuilding of that temple was bringing, as it were, this question to direct issue; it was an appeal to God, whether he had or had not finally rejected the people of Israel, and admitted the Christians to all their great and exclusive privileges. At all events, the elevation of Judaism was the depression of Christianity. It set the Old Testament, to which the Christians appealed, in 'direct and hostile opposition to the New.

Julian courts the Jews.

The profound interest awakened in the Jewish mind showed that the race of Israel embraced, with eager fervour, this solemn appeal to Heaven. With the joy which animated the Jew, at this unexpected summons to return to his native land and to rebuild his fallen temple, mingled, no doubt, some natural feeling of triumph and of gratified animosity over the Christian. In every part of the empire the Jews awoke from their slumber of abasement and of despondency. It was not for them to repudiate the overtures of Paganism. The Emperor acknowledged their God by the permission to build again the temple to his glory; and, if not as the sole and supreme God, yet Julian's language affected a monotheistic tone, and they might indulge the fond hope that the re-establishment of the temple upon Mount Moriah might be preparatory to the final triumph of their faith, in the awe-struck veneration of the whole world; the commencement of the Messiah's kingdom; the dawn of

Determines to rebuild the temple at Jerusalem.

their long-delayed, but, at length, approaching millennium of empire and of religious supremacy. Those who could not contribute their personal labour devoted their wealth to the national work. The extent of their sacrifices, the eagerness of their hopes, rather belong to the province of Jewish history. But every precaution was taken to secure the uninterrupted progress of the work. It was not an affair of the Jewish nation, but of the imperial government. It was entrusted to the ruler of the province, as the delegate of the Emperor. Funds were advanced from the public treasury; and, if the Jews themselves, of each sex and of every age, took pride in hallowing their own hands by assisting in heaping up the holy earth, or hewing the stone to be employed in this sacred design; if they wrought their wealth into tools of the precious metals, shovels and spades of silver, which were to become valued heirlooms as consecrated by this pious service, the Emperor seemed to take a deep personal interest in the design, which was at once to immortalize his magnificence, and to assist his other glorious undertakings. The Jews, who acknowledged that it was not lawful to offer sacrifice except on that holy place, were to propitiate their God, during his expedition into Persia; and on his triumphant return from that region, he promised to unite with them in adoration in the restored city and in the reconstructed fane of the great God of the Jews."

Judaism and Paganism had joined in this solemn adjuration, as it were, of the Deity. Their vows were met with discomfiture and disappointment. The simple fact of the interruption of their labours,

Interrupted.

---

* In his letter to the Jews, he calls the God of the Jews, ὑψίστου; in his Theologic Fragment (p. 295), μέγας Θεός.

by an event, which the mass of mankind could not but consider præternatural, even as recorded by the Pagan historians, appeared, in the more excited and imaginative minds of the Christians, a miracle of the most terrific and appalling nature. Few, if any, of the Christians could have been eye-witnesses of the scene. The Christian world would have averted its face in horror from the impious design. The relation must, in the first instance, have come from the fears of the discomfited and affrighted workmen. The main fact is indisputable, that, as they dug down to the foundations, terrific explosions took place; what seemed balls of fire burst forth; the works were shattered to pieces; clouds of smoke and dust enveloped the whole in darkness, broke only by the wild and fitful glare of the flames. Again the work was renewed by the obstinate zeal of the Jews; again they were repelled by this unseen and irresistible power, till they cast away their implements, and abandoned the work in humiliation and despair. How far natural causes—the ignition of the foul vapours, confined in the deeply excavated recesses of the hill of the temple, according to the recent theory—will account for the facts, as they are related in the simpler narrative of Marcellinus, may admit of some question; but the philosophy of the age, whether Heathen or Christian, was as unable as it was unwilling to trace such appalling events to the unvarying operations of nature.[o]

---

[o] See M. Guizot's note on Gibbon, with my additional observations. There seems a strong distinction in point of credibility between miracles addressed to the terror and those which appeal to the calmer emotions of the mind, such as most of those recorded in the Gospel. The former, in the first place, are usually momentary, or, if prolonged, endure but a short time. But the passion of fear so completely unhinges and disorders the mind, as to deprive it of all trustworthy power of observation or discrimination. In

Christianity may have embellished this wonderful event, but Judaism and Paganism confessed by their terrors the prostration of their hopes. The work was abandoned; and the Christians of later ages could appeal to the remains of the shattered works and unfinished excavations, as the unanswerable sign of the divine wrath against their adversaries, as the public and miraculous declaration of God in favour of their insulted religion.

But it was not as Emperor alone that the indefatigable Julian laboured to overthrow the Christian religion. It was not by the public edict, the more partial favour shown to the adherents of Paganism, the insidious disparagement of Christianity by the depression of its ministers and apostles, and the earnest elevation of Heathenism, to a moral code and an harmonious religion, with all the pomp of a sumptuous ritual; it was not in the council, or the camp, or the temple alone, that Julian stood forth as the avowed antagonist of Christianity. He was ambitious, as a writer, of confuting its principles and disproving its veracity: he passed in his closet the long nights of the winter, and continued, during his Persian campaign, his elaborate work against the faith of Christ. He seemed, as it were, possessed with an equal hatred of those whom he considered the two most dangerous enemies of the Roman empire, the Persians and the Christians. While oppressed by all the serious cares of

Writings of Julian.

---

themselves, therefore, I should venture to conclude that terrific miracles, resting on human testimony, are less credible than those of a less appalling nature. Though the other class of emotions, those of joy or gratitude, or religious veneration, likewise disturb the equable and dispassionate state of mind requisite for cool reasoning, yet such miracles are in general both more calmly surveyed, and more permanent in their effects.

organising and moving such an army as might bring back the glorious days of Germanicus or of Trajan; while his ambition contemplated nothing less than the permanent humiliation of the great Eastern rival of the empire; his literary vanity found time for its exercise, and in all his visions of military glory and conquest, Julian never lost sight of his fame as an author.[*] It is difficult to judge from the fragments of this work, selected for confutation after his death by Cyril of Alexandria, of the power, or even of the candour, shown by the imperial controversialist. But it appears to have been composed in a purely polemic spirit; with no lofty or comprehensive views of the real nature of the Christian religion, no fine and philosophic perception of that which in the new faith had so powerfully and irresistibly occupied the whole soul of man; with no consciousness of the utter inefficiency of the cold and incoherent Pagan mysticism, which he endeavoured to substitute for the Gospel.

Work against Christianity.

But, at least, this was a grave and serious employment. Whatever might be thought of his success as a religious disputant, there was no loss of dignity in the Emperor condescending to enlighten his subjects on such momentous questions. But, when he stooped to be the satirist of the inhabitants of a city which had ridiculed his philosophy and rejected his religion, the finest and most elegant irony, the keenest and most delicate wit, would scarcely have justified this compromise of the imperial majesty. But in the Misopogon—the apology for his philosophic beard—Julian mingled the coarseness of the Cynic with

Misopogon.

---

[*] "Julianus Augustus septem li- Christum evomuit." Hieronym. Oper. bros in expositione Pauthicâ adversus | Epist. lxx.

the bitterness of personal indignity. The vulgar ostentation of his own filthiness, the description of the vermin which peopled his thick beard, ill accord with the philosophic superiority with which Julian rallies the love of amusement and gaiety among his subjects of Antioch. Their follies were at least more graceful and humane than this rude pedantry. There is certainly much felicity of sarcasm, doubtless much justice, in his animadversions on the dissolute manners of the Antiochenes, their ingratitude for his liberality, their dislike of his severe justice, the insolence of their contempt for his ruder manners, throughout the Misopogon; but it lowers Julian from a follower of Plato, to a coarse imitator of Diogenes; it exhibits him as borrowing the worst part of the Christian monkish character, the disregard of the decencies and civilities of life, without the high and visionary enthusiasm, or the straining after superiority to the low cares and pursuits of the world. It was singular to hear a Grecian sophist, for such was undoubtedly the character of Julian's writings, extolling the barbarians, the Celts and Germans, above the polished inhabitants of Greece and Syria.

Paganism followed with faithful steps, and with eager hopes, the career of Julian on the brilliant outset of his Persian campaign. Some of the Syrian cities through which he passed, Batnæ and Hierapolis, and Carrhæ, seemed to enter into his views, and endeavoured, with incense and sacrifice, to propitiate the gods of Julian.⁴ For the last time the Etruscan haruspices accompanied a Roman Emperor; but by a singular fatality, their adverse interpretation of the signs of heaven was disdained, and Julian fol-

Julian sets forth on his Persian expedition.

---

⁴ Julian. Epist. xxvii. p. 399. Amm. Marc. xxiii. 2.

lowed the advice of the philosophers, who coloured their predictions with the bright hues of the Emperor's ambition.[f]

The death of Julian did greater honour to his philosophy. We may reject as in itself improbable, and as resting on insufficient authority, the bitter sentence ascribed to him when he received his fatal wound. "Thou hast conquered, O Galilean."[g] He comforted his weeping friends; he expressed his readiness to pay the debt of nature, and his joy that the purer and better part of his being was so soon to be released from the gross and material body. "The gods of heaven sometimes bestow an early death as the best reward of the most pious." His conscience uttered no reproach; he had administered the empire with moderation, firmness and clemency; he had repressed the licence of public manners; he had met danger with firmness. His prescient spirit had long informed him that he should fall by the sword. And he thanked the everlasting deity that he thus escaped the secret assassination, the slow and wasting disease, the ignominious death; and departed from the world in the midst of his glory and prosperity. "It is equal cowardice to seek death before our time, and to attempt to avoid it when our time is come." His calmness was only disturbed by the intelligence of the loss of a friend. He who despised his own death lamented that of another. He reproved the distress of his attendants, declaring that it was humiliating to mourn over a prince already reconciled to the heavens and to the stars; and thus calmly discoursing with the philosophers Priscus and Maximus

Death of Julian.

---

[f] Amm. Marc. xxiii. 5.
[g] Νενίκηκας, Γαλιλαιε. Theodoret, Hist. Eccl. iii., 25.

on the metaphysics of the soul, expired Julian, the philosopher and Emperor.¹

Julian died, perhaps happily for his fame. Perilous as his situation was, he might still have extricated himself by his military skill and courage, and eventually succeeded in his conflict with the Persian empire; he might have dictated terms to Sapor, far different from those which the awe of his name and the vigorous organisation of his army, even after his death, extorted from the prudent Persian. But in his other, his internal conflict, Julian could have obtained no victory, even at the price of rivers of blood shed in persecution, and perhaps civil wars throughout the empire. He might have arrested the fall of the empire, but that of Paganism was beyond the power of man.² The invasion of arms may be resisted or repelled, the silent and profound encroachments of opinion and religious sentiment will not retrograde. Already there had been ominous indications that the temper of Julian would hardly maintain its more moderate policy; nor would Christianity in that age have been content with opposing him with passive courage. The insulting fanaticism of the violent, no less than the stubborn contumacy of the disobedient, would have goaded him by degrees to severer measures.

<small>Amm. Marc. *ibid.* Even the Christians, at a somewhat later period, did justice to the great qualities of Julian. The character drawn by the Pagan, Aurelius Victor, is adopted by Prudentius, who kindles into unusual vigour. "Cupido laudis immodicæ; cultus numinum superstitiosus; audax plus, quam imperatorem decet, cui salus propria cum semper ad securita-

tem omnium, maximè in bello, conservanda est." Epit. p. 228.

Ductor fortissimus armis;
Conditor et legum celeberrimus; ore ma-
nuque
Consultor patriæ, sed non consultor habendæ
Religionis; amans ter centum millia Divûm;
Perfidus ille Deo, sed non et perfidus orbi.
Apoth. 450.

² Julian's attempt to restore Paganism was like that of Rienzi to restore the liberties of Rome.</small>

The whole empire would have been rent by civil dissensions. The bold adventurer would scarcely have been wanting, who, either from ambition or enthusiasm, would have embraced the Christian cause; and the pacific spirit of genuine Christianity, its high notions of submission to civil authority, would scarcely, generally or constantly, have resisted the temptation of resuming its seat upon the throne. Julian could not have subdued Christianity, without depopulating the empire; nor contested with it the sovereignty of the world, without danger to himself and to the civil authority; nor yielded, without the disgrace and bitterness of failure. He who stands across the peaceful stream of progressive opinion, by his resistance maddens it to an irresistible torrent, and is either swept away by it at once, or diverts it over the whole region in one devastating deluge.ˣ

ˣ Theodoret describes the rejoicings at Antioch on the news of the death of Julian. There were not only festal dancings in the churches and cemeteries of the martyrs, but in the theatres they celebrated the triumph of the cross, and mocked at his vaticinations. Ἡ δὲ Ἀντιόχου πόλις τὴν ἐκείνου μεμαθηκυῖα σφαγὴν, δημοθοινίας ἐπετέλει καὶ πανηγύρεις καὶ οὐ μόνον ἐν ταῖς ἐκκλησίαις ἐχόρευον καὶ τοῖς μαρτύρων σηκοῖς, ἀλλὰ καὶ ἐν τοῖς θεάτροις τοῦ σταυροῦ τὴν νίκην ἐκήρυττον, καὶ τοῖς ἐκείνου μαντεύμασιν ἐπετώθαζον. E. H. iii. 27.

CHAPTER VII.

Valentinian and Valens.

Lamentations of the Pagans at the death of Julian.

IT is singular to hear the Pagans taking up, in their altered position, the arguments of the Christians. The extinction of the family of Constantine was a manifest indication of the divine displeasure at the abandonment of Paganism.[a] But this was the calmer conclusion of less recent sorrow and disappointment. The immediate expression of Pagan regret was a bitter and reproachful complaint against the ingratitude of the gods, who made so bad a return for the zealous services of Julian. "Was this the reward for so many victims, so many prayers, so much incense, so much blood, shed on the altar by night as well as by day? Julian, in his profuse and indiscriminate piety, had neglected no deity; he had worshipped all who lived in the tradition of the poets,—fathers and children, gods and goddesses, superior and subordinate deities; and they, instead of hurling their thunderbolts and lightnings, and all the armoury of Heaven, against the hostile Persians, had thus basely abandoned their sacred charge. The new Salmoneus, the more impious Lycurgus, the senseless image of a man (such were the appellations with which the indignant rhetorician alluded to Constantius), who had waged implacable warfare with the gods, quenched the sacred fires, trampled on the altars,

---

[a] Liban. pro Templis, ii. 184.

CHAP. VII.   REIGN OF JOVIAN.   31

closed or demolished or profaned the temples, or
alienated them to loose companions,—this man had
been permitted to pollute the earth for fifty years,
and then departed by the ordinary course of nature;
while Julian, with all his piety and all his glory, had
only given to the world a hasty glimpse of his greatness, and suddenly departed from their unsatisfied
sight."[b] On the other hand the Christians raised a shout
of undissembled triumph; Antioch was in a tumult
of joy.[c] Gregory of Nazianzum poured forth from the
pulpit his bitter eloquence on the head of the apostate.[d]
Christian legend is full of predictions of the death of
Julian. The most striking is the answer attributed
to a grammarian of Antioch, whom Libanius accosted
with a sneer, "What is the carpenter's son doing
now?" "He is making a coffin."[e] But, without regarding the vain lamentations of Paganism, Christianity
calmly resumed its ascendancy. The short reign of
Jovian sufficed for its re-establishment; and, Reign of
as yet, it exacted no revenge for its sufferings Jovian.
and degradation under Julian.[f] There may have been

---

[b] Libanius insults, in this passage, every man free to follow that form of
the worship of the dead man, whose religion which seems best to him."
sarcophagus (he seems to allude to the Ad Jovian. p. 81., ed. Dindorf. He
pix or consecrated box in which the proceeds to assert, that the general
sacramental symbol of our Saviour's piety will be increased by the rivalry
body was enclosed) is introduced into of different religions. "The Deity
the κλῆρος of the gods. Monod. in does not demand uniformity of faith."
Julian. i. p. 509. He touches on the evils which had
[c] Theodoret lii. 38. arisen out of religious factions, and
[d] Greg. Orat. iv. c. 124. urges Jovian to permit supplications
[e] Theodoret iii. 23. to ascend to Heaven from all parts of
[f] Themistius praises highly the the empire for his prosperous reign.
toleration of Jovian. "Thy law, and He praises him, however, for suppress-
that of God, is eternal and unchange- ing magic and Gostic sacrifices.
able; that which leaves the soul of

policy as well as moderation in the toleration of Jovian. The empire had been first offered to the Prefect Sallust, a Pagan. It was Procopius, probably another Pagan, who laid the diadem at the feet of Jovian. Sacrifices to the gods were still performed at Constantinople,[e] the entrails of victims were consulted by the haruspices on the fate of the army.[h] Yet during his eight months' reign Jovian had time to declare himself not only a Christian but an orthodox emperor.[i] He received Athanasius, who had emerged from his concealment, with distinguished favour, and repelled the Arian bishop with scorn.[k] The character of the two brothers who succeeded to the empire, Valentinian and Valens, and their religious policy, were widely at variance. Valentinian ascended the throne with the fame of having rejected the favour of Julian and the prospects of military distinction, for the sake of his religion. He had withdrawn from the army rather than offer even questionable adoration to standards decorated with the symbols of idolatry. But Valentinian was content to respect those rights of conscience which he had so courageously asserted.

The Emperor of the West maintained a calm and uninterrupted toleration, which incurred the reproach of indifference from the Christian party, but has received the respectful homage of the Pagan historian.[m] The immunities and the privileges of the Pagan priesthood were confirmed;[n] the rites of

---

[e] La Bleterie, Vie de Jovien, p. 118.
[h] Amm. Marcell. xxv. 6.
[i] Julian died June 26, A.D. 363. Jovian, Feb. 17, A.D. 364.
[k] Athanasius ii. 622.
[m] Ammianus Marcellinus, l. xxx. c.9.

"Testes sunt leges a me in exordio imperii mei datæ; quibus unicuique quod animo imbibisset, colendi libera facultas tributa est." Cod. Theod. l. ix. tit. 16, l. 9.
[n] Cod. Theod. xii. 1, 60, 75.

divination were permitted, if performed without malicious intent.° The prohibition of midnight sacrifices, which seemed to be required by the public morals, threatened to deprive the Greeks of their cherished mysteries. Prætextatus, then proconsul of Achaia, the head of the Pagan party, a man of high and unblemished character, represented to the Emperor that these rites were necessary to the existence of the Greeks. The law was relaxed in their favour, on the condition of strict adherence to ancient usage. In Rome, the vestal virgins maintained their sanctity; the altar of Victory, restored by Julian, preserved its place; a military guard protected the temples from insult, but a tolerant as well as prudent provision, forbade the employment of Christian soldiers on this service.[p] On the other hand, Valentinian appears to have revoked some of the lavish endowments conferred by Julian on the Heathen temples. These estates were re-incorporated with the private treasure of the sovereign.[q] At a later period of his reign, there must have been some general prohibition of animal sacrifice; the Pagan worship was restricted to the offering of incense to the gods.[r] But, according to the expression of Libanius, they dured not execute this law in Rome, so fatal would it have been considered to the welfare of the empire.[s]

Valens, in the East, as Valentinian, in the West, allowed perfect freedom to the public ritual of Paganism. But both in the East, and in the West, the persecution against magic and unlawful

---

° God. Theod. ix. 16, 9.
[p] Cod. Theod. xvi. 1, 1.
[q] Cod. Theod. x. 1, 8. The law reads as if it were a more general and indiscriminate confiscation.

[r] Lib. pro Templis, vii. p. 163. ed. Reiske. This arose out of some recent and peculiar circumstances.
[s] Liban. vol. ii. p. 180.

divination told with tremendous force against the Pagan cause. It was the more fatal, because it was not openly directed against the religion, but against practices denounced as criminal, and believed to be real, by the general sentiment of mankind, and prosecuted by that fierce animosity which is engendered by fear. Some compassion might be felt for innocent victims, supposed to be unjustly implicated in such charges; the practice of extorting evidence or confession by torture, might be revolting, to those especially who looked back with pride and with envy to the boasted immunity of all Roman citizens from such cruelties; but where strong suspicion of guilt prevailed, the public feeling would ratify the stern sentence of the law against such delinquents; the magician or the witch would pass to execution amid the universal abhorrence. The notorious connexion of any particular religious party with such dreaded and abominated proceedings, especially if proved by the conviction of a considerable majority of the condemned from their ranks, would tend to depress the religion itself. This sentiment was not altogether unjust. Paganism had, as it were, in its desperation, thrown itself upon the inextinguishable superstition of the human mind. The more the Pagans were depressed, the hope of regaining their lost superiority, the desire of vengeance, would induce them to seize on every method of awing or commanding the minds of their wavering votaries. Nor were those who condescended to these arts, or those who in many cases claimed the honours annexed to such fearful powers, only the bigoted priesthood, or mere itinerant traders in human credulity; the high philosophic party, which had gained such predominant influence during the reign of Julian, now wielded the terrors and incurred the penalties, of these dark and forbidden practices. It is impossible to read their writings without remarking a boastful display of intercourse with supernatural agents, which to the Christian would appear an illicit communion with malignant spirits. This was not indeed magic, but it was the groundwork of it. The theurgy, or mysterious dealings of the Platonic philosopher with the dæmons or still higher powers, was separated by a thin and imperceptible distinction from Goetic or unlawful enchantment. Divination, indeed, or the foreknowledge of futurity by different arts, was an essential part of the Greek and Roman religion. But divination had, in Greece at least, withdrawn from its public office. It had retired from the silenced oracles of Delphi or Dodona. The gods, rebuked according to the Christian, offended according to the Pagan, had withdrawn their presence. In Rome the Etruscan soothsayers, as part of the great national ceremonial, maintained their place, and to a late period preserved their influence over the public mind. But, in general, it was only in secret, and to its peculiar favourites, that the summoned or spontaneous deity revealed the secrets of futurity; it was by the dream, or the private omen, the sign in the heavens, vouchsafed only to the initiate; or the direct inspiration; or, if risked, it was by the secret, mysterious, usually the nocturnal rite, that the reluctant god was compelled to disclose the course of fate.

The persecutions of Valentinian in Rome were directed against magical ceremonies. The Pagans, who <small>Cruelty of Valentinian.</small> remembered the somewhat ostentatious lenity and patience of Julian on the public tribunal, might contrast the more than inexorable, the inquisitorial and sanguinary, justice of the Christian Valentinian, even in ordinary cases, with the benignant precepts of his religion. But justice with Valentinian, in all cases, more particularly in these persecutions, degenerated into savage tyranny. The Emperor kept two fierce bears by his own chamber, to which the miserable criminals were thrown in his presence, while the unrelenting Valentinian listened with ferocious delight to their groans. One of these animals, as a reward for his faithful service to the state, received his freedom, and was let loose into his native forest.[1]

Maximin, the representative of Valentinian at Rome, *Trials in Rome before Maximin.* administered the laws with all the vindictive ferocity, but without the severe dignity, of his imperial master. Maximin was of an obscure and barbarian family, settled in Pannonia. He had attained the government of Corsica and Sardinia, and subsequently of Tuscany. He was promoted in Rome to the important office of superintendent of the markets of the city. During the illness of Olybius, the prefect of Rome, the supreme judicial authority had been delegated to Maximin. Maximin was himself rumoured to have dabbled in necromantic arts; and lived in constant terror of accusation till released by the death of his accomplice. This rumour may create a suspicion that Maximin was, at least at the time at which the accusation pointed, a Pagan. The Paganism of a large proportion of his victims is more evident. The first trial over which Maximin presided was a charge made by Chilon, vicar of the prefects, and his wife, Maximia, against three

---

[1] The Christians did not escape these legal murders, constantly perpetrated by the orders of Valentinian. In Milan the place where three obscure victims were buried was called *ad Innocentes*. When he had condemned the decurions of three towns to be put to death, in a remonstrance against their execution, it was stated that they would be worshipped as martyrs by the Christians. Amm. Marc. xxvii. 7.

obscure persons for attempting their lives by magical arts: of these, one was a soothsayer.[u] Cruel tortures extorted from these miserable men a wild string of charges at once against persons of the highest rank and of the basest degree. All had tampered with unlawful arts, and had mingled with them the crimes of murder, poisoning, and adultery. A general charge of magic hung over the whole city. Maximin poured these dark rumours into the greedy ear of Valentinian, and obtained the authority which he coveted, for making a strict inquisition into these offences, for exacting evidence by torture from men of every rank and station, and for condemning them to a barbarous and ignominious death. The crime of magic was declared of equal enormity with treason; the rights of Roman citizenship, and the special privileges granted by the imperial edicts, were suspended;[v] neither the person of senator or dignitary was sacred against the scourge or the rack. The powers of this extraordinary commission were exercised with the utmost latitude and most implacable severity. Anonymous accusations were received; Maximin was understood to have declared that no one should be esteemed innocent whom he chose to find guilty.

But the details of this persecution belong to our history only as far as they relate to religion. On general grounds, it may be inferred, that the chief brunt of this sanguinary persecution fell on the Pagan party. Magic—although, at that time, perhaps, the insatiate curiosity about the future, the indelible passion for supernatural excitement, and even more criminal designs, might betray

---

[u] Haruspex.
[v] Juris prisci justitia et divorum arbitria. Amm. Marc.

some few professed Christians into this direct treason
against their religion—was an offence which, in general,
would have been held in dread and abhorrence by the
members of the church. In the laws it is invariably
denounced as a Pagan crime. The aristocracy of Rome
were the chief victims of Maximin's cruelty, and in
this class, till its final extinction, was the stronghold of
Paganism. It is not assuming too much influence for the
Christianity of that age, to consider the immoralities and crimes, the adulteries and the poisonings, which were mingled up with these charges
of magic, as the vestiges of the old unpurified Roman
manners. The Christianity of that period ran into the
excess of monastic asceticism, for which the enthusiasm,
to judge from the works of St. Jerome, was at its height;
and this violation of nature had not yet produced its
remote but apparently inevitable consequence—dissoluteness of morals. In almost every case recorded by
the historian may be traced indications of Pagan religious usages. A soothsayer, as it has appeared, was
involved in the first criminal charge. While his meaner
accomplices were beaten to death by straps loaded with
lead, the judge having bound himself by an oath that
they should neither die by fire nor steel, the soothsayer,
to whom he had made no such pledge, was burned alive.
The affair of Hymettius betrays the same connexion
with the ancient religion. Hymettius had been accused, seemingly without justice, of malversation in his
office of proconsul of Africa, in the supplies of corn to
the metropolis. A celebrated soothsayer (haruspex),
named Amantius, was charged with offering sacrifices,
by the command of Hymettius, with some unlawful or
treasonable design. Amantius resisted the torture with
unbroken courage; but among his papers was found a

Connexion of these crimes with Paganism.

writing of Hymettius, of which one part contained bitter invectives against the avaricious and cruel Valentinian; the other implored Amantius, by sacrifices, to induce the gods to mitigate the anger of both the Emperors. Amantius suffered capital punishment. A youth named Lollianus, convicted of inconsiderately copying a book of magical incantations and condemned to exile, had the rashness to appeal to the Emperor, and suffered death. Lollianus was the son of Lampadius, formerly prefect of Rome,* and, for his zeal for the restoration of the ancient buildings, and his vanity in causing his own name to be inscribed on them, was called the Lichen. Lampadius, was probably a Pagan. The leader of that party, Prætextatus, whose unimpeachable character maintained the universal respect of all parties, was the head of a deputation to the Emperor,^y entreating him that the punishment might be proportionate to the offences, and claiming for the senatorial order their immemorial exemption from the unusual and illegal application of torture. On the whole, this relentless and sanguinary inquisition into the crime of magic, enveloping in one dreadful proscription a large proportion of the higher orders of Rome and of the West, even if not directly, must, incidentally, have weakened the cause of Paganism; connected it in many minds with dark and hateful practices; and altogether increased the deepening animosity against it.

In the East, the fate of Paganism was still more adverse. There is strong ground for supposing that the rebellion of Procopius was connected with the revival of Julian's party. It was assiduously rumoured abroad that Procopius had

In the East, rebellion of Procopius. A.D. 365.

---

* Tillemont thinks Lampadius to have been a Christian; but his reasons are to me inconclusive.
^y Amm. Marc. xxvii. 1, &c.

been designated as his successor by the expiring Julian. Procopius, before the soldiery, proclaimed himself the relative and heir of Julian.[a] The astrologers had predicted the elevation of Procopius to the greatest height—of empire, as his partisans fondly hoped,—of misery, as the ingenious seers expounded the meaning of their oracle after his death.[b] The Pagan and philosophic party were more directly and exclusively implicated in the fatal event, which was disclosed to the trembling Valens at Antioch, and brought as wide and relentless desolation on the East as the cruelty of Maximin on the West. It was mingled up with treasonable designs against the throne and the life of the Emperor. The magical ceremony of divination, which was denounced before Valens, was Pagan throughout all its dark and mysterious circumstances.[c] The tripod on which the conspirators performed their ill-omened rites was modelled after that at Delphi; it was consecrated by magic songs and frequent and daily ceremonies, according to the established ritual. The house where the rite was held was purified by incense: a kind of charger made of mixed metals was placed upon the altar, around the rim of which were letters at certain intervals. The officiating diviner wore the habit of a Heathen priest, the linen garments, sandals, and a fillet wreathed round his head, and held

A.D. 368.

---

[a] Amm. Marc. xxvi. 6.
[b] See Le Beau, iii. p. 250.
"Ὥστε αὐτὸν τῶν ἐπὶ ταῖς μεγίσταις ἀρχαῖς γνωρισθέντων, ἐν τῷ μεγέθει τῆς συμφορᾶς γενέσθαι διασημότερον. He was deceived by the Genethliaci. Greg. Nyss. de Fato.
[c] Philostorgius describes it as a prediction of the Gentile oracles. Τῶν Ἑλληνικῶν χρηστηρίων, lib. viii. c. 15.

I cannot but suspect that the prohibition of sacrifice mentioned by Libanius, which seems contrary to the general policy of the brothers, and was but partially carried into execution, may have been connected with these transactions.

a sprig of an auspicious plant in his hand; he chanted the accustomed hymn to Apollo, the god of prophecy. The divination was performed by a ring running round on a slender thread and pointing to certain letters, which formed an oracle in heroic verse, like those of Delphi. The fatal prophecy then pointed to the three first and the last letters of a name, like *Theodorus*, as the fated successor of Valens.

Among the innumerable victims to the fears and the vengeance of Valens, whom the ordinary prisons were not capacious enough to contain, those who either were, or were suspected of having been entrusted with the fatal secret, were almost all the chiefs of the philosophic party. Hilarius of Phrygia, with whom are associated, by one historian, Patricius of Lydia, and Andronicus of Caria, all men of the most profound learning,[c] and skilled in divination, were those who had been consulted on that unpardoned and unpardonable offence, the enquiring the name of the successor to the reigning sovereign. They were, in fact, the conductors of the magic ceremony; and in their confession betrayed the secret circumstances of the incantation. Some, among whom appears the name of Iamblichus, escaped by miracle from torture and execution.[d] Libanius himself (this may be observed as evidence how closely magic and philosophy were mingled up together in the popular opinion) had already escaped with difficulty two charges of unlawful practices;[e] on this occasion, to the general surprise, he had the same good fortune: either the favour or the clemency of the Emperor, or some interest with the general accusers of his friends, exempted him from the common peril. Of those whose

---

[c] Zosimus, iv. 15   [d] See Zonaras, 13, 2   [e] Vit. i. 114.

sufferings are recorded, Pasiphilus resisted the extremity of torture rather than give evidence against an innocent man: that man was Eutropius, who held the rank of proconsul of Asia. Simonides, though but a youth, was one of the most austere disciples of philosophy. He boldly admitted that he was cognisant of the dangerous secret, but he kept it undivulged. Simonides was judged worthy of a more barbarous death than the rest; he was condemned to be burned alive; and the martyr of philosophy calmly ascended the funeral pile.

The fate of Maximus, since the death of Julian, had been marked with strange vicissitude. With Priscus, on the accession of Valentinian, he was summoned before the imperial tribunal; the blameless Priscus was dismissed, but Maximus, who, according to his own friends, had displayed, during the life of Julian, a pomp and luxuriousness unseemly in a philosopher, was sent back to Ephesus and amerced in a heavy fine, utterly disproportioned to philosophic poverty. The fine was mitigated, but, in its diminished amount, exacted by cruel tortures. Maximus, in his agony, entreated his wife to purchase poison to rid him of his miserable life. The wife obeyed, but insisted on taking the first draught:—she drank, expired, and Maximus—declined to drink. He was so fortunate as to attract the notice of Clearchus, proconsul of Asia; he was released from his bonds; rose in wealth and influence, returned to Constantinople; and resumed his former state. The fatal secret had been communicated to Maximus. He had the wisdom, his partisans declared the prophetic foresight, to discern the perilous consequences of the treason. He predicted the speedy death of himself and of all who were in possession of the secret. He added, it is said, a more wonderful oracle; that the Emperor himself would soon perish by a strange death, and not even find burial. Maximus was apprehended and carried to Antioch. After a hasty trial, in which he confessed his knowledge of the oracle, but declared that he esteemed it unworthy of a philosopher to divulge a secret entrusted to him by his friends, he was taken back to Ephesus, and there executed with all the rest of his party who were implicated in the conspiracy. Festus, it is said, who presided over the execution, was haunted in after life by a vision of Maximus dragging him to judgement before the infernal deities.[f] Though a despiser of the gods, a Christian, Festus was compelled by his terrors to sacrifice to the Eumenides, the avengers of blood; and having so done, he fell down dead. So completely did the cause of the Pagan deities appear involved with that of the persecuted philosophers.

Nor was this persecution without considerable influence on the literature of Greece. So severe an inquisition was instituted into the possession of magical books, that, in order to justify their sanguinary proceedings, vast heaps of manuscripts relating to law and general literature were publicly burned, as if they contained unlawful matter. Many men of letters throughout the East in their terror destroyed their whole libraries, lest some innocent or unsuspected work should be seized by the ignorant or malicious informer, and bring them unknowingly within the relentless penalties of the law.[g] From this period, philosophy is

---

[f] Eunap. Vit. Maxim. Amm. Marc. xxix. 1.
[g] Amm. Marcell. xxix. 1. Inde factum est per Orientales provincias, ut omnes metu similium exurerent libraria omnia; tantus universos invaserat terror, xxix. 2. Compare Heyne, note on Zosimus.

almost extinct, and Paganism, in the East, drags on its
silent and inglorious existence, deprived of its literary
aristocracy, and opposing only the inert resistance of
habit to the triumphant energy of Christianity.

Arianism, under the influence of Valens, maintained
its ascendancy in the East. Throughout the
whole of that division of the empire, the two
forms of Christianity still subsisted in irreconcilable
hostility. Almost every city had two prelates, each at
the head of his separate communion; the one, according
to the powers or the numbers of his party, assuming
the rank and title of the legitimate bishop, and looking
down, though with jealous animosity, on his factious
rival. During the life of Athanasius the see of
Alexandria remained faithful to the Trinitarian doctrines.
For a short period, indeed, the prelate was obliged to
retire, during what is called his fifth exile, to the tomb
of his father; but he was speedily welcomed back by
the acclamations of his followers, and the baffled
imperial authority acquiesced in his peaceful rule till
his decease. But at his death, five years afterwards,
were renewed the old scenes of discord and bloodshed.

Palladius, the prefect of Egypt, received the
imperial commission to install the Arian
prelate, Lucius, on the throne of Alexandria. Palladius
was a Pagan, and the Catholic writers bitterly reproach
their rivals with this monstrous alliance. It was
rumoured that the Pagan population welcomed the
Arian prelate with hymns of gratulation as the friend of
the god Serapis, as the restorer of his worship.

In Constantinople, Valens had received baptism from
Eudoxus, the aged Arian prelate of that see.
Sacerdotal influence once obtained over the
feeble mind of Valens, was likely to carry him to any

extreme; yet, on the other hand, he might be restrained and overawed by calm and dignified resistance. In general, therefore, he might yield himself up as an instrument to the passions, jealousies, and persecuting violence of his own party; while he might have recourse to violence to place Demophilus on the episcopal throne of Constantinople, he might be awed into a more tolerant and equitable tone by the eloquence and commanding character of Basil. It is unjust to load the memory of Valens with the most atrocious crime which has been charged upon him by the vindictive exaggeration of his triumphant religious adversaries. As a deputation of eighty Catholic ecclesiastics of Constantinople were returning from Nicomedia, the vessel was burned, the crew took to the boat, the ecclesiastics perished to a man. As no one escaped to tell the tale, and the crew, if accomplices, were not likely to accuse themselves, we may fairly doubt the assertion that orders had been secretly issued by Valens to perpetrate this wanton barbarity.

The memorable interview with Saint Basil, as it is related by the Catholic party, displays, if the weakness, certainly the patience and toleration, of the sovereign—if the uncompromising firmness of the prelate, some of that leaven of pride with which he is taunted by Jerome. *Interview with Basil.*

During his circuit through the Asiatic provinces, the Emperor approached the city of Cæsarea in Cappadocia. Modestus, the violent and unscrupulous favourite of Valens, was sent before, to persuade the bishop to submit to the religion of the Emperor. Basil was inflexible. "Know you not," said the offended officer, "that I have power to strip you of all your possessions, to banish you, to deprive you of life?" *A.D. 371.*

"He," answered Basil, "who possesses nothing can lose nothing; all you can take from me is the wretched garments I wear, and the few books, which are my only wealth. As to exile, the earth is the Lord's; everywhere it will be my country, or rather my place of pilgrimage. Death will be a mercy; it will but admit me into life: long have I been dead to this world." Modestus expressed his surprise at this unusual tone of intrepid address. "You have never, then," replied the prelate, "before conversed with a bishop?" Modestus returned to his master. "Violence will be the only course with this man, who is neither to be appalled by menaces nor won by blandishments." But the Emperor shrunk from such harsh measures. His humbler supplication confined itself to the admission of Arians into the communion of Basil; but he implored in vain. The Emperor mingled with the crowd of undistinguished worshippers; but he was so impressed by the solemnity of the Catholic service, the deep and full chanting of the psalms, the silent adoration of the people, the order and the majesty, as well as by the calm dignity of the bishop and of his attendant clergy, which appeared more like the serenity of angels than the busy scene of mortal men, that, awe-struck and overpowered, he scarcely ventured to approach to make his offering. The clergy stood irresolute, whether they were to receive it from the infectious hand of an Arian; Basil, at length, while the trembling Emperor leaned for support on an attendant priest, condescended to advance and accept the oblation. But neither supplications, nor bribes, nor threats, could induce the bishop to admit the sovereign to the communion. In a personal interview, instead of convincing the bishop, Valens was so overpowered by the eloquence of Basil, as to bestow an endowment on the church for the use of the poor. A scene of mingled intrigue and asserted miracle ensued. The exile of Basil was determined, but the mind of Valens was alarmed by the dangerous illness of his son. The prayers of Basil were said to have restored the youth to life; but a short time after, having been baptized by Arian hands, he relapsed and died. Basil, however, maintained his place and dignity to the end.[h]

But the fate of Valens drew on; it was followed by the first permanent establishment of the barbarians within the frontiers of the Roman empire. Christianity now began to assume a new and important function, that assimilation and union between the conquerors and the conquered, which prevented the total extinction of the Roman civilisation, and the oppression of Europe by complete and almost hopeless barbarism. However Christianity might have disturbed the peace, and therefore, in some degree, the stability of the empire by the religious factions which distracted the principal cities; however that foreign principle of celibacy, which had now become completely identified with it, by withdrawing so many active and powerful minds into the cloister or the hermitage, may have diminished the civil energies, and even have impaired the military forces of the empire,[i] yet the enterprising and victorious religion amply repaid those injuries by its influence in remodelling the new

Effect of Christianity in mitigating the evils of barbarian invasion.

---

[h] Greg. Naz. Orat. xx.; Greg. Nyss. contra Eunom.; and the ecclesiastical historians in loco.

[i] Valens, perceiving the actual operation of this unwarlike dedication of so many able-bodied men to useless inactivity, attempted to correct the evil by law, and by the strong interference of the government. He invaded the monasteries and solitary hermitages of Egypt, and swept the monks by thousands into the ranks of his army. But a reluctant Egyptian monk would, in general, make but an indifferent soldier.

state of society. If treacherous to the interests of the Roman empire, it was true to those of mankind. Throughout the whole process of the resettling of Europe and the other provinces of the empire, by the migratory tribes from the north and east, and the vast system of colonisation and conquest, which introduced one or more new races into every province, Christianity was the one common bond, the harmonising principle, which subdued to something like unity the adverse and conflicting elements of society. Christianity, no doubt, while it discharged this lofty mission, could not but undergo a great and desecrating change. It might repress, but could not altogether subdue, the advance of barbarism; it was constrained to accommodate itself to the spirit of the times; while struggling to counteract barbarism, itself became barbarised. It lost at once much of its purity and its gentleness; it became splendid and imaginative, warlike, and at length chivalvous.

When a country in a comparatively high state of civilisation is overrun by a foreign and martial horde, in numbers too great to be absorbed by the local population, the conquerors usually establish themselves as a kind of armed aristocracy, while the conquered are depressed into a race of slaves. Where there is no connecting, no intermediate power, the two races co-exist in stern and implacable hostility. The difference in privilege, and often in the territorial possession of the land, is increased and rendered more strongly marked by the total want of communion in blood. Intermarriages, if not, as commonly, prohibited by law, are almost entirely discountenanced by general opinion. Such was, in fact, the ordinary process in the formation of the society which arose out of the ruins of the Roman empire. The conquerors became usually a military aristocracy; assumed the property in the conquered lands, or, at least, a considerable share in the landed estates, and laid the groundwork for that feudal system which was afterwards developed with more or less completeness in different countries of Europe.

One thing alone in some cases, tempered, during the process of conquest, the irreclaimable hostility; in all, after the final settlement, moulded up together in some degree the adverse powers. Where, as in the Gothic invasion, it had made some previous impression on the invading race, Christianity was constantly present, silently mitigating the horrors of the war, and afterwards blending together, at least to a certain extent, the rival races. At all times, it became the connecting link, the intermediate power, which gave some community of interest, some similarity of feeling, to the master and the slave. They worshipped at least the same God, in the same church; and the care of the same clergy embraced both with something of an harmonising and equalising superintendence. The Christian clergy occupied a singular position in this new state of society. At the earlier period, they were, in general, Roman; later, though sometimes barbarian by birth, they were Roman in education. When the prostration of the conquered people was complete, there was still an order of people, not strictly belonging to either race, which maintained a commanding attitude, and possessed certain authority. The Christian bishop confronted the barbarian sovereign or took his rank among the leading nobles. During the invasion, the Christian clergy, though their possessions were ravaged in the indiscriminate warfare; though their persons were not always secure from insult, or from slavery;

yet, on the whole, retained, or very soon resumed, a
certain sanctity, and hastened, before long, to wind
their chains around the minds of the conquerors. Before
a new invasion, Christianity had, in general, mingled
the invaders with the invaded; till at length Europe,
instead of being a number of disconnected kingdoms,
hostile in race, in civil polity, in religion, was united in
a kind of federal Christian republic, on a principle of
unity, acknowledging the supremacy of the Pope.

<small>Their im-
portance in
this new state
of things.</small> The overweening authority claimed and exercised by
the clergy; their existence as a separate and
exclusive caste, at this particular period in the
progress of civilisation, became of the highest
utility. A religion without a powerful and separate
sacerdotal order, even, perhaps, if that order had not in
general been bound to celibacy and so prevented from
degenerating into an hereditary caste, would have been
absorbed and lost in the conflict and confusion of the
times. Religion, unless invested by general opinion in
high authority, and that authority asserted by an active
and incorporated class, would scarcely have struggled
through this complete disorganisation of all the existing
relations of society. The respect which the clergy
maintained was increased by their being almost the exclusive possessors of that learning which commands the
reverence even of barbarians, when not actually engaged
in war. A religion which rests on a written record,
however that record may be but rarely studied, and by
a few only of its professed interpreters, enforces general
respect to literary attainment. Though the traditional commentary may overload or supersede the
original book, the commentary itself is necessarily
committed to writing, and becomes another subject of
honoured and laborious study. All other kinds of litera-

ture, as far as they survive, gladly rank themselves under the protection of that which commands reverence for its religious authority. The cloister or the religious foundation thus became the place of refuge to all that remained of letters or of arts. Knowledge brooded in secret, though almost with unproductive, yet with life-sustaining warmth, over these secluded treasures. But it was not merely an inert and quiescent resistance which was thus offered to barbarism; it was perpetually extending its encroachments, as well as maintaining its place. Perhaps the degree to which the Roman language modified the Teutonic tongues may be a fair example of the extent to which the Roman civilisation generally leavened the manners and the laws of the Northern nations.

The language of the conquered people lived in the religious ritual. Throughout the rapid succession of invaders who passed over Europe, seeking their final settlement, some in the remotest province of Africa, before the formation of other dialects, the Latin was kept alive as the language of Western Christianity. The clergy were its conservators, the Vulgate Bible and the offices of the church its depositaries, unviolated by any barbarous interruption, respected as the oracles of divine truth. But the constant repetition of this language in the ears of the mingled people can scarcely have been without influence in increasing and strengthening the Roman element in the common language, which gradually grew up from mutual intercourse, intermarriage, and all the other bonds of community which blended together the various races.

The old municipal institutions of the empire probably owed their permanence, in no inconsiderable degree, to

Christianity. It has been observed in what manner

<small>on the municipal institutions.</small> the decurionate, the municipal authorities of each town, through the extraordinary and oppressive system of taxation, from guardians of the liberties of the people, became mere passive and unwilling agents of the Government. Responsible for payments which they could not exact, men of opulence, men of humanity, shrunk from the public offices. From objects of honourable ambition, these functions had become burdens, loaded with unrepaid unpopularity, assumed by compulsion, and exercised with reluctance. The *defensors*, instituted by Valentinian and Valens, however they might afford temporary protection and relief to the lower orders, scarcely exercised any long or lasting influence on the state of society. Yet the municipal authorities at least retained the power of administering the laws; and, as the law became more and more impregnated with Christian sentiment, it assumed something of a religious as well as civil authority. The magistrate became, as it were, an ally of the Christian bishop; the institutions had a sacred character, besides that of their general utility. Whatever remained of commerce and of art subsisted chiefly among the old Roman population of the cities, which was already Christian; and hence, perhaps, the guilds and fraternities of the trades, which may be traced up to an early period, gradually assumed a sort of religious bond of union. In all points, the Roman civilisation and Christianity, when the latter had completely pervaded the various orders of men, began to make common cause; and during all the time that this disorganisation of conquest and new settlement was taking place in this groundwork of the Roman social system, and the loose elements of society were severing

by gradual disunion, a new confederative principle arose in these smaller aggregations, as well as in the general population of the empire. The church became another centre of union. Men incorporated themselves together, not only, nor so much, as fellow-citizens, as fellow-Christians. They submitted to an authority co-ordinate with the civil power, and united as members of the same religious fraternity.

Christianity, to a certain degree, changed the general habits of men. For a time, at least, they were less public, more private and domestic men. The tendency of Christianity, while the Christians composed a separate and distinct community, to withdraw men from public affairs; their less frequent attendance on the courts of law, which were superseded by their own peculiar arbitration; their repugnance to the ordinary amusements, which soon, however, in the large cities, such as Antioch and Constantinople, wore off—all these principles of disunion ceased to operate when Christianity became the dominant, and at length the exclusive, religion. The Christian community became the people; the shows, the pomps, the ceremonial of the religion, replaced the former seasons of periodical popular excitement; the amusements,—which were not extirpated by the change of sentiment, some theatrical exhibitions, and the chariot race,—were crowded with Christian spectators; Christians ascended the tribunals of law: not only the spirit and language of the New Testament, but likewise of the Old, entered both into the Roman jurisprudence and into the various barbarian codes, in which the Roman law was mingled with the old Teutonic usages. Thus Christianity was perpetually discharging the double office of conservator, with regard to the social institutions with which she had entered into alliance; and of mediator between the conflicting races which she was gathering together under her own wing. Where the relation between the foreign conqueror and the conquered inhabitant of the empire was that of master and slave, the Roman ecclesiastic still maintained his independence, and speedily regained his authority; he only admitted the barbarian into his order on the condition that he became to a certain degree Romanised; and there can be no doubt that the gentle influence of Christian charity and humanity was not without its effect in mitigating the lot, or at least in consoling the misery of the change from independence or superiority, to humiliation and servitude. Where the two races mingled, as seems to have been the case in some of the towns and cities, on more equal terms, by strengthening the municipal institutions with something of a religious character, and by its own powerful federative principle, it condensed them much more speedily into one people, and assimilated their manners, habits, and usages.

Christianity had early, as it were, prepared the way for this amalgamation of the Goths with the Roman empire. In their first inroads during the reign of Gallienus, when the Goths ravaged a large part of the Roman empire, they carried away numbers of slaves, especially from Asia Minor and Cappadocia. Among these were many Christians. The slaves subdued the conquerors; the gentle doctrines of Christianity made their way to the hearts of the barbarous warriors. The families of the slaves continued to supply the priesthood to this growing community. A Gothic bishop,[k] with a Greek name, Theophilus,

Early Christianity among the Goths.

---

[k] Philostorgius, ii. 5.

CHAP. VII.   THE GOTHIC OF ULPHILAS.   55

attended at the council of Nicæa; Ulphilas, at the time of the invasion in the reign of Valens, consecrated bishop of the Goths during an embassy to Constantinople, was of Cappadocian descent.[m] Among the Goths, Christianity first assumed its new office, the advancement of general civilisation, as well as of purer religion. It is difficult to suppose that the art of writing was altogether unknown to the Goths before the time of Ulphilas. The language seems to have attained a high degree of artificial perfection before it was employed by that prelate in the translation of the Scriptures.[n] Still the Mœso-Gothic alphabet, of which the Greek is by far the principal element, was generally adopted by the Goths.[o] It was universally disseminated; it was perpetuated, until the extinction or absorption of the Gothic race in other tribes, by the translation of the sacred writings. This was the work of Ulphilas, who, in his version of the Scriptures,[p] is reported to have omitted,

Ulphilas's version of the Scriptures.

---

[m] Socrates, ii. 41.
[n] The Gothic of Ulphilas is the link between the East and Europe, the transition state from the Sanscrit to the modern Teutonic languages. It is possible that the Goths, after their migration from the East to the north of Germany, may have lost the art of writing, partly from the want of materials. The German forests would afford no substitute for the palm-leaves of the East; they may have been reduced to the barbarous runes of the other Heathen tribes. Compare Bopp., Conjugations System.
[o] The Mœso-Gothic alphabet has twenty-five letters, of which fifteen are evidently Greek, eight Latin. The two, th and hw, to which the Greek and Latin have no corresponding sound, are derived from some other quarter. They are most likely ancient characters. The th resembles closely the runic letter, which expresses the same sound. See St. Martin, note on Le Beau, lii. p. 120.
[p] The greater part of the fragments of Ulphilas's version of the Scriptures now extant is contained in the celebrated Codex Argenteus, now at Upsala. This splendid MS., written in silver letters, on parchment of a purple ground, contains almost the whole four Gospels. Knittel, in 1762, discovered five chapters of St. Paul's Epistle to the Romans, in a Palimpsest MS. at Wolfenbuttel. The best edition of the whole of this is by J. Christ.

with a Christian, but vain, precaution, the books of Kings, lest, being too congenial to the spirit of his countrymen, they should inflame their warlike enthusiasm. Whether the genuine mildness of Christianity, or some patriotic reverence for the Roman empire, from which he drew his descent, influenced the pious bishop, the martial ardour of the Goths was not the less fatal to the stability of the Roman empire. Christianity did not even mitigate the violence of the shock with which, for the first time, a whole host of Northern barbarians was thrown upon the empire, never again to be shaken off. This Gothic invasion, which first established a Teutonic nation within the frontier of the empire, was conducted with all the ferocity—provoked indeed on the part of the Romans by the basest treachery—of hostile races with no bond of connection.⁴

The pacificatory effect of the general conversion of the Goths to Christianity was impeded by the form of faith which they embraced. The Gothic prelates, Ulphilas among the rest, who visited the court of Constantinople, found the Arian bishops in possession of the chief authority; they were the recognised prelates of the empire. Whether their less

---

Zahn, Weissenfels, 1805. Since that time, M. Mai has published, from Milan Palimpsests, several other fragments, chiefly of the other Epistles of St. Paul. Milan, 1819. St. Martin, notes to Le Beau, III. 100. On the Gothic translation of the Scriptures. See Socrat. iv. 33, Sozom. vi. 37. Philostorgius, ii. 5. Compare Throdoret, v. 30-31. A complete edition of the remains of the Bible of Ulphilas was published by Dr. Gabelentz and Dr. Löbe, 1836, but the most useful edition is that of Massmann, Stuttgart, 1857.

⁴ It is remarkable to find a Christian priest employed as an ambassador between the Goths and the Romans, and either the willing or undesigning instrument of that stratagem of the Gothic general which was so fatal to Valens. Amm. Marc. xxxi. 12.

cultivated minds were unable to comprehend, or their language to express, the fine and subtle distinctions of the Trinitarian faith, or they were persuaded, as it was said, by the Arian bishops that it was mere verbal dispute, these doctrines were introduced among the Goths before their passage of the Danube, or their settlement within the empire. The whole nation received this form of Christianity; from them it appears to have spread, first embracing the other branch of the nation, the Ostrogoths, among the Gepidæ, the Vandals, and the Burgundians.* Among the barbaric conquerors was the stronghold of Arianism; while it was gradually repudiated by the Romans both in the East and in the West, it raised its head, and obtained a superiority which it had never before attained, in Italy and Spain. Whether more congenial to the simplicity of the barbaric mind, or in some respects cherished on one side by the conqueror as a proud distinction, and more cordially detested by the Roman population, as the creed of their barbarous masters, Arianism appeared almost to make common cause with the Teutonic invaders, and only fell with the Gothic monarchies in Italy and in Spain. While Gratian and Valentinian the Second espoused the cause of Trinitarianism in the West (we shall hereafter resume the Christian history of that division of the empire), by measures which show that their sacerdotal advisers were men of greater energy and decision than their civil ministers,

---

* "Sic quoque Visigothi a Valente Imperatore Ariani potius quam Christiani effecti. De cætero tam Ostrogothis, quam Gepidis parentibus suis per affectionis gratiam evangelizantes, hujus perfidiæ culturam docentes omnem ubique linguæ hujus nationem ad culturam hujus sectæ incitavere." Jornand. c. 25.

Arianism subsisted almost as a foreign and barbarous form of Christianity.*

---

* The Bible of Ulphilas was the Bible of all the Gothic races. Massmann, Die Unruhe wie die Nothdrang des äusseren Lebens, der inwohnenden Thatkreich des einheitlichen nordischen Menschengeschlechtes, das die Welt erneuen und befreien sollte, führte dasselbe von den friedlichen Ufern der Ostsee über die Donau vielmals bis vor die Thore des Constantinopel, zu den blutbetränkten Gestaden des Schwarzsee wie des Mittelmeeres, bis tief nach Asien, in und über Italien und Frankreich bis nach Spanien und Africa, überall aber trugen sie Ulfilas Bibel mit sich."—Einleitung X. Massmann observes, p. xliii., that there is no trace of Arianism in the surviving remains of the Gothic translation of the New Testament. The Gothic of Philip ii. 6. has been misunderstood. The Arian Goths professed to adhere to the words of Scripture, they avoided the Homoiousios and Homoousios; they called themselves Catholics, and were singularly tolerant of the orthodox tenets and of the Catholic clergy. Compare Latin Christianity, Book III. c. 2.

CHAPTER VIII.

Theodosius. Abolition of Paganism.

THE fate of Valens summoned to the empire a sovereign not merely qualified to infuse a conservative vigour into the civil and military administration of the empire, but to compress into one uniform system the religion of the Roman world. It was necessary that Christianity should acquire a complete predominance, and that it should be consolidated into one vigorous and harmonious system. The relegation, as it were, of Arianism among the Goths and other barbarous tribes, though it might thereby gain a temporary accession of strength, did not permanently impede the final triumph of Trinitarianism. While the imperial power was thus lending its strongest aid for the complete triumph and concentration of Christianity, from the peculiar character of the mind of Theodosius, the sacerdotal order, on the strength and unity of which was to rest the permanent influence of Christianity during the approaching centuries of darkness, assumed new energy. A religious emperor, under certain circumstances, might have been the most dangerous adversary of the priestly power; he would have asserted with vigour, which could not at that time be resisted, the supremacy of the civil authority. But the weaknesses, the vices, of the great Theodosius, bowed him down before the aspiring priesthood, who, in asserting and advancing their own authority, were asserting the cause of humanity. The passionate tyrant, at the feet of the Christian prelate, deploring the rash resentment which had condemned a whole city to massacre; the prelate exacting the severest penance for the outrage on justice and on humanity, stand in extraordinary contrast with the older Cæsars, themselves the priesthood, without remonstrance or without humiliation, glutting their lusts or their resentment with the misery and blood of their subjects.

The accession of Theodosius was hailed with universal enthusiasm throughout the empire. The pressing fears of barbaric invasion on every frontier silenced for a time the jealousies of Christian and Pagan, of Arian and Trinitarian. On the shore of each of the great rivers which bounded the empire, appeared a host of menacing invaders. The Persians, the Armenians, the Iberians, were prepared to pass the Euphrates or the eastern frontier; the Danube had already afforded a passage to the Goths; behind them were the Huns in still more formidable and multiplying swarms; the Franks and the rest of the German nations were crowding to the Rhine. Paganism, as well as Christianity, hastened to pay its grateful homage to the deliverer of the empire; the eloquent Themistius addressed Theodosius in the name of the imperial city; Libanius ventured to call on the Christian Emperor to revenge the death of Julian, that crime for which the gods were exacting just retribution. Pagan poetry awoke from its long silence; the glory of Theodosius and his family inspired its last noble effort in the verse of Claudian.

Theodosius was a Spaniard. In that province Christianity had probably found less resistance from the feeble provincial Paganism; nor was there, as in Gaul, an old national religion which lingered in the minds of the native population. Christianity was early and permanently established in the Peninsula. To Theodosius, who was but slightly tinged with the love of letters or the tastes of a more liberal education, the colossal temples of the East, or the more graceful and harmonious fabrics of Europe, would probably create no feeling but that of aversion from the shrines of idolatry. His Christianity was pure from any of the old Pagan associations; unsoftened, it may, perhaps, be said, by any feeling for art, and unawed by any reverence for the ancient religion of Rome: he was a soldier, a provincial, an hereditary Christian of a simple and unquestioning faith; and he added to all this the consciousness of consummate vigour and ability, and a choleric and vehement temperament.

Spain, throughout the Trinitarian controversy, perhaps from the commanding influence of Hosius, had firmly adhered to the Athanasian doctrines. The Manichean tenets, for which Priscillian and his followers suffered (the first heretics condemned to death for their opinions), were but recently introduced into the province.

Thus, by character and education, deeply impressed with Christianity, and that of a severe and uncompromising orthodoxy, Theodosius undertook the sacred obligation of extirpating Paganism, and of restoring to Christianity its severe and inviolable unity. Without tracing the succession of events throughout his reign, we may survey the Christian Emperor in his acts; first, as commencing, if not completing, the forcible extermination of Paganism; secondly, as confirming Christianity, and extending the authority of the sacerdotal order; and thirdly, as establishing the uniform orthodoxy of the Western Roman Church.

The laws of Theodosius against the Pagan sacrifices grew insensibly more and more severe. The inspection of the entrails of victims, and magic rites, were made capital offences. In A.D. 391, issued an edict prohibiting sacrifices, and even the entering into the temples. In the same year, a rescript was addressed to the court and prefect of Egypt, fining the governors of provinces who should enter a temple fifteen pounds of gold, and giving a kind of authority to the subordidinate officers to prevent their superiors from committing such offences. The same year, all unlawful sacrifices are prohibited by night or day, within or without the temples. In 392, all immolation is prohibited under the penalty of death, and all other acts of idolatry under forfeiture of the house or land in which the offence shall have been committed.[a]

The Pagan temples, left standing in all their majesty, but desecrated, deserted, overgrown, would have been the most splendid monument to the triumph of Christianity. If, with the disdain of conscious strength, she had allowed them to remain without victim, without priest, without worshipper, but uninjured and only exposed to natural decay from time and neglect, posterity would not merely have been grateful for the preservation of such stupendous and graceful models of art, but would have been strongly impressed with admiration of her magnanimity. But such magnanimity was neither to be expected from the age or the state of the religion. The Christians believed in the existence of the Heathen deities, with, perhaps, more undoubting faith than the Heathens themselves. The dæmons who inhabited the temples were spirits of malignant and pernicious power, which it was no less the interest than the duty of the Christian to expel from their proud and attractive

---

[a] Cod. Theod. xvi. 10, 7, 11, 12.

mansions.[b] The temples were the strongholds of the vigilant and active adversaries of Christian truth and Christian purity, of the enemies of God and man. The idols, it is true, were but wood and stone, but the beings they represented were real; they hovered, perhaps, in the air; they were still present in the consecrated spot, though rebuked and controlled by the mightier name of Christ, yet able to surprise the careless Christian in his hour of supineness or negligent adherence to his faith or his duty. When zeal inflamed the Christian populace to aggression upon any of these ancient and time-hallowed buildings, no doubt some latent awe lingered within; something of the suspense of doubtful warfare watched the issue of the strife. However they might have worked themselves up to the conviction that their ancient gods were but of this inferior and hostile nature, they would still be haunted by some apprehensions, lest they should not be secure of the protection of Christ, or of the angels and saints in the new tutelar hierarchy of Heaven. The old deities might not have been so completely rebuked and controlled as not to retain some power of injuring their rebellious votaries. It was at last, even to the faithful, a conflict between two unequal supernatural agencies; unequal indeed, particularly where the faith of the Christian was fervent and sincere, yet dependent for its event on the confidence of that faith which sometimes trembled at its own insufficiency, and feared lest it should be abandoned by the divine support in the moment of strife.

Throughout the East and West, the monks were the chief actors in this holy warfare. They are constantly

---

[b] " Dii enim Gentium dæmonia, ut Scriptura docet." Ambros. Epist. Imp. at Symmach. in Init.

spoken of by the Heathen writers in terms of the bitterest reproach and contempt. The most particular accounts of their proceedings relate to the East. Their desultory attacks were chiefly confined to the country, where the numberless shrines, images, and smaller temples were at the same time less protected, and more dear to the feelings of the people. In the towns, the larger fanes, if less guarded by the reverence of their worshippers, were under the protection of the municipal police.[c] Christianity was long almost exclusively the religion of the towns; and the term Paganism (notwithstanding the difficulties which embarrass this explanation) appears to owe its origin to this general distinction. The agricultural population, liable to frequent vicissitudes, trembled to offend the gods, on whom depended the plenty or the failure of the harvest. Habits are more intimately enwoven with the whole being in the regular labours of husbandry, than in the more various and changeable occupations of the city. The whole Heathen ritual was bound up with the course of agriculture: this was the oldest part both of the Grecian and Italian worship, and had experienced less change from the spirit of the times. In every field, in every garden, stood a deity; shrines and lesser temples were erected in every grove, by every fountain. The drought, the mildew, the murrain, the locusts,—whatever was destructive to the harvest or to the herd, was in the power of these capricious deities.[d] Even when converted to Christianity, the peasant trembled at the consequences of his own apostasy; and it is probable,

---

[c] Τολμᾶται μὲν οὖν κἂν ταῖς πόλεσι, τὸ πολὺ δὲ ἐν τοῖς ἀγροῖς. Liban. pro Templis.

[d] Καὶ τοῖς γεωργοῦσιν ἐν αὐτοῖς αἱ ἐλπίδες, ὅσαι περὶ τε ἀνδρῶν καὶ γυναικῶν, καὶ τέκνων καὶ βοῶν, καὶ τῆς σπειρομένης γῆς καὶ πεφυτευμένης. Liban. pro Templ.

that until the whole of this race of tutelary deities had been gradually replaced by what we must call the inferior divinities of Paganising Christianity, saints, martyrs, and angels, Christianity was not extensively or permanently established in the rural districts.[e]

During the reign of Constantine, that first sign of a decaying religion, the alienation of the property attached to its maintenance, began to be discerned. Some estates belonging to the temples were seized by the first Christian Emperor, and appropriated to the building of Constantinople. The favourites of his successor, as we have seen, were enriched by the donation of other sacred estates, and even of the temples themselves.[f] Julian restored the greater part of these prodigal gifts; but they were once more resumed under Valentinian, and the estates escheated to the imperial revenue. Soon after the accession of Theodosius, the Pagans, particularly in the East, saw the storm gathering in the horizon. The monks, with perfect impunity, traversed the rural districts, demolishing all the unprotected edifices. In vain did the Pagans appeal to the episcopal authority; the bishops declined to repress the over-active, perhaps, but pious zeal of their adherents. Already much destruction had taken place among the smaller rural shrines; the temples in Antioch, of Fortune, of Jove, of Athene, of Dionysus, were still standing; but the demolition of one stately temple, either at Edessa or

---

[e] This difference prevailed equally in the West. Fleury gives an account of the martyrdom of three missionaries by the rural population of a district in the Tyrol, who resented the abolition of their deities and their religious ceremonies. Hist. Eccles. v. 64.

[f] They were bestowed, according to Libanius, with no more respect than a horse, a slave, a dog, or a golden cup. The position of the slave between the horse and the dog, as cheap gifts, is curious enough. Liban. Op. v. ii. p. 185.

Palmyra, and this under the pretext of the imperial authority, had awakened all the fears of the Pagans. Libanius addressed an elaborate oration to the Emperor, "For the Temples."[g] Like Christianity under the Antonines, Paganism is now making its apology for its public worship. Paganism is reduced to still lower humiliation; one of its modest arguments against the destruction of its temples, is an appeal to the taste and love of splendour, in favour of buildings at least as ornamental to the cities as the imperial palaces.[h] The orator even stoops to suggest that, if alienated from religious uses, and let for profane purposes; they might be a productive source of revenue. But the eloquence and arguments of Libanius were wasted on deaf and unheeding ears. The war against the temples commenced in Syria; but it was not conducted with complete success. In many cities the inhabitants rose in defence of their sacred buildings, and, with the Persian on the frontier, a religious war might have endangered the allegiance of these provinces. The splendid temples, of which the ruins have recently been discovered, at Petra,[i] were defended by the zealous worshippers; and in those, as well as at Areopolis and Raphia, in Palestine, the Pagan ceremonial continued without disturbance. In Gaza, the temple of the tutelar deity, Marnas, the lord of men, was closed; but the Christians did not venture to violate it. The form of some of the Syrian edifices allowed their transformation into Christian churches; they were enclosed, and made

Oration of Libanius

Syrian temples destroyed.

---

[g] This oration was probably not delivered in the presence of Theodosius.
[h] Liban. pro Templis, p. 190.
[i] Laborde's Journey. In most of these buildings Roman architecture of the age of the Antonines is manifest, raised in general on the enormous substructions of much earlier ages.

to admit sufficient light for the services of the church. A temple at Damascus, and another at Heliopolis or Baalbec,[k] were consecrated to the Christian worship. Marcellus of Apamea was the martyr in this holy warfare. He had signalised himself by the destruction of the temples in his own city, particularly that of Jupiter, whose solid foundations defied the artificers and soldiery employed in the work of demolition, and required the aid of miracle to undermine them. But, on an expedition into the district of Apamea, called the Aulon, the rude inhabitants rose in defence of their sacred edifice, seized Marcellus, and burned him alive. The synod of the province refused to revenge on his barbarous enemies a death so happy for Marcellus and so glorious for his family.[m]

The work of demolition was not long content with these less famous edifices, these outworks of Paganism; it aspired to attack its strongest citadels, and, by the public destruction of one of the most celebrated temples in the world, to announce that Polytheism had for ever lost its hold upon the minds of men.[n]

It was considered the highest praise of the magnificent temple in Edessa, of which the roof was of re- Temple of markable construction, and which contained in Alexandria. its secret sanctuary certain very celebrated statues of wrought iron, and whose fall had excited the indignant

---

[k] If this (as indeed is not likely) was the vast Temple of the Sun, the work of successive ages, it is probable that a Christian church was enclosed in some part of its precincts. The sanctuary was usually taken for this purpose.

[m] Sozomen, vii. 15. Theodoret, v. 21.

[n] Compare throughout, Histoire de la Destruction du Paganisme dans l'Empire d'Orient, par Etienne Chastel, Paris, 1850. This work, crowned by the Institute, is perhaps not quite of so high order as that of M. Beugnot on the destruction of Paganism in the West, but is still a very valuable book.

F 2

eloquence of Libanius, to compare it to the Serapion in Alexandria. The Serapion, at that time, appeared secure in the superstition, which connected its inviolable sanctity, and the honour of its god,[a] with the rise and fall of the Nile, with the fertility and existence of Egypt, and, as Egypt was the granary of the East, the existence of Constantinople. The Pagans had little apprehension that the Serapion itself, before many years, would be levelled to the ground.

The temple of Serapis, next to that of Jupiter in the Capitol, was the proudest monument of Pagan religious architecture.[b] Like the more celebrated structures of the East, and that of Jerusalem in its glory, it comprehended within its precincts a vast mass of buildings, of which the temple itself formed the centre. It was built on an artificial hill, in the old quarter of the city, called Rhacotis. The ascent to it was by a hundred steps. All the substructure was vaulted over; and in these dark chambers, which communicated with each other, were supposed to be carried on the most fearful, and, to the Christian, abominable mysteries. All around the spacious level platform were the habitations of the priests, and of the ascetics dedicated to the worship of the god. Within these outworks of this city rather than temple, was a square, surrounded on all sides with a magnificent portico. In the centre arose the temple, on pillars of enormous magnitude and beautiful proportion. The work either of Alexander himself or of the first Ptolemy, aspired to unite the colossal grandeur of Egyptian with

---

[a] Libanius expresses himself to this ! bilis Roma in æternum attollit, nihil effect. orbis terrarum ambitiosius cernat."
[b] "Post Capitolium, quo se venera- Ammian. Marcell. xxii. 16.

the fine harmony of Grecian art. The god himself was the especial object of adoration throughout the whole country, and throughout every part of the empire into which the Egyptian worship had penetrated,[q] but more particularly in Alexandria; and the wise policy of the Ptolemies had blended together, under this pliant and all-embracing religion, the different races of their subjects. Egyptian and Greek met as worshippers of Serapis. The Serapis of Egypt was said to have been worshipped for ages at Sinope; he was transported from that city with great pomp and splendour, to be reincorporated, as it were, and reidentified with his ancient prototype. While the Egyptians worshipped in Serapis the great vivific principle of the universe, the fecundating Nile, holding the Nilometer for his sceptre, the Lord of Amen-ti, the President of the regions beyond the grave,—the Greeks, at the same time, recognised the blended attributes of their Dionysus, Helios, Æsculapius, and Hades.[r]

Worship of Serapis.

The colossal statue of Serapis embodied these various attributes.[s] It filled the sanctuary: its outstretched and all-embracing arms touched the walls; the right the one, the left the other. It was said to have been the work of Sesostris; it was made of all the metals fused together, gold, silver, copper, iron, lead, and tin; it was inlaid with all kinds of precious stones; the whole was polished, and appeared of an

Statue of Serapis.

---

[q] In Egypt alone he had forty-two temples; innumerable others in every part of the Roman empire. Aristid. Orat. in Canop.

[r] This appears to me the most natural interpretation of the celebrated passage in Tacitus. Compare De Guigniaut, Le Dieu Serapis et son Origine, originally written as a note for Bournouf's Translation of Tacitus.

[s] The statue is described by Macrobius, Saturn. l. 20.; Clemens Alexandrin. Exhortat. ad Gent. l. p. 42.; Rufinus, E. H. xi. 23.

azure colour. The measure or bushel, the emblem of productiveness or plenty, crowned its head. By its side stood the symbolic three-headed animal, one the fore-part of a lion, one of a dog, one of a wolf. In this the Greeks saw the type of their poetic Cerberus.[1] The serpent, the symbol of eternity, wound round the whole, and returned resting its head on the hand of the god.

The more completely the adoration of Serapis had absorbed the worship of the whole Egyptian pantheon, the more eagerly Christianity desired to triumph over the representative of Polytheism. However, in the time of Hadrian, the philosophic party may have endeavoured to blend and harmonise the two faiths,[u] they stood now in their old direct and irreconcileable opposition. The suppression of the internal feuds between the opposite parties in Alexandria, enabled Christianity to direct all its concentrated force against Paganism. Theophilus, the archbishop, was a man of boldness and activity, eager to seize and skilful to avail himself of every opportunity to inflame the popular mind against the Heathens. A priest of Serapis was accused and convicted of practising those licentious designs against the virtue of the female worshippers, so frequently attributed to the priesthood of the Eastern religions. The noblest and most beautiful women were persuaded to submit to the embraces of the god, whose place, under the favourable darkness caused by the sudden extinction of the lamps in the temple, was filled by the priest. These inauspicious

The first attacks on Paganism.

---

[1] According to the interpretation of Macrobius, the three heads represented the past, the present, and the future; the rapacious 'wolf' the past, the central lion the intermediate present, the fawning dog the hopeful future. * See the Letter of Hadrian, Vol. II. p. 106.

rumours prepared the inevitable collision. A neglected temple of Osiris or Dionysus had been granted by Constantius to the Arians of Alexandria. Theophilus obtained from the Emperor a grant of the vacant site for a new church, to accommodate the increasing numbers of the Catholic Christians. On digging the foundation, there were discovered many of the obscene symbols, used in the Bacchic or Osirian mysteries. Theophilus, with more regard to the success of his cause than to decency, exposed these ludicrous or disgusting objects, in the public market place, to the contempt and abhorrence of the people. The Pagans, indignant at this treatment of their sacred symbols, and maddened by the scorn and ridicule of the Christians, took up arms. The streets ran with blood; and many Christians who fell in this tumultuous fray received the honours of martyrdom. A philosopher, named Olympus, placed himself at the head of the Pagan party. Olympus had foreseen and predicted the ruin of the external worship of Polytheism. He had endeavoured to implant a profound feeling in the hearts of the Pagans which might survive the destruction of their ordinary objects of worship. "The statues of the gods are but perishable and material images; the eternal intelligences, which dwelt within them, have withdrawn to the heavens,"[1] Yet Olympus hoped, and at first with his impassioned eloquence succeeded, in rousing his Pagan compatriots to a bold defiance of the public authorities in support of their religion. Faction and rivalry supplied what was wanting to faith; and it appeared that Paganism would likewise boast its army

Olympus the philosopher.

[1] "Τλην ἑβαρτὴν καὶ ἰνδάλματα, δί τινα ἐνοικῆσαι αὐτοῖς, καὶ εἰς λόγων εἶναι τὰ ἀγάλματα, καὶ διὰ τοῦτο ἀφανισμὸν θνητότερον δοκιμεῖς· οὐρανὸν ἀνοστῆσαι. Sozom. H. E. vii. 15.

of martyrs,—martyrs, not indeed through patient submission to the persecutor, but in heroic despair perishing with their gods.

War in the city. The Pagans at first were the aggressors; they sallied from their fortress, the Serapion, seized the unhappy Christians whom they met, forced them to sacrifice on their altar, or slew them upon it, or threw them into the deep trench defiled with the blood and offal of sacrifice. In vain Evagrius, the prefect of Egypt, and Romanus, the commander of the troops, appeared before the gates of the Temple, remonstrated with the garrison, who appeared at the windows, against their barbarities, and menaced them with the just vengeance of the law. They were obliged to withdraw, baffled and disregarded, and to await the orders of the Emperor. Olympus exhorted his followers to the height of religious heroism. "Having made a glorious sacrifice of our enemies, let us immolate ourselves and perish with our gods." But before the rescript arrived,

Flight of Olympus. Olympus had disappeared: he had stolen out of the Temple, and embarked for Italy. The Christian writers do honour to his sagacity or to his prophetic powers, at the expense of his courage and fidelity to his party. In the dead of night, when all was slumbering around, and all the gates closed, he had heard the Christian Alleluia pealing from a single voice through the silent Temple. He acknowledged the sign, or the omen, and anticipated the unfavourable sentence of the Emperor, the fate of his faction and of his gods.

The eastern Pagans, it should seem, were little acquainted with the real character of Theodosius. When the rescript arrived they laid down their arms, and assembled in peaceful array before the Temple, as if they expected the sentence of the Emperor in their own favour.⁷ The officer began; the first words of the rescript plainly intimated the abhorrence of Theodosius against idolatry. Cries of triumph from the Christians interrupted the proceedings; the panic-stricken Pagans, abandoning their temple and their god, silently dispersed; they sought out the most secret places of refuge; they fled their country. Two of the celebrated pontiffs, one of Amoun, one of "the Ape," retired to Constantinople, where the one, Ammonius, taught in a school, and continued to deplore the fall of Paganism; Helladius, the other, was known to boast the part he had taken in the sedition of Alexandria, in which, with his own hand, he had slain nine Christians.⁸

Rescript of Theodosius.

The imperial rescript at once went beyond and fell short of the fears of the Pagans. It disdained to exact vengeance for the blood of the Christian martyrs, who had been so happy as to lay down their lives for their Redeemer; but it commanded the destruction of the idolatrous temples; it confiscated all the ornaments, and ordered the statues to be melted or broken up for the benefit of the poor.

Theophilus hastened in his triumphant zeal to execute the ordinance of the Emperor. Marching, with the prefect at the head of the military, the invaders

---

⁷ If the oration of Libanius, exhorting the Emperor to revenge the death of Julian, was really presented to Theodosius, it betrays something of the same ignorance. He seems to think his arguments not unlikely to meet with success; at all events, he appears not to have the least notion that Theodosius would not respect the memory of the apostate. ⁸ Socrat. Eccl. Hist. v. 16. Helladius is mentioned in a law of Theodosius the younger, as a celebrated grammarian elevated to certain honours. This law is, however, dated 425; at least five and thirty years after this transaction.

ascended the steps to the temple of Serapis. They
surveyed the vacant chambers of the priests
and the ascetics; they paused to pillage the
library;[a] they entered the deserted sanctuary; they
stood in the presence of the god. The sight of this
colossal image, for centuries an object of
worship, struck awe to the hearts of the
Christians themselves. They stood silent, inactive,
trembling. The archbishop alone maintained his
courage: he commanded a soldier to proceed to the
assault. The soldier struck the statue with his hatchet
on the knee. The blow echoed through the breathless
hall, but no sound or sign of divine vengeance ensued;
the roof of the Temple fell not to crush the sacrilegious
assailant nor did the pavement heave and quake
beneath his feet. The emboldened soldier climbed up to
the head and struck it off; it rolled upon the ground.
Serapis gave no sign of life, but a large colony of rats,
disturbed in their peaceful abode, ran about on all sides.
The passions of the multitude are always in extremes.
From breathless awe they passed at once to ungovernable mirth. The work of destruction went on amid
peals of laughter, coarse jests, and shouts of acclamation; and as the fragments of the huge body of Serapis
were dragged through the streets, the Pagans, with
that revulsion of feeling common to the superstitious
populace, joined in the insult and mockery against
their unresisting and self-abandoned god.[b]

---

[a] "Nos vidimus armaria librorum; quibus direptis, exinanita ea a nostris hominibus, nostris temporibus memorant." Oros. vi. 15.

[b] They were said to have discovered several of the tricks by which the priests of Serapis imposed on the credulity of their worshippers. An aperture of the wall was so contrived, that the light of the sun, at a particular time, fell on the face of Serapis. The sun was then thought to visit Serapis; and at the moment of their meeting, the flashing light threw a

CHAP. VIII. DEMOLITION OF THE TEMPLE.

The solid walls and deep foundations of the Temple offered more unsurmountable resistance to the baffled zeal of the Christians; the work of demolition proceeded but slowly with the massive architecture;* and some time after a church was erected in the precincts, to look down upon the ruins of idolatry, which still frowned in desolate grandeur upon their conquerors.[d]

Yet the Christians, even after their complete triumph, were not without some lingering terrors; the Pagans not without hopes that a fearful vengeance would be exacted from the land for this sacrilegious extirpation of their ancient deities. Serapis was either the Nile, or the deity who presided over the periodical inundations of the river. The Nilometer, which measured the rise of the waters, was kept in the Temple. Would the indignant river refuse its fertilising moisture; keep sullenly within its banks, and leave the ungrateful land blasted with perpetual drought and barrenness? As the time of the inundation approached, all Egypt was in a state of trembling suspense. Long beyond the accustomed day the waters remained at their usual level; there was no sign of overflowing. The people began to murmur; the murmurs swelled into indignant remonstrances; the usual rites and sacrifices were demanded from the reluctant prefect, who despatched a

---

smile on the lips of the Deity. There is another story of a magnet on the roof, which, as in the fable about Mohammed's coffin, raised either a small statue of the Deity, or the sun in a car with four horses, to the roof, and there held it suspended. A Christian withdrew the magnet, the car fell, and was dashed to pieces on the pavement.

* Compare Eunap. Vit. Ædesil, p. 44. edit. Boissonade.

[d] The Christians rejoiced in discovering the cross in various parts of the building; they were inclined to suppose it miraculous or prophetic of their triumph. But, in fact, the crux ansata is a common hieroglyphic, a symbol of life.

hasty messenger to the Emperor for instructions. There was every appearance of a general insurrection; the Pagans triumphed in their turn; but before the answer of the Emperor arrived, which replied, in uncompromising faith, "that if the inundation of the river could only be obtained by magic and impious rites, let it remain dry; the fertility of Egypt must not be purchased by an act of infidelity to God"[e]—suddenly, the waters began to swell, an inundation more full and extensive than usual spread over the land, and the versatile Pagans had now no course but to join again with the Christians in mockeries against the impotence of their gods.

But Christianity was not content with the demolition of the Serapion; its predominance throughout Egypt may be estimated by the bitter complaint of the Pagan writer: "Whoever wore a black dress (the monks are designated by this description) was invested in tyrannical power; philosophy and piety to the gods were compelled to retire into secret places, and to dwell in contented poverty and dignified meanness of appearance. The temples were turned into tombs for the adoration of the bones of the basest and most depraved of men who had suffered the penalty of the law, whom they made their gods."[f] Such was the light in which the martyr-worship of the Christians appeared to the Pagans.

The demolition of the Serapion was a penalty inflicted

---

[e] Improbable as it may seem, that such an answer should be given by a statesman like Theodosius, yet it is strongly characteristic of the times. The Emperor neither denies the power of the malignant dæmons worshipped by the idolaters, nor the efficacy of enchantments, to obtain their favour, and to force from them the retarded overflow of the river.

[f] Eunap. Vit. Ædesii, loc. cit.

on the Pagans of Alexandria for their sedition and sanguinary violence; but the example was too encouraging, the hope of impunity under the present government too confident, not to spread through other cities of Egypt. It moved on to Canopus, where the principle of humidity was worshipped in the form of a vase, with a human head. Theophilus, who considered Canopus within his diocese, marched at the head of his triumphant party, demolished the temples, abolished the rites, which were distinguished for their dissolute licence, and established monasteries in the place. Canopus, from a city of revel and debauchery, became a city of monks.*

The persecution extended throughout Egypt; but the vast buildings which even now subsist, the successive works of the Pharaohs, the Ptolemies, and the Roman Emperors, having triumphed alike over time, Christianity, and Mahommedanism, show either some reverent reluctance to deprive the country of its most magnificent ornaments, or the inefficiency of the instruments which they employed in the work of devastation. For once it was less easy for men to destroy than to preserve; the power of demolition was rebuked before the strength and solidity of these erections of primeval art.

The war, as we have seen, raged with the same partial and imperfect success in Syria; with less, probably, in Asia Minor; least of all in Greece. The demolition was nowhere general or systematic. Wherever monastic Christianity was completely predominant, there emulous zeal excited the laity to these

---

* The Christians laughed at Canopus being called "the conqueror of the gods." The origin of this name was, that the principle of fire, the god of the Chaldeans, had been extinguished by the water within the statue of Canopus, the principle of humidity.

aggressions on Paganism. But in Greece the noblest buildings of antiquity, at Olympia, Eleusis, Athens,[b] show in their decay the slower process of neglect and time, of accident and the gradual encroachment of later barbarism, rather than the iconoclastic destructiveness of early religious zeal.[i]

In the West, the task of St. Martin of Tours, the great extirpator of idolatry in Gaul, was comparatively easy; and his achievements by no means so much to be lamented as those of the destroyers of the purer models of architecture in the East. The life of this saint by Sulpicius, in which the comparatively polished and classical style singularly contrasts with the strange and legendary incidents which it relates, describes St. Martin as making regular campaigns into all the region, destroying, wherever he could, the shrines and temples of the Heathen, and replacing them by churches and monasteries. So completely was his excited imagination full of his work, that he declared that Satan often assumed the visible form of Jove, of Mercury, of Venus, or of Minerva, to divert him, no doubt, from his holy design, and to protect their trembling fanes.[k]

---

[b] The Parthenon, it is well known, was entire, till towards the close of the sixteenth century. Its roof was destroyed during the siege by the Venetians. See Spon. and Wheler's Travels.

[i] The council of Illiberis refused the honours of martyrdom to those who were killed while breaking idols Can. lx.

The invasion of the Goths (Eunapius accuses the black monks of having betrayed Thermopylæ to them) carried devastation into Greece and Peloponnesus. These newly-converted barbarians had no feeling for art. They burned Corinth, Amyclæ, Lacedæmon, Olympia, (from that time the games ceased) with all their glorious temples and noble statues. Zosimus asserts that Minerva preserved Athens. Her apparition appalled Alaric. But Ceres did not protect Eleusis. There was a frightful massacre of the Hierophants among the ruins of the temple. (Eunapius, in loc., I.ex. v. 0.) Compare Chastel, p. 215. Fahmerayer, Geschichte der Morea, 136.

[k] Sulpic. Sever. VII. B. Martini. p. 469.

CHAP. VIII.   PAGANISM AT ROME.   79

But the power and the majesty of Paganism were still concentred at Rome; the deities of the ancient faith found their last refuge in the capital of the empire. To the stranger, Rome still offered the appearance of a Pagan city: it contained one hundred and fifty-two temples, and one hundred and eighty smaller chapels or shrines, still sacred to their tutelary God, and used for public worship.[m] Christianity had neither ventured to usurp those few buildings which might be converted to her use, still less had she the power to destroy them. The religious edifices were under the protection of the prefect of the city, and the prefect was usually a Pagan; at all events, he would not permit any breach of the public peace, or violation of public property. Above all still towered the Capitol, in its unassailed and awful majesty, with its fifty temples or shrines, bearing the most sacred names in the religious and civil annals of Rome, those of Jove, of Mars, of Janus, of Romulus, of Cæsar, of Victory. Some years after the accession of Theodosius to the Eastern empire, the sacrifices were still performed as national rites at the public cost; the pontiffs made their offerings in the name of the whole human race. The Pagan orator ventures to assert that the Emperor dared not to endanger the safety of the empire by their abolition.[n] The Emperor still bore the title and insignia of the supreme Pontiff; the consuls before they entered upon their functions, ascended the Capitol;

Paganism at Rome.

---

[m] See the Descriptiones Urbis, which bear the names of Publicus Victor, and Sextus Rufus Festus. These works could not have been written before or long after the reign of Valentinian. Compare Beugnot, Histoire de la Destruction du Paganisme en Occident. M. Beugnot has made out, on more or less satisfactory evidence, a list of the deities still worshipped in Italy. t. i. L. viii. c. 9. St. Augustin, when young, was present at the rites of Cybele, about A. D. 374.

[n] Liban. pro Templis.

the religious processions passed along the crowded streets; and the people thronged to the festivals and theatres, which still formed part of the Pagan worship.

But the edifice had begun to tremble to its founda-
<small>Gratian, Emperor, A.D. 367. Valentinian II., A.D. 375. Theodosius, A.D. 379.</small> tions. The Emperor had ceased to reside at Rome; the mind of Theodosius, as afterwards that of Gratian, and that of the younger Valentinian, was free from those early inculcated and daily renewed impressions of the majesty of the ancient Paganism which still enthralled the minds of the Roman aristocracy. Of that aristocracy, the flower and the pride was Vettius Agorius Prætextatus.[a] In him the wisdom of Pagan philosophy blended with the serious piety of Pagan religion: he lived to witness the commencement of the last fatal change which he had no power to avert; he died, and his death was deplored as a public calamity, in time to escape the final extinction, or rather degradation, of
<small>A.D. 374.</small> Paganism. Only eight years before the fatal accession of Gratian, and the year of his own death, he had publicly consecrated twelve statues in the Capitol, with all becoming splendour, to the Dii curantes, the great guardian deities of Rome.[b] It was not only the ancient religion of Rome which still maintained some part of its dignity, all the other religions of the empire, which still publicly celebrated their rites, and retained their temples in the metropolis, concentred all their honours on Prætextatus, and took refuge, as it were, under the protection of his blameless

---

[a] See on Prætextatus, Macrob. Saturn. l. 2. Symmachi Epistolæ, l. 40. 43. 45., ii. 7. 34. 36. 53. 59. Hieronym. Epistolæ, xxiii.

[b] This appears from an inscription recently discovered (A.D. 1835), and published in the Bolletino of the Archæological Society of Rome. Compare Bunsen, Roms Beschreibung, vol. iii. p. 9.

CHAP. VIII.   PRÆTEXTATUS.   81

and venerable name. His titles in an extant inscription announce him as having attained, besides the countless honours of Roman civil and religious dignity, the highest rank in the Eleusinian, Phrygian, Syrian, and Mithriac mysteries.[a] His wife boasted the same religious titles; she was the priestess of the same mysteries, with the addition of some peculiar to the female sex.[b] She celebrated the funeral, even the apotheosis, of her noble husband with the utmost pomp: he was the last Pagan, probably, who received the honours of deification.[c] All Rome crowded, in sorrow and profound reverence, to the ceremony. In the language of the vehement Jerome there is a singular mixture of enforced respect and of aversion; he describes (to moralise at the awful change) and contrasts with his funeral the former triumphant ascent of the Capitol by Prætextatus amid the acclamations of the whole city; he admits the popularity of his life, but condemns him, without remorse, to eternal misery.[d]

A.D. 384.

---

[a] Augur, Pontifex Vestæ, Pontifex Solis, Quindecemvir, Curialis Herculis, sacratus Libero et Eleusiniis, Hierophanta, Neocorus, Taurobollatus, Pater Patrum. Gruter, p. 1102. No. 2.

[b] Sacrata apod Eleusinam Deo Baccho, Cereri, et Coræ, apud Lernam: Deo Libero, et Cereri, et Coræ, sacratæ apud Æginam Deabus; Taurobolitæ, Isiacæ, Hierophantia Deæ Hecatæ, sacratæ Deæ Cereris. Gruter, 309.

[c] Read the two beautiful poems, one a short one addressed by Vettius Agorius Prætextatus to his wife Aconia Fabia Paulina, the other, longer, by Paulina to her husband. I subjoin some lines from that of

Paulina,—

Te nam, marite, disciplinarum bono Purum ac pudicum sorte nactis eximens, In templa docts ac familiam divis dicas, Te teste cunctis imbuor mysteriis, Tu Dindymenes Attisooque antistitem Teletis honoras taurels consors piis, Hecates ministram trina secreta edoces, Cererisque Graiæ ta sacris dignari paras. Te propter omnes me beatam, me piam Cel-brant, quod ipse me bonam disseminas Totum per orbem. Ignota noscor omnibus, Nam te marito cui placere non queam. Exempla de me Romulæ matres petunt. Sobolemque pulchram, si tuæ similis, putant Optant probantque uuno viri nomo formosæ.

Apud Meyer Anthologia Latina, II. 198.

[d] ' O quanta rerum mutatio ! Ille quem ante paucos dies dignitatum omnium culmina precedebant, qui quasi de subjectis hostibus triumphavit, Capitolinas ascendit arces; quem

VOL. III.   G

Up to the accession of Gratian, the Christian Emperor had assumed, as a matter of course, the supremacy over the religion, as well as the state, of Rome. He had been formally arrayed in the robes of the sovereign Pontiff. For the first few years of his reign, Gratian maintained the inaggressive policy of his father Valentinian.ᵘ But the masculine mind of Ambrose obtained, and indeed had deserved by his public services, the supremacy over the feeble youth; and the influence of Ambrose began to reveal itself in a succession of acts, which plainly showed that the fate of Paganism drew near. When Gratian was in Gaul, the senate of Rome remembered that he had not been officially arrayed in the dignity of the supreme Pontificate. A solemn deputation from Rome attended to perform the customary ceremonial. The idolatrous honour was disdainfully rejected. The event was heard in Rome with consternation; it was the first overt act of separation between the religious and the civil power of the empire.ˣ The next hostile measure was still more unexpected. Notwithstanding the manifest authority assumed by Christianity, and by one of the Christian prelates, best qualified by his own determined character to wield at his will the weak and irresolute Gratian; notwithstanding the long ill-suppressed murmurs, and now bold and authoritative

---

plausu quodam et tripudio populus Romanus excepit, ad cujus intentum urbs universa commota est,—nunc desolatus et nudus, . . . non in lacteo cœli palatio ut uxor mentitur infelix, sed in sordentibus tenebris continetur. Hieronym. Epist. xxiii. vol. i. p. 135.

ˣ M. Beugnot considers that Gratian was tolerant of Paganism from his accession, A.D. 367 to 382. He was sixteen when he ascended the throne, and became the first Augustus on the death of Valens, A.D. 378.

ᵘ Zosimus, iv. 36. The date of this transaction is conjectural. The opinion of La Bastie, Mém. des Inscrip. xv. 141, is followed.

remonstrances, against all toleration, and all connivance at Heathen idolatry, it might have been thought that any other victim would have been chosen from the synod of gods; that all other statues would have been thrown prostrate, all other worship proscribed, before that of Victory. Constantius, though he had calmly surveyed the other monuments of Roman superstition, admired their majesty, and read the inscriptions over the porticos of the temples, had nevertheless given orders for the removal of this statue, and this alone,—its removal, it may be suspected not without some superstitious reverence—to the rival capital.[r] Victory had been restored by Julian to the Senate-house at Rome, where she had so long presided over the counsels of the conquering republic and of the empire. She had maintained her place during the reign of Valentinian. The decree that the statue of Victory was to be ignominiously dragged from its pedestal in the Senate-house, that the altar was to be removed, and the act of public worship, with which the Senate had for centuries of uninterrupted prosperity and glory commenced and hallowed its proceedings, discontinued, fell, like a thunderbolt, among the partisans of the ancient worship. Surprise yielded to indignation. By the advice of Prætextatus, a solemn deputation was sent to remonstrate with the Emperor. The Christian party in the Senate were strong enough to forward, through the Bishop Damasus, a counter-petition, declaring their resolution to abstain from attendance in the Senate so long as it should be defiled

Statue of Victory.

A.D. 392.

---

[r] Constantius (the whole account of this transaction is vague and uncircumstantial), acting in the spirit of his father, who collected a great number of the best statues to adorn the new capital, perhaps intended to transplant Victory to Constantinople.

by an idolatrous ceremonial. Gratian coldly dismissed the deputation though headed by the eloquent Symmachus, as not representing the unanimous sentiments of the Senate.

This first open aggression on the Paganism of Rome was followed by a law which confiscated at once all the property of the temples, and swept away the privileges and immunities of the priesthood. The fate of the Vestal virgins excited the strongest commiseration. They now passed unhonoured through the streets. The violence done to this institution, coeval with Rome itself, was aggravated by the bitter mockery of the Christians at the importance attached to those few and rare instances of chastity by the Pagans. They scoffed at the small number of the sacred virgins; at the occasional delinquencies (for it is singular that almost the last act of Pagan pontifical authority was the capital punishment of an unchaste Vestal); the privilege they possessed, and sometimes claimed, of marriage after a certain period of service, when, according to the severer Christians, such unholy desires should have been long extinct.[a] If the state is to reward virginity (said the vehement Ambrose), the claims of the Christians would exhaust the treasury.

By this confiscation of the sacerdotal property, which

---

[a] It is very singular that, even at this very time, severe laws seem to have been necessary to punish apostates from Christianity. In 381, Theodosius deprived such persons of the right of bequeathing their property. Similar laws were passed in 383 and 391, against those qui ex Christianis Pagani facti sunt; qui ad Paganos ritus cultusque migrarunt;— qui venerabili religione neglectâ ad aras et templa transierint. Cod. Theodos. xvi. 7. 1, 2, 4, 5.

[b] Prudentius, though he wrote later, expresses this sentiment:—

Nobis anus veterana, sacro perfuncta labore, Deserviisque focis, quibus est famulata juventus,
Transfert invitae ad felcris jugalis rogos, Discit et in gelido nova nupta calescere lecto.
Adv. Symm. lib. ii.

had hitherto maintained the priesthood in opulence, the temples and the sacrificial rites in splendour, the Pagan hierarchy became stipendiaries of the state, the immediate step to their total dissolution. The public funds were still charged with a certain expenditure[b] for the maintenance of the public ceremonies. This was not abrogated till after Theodosius had again united the whole empire under his conquering sway, and shared with Christianity the subjugated world.

In the interval, Heathenism made perhaps more than one desperate though feeble struggle for the ascendancy. Gratian was murdered in the year 383. Valentinian II. succeeded to the sole empire of the West. The celebrated Symmachus became prefect of Rome. Symmachus commanded the respect, and even deserved the common attachment, of all his countrymen; he ventured (a rare example in those days) to interfere between the tyranny of the sovereign and the menaced welfare of the people. An uncorrupt magistrate, he deprecated the increasing burdens of unnecessary taxes which weighed down the people; he dared to suggest that the eager petitions for office should be at once rejected and the worthiest chosen out of the unpretending multitude. Symmachus inseparably connected, in his Pagan patriotism, the ancient religion with the welfare of Rome. He mourned in bitter humiliation over the acts of Gratian; the removal of the statue of Victory; the abrogation of the immunities of the Pagan priesthood. He hoped to obtain from the justice, or perhaps the fears, of the young Valentinian, that which had been refused by Gratian. The senate met under his authority; a petition was drawn up and presented in the

---

[b] This was called the Annona.

name of that venerable body to the Emperor. On this composition Symmachus lavished all his eloquence. His oration is written with vigour, with dignity, with elegance. It is in this respect, perhaps, superior to the reply of Saint Ambrose.[c] But in the feeble and apologetic tone, we perceive at once, that it is the artful defence of an almost hopeless cause; it is cautious to timidity; dexterous; elaborately conciliatory; moderate from fear of offending rather than from tranquil dignity. Ambrose, on the other hand, writes with all the fervid and careless energy of one confident in his cause and who knows that he is appealing to an audience already pledged by their own feelings to his side; he has not to obviate objections, to reconcile difficulties, to sue or to propitiate; his contemptuous and criminating language has only to inflame zeal, to quicken resentment and scorn. He is flowing down on the full tide of human passion, and his impulse but accelerates and strengthens the rapid current.

The personification of Rome, in the address of Symmachus, is a bold stroke of artificial rhetoric, but it is artificial; and Rome pleads instead of commanding; intreats for indulgence, rather than menaces for neglect. "Most excellent Princes, Fathers of your country, respect my years, and permit me still to practise the religion of my ancestors, in which I have grown old. Grant me but the liberty of living according to my

---

[c] Heyne has expressed himself strongly on the superiority of Symmachus, Argumentorum delectu, vi. pondere, aculeis, non minus admirabilis illa est quam prudentiâ, cautione, ac verecundiâ; quam tanto magis sentias si verbosam et inanem, interdum calumniosam et veratoriam declamationem Ambrosii comparas. Censur. Ingen, et mor. Q. A. Symmachi, in Heyne Opuscul.

The relative position of the parties influenced, no doubt, the style, and will, perhaps, the judgement, of posterity on the merit, of the compositions.

ancient usage. This religion has subdued the world to my dominion; these rites repelled Hannibal from my walls, the Gauls from the Capitol. Have I lived thus long, to be rebuked in my old age for my religion? It is too late; it would be discreditable to amend in my old age. I intreat but peace for the gods of Rome, the tutelary gods of our country." Rome condescends to that plea, which a prosperous religion neither uses nor admits, but to which a falling faith always clings with desperate energy. "Heaven is above us all: we cannot all follow the same path; there are many ways by which we arrive at the great secret. But we presume not to contend, we are humble suppliants!" The end of the third century had witnessed the persecutions of Diocletian; the fourth had not elapsed when this is the language of Paganism, uttered in her strongest hold by the most earnest and eloquent of her partisans. Symmachus remonstrates against the miserable economy of saving the maintenance of the vestal virgins; the disgrace of enriching the imperial treasury by such gains; he protests against the confiscation of all legacies bequeathed to them by the piety of individuals. "Slaves may inherit; the Vestal virgins alone, and the ministers of religion, are precluded from this common privilege." The orator concludes by appealing to the deified father of the Emperor, who looks down with sorrow from the starry citadel, to see that toleration violated which he had maintained with willing justice.

But Ambrose was at hand to confront the eloquent Pagan, and to prohibit the fatal concession. Far different is the tone and manner of the Archbishop of Milan. He asserts, in plain terms, the unquestionable obligation of a Christian sovereign to permit no part of the public revenue to be devoted

Reply of Ambrose.

to the maintenance of idolatry. Their Roman ancestors were to be treated with reverence; but in a question of religion they were to consider God alone. He who advises such grants as those demanded by the suppliants is guilty of sacrifice. Gradually he rises to still more imperious language, and unveils all the terrors of the sacerdotal authority. "The Emperor who shall be guilty of such concessions will find that the bishops will neither endure nor connive at his sin. If he enters a church, he will find no priest, or one who will defy his authority. The church will indignantly reject the gifts of him who has shared them with Gentile temples. The altar disdains the offerings of him who has made offerings to images. It is written, 'Man cannot serve two masters.'" Ambrose, emboldened, as it were, by his success, ventures in his second letter to treat the venerable and holy traditions of Roman glory with contempt. "How long did Hannibal insult the gods of Rome? It was the goose and not the deity that saved the Capitol. Did Jupiter speak in the goose? Where were the gods in all the defeats, some of them but recent, of the Pagan emperors? Was not the altar of Victory then standing?" He insults the number, the weaknesses, the marriages of the vestal virgins. "If the same munificence were shown to Christian virgins, the beggared treasury would be exhausted by the claims." "Are not the baths, the porticos, the streets, still crowded with images? Must they still keep their place in the great council of the empire? You compel to worship if you restore the altar. And who is this deity? Victory is a gift, and not a power; she depends on the courage of the legions, not on the influence of the religion,—a mighty deity, who is bestowed by the numbers of an army, or the doubtful issue of a battle!"

ACCESSION OF EUGENIUS.

Foiled in argument, Paganism vainly grasped at other arms, which she had as little power to wield. On the murder of Valentinian, Arbogastes the *Murder of Valentinian, A.D. 392.* Gaul, whose authority over the troops was without competitor, hesitated to assume the purple which had never yet been polluted by a barbarian. He placed Eugenius, a rhetorician, on the throne. The elevation of Eugenius was an act of military violence; but the Pagans of the West hailed *Accession of Eugenius.* his accession with the most eager joy and the fondest hopes. The Christian writers denounce the apostasy of Eugenius, not without justice if Eugenius ever professed Christianity.[4] Throughout Italy the temples were re-opened; the smoke of sacrifice ascended from all quarters; the entrails of victims were explored for the signs of victory. The frontiers were guarded by all the terrors of the old religion. The statue of Jupiter the Thunderer, sanctified by magical rites of the most awful significance, and placed on the fortifications amid the Julian Alps, looked defiance on the advance of the Christian Emperor. The images of the gods were unrolled on the banners, and Hercules was borne in triumph at the head of the army. Ambrose fled from Milan, for the soldiery boasted that they would stable their horses in the churches and press the clergy to fill their legions.

In Rome, Eugenius consented, without reluctance, to the restoration of the altar of Victory, but he had the wisdom to foresee the danger which his cause might incur by the resumption of the temple estates, many of which had been granted away: he yielded with undis-

---

[4] Compare the letter of Ambrose to Eugenius. He addresses Eugenius apparently as a Christian, but one in the hands of more powerful Pagans.

guised unwillingness to the irresistible importunities of Arbogastes and Flavianus.

While this reaction was taking place in the West, perhaps irritated by the intelligence of this formidable conspiracy of Paganism, with the usurpation of the throne, Theodosius published in the East the last and most peremptory of those edicts which, gradually rising in the sternness of their language, proclaimed the ancient worship a treasonable and capital crime. In its minute and searching phrases this statute seemed eagerly to pursue Paganism to its most secret and private lurking-places. Thenceforth no man of any station, rank, or dignity, in any place in any city, was to offer an innocent victim in sacrifice; the more harmless worship of the household gods, which lingered, probably, more deeply in the hearts of the Pagans than any other part of their system, was equally forbidden, not merely the smoke of victims, but even lamps, incense, and garlands. To sacrifice, or to consult the entrails of victims, was constituted high treason, and thereby a capital offence, although with no treasonable intention of calculating the days of the Emperor. It was a crime of the same magnitude to infringe the laws of nature, to pry into the secrets of futurity, or to inquire concerning the death of any one. Whoever permitted any Heathen rite—hanging a tree with chaplets, or raising an altar of turf—forfeited the estate on which the offence was committed. Any house profaned with the smoke of incense was confiscated to the imperial exchequer. Whoever violated this prohibition, and offered sacrifice either in a public temple, or on the estate of another, was amerced in a fine of twenty-five pounds of gold (a thousand pounds of our money); and whoever connived at the offence

A.D. 394.

was liable to the same fine: the magistrate who neglected to enforce it, to a still heavier penalty.ᵉ This law, stern and intolerant as it was, spoke, no doubt, the dominant sentiment of the Christian world;ᶠ but its repetition by the successors of Theodosius, and the employment of avowed Pagans in many of the high offices of the state and army, may permit us charitably to doubt whether the exchequer was much enriched by the forfeitures, or the sword of the executioner deeply stained with the blood of conscientious Pagans. Polytheism boasted no martyrs; and we may still hope that if called upon to carry its own decrees into effect, its native clemency—though, unhappily, Christian bigotry had already tasted of heretical blood—would have revolted from the sanguinary deed,ᵍ and yet have seen the inconsistency of these acts (which it justified in theory, on the authority of the Old Testament) with the vital principles of the Gospel.

The victory of Theodosius in the West dissipated at once the vain hopes of Paganism; the pageant vanished away. Rome heard of the triumph, perhaps witnessed the presence of the great conqueror, who, in the East, had already countenanced the most destructive attacks against the temples of the gods. The Christian poet describes a solemn debate of the Senate

---

ᵉ Cod. Theod. xvi. 10, 12.

ᶠ Gibbon has quoted from Le Clerc a fearful sentence of St. Augustine, addressed to the Donatists. "Quis nostrûm, quis vestrûm non laudat leges ab Imperatoribus datas adversus sacrificia Paganorum? Et certè longè ibi pœna æterior constituta est; illius quippe impietatis capitale supplicium est." Epist. xciii. But passages amiably inconsistent with this fierce tone might be quoted on the milder side. Compare Editor's note on Gibbon, v. p. 114.

ᵍ Quis eorum comprehensus est in sacrificio (cum his legibus ista prohiberentur) et non negavit. Augustin, in Psalm cxx., quoted by Gibbon from Lardner.

on the claims of Jupiter and of Christ to the adoration of the Roman people. According to his account, Jupiter was outvoted by a large number of suffrages; the decision was followed by a general desertion of their ancestral deities by the obsequious minority; the old hereditary names, the Annii and the Probi, the Anicii and Olybii, the Paulini and Bassi, the popular Gracchi, six hundred families, at once passed over to the Christian cause.[b] The Pagan historian to a certain degree confirms the fact of the deliberate discussion, but differs as to the result. The senate, he states, firmly, but respectfully, adhered to their ancient deities.[i] But the last argument of the Pagan advocates was fatal to their cause. Theodosius refused any longer to assign funds from the public revenue to maintain the charge of the idolatrous worship. The senate remonstrated, that if they ceased to be supported at the national cost, they would cease to be national rites. This argument was more likely to confirm than to shake the determination of the Christian Emperor. From this time the temples were deserted; the priests and priestesses, deprived of their maintenance, were scattered abroad. The public temples still stood, nor was it forbidden to worship within their walls, without sacrifice; the private, and family, or Gentile, deities, still preserved their influence.

Theodosius died the year after the defeat of Eugenius. We pursue to its close the history of Western Paganism, which was buried at last in the ruins of the empire. Gratian had dissevered the supremacy of the national religion from the imperial

A.D. 394.

---

[b] Sexcentas numerare domus de sanguine prisco
Nobilium licet, ad Christi signacula versas,
Turpis ab idoli vasto emersisse profundo.
Prud. ad Symmach.

Prudentius has probably amplified some considerable desertion of the wavering and dubious believers.
[i] Zosim. Hist. iv. 59.

dignity; he had confiscated the property of the temples; Theodosius had refused to defray the expense of public sacrifices from the public funds. Still, however, the outward form of Paganism remained. Some priesthoods were still handed down in regular descent; the rites of various deities, even of Mythra and Cybele, were celebrated without sacrifice, or with sacrifice furtively performed; the corporation of the haruspices was not abolished. There still likewise remained a special provision for certain festivals and public amusements.[k] The expense of the sacred banquets and of the games was defrayed by the state: an early law of Honorius respected the common enjoyments of the people.[m]

The poem of Prudentius[n] acknowledges that the enactments of Theodosius had been far from altogether successful;[o] his bold assertion of the universal adoption of Christianity by the whole senate is in some degree contradicted by his admission that the old pestilence of idolatry had again broken out in Rome.[p] It implies that the restoration of the statue of Victory had again been urged, and by the indefatigable Symmachus, on the sons of Theodosius.[q] The poem was written after

---

[k] It was called the vectigal templorum.

[m] Communis populi lætitia.

[n] The poem of Prudentius is by no means a recapitulation of the arguments of St. Ambrose; it is original, and in some parts very rigorous.

[o] Inclitus ergo parens patriæ, moderator et orbis,
Id epit prohibendo, vagus ne pristinus error
Crederet esse Deûm migrantis sub aere formas.

[p] Sed quoniam renovata lues tartaro salutem
Tantæ Romulidum.

[q] Armorum dominos, vernantes flore juventæ,
Inter castra patris genitos, sub imagine avitâ
Eductos, exempla domi congesta tenebiea,
frater catus instigat.
Si vobis vel patria, viri, victoria cordi est,
Vel parientis debitae, templum Dea virgo sacratum
Obtineat, vobis regnantibus.

The orator catus, is Symmachus; the parta victoria, that of Pollentia; the Dea virgo, Victory.

the battle of Pollentia, as it triumphantly appeals to the glories of that day against the argument that Rome was indebted for the victories of former times to her ancient gods. It closes with an earnest admonition to the son of Theodosius to fulfil the task which was designedly left to him by the piety of his father,' to suppress at once the Vestal virgins, and, above all, the gladiatorial shows, which they were accustomed to countenance by their presence.

In the year 408 came forth the edict which aimed at the direct and complete abolition of Paganism throughout the Western empire. The whole of this reserved provision for festivals was swept away; it was devoted to the more useful purpose, the pay of the loyal soldiery.' The same edict proceeded to actual violence, to invade and take possession of the sanctuaries of religion. All images were to be thrown down; the edifices, now useless and deserted, to be occupied by the imperial officers, and appropriated to useful purposes.' The government, wavering between demolition and desecration, devised this plan for the preservation of these great ornaments of the cities, which thus, taken under the protection of the magistracy as public property, were secured from the destructive zeal of the more fanatical Christians. All sacrilegious rites, festivals, and ceremonies were prohibited. The bishops of the towns were invested with

---

' Quam ubi suppicandam Deus, et gentiorts amica.
Servavit pietas: solus ne praescia tantis
Virtutis caperet "partem, tibi, nate reservo."
Dias, et integrum decus intactumque reliquit. Sub ita.
' Expensis devotissimorum militum profutura.
' Augustine (though not entirely consistent) disapproved of the forcible demolition of the temples. "Let us first extirpate the idolatry of the heathen; and they will either themselves invite us, or anticipate us in the execution of this good work." Tom. v. p. 62.

power to suppress these forbidden usages, and the civil authorities, as though the government mistrusted their zeal, were bound, under a heavy penalty, to obey the summons, and to assist the prelates in the extirpation of idolatry. Another edict excluded all enemies of the Christian faith from the great public offices in the state and in the army, and this, if fully carried into effect, would have transferred the whole power throughout the empire into the hands of the Christians. But the times were not yet ripe for this measure. Generides, a Pagan, in a high command in the army, threw up his commission. The edict was repealed.[a]

---

[a] Prudentius ventures to admire the tolerant impartiality of Theodosius, in admitting both parties alike to civil and military honours. He urges this argumentum ad hominem against Symmachus:—

Denique pro meritis terrestribus aequa rependens
Munera, sacricolis summas impertit honores
Dux bonus, et certare sinit cum laude suorum.
Nec pago implicitos per debita culmina mitti
Ire vetat,
Ipse magistratum tibi consulis, ipse tribunal
Contulit.

In the East, the Pagan Themistius had been appointed prefect of Constantinople by Theodosius. It is curious to read his flatteries of the orthodox Christian Emperor; he praises his love of philosophy in the most fervent language.

The most remarkable instance of this inconsistency, at a much later period, occurs in the person of Merobaudes, a general and a poet, who flourished in the first half of the fifth century. A statue in honour of Merobaudes was placed in the Forum of Trajan, of which the inscription is still extant. Fragments of his poems have been discovered by the industry and sagacity of Niebuhr. In one passage, Merobaudes, in the genuine Heathen spirit, attributes the ruin of the empire to the abolition of Paganism, and almost renews the old accusation of Atheism against Christianity. He impersonates some deity, probably Discord, who summons Bellona to take arms for the destruction of Rome; and, in a strain of fierce irony, recommends to her, among other fatal measures, to extirpate the gods of Rome:

Roma, ipsique tremant furialia murmura regna.
Jam superos terris, atque hospita numina pelle:
Romanos populare Deos, si nullus in aris
Vestas exoriatur, totus atroz, pallleat ignis.
His instructa dolis palatia celsa subibo,
Majorum mores, et pectora prisca fugabo
Funditus, atque simul, nullo discrimine rerum,
Spernantur fortes, nec ali reverentia justis.
Attica neglecto pereat facundia Phoebo,
Indigenis contingat honos, et pondera rerum;
Non virtus aut casus agat, tristisque cupido;

Rome once more beheld the shadow of a Pagan Emperor, Attalus, while the Christian Emperor maintained his court at Ravenna; and both stood trembling before the victorious Alaric. When that triumphant Goth formed the siege of Rome, Paganism, as if grateful for the fidelity of the imperial city, made one last desperate effort to avert the common ruin. Pagan magic was the last refuge of conscious weakness. The Etrurian soothsayers were called forth from their obscurity, with the concurrence of the whole city (the Pope himself is said to have assented to the idolatrous ceremony), to blast the barbaric invader with the lightnings of Jupiter. The Christian historian saves the credit of his party, by asserting that they kept away from the profane rite.[a] But it may be doubted, after all, whether the ceremony really took place; both parties had more confidence in the power of a large sum of money, offered to arrest the career of the triumphant barbarian.

The impartial fury of Alaric fell alike on church and temple, on Christian and Pagan. But the capture of Rome consummated the ruin of Paganism. The temples, indeed, were for the most part left standing, but their worshippers had fled. The Roman aristocracy, in whom alone Paganism still retained its most powerful adherents, abandoned the city, and, scattered in the provinces of the empire, were absorbed in the rapidly Christianising population. The deserted buildings had now neither public authority nor private zeal and munificence to maintain them against the encroachments of time or accident, to support the tottering roof, or repair the broken column. There was neither public fund, nor private contribution, for their preservation, till at length the Christians, in many instances, took possession of the abandoned edifice, converted it to their own use, and hallowed it by a new consecration.[y] Thus, in many places, though marred and disfigured, the monuments of architecture survived, with no great violation of the ground plan, distribution, or general proportions.[z]

Paganism was, in fact, left to die out by gradual dissolution.[a] The worship of the Heathen deities lingered in many temples, till it was superseded by the new form of Christianity, which, at least in its outward appearance, approximated to Polytheism: the Virgin gradually supplanted many of the local deities. In Sicily, which long remained obstinately wedded to the ancient faith, eight celebrated temples were dedicated to the Mother of God.[b] It was not till the seventh century, that the Pantheon was dedicated by Pope Boniface IV. to the

---

[y] There are many churches in Rome, which, like the Pantheon, are ancient temples; thirty-nine built on the foundations of temples. Four retain Pagan names. S. Maria sopra Minerva, S. Maria Aventina, S. Lorenzo in Matuta, S. Stefano in Cacco. At Sienna, the temple of Quirinus became the church of S. Quirino. Beugnot, ii. p. 266. See in Bingham, book vili. c. 4., references to several churches in the East, converted into temples. But this passage must be read with caution.

[z] In some cases, by a more destructive appropriation, they converted the materials to their own use, and worked them up into their own barbarous churches.

[a] The fifth council of Carthage (A. D. 398), can. xv., petitioned the most glorious Emperors to destroy the remains of idolatry, not merely "in simulacris," but in other places, groves, and trees.

[b] Beugnot, ii. 271; from Aprile, Chronologia Universale de Sicilià.

Holy Virgin. Of the public festivals, the last which clung with tenacious grasp to the habits of the Roman people, was the Lupercalia. It was suppressed towards the close of the fifth century by Pope Gelasius. The rural districts were not completely Christianised until the general introduction of monasticism. Heathenism was still prevalent in many parts of Italy, especially in the neighbourhood of Turin, in the middle of the fifth century.* Its conqueror was the missionary from the convent who wandered through the villages, or who, from his monastery, regularly discharged the duties of a village pastor. St. Benedict of Nursia destroyed the worship of Apollo on Mount Casino.⁴

Every where the superstition survived the religion, and that which was unlawful under Paganism, continued to be unlawfully practised under Christianity. The insatiable propensity of men to enquire into futurity, and to deal with secret and invisible agencies, which reason condemns, and often, while it condemns, consults, retained its old formularies, some religious, some pretending to be magical or theurgic. Divination and witchcraft have never been extinct in Italy, or, perhaps, in any part of Europe. The descendants of Canidia or Erictho, the seer and the magician, have still

---

* See the sermons of Maximus, bishop of Turin, quoted in Beugnot, ii. 253.

⁴ Greg. M. Dialog. Lib. 2, p. 262. He converted many worshippers of idols in a village near his monastery. Ibid. ch. xix. 60, he mentions *idolorum cultores* in an epistle to the Bishop of Tyndaris in Sicily. So in Sardinia, iii.

23 and 26. The peasants belonging to the church were to be heavily taxed till they ceased to be Paganise, also he names 29 worshippers of trees, &c. near Terracina, vii. 20. Idolatrous Aruspices and Sortilegi in Sardinia to be preached to; if obstinate, slaves to be scourged, free men imprisoned till they repent. vii. 2. 67.

practised their arts, to which the ignorant, including at times all mankind, have listened with unabated credulity.

We must resume our consideration of Paganising Christianity, as the parent of Christian art and poetry, and, in fact, as the ruler of the human mind for many ages.

CHAPTER IX.

Theodosius. Triumph of Trinitarianism. The great Prelates of the East.

But the unity, no less than the triumph, of Christianity occupied the vigorous mind of Theodosius. He had been anticipated in this design in the West by his feeble predecessors and his colleagues, Gratian and Valentinian the younger. The laws began to speak the language not only of the exclusive establishment of Christianity, but of Christianity under one rigorous and unaccommodating creed and discipline.

Almost the first act of Theodosius was the edict for the universal acceptance of the Catholic faith.[a] It appeared under the name, and with the conjoint authority of the three Emperors, Gratian, Valentinian II., and Theodosius. It was addressed to the inhabitants of Constantinople. "We, the three Emperors, *will* that all our subjects follow the religion taught by St. Peter to the Romans, professed by those saintly prelates, Damasus Pontiff of Rome, and Peter Bishop of Alexandria, that we believe the one divinity of the Father, Son, and Holy Spirit, of majesty coequal, in the Holy Trinity. We *will* that those who embrace this creed be called Catholic Christians; we brand all the senseless followers of other religions by the infamous name of heretics, and forbid their conventicles to assume the name of

---

[a] Codex Theodos. xvi. 1, 2.

churches; we reserve their punishment to the vengeance of heaven, and to such measures as divine inspiration shall dictate to us."[b] Thus the religion of the whole Roman world was enacted by two feeble boys, and a rude Spanish soldier.[c] The next year witnessed the condemnation of all heretics, particularly the Photinians, Arians, and Eunomians, and the expulsion of the Arians from the churches of all the cities in the East,[d] and their surrender to the only *lawful* form of Christianity. On the assembling of the council of Chalcedon, two severe laws were issued against Apostates and Manicheans, prohibiting them from making wills. During its sitting, the Emperor promulgated an edict, prohibiting the Arians from building churches either in the cities or in the country, under pain of the confiscation of the funds devoted to the purpose.[e]

The circumstances of the times happily coincided with the design of Theodosius to concentrate the whole Christian world into one vigorous and consistent system. The more legitimate influence of argument and intellectual and religious superiority concurred with the stern mandates of the civil power. All the great and commanding minds of the age were on the same side as to the momentous and strongly agitated questions of

All the more powerful ecclesiastical writers favourable to Trinitarianism.

---

[b] Post etiam motus nostri, quam ex cœlesti arbitrio sumpserimus, ultione plectendas. Godefroy supposes these words not to mean "cœleste oraculum," but, "Dei arbitrium, regulam et formulam juris divini."

[c] Baronius, and even Godefroy, call this law a golden, pious, and wholesome statute. Happily it was on the right side.

[d] On the accession of Theodosius, according to Sozomen, the Arians possessed all the churches of the East, except Jerusalem. H. E. vii. 2.

[e] Sozomen mentions these severe laws; but asserts that they were enacted merely in terrorem, and with no design of carrying them into execution. H. E. vii. 12.

the faith. The productive energies of Arianism seemed, as it were, exhausted; its great defenders had passed away, and left, apparently, no heirs to their virtues or abilities. It was distracted with schisms, and had to bear the unpopularity of the sects, which seemed to have sprung from it in the natural course, the Eunomians, Macedonians, and a still multiplying progeny of heresies. Everywhere the Trinitarian prelates rose to ascendancy, not merely from the support of the government, but from their pre-eminent character or intellectual powers. Each province seemed to have produced some man adapted to the particular period and circumstances of the time, who devoted himself to the establishment of the orthodox opinions. The intractable Egypt, more especially turbulent Alexandria, was ruled by the strong arm of the bold and unprincipled Theophilus. The dreamy mysticism of Syria found a congenial representative in St. Ephrem. A more intellectual, yet still somewhat imaginative, Orientalism animates the writings of St. Basil; in a less degree, those of Gregory of Nazianzum; still less, those of Gregory of Nyssa. The more powerful and Grecian eloquence of Chrysostom swayed the popular mind in Constantinople. Jerome, a link, as it were, between the East and the West, transplanted the monastic spirit and opinions of Syria into Rome; and brought into the East much of the severer thought, and more prosaic reasoning, of the Latin world. In Gaul, where Hilary of Poictiers had long maintained the cause of Trinitarianism, on the borders of civilisation, St. Martin of Tours acted the part of a bold and enterprising missionary; while in Milan, the court-capital of the West, the strong practical character of Ambrose, his sternly conscientious moral energy, though hardening at times into rigid intolerance, with the masculine strength of his style, confirmed the Latin church in that creed to which Rome had adhered with almost unshaken fidelity. If not the greatest, the most permanently influential of all, Augustine, united the intense passion of the African mind with the most comprehensive and systematic views and intrepid dogmatism on the darkest subjects. United in one common cause, acting in their several quarters according to their peculiar temperaments and characters, these strong-minded and influential ecclesiastics almost compelled the world into a temporary peace, till first Pelagianism, and afterwards Nestorianism, unsettled again the restless elements; the controversies, first in the West concerning grace, free-will, and predestination, then in the East on the Incarnation and two natures of Christ, succeeded to the silenced and exhausted feud concerning the Trinity of persons in the Godhead.

Theophilus of Alexandria[f] performed his part in the complete subjection of the world by his energy as a ruler, not by the slower and more legitimate influence of moral persuasion through his preaching or his writings.[g] He suppressed Arianism by the same violent and coercive means with which he extirpated Paganism. The tone of this prelate's epistles is invariably harsh and criminatory. He appears in the best light as opposing the vulgar anthropomorphism of the monks in the neighbourhood of Alexandria, and insisting on the pure spiritual nature of the Deity. Yet he condescended to appease these turbulent adversaries by an unmanly

Theophilus of Alexandria, bishop, from 385 to 412.

---

[f] I have not placed these writers in their strict chronological order, but according to the countries in which they lived.

[g] The Trinitarian doctrines had been maintained in Alexandria by the virtues and abilities of Didymus the Blind.

artifice. He consented to condemn the doctrines of Origen, who, having reposed quietly in his tomb for many years, in general respect, if not in the odour of sanctity, was exhumed, as it were, by the zeal of later times, as a dangerous heresiarch. The Oriental doctrines with which Origen had impregnated his system were unpopular, and perhaps not clearly understood.[b] The notion that the reign of Christ was finite was rather an inference from his writings than a tenet of Origen. For if all bodies were to be finally annihilated (according to his anti-materialistic system), the humanity of Christ, and consequently his personal reign, must cease. The possibility that the devil might, after long purification, be saved, and the corruptibility of the body after the resurrection, grew out of the same Oriental cast of opinions. But the perfectly pure and immaterial nature of the Deity was the tenet of Origen which was the most odious to the monks; and Theophilus, by anathematising Origenism in the mass, while he himself held certainly the sublimest, but to his adversaries most objectionable part of the system, adopted a low and undignified deception. The persecution of Isidore, and the heads of the monasteries who befriended his cause (the tall brethren, as they were called), from personal motives of animosity, display the Alexandrian prelate in his ordinary character. We shall again encounter Theophilus in the lamentable intrigues against the advancement and influence of Chrysostom.

The character of Ephrem,[1] the Syrian, was the exact counterpart to that of the busy and worldly Theophilus. A native of Nisibis, or rather of its neighbourhood, Ephrem passed the greater part of

S. Ephrem.
the Syrian,
died 379.

---

[b] Socrates, vi. 10. Sozomen. viii. 13. [1] See the Life of Ephrem prefixed to his works; and in Tillemont.

his life at Edessa, and in the monastic establishments which began to abound in Mesopotamia and Syria, as in Egypt. His genius was that of the people in whose language he wrote his numerous compositions in prose and verse.[k] In Ephrem something of the poetic mysticism of the Gnostic was allied with the most rigid orthodoxy of doctrine. But with his imaginative turn were mingled a depth and intensity of feeling, which gave him his peculiar influence over the kindred minds of his countrymen. Tears were as natural to him as perspiration; day and night, in his devout seclusion, he wept for the sins of mankind and for his own; his very writings, it was said, weep; there is a deep and latent sorrow even in his panegyrics or festival homilies.[l]

Ephrem was a poet, and his hymns, poured forth in the prodigality of his zeal, succeeded at length in entirely disenchanting the popular ear from the heretical strains of Bardesanes and his son Harmonius, which lingered after the general decay of Gnosticism.[m] The hymns of Ephrem were sung on the festivals of the martyrs. His psalms, the constant occupation which he enjoins upon his monkish companions, were always of a sorrowful and contrite tone. Laughter was the source and the indication of all wickedness, sorrow of all virtue. During the melancholy psalm, God was present with his angels; all more joyous strains belonged to heathenism and idolatry.

[k] According to Theodoret, he was unacquainted with Greek. Παιδείας γὰρ οὐ γεγευμένος ἑλληνικῆς, τοὺς τε πολυσχιδεῖς τῶν Ἑλλήνων διελέγξε πλάνους καὶ πάσης αἱρετικῆς κακοτεχνίας ἐγύμνωσε τὴν ἀσέβειαν. The refutation of Greek heresy in Syriac must have been curious.

[l] See the two treatises in his works, vol. i. p. 94-107. Non eme ridendum sed lugendum potius atque plorandum; and, Quod ludicris rebus abstinendum sit Christianis.

[m] Theodoret, iv. 29.

The monasticism, as well as the Trinitarianism, of Syria received a strong impulse from Ephrem; and in Syria monasticism began to run into its utmost extravagance. There was one class of ascetics who, at certain periods, forsook their cities, and retired to the mountains to browse on the herbage which they found, as their only food. The writings of Ephrem were the occupation and delight of all these gentle and irreproachable fanatics; and, as Ephrem was rigidly Trinitarian, he contributed to fix the doctrinal language of the various cœnobitic institutions and solitary hermitages. In fact, the quiescent intellect probably rejoiced in being relieved from these severe and ungrateful enquiries: and full freedom being left to the imagination and ample scope to the language in the vague and fervent expressions of divine love, the Syrian mind felt not the restriction of the rigorous creed, and passively surrendered itself to ecclesiastical authority. Absorbed in its painful and melancholy struggles with the internal passions and appetites, it desired not to provoke, but rather to repress, the dangerous activity of the reason. The orthodoxy of Ephrem himself savours perhaps of timidity and the disinclination to agitate such awful and appalling questions. He would elude and escape them, and abandon himself altogether to the more edifying emotions which it is the chief object of his writings to excite and maintain. The dreamer must awake in order to reason, and he prefers the passive tranquillity of the half-slumbering state.

Greece, properly so called, contributed none of the more distinguished names in Eastern Christianity. Even the Grecian part of Asia Minor was by no means fertile in names which survive in the annals of the Church. In Athens philosophy still lingered, and struggled to maintain its predominance. Many of the more eminent ecclesiastics had visited its schools in their youth, to obtain those lessons of rhetoric and profane knowledge which they were hereafter to dedicate to their own sacred uses. But they were foreigners; and, in the old language of Greece, would have been called barbarians.

The rude and uncivilised Cappadocia gave birth to Basil and the two Gregories. The whole of the less dreamy, and still active and commercial, part of Asia was influenced by Basil, on whose character and writings his own age lavished the most unbounded praise. The name of Basil is constantly united with those of the two Gregories. One, Gregory of Nyssa, was his brother; the other, named from his native town of Nazianzum, of which his father was bishop, was the intimate friend of his boyhood and of his later years. The language, the eloquence, the opinions of these writers retain, in different degrees, some tinge of Asiatic colouring. Far more intelligible and practical than the mystic strains and passionate homilies of Ephrem, they delight in agitating, though in a more modest spirit, the questions which had inflamed the imagination of the Gnostics. But with them, likewise, enquiry proceeds with cautious and reverent steps. On these subjects they are rigorously orthodox, and assert the exclusive doctrines of Athanasius with the most distinct and uncompromising energy. Basil maintained the cause of Trinitarianism with unshaken fidelity during its days of depression and adversity. His friend Gregory of Nazianzum lived to witness and bear a great part of its triumph. Both Basil and Gregory were ardent admirers, and in themselves transcendent models, of the more monastic Christianity. The influence of Basil crowded that part of Asia with cœnobitic institutions: but in his monasteries labour and useful industry prevailed to a greater extent than in the the Syrian deserts.

Basil was a native of the Cappadocian Cæsarea.[a] He was an hereditary Christian. His grandfather had retired during the Diocletian persecution to a mountain-forest in Pontus. His father was a man of estimation as a lawyer, possessed considerable property, and was remarkable for his personal beauty. His mother, in person and character, was worthy of her husband. The son of such parents received the best education which could be bestowed on a Christian youth. Having exhausted the instruction to be obtained in his native city of Cæsarea, he went to Constantinople, where he is reputed to have studied the art of rhetoric under the celebrated Libanius. But Athens was still the centre of liberal education, and, with other promising youths from the Eastern provinces, Basil and his friend Gregory resided for some time in that city. But with all his taste for letters and eloquence (and Basil always spoke even of profane learning with generous respect, far different from the tone of contempt and animosity expressed by some writers), Christianity was too deeply rooted in his heart to be endangered either by the studies or the society of Athens. On his return to Cæsarea, he embraced the ascetic faith of the times with more than ordinary fervour. He abandoned his property; he practised such severe austerities as to injure his health, and to reduce his bodily form to the extreme of meagreness and weakness. He was "without wife, without property, without flesh, almost without blood." He fled into the desert; his fame collected, as it were, a city around him; he built a monastery, and

S. Basil.

---

[a] Life of Basil, prefixed to his works: and Tillemont, Vie de S. Basile.

monasteries sprang up on every side. Yet the opinions of Basil concerning the monastic life were far more moderate and practical than the wilder and more dreamy asceticism which prevailed in Egypt and in Syria. He admired and persuaded his followers to cœnobitic, not to eremitical, life. It was the life of the industrious religious community, not of the indolent and solitary anchorite, which to Basil was the perfection of Christianity. All ties of kindred were indeed to give place to that of spiritual association. He that loves a brother in blood more than a brother in the religious community is still a slave to his carnal nature." The indiscriminate charity of these institutions was to receive orphans of all classes for education and maintenance, but other children only with the consent, or at the request of parents, certified before witnesses; and vows of virginity were by no means to be enforced upon these youthful pupils.[p] Slaves who fled to the monasteries were to be admonished, and sent back to their owners. There is one reservation, that slaves were not bound to obey their master, if he should order what is contrary to the laws of God.[q] Industry was to be the animating principle of these settlements. Prayer and psalmody were to have their appointed hours; but by no means to intrude upon those devoted to useful labour. These labours were strictly defined, such as were of real use to the community, not those which might contribute to vice or luxury. Agriculture was especially recommended. The life was in no respect to be absorbed in a perpetual mystic communion with the Deity.

Basil lived in his monastic retirement during a great

---

* Basil. Opera, ii. 325. Sermo Asceticus.
p Basil. Opera, ii. 355.
q Basil. Opera, ii. 357.

part of the triumphant period of Arianism in the East; but during the reign of Valens, he was recalled to Cæsarea, to be the champion of Trinitarianism against the Emperor and his Arian partisans. The firmness of Basil, as we have seen, commanded the respect even of his adversaries. In the midst of the raging controversy, he was raised to the archepiscopal throne of Cæsarea. He governed the see with activity and diligence: not only the influence of his writings, but his actual authority (his pious ambition of usefulness induced him perhaps to overstep the limits of his diocese) extended beyond Cappadocia, into Armenia and parts of Asia Minor. He was the firm supporter of the Nicene Trinitarianism, but did not live to behold its final triumph. His decease followed immediately upon the defeat and death of Valens. The style of Basil did no discredit to his Athenian education; in purity and perspicuity he surpasses most of the Heathen as well as the Christian writers of his age.

Gregory of Nazianzum, as he shared the friendship, so he has constantly participated in the fame of Basil. He was born in a village, Arianza, within the district of Nazianzum, his father was bishop of that city.* With Basil he passed a part of his youth at Athens, and predicted, according to his own account, the apostasy of Julian, from the observation of his character, and even of his person. Gregory is his own biographer; one or rather two poems, the first consisting of above two thousand iambics, the second of hexameters, describe the whole course of his

---

* Tillemont is grievously embarrassed by the time of Gregory's birth. The stubborn dates insist upon his having been born after his father had attained the episcopate. Tillemont is forced to acknowledge the laxity of ecclesiastical discipline on this head, at this period of the church.

early life. But Grecian poetry was not to be awakened from its long slumber by the voice of a Christian poet: it was faithful to its ancient source of inspiration. Christian thoughts and images will not blend with the language of Homer and the tragedians. Yet the autobiographical poems of Gregory illustrate a remarkable peculiarity which distinguishes modern and Christian from the older, more particularly the Grecian, poetry. In the Grecian poetry, as in Grecian life, the public absorbed the individual character. The person of the poet rarely appears, unless occasionally as the poet, as the objective author or reciter, not as the subject of the poem. The Elegiac poets of Greece, if we may judge from the few surviving fragments, and the amatory writers of Rome, speak in their proper persons, utter their individual thoughts, and embody their peculiar feelings. In the shrewd common-life view of Horace, and, indeed in some of his higher lyric poetry, the poet is more prominent; and the fate of Ovid, one day basking in the imperial favour, the next, for some mysterious offence, banished to the bleak shores of the Euxine, seemed to give him the privilege of dwelling upon his own sorrows; his strange fate invested his life in peculiar interest. These however are rare and exceptional instances in Greek and Roman poetry. But by the Christian scheme, the individual man has assumed a higher importance; his actions, his opinions, the emotions of his mind, as connected with his immortal state, have acquired a new and commanding interest, not only to himself, but to others. The poet profoundly scrutinises, and elaborately reveals, the depths of his moral being. The psychological history of the man, in all its minute particulars, becomes the predominant matter of the poem. In

this respect, these autobiographical poems of Gregory,
loose as they are in numbers, spun out with
a wearisome and garrulous mediocrity, and
wanting that depth and passion of religion which has
made the Confessions of Augustine one of the most
permanently popular of Christian writings, possess nevertheless
some interest, as indicating the transition state
in poetry, as well as illustrating the thought and feeling
prevalent among the Christian youth of the period.
The one great absorbing question was the comparative
excellence of the secular and the monastic life, the state
of marriage or of virginity. The enthusiasm of the
East scarcely deigned to submit this point to discussion.
In one of Gregory's poems, Marriage and Virginity each
pleads his cause; but there can be no doubt, from the
first, to which will be assigned the victory. The Saviour
gives to Virginity the place of honour on his right hand.
Gregory had never entangled himself with marriage,
that fatal tie which enthralls the soul in the bonds of
matter. For him silken robes, gorgeous banquets,
splendid palaces, music and perfumes, had no charm.
He disregarded wealth, and feasted contentedly on
bread with a little salt, and water for his only drink.
The desire of supporting the declining age of his parents
thwarted his holy ambition of withdrawing from all
worldly intercourse: but this became a snare. He was
embarrassed by refractory servants, by public and
private business. The death of his brother involved
him still more inextricably in affairs arising out of his
contested property. But the faithless friendship of
Basil, which he deplores in the one touching passage
of his whole poem,[1] still further endangered his peace.

---

[1] Gibbon's selection of this passage, and his happy illustration from Shakespeare, do great credit to his poetical taste.

In the zeal of Basil to fill the bishoprics of his metropolitan diocese, calculating perhaps that Gregory, like himself, would generously sacrifice the luxury of religious quietude for the more useful duties of a difficult active position, he imposed upon his reluctant friend the charge of the newly created see of Sasima. This was a small and miserable town, at the meeting of three roads, in a country at once arid, marshy, and unwholesome, noisy and dusty from the constant passage of travellers, the disputes with extortionate custom-house officers, and all the tumult and drunkenness belonging to a town inhabited by loose and passing strangers. With Basil, Gregory had passed the tranquil days of his youth, the contemplative period of his manhood; together they had studied at Athens, together they had twice retired to monastic solitude; and this was the return for his long and tried attachment! Gregory, in the bitterness of his remonstrance, at one time assumes the language of an Indian faquir. Instead of rejoicing in the sphere opened to his activity, he boldly asserts his supreme felicity to be total inaction.* He submitted with the strongest repugnance to the office, and abandoned it, almost immediately, on the first opposition. He afterwards administered the see of Nazianzum under his father, and even after his father's decease, without assuming the episcopal title.

Gregory, bishop of Sasima. A.D. 372.

Πάντα κοινά λέγων
'Ομοστεγίαν τε, καὶ σωσεστίαν βίου.
Ναῶν εἰς ἐν ἀμφοῖν * * * *
Διεσπάκασται πάντα, ἐρρίφθαι χαμαὶ
Ἀθμα φέρουσι τὰς παλαιὰς ἐλπίδας.
Is all the counsel that we two have shared.
The sisters' vows, &c.
Helena, in the Midsummer Night's Dream.

See Gibbon, c. xxvii. vol. v. p. 18.

* 'Εμοὶ δὲ μεγίστη πρᾶξις ἐστιν ἡ ἀπραξία. Epist. xxiii. p. 797.

But Gregory was soon compelled by his own fame for eloquence and for orthodoxy to move in a more arduous and tumultuous sphere. For forty years Arianism had been dominant in Constantinople. The Arians mocked at the small number which still lingered in the single religious assemblage of the Athanasian party.[u] Gregory is constrained to admit this humiliating fact, and indignantly inquires, whether the sands are more precious than the stars of heaven, or the pebbles than pearls, because they are more numerous.[x] But the accession of Theodosius opened a new æra to the Trinitarians. The religion of the Emperor would no longer condescend to this humble and secondary station. Gregory was invited to take charge of the small community which was still faithful to the doctrines of Athanasius. Gregory was already bowed with age and infirmity; his bald head stooped to his bosom; his countenance was worn by his austerities and his inward spiritual conflicts, when he reluctantly sacrificed his peace for this great purpose.[y] The Catholics had no church; they met in a small house, on the site of which afterwards arose the celebrated church of St. Anastasia. The eloquence of Gregory wrought wonders in the busy and versatile capital. The Arians themselves crowded to hear him. His adversaries were reduced to violence; the Anastasia was attacked; the Arian monks, and even the virgins, mingled in the furious fray: many lives were lost, and Gregory was accused as the cause of the tumult. His innocence, and the known favour of the Emperor, secured his acquittal; his eloquence was seconded by the imperial edicts. The law had been promulgated which

---

[u] In the reign of Valentinian, they met *ἐν μικρῷ οἰκίσκῳ*. Socrates, iv. 1. [x] Orat. xiv. p. 431. [y] Tillemont, art. xlvi.

denounced as heretics all who rejected the Nicene Creed.

The influence of Gregory was thwarted and his peace disturbed, by the strange intrigues of one Maximus to possess himself of the episcopal throne of Constantinople. Maximus was called the Cynic, from his attempt to blend the rude manners, the coarse white dress, his enemies added, the vices, of that sect, with the profession of Christianity. His memory is loaded with every kind of infamy; yet by dexterous flattery and assiduous attendance on the sermons of Gregory, he had stolen into his unsuspecting confidence, and received his public commendations in a studied oration.[a] Constantinople and Gregory himself were suddenly amazed with the intelligence that Maximus had been consecrated the Catholic bishop of the city. This extraordinary measure had been taken by seven Alexandrians of low birth and character,[a] with some bishops deputed by Peter the orthodox Archbishop of Alexandria.[b] A number of mariners, probably belonging to the corn fleet, had assisted at the ceremony and raised the customary acclamations. A great tumult of all orders arose; all rushed to the church, from which Maximus and his party withdrew, and hastily completed a kind of tonsure (for the cynic prided himself on his long hair) in the private dwelling of a flute-player. Maximus seems to have been rejected with indignation by the Athanasians

---

[a] The panegyric on the philosopher Heron.

[a] Some of their names were whimsically connected with the Egyptian mythology, Ammon, Anubis, and Hermanubis.

[b] The interference of the Egyptians is altogether remarkable. Could there be a design to establish the primacy of Alexandria over Constantinople, and so over the East? It is observable that in his law, Theodosius names as the examples of doctrine, the Bishop of Rome in the West, of Alexandria in the East. The intrigues of Theophilus against Chrysostom rather confirm this notion of an attempt to erect an Eastern papacy.

of Constantinople, who adhered with unshaken fidelity to Gregory; he fled to the court of Theodosius, but the earliest measure adopted by the Emperor to restore strength to the orthodox party, was the rejection of the intrusive prelate.

The first act of Theodosius on his arrival at Constantinople, was to issue an edict, expelling the Arians from the churches, and summoning Demophilus, the Arian bishop, to conform to the Nicene doctrine. Demophilus refused. The Emperor commanded that those who would not unite to establish Christian peace should retire from the houses of Christian prayer. Demophilus assembled his followers, and quoting the words of the Gospel, "If you are persecuted in one city, flee unto another," retired before the irresistible authority of the Emperor. The next step was the appointment of the reluctant Gregory to the see, and his enthronisation in the principal church of the metropolis. Environed by the armed legionaries, in military pomp, accompanied by the Emperor himself, Gregory, amazed and bewildered, and perhaps sensible of the incongruity of the scene with the true Christian character, headed the triumphal procession. All around he saw the sullen and menacing faces of the Arian multitude, and his ear might catch their suppressed murmurs; even the heavens, for the morning was bleak and cloudy, seemed to look down with cold indifference on the scene. No sooner, however, had Gregory, with the Emperor, passed the rails which divided the sanctuary from the nave of the church, than the sun burst forth in his splendour, the clouds were dissipated, and the glorious light came streaming in upon the applauding congregation. At once a shout of acclamation demanded the enthronisation of Gregory.

But Gregory, commanding only in his eloquence from the pulpit, seems to have wanted the firmness and vigour necessary for the prelate of a great metropolis. Theodosius summoned the council of Constantinople; and Gregory, embarrassed by the multiplicity of affairs; harassed by objections to the validity of his own election; entangled in the feuds which arose out of the contested election to the see of Antioch, entreated, and obtained, apparently the unreluctant, assent of the bishops and the Emperor to abdicate his dignity and to retire to his beloved privacy. His retreat, in some degree disturbed by the interest which he still took in the see of Nazianzum, gradually became more complete, till, at length, he withdrew into solitude, and ended his days in that peace, which perhaps was not less sincerely enjoyed from his experience of the cares and vexations of worldly dignity. Arianza, his native village, was the place of his seclusion; the gardens, the trees, the fountain, familiar to his youth, welcomed his old age. But Gregory had not exhausted the fears, the dangers, or the passions of life. The desires of youth still burned in his withered body and demanded the severest macerations. The sight or even the neighbourhood of females afflicted his sensitive conscience; and instead of allowing ease or repose to his aged frame, his bed was a hard mat, his coverlid sackcloth, his dress one thin tunic; his feet were bare; he allowed himself no fire, and here, in the company of the wild beasts, he prayed with bitter tears, he fasted, and devoted his hours to the composition of poetry, which, from its extreme difficulty, he considered as an act of penitence. His painful existence was protracted to the age of ninety.

The complete restoration of Constantinople to the

orthodox communion demanded even more powerful eloquence, and far more vigorous authority, than that of Gregory. If it was not finally achieved, its success was secured, by the most splendid orator who had ever adorned the Eastern church. Sixteen years after the retirement of Gregory, the fame of Chrysostom designated him as the successor to that important dignity.

Chrysostom was the model of a preacher for a great capital.[c] Clear rather than profound, his dogmatic is essentially moulded up with his moral teaching. He is the champion, not so exclusively of any system of doctrines, as of Christian holiness against the vices, the dissolute manners, the engrossing love of amusement, which prevailed in the new Rome of the East. His doctrines flow naturally from his subject or from the passage of Scripture under discussion; his illustrations are copious and happy; his style free and fluent; while he is an unrivalled master in that rapid and forcible application of incidental occurrences, which gives such life and reality to eloquence. He is, at times, in the highest sense, dramatic in his manner.

Chrysostom, like all the more ardent spirits of his age, was enamoured in his early youth of monasticism. But this he had gradually thrown off, even while he remained at Antioch. Though by no means formally abandoning these principles, or lowering his admiration of this imaginary perfection of religion, in his later works he is more free, popular, and practical. His ambition is not so much to elevate a few enthusiastic spirits to a high-toned and mystic piety, as to impregnate

[c] Compare the several lives of volume of Neander's Joannes Chrysostom by Palladius, that in the tomus. The second has since appeared. Benedictine edition of his works, and in Tillemont. I have only the first.

the whole population of a great capital with Christian virtue and self-denial.

John, who obtained the name of Chrysostom, the golden-mouthed, was born at Antioch, about the year 347. He was brought up by his mother in the Christian faith; he studied rhetoric under the celebrated Libanius, who used his utmost arts, and displayed all that is captivating in Grecian poetry and philosophy, to enthral the imagination of his promising pupil. Libanius, in an extant epistle, rejoices at the success of Chrysostom at the bar in Antioch. He is said to have lamented on his death-bed the sacrilegious seduction of the young orator by the Christians; for to Chrysostom, he had intended to bequeath his school and the office of maintaining the dignity of Paganism.

But the eloquence of Chrysostom was not to waste itself in the barren litigations of the courts of justice in Antioch, or in the vain attempt to infuse new life into the dead philosophy and religion of Greece. He felt himself summoned to a nobler field. At the age of eighteen, Chrysostom began to study that one source of eloquence to which the human heart responded, the sacred writings of the Christians. The church was not slow in recognising the value of such a proselyte. He received the strongest encouragement from Meletius, Bishop of Antioch; he was appointed a reader in the church. But the soul of Chrysostom was not likely to embrace these stirring tenets with coolness or moderation. A zealous friend inflamed, by precept and emulation, the fervour of his piety: they proposed to retire to one of the most remote hermitages in Syria; and the great Christian orator was almost self-doomed to silence, or to exhaust his power of language in prayers and ejaculations heard by no human ear. The mother of Chrysostom saved the Christian church from this fatal loss. There is something exquisitely touching in the traits of domestic affection which sometimes gleam through the busy pages of history. His mother had become a widow at the age of twenty; to the general admiration, she had remained faithful to the memory of her husband and to her maternal duties. As soon as she heard the determination of her son to retire to a distant region (Chrysostom himself relates the incident), she took him by the hand, she led him to her chamber, she made him sit by her on the bed in which she had borne him, and burst out into tears and into language more sad than tears. She spoke of the cares and troubles of widowhood; grievous as they had been, she had ever one consolation, the gazing on his face, and beholding in him the image of his departed father. Before he could speak, he had thus been her comfort and her joy. She reminded him of the fidelity with which she had administered the paternal property. "Think not that I would reproach you with these things. I have but one favour to entreat—make me not a second time a widow; awaken not again my slumbering sorrows. Wait, at least, for my death; perhaps I shall depart before long. When you have laid me in the earth, and reunited my bones to those of your father, then travel wherever thou wilt, even beyond the sea; but, as long as I live, endure to dwell in my house, and offend not God by afflicting your mother, who is at least blameless towards thee."[d]

Whether released by the death of his mother, or hurried away by the irresistible impulse which would

---

[d] M. Villemain, in his Essai sur l'Eloquence Chrétienne dans le Quatrième Siècle, has pointed out the exquisite simplicity and tenderness of this passage. De Sacerdotio, l.

not allow him to withhold himself from what he calls "the true philosophy," Chrysostom, some years afterwards, entered into one of the monasteries in the neighbourhood of Antioch. He had hardly escaped the episcopal dignity, which was almost forced upon him by the admirers of his early piety. Whether he considered this gentle violence lawful to compel devout Christians to assume awful dignity, he did not hesitate to practise a pious fraud on his friend Basilius, with whom he promised to submit to consecration. Basilius found himself a bishop, but looked in vain for his treacherous friend who had deceived him into this momentous step, but deserted him at the appointed hour.

But the voice of Chrysostom was not doomed to silence even in his seclusion. The secession of so many of the leading youths from the duties of civil life, from the municipal offices and the service of the army, had awakened the jealousy of the government. Valens issued his edict against those "followers of idleness."[e] The monks were, in some instances, assailed by popular outrage; parents, against whose approbation their children had deserted their homes and retired into the desert, appealed to the imperial authority to maintain their own. Chrysostom came forward as the zealous, the vehement, advocate of the "true philosophy."[f] He threatened misery in this life, and all the pains of hell (of which he is prodigal in his early writings) against the unnatural, the soul-slaying fathers, who forced their sons to expose themselves to the guilt and danger of the world, and forbade them to enter into the earthly society of angels; by this phrase he describes the

[e] Ignaviæ sectatores.   [f] Adversus Oppugnatores Vitæ Monasticæ.

monasteries near Antioch. He relates, with triumph, the clandestine conversion of a noble youth, through the connivance of his mother, whom the father, himself a soldier, had destined to serve in the armies of the empire.

But Chrysostom himself, whether he considered that the deep devotion of the monastery for some years had braced his soul to encounter the more perilous duties of the priesthood, appeared again in Antioch. His return was hailed by Flavianus, the bishop, who had succeeded to Meletius. He was ordained deacon, and then presbyter, and at once took his station in that office, which was sometimes reserved for the Bishop, as the principal preacher in that voluptuous and effeminate city.

The fervid imagination and glowing eloquence of Chrysostom, which had been lavished on the angelic immunity of the cœnobite or the hermit from the passions, ambition, and avarice inseparable from a secular life, now arrayed his new office in a dignity and saintly perfection, which might awake the purest ambition of the Christian. Chrysostom has the most exalted notion of the majesty, at the same time of the severity, of the sacerdotal character. His views of the office, of its mission and authority, are the most sublime; his demands upon their purity, blamelessness, and superiority to the rest of mankind, proportionably rigorous.[1]

Nor, in the loftiness of his tone as a preacher or his sanctity as a man, did he fall below his own standard of the Christian priesthood. His preaching already took its peculiar character. It was not so much addressed to

---

[1] The treatise de Sacerdotio passim.

the opinions as to the conscience of man. He threw aside the subtleties of speculative theology and repudiated, in general, the fine-drawn allegory in which the interpreters of Scripture had displayed their ingenuity, and amazed and fruitlessly wearied their unimproved audience. His scope was plain, severe, practical. Rigidly orthodox in his doctrine, he seemed to dwell more on the fruits of a pure theology (though at times he could not keep aloof from controversy) than on theology itself.

If, in her ordinary course of voluptuous amusement, of constant theatrical excitement, Antioch could not but listen to the commanding voice of the Christian orator, it is no wonder that in her hour of danger, possibly of impending ruin, the whole city stood trembling and awestruck beneath his pulpit. Soon after he had assumed the sacerdotal office, Chrysostom was placed in an extraordinary position as the representative of the bishop.

In one of those sudden tumultuous insurrections which take place among the populace of large cities, Antioch had resisted the exorbitant demands of a new taxation, maltreated the imperial officers, and thrown down and dragged about, with every kind of insult, the statues of Theodosius, his empress, and their two sons.[b] The stupor of fear succeeded to this momentary outbreak of mutiny,

A.D. 387

---

[b] It is curious to observe the similarity between the Pagan and Christian accounts of this incident which we have the good fortune to possess. Both ascribe the guilt to a few strangers, under the instigation of diabolic agency. Τοιούτοις ὑπηρέταις ὁ κακὸς χρώμενος δαίμων, ἐπραξεν, ἃ συντᾶν ἐβουλόμην. This is a sentence of Libanius (ad Theodos. iv. p. 638), not of Chrysostom. Flavianus exhorts Theodosius to pardon Antioch, in order that he may disappoint the malice of the devils, to whom he ascribes the guilt. Chrys. Hom. xvi. ad Antioch.

which had been quelled by a single troop of archers. For days the whole people awaited in shuddering agitation the sentence of the Emperor. The anger of Theodosius was terrible; he had not yet, it is true, ordered the massacre of the whole population of Thessalonica, but his stern and relentless character was too well known. Dark rumours spread abroad that he had threatened to burn Antioch, to exterminate its inhabitants, and to pass the ploughshare over its ruins. Multitudes fled destitute from the city; others remained shut up in their houses, for fear of being seized. Instead of the forum crowded with thousands, one or two persons were seen timidly wandering about. The gay and busy Antioch had the appearance of a captured and depopulated city. The theatres, the circus, were closed; no marriage-song was heard; even the schools were shut up.[1] In the mean time the government resumed its unlimited and unresisted authority, which it administered with the sternest severity and rigorous inquisition into the guilt of individuals. The prisons were thronged with criminals of every rank and station; confiscation swept away their wealth, punishments of every degree were inflicted on their persons. Citizens of the highest rank were ignominiously scourged; those who confessed their guilt were put to the sword, burned alive, or thrown to the wild beasts.[k] Chrysostom's description of the agony of those days is in the highest style of dramatic oratory. Women of the highest rank, brought up with the utmost delicacy and accustomed to every luxury, were seen crowding around the gates, or

---

[1] Liban. ad Theod. in fin.
[k] Chrysostom asserts this in a fine passage, in which he reminds his hearers of their greater offences against (God. Καὶ οἱ μὲν σιδήρῳ, οἱ δὲ πυρί, οἱ δὲ θηρίοις παραδοθέντες ἀνάλωντο. Hom. iii. 6, p. 45.

in the outer judgement hall, unattended, repelled by the rude soldiery, but still clinging to the doors or prostrate on the ground, listening to the clash of the scourges, the shrieks of the tortured victims, and the shouts of the executioners; one minute supposing that they recognised the familiar voices of fathers, husbands, or brothers; or trembling lest those who were undergoing torture should denounce their relatives and friends. Chrysostom passes from this scene, by a bold but natural transition, to the terrors of the final Judgement, and the greater agony of that day.

Now was the time to put to the test the power of Christianity, and to ascertain whether the orthodox opinions of Theodosius were altogether independent of that humanity which is the essence of the Gospel. Would the Christian Emperor listen to the persuasive supplications of the Christian prelate—that prelate for whose character he had expressed the highest respect?

While Flavianus, the aged and feeble bishop, quitting the bedside of his dying sister, set forth on his pious mission to the West, on Chrysostom devolved the duty of assuaging the fears, of administering consolation, and of profiting by this state of stupor and dejection to correct the vices and enforce serious thoughts upon the light and dissolute people. Day after day he ascended the pulpit; the whole population, deserting the forum, forgetting the theatre and the circus, thronged the churches. There was even an attendance (an unusual circumstance) after the hour of dinner. The whole city became a church. There is wonderful skill and judgement in the art with which the orator employs the circumstances of the time for his purpose; in the manner in which he allays the

Flavianus sets forth to intercede for mercy.

terror, without too highly encouraging the hopes, of the people: "The clemency of the Emperor *may* forgive their guilt, but the Christians ought to be superior to the fear of death; they cannot be secure of pardon in this world, but they may be secure of immortality in the world to come."

Sentence of Theodosius. Long before the success of the bishop's intercession could be known, the delegates of the Emperor, Hellabichus and Cæsarius, arrived with the sentence of Theodosius, which was merciful, if compared with what they had feared,—the destruction of the city, and the massacre of its inhabitants. But it was fatal to the pleasures, the comforts, the pride of Antioch. The theatres and the circus were to be closed; Antioch was no longer to enjoy theatrical representations of any kind; the baths, in an Eastern city not objects of luxury alone, but of cleanliness and health, were to be shut; and Antioch was degraded from the rank of a metropolitan city, to a town under the jurisdiction of Laodicea.

The city was in the deepest depression, but Chrysostom maintained his lofty tone of consolation. Antioch ought to rejoice at the prohibition of those scenes of vice and dissipation which disgraced the theatres: the baths tended to effeminacy and luxury, they were disdained by true philosophy—the monastic system; the dignity of the city did not depend on its rank in the empire, but on the virtue of its citizens; it might be a heavenly, if no longer an earthly, metropolis.

The inquisition into the guilt of those who had actually assisted, or had looked on in treasonable indifference, while the statues of the Emperor and his family were treated with such unseemly contumely, had commenced under the regular authorities; it was now carried on with stern and indiscriminate impartiality. The prisoners were crowded together in a great open enclosure, in one close and agonising troop, which comprehended the whole senate of the city. The third day of the inquiry was to witness the execution of the guilty, and no one, not the relatives or kindred of the wealthiest, the noblest, or the highest in station, knew whether the doom had not fallen on their fathers or husbands.

But Hellabichus and Cæsarius were men of humanity, and ventured to suspend the execution of the sentence. They listened to the supplications of the people. One mother, especially, seized and clung to the reins of the horse of Hellabichus. The monks who, while the philosophers, as Chrysostom asserts, had fled the city, had poured down from their mountain solitudes, and during the whole time had endeavoured to assuage the fear of the people, and to awaken the compassion of the government, renewed, not without effect, their pious exertions.[m] They crowded round the tribunal, and one, named Macedonius, was so courageous as boldly to remonstrate against the crime of avenging the destruction of a few images of brass by the destruction of the image of God in so many human beings. Cæsarius himself undertook a journey to Constantinople for farther instructions.

At length Chrysostom had the satisfaction to announce to the people the return of the bishop with an act of unlimited amnesty. He described the interview of Flavianus with the Emperor; his silence, his shame, his tears, when Theodosius gently reminded him of his benefactions

[m] Chrysostom, Hom. xvii. vol. II. p. 172.

to the city which enhanced their heinous ingratitude. The reply of Flavianus, though the orator professes to relate it on the authority of one present at the interview, is no doubt coloured by the eloquence of Chrysostom. The Bishop acknowledged the guilt of the city in the most humiliating language. But he urged, that the greater that guilt, the greater would be the magnanimity of the Emperor if he should pardon it. He would raise statues, not of perishable materials, in the hearts of all mankind. It is not the glory of Theodosius, he proceeded, but Christianity itself, which is put to the test before the world. The Jews and Greeks, even the most remote barbarians, are anxiously watching whether this sentence will be that of Christian clemency. How will they all glorify the Christian's God if he shall restrain the wrath of the master of the world, and subdue him to that humanity which would be magnanimous even in a private man. Inexorable punishment might awe other cities into obedience, but mercy would attach mankind by the stronger bonds of love. It would be an imperishable example of clemency, and all future acts of other sovereigns would be but the fruit of this, and would reflect their glory on Theodosius. What glory to concede that to a single aged priest, from the fear of God, which he had refused to all other suppliants. For himself, Flavianus could never bear to return to his native city; he would remain an exile, until that city was reconciled with the Emperor. Theodosius, it is said, called to mind the prayer of the Saviour for his enemies, and satisfied his wounded pride that in his mercy he imitated his Redeemer. He was even anxious that Flavianus should return to announce the full pardon before the festival of Easter. "Let the Gentiles," exclaims the ardent preacher, "be confounded, or rather, let them be instructed by this unexampled instance of imperial clemency and episcopal influence."[a]

Theodosius had ceased to reign many years before Chrysostom was summoned to the pontifical throne of Constantinople. The East was now governed by women and eunuchs. In assuming the episcopal throne of the metropolis, to which he is said to have been transported almost by force, Chrysostom, who could not but be conscious of his power over the minds of men, might entertain visions of the noblest and purest ambition. His views of the dignity of the sacerdotal character were as lofty as those of his contemporaries in the West; while he asserted their authority, which set them apart and far above the rest of mankind, he demanded a moral superiority and entire devotion to their calling, which could not but rivet their authority upon the minds of men. The clergy, such as his glowing imagination conceived them, would unite the strongest corporate spirit with the highest individual zeal and purity. The influence of the bishop in Antioch, the deference which Theodosius had shown to the intercession of Flavianus, might encourage Chrysostom in the fallacious hope of restoring peace, virtue, and piety, as well as orthodoxy, in the imperial city.

But in the East, more particularly in the metropolis, the sacerdotal character never assumed the unassailable sanctity, the awful inviolability, which it attained in the West. The religion of Constantinople was that of the Emperor. Instead of growing up, like the Bishop of Rome, first to

---

[a] Chrysostom had ventured to assert—"Ἀνὴρ οὐδενὶ ἑτέρῳ, ταῦτα χαρίεται τοῖς ἱερεῦσι. Hom. xi. 3.

independence, afterwards to sovereignty, the religious supremacy was overawed and obscured by the presence of the Imperial Government. In Rome, the Pope was subject at times to the rebellious control of the aristocracy, or exposed to the irreverent fury of the populace; but he constantly emerged from his transient obscurity and resumed his power. In Constantinople, a voluptuous court, a savage populace, at this period multitudes of concealed Arians, and heretics of countless shades and hues at all periods, thwarted the plans, debased the dignity, and desecrated the person of the Patriarch of Constantinople.

In some respects, Chrysostom's character wanted the peculiar, and perhaps inconsistent qualifications requisite for his position. He was the preacher, but not the man of the world. A great capital is apt to demand that magnificence in its prelate at which it murmurs. It will not respect less than splendid state and the show of authority, while at the same time it would have the severest austerity and the strongest display of humility,—the pomp of the Pontiff with the poverty and lowliness of the Apostle. Chrysostom carried the asceticism of the monk not merely into his private chamber but into his palace and his hall. The great prelates of the West, when it was expedient, could throw off the monk and appear as statesmen or as nobles in their public transactions; though this, indeed, was much less necessary than in Constantinople. But Chrysostom cherished all these habits with zealous, perhaps with ostentatious, fidelity. Instead of munificent hospitality, he took his scanty meal in his solitary chamber. His rigid economy endured none of that episcopal sumptuousness with which his predecessor Nectarius had dazzled the public eye: he proscribed all the carpets, all the silken dresses; he sold the costly furniture and the rich vessels of his residence; he was said even to have retrenched from the church some of its gorgeous plate, and to have sold some rich marbles and furniture designed for the Anastasia. He was lavish, on the other hand, in his expenditure on the hospitals and charitable institutions. But even the uses to which they were applied, did not justify to the general feeling the alienation of those ornaments from the service of the church. The populace, who, no doubt, in their hours of discontent, had contrasted the magnificence of Nectarius with apostolical poverty, were now offended by the apostolical poverty of Chrysostom, which seemed unworthy of his lofty station.

But the Bishop of Constantinople had even a more difficult task in prescribing to himself the limits of his interference with secular affairs. *Political difficulties of Chrysostom.* It is easy to imagine, in the clergy, a high and serene indifference to the political tumults of society. This is perpetually demanded by those who find the sacerdotal influence adverse to their own views; but to the calm inquirer, *Interference of the clergy in secular affairs.* this simple question becomes the most difficult and intricate problem in religious history. If religion consisted solely in the intercourse between man and his Creator; if the Christian minister were merely the officiating functionary in the ceremonial of the church, —the human mediator between the devotion of man and the providence of God,—the voice which expresses the common adoration,—the herald who announces the gracious message of revelation to mankind,—nothing could be more clear than the line which might exclude him from all political, or even all worldly affairs. But Christianity is likewise a moral power; and as that

moral power or guide, religion, and the minister of
religion, cannot refrain from interposing in all questions
of human conduct; as the interpreter of the divine law
to the perplexed and doubting conscience, it cannot but
spread its dominion over the whole field of human
action. In this character religion embraced the whole
life of man, public as well as private. How was the
minister of that religion to pause and discriminate as to
the extent of his powers, particularly since the public
acts of the most eminent in station possessed such
unlimited influence over the happiness of society and
even the eternal welfare of the whole community?
What public misconduct was not at the same time an
unchristian act? Were the clergy, by connivance, to
become accomplices in vices which they did not
endeavour to counteract? Christianity on the throne
as in the cottage, was equally bound to submit on every
point in which religious motive or principle ought to
operate, in every act, therefore, of life, to the admitted
restraints of the Gospel; and the general feeling of
Christianity at this period had invested the clergy with
the right, or rather the duty, of enforcing the precepts
of the Gospel on every professed believer. How, then,
were the clergy to distinguish between the individual
and political capacity of the man; to respect the
prince, yet to advise the Christian; to look with indifference on one set of actions as secular, to admonish
on the danger of another as affairs of conscience?

Nor at this early period of its still aggressive, still
consciously beneficial influence, could the hierarchy be
expected to anticipate with coldly prophetic prudence
the fatal consequence of some of its own encroachments
on worldly authority. The bishop of a great capital
was the conductor, the representative, of the moral

power of the Gospel, which was perpetually striving to obtain its ascendancy over brute force, violence, and vice; and of necessity, perhaps, was not always cautious or discreet in the means to which it resorted. It became contaminated in the incessant strife, and forgot its end, or rather sought for the mastery as its end, rather than as the legitimate means of promoting its beneficial objects. Under the full, and no doubt, at first, warrantable persuasion, that it was advancing the happiness and virtue of mankind, where should it arrest its own course, or set limits to its own humanising and improving interpositions? Thus, under the constant temptation of assuming, as far as possible, the management of affairs which were notoriously mismanaged through the vices of public men, the administration even of public matters by the clergy might seem, to them at least, to insure justice, disinterestedness, and clemency. Till tried by the possession of power, they would be the last to discern the danger of being invested in that power.

The first signal interposition of Chrysostom in the political affairs of Constantinople was an act not merely of humanity but of gratitude. *Eutropius the eunuch.* Eutropius the eunuch, minister of the feeble Arcadius, is condemned to immortal infamy by the vigorous satire of Claudian. Among his few good deeds, had been the advancement of Chrysostom to the see of Constantinople. Eutropius had found it necessary to restrict the right of asylum, which began to be generally claimed by all the Christian churches, little foreseeing that to the bold assertion of that right he would owe his life.

There is something sublime in the first notion of the right of asylum. It is one of those institutions based in the universal religious sentiment of man; it is found in almost all religions. In the Greek, as in the Jewish, man took refuge from the vengeance, often from the injustice, of his fellow-men, in the presence of the gods. Not merely private revenge, but the retributive severity of the law, stands rebuked before the dignity of the divine court, in which the criminal has lodged his appeal. The lustrations in the older religions, the rites of expiation and reconciliation performed in many of the temples, the appellations of certain deities, as the reconcilers or pacifiers of man,* were enwoven with their mythology, and embodied in their poetry. But Christianity, in a still higher and more universal sense, might assume to take under its protection, in order to amend and purify, the outcast of society, whom human justice followed with relentless vengeance. As the representative of the God of mercy it excluded no human being from the pale of repentance, and would protect the worst, when disposed to that salutary change, if it could possibly be made consistent with the public peace and safety. The merciful intervention of the clergy between the criminal and his sentence, at a period when the laws were so implacable and sanguinary, was at once consistent with Christian charity and tended to some mitigation of the ferocious manners of the age. It gave time at least for exasperated justice to reconsider its sentence, and checked that vindictive impulse, which if it did not outrun the law, hurried it to instantaneous and irrevocable execution.⁹ But that which commenced in pure

---

* The ἀποτροπαιοι, or averruncators. the right of asylum had been granted by the Heathen to their altars, and to
⁹ In a law which is extant in Greek, the statues of the Emperors, it ought there is an elaborate argument, that if to belong to the temples of God.

See

benevolence had already, it should seem, begun to degenerate into a source of power. The course of justice was impeded, but not by a wise discrimination between the more or less heinous delinquents, or a salutary penitential system, which might reclaim the guilty and safely restore him to society.

Like other favourites of arbitrary sovereigns, Eutropius was suddenly precipitated from the height of power. The army forced the sentence of his dismissal from the timid Emperor; and the furious populace, as usual, thirsted for the blood of him to whose unbounded sway they had so long submitted in humble obedience. Eutropius fled in haste to that asylum, the sanctity of which had been limited by his own decree; and the courage and influence of Chrysostom protected that most forlorn of human beings, the discarded favourite of a despot. The armed soldiery and the raging populace were met at the door of the church by the defenceless ecclesiastic. His demeanour and the sanctity of the place arrested the blind fury of the assailants. Chrysostom before the Emperor pleaded the cause of Eutropius with the same fearless freedom; and for once the life of a fallen minister was spared, his sentence was commuted for banishment. His fate indeed was only delayed; he was afterwards brought back from Cyprus, his place of exile, and beheaded at Chalcedon.

A.D. 399.

Chrysostom saves the life of Eutropius.

See the laws which defined the right of asylum, Cod. Theodos. lx. 45. 3, et seqq. The sacred space extended to the outer gates of the church. But those who took refuge in the church were on no account to be permitted to profane the holy building itself by eating or sleeping within it. "Quibus si perfuga non admit, neque consentit, præferenda humanitati religio est." There was a strong prohibition against introducing arms into the churches; a prohibition which the Emperors themselves did not scruple to violate on more than one occasion.

But with all his courage, his eloquence, his moral dignity, Chrysostom, instead of establishing a firm and permanent authority over Constantinople, became himself the victim of intrigue and jealousy. Besides his personal habits and manners, the character of Chrysostom, firm on great occasions and eminently persuasive when making a general address to the multitude, was less commanding and authoritative in his constant daily intercourse with the various orders. Calm and self-possessed as an orator, he was accused of being passionate and overbearing in ordinary business: the irritability of feeble health may have caused some part of this infirmity. Men, whose minds, like that of Chrysostom, are centered on one engrossing object, are apt to abandon the details of business to others, who thus become necessary to them, and at length, if artful and dextrous, rule them with inextricable sway: they have much knowledge of mankind, little practical acquaintance with individual men. Thus, Chrysostom was completely governed by his deacon Serapion who managed his affairs, and like all men of address in such stations, while he exercised all the power, and secured the solid advantages, left the odium and responsibility upon his master. On the whole, the character of Chrysostom retained something of the unworldly monastic enthusiasm, and wanted decisive practical wisdom, when compared, for instance, with Ambrose in the West; and thus his character powerfully contributed to his fall.[q]

But the circumstances of his situation might have

---

[q] The unfavourable view of Chrysostom's character is brought out perhaps with more than impartiality by the ecclesiastical historian Sozomen, who wrote at Constantinople, and may have preserved much of the hostile tradition relating to him.

embarrassed even Ambrose himself. All orders and interests conspired against him. The court would not endure the grave and severe censor; the clergy rebelled against the rigour of the prelate's discipline; the populace, though when under the spell of his eloquence, fondly attached to his person, no doubt, in general resented his implacable condemnation of their amusements. The Arians, to whom, in his uncompromising zeal, he had persuaded the Emperor to refuse a single church, though demanded by the most powerful subject of the empire, Gainas the Goth, were still no doubt secretly powerful. A Pagan prefect, Optatus, seized the opportunity of wreaking his animosity towards Christianity itself upon its powerful advocate. Some wealthy females are named as resenting the severe condemnation of their dress and manners.[7]

Of all these adversaries, the most dangerous, the most persevering, and the most implacable, were those of his own order and his own rank.[8] The sacerdotal authority in the East was undermined by its own divisions. The imperial power, which, in the hands of a violent, and not irreproachable woman, the Empress Eudoxia, might, perhaps, have quailed before the energy of a blameless and courageous prelate, allied itself with one section of the church, and so secured its triumph over the whole. The more Chrysostom endeavoured to carry out by episcopal authority those exalted notions of the sacerdotal character which he had developed in his work upon the priesthood, the more he estranged many of his natural supporters. He visited the whole of Asia Minor; degraded bishops; exposed with unsparing indignation the vices and venality of the clergy; and involved them

[7] Tillemont, p. 180.
[8] The good Tillemont confesses this humiliating truth with shame and reluctance. Vie de Chrysostome, p. 181.

all in one indiscriminate charge of simony and licentiousness. The assumption of this authority was somewhat questionable; the severity with which it was exercised did not reconcile the reluctant province to submission. Among the malcontent clergy, four bishops took the lead; but the head of this unrelenting faction was Theophilus, the violent and unscrupulous Prelate of Alexandria. The apparently trivial causes which inflamed the hostility of Theophilus confirm a suspicion, previously suggested, that the rivalry of the two principal sees in the East mingled with the personal animosity of Theophilus against the Bishop of Constantinople. Chrysostom had been accused of extending his jurisdiction beyond its legitimate bounds. Certain monks of Nitria had fled from the persecutions of Theophilus, and taken refuge in Constantinople; and Chrysostom had extended his countenance, if not his protection, to these revolted subjects of the Alexandrian prelate. But he had declined to take legal cognisance of the dispute as a superior prelate, or as the head of a council; partly, he states,[1] out of respect for Theophilus, partly because he was unwilling to interfere in the affairs of another province. But Theophilus was not so scrupulous; he revenged himself for the supposed invasion of his own province by a most daring inroad on that of his rival. He assumed for the Patriarch of Alexandria the right of presiding over the Eastern bishops, and of summoning the Bishop of Constantinople before this irregular tribunal. Theophilus, with the sanction, if not by the invitation, of the Empress, landed at Constantinople. He was accompanied by a band of Alexandrian

---

[1] Epist. ad Innocentium Papam, vol. iii. p. 516.

mariners as a protection against the populace of the city.

The council was held, not in Constantinople, but at a place called the Oak, in the suburb of Chalcedon. It consisted for the most part of Egyptian bishops, under the direct influence of Theophilus, and of Asiatic prelates, the personal enemies of Chrysostom.* For fourteen days it held its sessions, and received informations, which gradually grew into twenty-nine grave and specific charges. Four times was Chrysostom summoned to appear before this self-appointed tribunal, of which it was impossible for him to recognise the legal authority. In the mean time, he was not inactive in his peculiar sphere—the pulpit. Unfortunately, the authenticity of the sermon ascribed to him at this period is not altogether certain, nor the time at which some extant discourses, if genuine, were delivered, conclusively settled. One, however, bears strong indications of the manner and sentiments of Chrysostom; and it is generally acknowledged that he either did boldly use, or was accused of using, language full of contumelious allusion to the Empress. This sermon, therefore, if not an accurate report of his expressions, may convey the sense of what he actually uttered, or which was attributed to him by his adversaries.ˣ "The billows," said the energetic prelate, "are

Council of the Oak.

---

* It is contested whether there were thirty or forty-six bishops.

ˣ It is singularly characteristic of the Christianity of the times to observe the charges against which Chrysostom protests with the greatest vehemence; and this part of the oration in question is confirmed by one of his letters to Cyriacus. Against that of personal impurity with a female, he calmly offers the most unquestionable evidence. But he was likewise accused of having administered baptism after he had eaten. On this he breaks out :—"If I have done this, Anathema upon me; may I be no longer counted among bishops, nor be admitted among the angels accepted

mighty, and the storm furious; but we fear not to be wrecked, for we are founded on a rock. What can I fear? Death? *To me to live is Christ, and to die is gain.* Exile? *The earth is the Lord's and the fulness thereof.* Confiscation? *We brought nothing into this world, and it is certain we can carry nothing out of it.* I scorn the terrors, and smile at the advantages of life. I fear not death. I desire to live only for your profit. The church against which you strive, dashes away your assaults into idle foam. It is fixed by God, who shall revoke it? The church is stronger than Heaven itself! *Heaven and earth shall pass away, but my words shall not pass away.* * * * But you know, my brethren, the true cause of my ruin. Because I have not strewn rich carpets on my floors, nor clothed myself in silken robes; because I have discountenanced the sensuality of certain persons. The seed of the serpent is still alive, but grace is still on the side of Elijah." Then follows in obscure and embarrassed language, as though, if genuine, the preacher were startled at his own boldness, an allusion to the fate of John the Baptist, and to the hostility of Herodias:—"It is a time of wailing—lo, all things tend to "*disgrace;* but time judgeth all things." The fatal word, "*disgrace,*" (ἀδοξία) was supposed to be an allusion to Eudoxia, the Empress.

There was a secret understanding between the court and the council. The court urged the proceedings of the council, and the council pronounced the sentence of deposition, but left to the

---

of God." He was said to have administered the sacrament to those who had in like manner broken their fast. "If I have done so, may I be rejected of Christ." He then justifies himself, even if guilty, by the example of Paul, and even of Christ himself, but still seems to look on this breach of discipline with the utmost horror.

court to take cognisance of the darker charge of high treason, of which they asserted Chrysostom to be guilty, but which was beyond their jurisdiction. The alleged treason was the personal insult to the Empress Eudoxia, which was construed into exciting the people to rebellion. But the execution of this sentence embarrassed the council and the irresolute government. Chrysostom now again ruled the popular mind with unbounded sway. It would have been dangerous to have seized him in the church, environed, as he constantly was, by crowds of admiring hearers, whom a few fervent words might have maddened into insurrection.

Chrysostom, however, shrunk, whether from timidity or Christian peacefulness of disposition, from being the cause, even innocently, of tumult and bloodshed. *Chrysostom leaves Constantinople.* He had neither the ambition, the desperate recklessness, nor perhaps the resolution, of a demagogue. He would not be the Christian tribune of the people. He seized the first opportunity of the absence of his hearers quietly to surrender himself to the imperial officers. He was cautiously transported by night, though the jealous populace crowded the streets in order to release their prelate from the hands of his enemies, to the opposite side of the Bosphorus and confined in a villa on the Bithynian shore.

The triumph of Chrysostom's enemies was complete. Theophilus entered the city, and proceeded to wreak his vengeance on the partisans of his adversary; the Empress rejoiced in the conscious assurance of her power; the people were overawed into gloomy and sullen silence.

The night of the following day, strange and awful sounds were heard throughout the city. The palace, the whole of Constantinople, shook with an earthquake. The Empress, as superstitious as she was violent, when she felt her chamber rock beneath her, shuddering at the manifest wrath of Heaven, fell on her knees, and entreated the Emperor to revoke the fatal sentence. She wrote a hasty letter, disclaiming all hostility to the banished prelate, and protesting that she was "innocent of his blood." The next day, the palace was surrounded by clamorous multitudes, impatiently demanding his recall. The voice of the people and the voice of God seemed to join in the vindication of Chrysostom. The edict of recall was issued; the Bosphorus swarmed with barks, eager to communicate the first intelligence, and to obtain the honour of bringing back the guardian and the pride of the city. He was met on his arrival by the whole population, men, women, and children; all who could, bore torches in their hands, and hymns of thanksgiving, composed for the occasion, were chanted before him, as he proceeded to the great church. His enemies fled on all sides. Soon after, Theophilus, on the demand of a free council, left Constantinople, at the dead of the night, and embarked for Alexandria.

There is again some doubt as to the authenticity of the first discourse delivered by Chrysostom on this occasion,—none of the second. But the first was an extemporaneous address, to which the extant speech appears to correspond. "What shall I say? Blessed be God! These were my last words on my departure, these the first on my return. Blessed be God! because he permitted the storm to rage; Blessed be God! because he has allayed it. Let my enemies behold how their conspiracy has advanced my peace, and redounded to my glory. Before, the church alone was crowded, now, the whole forum is become a church. The games are celebrating in the circus, but the whole people pour like a torrent to the church. Your prayers in my behalf are more glorious than a diadem,—the prayers both of men and women; for in *Christ there is neither male nor female.*"

In the second oration he draws an elaborate comparison between the situation of Abraham in Egypt and his own. The barbarous Egyptian (this struck, no doubt, at Theophilus) had endeavoured to defile his Sarah, the church of Constantinople; but the faithful church had remained, by the power of God, uncontaminated by this rebuked Abimelech. He dwelt with pardonable pride on the faithful attachment of his followers. They had conquered; but how? by prayer and submission. The enemy had brought arms into the sanctuary, they had prayed; like a spider's web the enemy had been scattered, the faithful remained firm as a rock. The Empress herself had joined the triumphal procession, when the sea became, as the city, covered with all ranks, all ages, and both sexes.[y]

But the peace and triumph of Chrysostom were not lasting. As the fears of the Empress were allayed, the old feeling of hatred to the Bishop, embittered by the shame of defeat, and the constant suspicion that either the preacher or his audience pointed at her his most vigorous declamation, rankled in the mind of Eudoxia. It had become a strife for ascendancy, and neither could recede with safety and honour. Opportunities could not but occur to enrage and exasperate; nor

---

[y] Chrysostom, in both these discourses, states a curious circumstance, that the Jews of Constantinople took great interest in his cause.

would ill-disposed persons be wanting to inflame the passions of the Empress, by misrepresenting and personally applying the bold and indignant language of the prelate.

A statue of the Empress was about to be erected; and on these occasions of public festival the people were wont to be indulged in dances, pantomimes, and every kind of theatrical amusement. The zeal of Chrysostom was always especially directed against these idolatrous amusements, which often, he confesses, drained the church of his hearers. This, now ill-timed, zeal was especially awakened, because the statue was to be erected, and the rejoicings to take place, in front of the entrance to the great church, the St. Sophia. His denunciations were construed into personal insults to the Empress; she threatened a new council. The prelate threw off the remaining restraints of prudence; repeated more explicitly the allusion which he had before but covertly hinted. He thundered out a homily, with the memorable exordium, "Herodias is maddening, Herodias is dancing, Herodias demands the head of John." If Chrysostom could even be suspected of such daring outrage against the temporal sovereign; if he ventured on language approaching to such unmeasured hostility; it was manifest that either the imperial authority must quail and submit to the sacerdotal domination, or employ, without scruple, its power to crush the bold usurpation.

An edict of the Emperor suspended the prelate from his functions. Though forty-two bishops adhered, with inflexible fidelity, to his cause, he was condemned by a second hostile council, not on any new charge, but for contumacy in resisting the decrees of the former assembly, and for a breach of the ecclesiastical laws, in resuming his authority while under the condemnation of a council.

The soldiers of the Emperor were more dangerous enemies than the prelates. In the midst of the solemn celebration of Good Friday, in the great church of Santa Sophia, the military forced their way, not merely into the nave, but up to the altar, on which were placed the consecrated elements. Many worshippers were trodden under foot; many wounded by the swords of the soldiers; the clergy were dragged to prison; some females, who were about to be baptized, were obliged to fly with their disordered apparel: the waters of the font were stained with blood; the soldiers pressed up to the altar; seized the sacred vessels as their plunder: the sacred elements were scattered about; their garments were bedewed with the blood of the Redeemer.[a] Constantinople for several days had the appearance of a city which had been stormed. Wherever the partisans of Chrysostom were assembled, they were assaulted and dispersed by the soldiery; females were exposed to insult, and one frantic attempt was made to assassinate the prelate.[b]

Chrysostom at length withdrew from the contest; he escaped from the friendly custody of his adherents, and surrendered himself to the imperial officers. He was immediately conveyed by night to the Asiatic shore. At the instant of his departure, another fearful calamity agitated the public

---

[a] Chrysostom, Epist. ad Innocentium, c. iii. v. iii. p. 519. Chrysostom exempts the Emperor from all share in this outrage; but attributes it to the hostile bishops.

[b] See Letter to Olympias, p. 548.

mind. The church which he left burst into flames, and the conflagration, said to have first broken out in the episcopal throne, reached the roof of the building, and spread from thence to the senate-house. These two magnificent edifices, the latter of which contained some noble specimens of ancient art, became in a few hours a mass of ruins. The partisans of Chrysostom, and Chrysostom himself, were, of course, accused of this act, the author of which was never discovered, and in which no life was lost. But the bishop was charged with the horrible design of destroying his enemies in the church; his followers were charged with the guilt of incendiarism with a less atrocious object, that no bishop after Chrysostom might be seated in his pontifical throne.[b]

The prelate was not permitted to choose his place of exile. The peaceful spots which might have been found in the more genial climate of Bithynia, or in the adjacent provinces, would have been too near the capital. He was transported to Cucusus, a small town in the mountainous and savage district of Armenia. On his journey thither of several days, he suffered much from fever and disquiet of mind, and from the cruelty of the officer who commanded the guard.[c]

Yet his influence was not extinguished by his

---

[b] There are three laws in the Theodosian Code against unlawful and seditious meetings (conventicula), directed against the followers of Chrysostom,—the Joannitæ, as they were called, "qui sacrilego animo auctoritatem nostri numinis sui fuerint expugnare." The *deity* is the usual term, but the deity of the feeble Arcadius, and of the passionate Eudoxia, reads strangely.

[c] The zeal of Chrysostom did not slumber even in this remote retreat. In his power he had caused to be destroyed all the temples of Cybele in Phrygia. He now urged the tardy monks to the destruction of all the Heathen Temples in the neighbouring districts. Epist. 129. 126. Compare Chastel, p. 220.

absence. The Eastern Church was almost governed from the solitary cell of Chrysostom. He corresponded in all quarters; women of rank and opulence sought his solitude in disguise. The bishops of many distant sees sent him assistance, and coveted his advice. The Bishop of Rome received his letters with respect, and wrote back ardent commendations of his patience. The exile of Cucusus exercised perhaps more extensive authority than the Patriarch of Constantinople.[d]

His retreat.

He was not, however, permitted to remain in peace in this miserable seclusion: sometimes his life was endangered by the invasions of the Isaurian marauders; and he was obliged to take refuge in a neighbouring fortress, named Ardissa. He encouraged his ardent disciples with the hope, the assurance, of his speedy return; but he miscalculated the obstinate and implacable resentment of his persecutors. At length an order came to remove him to Pityus, on the Euxine, a still more savage place on the verge of the empire. He died on the journey, near Comana, in Pontus.

Some years afterwards, the remains of Chrysostom were transported to Constantinople with the utmost reverence, and received with solemn pomp. Constantinople, and the imperial family, submitted with eager zeal to worship

His remains transported to Constantinople.

---

[d] Among his letters may be remarked those written to the celebrated Olympias. This wealthy widow, who had refused the solicitations or commands of Theodosius to marry one of his favourites, had almost washed away, by her austerities and virtues, the stain of her nuptials, and might rank in Christian estimation with those unsullied virgins who had never been contaminated by marriage. She was the friend of all the distinguished and orthodox clergy,—of Gregory of Nazianzum, and of Chrysostom. Chrysostom records to her *proter*, that by her austerities, she had brought on painful diseases, which baffled the art of medicine. Chrysost. Epist. viii. p. 540.

as a saint him whom they would not endure as a prelate.

The remarkable part in the whole of this persecution of Chrysostom is that it arose not out of difference of doctrine or polemic hostility. No charge of heresy darkened the pure fame of the great Christian orator. His persecution had not the dignity of conscientious bigotry; it was a struggle for power between the temporal and ecclesiastical supremacy; but the passions and the personal animosities of ecclesiastics, the ambition, and perhaps the jealousy of the Alexandrian Patriarch as to jurisdiction, lent themselves to the degradation of the episcopal authority in Constantinople, from which it never rose. No doubt the choleric temper, the overstrained severity, the monastic habits, the ambition to extend his authority, perhaps beyond its legitimate bounds, and the indiscreet zeal of Chrysostom, laid him open to his adversaries; but in any other station, in the episcopate of any other city, these infirmities would have been lost in the splendour of his talents and his virtues. Though he might not have weaned the general mass of the people from their vices or their amusements, which he proscribed with equal severity, yet he would have commanded general respect; and nothing less than a schism, arising out of religious difference, would have shaken or impaired his authority.

At all events, the fall of Chrysostom was an inauspicious omen, and a warning which might repress the energy of future prelates; and, doubtless, the issue of this conflict materially tended to degrade the office of the chief bishop in the Eastern empire. It may be questioned whether the proximity of the court, and such a court as that of the East, would, under any circumstances, have allowed the episcopate to assume its legitimate power, far less to have encroached on the temporal sovereignty. But after this time, the Bishop of Constantinople almost sank into a high officer of state; appointed by the influence, if not directly nominated by the Emperor, his gratitude was bound to reverence, or his prudence to dread, that arbitrary power which had raised him from nothing, and might dismiss him to his former insignificance. Except on some rare occasions, he bowed with the rest of the empire before the capricious will of the sovereign or the ruling favourite; he was content if the Emperor respected the outward ceremonial of the church, and did not openly espouse any heretical doctrine.

Christianity thus remained, in some respects, an antagonist principle, counteracting by its perpetual remonstrance, and rivalling by its attractive ceremonial, the vices and licentious diversions of the capital; but its moral authority was not allied with power; it quailed under the universal despotism, and was entirely inefficient as a corrective of imperial tyranny. It thus escaped the evils inseparable from the undue elevation of the sacerdotal character, and the temptations to encroach beyond its proper limits on the civil power; but it likewise gradually sank far below that uncompromising independence, that venerable majesty, which might impose some restraint on the worst excesses of violence, and infuse justice and humanity into the manners of the court and of the people.

CHAPTER X.

The great Prelates of the West.

THE character and the fate of Ambrose offer the
strongest contrast with that of Chrysostom.
Ambrose was no dreaming solitary brought
up in the seclusion of the desert or among a fraternity
of religious husbandmen. He had been versed in civil
business from his youth; he had already obtained a
high station in the Imperial service. His eloquence
had little of the richness, imaginative variety, or
dramatic power of the Grecian orator; hard but
vigorous, it was Roman, forensic, practical—I mean
where it related to affairs of business, or addressed men
in general; it has, as we shall hereafter observe, a very
different character in some of his theological writings.

In Ambrose the sacerdotal character assumed a
dignity and an influence as yet unknown; it first began
to confront the throne not only on terms of equality,
but of superior authority, and to exercise a spiritual
dictatorship over the supreme magistrate. The resistance of Athanasius to the Imperial authority had
been firm but deferential, passive rather than aggressive.
In his *public* addresses he had respected the majesty of
the empire; at all events, the hierarchy of that period
only questioned the authority of the sovereign in
matters of faith. But in Ambrose the episcopal power
acknowledged no limits to its moral dominion, and
admitted no distinction of persons. While the bishops
of Rome were comparatively without authority, and

Ambrose Archbishop of Milan.

still partially obscured by the concentration of Paganism in the aristocracy of the Capitol, the Archbishop of Milan began to develop papal power and papal imperiousness. Ambrose was the spiritual ancestor of the Hildebrands and the Innocents. Like Chrysostom, Ambrose had to strive against the passionate animosity of an empress, not merely exasperated against him by his suspected disrespect and disobedience, but by the bitterness of religious difference. Yet how opposite the result! And Ambrose had to assert his religious authority, not against the feeble Arcadius, but against his father, the great Theodosius. We cannot, indeed, but recognise something of the undegraded Roman or the West in Ambrose; Chrysostom has something of the feebleness and degeneracy of the Byzantine.

The father of Ambrose, who bore the same name, had administered the province of Gaul as prætorian prefect. The younger Ambrose, while pursuing his studies at Rome, had attracted the notice of Probus, prætorian prefect of Italy. Ambrose, through his influence, was appointed to the administration of the provinces of Æmilia and Liguria.[a] Probus was a Christian, and his parting admonition to the young civilian was couched in these prophetic words— "Rule the province, not as a judge, but as a bishop."[b] Milan was within the department assigned to Ambrose. This city had now begun almost to rival or eclipse Rome as the capital of the Occidental empire, and from the celebrity of its schools it was called the Athens of the West. The Church of Milan was rent with

---

[a] Chiefly from the life of Ambrose affixed to the Benedictine edition of his works; the Life by Paulinus; and Tillemont.
[b] Paul. Vit. Ambros. 8.

divisions. On a vacancy caused by the death of Auxentius, the celebrated Arian, the two parties, the Arian and the Athanasian, violently contested the appointment of the bishop.

Ambrose appeared in his civil character to allay the tumult, by the awe of his presence and by the persuasive force of his eloquence. He spoke so wisely, and in such a Christian spirit, that a general acclamation suddenly broke forth, "Ambrose, be bishop—Ambrose, be bishop." Ambrose was yet only a catechumen; he attempted in every way, by assuming a severe character as a magistrate, and by flight, to elude the unexpected honour.[c] The ardour of the people, and the approbation of the Emperor,[d] compelled him to assume the office. Ambrose cast off at once the pomp and majesty of his civil state; but that which was in some degree disadvantageous to Chrysostom, his severe simplicity of life, only increased the admiration and attachment of the less luxurious, or at least less effeminate, West, to their pious prelate; for Ambrose assumed only the austerity, nothing of the inactive and contemplative seclusion of the monastic system. The only Eastern influence which fettered his strong mind was his earnest admiration of celibacy; in all other respects he was a Roman statesman, not a meditative Oriental, or rhetorical Greek. The strong contrast of this doctrine with the dissolute manners of Rome, which no doubt extended to Milan, made it the more impressive: it was received with all the ardour of novelty, and the impetuosity of the Italian character; it captivated all ranks and all

_{Ambrose Bishop A.D. 374.}

_{Ambrose advocate of celibacy.}

---

[c] De Offic.; Vita S. Ambros.; Epist. xxi. p. 865; Epist. lxiii.

[d] Compare the account of Valentinian's conduct in Theodoret, iv. 7.

orders. Mothers shut up their daughters, lest they should be exposed to the chaste seduction of the bishop's eloquence; and, binding themselves by rash vows of virginity, forfeit the hope of becoming Roman matrons. Ambrose, immediately on his appointment, under Valentinian I., asserted that ecclesiastical power which he confirmed under the feeble reign of Gratian and Valentinian II.;* he maintained it when he was confronted by a nobler antagonist, the great Theodosius. He assumed the office of director of the royal conscience, and he administered that office with all the uncompromising moral dignity which had no indulgence for unchristian vices, for injustice, or cruelty, even in an emperor; and with all the stern and conscientious intolerance of one, with whom hatred of paganism and of heresy was a prime article of his creed. The Old and the New Testament met in the person of Ambrose —the implacable hostility to idolatry, the abhorrence of every deviation from the established formulary of belief; the wise and courageous benevolence, the generous and unselfish devotion to the great interests of humanity.

If Christianity assumed a haughtier and more rigid tone in the conduct and writings of Ambrose, it was by no means forgetful of its gentler duties, in allaying human misery and extending its beneficent care to the utmost bounds of society. With Ambrose it began its high office of mitigating the horrors of slavery, which now that war raged in turn on every frontier, might seem to threaten individually the whole free population of the empire. Rome, who had drawn new supplies of slaves from almost every frontier of her dominions, now

---

* Theodoret, iv. 7.

suffered fearful reprisals; her free citizens were sent into captivity and sold in the markets by the barbarians, whose ancestors had been bought and bartered by her insatiable slave trade. The splendid offerings of piety, the ornaments, even the consecrated vessels of the churches, were prodigally expended by the Bishop of Milan, in the redemption of captives.[f] "The church possesses gold, not to treasure up, but to distribute it for the welfare and happiness of men. We are ransoming the souls of men from eternal perdition. It is not merely the lives of men and the honour of women, which are endangered in captivity, but the faith of their children. The blood of redemption which has gleamed in those golden cups has sanctified them, not for the service alone, but for the redemption of man."[g] These arguments may be considered as a generous repudiation of the ecclesiastical spirit for the nobler ends of beneficence; and, no doubt, in that mediation of the church between mankind and the miseries of slavery, which was one of her most constant and useful ministrations during the darker period of human society, the example and authority of Ambrose perpetually encouraged the generosity of the more liberal, and repressed the narrow view of those who considered the consecrated treasures of the church inviolable, even for these more sacred objects.[h]

The ecclesiastical zeal of Ambrose, like that of Chrysostom, scorned the limits of his own diocese. The see of Sirmium was vacant; Ambrose appeared

[f] Numerent quos redemerint templa captivos. So Ambrose appeals, in execrable pride, to the heathen orator, Ambros. Epist. ii. in Symmachum.

[g] Offic. c. 15. c. 28. Compare Greg. M. Epist. vi. 35. vii. 2. 14.
[h] Even Fleury argues that these could not be consecrated vessels.

in that city to prevent the election of an Arian, and to secure the appointment of an orthodox bishop. The strength of the opposite party lay in the zeal and influence of the Empress Justina. Ambrose defied both, and made himself a powerful and implacable enemy.

A.D. 373.

But, for a time, Justina was constrained to suppress her resentment. In a few years, Ambrose appears in a new position for a Christian bishop, as the mediator between rival competitors for the empire. The ambassador sent to Maximus (who had assumed the purple in Gaul, and, after the murder of Gratian, might be reasonably suspected of hostile designs on Italy), was no distinguished warrior, or influential civilian; the difficult negociation was forced upon the bishop of Milan. The character and weight of Ambrose appeared the best protection of the young Valentinian. Ambrose is said to have refused to communicate with Maximus, the murderer of his sovereign. The interests of his earthly monarch or of the empire would not induce him to sacrifice for an instant those of his heavenly Master; he would have no fellowship with the man of blood.[1] Yet so completely, either by his ability as a negociator or by his dignity and sanctity as a prelate, did he overawe the usurper, as to avert the evils of war, and to arrest the hostile invasion of his diocese and of Italy. He succeeded in establishing peace.

A.D. 383.

A.D. 875.

But the gratitude of Justina for this essential service could not avert the collision of hostile religious creeds. The Empress demanded one of the churches in Milan for the celebration of the Arian

Dispute with the Empress Justina.

---

[1] The seventeenth Epistle of Ambrose relates the whole transaction, p. 852.

service. The first and more modest request named the Porcian Basilica without the gates, but these demands rose to the new and largest edifice within the walls.[b] The answer of Ambrose was firm and distinct; it asserted the inviolability of all property in the possession of the church—"A bishop cannot alienate that which is dedicated to God." After some fruitless negociation, the officers of the Emperor proceeded to take possession of the Porcian Basilica. Where these buildings had belonged to the state, the Emperor might still, perhaps, assert the right of property. Tumults arose: an Arian priest was severely handled and only rescued from the hands of the populace by the influence of Ambrose. Many wealthy persons were thrown into prison by the government, and heavy fines exacted on account of these seditions. But the inflexible Ambrose persisted in his refusal to acknowledge the imperial authority over things dedicated to God. When he was commanded to allay the populace, "it is in my power," he answered, "to refrain from exciting their violence, but it is for God to appease it when excited."[m] The soldiers surrounded the building; they threatened to violate the sanctity of the church in which Ambrose was performing the usual solemnities. The bishop calmly continued his functions, and his undisturbed countenance seemed as if his whole mind was absorbed in its devotion. The soldiers entered the church; the affrighted females began to fly; but the rude and armed men fell on their knees and assured Ambrose that they came to pray and not to fight.[n] Ambrose ascended the pulpit; his

---

[b] Paul. Vit. Ambros. Ambros. Epist. xx.

[m] Referebam in meo jure esse, ut non excitarem, in Dei manu, uti mitigaret.

[n] It would be curious if we could ascertain the different constitution of the troops employed in the irreverent

sermon was on the Book of Job; he enlarged on the conduct of the wife of the patriarch, who commanded him to blaspheme God; he compared the Empress with this example of impiety; he went on to compare her with Eve, with Jezebel, with Herodias. "The Emperor demands a church—what has the Emperor to do with the adulteress, the church of the heretics?" Intelligence arrived that the populace were tearing down the hangings of the church on which was the sacred image of the sovereign, and which had been suspended in the Porcian Basilica, as a sign that the church had been taken into the possession of the Emperor. Ambrose sent some of his priests to allay the tumult, but went not himself. He looked triumphantly around on his armed devotees: "The Gentiles have entered into the inheritance of the Lord; but the armed Gentiles have become Christians and co-heirs of God. My enemies are now my defenders."

A confidential secretary of the Emperor appeared, not to expel or degrade the refractory prelate, but to deprecate his *tyranny*. "Why do ye hesitate to strike down *the tyrant*," replied Ambrose, "my only defence is in my power of exposing my life for the honour of God." He proceeded with proud humility, "Under the ancient law, priests have bestowed, they have not condescended to assume empire; kings have desired the priesthood rather than priests the royal power." He appealed to his influence over Maximus, The Emperor which had averted the invasion of Italy. The Ambrose. imperial authority quailed before the resolute prelate;

---

scenes in the churches of Alexandria | cities, the latter partly composed
and Constantinople, and here at Milan. | of barbarians? How much is justly
Were the former raised from the | to be attributed to the character of
vicious population of the Eastern | the prelate?

the soldiers were withdrawn, the prisoners released, and the fines annulled.° When the Emperor himself was urged to confront Ambrose in the church, the timid or prudent youth replied, "His eloquence would compel yourselves to lay me bound hand and foot before his throne." To such a height had the sacerdotal power attained in the West, when wielded by a man of the energy and determination of Ambrose.ᵖ

But the pertinacious animosity of the Empress was not yet exhausted. A law was passed authorising the assemblies of the Arians. A second struggle took place; a new triumph for Ambrose; a new defeat for the Imperial power. From his inviolable citadel, his church, Ambrose uttered in courageous security his defiance. An emphatic sentence expressed the prelate's notion of the relation of the civil and religious power, and proclaimed the subordination of the Emperor within the mysterious circle of sacerdotal authority—"The Emperor is of the church, and in the church, but not above the church."

Was it to be supposed that the remonstrances of expiring Paganism would make any impression upon a court thus under subjection to one, who, by exercising the office of protector in the time of peril, assumed the right to dictate on subjects which appeared more completely within his sphere of jurisdiction? If

---

° Certatim hoc nuntiare milites, irruentem in altaria, oculis significare pacis insigna. Ambrose perceived that God had stricken Lucifer, the great Dragon (vermem antelucanum).

ᵖ Ambrose relates that one of the officers of the court, more daring than the rest, presumed to resent this outrage, as he considered it, on the Emperor. "While I live, dost thou thus treat Valentinian with contempt? I will strike off thy head." Ambrose replied, "God grant that thou mayest fulfil thy menace. I shall suffer the fate of a bishop, thou wilt do the act of an eunuch" (ta facies, quod spadones).

Arianism in the person of the Empress was compelled to bow, Paganism could scarcely hope to obtain even a patient hearing.

We have already related the contest between expiring Polytheism and ascendant Christianity in the persons of Symmachus and of Ambrose. The more polished periods and the gentle dignity of Symmachus might delight the old aristocracy of Rome. But the full flow of the more vehement eloquence of Ambrose, falling into the current of popular opinion at Milan, swept all before it.[q] By this time the Old Testament language and sentiment with regard to idolatry were completely incorporated with the Christian feeling; and when Ambrose enforced on a Christian Emperor the sacred duty of intolerance against opinions and practices which scarcely a century before had been the established religion of the Empire, his zeal was supported by almost the unanimous applause of the Christian world.

Ambrose did not rely on his eloquence alone, or on the awfulness of his sacerdotal character, to control the public mind. The champion of the Church was invested by popular belief, perhaps by his own ardent faith, with

---

[q] The most curious fact relating to Ambrose, is the extraordinary contrast between his vigorous, practical, and statesmanlike character as a man, as well as that of such among his writings as may be called public and popular, and the mystic subtlety which fills most of his theological works. He treats the Scripture as one vast allegory, and propounds his own fanciful interpretation, or corollaries, with as much authority as if they were the plain sense of the sacred writer. No retired schoolman follows out the phantastic analogies and recondite significations which he perceives in almost every word, with more vain ingenuity than Ambrose. Every word or number reminds him of every other place in the Scripture in which the same word or number occurs; and stringing them together with this loose connexion, he works out some latent mystic signification, which he would suppose to have been within the intention of the inspired writer. See particularly the Hexaemeron.

miraculous power, and the high state of religious excitement was maintained in Milan by the increasing dignity and splendour of the ceremonial, and by the pompous installation of the reliques of saints within the principal church.

It cannot escape the observation of a calm inquirer into the history of man, or be disguised by an admirer of a rational, pious, and instructive Christian ministry, that whenever, from this period, the clergy possessed a full and dominant power, the claim to supernatural power is more frequently and ostentatiously made, while where they possess a less complete ascendency, miracles cease. While Ambrose was at least availing himself of, if not encouraging, this religious credulity, Chrysostom, partly, no doubt, from his own good sense, partly from respect for the colder and more inquisitive character of his audience, not merely distinctly disavows miraculous powers in his own person, but asserts that long ago they had come to an end.[r] But in Milan the arch-

---

[r] Διὰ τοῦτο παρὰ μὲν τὴν ἀρχὴν καὶ ἀναξίοις χαρίσματα ἐδίδοτο· χρεία γὰρ εἶχε τὸ παλαιὸν, τῆς πίστεως ἕνεκα, ταύτης τῆς βοηθείας· νῦν δὲ οὐδὲ ἀξίοις δίδοται. In Act. vol. iii. 65. Μὴ τοίνυν τὸ μὴ γίνεσθαι νῦν σημεῖα, τεκμήριον ποιοῦ τοῦ μὴ γενῆσθαι τότε, καὶ γὰρ δὴ τότε χρησίμως ἐγίνετο, καὶ νῦν χρησίμως οὐ γίνεται. See the whole passage in Cor. Hom. vi. xi. 45. On Psalm cx., indeed, vol. v. p. 271, he seems to assert the continuance of miracles, particularly during the reign of Julian and of Maximin. But he gives the death of Julian as one of those miracles. Καὶ γὰρ καὶ διὰ τοῦτο, καὶ δι᾽ ἕτερον τὰ σημεῖα ἔπαυσεν ὁ Θεός, in Matt. vii. 375. Compare also vol. i. p. 411; xi. 397, in Coloss.; on Psalm cxli. vol. v. p. 455. Middleton has dwelt at length on this subject. Works, vol. i. p. 103.

Augustine denies the continuance of miracles with equal distinctness. Cum enim Ecclesia Catholica per totum orbem diffusa atque fundata sit, nec miracula illa in nostra tempora durare permissa sunt, ne animus semper visibilia quæreret, et eorum consuetudine frigesceret genus humanum, quorum novitate flagravit. De Verâ Relig. c. 47. Oper. l. 765. Yet Fleury appeals, and not without ground, to the repeated testimony of St. Augustine, as eye-witness of this miracle; and the reader of St. Augustine's works, even his noblest

bishop asserts his belief in, and the eager enthusiasm of the people did not hesitate to embrace as unquestionable truth, the public display of preternatural power in the streets of the city. A dream revealed to the pious prelate the spot, where rested the reliques of the martyrs, SS. Gervaise and Protadius. As they approached the place, a man possessed by a demon was seized with a paroxysm which betrayed his trembling consciousness of the presence of the holy remains. The bones of two men of great stature were found, with much blood.¹ The bodies were disinterred, and conveyed in solemn pomp to the Ambrosian Church. They were reinterred under the altar; they became the tutelary Saints of the spot.² A blind butcher, named Severus, recovered his eyesight by the application of a handkerchief, which had touched the reliques, and this was but one of the many wonders which were universally supposed to have been wrought by the smallest article of dress, which had imbibed the miraculous virtue of these sacred bones.

The awe-struck mind was never permitted to repose; more legitimate means were employed to maintain the

---

¹ see lib. xx. c. 8.), the City of God, cannot but call to mind perpetual instances of miraculous occurrences related with unhesitating faith. It is singular how often we hear at one time the strong intellect of Augustine, at another the age of Augustine, speaking in his works.

² The Arians denied this miracle, Ambrose, Epist. xxii. Invenimus miræ magnitudinis viros duos, ut prisca ætas ferebat. Did Ambrose suppose that the race of men had degenerated in the last two or three centuries? or that the heroes of the faith had been gifted with heroic stature? The sermon of Ambrose is a strange rhapsody, which would only salt an highly excited audience. He acknowledges that these martyrs were unknown, and that the church of Milan was before barren of reliques.

¹ "Succedunt victimæ triumphales in locum ubi Christus natus est; sed ille super altare qui pro omnibus passus est; isti sub altari qui illius revereri sunt passionem;" but Ambrose calls them the guardians and defenders of the Church.

ardent belief, thus enforced upon the multitude. The whole ceremonial of the church was conducted by Ambrose with unrivalled solemnity and magnificence. Music was cultivated with the utmost care, some of the noblest hymns of the Latin Church are attributed to Ambrose himself, and the Ambrosian service for a long period distinguished the Church of Milan by the grave dignity and simple fullness of its harmony.[a]

But the sacerdotal dignity of Ambrose might command a feeble boy: he had now to confront the imperial majesty in the person of one of the greatest men who had ever worn the Roman purple. Even in the midst of his irreconcileable feud with the heretical Empress, Ambrose had been again entreated to spread the shield of his protection over the youthful Emperor. He had undertaken a second embassy to the usurper Maximus. Maximus, as if he feared the awful influence of Ambrose over his mind, refused to admit the priestly ambassador, except to a public audience. Ambrose was considered as condescending from his dignity, in approaching the throne of the Emperor. The usurper reproached the prelate for his former interference, by which he had been arrested in his invasion of Italy, and had lost the opportunity of becoming master of the unresisting province. Ambrose answered with pardonable pride, that he accepted the honourable accusation of having saved the orphan Emperor. He then arrayed himself, as it were, in his priestly inviolability, reproached Maximus with the murder of Gratian, and demanded his remains. He again refused all spiritual communion with one guilty of innocent blood, for which as yet he had submitted

---

[a] This subject will recur at a later part of this volume.

to no ecclesiastical penance. Maximus, as might have been expected, drove from his court the daring prelate, who had thus stretched to the utmost the sanctity of person attributed to an ambassador and a bishop. Ambrose, however, returned not merely safe, but without insult or outrage, to his Italian diocese.*

The arms of Theodosius decided the contest, and secured the trembling throne of Valentinian the younger. But the accession of Theodosius, instead of obscuring the rival pretensions of the Church to power and influence, seemed to confirm and strengthen them. That such a mind as that of Theodosius should submit with humility to ecclesiastical remonstrance and discipline tended no doubt, beyond all other events, to overawe mankind. Everywhere else throughout the Roman world, the state, and even the Church, bowed at the foot of Theodosius; in Milan alone, in the height of his power, he was confronted and subdued by the more commanding mind and religious majesty of Ambrose. His justice as well as his dignity quailed beneath the ascendancy of the prelate. A synagogue of the Jews at Callinicum, in Osroene, had been burned by the Christians, it was said, at the instigation, if not under the actual sanction of the Bishop. The church of the Valentinian Gnostics had likewise been destroyed and plundered by the zeal of some monks. Theodosius commanded the restoration of the synagogue at the expense of the Christians, and fair compensation to the heretical Valentinians for their losses.

The pious indignation of Ambrose was not restrained either by the remoteness of these transactions from the

* Epist. xliv.

scene of his own labours or by the undeniable violence of the Christian party. He stood forward, designated, it might seem, by his situation and character, as the acknowledged champion of the whole of Christianity; the sacerdotal power was embodied in his person. In a letter to the Emperor, he boldly vindicated the Bishop; he declared himself, as far as his approbation could make him so, an accomplice in the glorious and holy crime. If martyrdom was the consequence, he claimed the honour of that martyrdom; he declared it to be utterly irreconcileable with Christianity, that it should in any way contribute to the restoration of Jewish or heretical worship.[y] If the Bishop should comply with the mandate, he would be an apostate, and the Emperor would be answerable for his apostasy. This act was but a slight and insufficient retaliation for the deeds of plunder and destruction perpetrated by the Jews and heretics against orthodox Christians. The letter of Ambrose did not produce the desired effect; but the Bishop renewed his address in public in the church, and at length extorted from the Emperor the impunity of the offenders. Then, and not till then, he condescended to approach the altar, and to proceed with the service of God.

Ambrose felt his strength; he feared not to assert that superiority of the altar over the throne which was

[y] Hac propositâ conditione, puto dicturum episcopum, quod ipse ignes sparserit, turbas compulerit, populos concluserit, ne amittat occasionem martyrii, ut pro invalido subjiciat validiorem. O beatum mendacium quo adquiritur sibi aliorum absolutio, sui gratia. Hoc est, Imperator, quod poposci et ego, ut in me magis vindicares, et hoc si crimen putares mihi adscriberes. Quid mavis in absentes judicium? Habes præsentem, habes confitentem reum. Proclamo, quod ego synagogam incenderim, certè quod ego illis mandaverim, ne esset locus, in quo Christus negaretur. Si objiciatur mihi, cur hic non incenderim? Divino jam cœpit cremari judicio; meam cessavit opus. Epist. xxiv. p. 561.

a fundamental maxim of his Christianity. There is no reason to ascribe to ostentation, or to sacerdotal ambition, rather than to the profound conviction of his mind, the dignity which he vindicated for the priesthood, the authority supreme and without appeal in all things which related to the ceremonial of religion. Theodosius endured, and the people applauded, the public exclusion of the Emperor from within the impassable rails, which fenced off the officiating priesthood from the profane laity. An exemption had usually been made for the sacred person of the Emperor, and, according to this usage, Theodosius ventured within the forbidden precincts. Ambrose, with lofty courtesy, pointed to the seat or throne reserved for the Emperor, at the head of the laity. Theodosius submitted to the rebuke, and withdrew to the lowlier station.

But if these acts of Ambrose might to some appear unwise or unwarrantable aggressions on the dignity of the civil magistrate; or if to the prophetic sagacity of others they might foreshow the growth of an enormous and irresponsible authority, and awaken well-grounded apprehension or jealousy, the Roman world could not withhold its admiration from another act of the Milanese prelate. It could not but hail the appearance of a new moral power, enlisted on the side of humanity and justice; a power which could bow the loftiest, as well as the meanest, under its dominion. For the first time since the establishment of the imperial despotism, the voice of a subject was heard in deliberate, public, and authoritative condemnation of a deed of atrocious tyranny and sanguinary vengeance; for the first time, an Emperor of Rome trembled before public opinion, and humbled himself to a contrite confession of guilt and cruelty.

With all his wisdom and virtue Theodosius was liable to paroxysms of furious and ungovernable anger. A dispute had arisen in Thessalonica about a favourite charioteer in the circus; out of the dispute a sedition, in which some lives were lost. The imperial officers, who interfered to suppress the fray, were wounded or slain, and Botheric, the representative of the Emperor, treated with indignity. Notwithstanding every attempt on the part of the clergy to allay the furious resentment of Theodosius, the counsels of the more violent advisers prevailed. Secret orders were issued; the circus, filled with the whole population of the city, was surrounded by troops, and a general and indiscriminate massacre of all ages and sexes, the guilty and the innocent, revenged the insult on the imperial dignity. Seven thousand lives were sacrificed in this remorseless carnage.

On the first intelligence of this atrocity, Ambrose, with prudent self-command, kept aloof from the exasperated Emperor. He retired into the country, and a letter from his own hand was delivered to the sovereign. The letter expressed the horror of Ambrose and his brother bishops at this inhuman deed, in which he should consider himself an accomplice if he could refrain from expressing his detestation of its guilt; if he should not refuse to communicate with a man stained with the innocent blood, not of one, but of thousands. He exhorts Theodosius to penitence; he promises to offer prayers in his behalf. He acted up to his declaration; the Emperor of the world found the doors of the church closed against him. For eight months he endured this ignominious exclusion. Even on the sacred day of the Nativity, Theodosius implored in vain to be admitted within those precincts which were open to the slave and to the beggar; those precincts which were the vestibule to heaven, for through the church alone was heaven to be approached. Submission and remonstrance were alike in vain; to an urgent minister of the sovereign, Ambrose calmly replied, that the Emperor might kill him and pass over his body into the sanctuary.

At length Ambrose consented to admit the Emperor to an audience; with difficulty he was persuaded to permit him to enter, not into the church itself, but into the outer porch, the place of the public penitents. At length the interdict was removed on two conditions; that the Emperor should issue an edict prohibiting the execution of capital punishments for thirty days after conviction, and that he should submit to public penance. Stripped of his imperial ornaments, prostrate on the pavement, beating his breast, tearing his hair, watering the ground with his tears, the master of the Roman empire, the conqueror in so many victories, the legislator of the world, at length received the hard-wrung absolution.

This was the culminating point of pure Christian influence. Christianity appeared before the world as the champion and vindicator of outraged humanity; as having founded a tribunal of justice, which extended its protective authority over the meanest, and suspended its retributive penalties over the mightiest of mankind.

Nearly at the same time (about four years before) had been revealed the latent danger from this new unlimited sovereignty over the human mind. *The first blood was judicially shed for religious opinion.* Far, however, from apprehending the fatal consequences which might arise out of their own exclusive and intolerant sentiments, or foreseeing that the sacerdotal authority, which they fondly and sincerely supposed they were strengthening for the unalloyed welfare of mankind, would seize and wield the sword of persecution with such remorseless and unscrupulous severity—this first fatal libation of Christian blood, which was the act of an usurping Emperor, and of a few foreign bishops—was solemnly disclaimed by all the more influential dignitaries of the Western Church.

Priscillian and his followers. Priscillian, a noble and eloquent Spaniard, had embraced some Manichean or rather Gnostic opinions. The same contradictory accusations of the severest asceticism and of licentious habits, which were so perpetually adduced against the Manicheans, formed the chief charge against Priscillian and his followers. The leaders of the sect had taken refuge, from the persecutions of their countrymen, in Gaul, and propagated their opinions to some extent in Aquitaine. They were pursued with unwearied animosity by the Spanish Bishops Ithacius and Idacius. Maximus, the usurping Emperor of Gaul, who then resided at Treves,

Martin of Tours. took cognisance of the case. In vain the celebrated Martin of Tours, whose life was almost an unwearied campaign against idolatry, and whose unrelenting hand had demolished every religious edifice within his reach—a prelate whose dread of heresy was almost as sensitive as of Paganism, urged his protest against these proceedings with all the vehemence of his character. During his absence, a capital sentence was extorted from the Emperor; Priscillian and some of his followers were put to death by the civil authority for the crime of religious error. The fatal precedent was disowned by the general voice of Christianity. It required another considerable period of ignorance and bigotry to deaden the fine moral sense of Christianity to the total abandonment of its spirit of love. When Ambrose reproached the usurper with the murder of his sovereign Gratian, he reminded him likewise of the unjust execution of the Priscillianists; he refused to communicate with the bishops who had any concern in that sanguinary and unchristian transaction.*

Ambrose witnessed and lamented the death of the young Valentinian, over whom he pronounced a funeral oration. On the usurpation of the Pagan Eugenius, he fled from Milan; but returned to behold and to applaud the triumph of Theodosius. The conquering Emperor gave a new proof of his homage to Christianity and to its representative. Under the influence of Ambrose, he refrained for a time from communicating in the Christian mysteries, because his hands were stained with blood, though that blood had been shed in a just and necessary war.* To Ambrose the dying Emperor commended his sons, and the Bishop of Milan pronounced the funeral oration over the last great Emperor of the world.

He did not long survive his imperial friend. It is related that, when Ambrose was on his deathbed, Stilicho, apprehending the loss of such a man to Italy and to Christendom, urged the principal inhabitants of Milan to entreat the effective prayers of the bishop for his own recovery. "I have not so lived among you," replied Ambrose, "as to be ashamed to live; I have so good a Master, that I am

---

* Ambros. Epist. xxlv. The whole transaction in Sulpicius Sever. E. H. and Life of St. Martin.
* Oratio de Obitu Theodos, 34.

not afraid to die." Ambrose expired in the attitude and in the act of prayer.

While Ambrose was thus assuming an unprecedented supremacy over his own age, and deepening and strengthening the foundation of the ecclesiastical power, Augustine was beginning gradually to consummate that total change in human opinion which was to influence the Christianity of the remotest ages.

Of all Christian writers since the Apostles, Augustine has maintained the most permanent and extensive influence. That influence, indeed, was unfelt, or scarcely felt, in the East; but as the East gradually became more estranged, till it was little more than a blank in Christian history, the dominion of Augustine over the opinions of the Western world was eventually over the whole of Christendom. Basil and Chrysostom spoke a language foreign or dead to the greater part of the Christian world. The Greek empire, after the reign of Justinian, gradually contracting its limits and sinking into abject superstition, forgot its own great writers on the more momentous subjects of religion and morality, for new controversialists on frivolous and insignificant points of difference. The more important feuds, as of Nestorianism, made little progress in the West; the West repudiated almost with one voice the iconoclastic opinions; and at length Mohammedanism swept away its fairest provinces, and limited the Greek church to a still narrowing circle. The Latin language thus became almost that of Christianity; Latin writers the sole authority to which men appealed, or from which they imperceptibly imbibed the tone of religious doctrine or sentiment. Of these, Augustine was the most universal, the most commanding, the most influential.

The earliest Christian writers had not been able or willing altogether to decline some of the more obvious and prominent points of the Augustinian theology; but in his works they were first wrought up into a regular system. Abstruse topics, which had been but slightly touched, or dimly hinted in the Apostolic writings, and of which the older creeds had been entirely silent, became the prominent and unavoidable tenets of Christian doctrine. Augustinianism has constantly revived, in all its strongest and most peremptory statements, in every period of religious excitement. In later days, it formed much of the doctrinal system of Luther; it was worked up into a still more rigid and uncompromising system by the severe intellect of Calvin; it was remoulded into the Roman Catholic doctrine by Jansenius; the popular theology of most of the Protestant sects is but a modified Augustinianism.

Christianity had now accomplished its divine mission, so far as impregnating the Roman world with its first principles, the unity of God, the immortality of the soul, and future retribution. These vital questions between the old Paganism and the new religion had been decided by their almost general adoption into the common sentiments of mankind. And now questions naturally and necessarily arising out of the providential government of that Supreme Deity, out of that conscious immortality, and out of that acknowledged retribution, had begun profoundly to agitate the human heart. The nature of man had been stirred in its inmost depths. The hopes and fears, now centered on another state of being, were ever restlessly hovering over the abyss into which they were forced to gaze. As men were not merely convinced, but deeply penetrated, with the belief that they had souls to be

Augustinian theology.

saved, the means, the process, the degree of attainable assurance concerning salvation, became subjects of anxious inquiry. Every kind of information on these momentous topics was demanded with importunity and hailed with eagerness. With the ancient philosophy, the moral condition of man was a much simpler and calmer subject of consideration. It could coldly analyse every emotion, trace the workings of every passion, and present its results; if in eloquent language, kindling the mind of the hearer, rather by that language, than by the excitement of the inquiry. It was the attractive form of the philosophy, the adventitious emotion produced by bold paradox, happy invention, acute dialectics, which amused and partially enlightened the inquisitive mind. But now mingled up with religion, every sensation, every feeling, every propensity, every thought, had become not merely a symptom of the moral condition, but an element in that state of spiritual advancement or deterioration which was to be weighed and examined in the day of Judgement. The ultimate and avowed object of philosophy, the *summum bonum*, the greatest attainable happiness, shrunk into an unimportant consideration. These were questions of spiritual life and death, and the solution was therefore embraced rather by the will and the passions, than by the cool and sober reason. This solution in all these difficulties was the more acceptable in proportion as it was peremptory and dogmatic. Any thing could be endured rather than uncertainty, and Augustine himself was, doubtless, urged more by the desire of peace to his own anxious spirit than by the ambition of dictating to Christianity on these abstruse topics. The influence of Augustine thus concentered the Christian mind on subjects to which Christianity led, but did not answer with fulness or precision. The Gospels and Apostolic writings paused within the border of attainable human knowledge; Augustine fearlessly rushed forward, or was driven by his antagonists; and partly from the reasonings of a new religious philosophy, partly by general inferences from limited and particular phrases in the sacred writings, framed a complete, it must be acknowledged, and as far as its own consistency, an harmonious system; but of which it was the inevitable tendency to give an overpowering importance to problems on which Christianity, wisely measuring, it should seem, the capacity of the human mind, had declined to utter any final or authoritative decrees. Almost up to this period in Christian history,[b] on these mysterious topics, all was unquestioned and undefined; and though they could not but cross the path of Christian reasoning, and could not but be incidentally noticed, they had, as yet, undergone no full or direct investigation. Nothing but the calmest and firmest philosophy could have avoided or eluded these points, on which, though the human mind could not attain to knowledge, it was impatient of ignorance. The immediate or more remote, the direct or indirect, the sensible or the imperceptible, influence of the divine agency (grace) on the human soul, with the inseparable consequences of necessity and free-will, thus became the absorbing and agitating points of Christian doctrine. From many causes, these inevitable questions had forced themselves, at this period, on the general attention. Manicheism on one hand, Pelagianism on

[b] In the Historia Pelagiana of Vossius may be found quotations expressive of the sentiments of the earlier Fathers on many of these points.

the other, stirred up their darkest depths. The Christian mind demanded on all these topics at once excitement and rest. Nothing could be more acceptable than the unhesitating and peremptory decisions of Augustine. His profound piety ministered perpetual emotion; his glowing and perspicuous language, his confident dogmatism, and the apparent completeness of his system, offered repose.

But the primary principle of the Augustinian theology was already deeply rooted in the awe-struck piety of the Christian world. In this state of the general mind, that which brought the Deity more directly and more perpetually in contact with the soul, at once enlisted all minds which were under the shadow of religious fears, or softened by any milder religious feeling. It was not a remote supremacy, a government through unseen and untraceable influences, a general reverential trust in the divine protection, which gave satisfaction to the agitated spirit; but an actually felt and immediate presence, operating on each particular and most minute part of the creation; not a regular and unvarying emanation of the divine will, but a special and peculiar intervention in each separate case. The whole course of human events, and the moral condition of each individual, were alike under the acknowledged, or conscious and direct, operation of the Deity. But the more distinct and unquestioned this principle, the more the problem which in a different form had agitated the Eastern world,—the origin of evil,—forced itself on the consideration. In the East it had taken a kind of speculative or theogonical turn, and allied itself with physical notions; in the West it became a moral and practical, and almost every-day question, involving the prescience of God and the freedom of the human soul.

Augustine had rejected Manicheism; the antagonistic and equally conflicting powers of that system had offended his high conception of the supremacy of God. Still his earlier Manicheism lent an unconscious colouring to his maturer opinions. In another form, he divided the world into regions of cloudless light and total darkness. But he did not mingle the Deity in any way in the darkness which enveloped the whole of mankind, a chosen portion of which alone were rescued, by the gracious intervention of the Redeemer and the Holy Spirit. The rest were separated by an insuperable barrier, that of hereditary evil; they bore within, the fatal and inevitable proscription. Within the pale of Election was the world of Light, without, the world of Perdition; and the human soul was so reduced to a subordinate agent before the mysterious and inscrutable power, which, by the infusion of faith, rescued it from its inveterate hereditary propensity, as to become entirely passive, altogether annihilated, in overleaping the profound though narrow gulph, which divided the two kingdoms of Grace and of Perdition.

Thus that system which assigned the most unbounded and universal influence to the Deity was seized upon by devout piety as the truth which it would be an impious limitation of Omnipotence to question. Man offered his free agency on the altar of his religion, and forgot that he thereby degraded the most wonderful work of Omnipotence, a being endowed with free agency. While the internal consciousness was not received as sufficient evidence of the freedom of the will, it was considered as unquestionable testimony to the operations of divine grace.

At all events, these questions now became unavoidable articles of the Christian faith. From this time the simpler Apostolic Creed, and the splendid amplifications of the divine attributes of the Trinity, were enlarged, if not by stern definitions, by dictatorial axioms on original sin, on grace, predestination, the total depravity of mankind, election to everlasting life, and final reprobation. To the appellations which awoke what was considered righteous and legitimate hatred in all true believers, Arianism and Manicheism, was now added as a term of equal obloquy,—Pelagianism.*

* The doctrines of Pelagius have been represented as arising out of the monastic spirit, or at least out of one form of its influence. The high ideal of moral perfection (it has been said) which the monk set before himself, the conscious strength of will which was necessary to aspire to that height, the proud impatience and disdain of the ordinary excuse for infirmity, the inherited weakness and depravity of human nature, induced the colder and more severe Pelagius to embrace his peculiar tenets; the rejection of original sin; the assertion of the entire freedom of the will; the denial or limitation of the influence of divine grace. Of the personal history of Pelagius little is known, except that he was a British or French monk (his name is said, in one tradition, to have been Morgan), but neither he nor his colleague Cælestius appears to have been a secluded ascetic; they dwelt in Rome for some time, where they propagated their doctrines. Of his character perhaps still less is known, unless from his tenets, and some fragments of his writings, preserved by his adversaries; excepting that the blamelessness of his manners is admitted by his adversaries (the term egregiè Christianus is the expression of St. Augustine); and even the violent Jerome bears testimony to his innocence of life.

But the tenets of Augustine appear to flow more directly from the monastic system. His doctrines (in his controversy with Pelagius, for in his other writings he holds another tone) are tinged with the Encratite or Manichean notion, that there was a *physical* transmission of sin in the propagation of children, even in lawful marriage. (See, among other writers, Jer. Taylor's Vindication of his Deus Justificatus.) Even this concupiscentia carnis peccatum est, quia inest illi inobedientia contra dominatum mentis, De Pecc. Remis. l. 3. This is the old doctrine of the inherent evil of matter. We are astonished that Augustine, who had been a father and a fond father, though of an illegitimate son, could be driven by the stern logic of polemics to the damnation of unbaptised infants, a *milder* damnation, it is true, to eternal fire. This was the more genuine doctrine of

Augustine, by the extraordinary adaptation of his genius to his own age, the comprehensive grandeur of his views, the intense earnestness of his character, his inexhaustible activity, the vigour, warmth, and perspicuity of his style, had a right to command the homage of Western Christendom. He was at once the first universal, and the purest and most powerful of the Latin Christian writers. It is singular that almost all the earlier Christian authors in the West were provincials, chiefly of Africa. But the works of Tertullian were, in general, brief treatises on temporary subjects of controversy; if enlivened by the natural vehemence and strength of the man, disfigured by the worst barbarisms of style. The writings of Cyprian were chiefly short epistles or treatises on subjects of immediate or local interest. Augustine retained the fervour and energy of the African style with much

---

men in whose hearts all the sweet charities of life had been long seared up by monastic discipline; men like Fulgentius, to whose name the title of saint is prefixed, and who lays down this benignant and Christian axiom: "Firmissime tene et nullatenus dubites, parvulos, sive in uteris matrum vivere incipiunt, et ibi moriuntur, sive cum de matribus nati, sine sacramento sancto baptismatis de hac seculo transeunt, ignis æterni sempiterno supplicio puniendos." Fulgentius de Fide, quoted in Vossius, Hist. Pelag. p. 257.

The assertion of the entire freedom of the will, and the restricted sense in which Pelagius appears to have received the doctrine of divine grace, confining it to the influences of the divine revelation, appear to arise out of philosophical reasonings rather than out of the monastic spirit. The severe monastic discipline was more likely to infuse the sense of the slavery of the will; and the brooding over bodily and mental emotions, the general cause and result of the monastic spirit, would tend to exaggerate rather than to question or limit the actual, and even sensible workings of the divine spirit within the soul. The calmer temperament, indeed, and probably more peaceful religious developement of Pelagius, may have disposed him to his system; as the more vehement character, and agitated religious life of Augustine, to his vindication, founded on his internal experience, of the constant divine agency upon the heart and the soul.

purer and more perspicuous Latinity. His ardent imagination was tempered by reasoning powers which boldly grappled with every subject. He possessed and was unembarrassed by the possession of all the knowledge which had been accumulated in the Roman world. He commanded the whole range of Latin literature, and perhaps his influence over his own hemisphere was not diminished by his ignorance, or at best imperfect and late-acquired acquaintance with Greek.[4] But all his knowledge and all his acquirements fell into the train of his absorbing religious sentiments or passions. On the subjects with which he was conversant, a calm and dispassionate philosophy would have been indignantly repudiated by the Christian mind, and Augustine's temperament was too much in harmony with that of the time to offend by deficiency in fervour. It was profound religious agitation, not cold and abstract truth, which the age required; the emotions of piety, rather than the convictions of severe logical inquiry; and in Augustine, the depth or abstruseness of the matter never extinguished or allayed the passion, or in one sense, the popularity, of his style. At different periods of his life, Augustine aspired to and succeeded in enthralling all the various powers and faculties of the human mind. That life was the type of his theology; and as it passed through its various changes of age, of circumstance, and of opinion, it left its own impressions strongly and permanently stamped upon the whole of Latin Christianity. The gentleness of his childhood, the passions of his youth, the studies of his adolescence, the wilder dreams of his immature Chris-

[4] On St. Augustine's knowledge of Greek, compare Tillemont, in his Life, p. 7. Punic was still spoken by the common people in the neighbourhood of Carthage.

tianity, the Manicheism, the intermediate stage of Platonism, through which he passed into orthodoxy, the fervour with which he embraced, the vigour with which he developed, the unhesitating confidence with which he enforced his final creed—all affected more or less the general mind. His Confessions became the manual of all those who were forced by their temperament or inclined by their disposition to brood over the inward sensations of their own minds; to trace within themselves all the trepidations, the misgivings, the agonies, the exultations, of the religious conscience; the gradual formation of opinions till they harden into dogmas, or warm into objects of ardent passion. Since Augustine, this internal autobiography of the soul has always had the deepest interest for those of strong religious convictions; it was what multitudes had felt, but no one had yet embodied in words; it was the appalling yet attractive manner in which men beheld all the conflicts and adventures of their own spiritual life reflected with bold and speaking truth. Men shrunk from the divine and unapproachable image of Christian perfection in the life of the Redeemer, to the more earthly, more familiar picture of the developement of the Christian character, crossed with the light and shade of human weakness and human passion.

The religious was more eventful than the civil life of St. Augustine. He was born A.D. 354, in Tagasta, an episcopal city of Numidia. His parents were Christians of respectable rank. In his childhood, he was attacked by a dangerous illness; he entreated to be baptized. His mother Monica took the alarm; all was prepared for that solemn ceremony; but on his recovery, it was deferred, and Augustine remained for some years in the

humbler rank of catechumen. He received the best
education, in grammar and rhetoric, which the neighbouring city of Madaura could afford. At
seventeen, he was sent to Carthage to finish
his studies. Augustine has, perhaps, highly coloured
both the idleness of his period of study in Madaura,
and the licentious habits to which he abandoned himself in the dissolute city of Carthage. His ardent mind
plunged into the intoxicating enjoyments of the theatre,
and his excited passions demanded every kind of
gratification. He had a natural son, called by the
somewhat inappropriate name A-deo-datus. He was
first arrested in his sensual course, not by the solemn
voice of religion, but by the gentler remonstrances of
Pagan literature. He learned from Cicero, not from
the Gospel, the higher dignity of intellectual attainments. From his brilliant success in his studies, it
is clear that his life, if yielding at times to the
temptations of youth, was not a course of indolence
or total abandonment to pleasure. It was the Hortensius of Cicero which awoke his mind to nobler
aspirations and to the contempt of worldly enjoyments.

But philosophy could not satisfy the lofty desires
which it had awakened: Augustine panted for some
better hopes, and more satisfactory objects of study.
He turned to the religion of his parents, but his mind
was not subdued to a feeling for the inimitable beauty
of the New Testament. Its simplicity of style appeared
rude, after the stately march of Tully's eloquence.
But Manicheism seized at once upon his kindled imagination. For nine years, from the age of nineteen to
twenty-eight, the mind of Augustine wandered among
the vague and fantastic reveries of Oriental theology.

The virtuous and holy Monica, with the anxious apprehensions and prescient hopes of a mother's heart, watched over the irregular development of his powerful faculties. Her distress at his Manichean errors was consoled by an aged bishop, who had himself been involved in the same opinions. "Be of good cheer, the child of so many tears cannot perish." The step against which she remonstrated most strongly, led to that result which she scarcely dared to hope. Augustine grew discontented with the wild Manichean doctrines, which neither satisfied the religious yearnings of his heart nor the philosophical demands of his understanding. He was in danger of falling into a desperate Pyrrhonism, or at best the proud indifference of an Academic. He determined to seek a more distinguished sphere for his talents as a teacher of rhetoric; and, notwithstanding his mother's tears, he left Carthage for Rome. The fame of his abilities obtained him an invitation to teach at Milan. He was there within the magic circle of the great ecclesiastic of the West. But we cannot pause to trace the throes and pangs of his final conversion. The writings of St. Paul accomplished what the eloquence of Ambrose had begun. In one of the paroxysms of his religious agony, he seemed to hear a voice from heaven,—"Take and read, take and read." Till now he had rejected the writings of the Apostle; he opened on the passage which contains the awful denunciations of Paul against the dissolute morals of the Heathen. The conscience of Augustine recognised "in the chambering and wantonness" the fearful picture of his own life; for though he had abandoned the looser indulgences of his youth (he had lived in strict fidelity, not to a lawful wife indeed, but to a concubine) even his mother was anxious to disengage him, by an honourable marriage, from the bonds of a less legitimate connexion. But he burst at once his thraldom; shook his old nature from his heart; renounced for ever all, even lawful indulgences, of the carnal desires; forswore the world, and withdrew himself, though without exciting any unnecessary astonishment among his hearers, from his profaner function as teacher of rhetoric. His mother, who had followed him to Milan, lived to witness his baptism as a Catholic Christian by the hands of Ambrose; and in all the serene happiness of her accomplished hopes and prayers, expired in his arms before his return to Africa. His son, Adeodatus, who died a few years afterwards, was baptized at the same time.

<small>Baptism of Augustine, A.D. 387.</small>

To return to the writings of St. Augustine, or rather to his life in his writings. In his controversial treatises against the Manicheans and against Pelagius, Augustine had the power of seemingly at least, bringing down those abstruse subjects to popular comprehension. His vehement and intrepid dogmatism hurried along the unresisting mind, which was allowed no pause for the sober examination of difficulties, or was awed into acquiescence by the still suspended charge of impiety. The imagination was at the same time kept awake by a rich vein of allegoric interpretation, dictated by the same bold decision, and enforced as necessary conclusions from the sacred writings, or as latent truths intentionally wrapped up in those mysterious phrases.

<small>Controversial writings.</small>

The City of God was unquestionably the noblest work, both in its original design, and in the fulness of its elaborate execution, which the genius of man had as yet contributed to the support of

<small>City of God.</small>

Christianity. Hitherto the Apologies had been framed to meet particular exigences: they were either brief and pregnant statements of the Christian doctrines; refutations of prevalent calumnies; invectives against the follies and crimes of Paganism; or confutations of anti-Christian works like those of Celsus, Porphyry, or Julian, closely following their course of argument, and rarely expanding into general and comprehensive views of the great conflict. The City of God, in the first place, indeed, was designed to decide for ever the one great question, which alone kept in suspense the balance between Paganism and Christianity, the connection between the fall of the empire and the miseries under which the whole Roman society was groaning, with the desertion of the ancient religion of Rome. Even this part of his theme led Augustine into a full, and, if not impartial, yet far more comprehensive survey of the whole religion and philosophy of antiquity than had been yet displayed in any Christian work. It has preserved more on some branches of these subjects than the whole surviving Latin literature. The City of God was not merely a defence, it was likewise an exposition of Christian doctrine. The last twelve books developed the whole system with a regularity and copiousness, as far as we know, never before attempted by any Christian writer. It was the first complete Christian theology.

The immediate occasion of this important work of Augustine was worthy of this powerful concentration of his talents and knowledge. The capture of Rome by the Goths had appalled the whole empire. So long as the barbarians only broke through the frontiers, or severed province after province from the dominion of the Emperor, men

could close their eyes to the gradual declension and
decay of the Roman supremacy; and in the rapid
alternations of power, the empire, under some new
Cæsar or Constantine, might again throw back the
barbaric inroads; or where the barbarians were settled
within the frontiers, awe them into peaceful subjects,
or array them as valiant defenders of their dominions.
As long as both Romes, more especially the ancient
city of the West, remained inviolate, so long the fabric
of the Roman greatness seemed unbroken, and she
might still assert her title as Mistress of the World.
The capture of Rome dissipated for ever these proud
illusions; it struck the Roman world to the heart;
and in the mortal agony of the old social system, men
wildly grasped at every cause which could account
for this unexpected, this inexplicable, phenomenon.
They were as much overwhelmed with dread and
wonder as if there had been no previous omens of
decay, no slow and progressive approach to the sacred
walls; as if the fate of the city had not been already
twice suspended by the venality, the mercy, or the
prudence of the conqueror. Murmurs were again heard
impeaching the new religion as the cause of this disastrous consummation: the deserted gods had deserted
in their turn the apostate city.*

There seems no doubt that Pagan ceremonies took
place in the hour of peril, to avert, if possible, the
imminent ruin. The respect paid by the barbarians

---

* Orosius attempted the same theme: the Pagans, he asserts, "præ-sentia tantum tempore, veluti malis extra solitum infestissima, ob hoc solum, quod creditur Christus, et colitur, idola autem minus coluntur, infamant." Heyne has well observed on this work of Orosius,—Excitavenat Augustini vibrantia arma exemplum Orosium, discipulum, ut et ipse arma sumeret, etsi imbellibus manibus. Opuscula, vi. p. 130.

to the churches might, in the zealous or even the wavering votaries of Paganism, strengthen the feeling of some remote connexion between the destroyer of the civil power and the destroyer of the ancient religions. The Roman aristocracy, which fled to different parts of the world, more particularly to the yet peaceful and uninvaded province of Africa; and among whom the feelings of attachment to the institutions and to the gods of Rome were still the strongest, were not likely to suppress the language of indignation and sorrow, or to refrain from the extenuation of their own cowardice and effeminacy, by ascribing the fate of the city to the irresistible power of the alienated deities.

Augustine dedicated thirteen years to the completion of this work, which was for ever to determine this solemn question, and to silence the last murmurs of expiring Paganism. The City of God is at once the funeral oration of the ancient society and the gratulatory panegyric on the birth of the new. It acknowledged, it triumphed in the irrevocable fall of the Babylon of the West, the shrine of idolatry: it hailed at the same time the universal dominion which awaited the new theocratic policy. The earthly city had undergone its predestined fate;. it had passed away with all its vices and superstitions, with all its virtues and its glories (for the soul of Augustine was not dead to the noble reminiscences of Roman greatness), with its false gods and its Heathen sacrifices. Its doom was sealed, and for ever. But in its place had arisen the City of God, the Church of Christ; a new social system had emerged from the ashes of the old; that system was founded by God, was ruled by divine laws, and had the divine promise of perpetuity.

A.D. 413 to 426.

The first ten books of the City of God are devoted to the question of the connection between the prosperity and the religion of Rome; five of them to the influence of Paganism in this world; five to that in the world to come. Augustine appeals in the five first to the mercy shown by the conqueror as the triumph of Christianity. Had the *Pagan* Radagaisus taken Rome, not a life would have been spared, no place would have been sacred. The *Christian* Alaric had been checked and overawed by the sanctity of the Christian character and his respect for his Christian brethren. He denies that worldly prosperity is an unerring sign of the divine favour; he denies the exemption of the older Romans from disgrace and distress, and recapitulates the crimes and the calamities of their history during their worship of their ancient gods. He ascribes their former glory to their valour, their frugality, their contempt of wealth, their fortitude, and their domestic virtues; he assigns their vices, their frightful profligacy of manners, their pride, their luxury, their effeminacy, as the proximate causes of their ruin. Even in their ruin they could not forget their dissolute amusements; the theatres of Carthage were crowded with the fugitives from Rome. In the five following books he examines the pretensions of Heathenism to secure felicity in the world to come; he dismisses with contempt the old popular religion, but seems to consider the philosophic Theism, the mystic Platonism of the later period, a worthier antagonist. He puts forth all his subtlety and power in refutation of these tenets.

The last twelve books place in contrast the origin, the pretensions, the fate, of the new city, that of God. He enters at large into the evidences of Christianity; he describes the sanctifying effects of the faith; but pours forth all the riches of his imagination and eloquence on the destinies of the church at the Resurrection. Augustine had no vision of the worldly power of the new city; he foresaw not the spiritual empire of Rome which would replace the new fallen Rome of Heathenism. With him the triumph of Christianity is not complete till the world itself,—not merely its outward framework of society and the constitution of its kingdoms,—has experienced a total change. In the description of the final kingdom of Christ, he treads his way with great dexterity and address between the grosser notions of the Millenarians with their kingdom of earthly wealth, and power, and luxury (this he repudiates with devout abhorrence); and that finer and subtler spiritualism, which is ever approaching to Pantheism, and by the rejection of the bodily resurrection, renders the existence of the disembodied spirit too fine and impalpable for the general apprehension.

The uneventful personal life of St. Augustine, at least, till towards its close, contrasts with that of Ambrose and that of Chrysostom. After the first throes and travail of his religious life, described with such dramatic fidelity in his Confessions, he subsided into a peaceful bishop in a remote and rather inconsiderable town.[1] He had not, like Ambrose, to interpose between rival Emperors, or to rule the conscience of the universal sovereign. He had not, like Chrysostom, to enter into a perilous conflict with the vices of a capital and the intrigues of a court. Forced by the devout admiration of the people to assume the

---

[1] He was thirty-five before he was ordained presbyter, A.D. 389: he was chosen coadjutor to the Bishop of Hippo, A.D. 395.

episcopate in the city of Hippo, he was faithful to his first bride, his earliest, though humble, see. Not that his life was that of contemplative inactivity, or tranquil literary exertion; his personal conferences with the leaders of the Donatists, the Manicheans, the Arians, and Pelagians, and his presence in the councils of Carthage, displayed his power of dealing with men. His letter to Count Boniface showed that he was not unconcerned with the public affairs, and his former connection with Boniface, who at one time had expressed his determination to embrace the monastic life, might warrant his remonstrance against the fatal revolt which involved Boniface and Africa in ruin.

At the close of his comparatively peaceful life, Augustine was exposed to the trial of his severe and lofty principles. His faith and his superiority to the world were brought to the test in the fearful calamities which desolated the whole African province. No part of the empire had so long escaped; no part was so fearfully visited, as Africa by the invasion of the Vandals. The once prosperous and fruitful region presented to the view only ruined cities, burning villages, a population thinned by the sword, bowed to slavery, and exposed to every kind of torture and mutilation. With these fierce barbarians, the awful presence of Christianity imposed no respect. The churches were not exempt from the general ruin, nor the bishops and clergy from cruelty and death, nor the dedicated virgins from worse than death. In many places the services of religion entirely ceased from the extermination of the worshippers or the flight of the priests. To Augustine, as the supreme authority in matters of faith or conduct, was submitted the grave question of the course to be pursued by the clergy;

whether they were to seek their own security or to confront the sword of the ravager. The advice of Augustine was at once lofty and discreet. Where the flock remained it was cowardice, it was impiety, in the clergy to desert them and to deprive them in those disastrous times of the consolatory offices of religion, their children of baptism, themselves of the holy Eucharist. But where the priest was an especial object of persecution and his place might be supplied by another; where the flock was massacred or dispersed or had abandoned their homes, the clergy might follow them, and if possible, provide for their own security.

Augustine did not fall below his own high notions of Christian, of episcopal duty. When the Vandal army gathered around Hippo, one of the few cities which still afforded a refuge for the persecuted provincials, he refused, though more than seventy years old, to abandon his post. In the third month of the siege he was released by death, and escaped the horrors of the capture, the cruelties of the conqueror, and the desolation of his church.[e]

A.D. 430.

---

[e] In the life of Augustine, I have chiefly consulted that prefixed to his works, and Tillemont, with the passages in his Confessions and Epistles.

CHAPTER XL

Jerome.—The Monastic System.

THOUGH not so directly or magisterially dominant over the Christianity of the West, the influence of Jerome has been of scarcely less importance than that of Augustine. Jerome was the connecting link between the East and the West; through him, as it were, passed over into the Latin hemisphere of Christendom that which was still necessary for its permanence and independence during the succeeding ages. The time of separation approached, when the Eastern and Western empires, the Latin and the Greek languages, were to divide the world. Western Christianity was to form an entirely separate system. The different nations and kingdoms which were to arise out of the wreck of the Roman empire were to maintain, each its national church, but there was to be a permanent centre of unity in that of Rome, considered as the common parent and federal head of Western Christendom. But before this vast and silent revolution took place, certain preparatives, in which Jerome was chiefly instrumental, gave strength, and harmony, and vitality to the religion of the West, from which the precious inheritance has been secured to modern Europe.

The two leading transactions in which Jerome took the effective part, were—1st, the introduction, or at least the general reception, of Monachism in the West; 2nd, the establishment of an authoritative and universally recognised version of the sacred writings into the

Latin language. For both these important services, Jerome qualified himself by his visits to the East. He was probably the first occidental (though born in Dalmatia, he may be almost considered a Roman, having passed all his youth in that city) who became completely naturalised and domiciliated in Judæa: and his example, though it did not originate, strengthened to an extraordinary degree the passion for pilgrimages to the Holy Land; a sentiment in later times productive of such vast and unexpected results. In the earlier period, the repeated devastations of that devoted country, and still more its occupation by the Jews, had overpowered the natural veneration of the Christians for the scene of the life and sufferings of the Redeemer. It was an accursed rather than a holy region, desecrated by the presence of the murderers of the Lord, rather than endeared by the reminiscences of his personal ministry and expiatory death. The total ruin of the Jews, and their expulsion from Jerusalem by Hadrian; their dispersion into other lands, with the simultaneous progress of Christianity in Palestine, and their settlement in Ælia, the Roman Jerusalem, notwithstanding the profanation of that city by idolatrous emblems, allowed those more gentle and sacred feelings to grow up in strength and silence.* Already, before the time of Jerome, pilgrims had flowed from all quarters of the

---

* Augustine asserts that the *whole world* flocked to Bethlehem to see the place of Christ's nativity. t. l. p. 561. Pilgrimages, according to him, were undertaken to Arabia, to see the dungheap on which Job sat. t. ii. p. 59. For 180 years, according to Jerome, from Hadrian to Constantine, the statue of Jupiter occupied the place of the resurrection, and a statue of Venus was worshipped on the rock of Calvary. But as the object of Hadrian was to insult the Jewish, not the Christian, religion, it seems not very credible that these two sites should be chosen for the Heathen temples. Hieronym. Oper. Epist. xlix. p. 505.

world; and during his life, whoever had attained to any proficiency in religion, in Gaul, or in the secluded island of Britain, was eager to obtain a personal knowledge of these hallowed places. They were met by strangers from Armenia, Persia, India (the Southern Arabia), Æthiopia, the countless monks of Egypt, and from the whole of Western Asia.[b] Yet Jerome was, no doubt, the most influential pilgrim to the Holy Land; the increasing and general desire to visit the soil printed, as it were, with the footsteps, and moist with the redeeming blood of the Saviour, may be traced to his writings, which opened as it were a constant and easy communication, and established an intercourse, more or less regularly maintained, between Western Europe and Palestine.[c]

[b] Quicunque in Galliâ fuerat primas huc properat, Divisus ab orbe nostro Britannus, si in religione processerit, occiduo sole dimisso, quaerit locum famâ sibi tantum, et Scripturarum relatione cognitum. Quid referamus Armenios, quid Persas, quid Indos, quid Æthiopiæ populos, ipsamque juxta Ægyptum, fertilem monachorum, Pontum et Cappadociam, Syriam, Cretam, et Mesopotamiam cunctaque orientis examina. This is the letter of a Roman female, Paula. Hieronym. Oper. Epist. xliv. p. 551.

[c] See the glowing description of all the religious wonders in the Holy Land in the Epitaphium Paulæ. An epistle, however, of Gregory of Nyssa strongly remonstrates against pilgrimages to the Holy Land, even from Cappadocia. He urges the dangers and suspicions to which pious recluses, especially women, would be subject with male attendants, either strangers or friends, on a lonely road; the dissolute words and sights which may be unavoidable in the inns; the dangers of robbery and violence in the Holy Land itself, of the moral state of which he draws a fearful picture. He asserts the religious superiority of Cappadocia, which had more churches than any part of the world; and inquires, in pain terms, whether a man will believe the virgin birth of Christ the more by seeing Bethlehem, or his resurrection by visiting his tomb, or his ascension by standing on the Mount of Olives. Greg. Nyss. de eunt. Hieros.

The authenticity of this epistle is indeed contested by Roman Catholic writers; but I can see no internal evidence against its genuineness. Jerome's more sober letter to Paulinus, Epist. xxix. vol. iv. p. 563., should also be compared.

But besides this subordinate, if indeed subordinate, effect of Jerome's peculiar position between the East and West, he was thence both incited and enabled to accomplish his more immediately influential undertakings. In Palestine and in Egypt, Jerome became himself deeply imbued with the spirit of Monachism, and laboured with all his zeal to awaken the more tardy West to rival Egypt and Syria in displaying this sublime perfection of Christianity. By his letters, descriptive of the purity, the sanctity, the total estrangement from the deceitful world in these blessed retirements, he kindled the holy emulation, especially of the females, in Rome. Matrons and virgins of patrician families embraced with contagious fervour the monastic life; and though the populous districts in the neighbourhood of the metropolis were not equally favourable for retreat, yet they attempted to practise the rigid observances of the desert in the midst of the busy metropolis.

For the second of his great achievements, the version of the sacred Scriptures, Jerome derived inestimable advantages, and acquired unprecedented authority, by his intercourse with the East. His residence in Palestine familiarised him with the language and peculiar habits of the sacred writers. He was the first Christian writer of note who thought it worth while to study Hebrew. Nor was it the language alone; the customs, the topography, the traditions, of Palestine were carefully collected, and applied by Jerome, if not always with the soundest judgement, yet occasionally with great felicity and success to the illustration of the sacred writings.

The influence of Monachism upon the manners, opinions, and general character of Christianity, as well as that of the Vulgate translation of the Bible, not only on the religion, but on the literature of Europe, appear to demand a more extensive investigation; and as Jerome, if not the representative, was the great propagator of Monachism in the West, and as about this time this form of Christianity overshadowed and dominated throughout the whole of Christendom, it will be a fit occasion, although I have in former parts of this work not been able altogether to avoid it, to develope more fully its origin and principles.

Monachism.

It is singular to see this oriental influence successively enslaving two religions in their origin and in their genius so totally opposite to Monachism as Christianity and the religion of Mohammed. Both gradually and unreluctantly yield to the slow and inevitable change. Christianity, with very slight authority from the precepts, and none from the practice of the Author and first teachers of the faith, admitted this without inquiry as the perfection and consummation of its own theory. Its advocates and their willing auditors equally forgot that if Christ and his apostles had retired into the desert, Christianity would never have spread beyond the wilderness of Judæa. The transformation which afterwards took place of the fierce Arab marauder, or the proselyte to the martial creed of the Koran, into a dreamy dervish, was hardly more violent and complete, than that of the disciple of the great example of Christian virtue, or of the active and popular Paul, into a solitary anchorite.

Still that which might appear most adverse to the universal dissemination of Christianity eventually tended to its entire and permanent incorporation with the whole of society. When Eremitism gave place to Cœnobitism; when the hermitage grew up into a convent, the establishment of these religious

Cœnobitism.

fraternities in the wildest solitudes gathered round them a Christian community, or spread, as it were, a gradually increasing belt of Christian worship, which was maintained by the spiritual services of the monks. The monks, though not generally ordained as ecclesiastics, furnished a constant supply for ordination. In this manner, the rural districts, which, in most parts, long after Christianity had gained the predominance in the towns, remained attached by undisturbed habit to the ancient superstition, were slowly brought within the pale of the religion. The monastic communities commenced, in the more remote and less populous districts of the Roman world, that ameliorating change which, at later times, they carried on beyond the frontiers. As afterwards they introduced civilisation and Christianity among the barbarous tribes of North Germany or Poland, so now they continued in all parts a quiet but successful aggression on the lurking Paganism.

Monachism was the natural result of the incorporation of Christianity with the prevalent opinions of mankind, and in part of the state of profound excitement into which it had thrown the human mind. We have traced the universal predominance of the great principle, the inherent evil of matter. This primary tenet, as well of the Eastern religions as of the Platonism of the West, coincided with the somewhat ambiguous use of the term "world" in the sacred writings. Both were alike the irreclaimable domain of the Adversary of good. The importance assumed by the soul, now through Christianity become profoundly conscious of its immortality, tended to the same end. The deep and serious solicitude for the fate of that everlasting part of our being, the concentration of all its energies on its own individual welfare, withdrew it entirely

Origin of Monachism.

within itself. A kind of sublime selfishness excluded all subordinate considerations.[4] The only security against the corruption which environed it on all sides seemed entire alienation from the contagion of matter; the constant mortification, the extinction, if possible, of those senses which were necessarily keeping up a dangerous and treasonable correspondence with the external universe. On the other hand, entire estrangement from the rest of mankind, included in the proscribed and infectious *world*, appeared no less indispensable. Communion with God alone was at once the sole refuge and perfection of the abstracted spirit; prayer the sole unendangered occupation, alternating only with that coarse industry which might give employment to the refractory members, and provide that scanty sustenance required by the inalienable infirmity of corporeal existence. The fears and the hopes were equally wrought upon—the fear of defilement and consequently of eternal perdition; the hope of attaining the serene enjoyment of the divine presence in the life to come. If any thought of love to mankind, as an unquestionable duty entailed by Christian brotherhood, intruded on the isolated being, thus labouring on the single object, his own spiritual perfection, it found a vent in prayer for their happiness, which excused all more active or effective benevolence.

---

[4] It is remarkable how rarely, if ever (I cannot call to mind an instance), in the discussions on the comparative merits of marriage and celibacy, the social advantages appear to have occurred to the mind; the benefit to mankind of raising up a race born from Christian parents and brought up in Christian principles. It is always argued with relation to the interests and the perfection of the individual soul; and even with regard to that, the writers seem almost unconscious of the softening and humanising effect of the natural affections, the beauty of parental tenderness and filial love.

CELIBACY.

On both principles, of course, marriage was inexorably condemned.* Some expressions in the writings of St. Paul,† and emulation of the Gnostic sects, combining with these general sentiments, had very early raised celibacy into the highest of Christian virtues: marriage was a necessary evil, an inevitable infirmity of the weaker brethren. With the more rational and earlier writers, Cyprian, Athanasius, and even in occasional passages in Ambrose or Augustine, it had its own high and peculiar excellence; but even with them, virginity, the absolute estrangement from all sensual indulgence, was the transcendant virtue, the pre-assumption of the angelic state, the approximation to the beatified existence.‡

---

* There is a sensible and judicious book, entitled "Die Einführung der erzwungenen Ehelosigkeit bei den Christlichen Geistlichen und ihre Folge," von J. A. und Aug. Theiner, Altenburg, 1828, which enters fully into the origin and consequences of celibacy in the whole church. This is an early work of Theiner, now become a Roman Catholic, and labouring in the library of the Vatican, as the Continuator of Baronius.

† I agree with Theiner (p. 24) in considering these precepts local and temporary, relating to the especial circumstances of those whom St. Paul addressed.

‡ The general tone was that of the vehement Jerome. There must not only be vessels of gold and silver, but of wood and earthenware. This contemptuous admission of the necessity of the married life distinguished the orthodox from the Manichean, the Montanist, and the Encratite. Jerom. adv. Jovin. p. 148.

The sentiments of the Fathers on marriage and virginity may be thus briefly stated. I am not speaking with reference to the marriage of the clergy, which will be considered hereafter.

The earlier writers, when they are contending with the Gnostics, though they elevate virginity above marriage, speak very strongly on the folly, and even the impiety, of prohibiting or disparaging lawful wedlock. They acknowledge and urge the admitted fact that several of the Apostles were married. This is the tone of Ignatius (Cotel, Pat. Apost. ii. 77), of Tertullian (licebat et Apostolis nubere et uxores circumducere. De Exhort. Castit.), above all, of Clement of Alexandria.

In the time of Cyprian, vows of virginity were not irrevocable. Si

Every thing conspired to promote, nothing remained to counteract, this powerful impulse. In the East this seclusion from the world was by no means uncommon. Even among the busy and restless Greeks some of the philosophers had asserted the privilege of wisdom to stand aloof from the rest of mankind; the question of the superior excellence of the active or the contemplative life had been agitated on equal terms. But in some regions of the East, the sultry and oppressive heats, the general relaxation of the physical system, dispose constitutions of a certain temperament to a dreamy inertness. The indolence and prostration of the body produce a kind of activity in the mind, if that may properly be called activity which is merely giving loose to the imagination and the

---

autem perseverare nolunt, vel non possunt, melius est ut nubant, quam in ignem delictis suis cadant. Epist. 62. And his general language, more particularly his tract de Habitu Virginum, implies that strong discipline was necessary to restrain the dedicated virgins from the vanities of the world.

But in the fourth century the eloquent Fathers vie with each other in exalting the transcendant, holy, angelic virtue of virginity. Every one of the more distinguished writers, —Basil, the two Gregories, Ambrose, Augustine, Chrysostom, has a treatise or treatises upon virginity, on which he expands with all the glowing language which he can command. It became a common doctrine that sexual intercourse was the sign and the consequence of the Fall; they forgot that the command to "increase and multiply" is placed in the Book of Genesis (l. 28) before the Fall.

We have before (p. 190) quoted passages from Greg. of Nazianzum. Gregory of Nyssa says,—ἤδοτη δὲ ανάγκης ἐγγινόμενη τῆς ἐκντεύσεως ἤρξατο—ἐν ἀνομίαις ἐστὶν ἡ σύλληψις, ἐν ἁμαρτίαις ἡ κύησις. Greg. Nyss. de Virgin. c. 12, c. 13. But Jerome is the most vehement of all:— Nuptiae terram replent, virginitas Paradisum. The unclean beasts went by pairs into the ark, the clean by seven. Though there is another mystery in the pairs, even the unclean beasts were not to be allowed a second marriage:—Ne in bestiis quidem et immundis avibus digamia comprobatur sit. Adv. Jovin. vol. iv. p. 160. Laudo nuptias, laudo conjugium, sed quia mihi virgines generat. Ad Eustoch. p. 36.

emotions, as they follow out a wild train of incoherent thought, or are agitated by impulses of spontaneous and ungoverned feeling. Ascetic Christianity ministered new aliment to this common propensity; it gave an object both vague and determinate enough to stimulate, yet never to satisfy or exhaust. The regularity of stated hours of prayer, and of a kind of idle industry, weaving mats, or plaiting baskets, alternated with periods of morbid reflection on the moral state of the soul, and of mystic communion with the Deity.[h] It cannot, indeed, be wondered that the new revelation, as it were, of the Deity; this profound and rational certainty of his existence; this infelt consciousness of his perpetual presence; these yet unknown impressions of his infinity, his power, and his love, should give a higher character to this eremitical enthusiasm, and attract men of loftier and more vigorous minds within its sphere. It was not merely the pusillanimous dread of encountering the trials of life which urged the humbler spirits to seek the safe retirement, or the natural love of peace and the weariness and satiety of life, which commended this seclusion to those who were too gentle to mingle in, or who were exhausted with, the unprofitable turmoil of the world. Nor was it always the anxiety to mortify the rebellious and refractory body with more advantage. The one absorbing idea of the majesty of the Godhead almost seemed to swallow up all other considerations; the transcendant nature of the Triune Deity, the rela-

[h] Nam pariter exercentes corporis animæque virtutes, exterioris hominis stipendia cum emolumentis interioris exæquant, lubricis motibus cordis, et fluctuationi cogitationum instabili, operum pondera, velut quandam tenacem atque immobilem anchoram præfigentes, cui volubilitas ac pervagatio cordis inoexa intra cellæ claustra, velut in portu fidissimo valet contineri. Cassian. Instit. ii. 13.

tion of the different persons in the Godhead to each
other, seemed the only worthy objects of man's contemplative faculties. If the soul never aspired to that
Pantheistic union with the spiritual essence of being
which is the supreme ambition of the higher Indian
mysticism, their theory seemed to promise a sublime
estrangement from all sublunary things, an occupation
for the spirit, already, as it were, disembodied and
immaterialised by its complete concentration on the
Deity.

In Syria and in Egypt, as well as in the remoter
East, the example had already been set both of solitary
retirement and of religious communities. The Jews
had both their hermitages and their cœnobitic institutions. Anchorites swarmed in the deserts near the
Dead Sea;[1] and the Essenes, in the same district, and
the Egyptian Therapeutæ, were strictly analogous to
the Christian monastic establishments. In the neighbourhood of many of the Eastern cities were dreary and
dismal wastes, incapable of, or unimproved by, cultivation, which seemed to allure the enthusiast to abandon
the haunts of men and the vices of society. Egypt
especially, where everything excessive and extravagant
found its birth or ripened with unexampled vigour,
seemed formed for the encouragement of the wildest
anchoritism. It is a long narrow valley, closed in on
each side by craggy or by sandy deserts. The rocks
were pierced either with natural caverns, or hollowed
out by the hand of man into long subterranean cells
and galleries for various uses, either of life, or of superstition, or of sepulture. The Christian, sometimes
driven out by persecution (for persecution no doubt

---

[1] Josephi Vita.

greatly contributed to people these solitudes),[k] or prompted by religious feelings to fly from the face of man, found himself, with no violent effort, in a dead and voiceless wilderness, under a climate which required no other shelter than the ceiling of the rock-hewn cave, and where actual sustenance might be obtained with little difficulty.

St. Antony is sometimes described as the founder of the monastic life; it is clear, however, that he only imitated and excelled the example of less famous anchorites. But he may fairly be considered as its representative. [Antony.]

Antony[m] was born of Christian parents, bred up in the faith, and before he was twenty years old, found himself master of considerable wealth, and charged with the care of a younger sister. He was a youth of ardent imagination, vehement impulses, and so imperfectly educated as to be acquainted with no language but his native Egyptian.[n] A constant attendant on Christian worship, he had long looked back with admiration on those primitive times when the Christians laid all their worldly goods at the feet of the Apostles. One day he heard the sentence, "Go, sell all thou hast, and give to the poor, ... and come, and follow me." It seemed personally addressed to himself by the voice of God. He returned home, distributed his lands among his

---

[k] Paul, the first Christian hermit, fled from persecution. Hieronym. Vit. Paul, p. 69.

[m] The fact that the great Athanasius paused in his polemic warfare to write the life of Antony, may show the general admiration towards the monastic life.

[n] Jerome claims the honour of being the first hermit for Paul, in the time of Decius or Valerian, (Vit. Paul. p. 68); but the whole life of Paul, and the visit of Antony to him, read like religious romance; and, it appears from the preface of Jerome to the Life of Hilarion, did not find implicit credit in his own day.

neighbours, sold his furniture and other effects, except a small sum reserved for his sister, whom he placed under the care of some pious Christian virgins. Another text, "Take no thought for the morrow," transpierced his heart, and sent him forth for ever from the society of men. He found an aged solitary, who dwelt without the city. He was seized with pious emulation, and from that time devoted himself to the severest asceticism. There was still, however, something gentle and humane about the asceticism of Antony. His retreat (if we may trust the romantic life of St. Hilarion, in the works of St. Jerome), was by no means of the horrid and savage character affected by some other recluses: it was at the foot of a high and rocky mountain, from which welled forth a stream of limpid water, bordered by palms, which afforded an agreeable shade. Antony had planted this pleasant spot with vines and shrubs; there was an enclosure for fruit trees and vegetables, and a tank from which the labour of Anthony irrigated his garden. His conduct and character seemed to partake of this less stern and gloomy tendency.* He visited the most distinguished anchorites, but only to observe, that he might imitate, the peculiar virtue of each; the gentle disposition of one; the constancy of prayer in another; the kindness, the patience, the industry, the vigils, the macerations, the love of study, the passionate contemplation of the Deity, the charity towards mankind. It was his devout ambition to equal or transcend each in his particular austerity or distinctive excellence.

But man does not violate nature with impunity; the solitary state had its passions, its infirmities, its perils. The hermit could fly from his fellow men, but not from

---

* Vita St. Hilarion. p. 85.

himself. The vehement and fervid temperament which drove him into the desert was not subdued; it found now ways of giving loose to its suppressed impulses. The self-centred imagination began to people the desert with worse enemies than mankind. Dæmonology, in all its multiplied forms, was now an established part of the Christian creed, and embraced with the greatest ardour by men in such a state of religious excitement as to turn hermits. The trials, the temptations, the agonies, were felt and described as personal conflicts with hosts of impure, malignant, furious, fiends. In the desert, these beings took visible form and substance; in the day-dreams of profound religious meditation, in the visions of the agitated and exhausted spirit, they were undiscernible from reality.[p] It is impossible, in the wild legends which became an essential part of Christian literature, to decide how much is the disordered imagination of the saint, the self-deception of the credulous, or the fiction of the zealous writer. The very effort to suppress certain feelings has a natural tendency to awaken and strengthen them. The horror of carnal indulgence would not permit the sensual desires to die away into apathy. Men are apt to find what they seek in their own hearts, and by anxiously searching for the guilt of lurking lust, or desire of worldly wealth or enjoyment, the conscience, as it were, struck forcibly upon the chord which it wished to deaden, and made it vibrate with a kind of morbid, but more than ordinary, energy. Nothing was so licentious or so terrible as not to find its way to the cell of the recluse. Beautiful women danced around him; wild beasts of every shape, and monsters with no shape at all, howled

---

[p] Compare Jerome's Life of St. Hilarion, p. 76.

and yelled and shrieked about him, while he knelt in prayer, or snatched his broken slumbers. "Oh how often in the desert," says Jerome, "in that vast solitude, which, parched by the sultry sun, affords a dwelling to the monks, did I fancy myself in the midst of the luxuries of Rome. I sat alone; for I was full of bitterness. My misshapen limbs were rough with sackcloth; and my skin was so squalid that I might have been taken for a negro. Tears and groans were my occupation every day, and all day; if sleep surprised me unawares, my naked bones, which scarcely held together, clashed on the earth. I will say nothing of my food or beverage: even the rich have nothing but cold water; any warm drink is a luxury. Yet even I, who for the fear of hell had condemned myself to this dungeon, the companion only of scorpions and wild beasts, was in the midst of girls dancing. My face was pale with fasting, but the mind in my cold body burned with desires; the fires of lust boiled up in the body, which was already dead. Destitute of all succour, I cast myself at the feet of Jesus, washed them with my tears, dried them with my hair, and subdued the rebellious flesh by a whole week's fasting." After describing the wild scenes into which he fled, the deep glens and shaggy precipices,—"The Lord is my witness," he concludes; "sometimes I appeared to be present among the angelic hosts, and sang, 'We will haste after thee for the sweet savour of thy ointments.'"[1] For at times, on the other hand, gentle and more than human voices were heard consoling the constant and devout recluse; and sometimes the baffled dæmon would humbly acknowledge himself to be rebuked before the hermit. But this was

---

[1] Song of Solomon. Hieronym. Epist. xxii.

CHAP. XI.   SELF-TORTURE.   205

in general after a fearful struggle. Desperate diseases require desperate remedies. The severest pain could alone subdue or distract the refractory desires or the preoccupied mind. Human invention was exhausted in self-inflicted torments. The Indian faquir was rivalled in the variety of distorted postures and of agonising exercises. Some lived in clefts and caves; some in huts, into which the light of day could not penetrate; some hung huge weights to their arms, necks, or loins; some confined themselves in cages; some on the tops of mountains, exposed to the sun and weather. The most celebrated hermit at length for life condemned himself to stand in a fiery climate, on the narrow top of a pillar.[r] Nor were these always rude or uneducated fanatics. St. Arsenius had filled, and with universal respect, the dignified post of tutor to the Emperor Arcadius. But Arsenius became an hermit; and, among other things, it is related of him, that, employing himself in the common occupation of the Egyptian monks, weaving baskets of palm-leaves, he changed only once a year the water in which the leaves were moistened. The smell of the fœtid water was a just penalty for the perfumes which he had inhaled during his worldly life. Even sleep was a sin; an hour's un-

---

[r] The language of Evagrius (H. E. l. 13) about Simeon vividly expresses the effect which he made on his own age. "Rivalling, while yet in the flesh, the conversation of angels, he withdrew himself from all earthly things, and doing violence to nature, which always has a downward tendency, he aspired after that which is on high; and standing midway between earth and heaven, he had communion with God, and glorified God with the angels; from the earth offering supplications (προσβείας προσγων) as an ambassador to God; bringing down from heaven to men the divine blessing." The influence of the most holy martyr in the air (πανυγίου και ἀερίου μάρτυρος) on political affairs, lies beyond the range of the present history.

broken slumber was sufficient for a monk. On Saturday evening, Arsenius lay down with his back to the setting sun, and continued awake, in fervent prayer, till the rising sun shone on his eyes;[a] so far had Christianity departed from its humane and benevolent and social simplicity.

It may be a curious question how far enthusiasm repays its votaries as far as the individual is concerned; in what degree these self-inflicted tortures added to or diminished the real happiness of man; how far these privations and bodily sufferings, which to the cool and unexcited reason appear intolerable, either themselves produced a callous insensibility, or were met by apathy arising out of the strong counter-excitement of the mind; to what extent, if still felt in unmitigated anguish, they were compensated by inward complacency from the conscious fulfilment of religious duty; the stern satisfaction of the will at its triumph over nature; the elevation of mind from the consciousness of the great object in view, or the ecstatic pre-enjoyment of certain reward. In some instances, they might derive some recompense from the respect, veneration, almost adoration, of men. Emperors visited the cells of these ignorant, perhaps superstitious, fanatics, revered them as oracles, and conducted the affairs of empire by their advice. The great Theodosius is said to have consulted John the Solitary on the issue of the war with Eugenius.[b] His feeble successors followed faithfully the example of his superstition.

Antony appeared at the juncture most favourable for the acceptance of his monastic tenets.[c] His fame and

---

[a] Compare Fleury, xx. 1, 2.
[b] Evagr. Vit. St. Paul, c. 1. Theodoret, v. 24. See Flechier, Vie de Theodose, iv. 43.
[c] Hujus vitæ auctor Paulus, illustrator Antonius. Jerom. p. 46.

his example tended still further to disseminate the spreading contagion. In every part the desert began to swarm with anchorites, who found it difficult to remain alone. Some sought out the most retired chambers of the ancient cemeteries; some those narrow spots which remained above water during the inundations, and saw with pleasure the tide arise which was to render them unapproachable to their fellow-creatures. But in all parts the determined solitary found himself constantly obliged to recede farther and farther; he could scarcely find a retreat so dismal, a cavern so profound, a rock so inaccessible, but that he would be pressed upon by some zealous competitor or invaded by the humble veneration of some disciple.

It is extraordinary to observe this infringement on the social system of Christianity, this disconnecting principle, which, pushed to excess, might appear fatal to that organisation in which so much of the strength of Christianity consisted, gradually self-expanding into a new source of power and energy, so wonderfully adapted to the age. The desire of the anchorite to isolate himself in unendangered seclusion was constantly balanced and corrected by the holy zeal or involuntary tendency to proselytism. The farther the saint retired from the habitations of men, the brighter and more attractive became the light of his sanctity; the more he concealed himself, the more was he sought out by a multitude of admiring and emulous followers. Each built or occupied his cell in the hallowed neighbourhood. A monastery was thus imperceptibly formed around the hermitage; and nothing was requisite to the incorporation of a regular community, but the formation of rules for common intercourse, stated meetings for worship, and something of uniformity in dress, food, and daily occupations. Some monastic establishments were no doubt formed at once, in imitation of the Jewish Therapeutæ; but many of the more celebrated Egyptian establishments gathered, as it were, around the central cell of an Antony or a Pachomius.*

Something like an uniformity of usage appears to have prevailed in the Egyptian monasteries. The brothers were dressed, after the fashion of the country, in long linen tunics, with a woollen girdle, a cloak, and over it a sheep-skin. They usually went barefooted, but at certain very cold or very parching seasons, they wore a kind of sandal. They did not wear the hair-cloth.ʸ Their food was bread and water; their luxuries, occasionally a little oil or salt, a few olives, peas, or a single fig: they ate in perfect silence, each decury by itself. They were bound to strict obedience to their superiors; they were divided into decuries and centenaries, over whom the decurions and centurions presided: each had his separate cell.ˢ The furniture of their cells was a mat of palm-leaves and a bundle of the papyrus, which served for a pillow by night and a seat by day. Every evening and every night they were summoned to prayer by the sound of a horn. At each meeting were sung twelve psalms, pointed out, it was believed, by an angel. On certain occasions, lessons

Cœnobitic establishments.

---

* Pachomius was, strictly speaking, the founder of the cœnobitic establishments in Egypt; Eustathius in Armenia; Basil in Asia. Pachomius had 1400 monks in his establishment; 7000 acknowledged his jurisdiction.

ʸ Jerome speaks of the cilicium as common among the Syrian monks, with whom he lived. Epist. i. Hereunt sacco membra deformi. Even

women assumed it. Epitaph. Paulæ, p. 678. Cassian is inclined to think it often a sign of pride. Instit. I. 3.

ˢ The accounts of Jerome (in Eustochium, p. 45) and of Cassian are blended. There is some difference as to the hours of meeting for prayers, but probably the cœnobitic institutes differed as to that and on some points of diet.

were read from the Old or New Testament. The assembly preserved total silence; nothing was heard but the voice of the chanter or reader. No one dared even to look at another. The tears of the audience alone, or if he spoke of the joys of eternal beatitude, a gentle murmur of hope, was the only sound which broke the stillness of the auditory. At the close of each psalm, the whole assembly prostrated itself in mute adoration.[a] In every part of Egypt, from the Cataracts to the Delta, the whole land was bordered by these communities; there were 5000 coenobites in the desert of Nitria alone;[b] the total number of male anchorites and monks was estimated at 76,000; the females at 27,700. Parts of Syria were, perhaps, scarcely less densely peopled with ascetics. Cappadocia and the provinces bordering on Persia boasted of numerous communities, as well as Asia Minor and the eastern parts of Europe. Though the monastic spirit was in its full power, the establishment of regular communities in Italy must be reserved for Benedict of Nursia, and lies beyond the bounds of our present history. The enthusiasm pervaded all orders. Men of rank, of family, of wealth, of education, suddenly changed the luxurious palace for the howling wilderness, the flatteries of men for the total silence of the desert. They voluntarily abandoned their estates,

---

[a] Tantum a cunctis præbetur silentium, ut cum in unum tam numerosa fratrum multitudo conveniat, præter illum, qui consurgens psalmum decantat in medio, nullus hominum penitus adesse credatur. No one was heard to spit, to sneeze, to cough, or to yawn—there was not even a sigh or a groan—nisi forth hæc quæ per excessum mentis claustra oris effugerit, quæque maenaibiliter cordi obrepserit, immoderato scilicet atque intolerabili spiritûs fervore successo, dum ea quæ lgnita mens in semetipsâ non prævalet continere, per ineffabilem quendam gemitum pectoris sui conclavibus erumpere conatur. Cassian. Instit. ii. 10.

[b] Jerom. ad Eustoch. p. 44.

their connections, their worldly prospects. The desire of fame, of power, of influence, which might now swell the ranks of the ecclesiastics, had no concern in their sacrifice. Multitudes must have perished without the least knowledge of their virtues or their fate transpiring in the world. Few could obtain or hope to obtain the honour of canonisation, or that celebrity which Jerome promises to his friend Blesilla, to live not merely in heaven, but in the memory of man; to be consecrated to immortality by his writings.[c]

But the coenobitic establishments had their dangers no less than the cell of the solitary hermit. Besides those consequences of seclusion from the world, the natural results of confinement in this close separation from mankind and this austere discharge of stated duties, were too often found to be the proscription of human knowledge and the extinction of human sympathies. Christian wisdom and Christian humanity could find no place in their unsocial system. A morose, and sullen, and contemptuous ignorance could not but grow up where there was no communication with the rest of mankind, and the human understanding was rigidly confined to certain topics. The want of objects of natural affection could not but harden the heart; and those who, in their stern religious austerity are merciless to themselves, are apt to be merciless to others:[d] their callous and insensible hearts have no sense of the exquisitely delicate and

Dangers of coenobitism.

Bigotry.

---

[c] Quæ cum Christo vivit in cœlis, in hominum quoque ore victura est. . . . . Nunquam in meis moriturа est libris. Epist. xxiii. p. 60.

[d] There is a cruel history of an abbot, Mucius, in Cassian. Mucius entreated admission into a monastery. He had one little boy with him of eight years old. They were placed in separate cells, lest the father's heart should be softened and indisposed to total renunciation of all earthly joys.

poignant feelings which arise out of the domestic affections. Bigotry has always found its readiest and sternest executioners among those who have never known the charities of life.

These fatal effects seem inherent consequences of Monasticism; its votaries could not but degenerate from their lofty and sanctifying purposes. That which in one generation was sublime enthusiasm, in the next became sullen bigotry, or sometimes wrought the same individual into a stern forgetfulness not only of the vices and follies but of all the more generous and sacred feelings of humanity. In the cœnobitic institutes was added a strong corporate spirit, and a blind attachment to their own opinions, which were identified with religion and the glory of God. The monks of Nitria, from simple and harmless enthusiasts, became ferocious bands of partisans; instead of remaining aloof in jealous seclusion from the factions of the rest of the world, they rushed down armed into Alexandria: what they considered a sacred cause inflamed and warranted a ferocity not surpassed by the turbulent and blood-thirsty rabble of that city. In support of a favourite doctrine or in defence of a popular prelate,

<small>Fanaticism.</small>

<small>by the sight of his child. That he might still further prove his Christian obedience [!] and self-denial, the child was systematically neglected, dressed in rags, and so dirty, as to be disgusting to the father; he was frequently beaten, to try whether it would force tears down the parent's squalid cheeks. "Nevertheless, for the love of Christ!!! and from the virtue of obedience, the heart of the father remained hard and unmoved;" he thought little of his child's tears, only of his own humility and perfection. He at length was urged to show the last mark of his submission by throwing the child into the river. As if this was a commandment of God, he seized the child, and "the work of faith and obedience" would have been accomplished, if the brethren had not interposed, "and, as it were, rescued the child from the waters." And Cassian relates this as an act of the highest religious heroism! Lib. iv. 27.</small>

they did not consider that they were violating their own first principles, in yielding to all the savage passions, and mingling in the bloody strife of that world which they had abandoned.

Total seclusion from mankind is as dangerous to enlightened religion as to Christian charity. We might have expected to find among those who separated themselves from the world, to contemplate, undisturbed, the nature and perfections of the Deity, in general, the purest and most spiritual notions of the Godhead. Those whose primary principle was dread of the corruption of matter would be the last coarsely to materialise their divinity. But those who could elevate their thoughts or could maintain them at this height, were but a small part of the vast numbers, whom the many-mingled motives of zeal, superstition, piety, pride, emulation, or distaste for the world, led into the desert. They required something more gross and palpable than the fine and subtle conception of a spiritual being. Superstition, not content with crowding the brain with imaginary figments, spread its darkening mists over the Deity himself.

It was among the monks of Egypt that anthropomorphism assumed its most vulgar and obstinate form. They would not be persuaded that the expressions in the sacred writings which ascribe human acts, and faculties, and passions to the Deity were to be understood as a condescension to the weakness of our nature; they seemed disposed to compensate to themselves for the loss of human society by degrading the Deity, whom they professed to be their sole companion, to the likeness of man. Imagination could not maintain its flight, and they could not summon reason, which they surrendered with the rest of their dangerous freedom, to supply its place; and generally superstition demanded and received the same implicit and resolute obedience as religion itself. Once having humanised the Deity, they could not be weaned from the object of their worship. The great cause of quarrel between Theophilus, the Archbishop of Alexandria, and the monks of the adjacent establishments, was his vain attempt to enlighten them on those points to which they obstinately adhered, as the vital and essential part of their faith.

Pride, moreover, is almost the necessary result of such distinctions as the monks drew between themselves and the rest of mankind; and prejudice and obstinacy are the natural fruits of pride. Once having embraced opinions, however, as in this instance, contrary to their primary principles, small communities are with the utmost difficulty induced to surrender those tenets in which they support and strengthen each other by the general concurrence. The anthropomorphism of the Egyptian monks resisted alike argument and authority. The bitter and desperate remonstrance of the aged Serapion, when he was forced to surrender his anthropomorphic notions of the Deity,—" You have deprived me of my God,"* shows not merely the degraded intellectual state of the monks of Egypt, but the incapacity of the mass of mankind to keep up such high-wrought and imaginative conceptions. Enthusiasm of any particular kind wastes itself as soon as its votaries become numerous. It may hand down its lamp from individual to individual for many generations; but when it would include a whole section of society, it substitutes some new incentive, strong party or corporate feeling, habit,

---

* Cassian Collat. x. 1.

advantage, or the pride of exclusiveness, for its original disinterested zeal; and can never for a long period adhere to its original principles.

The effect of Monachism on Christianity, and on society at large, was of a very mingled character. Its actual influence on the population of the empire was probably not considerable, and would scarcely counterbalance the increase arising out of the superior morality, as regards sexual intercourse, introduced by the Christian religion.[f] Some apprehensions, indeed, were betrayed on this point, and when the opponents of Monachism urged, that if such principles were universally admitted, the human race would come to an end, its resolute advocates replied, that the Almighty, if necessary, would appoint new means for the propagation of mankind.

The withdrawal of so much ardour, talent, and virtue into seclusion, which, however elevating to the individual, became altogether unprofitable to society, might be considered a more serious objection. The barren world could ill spare any active or inventive

---

[f] There is a curious passage of St. Ambrose on this point. "Si quis igitur putat, conservatione virginum minui genus humanum, consideret, quia, ubi paucæ virgines, ibi etiam pauciores homines: ubi virginitatis studia crebriora, ibi numerum quoque hominum esse majorem. Dicite, quantas Alexandrina, totiusque Orientis, et Africana ecclesia, quotannis sacrare consueverint. Pauciores hic homines prudeunt, quam illic virgines consecrantur." We should wish to know whether there was any statistical ground for this singular assertion, that, in those regions in which celibacy was most practised, the population increased—or whether Egypt, the East, and Africa, were generally more prolific than Italy. The assertion that the vows of virginity in those countries exceeded the births in the latter is, most probably, to be set down to antithesis. Compare a good Essay of Zumpt, in the Transactions of the Berlin Academy, 1840, on this subject. He concludes that Christianity generally tended to diminish the population of the Empire. (1843.)

mind. Public affairs, at this disastrous period, demanded the best energies which could be combined from the whole Roman empire for their administration. This dereliction of their social duties by so many, could not but leave the competition more open to the base and unworthy; particularly as the actual abandonment of the world, and the capability of ardent enthusiasm, in men of high station, or of commanding intellect, displayed a force and independence of character which might, it should seem, have rendered important active service to mankind. If barbarians were admitted by a perilous, yet inevitable policy, into the chief military commands, was not this measure at least hastened, not merely by the general influence of Christianity, which reluctantly permitted its votaries to enter into the army, but still more by Monachism, which withdrew them altogether into religious inactivity? The civil and fiscal departments, and especially that of public education conducted by salaried professors, might also be deprived of some of the most eligible and useful candidates for employment. At a time of such acknowledged deficiency, it may have appeared little less than treasonable indifference to the public welfare, to break all connection with mankind, and to dwell in unsocial seclusion entirely on individual interests. Such might have been the remonstrance of a sober and dispassionate Pagan,[t] and in part of those few more rational Christians, who could not consider the rigid monastic Christianity as the original religion of its divine founder.

If, indeed, this peaceful enthusiasm had counteracted any general outburst of patriotism, or left vacant or abandoned to worthless candidates posts in the public

---

[t] Compare the law of Valens, de Monachis, quoted above.

service which could be commanded by great talents and honourable integrity, Monachism might fairly be charged with weakening the energies and deadening the resistance of the Roman empire to its gathering and multiplying adversaries. But the state of public affairs probably tended more to the growth of Monachism than Monachism to the disorder and disorganisation of public affairs. The partial and unjust distribution of the rewards of public service; the uncertainty of distinction in any career, in which success entirely depended on the favouritism and intrigue within the narrow circle of the court; the difficulty of emerging to eminence under a despotism by fair and honourable means; disgust and disappointment at slighted pretensions and baffled hopes; the general and apparently hopeless oppression which weighed down all mankind; the total extinction of the generous feelings of freedom; the conscious decrepitude of the human mind; the inevitable conviction that its productive energies in knowledge, literature, and arts, were extinct and effete, and that every path was preoccupied,—all these concurrent motives might naturally, in a large proportion of the most vigorous and useful minds, generate a distaste and weariness of the world. Religion, then almost universally dominant, would seize on this feeling, and enlist it in her service: it would avail itself of, not produce, the despondent determination to abandon an ungrateful world; it would ennoble and exalt the preconceived motives for seclusion; give a kind of conscious grandeur to inactivity, and substitute a dreamy but elevating love for the Deity for contemptuous misanthropy, as the justification for the total desertion of social duty. Monachism, in short, instead of precipitating the fall of the Roman empire, by enfeebling in any great degree its powers of resistance, enabled some portion of mankind to escape from the feeling of shame and misery. Amid the irremediable evils and the wretchedness that could not be averted, it was almost a social benefit to raise some part of mankind to a state of serene indifference, to render some at least superior to the general calamities.

Monachism, indeed, directly secured many in their isolation from all domestic ties, from that worst suffering inflicted by barbarous warfare, the sight of beloved females outraged, and innocent children butchered. In those times, the man was happiest who had least to lose, and who exposed the fewest vulnerable points of feeling or sympathy. The natural affections, in which, in ordinary times, consists the best happiness of man, were in those days such perilous indulgences, that he who was entirely detached from them embraced, perhaps, considering temporal views alone, the most prudent course. The solitary could but suffer in his own person; and though by no means secure in his sanctity from insult, or even death, his self-inflicted privations hardened him against the former, his high-wrought enthusiasm enabled him to meet the latter with calm resignation: he had none to leave whom he had to lament, none to lament him after his departure. The spoiler who found his way to his secret cell was baffled by his poverty; and the sword which cut short his days but shortened his painful pilgrimage on earth, and removed him at once to an anticipated heaven. With what different feelings would he behold, in his poor, and naked, and solitary cell, the approach of the blood-thirsty barbarians, from the father of a family, in his splendid palace, or his more modest and comfortable private dwelling, with a wife in his arms, whose death he would desire to see rather than that worse than death to which she might first be doomed in his presence; with helpless children clinging around his knees: the blessings which he had enjoyed, the wealth or comfort of his house, the beauty of his wife, of his daughters, or even of his sons, being the strongest attraction to the spoiler, and irritating more violently that spoiler's merciless and unsparing passions. If to some the monastic state offered a refuge for the sad remainder of their bereaved life, others may have taken warning in time, and with deliberate forethought refused to implicate themselves in tender connections, which were threatened with such deplorable end. Those, who secluded themselves from domestic relations, from other motives, at all events, were secured from such miseries, and might be envied by those who had played the game of life for a higher stake and ventured on its purest pleasures, with the danger of incurring all its bitterest reverses.

Monachism tended powerfully to keep up the vital enthusiasm of Christianity. Allusion has been made to its close connection with the conversion both of the Roman and the Barbarian; and to the manner in which, from its settlement in some retired Pagan district, it gradually disseminated the faith, and sometimes the industrious, always the moral, influence of Christianity through the neighbourhood in a gradually expanding circle. Its peaceful colonies, within the frontier of Barbarism, slowly but uninterruptedly subdued the fierce or indolent savages to the religion of Christ and the manners and habits of civilisation. But its internal influence was not less visible, immediate, and inexhaustible. The more extensive dissemination of Christianity naturally weakened its authority. When the small primitive assembly of the Christians grew into an universal church; when the village, the town, the city, the province, the empire, became in outward form and profession Christian, the practical Heathenism only retired to work more silently and imperceptibly into the Christian system. The wider the circle, the fainter the line of distinction from the surrounding waters. Small societies have a kind of self-acting principle of conservation within. Mutual inspection generates mutual awe; the generous rivalry in religious attainment keeps up regularity in attendance on the sacred institutions, and at least propriety of demeanour. Such small communities may be disturbed by religious faction, but are long before they degenerate into unchristian licentiousness or languish into religious apathy. But when a large proportion of Christians received the faith as an inheritance from their fathers rather than from personal conviction; when hosts of deserters from Paganism passed over into the opposite camp, not because it was the best, but because it was the most flourishing cause; it became inexpedient, as well as impossible, to maintain the severer discipline of former times. But Monachism was constantly reorganising small societies, in which the bond of aggregation was the common religious fervour, in which emulation continually kept up the excitement, and mutual vigilance exercised unresisted authority. The exaggeration of their religious sentiments was at once the tenure of their existence and the guarantee for their perpetuity. Men would never be wanting to enrol themselves in their ranks, and their constitution prevented them from growing to an unmanageable size. When one establishment or institution wore out, another was sure to spring up. The republics of Monachism were constantly reverting to their first principles, and undergoing a vigorous and thorough reformation. Thus, throughout the whole of Christian history, until, or even after, the Reformation, within the church of Rome, we find either new monastic orders rising, or the old remodelled and regulated by the zeal of some ardent enthusiast. The associatory principle, that great political and religious engine which is either the conservative or the destructive power in every period of society, was constantly embracing a certain number of persons devoted to a common end; and the new sect, distinguished by some peculiar badge of dress, of habit, or of monastic rule, re-embodied some of the fervour of primitive Christianity, and awakened the growing lethargy, by the example of unusual austerities or rare and exemplary activity in the dissemination of the faith.

The beneficial tendency of this constant formation of young and vigorous societies in the bosom of Christianity was of more importance in the times of desolation and confusion which impended over the Roman empire. In this respect, likewise, their lofty pretensions insured their utility. Where reason itself was about to be in abeyance, rational religion would have had but little chance: it would have commanded no respect. Christianity, in its primitive simple and unassuming form, might have imparted its holiness, and peace, and happiness, to retired families, whether in the city or the province, but its modest and retiring dignity would have made no impression on the general tone and character of society. There was something in the seclusion of religious men from mankind, in their standing aloof from the rest of the world, calculated to impress barbarous minds with a feeling of their peculiar sanctity. The less they were like to ordinary men, the more, in the ordinary estimation, they were approximated to the divinity. At all events, this apparently broad and manifest evidence of their religious sincerity would be more impressive to unreasoning minds than the habits of the clergy, which approached more nearly to those of the common laity.[b]

The influence of this continual rivalry of another sacred, though not decidedly sacerdotal class, upon the secular clergy, led to important results. We may perhaps ascribe to the constant presence of Monachism the continuance and the final recognition of the celibacy of the clergy, the vital principle of the ecclesiastical power in the middle ages. Without the powerful direct support which they received from the monastic orders; without the indirect authority over the minds of men which flowed from their example, and inseparably connected, in the popular mind, superior sanctity with the renunciation of marriage, the ambitious Popes would never have been able, particularly in the north, to part the clergy by this strong line of demarcation from the profane laity. As it was, it required the most vigorous and continued effort to establish, by ecclesiastical regulation and papal power, that which was no longer in accordance with the religious sentiments of the clergy themselves. The general practice of marriage, or of a kind of legalised concubinage, among the northern clergy, showed the tendency, if it had not been thus counteracted by the rival order, and by the dominant *ecclesiastical* policy of

Influence on the clergy.

In promoting celibacy.

---

[b] The monks were originally laymen (Cassian, v. 26); gradually churches were attached to the monasteries, but these were served by regularly ordained clergy.—(Pallad. Hist. Lausiac.); but their reputation for sanctity constantly exposed them to be seized and consecrated by the ardent admiration of their followers. Theiner has collected with considerable labour a long list of the more celebrated prelates of the church who had been monks, p. 106. Ita ergo age et vive in monasterio, ut clericus esse merearis. Hieron. Epist. ad Rustic. 95.

the Church.[1] But it is impossible to calculate the effect of that complete blending up of the clergy with the rest of the community which would probably have ensued from the gradual abrogation of this single distinction at this juncture. The interests of their order, in men connected with the community by the ordinary social ties, would have been secondary to their own personal advancement, or that of their families. They would have ceased to be a peculiar and separate caste, and sunk down into the common penury, rudeness, and ignorance. Their influence would be closely connected with their wealth and dignity, which, of course, on the other hand, would tend to augment their influence; but that corporate ambition which induced them to consider the cause of their order as their own; that desire of riches, which wore the honorable appearance of personal disinterestedness, and zeal for the splendour of religion, could not have existed but in a class completely insulated from the common feelings and interests of the community. Individual members of the clergy might have become wealthy, and obtained authority over the ignorant herd, but there would have been no opulent and powerful Church, acting with vigorous unity, and arranged in simultaneous hostility against Barbarism and Paganism.

Our history must hereafter trace the connection of the independence and separate existence of the clergy with the maintenance and the authority of Christianity. But even as conservators of the lingering remains of science, arts, and letters, as the sole order to which

---

[1] The general question of the celibacy of the clergy will be subsequently examined. Compare Latin Christianity, especially the great struggle at Milan. Book vi. c. iii.

some kind of intellectual education was necessary, when knowledge was a distinction which alone commanded respect, the clergy were, not without advantage, secured by their celibacy from the cares and toils of social life. In this respect, Monachism acted in two ways; as itself the most efficient guardian of what was most worth preserving in the older civilisation, and as preventing, partly by emulation, partly by this enforcement of celibacy, the secular clergy from degenerating universally into that state of total ignorance which prevailed among them in some quarters.

It is impossible to survey Monachism in its general influence, from the earliest period of its interworking into Christianity, without being astonished and perplexed with its diametrically opposite effects. Here, it is the undoubted parent of the blindest ignorance and the most ferocious bigotry, sometimes of the most debasing licentiousness; there, the guardian of learning, the author of civilisation, the propagator of humble and peaceful religion. To the dominant spirit of Monachism may be ascribed some part at least of the gross superstition and moral inefficiency of the church in the Byzantine empire; to the same spirit much of the salutary authority of Western Christianity, its constant aggressions on barbarism, and its connection with the Latin literature. Yet neither will the different genius of the East and West account for this contradictory operation of the monastic spirit in the two divisions of the Roman empire. If human nature was degraded by the filth and fanatic self-torture, the callous apathy, and the occasional sanguinary violence, of the Egyptian or Syrian monk, yet the monastic retreat sent forth its Basils and Chrysostoms, who seemed to have braced their strong intellects by the air of the desert. Their intrepid and disinterested devotion to their great cause, the complete concentration of their whole faculties on the advancement of Christianity, seemed strengthened by this entire detachment from mankind.

Nothing can be conceived more apparently opposed to the designs of the God of nature, and to the mild and beneficent spirit of Christianity; nothing more hostile to the dignity, the interests, the happiness, and the intellectual and moral perfection of man, than the monk afflicting himself with unnecessary pain, and thrilling his soul with causeless fears; confined to a dull routine of religious duties, jealously watching, and proscribing every emotion of pleasure as a sin against the benevolent Deity; dreading knowledge as an impious departure from the becoming humility of man.

On the other hand, what generous or lofty mind can refuse to acknowledge the grandeur of that superiority to all the cares and passions of mortality; the felicity of that state which is removed far above the fears or the necessities of life; that sole passion of admiration and love of the Deity, which no doubt was attained by some of the purer and more imaginative enthusiasts of the cell or the cloister? Who still more will dare to depreciate that heroism of Christian benevolence, which underwent this self-denial of the lawful enjoyments and domestic charities of which it had neither extinguished the desire, nor subdued the regret—not from the slavish fear of displeasing the Deity, or the selfish ambition of personal perfection—but from the genuine desire of advancing the temporal and eternal improvement of mankind; of imparting the moral amelioration and spiritual hopes of Christianity to the wretched and the barbarous; of being the messengers of Christian faith, and the ministers of Christian charity, to the Heathen, whether in creed or in character?

We return from this long, but not unnecessary, digression, to the life of Jerome, the great advocate of Monachism in the West. Jerome began and closed his career as a monk of Palestine: he attained, he aspired to, no dignity in the church. Though ordained a presbyter against his will, he escaped the episcopal dignity which was forced upon his distinguished contemporaries. He left to Ambrose, to Chrysostom, and to Augustine, the authority of office, and was content with the lower, but not less extensive influence of personal communication, or the effect of his writings. After having passed his youth in literary studies in Rome, and in travelling throughout the West, he visited Palestine. During his voyage to the East, he surveyed some great cities, and consulted their libraries; he was received in Cyprus by the Bishop Epiphanius. In Syria, he plunged at once into the severest austerities of asceticism. I have already inserted the lively description of the inward struggles and agonies which tried him during his first retreat in the Arabian desert.

But Jerome had other trials peculiar to himself. It was not so much the indulgence of the coarser passions, the lusts and ambition of the world, which distressed his religious sensibilities,[b] it was the nobler and more intellectual part of his being which was endangered by the fond reminiscences of his former

---

[a] Jerome says,—"Prima est virginitas à nativitate; secunda virginitas à secundâ nativitate;" he ingenuously confesses that he could only boast of the second. Epist. xxv. iv. p. 242; Oper. iv. p. 459.

days. He began to question the lawfulness of those literary studies which had been the delight of his youth. He had brought with him, his sole companions, besides the sacred books of his religion, the great masters of poetry and philosophy, of Greek and Latin style; and the magic of Plato's and Cicero's language, to his refined and fastidious ear, made the sacred writings of Christianity, on which he was intently fixed, appear rude and barbarous. In his retreat in Bethlehem he had undertaken the study of Hebrew,[m] as a severe occupation to withdraw him from those impure and worldly thoughts which his austerities had not entirely subdued; and in the weary hours when he was disgusted with his difficult task, he could not refrain from recurring, as a solace, to his favourite authors. But even this indulgence alarmed his jealous conscience; though he fasted before he opened his Cicero, his mind dwelt with too intense delight on the language of the orator; and the distaste with which he passed from the musical periods of Plato to the verses of the Prophets, of which his ear had not yet perceived the harmony, and his Roman taste had not perhaps imbibed the full sublimity, appeared to him as an impious offence against his religion.[n] The inward struggles of his mind threw him into a fever, he was thought to be dead, and in the lethargic dream of his distempered imagination, he thought that he beheld himself before the throne of the

---

[m] His description of Hebrew, as compared with Latin, is curious:— "Ad quam edomandam, cuidam fratri, qui ex Hebræis crediderat, me in disciplinam dedi ut post Quintiliani acumina, gravitatemque Frontonis, et levitatem Plinii, alphabetum discerem et stridentia anhelaque verba meditarer—quid ibi laboris insumserim?" Epist. xcv. ad Rusticum, p. 774.

[n] "Si quando in memet reversus, Prophetas legere cœpissem, sermo horrebat incultus. Epist. xviii. ad Eustoch. ir. p. 42.

great Judge, before the brightness of which he dared not lift up his eyes. "Who art thou?" demanded the awful voice.—"A Christian," answered the trembling Jerome.[*] "'Tis false," sternly replied the voice, "thou art no Christian, thou art a Ciceronian. Where the treasure is, there is the heart also." Yet, however the scrupulous conscience of Jerome might tremble at this profane admixture of sacred and heathen studies, he was probably qualified in a high degree by this very discordant collision of opposite tastes for one of the great services which he was to render to Christianity. No writer, without that complete mastery over the Latin language, which could only be attained by constant familiarity with its best models, could so have harmonised its genius with the foreign elements which were to be mingled with it, as to produce the vivid and glowing style of the Vulgate Bible. That this is far removed from the purity of Tully, no one will question : I shall hereafter consider more at length its genius and its influence; but we may conjecture what would have been the harsh, jarring, and inharmonious discord of the opposing elements, if the translator had only been conversant with the African Latinity of Tertullian, or the elaborate obscurity of writers like Ammianus Marcellinus.

Jerome could not, in the depths of his retreat, or in the absorbing occupation of his studies, escape being

---

[*] Interim parantur exequiæ, et vitalis animæ calor, toto frigescerate jam corpore, in solo tantum tepente pulviculo, palpitabat; quum subitò raptus in spiritu, ad tribunal judicis pertrahor; ubi tantum luminis, et tantum erat ex circumstantium claritate fulgoris, ut projectus in terram, sursum aspicere non auderem. Interrogatus de conditione, Christianum me esse respondi. Et ille qui præsidebat mortuus ait, Ciceronianus es, non Christianus; ubi enim thesaurus tuus, ibi et cor tuum. Ad Eustoch. Epist. xviii. lv. p. 42.

involved in those controversies which distracted the
Eastern churches, and penetrated to the cell of
the remotest anchorite. He returned to the
West to avoid the restless polemics of his brother monks.
On his return to Rome, the fame of his piety and
talents commended him to the confidence of the Pope
Damasus,[p] by whom he was employed in the most important
affairs of the Roman see. But either the
influence or the opinions of Jerome excited
the jealousy of the Roman clergy, whose vices
Jerome paints in no softened colours. We almost, in
this contest, behold a kind of prophetic prelude to the
perpetual strife, which has existed in almost all ages,
between the secular and regular clergy, the hierarchical
and monastic spirit. Though the monastic opinions and
practices were by no means unprecedented in Italy
(they had been first introduced by Athanasius in his
flight from Egypt); though they were maintained by
Ambrose, and practised by some recluses; yet the
pomp, the wealth, and the authority of the Roman
ecclesiastics, which is described by the concurrent testimony
of the Heathen historian[q] and the Christian
Jerome, would not humbly brook the greater popularity
of these severer doctrines, nor patiently submit to the
estrangement of some of their more opulent and distinguished
proselytes, particularly among the females.
Jerome admits, indeed, with specious, but doubtful
humility, the inferiority of the unordained monk to the
ordained priest. The clergy were the successors of
the Apostles; their lips could make the body of Christ;
they had the keys of heaven, until the day of judgement;

[p] Epist. xii. p. 744. Tillemont, Vie de Jerome.   [q] Ammianus Marcellinus. See postea.

they wore the shepherds, the monks only part of the flock. Yet the clergy, no doubt, had the sagacity to foresee the dangerous rival, as to influence and authority, which was rising up in Christian society. The great object of contention now was the command over the high-born and wealthy females of Rome. Jerome, in his advice to the clergy, cautiously warns them against the danger of female intimacy.[r] He, however, either considered himself secure, or under some peculiar privilege, or justified by the prospect of greater utility, to suspend his laws on his own behalf. He became a kind of confessor, he directed the sacred studies, he overlooked the religious conduct of more than one of these pious ladies. The ardour and vehemence with which his ascetic opinions were embraced, and the more than usually familiar intercourse with matrons and virgins of rank, may perhaps have offended the pride, if not the propriety, of Roman manners. The more temperate and rational of the clergy, in their turn, may have thought the zeal with which these female converts of Jerome were prepared to follow their teacher to the Holy Land, by no means a safe precedent; they may have taken alarm at the unusual fervour of language with which female ascetics were celebrated as united, by the nuptial tie, to Christ,[s] and exhorted, in

---

[r] Epist. ad Heliodorum, p. 10.

[s] See the Epistle ad Eustochium. The whole of this letter is a singular union of religious earnestness and what, to modern feeling, would seem strange indelicacy if not immodesty, and still stranger liberty with the language of Scripture. He seems to say that Eustochium was the first noble Roman maiden who embraced virginity:—"Quæ ... prima Romanæ urbis virgo nobilis esse cœpisti." He says, however, of Marcella,—"Nulla eo tempore nobilium feminarum noverat Romæ propositum monacharum, nec audebat propter rei novitatem, ignominiosum, ut tunc putabatur, et vile in populis, nomen assumere." Marcellæ Epitaph, p. 780.

the glowing imagery of the Song of Solomon, to devote themselves to their spiritual spouse. They were the brides of Christ;—Christ, worshipped by angels in heaven, ought to have angels to worship him on earth.[1] With regard to Jerome and his high-born friends, their suspicions were, doubtless, unjust.

Character of Roman females. It is singular, indeed, to contrast the different descriptions of the female aristocracy of Rome at the various periods of her history; the secluded and dignified matrons, the Volumnias or Cornelias, employed in household duties, and educating with severe discipline, for the military and civil service of the state, her future consuls and dictators; the gorgeous luxury, the almost incredible profligacy, of the later days of the republic and of the empire, the Julias and Messalinas, so darkly coloured by the satirists of the times; the active charity and the stern austerities of the Paulas and Eustochiums of the present period. It was not, in general, the severe and lofty Roman matron of the age of Roman virtue whom Christianity induced to abandon her domestic duties, and that highest of all duties to her country, the bringing up of noble and virtuous citizens; it was the soft, and at the same time, the savage female, who united the incongruous, but too frequently reconciled, vices of sensuality and cruelty; the female, whom the facility of divorce, if she abstained from less lawful indulgence, enabled to gratify in a more decent manner her inconstant passions; who had been inured from her most tender age, not merely to theatrical shows of questionable modesty, but to the

---

[1] In Jerome's larger interpretation of Solomon's Song (adv. Jovin. p. 171) is a very curious and whimsical passage, alluding to the Saviour as the spouse. There is one sentence, however, in the letter to Eustochium, so blasphemously indecent that it must not be quoted even in Latin. p. 38.

bloody scenes of the arena, giving the signal perhaps with her own delicate hand for the mortal blow to the exhausted gladiator. We behold with wonder, not unmixed with admiration, women of the same race and city either forswearing from their earliest youth all intercourse with men, or preserving the state of widowhood with irreproachable dignity; devoting their wealth to the foundation of hospitals, and their time to religious duties and active benevolence. These monastic sentiments were carried to that excess which seemed inseparable from the Roman character. At twelve years old, the young Asella devoted herself to God; from that time she had never conversed with a man; her knees were as hard as a camel's, by constant genuflexion and prayer.[a] Paula, the fervent disciple of Jerome, after devoting the wealth of an ancient and opulent house to charitable uses,[b] to the impoverishment of her own children, deserted her family. Her infant son and her marriageable daughter watched, with entreating looks, her departure; she did not even turn her head away to hide her maternal tears, but lifted up her unmoistened eyes to heaven, and continued her pilgrimage to the Holy Land. Jerome celebrates

Paula.

---

[a] Hieronym. Epist. xxi.

[b] Jerome thus describes the charity of Paula:—Quid ego referam, amplæ et nobilis domus, et quondam opulentissimæ, omnes pene divitias in pauperes erogatas. Quid in cunctos clementissimum animum, et bonitatem etiam in eos quos nunquam viderat, evagantem. Quis inopum moriens, non illius vestimentis obvolutus est? Quis clinicorum non ejus facultatibus sustentatus est? Quos curiosissimè totâ urbe perquirens, damnum putabat, si quis debilis et esuriens cibo sustentaretur alterius. Spoliabat filios, et inter objurgantes propinquos, majorem se eis hæreditatem, Christi misericordiam dimittere loquebatur. Epitaph. Paulæ, p. 671. At her death, Jerome relates, with great pride, that she did not leave a penny to her daughter, but a load of debts (magnum æs alienum).

this sacrifice of the holiest charities of life as the height of female religious heroism.[7]

Controversies of Jerome. The vehement and haughty temper of Jerome was not softened by his monastic austerities, nor humbled by the severe proscription of the gentler affections. His life, in the capital and in the desert, was one long warfare. After the death of his friend and protector, Damasus, the growing hostility of the clergy, notwithstanding the attachment of his disciples, rendered his residence in Rome disagreeable. Nor was the peace of the monastic life his reward for his zealous exertions in its cause. He retired *Retreat to Palestine.* to Palestine, where he passed the rest of his days in religious studies, and in polemic disputes. Wherever any dissentient from the doctrine or the practice of the dominant Christianity ventured to express his opinions, Jerome launched the thunders of his interdict from his cell at Bethlehem. No one was more perpetually involved in controversy, or opposed with greater rancour of personal hostility, than this earnest advocate of unworldly religious seclusion. He was engaged in a vehement dispute with St. Augustine on

---

[7] It is a passage of considerable beauty:—Descendit ad portum, fratre, cognatis, affinibus, et (quod his majus est) liberis prosequentibus, et clementissimam matrem pietate vincere cupientibus, Jam carbasa tendebantur, et remorum ductu navis in altum protrahebatur. Parvus Toxotius supplices manus tendebat in littora. Rufina, jam nubilis, ut suas expectaret nuptias, tacens fletibus obsecrabat, et tamen illa siccos ad cœlum oculos, pietatem in filios, pietate in Deum superans, nesciebat se matrem ut Christi probaret ancillam. . . . . Et contra jura naturæ plena fides petebatur, imo gaudens animus appetebat. Epitaph. Paulæ 672.

This was her epitaph:—

Aspicis angustum præcisa rupe sepulcrum?
Hospitium Paulæ est, cœlestia regna tenentis.
Fratrem, cognatos, Romam, patriamque relinquens,
Divitias, sobolem, Bethlehemite conditur antro.
Hic præsepe tuum, Christe, atque hic mystica Magi
Munera portantes, hominique, Deoque dedere.

the difference between St. Peter and St. Paul. But his repose was most embittered by the acrimonious and obstinate contest with Rufinus, which was rather a personal than a polemic strife.

In one controversy, Christendom acknowledged and hailed him as her champion. Jovinian and Vigilantius are involved in the dark list of heretics; but their error appears to have been that of unwisely attempting to stem the current of popular Christian opinion, rather than any departure from the important doctrines of Christianity. They were premature Protestants; they endeavoured, with vain and ill-timed efforts, to arrest the encroaching spirit of Monachism, which had now enslaved the whole of Christianity;[a] they questioned the superior merit of celibacy; they protested against the growing worship of relics.[b] Their effect upon the dominant sentiment of the times may be estimated by the language of wrath, bitterness, contempt, and abhorrence, with which Jerome assails these bold men, who thus presumed to encounter the spirit of their age. The four points of Jovinian's heresy, were,—1st, that virgins had no higher merit, unless superior in their good works, than widows and married women; 2nd, that there was no distinction of meats; 3rd, that those who had been baptized in full faith,

---

[a] Hieronym. adv. Vigilantium, p. 281.

[b] The observation of Fleury shows how mistimed was the attempt of Vigilantius to return to the simpler Christianity of former days: — "On ne voit pas que l'hérésie (de Vigilance), ait eu de suite; ni qu'on ait eu besoin d'aucun concile pour la condamner; mais elle étoit contraire à la tradition de l'Eglise Universelle." Tom. v. p. 278.

I have purposely, lest I should overstrain the *Protestantism* of these remarkable men, taken this view of their tenets from Fleury, perhaps the fairest and most dispassionate writer of his church. Tom. iv. p. 602; tom. v. p. 275.

would not be overcome by the Devil; and 4th, that those who had preserved the grace of baptism would meet with an equal reward in heaven. This last clause was perhaps a corollary from the first, as the panegyrists of virginity uniformly claimed a higher place in heaven for the immaculate than for those who had been polluted by marriage. To those doctrines Vigilantius added, if possible, more hated tenets. He condemned the respect paid to the martyrs and their relics; he questioned the miracles performed at their tombs; he condemned the lighting lamps before them as a Pagan superstition; he rejected the intercession of the saints; he blamed the custom of sending alms to Jerusalem, and the selling all property to give it to the poor; he asserted that it was better to keep it and distribute its revenues in charity; he protested against the whole monastic life, as interfering with the duty of a Christian to his neighbour. These doctrines were not without their followers; the resentment of Jerome was embittered by their effect on some of the noble ladies of Rome, who began to fall off to marriage. Even some bishops embraced the doctrines of Vigilantius, and, asserting that the high professions of continence led the way to debauchery, refused to ordain unmarried deacons.

The tone of Jerome's indignant writings against those new heretics is that of a man suddenly arrested in his triumphant career by some utterly unexpected opposition; his resentment at being thus crossed is mingled with a kind of wonder that men should exist who could entertain such strange and daring tenets. The length, it might be said the prolixity, to which he draws out his answer to Jovinian, seems rather the outpouring of his wrath and his learning, than as if he considered it necessary to refute such obvious errors. Throughout it is the master condescending to teach, not the adversary to argue. He fairly overwhelms him with a mass of scripture, and of classical learning: at one time he pours out a flood of allegorical interpretations of the scripture; he then confounds him with a clever passage from Theophrastus on the miseries of marriage. Even the friends of Jerome, the zealous Pammachius himself, were offended by the fierceness of his first invective against Jovinian,[b] and his contemptuous disparagement of marriage. The injustice of his personal charges is shewn and the charges refuted by the more temperate statements of Augustine and by his own admissions.[c] He was obliged, in his apology, to mitigate his vehemence, and reluctantly to fall into a milder strain; but even the Apology has something of the severe and contemptuous tone of an orator who is speaking on the popular side, with his audience already in his favour.

But his language to Jovinian is sober, dispassionate, and argumentative, in comparison with that to Vigilantius. He describes all the monsters ever invented

---

[b] Indignamini mihi, quod Jovinianum non docuerim, sed vicerim. Imo indignamur mihi qui illum anathematizatum dolent. Apolog. p. 236.

[c] Jerome admits that Jovinian did not assert the privilege which he vindicated; he remained a monk, though Jerome highly colours his luxurious habits. After his coarse tunic and bare feet, and food of bread and water, he has betaken himself to white garments, sweetened wine, and highly dressed meats: to the sauces of an Apicius or a Paxamus, to baths, and shampooings (fricticulæ,—the Benedictines translate this fritter shops), and cooks' shops, it is manifest that he prefers earth to heaven, vice to virtue, his belly to Christ, and thinks his rubicund colour (purpuram coloris ejus) the kingdom of heaven. Yet this handsome, this corpulent, smooth monk, always goes in white like a bridegroom; let him marry a wife to prove the equal value of virginity and marriage; but if he will not take a wife, though he is against us in his words, his actions are for us. He afterwards says,—Ille Romanæ ecclesiæ auctoritate damnatus inter fluviales aves, et carnes suillas, non tam emisit animam quam eructavit. p. 183.

by poetic imagination, the centaurs, the leviathan, the Nemean lion, Cacus, Geryon. Gaul, by her one monster, Vigilantius,[d] had surpassed all the pernicious and portentous horrors of other regions. "Why do I fly to the desert?—That I may not see or hear thee; that I may no longer be moved by thy madness, nor be provoked to war by thee; lest the eye of a harlot should captivate me, and a beautiful form seduce me to unlawful love." But his great and conclusive argument in favour of reverence for the dust of martyrs (that little dust which, covered with a precious veil, Vigilantius presumed to think but dust) is universal authority. "Was the Emperor Constantine sacrilegious, who transported the relics of Andrew, Luke, and Timothy to Constantinople, at whose presence the devils (such devils as inhabit the wretched Vigilantius) roar, and are confounded? or the Emperor Arcadius, who translated the bones of the holy Samuel to Thrace? Are all the bishops sacrilegious who enshrined these precious remains in silk, as a vessel of gold; and all the people who met them, and received them as it were the living prophet? Is the Bishop of Rome, who offers sacrifice on the altar under which are the venerable bones (the vile dust, would Vigilantius say?) of Peter and Paul; and not the bishop of one city alone, but the bishops of all the cities in the world who reverence these relics, around which the souls of the martyrs are constantly hovering to hear the prayers of the supplicant?"

---

[d] His brief sketch of the enormities of Vigilantius is as follows:— Qui immundo spiritu pugnat contra Christi spiritum, et martyrum negat sepulcra esse veneranda; damnandas dicit esse vigilias; nunquam nisi in Pascha Alleluia cantandum: continentiam hæresim, pudicitiam libidinis seminarium.

The great work of Jerome, the authoritative Latin version of the scriptures, will demand our attention, as one of the primary elements of Christian literature, a subject which must form one most important branch of our inquiry into the extent and nature of the general revolution in the history of mankind, brought about by the complete establishment of Christianity.*

---

* Compare Latin Christianity, book i. ch. 2. Note on Jerome. Especially the passages about the destruction of Rome by Alaric, vol. i. p. 101.

BOOK IV.

CHAPTER I.

The Roman empire under Christianity.

General survey of the change effected by Christianity. The period is now arrived when we may survey the total change in the habits and manners, as well as in the sentiments and opinions, of mankind, effected by the dominance of the new faith. Christianity is now the mistress of the Roman world; on every side the struggles of Paganism become more feeble; it seems resigned to its fate, or rather only hopes, by a feigned allegiance, and a simulation of the forms and language of Christianity, to be permitted to drag on a precarious and inglorious existence. The Christians are now no longer a separate people, founding and maintaining their small independent republics, fenced in by marked peculiarities of habits and manners from the rest of society; they have become to all outward appearance *the people;* the general manners of the world may be contemplated as the manners of Christendom. The monks, and in some respects the clergy, have, as it were, taken the place of the Christians as a separate and distinct body of men; the latter in a great degree, the former altogether, differing from the prevalent usages in their modes of life, and abstaining from the common pursuits and avocations of society. The Christian writers, therefore, become our leading, almost our only, authorities for the general habits and manners of mankind (for the notice of such matters in the Heathen writers are few and casual), except the Theodosian code. This indeed is of great value as a record of manners as well as a history of legislation; for that which demands the prohibition of the law, or is in any way of sufficient importance to require the notice of the legislature, may be considered as a prevalent custom: particularly as the Theodosian code is not a system of abstract and general law, but the register of the successive edicts of the Emperors, who were continually supplying, by their arbitrary acts, the deficiencies of the existing statutes, or as new cases arose, adapting those statutes to temporary exigences.

Sources of information.

Theodosian code.

But the Christian preachers are the great painters of Roman manners; Chrysostom of the East, more particularly of Constantinople; Jerome, and though much less copiously, Ambrose and Augustine, of Roman Christendom. Considerable allowance must, of course, be made in all these statements for oratorical vehemence; much more for the ascetic habits of the writers, particularly of Chrysostom, who maintained, and would have exacted, the rigid austerity of the desert in the midst of a luxurious capital. Nor must the general morality of the times be estimated from their writings without considerable discretion. It is the office of the preacher, though with a different design yet with something of the manner of the satirist, to select the vices of mankind for his animadversion, and to dwell with far less force on the silent and unpretending virtues. There might be, and probably was, an under-current of quiet Christian piety and gentleness

Christian writers.

and domestic happiness, which would not arrest the notice of the preacher who was denouncing the common pride and luxury, or, if kindling into accents of praise, was enlarging on the austere self-denial of the anchorite, or the more shining virtues of the saint.

Christianity disturbed not the actual relations of society, it interfered in no way with the existing gradations of rank. Though, as we shall see, it introduced a new order of functionaries,—what may be considered from the estimation in which they were held, a new aristocracy,—it left all the old official dignitaries in possession of their distinctions. With the great vital distinction between the freeman and the slave, as yet it made no difference.[a] It broke down none of the barriers which separated this race of men from the common rights of human kind; and in no degree legally brought up this Pariah caste of antiquity to the common level of the human race.

Slavery.

In the new relation established between mankind and the Supreme Being, the slave was fully participant; he shared in the redemption through Christ, he might receive all the spiritual blessings, and enjoy all the immortalising hopes of the believer; he might be dismissed from his death-bed to heaven by the absolving voice of the priest; and besides this inestimable consolation in misery and degradation, this religious equality, at least with the religious part of the community, could not fail to elevate his condition, and to strengthen that claim to the sympathies of mankind which was enforced by Christian humanity. The axiom of Clement of Alexandria that by the common law of

---

[a] The laws of Justinian, it must be remembered, are beyond this period.

Christian charity, we were to act to them as we would be acted by, because they were men,[b] though perhaps it might have been uttered with equal strength of language by some of the better philosophers, spoke with far more general acceptance to the human heart. The manumission, which was permitted by Constantine to take place in the Church, must likewise have tended indirectly to connect freedom with Christianity.[c]

Still, down to the time of Justinian, the inexorable law, which, as to their treatment, had already been wisely tempered by the Heathen Emperors, as to their *rights*, pronounced the same harsh and imperious sentence. It beheld them as an inferior class of human beings; their life was placed but partially under the protection of the law. If they died under a punishment of extraordinary cruelty, the master was guilty of homicide; if under more moderate application of the scourge, or any other infliction, the master was not accountable for their death.[d] While it refused to protect, the law inflicted on the slave punishments disproportionate to those of the freeman. If he accused his master for any crime, except high treason, he was to be burned;[e] if free women married slaves, they sank to the abject state of their husbands, and forfeited their rights as free women;[f] if a free woman intrigued with a slave, she was capitally punished, the slave was burned.[g]

The possession of slaves was in no degree limited by law. It was condemned as a mark of inordinate luxury,

---

[b] Clemens Alex. Pædagog. iii. 12.
[c] See Blair on Slavery, p. 268.
[d] Cod. Theodos. ix. 12, 1.
[e] Ibid. ix. 6, 2.
[f] Ibid. iv. 9, 1, 2, 3.

[g] Ibid. ix. 11, 1. Since the publication of this book has appeared the best and most comprehensive work on that subject—Wallon's 'Histoire de l'Esclavage dans l'Antiquité.'

but by no means as in itself contrary to Christian justice or equity.[b]

Manners of the court.
On the pomp and magnificence of the court, Christianity either did not aspire, or despaired of enforcing moderation or respect for the common dignity of mankind. The manners of the East, as the Emperor took up his residence in Constantinople, were too strong for the religion. With the first Christian Emperor commenced that Oriental ceremonial, which it might almost seem, that, rebuked by the old liberties of Rome, the imperial despot would not assume till he had founded another capital; or at least, if the first groundwork of this Eastern pomp was laid by Diocletian, Rome had already been deserted, and was not insulted by the open degradation of the first men in the empire to the language, attitudes, and titles of servitude.

Government of the eunuchs.
The eunuchs, who, however admitted in solitary instances to the confidence or favour of the earlier Emperors, had never formed a party or handed down to each other the successive administrations, now ruled in almost uncontested sovereignty, and except in some rare instances, seemed determined not to incur, without deserving, the antipathy and contempt of mankind. The luxury and prodigality of the court equalled its pomp and its servility. The parsimonious reformation introduced by Julian may exaggerate in its contemptuous expressions, the thousand cooks, the thousand barbers, and more than thousand cupbearers, with the host of eunuchs and drones of every description who

---

[b] Clemens Alex. Pædagog. iii. 12. It is curious to compare this passage of Clement with the beautiful essay of | Seneca. See likewise Chrysostom almost passim. Some had 2000 or 3000, t. vii. p. 633.

lived at the charge of the Emperor Constantius.[1] The character of Theodosius gave an imposing dignity to his resumption of that magnificence, of which Julian, not without affectation, had displayed his disdain. The Heathen writers, perhaps with the design of contrasting Theodosius with the severer Julian, who are the representatives, or at least, each the pride of the opposing parties, describe the Christian as immoderately indulging in the pleasures of the table, and of re-enlisting in the imperial service a countless multitude of cooks and other attendants on the splendour and indulgence of the court.[k]

That which in Theodosius was the relaxation or the reward for military services, and the cares and agitations of an active administration, degenerated with his feeble sons into indolent and effeminate luxury. The head of the empire became a secluded Asiatic despot. When, on rare occasions, Arcadius condescended to reveal to the public the majesty of the sovereign, he was preceded by a vast multitude of attendants, dukes, tribunes, civil and military officers, their horses glittering with golden ornaments, with shields of gold, set with precious stones, and golden lances. They proclaimed the coming of the Emperor, and commanded the ignoble crowd to clear the streets before him.[m] The Emperor stood or reclined on a gorgeous chariot surrounded by his immediate attendants distinguished by shields with golden bosses set round with golden eyes, and drawn by white

---

[1] Libanius, Epitaph. Julian. p. 565.
[k] Zosimus, iv. 28.
[m] Montfaucon, in an essay in the last volume of the works of Chrysostom, and in the twelfth vol. of the Memoirs of the Academy of Inscriptions, and Müller, in his treatise de Genio, Moribus, et Luxu Ævi Theodosiani, have collected the principal features of this picture, chiefly from Chrysostom.

mules with gilded trappings; the chariot was set with precious stones, and golden fans vibrated with the movement, and cooled the air. The multitude contemplated at a distance the snow-white cushions, the silken carpets with dragons enwoven upon them in rich colours. Those who were fortunate enough to catch a glimpse of the Emperor beheld his ears loaded with golden rings, his arms with golden chains, his diadem set with gems of all hues, his purple robes, which with the diadem were reserved for the Emperor, in all their sutures embroidered with precious stones. The wondering people, on their return to their homes, could talk of nothing but the splendour of the spectacle, the robes, the mules, the carpets, the size and splendour of the jewels. On his return to the palace, the Emperor walked on gold; ships were employed with the express purpose of bringing gold dust* from remote provinces, which was strewn by the officious care of a host of attendants, so that the Emperor rarely set his foot on the bare pavement.

The official aristocracy, which had succeeded to the hereditary patriciate of Rome, reflected in more moderate splendour, and less unapproachable seclusion, the manners of the court. The chief civil offices were filled by men of ignoble birth, often eunuchs. These, by the prodigal display of their ill-acquired wealth, insulted the people, who admired, envied, and hated their arrogant state. The military officers, in the splendour of their trappings and accoutrements, vied with the gorgeousness of the court-favourites; and even the barbarians, who began to force their way by their valour to these posts, in the capital caught the infection of luxury and pomp. As in all

---

* Χρύσττυ. See Müller, p. 10.

despotisms, especially in the East, there was a rapid rise and fall of unworthy favourites, whose vices, exactions, and oppressions, were unsparingly laid open by hostile writers, directly they had lost the protecting favour of the court. Men then found out that the enormous wealth, the splendour, the voluptuousness, in which an Eutropius or a Rufinus had indulged, had been obtained by the sale of appointments, by vast bribes from provincial governors, by confiscations, and every abuse of inordinate power.[a]

Christianity had not the power to elevate despotism into a wise and beneficent rule, or to dignify its inseparable consequence, court favouritism. Yet after all, feeble and contemptible as are many of the Christian Emperors, pusillanimous even in their vices; odious as was the tyranny of their ministers; they may bear no unfavourable comparison with the Heathen Emperors of Rome. Human nature is not so outraged; our belief in the possible depravity of man is not so severely tried, as by the monstrous vices and cruelties of a Tiberius, a Caligula, or a Nero. Theodora, even, if we credit the malignant satire of Procopius, maintained some decency upon the throne. The superstitions of the Emperors debased Christianity; the Christian bishop was degraded by being obliged at times to owe his promotion to an eunuch or a favourite; yet even the most servile and intriguing of the hierarchy could not be entirely for-

---

[a] "Hic Asiam villâ pactus regit; ille redemit
Conjugio ornata Syriam; dolet ille paterna
Bithynos mutâsse domo. Ruffius patevit
Vestibulo pretia distinguit regula gentium."—Claud. in Rufrop. l. 196.

". . . . . obtentan
Fallit, et ambitos à principe vendit honores.
. . . . .
Congestæ cumulantur opes, orbisque rapinæ
Accipit una domus. Populi servire coacti
Plenæque privatis succumbunt oppida regno."—In Rufin. l. 179-183.

getful of their high mission; there was still a kind of moral repugnance, inseparable from the character they bore, which kept them above the general debasement.

The aristocratical life, at this period, seems to have been characterised by gorgeous magnificence without grandeur, inordinate luxury without refinement, the pomp and prodigality of a high state of civilisation with none of its ennobling or humanising effects. The walls of the palaces were lined with marbles of all colours, crowded with statues of inferior workmanship, mosaics, of which the merit consisted in the arrangement of the stones; the cost, rather than the beauty or elegance, was the test of excellence, and the object of admiration. The nobles were surrounded with hosts of parasites or servants. "You reckon up," Chrysostom thus addresses a patrician, "so many acres of land, ten or twenty palaces, as many baths, a thousand or two thousand slaves, chariots plated with silver or overlaid with gold."[p]

Manners of the aristocracy.

Females.

Their banquets were merely sumptuous, without social grace or elegance. The dress of the females, the fondness for false hair, sometimes wrought up to an enormous height, and especially affecting the golden dye, and for paint, from which irresistible propensities they were not to be estranged even by religion, excite the stern animadversion of the ascetic Christian teacher. "What business have rouge and paint on a Christian cheek? Who can weep for her sins when her tears wash her face bare and mark furrows on her skin? With what trust can faces be lifted up towards heaven, which the Maker cannot recognise as his own workman-

---

[p] T. vii. p. 533.

ship?"⁴ Their necks, heads, arms, and fingers, were loaded with golden chains and rings; their persons breathed precious odours, their dresses were of gold stuff and silk; and in this attire they ventured to enter the church. Some of the wealthier Christian matrons gave a religious air to their vanity; while the more profane wore their thin silken dresses embroidered with hunting-pieces, wild beasts, or any other fanciful device, the more pious had the miracles of Christ, the marriage in Cana of Galilee, or the paralytic carrying his bed. In vain the preachers urged that it would be better to emulate these acts of charity and love, than to wear them on their garments.'

It might indeed be supposed that Christianity, by the extinction of that feeling for the beauty, grandeur, and harmony of outward form, which was a part of the religion of Greece, and was enforced by her purer and loftier philosophy, may have contributed to this total depravation of the taste. Those who had lost the finer feeling for the pure and noble in art and in social life, would throw themselves into the gorgeous, the sumptuous, and the extravagant. But it was rather the Roman character than the influence of Christianity which was thus fatal to the refinements of life. The degeneracy of taste was almost complete before the predominance of the new religion. The manners of ancient Rome had descended from the earlier empire,'

⁴ Hieronym. Epist. 54. Compare Epist. 19, vol. i. p. 284.

ʳ Müller, p. 112. There are several statutes prohibiting the use of gold brocade or dresses of silk in the Theodosian Code. x. tit. 20. Other statutes regulate the dress in Rome, xiv.

10, 1.

ˢ Compare the description of the manners and habits of the Roman nobles in Ammianus Marcellinus, so well transferred into English in the 31st chapter of Gibbon, vol. v. p. 258-268.

and the manners of Constantinople were in most respects an elaborate imitation of those of Rome.

The provincial cities, according to the national character, imitated the old and new Rome; and in all, no doubt, the nobility, or the higher order, were of the same character and habits.

On the appointment to the provincial governments, and the high civil offices of the empire, Christianity at this time exercised by no means a commanding, certainly no exclusive, influence. Either superior merit, or court intrigue, or favour, bestowed civil offices with impartial hand on Christian and Pagan. The Rufinus or the Eutropius cared little whether the bribe was offered by a worshipper in the church or in the temple. The Heathen Themistius was appointed prefect of Constantinople by the intolerant Theodosius; Prætextatus and Symmachus held the highest civil functions in Rome. The prefect who was so obstinate an enemy to Chrysostom was Optatus, a Pagan. At a later period, as I have observed, a statue was raised to the Heathen poet Merobaudes.

But, besides the officers of the imperial government, of the provinces and the municipalities, there now appeared a new order of functionaries, with recognised, if undefined powers, the religious magistrates of the religious community. In this magisterial character, the new hierarchy differed from the ancient priesthoods, at least of Greece and Rome. In Greece, these were merely the officiating dignitaries in the religious ceremonial; in Rome, the pontifical was attached to, and in effect merged in, the important civil function. But Christianity had its own distinct and separate aristocracy, which not merely officiated in the church, but ruled the public mind, and mingled itself with the various affairs of life, far beyond this narrow sphere of religious ministration.

The Christian hierarchy was completely organised and established in the minds of men before the great revolutions which, under Constantine, legalised Christianity, and, under Theodosius and his successors, identified the Church and State. The strength of the sacerdotal power was consolidated before it came into inevitable collision, or had to dispute its indefinable limits with the civil authority. Mankind was now submitted to a double dominion, the civil supremacy of the Emperor and his subordinate magistrates, and that of the Bishop with his inferior priesthood.

Up to the establishment of Christianity as the religion of the State, the clerical order had been the sole magistracy of the new communities. But it is not alone from the scantiness of authentic documents concerning the earliest Christian history, but from the inevitable nature of things, that the developement of the hierarchical power, as has already been partially shown,[1] was gradual and untraceable. In the infant Christian community, we have seen that the chief teacher and the ruler, almost immediately, if not immediately, became the same person. It was not so much that he was formally invested in authority, as that his advice, his guidance, his control, were sought on all occasions with timid diffidence, and obeyed with unhesitating submission. In the Christian, if it may be so said, the civil was merged in the religious being; he abandoned willingly his rights as a citizen, almost as a man, his independence of thought and action, in order to be taught conformity to the new doctrines which he

Gradual developement of the hierarchical power.

---
[1] Book ii. ch. 4.

had embraced, and the new rule of life to which he had submitted himself. Community of sentiment, rather than any strict federal compact, was the primary bond of the Christian republic; and this general sentiment, even prior, perhaps, to any formal nomination or ordination, designated the heads and the subordinate rulers, the Bishops, the Presbyters, and the Deacons; and therefore, where all agreed, there was no question in whom resided the right of conferring the title.*

The simple ceremonial of "laying on of hands," which dedicated the individual for his especial function, ratified and gave its religious character to this popular election which took place by a kind of silent acclamation; and without this sacred commission by the bishop, no one, from the earliest times of which we have any record, presumed, it should seem, to invest himself in the sacred office.¹ The civil and religious power of the hierarchy grew up side by side, or intertwined with each other, by the same spontaneous vital energy. Every thing in the primary formation of the communities tended to increase the power of their ecclesiastical superiors. The investiture of the blended teacher and ruler in a sacred, and at

---

* The growth of the Christian hierarchy, and the general constitution of the Church, are developed with learning, candour, and moderation, by Planck, in his Geschichte der Christlich-Kirchlichen Verfassung. Hanover, 1803.

¹ Gradually the admission to orders became a subject not merely of ecclesiastical, but of civil regulation. It has been observed that the decurion was prohibited from taking orders in order to obtain exemption from the duties of his station. Cod. Theod. xii. 1, 49. No slave, curialis, officer of the court, public debtor, procurator, or collector of the purple dye (murilegulus), or one involved in business, might be ordained, or, if ordained, might be reclaimed to his former state, Cod. Theod. ix. 45, 3. This was a law of the close of the fourth century, A.D. 398. The Council of Illiberis had made a restriction that no freedman, whose patron was a Gentile, could be ordained; he was still too much under control. Can. lxxx.

length in a sacerdotal character, the rigid separation of this sacred order from the mass of the believers, could not but arise out of the unavoidable developement of the religion. It was not their pride or ambition that withdrew them, but the reverence of the people which enshrined them in a separate sphere: they did not usurp or even assume their power and authority; it was heaped upon them by the undoubting and prodigal confidence of the community. The hopes and fears of men would have forced this honour upon them, had they been humbly reluctant to accept it. Man, in his state of religious excitement, imperiously required some authorised interpreters of those mysterious revelations from heaven which he could read himself but imperfectly and obscurely; he felt the pressing necessity of a spiritual guide. The privileges and distinctions of the clergy, so far from being aggressions on his religious independence, were solemn responsibilities undertaken for the general benefit. The Christian commonalty, according to the general sentiment, could not have existed without them, nor could such necessary but grave functions be entrusted to casual or common hands. No individual felt himself safe, except under their superintendence. Their sole right of entering the sanctuary arose as much out of the awe of the people as out of their own self-invested holiness of character. The trembling veneration for the mysteries of the sacrament must by no means be considered as an artifice to exalt themselves as the sole guardians and depositaries of these blessings; it was the genuine expression of their own profoundest feelings. If the clergy had not assumed the keys of heaven and hell; if they had not appeared legitimately to possess the power of pronouncing the eternal destiny of man, of suspending or excommunicating from those Christian privileges which were inseparably connected in Christian belief with the eternal sentence, or of absolving and readmitting into the pale of the Church and of salvation,—among the mass of believers, the uncertainty, the terror, the agony of minds fully impressed with the conviction of their immortality, and yearning by every means to obtain the assurance of pardon and peace, with heaven and hell constantly before their eyes, and agitating their inmost being, would have been almost insupportable. However the clergy might exaggerate their powers, they could not extend them beyond the ready acquiescence of the people. They could not possess the power of absolving without that of condemning; and men were content to brave the terrors of the gloomier award, for the indescribable consolations of confidence in their brighter and more ennobling promises.

The change in the relative position of Christianity to the rest of the world tended to the advancement of the hierarchy. At first there was no necessity to guard the admission into the society with rigid or suspicious jealousy, since the profession of Christianity in the face of a hostile world was in itself almost a sufficient test of sincerity. Expulsion from the society, or a temporary exclusion from its privileges, which afterwards grew into the awful forms of interdict or excommunication, must have been extremely rare or unnecessary,[7] since he who

---

[7] The case in St. Paul's Epistle to the Corinthians (1 Cor. v. 5), which seems to have been the first of forcible expulsion, was obviously an act of *Apostolic* authority. This, it is probable, was a Jewish convert, and these persons stood in a peculiar position; they would be ashamed, or would not be permitted, to return into the bosom of the Jewish community, which they had abandoned, and, if expelled from the Christian Church, would be complete outcasts. Not so the Heathen apostate, who might one day leave, and the next return to his old religion with all its advantages.

could not endure the discipline, or who doubted again the doctrines of Christianity, had nothing to do but to abandon a despised sect and revert to the freedom of the world. The older and more numerous the community, severer regulations were requisite for the admission of members, the maintenance of order, of unity in doctrine, and propriety of conduct, as well as for the ejection of unworthy disciples. Men began to be Christians, not from personal conviction, but from hereditary descent, as children of Christian parents. The Church was filled with doubtful converts, some from the love of novelty, others, when they incurred less danger and obloquy, from less sincere faith; some, no doubt, of the base and profligate, from the desire of partaking in the well-known charity of the Christians to their poorer brethren. Many became Christians, having just strength of mind enough to embrace its tenets, but not to act up to its duties. A more severe investigation, therefore, became necessary for admission into the society, a more summary authority for the expulsion of improper members.[*] These powers naturally devolved on the heads of the community, who had either originally possessed, and trans-

<small>Expulsion or excommunication.</small>

---

[*] It is curious to find that both ecclesiastical and civil laws against apostasy were constantly necessary. The Council of Elvira readmits an apostate to communion, who has not worshipped idols, after ten years' penance. The laws of Gratian and Theodosius, and even of Arcadius and Valentinian III., speak a more menacing language: the Christian who has become a Pagan forfeits the right of bequeathing by will—his will is null and void. Cod. Theod. xvi. 7. 1, 22. A law of Valentinian II. inflicts the same penalty (only with some limitation) on apostates to Judaism or Manicheism. The laws of Arcadius and Valentinian III. prove, by the severity of their prohibitions, not only that cases of apostasy took place, but that sacrifices were still frequently offered. Cod. Theodos. xvi. tit. de Apostatis.

mitted by regularly appointed descent, or held by general consent, the exclusive administration of the religious rites, the sacraments, which were the federal bonds of the community. Their strictly civil functions became likewise more extensive and important. All legal disputes had, from the first, been submitted to the religious magistracy, not as interpreters of the laws of the empire, but as best acquainted with the higher principles of natural justice and Christian equity. The religious heads of the communities were the supreme and universally recognised arbiters in all the transactions of life. When the magistrate became likewise a Christian, and the two communities were blended into one, considerable difficulty could not but arise, as we shall hereafter see, in the limits of their respective jurisdictions.

Increase in their civil influence.

But the magisterial or ruling part of the ecclesiastical function became thus more and more relatively important; government gradually became an affair of asserted superiority on one hand, of exacted submission on the other; but still the general voice would long be in favour of the constituted authorities. The episcopal power would be a mild, a constitutional, an unoppressive, and therefore unquestioned and unlimited sovereignty; for, in truth, in the earlier period, what was the bishop, and in a subordinate degree, the presbyter, or even the deacon?—He was the religious superior, elected by general acclamation, or at least, by general consent, as commanding that station by his unrivalled religious qualifications; he was solemnly invested in his office by a religious ceremony; he was the supreme arbiter in such civil matters as occurred among the members of the body, and thus the conservator of peace; he was the censor of morals, the minister in holy rites, the instructor in the doctrines of the faith, the adviser in all scruples, the consoler in all sorrows; he was the champion of the truth; in the hour of trial the first victim of persecution, the designated martyr. Of a being so sanctified, so ennobled to the thought, what jealous suspicion would arise, what power would be withholden from one whose commission would seem ratified by the Holy Spirit of God? Power might generate ambition, distinction might be attended by pride, but the transition would not be perceived by the dazzled sight of respect, of reverence, of veneration, and of love.

Above all, diversities of religious opinion would tend to increase the influence and the power of those who held the religious supremacy. It has been said, not without some authority, that the establishment of episcopacy in the Apostolic times arose for the control of the differences with the Judaising converts.* The multitude of believers would take refuge under authority from the doubts and perplexities thus cast among them; they would be grateful to men who would think for them, and in whom their confidence might seem to be justified by their station; a formulary of faith for such persons would be the most acceptable boon to the Christian society. This would be more particularly the case when, as in the Asiatic communities, these were not merely slight and unimportant, but vital points of difference. The Gnosticism, which the bishops of Asia Minor and of Syria had, to combat, was not a Christian sect or heresy, but

---

* No doubt this kind of constant and of natural appeal to the supreme religious functionary must have materially tended to strengthen and confirm this power. See vol. ii. page 28, and note.

another religion, although speaking in some degree Christian language. The justifiable alarm of those dangerous encroachments would induce the teachers and governors to assume a loftier and more dictatorial tone; those untainted by the new opinions would vindicate and applaud their acknowledged champions and defenders. Hence we account for the strong language in the Epistles of Ignatius, which appears to claim the extraordinary rank of actual representatives, not merely of the Apostles, but of Christ himself, for the bishops, precisely in this character, as maintainers of the true Christian doctrine.* In the pseudo-Apostolic Constitu-

---

* My own impression is decidedly in favour of the genuineness of these Epistles,—the shorter ones I mean—which are vindicated by Pearson; nor do I suspect that these passages, which are too frequent, and too much in the style and spirit of the whole, are later interpolations. Certainly the fact of the existence of two different copies of these Epistles throws doubt on the genuineness of both; but I receive them partly from an historical argument, which I have suggested, vol. II. p. 151, partly from internal evidence. Some of their expressions, *e. g.*, "Be ye subject to the bishop as to Jesus Christ " (ad Trall. c. 2); " Follow your bishop as Jesus Christ the Father, the presbytery as the Apostles; reverence the deacons as the ordinance of God " (ad Smyrn. c. 8); taken as detached sentences, and without regard to the figurative style and ardent manner of the writer, would seem so extraordinary a transition from the tone of the Apostles, as to throw still further doubts on the authenticity at least of these sentences. But it may be observed that in these strong expressions the object of the writer does not seem to be to raise the sacerdotal power, but rather to enforce Christian unity, with direct reference to these fatal differences of doctrine. In another passage he says, " Be ye subject to the bishop and to each other (τῷ ἐπισκόπῳ καὶ ἀλλήλοις), as Jesus Christ to the Father, and the Apostles to Christ, to the Father and to the Spirit."

I cannot indeed understand the inference that all the language or tenets of Christians who may have heard the Apostles are to be considered of Apostolic authority. Ignatius was a vehement and strongly figurative writer, very different in his tone, according to my judgement, to the Apostolic writings. His eager desire for martyrdom, his deprecating the interference of the Roman Christians in his behalf, is remarkably at variance with the sober dignity with which the Apostles did not seek, but submitted to death.

tions, which belong probably to the latter end of the third century, this more than Apostolic authority is sternly and unhesitatingly asserted.° Thus, the separation between the clergy and laity continually widened; the teacher or ruler of the community became the dictator of doctrine, the successor, not of the bishop appointed by Apostolic authority,⁴ or according to Apostolic usage, but of the Apostle; and at length took on himself a sacerdotal name and dignity. A strong corporate spirit, which arises out of associations formed for the noblest as well as for the most unworthy objects, could not but actuate the hierarchical college which was formed in each diocese or each city by the bishop and more or less numerous presbyters and deacons. The control on the autocracy of the bishop, which was exercised by this senate of presbyters, without whom he

---

That which may have been high-wrought metaphor in Ignatius, is repeated by the author of the Apostolic Constitutions, without reserve or limitation. This, I think, may be fairly taken as indicative of the language prevalent at the end of the third or beginning of the fourth century,—ὑμῶν ὁ ἐπίσκοπος εἰς Θεὸν τετιμήσθω. The bishop is to be honoured as God, ii. 80. The language of Psalm lxxxi. "Ye are Gods," is applied to them :— they are as much greater than the king as the soul is superior to the body—ἐνέργειαν ὀφείλετε ὡς ναοῖς, —φοβεῖσθαι ὡς βασιλέα,—1st Edit.

The question of the genuineness and authority of the Ignatian Epistles has been placed in an entirely new light, or perhaps has been enwrapped in a more indistinct haze, by the valuable publication of the Syriac Ignatius by Dr. Cureton. With this should be read some of the answers, especially Dr. Hussey's, and Baron Bunsen's Dissertation. My conclusion is, that I should be unwilling to claim historical authority for any passage not contained in Dr. Cureton's Syriac reprint. There is enough in Dr. Cureton's copy to justify the text, which I leave unaltered, though some of the quotations are probably not genuine. (1863.)

⁵ Οὗτος ὑμῖν ἐνέργειος Θεὸς μετὰ Θεοῦ. Lib. ii. c. 26.

⁴ The full Apostolic authority was claimed for the bishops, I think, first distinctly, at a later period. See the letter from Firmilianus to Cyprian's works, Epist. lxxv. "Potestas peccatorum remittendorum Apostolis data est * * et episcopis qui eis vicariâ ordinatione successerunt."

rarely acted, tended to strengthen, rather than to invalidate, the authority of the general body, in which all particular and adverse interests were absorbed in that of the clerical order.*

Language of the Old Testament. The language of the Old Testament, which was received perhaps with greater readiness, from the contemptuous aversion in which it was held by the Gnostics, on this as on other subjects, gradually found its way into the Church.[f] But the

Clergy and laity. strong and marked line between the ministerial or magisterial order (the clergy) and the inferior Christians, the people (the laity), had been drawn, before the bishop became a pontiff (for the Heathen names were likewise used), the presbyters the sacerdotal order, and the deacons, a class of men who shared in the indelible sanctity of the new priesthood. The common priesthood of all Christians, as distinguishing them by their innocent and dedicated character from the profane Heathen, asserted in the Epistle of St. Peter, was the only notion of the sacerdotal character at first admitted into the popular sentiment.[a] The appellation of the sacerdotal order began to be metaphorically applied to the Christian clergy,[b] but

---

* Even Cyprian enforces his own authority by that of his concurrent College of Presbyters:—"Quando à primordio episcopatûs mei statuerem, nihil sine consilio vestro, et cum consensu plebis, meâ privatim sententiâ gerere." Epist. v. In other passages he says, "Cui rei non potui me solum judicem dare." He had acted, therefore, "cum collegis meis, et cum plebe ipsâ universâ." Epist. xxviii.

[f] It is universally adopted in the Apostolic Constitutions. The crime of Korah is significantly adduced; tithes are mentioned, I believe, for the first time, ii. 25. Compare vi. 2.

[a] See the well-known passage of Tertullian:—"Nonne et laici sacerdotes sumus? * * Differentiam inter ordinem et plebem constituit ecclesiæ auctoritas." Tertullian evidently Montanises in this treatise, de Exhort. Castit. c. 7, yet seems to deliver these as maxims generally acknowledged.

[b] We find the first appearance of this in the figurative Ignatius. Ter-

soon became real titles; and by the close of the third
century, they were invested in the names and claimed
the rights of the Levitical priesthood in the Jewish
theocracy.[i] The Epistle of Cyprian to Cornelius, Bishop
of Rome, shows the height to which the episcopal power
had aspired before the religion of Christ had become
that of the Roman empire. The passages of the Old
Testament, and even of the New, in which honour or
deference are paid to the Hebrew pontificate, are recited
in profuse detail; implicit obedience is demanded for
the priest of God, who is the sole infallible judge or
delegate of Christ.[k]

Even if it had been possible that, in their state of
high-wrought attachment and reverence for the teachers
and guardians of their religion, any mistrust could have
arisen in the more sagacious and far-sighted minds of
the vast system of sacerdotal domination, of which they
were thus laying the deep foundations in the Roman
world, there was no recollection or tradition of any
priestly tyranny from which they could take warning or
imbibe caution. These sacerdotal castes were obsolete
or Oriental; the only one within their sphere of knowledge
was that of the Magians in the hostile kingdom

Tertullian uses the term "summi Sacerdotes."

[i] The passage in the Epistle of Clemens (ad Roman. c. 40), in which the analogy of the ministerial offices of the Church with the priestly functions of the Jewish temple is distinctly developed, is rejected as an interpolation by all judicious and impartial scholars.

[k] See his 66th Epistle, in which he draws the analogy between the legitimate bishop and the sacerdos of the law, the irregularly elected and Korah, Dathan, and Abiram:—"Neque enim aliunde haereses oborte sunt, aut nata sunt schismata, quam inde quod sacerdoti Dei non obtemperatur, nec unus in ecclesia ad tempus sacerdos, et ad tempus Judex, vice Christi cogitatur: cui si secundum magisteria divina obtemperaret fraternitas universa, nemo adversum sacerdotum collegium quicquam moveret." Ad Corael., Epist. lv.

of Persia. In Greece, the priesthood had sunk into the neglected ministers of the deserted temples; their highest dignity was to preside over the amusements of the people. The Emperor had now at length disdainfully cast off the supreme pontificate of the Heathen world, which had long been a title, and nothing more. Even among the Jews, the rabbinical hierarchy, which had gained considerable strength, even during our Saviour's time, but after the fall of the temple, and the publication of the Talmuds, had assumed a complete despotism over the Jewish mind, was not a priesthood. The Rabbins came promiscuously from all the tribes; their claims rested on learning and on knowledge of the traditions of the Fathers, not on Levitical descent.

Nor indeed could any danger be apparent, so long as the free voice of the community, guided by fervent piety and rarely perverted by less worthy motives, summoned the wisest and the holiest to these important functions. The nomination to the sacred office experienced the same, more gradual, perhaps, but not less inevitable, change from the popular to the self-electing form. The acclamation of the united, and seldom, if ever, discordant voices of the presbyters and the people, might be trusted with the appointment to the headship of a poor and devout community, whose utmost desire was to worship God, and to fulfil their Christian duties in uninterrupted obscurity. But as the episcopate became an object of ambition or interest, the disturbing forces which operate on the justice and wisdom of popular elections could not but be called forth; and slowly the clergy, by example, by influence, by recommendation, by dictation, by usurpation, identified their acknowledged right of consecration for a particular office with that of appointment to it. This was one of their last triumphs. In the days of Cyprian, and towards the close of the third century, the people had the right of electing, or at least of rejecting, candidates for the priesthood.[1] In the latter half of the fourth century, the streets of Rome ran with blood in the contest of Damasus and Ursicinus, for the bishopric of Rome; both factions arrayed against each other the priests and the people who were their respective partisans.[m] Thus the clergy had become a distinct and recognised class in society, consecrated by a solemn ceremony, the imposition of hands, which, however, does not yet seem to have been indelible.[n] But each church was still a separate and independent community; the bishop as its sovereign, the presbyters, and sometimes the deacons, as a kind of religious senate, conducted all its internal concerns. Great deference was paid from the first to the bishops of the more important sees: the number and wealth of the congregations would give them weight and dignity; and in general those prelates would be men of the highest character and attainments. Yet promotion to a wealthier or more distinguished see was looked upon as betraying worldly

---

[1] "Plebs ipsa maximè habeat potestatem vel eligendi dignos sacerdotes, vel indignos recusandi." Epist. lxvii. Cornelius was "testimonio cleri, ac suffragio populi electus." Compare Apostal. Constit. viii. 4. The Council of Laodicea (at the beginning of the fourth century) ordains that bishops are to be appointed by the metropolitans, and that the multitude, of ὄχλοι, are not to designate persons for the priesthood.

[m] Ammianus Marcell. xxvii. 3. Hieron. in Chron. Compare Gibbon, vol. iv. 259.

[n] A canon of the Council of Chalcedon (can. 7), prohibits the return of a spiritual person to the laity, and his assumption of lay offices in the state. See also Conc. Turon. i. c. 5. The laws of Justinian confiscate to the Church the property of any priest who has forsaken his orders. Cod. Just. l. tit. iii. 53; Nov. v. 4. 125 c. 15. This seems to imply that the practice was not uncommon even at that late period. Compare Planck, vol. i. 399.

ambition. The enemies of Eusebius, the Arian, or semi-Arian, bishop of Constantinople, bitterly taunted him with his elevation from the less important see of Nicomedia to the episcopate of the Eastern metropolis. This translation was prohibited by some councils.[o]

Metropolitan bishops. The level of ecclesiastical or episcopal dignity gradually broke up; some bishops emerged into a higher rank; the single community over which the bishop originally presided grew into the aggregation of several communities, and formed a diocese; the metropolitan rose above the ordinary bishop, the patriarch assumed a rank above the metropolitan, till at length, in the regularly graduated scale, the primacy of Rome was asserted, and submitted to by the humble and obsequious West.

The diocese grew up in two ways,—1. In the larger cities, the rapid increase of the Christians led *Formation of the diocese.* necessarily to the formation of separate congregations, which, to a certain extent, required each its proper organization, yet invariably remained subordinate to the single bishop. In Rome, towards the beginning of the fourth century, there were above forty churches, rendering allegiance to the prelate of the metropolis.

2. Christianity was first established in the towns and cities, and from each centre diffused itself with *Chorepiscopi.* more or less success into the adjacent country. In some of these country congregations, bishops appear to have been established, yet these chorepiscopi, or rural bishops, maintained some subordination to the head of the mother church;[p] or where the converts

---

[o] Synod. Nic. can. 15; Conc. Sard. c. 2; Conc. Arel. 21.
[p] See in Bingham, Ant. b. ii. c. 14, the controversy about the chorepiscopi or rural bishops.

were fewer, the rural Christians remained members of
the mother church in the city.⁴ In Africa, from the
immense number of bishops, each community seems to
have had its own superior; but this was peculiar to the
province. In general, the churches adjacent to the towns
or cities, either originally were, or became, the diocese
of the city bishop; for as soon as Christianity became
the religion of the state, the powers of the rural bishops
were restricted, and the office at length was either
abolished or fell into disuse.ʳ

The rank of the metropolitan bishop, who presided
over a certain number of inferior bishops, and the con-
vocation of ecclesiastical or episcopal synods, grew up
apparently at the same time and from the same causes.
The earliest authentic synods seem to have arisen out of
the disputes about the time of observing Easter;ˢ but
before the middle of the third century, these occasional
and extraordinary meetings of the clergy in certain
districts took the form of provincial synods. These
began in the Grecian provinces,ᵗ but extended throughout the Christian world. In some cases they seem to
have been assemblies of bishops alone, in others of the
whole clergy. They met once or twice in the year;
they were summoned by the metropolitan bishop, who
presided in the meeting, and derived from, or confirmed
his metropolitan dignity by this presidency.ᵘ

---

⁴ Justin Martyr speaks of the country converts: πάντων κατὰ πόλεις
ἢ ἀγροὺς μενόντων, ἐπὶ τὸ αὐτὸ
συνέλευσις γίνεται, Apolog. I. 67.

ʳ Concil. Antioch. can. 10; Concil.
Ancyr. c. 13; Canc. Laod. c. 57.

ˢ See the list of earlier synods
chiefly on this subject, Labbe, Con-

cilia, vol. I. pp. 595, 650, edit. Paris,
1671.

ᵗ See the remarkable passage in Tertullian, de Jejunio, with the ingenious
commentary of Mosheim, De Reb.
Christ. ante Const. M. pp. 264, 268.

ᵘ "Necessario apud nos fit, ut per
singulos annos seniores et praepositi in

As the metropolitans rose above the bishops, so the
Archbishops archbishops or patriarchs rose above the
and patri-
archs. metropolitans. These ecclesiastical dignities
seem to have been formed according to the civil divisions of the empire.[x] The Patriarchs of Antioch, Jerusalem, Alexandria, Rome, and by a formal decree of
the Council of Chalcedon, Constantinople, assumed
even a higher dignity. They asserted the right, in
some cases, of appointing, in others of deposing, even
metropolitan bishops.[y]

While Antioch, Alexandria, and Constantinople contested the supremacy of the East, the two former as
more ancient and Apostolic churches, the latter as the
imperial city, Rome stood alone, as in every respect
the most eminent church in the West. While other
churches might boast their foundation by a single
apostle (and those churches were always held in peculiar respect), Rome asserted that she had been founded
by, and preserved the ashes of two, and those the most
distinguished of the Apostolic body. Before the end
of the third century, the lineal descent of her bishops
from St. Peter was unhesitatingly claimed, and obse-
quiously admitted by the Christian world.[z] The name

---

unum conveniamus, ad disponenda ea,
quæ curæ nostræ commissa sunt."
Firm. ad Cyprian. Ep. 75.

[x] Bingham names thirteen or fourteen patriarchs: Alexandria, Antioch,
Cæsarea, Jerusalem, Ephesus, Constantinople, Thessalonica, Sirmium,
Rome, Carthage, Milan, Lyons, Toledo, York. But their respective
claims do not appear to have been
equally recognised, or at the same
period.

[y] Chrysostom deposed Gerontius,
metropolitan of Nicomedia. Sozomen, viii. 6.

[z] The passage of Irenæus (lib. ii. 115. ?c2
c. 3), as is well known, is the first
distinct assertion of any primacy in
Peter, and derived from him to the
see of Rome. This passage would be
better authority if it existed in the
original language; not in an indifferent
translation; if it were the language of
an Eastern, not a Western, prelate,

of Rome was still imposing and majestic, particularly in the West; the wealth of the Roman bishop probably surpassed that of other prelates; for Rome was still the place of general concourse and resort; and the pious strangers who visited the capital would not withhold their oblations to the metropolitan church. Within the city, he presided over above forty churches, besides the suburbicarian districts. The whole clerical establishment at Rome amounted to forty-six presbyters, seven deacons, seven sub-deacons, forty-two acolythes, fifty-two exorcists, readers, and doorkeepers. It comprehended fifteen hundred widows and poor brethren, with a countless multitude of the higher orders and of the people. No wonder that the name, the importance, the wealth, the accredited Apostolic foundation of Rome, arrayed her in pre-eminent dignity. Still, in his correspondence with the Bishop of Rome, the general tone of Cyprian, the great advocate of Christian unity is that of an equal; though he shows great respect to the Church of Rome, it is to the faithful guardian of an uninterrupted tradition, not as invested with superior authority.*

who might acknowledge a supremacy in Rome, which would not have been admitted by the older Asiatic sees; still more, if it did not assert what is manifestly untrue, the foundation of the Church of Rome by St. Peter and St. Paul (see vol. ii. p. 41); and, finally, if Irenæus could be conclusive authority on such a subject. Planck justly observes, that the potior principalitas of the city of Rome was the primary reason why a potior principalitas was recognised in the see of Rome.

* While I deliver my own conclusions, without fear or compromise, I would avoid all controversy on this as well as on other subjects. It is but right, therefore, for me to give the two apparently conflicting passages in Cyprian on the primacy of St. Peter:— "Nam nec Petrus quem primum Dominus elegit, et super quem ædificavit Ecclesiam suam * * vindicavit sibi aliquid insolenter aut arroganter assumpsit, ut diceret se primatum tenere, et obtemperari à novellis et præteris sibi potius oportere." Epist.

As the hierarchical pyramid tended to a point, its base spread out into greater width. The greater pomp of the services, the more intricate administration of affairs, the greater variety of regulations required by the increasing and now strictly separated classes of votaries, imposed the necessity for new functionaries, besides the bishops, priests, and deacons. These were the archdeacon and the five subordinate officiating ministers, who received a kind of ordination. 1. The sub-deacon, who, in the Eastern church, collected the alms of the laity and laid them upon the altar; and, in the Western, acted as a messenger, or bearer of despatches. 2. The reader, who had the custody of the sacred books, and, as the name implies, read them during the service. 3. The acolyth, who was an attendant on the bishop, carried the lamp before him, or bore the Eucharist to the sick. 4. The exorcist, who read the solemn forms over those possessed by dæmons, the energoumenoi, and sometimes at baptisms. 5. The ostiarius or doorkeeper, who assigned his proper place in the church to each member, and guarded against the intrusion of improper persons.

New sacred offices.

As Christianity assumed a more manifest civil existence, the closer correspondence, the more intimate sympathy between its remote and scattered members, became indispensable to its strength and consistency. Its uniformity of development in all parts of the world

---

laxi. "Hæc erant utique cæteri Apostoli, quod fuit Petrus, pari consortio præditi et honoris et potestatis; sed exordium ab unitate proficiscitur, et primatus Petro datur, ut una Christi ecclesia, et cathedra una monstretur." De Unit. Eccles. But this last passage is of more than doubtful authenticity; it is, no doubt, spurious. On the whole of this I have enlarged in the history of Latin Christianity.

arose out of, and tended to promote, this unity. It led to that concentration of the governing power in a few, which terminated at length in the West in the unrestricted power of one.

The internal unity of the Church, or universally disseminated body of Christians, had been maintained by the general similarity of doctrine, of sentiment, of its first simple usages and institutions, and the common dangers which it had endured in all parts of the world. It possessed its consociating principles in the occasional correspondence between its remote members, in those recommendatory letters with which the Christian who travelled was furnished to his brethren in other parts of the empire; above all, in the common literature, which, including the sacred writings, seems to have spread with more or less regularity through the various communities. Nothing, however, tended so much, although they might appear to exacerbate and perpetuate diversities of opinion, to the maintenance of this unity, as the assemblage and recognition of general Councils as the representatives of universal Christendom.[b] The bold impersonation,

Unity in the Church.

---

[b] The earliest councils (not Œcumenic) were those of Rome (1st and 2nd) and the seven held at Carthage, concerning the lapsi, the schism of Novatianus, and the re-baptising of heretics. The seventh in Routh, Reliquiæ Sacræ (Labbe, Concilia III.), is the first of which we have anything like a report; and from this time, either from the canons which they issue, or the opinions delivered by the bishops, the councils prove important authorities, not merely for the decrees of the Church, but for the dominant tone of sentiment, and even of manners. Abhorrence of heresy is the prevailing feeling in this council, which decided the validity of heretical baptism. "Christ," says one bishop, "founded the Church, the Devil heresy. How can the synagogue of Satan administer the baptism of the Church?" Another subjoins, "He who yields or betrays the baptism of the Church to heretics, what is he but a Judas of the spouse of Christ?" The Synod or Council of Antioch (A.D. 269) condemned Paul of Samo-

268   THE CHURCH A POWER.   Book IV.

General Councils. the Church, seemed now to assume a more imposing visible existence. Its vital principle was no longer that unseen and hidden harmony which had united the Christians in all parts of the world with their Saviour and with each other. By the assistance of the orthodox Emperors, and the commanding abilities of its great defenders, one dominant form of doctrine had obtained the ascendancy; Gnosticism, Donatism, Arianism, Manicheism, had been thrown aside; and the Church stood, as it were, individualised, or idealised, by the side of the other social impersonation, the State. The Emperor was the sole ruler of the latter, and at this period the aristocracy of the superior clergy, at a later the autocracy of the Pope, at least as

---

ents. The Council of Illiberis (Elvira, or Granada), A.D. 303, affords some curious notices of the state of Christianity in that remote province. Some of the Heathen flamines appear to have attempted to reconcile the performance of some of their religious duties, at least their presiding at the games, with Christianity. There are many moral regulations which do not give a high idea of Spanish virtue. The bishops and clergy were not to be itinerant traders; they might trade within the province (can. xviii.), but were on no account to take upon usury. The Jews were settled in great numbers in Spain (compare Hist. of the Jews): the taking food with them is interdicted, as also to permit them to reap the harvest. Gambling is forbidden. The Councils of Rome and of Arles were held to settle the Donatist controversy; but of the latter there are twenty-two canons chiefly of ecclesiastical regulations. The Council of Ancyra (A.D. 358) principally relates to the conduct of persons during the time of persecution. The Council of Laodicea (A.D. 365) has some curious general canons. The first Œcumenic council was that of Nicæa. See book iii. c. iv. It was followed by the long succession of Arian, and anti-Arian councils, at Tyre, Antioch, Rome, Milan, Sardica, Rimini, &c. The Arian Council of Antioch is very strict in its regulations for the residence of the bishops and the clergy, and their restriction of their labours to their own dioceses or cures (A.D. 341). Apud Labbe, vol. ii. 559. The first of Constantinople was the second Œcumenic council (A.D. 381). It re-established Trinitarianism as the doctrine of the East; it elevated the bishopric of Constantinople into a patriarchate, to rank after Rome. The two other Œcumenic councils are beyond the bounds of the present history.

THE STATE ECLIPSED.

the representative of the Western Church, became the supreme authority of the former. The hierarchical power, from exemplary, persuasive, amiable, was now authoritative, commanding, awful. When Christianity became the most powerful religion, when it became the religion of the many, of the Emperor, of the State, the convert, or the hereditary Christian had no strong Pagan party to receive him back into its bosom when outcast from the Church. If he ceased to believe, he no longer dared cease to obey. No course remained but prostrate submission, or the endurance of any penitential duty which might be enforced upon him; and on the penitential system, and the power of excommunication, to which we shall revert, rested the unshaken hierarchical authority over the human soul.

With the power of the clergy increased both those other sources of influence, pomp and wealth. Distinctions in station and in authority naturally lead to distinctions in manners, and those adventitious circumstances of dress and habits, which designate different ranks. Confederating upon equal terms, the superior authorities in the church began to assume an equal rank with those of the state. In the Christian city, the bishop became a personage of the highest importance; and the clergy, as a kind of subordinate religious magistracy, claimed, if a different kind, yet an equal share of reverence, with the civil authority. Where the civil magistrate had his insignia of office, the natural respect of the people, and the desire of maintaining his official dignity, would invest the religious functionary likewise with some peculiar symbol of his character. With their increased rank and estimation, the clergy could not but assume a more imposing demeanour; and that majesty in which they

Increase in pomp.

were arrayed during the public ceremonial could not be entirely thrown off when they returned to ordinary life. The reverence of man exacts dignity from those who are its objects. The primitive Apostolic meanness of appearance and habit was altogether unsuited to their altered position, as equal in rank, more than equal in real influence and public veneration, to the civil officers of the empire or municipality. The consciousness of power will affect the best disciplined minds, and the unavoidable knowledge that salutary authority is maintained over a large mass of mankind by imposing manners, dress, and mode of living, would reconcile many to that which otherwise might appear incongruous to their sacred character. There was, in fact, and always has been, among the more pious clergy, a perpetual conflict between a conscientious sense of the importance of external dignity, and a desire, as conscientious, of retaining something of outward humility. The monkish and ascetic waged implacable war against that secular distinction which, if in some cases eagerly assumed by pride and ambition, was forced upon others by the deference, the admiration, the trembling subservience of mankind. The prelate who looked the most imperious, and spoke most sternly, on his throne, fasted and underwent the most humiliating privations in his chamber or his cell. Some prelates supposed, that as ambassadors of the Most High, as supreme governors in that which was of greater dignity than the secular empire, the earthly kingdom of Christ, they ought to array themselves in something of imposing dignity. The bishops of Rome early affected a ate and magnificence. Chrysostom, on the other hand, in Constantinople, differing from his predecessors, considered poverty of dress, humility of demeanour, and the most severe austerity of life, as more becoming a Christian prelate, who was to set the example of the virtues which he inculcated, and to show contempt for those worldly distinctions which properly belonged to the civil power. Others, among whom was Ambrose of Milan, while in their own persons and in private they were the plainest, simplest, and most austere of men, nevertheless threw into the service of the Church all that was solemn and magnificent; and as officiating functionaries, put on for the time the majesty of manner, the state of attendance, the splendour of attire, which seemed to be authorised by the gorgeousness of dress and ceremonial pomp in the Old Testament.[c]

With the greater reverence, indeed, peculiar sanctity was exacted, and no doubt, in general, observed by the clergy. They were imperatively required to surpass the general body of Christians in purity of morals, and, perhaps even more, in all religious performances. As

[c] The clergy were long without any distinction of dress, except on ceremonial occasions. At the end of the fourth century, it was the custom for them in some churches to wear black. Socr. H. E. vi. 22. Jerome, however, recommends that they should neither be distinguished by too bright nor too sombre colours. Ad Nepot. The proper habits were probably introduced at the end of the fifth century, as they are recognised by councils in the sixth. Conc. Matisc. A.D. 581, can. l. 5; Trull. c. 27. The tonsure began in the fourth century. "Prima del iv. secolo i semplici preti non avevano alcun abito distinto dagli altri o Pagani o Cristiani, se non in quanto la professata loro umiltà faceva una certa pompa di abjezione e di povertà." Cicognara, Storia di Scultura, t. i. p. 27. Count Cicognara gives a curious account of the date and origin of the different parts of the clerical dress. The mitre is of the eighth century, the tiara of the tenth.

The fourth Council of Carthage (A.D. 398) has some restrictions on dress. The clericus was not to wear long hair or beard (nec comam habeat nec barbam. Can. xliv.); he was to approve his profession by his dress and walk, and not to study the beauty of his dress or sandals. He might obtain his sustenance by working as an artisan, or in agriculture, provided he did not neglect his duty. Can. li. lii.

the outward ceremonial, fasting, public prayer during almost every part of the day, and the rest of the ritual service, were more completely incorporated with Christianity, they were expected to maintain the public devotion by their example, and to encourage self-denial by their more rigid austerity.

Wealth as well as pomp followed in the train of power. The desire to command wealth (we must not yet use the ignoble term covetousness) not merely stole imperceptibly into intimate connexion with religion, but appeared almost a part of religion itself. The individual was content to be disinterested in his own person; the interest which he felt in the opulence of the Church, or even of his own order, appeared not merely excusable, but a sacred duty. In the hands of the Christian clergy, wealth, which seemed at that period to be lavished on the basest of mankind, and squandered on the most criminal and ignominious objects, might seem to be hallowed to the noblest purposes. It enabled Christianity to vie with Paganism in erecting splendid edifices for the worship of God, to provide an imposing ceremonial, lamps for midnight service, silver or golden vessels for the altar, veils, hangings, and priestly dresses; it provided for the wants of the poor, whom misgovernment, war, and taxation, independent of the ordinary calamities of human life, were grinding to the earth. To each church were attached numbers of widows and other destitute persons; the redemption of slaves was an object on which the riches of the Church were freely lavished: the sick in the hospitals and prisons, and destitute strangers were under their especial care. "How many captives has the wealth of the Pagan establishment released from bondage?" This is among the

CHAP. I.   CHRISTIANITY ASCENDANT.   273

triumphant questions of the advocates of Christianity.[d] The maintenance of children exposed by their parents, and taken up and educated by the Christians, was another source of generous expenditure. When, then, at first the munificence of the Emperor, and afterwards the gratitude and superstitious fears of the people, heaped up their costly offerings at the feet of the clergy, it would have appeared not merely ingratitude and folly, but impiety and uncharitableness to their brethren, to have rejected them. The clergy, as soon as they were set apart from the ordinary business of life, were maintained by the voluntary offerings of their brethren. The piety which embraced Christianity never failed in liberality. The payments seem chiefly to have been made in kind rather than in money; though on extraordinary occasions large sums were raised for some sacred or charitable object. One of the earliest acts of Constantine was to make munificent grants to the despoiled and destitute Church.[e] A certain portion of the public stores of corn and other produce, which was received in kind by the officers of the revenue, was assigned to the Church and clergy.[f] This was withdrawn by Julian, and when regranted by the Christian Emperors, was diminished one-third.

The law of Constantine which empowered the clergy of the Church to receive testamentary bequests, and to hold land, was a gift which would scarcely have been exceeded if he had granted them two provinces of the empire.[g] It became almost a sin to die without some bequest to pious uses; and before a century had elapsed, the mass

<small>Law of Constantine empowering the Church to receive bequests.</small>

---

[d] Ambros. contra Symmachum.
[e] Euseb. H. E. x. 6.
[f] Sozomen, H. E. v. 5.
[g] This is the observation of Planck.

VOL. III.   T

of property which had passed over to the Church was
so enormous, that the most pious of the Emperors were
obliged to issue a restrictive law, which the most ardent
of the Fathers were constrained to approve. Jerome
acknowledges, with the bitterness of shame, the necessity
of this check on ecclesiastical avarice.[b] "I
complain not of the law, but that we have
deserved such a law." The ascetic father and the
Pagan historian describe the pomp and avarice of the
Roman clergy in the fourth century. Ammianus, while
he describes the sanguinary feud which took place for
the prelacy between Damasus and Ursicinus,
intimates that the magnificence of the prize
may account for the obstinacy and ferocity with which it
was contested. He dwells on the prodigal offerings of
the Roman matrons to their bishop; his pomp, when in
elaborate and elegant attire he was borne in his chariot
through the admiring streets; the costly luxury of his
almost imperial banquets. But the just historian contrasts this pride and luxury of the Roman pontiff with
the more temperate life and dignified humility of the
provincial bishops.[i] Jerome goes on sternly to charge
the whole Roman clergy with the old vice of the
Heathen aristocracy, hæredipety or legacy hunting, and
asserts that they used the holy and venerable name of

Restrictive edict of Valentinian.

Pope Damasus.

---

[b] Valentinian II. de Episc. "Solis clericis et monachis hac lege prohibetor, et prohibetur non à persecutoribus sed à principibus Christianis; nec de lege coaqueror, sed doleo cur meruerimus hanc legem." Hieronym. ad Nepot. He speaks also of the "provida severaque legis cautio, et tamen non sic refrænatur avaritia." Ambrose (l. ii. adv. Symm.) admits the necessity of the law. Augustine, while he loftily disclaims all participation in such abuses, acknowledges their frequency. "Quicunque vult, exhæredato filio hæredem facere ecclesiam, quærat alterum qui suscipiat, non Augustinum, immo, Deo propitio, inveniat neminem." Serm. 49.

[i] Amm. Marcellinus, xxvii. 3.

the Church to extort for their own personal emolument, the wealth of timid or expiring devotees. The law of Valentinian justly withheld from the clergy and the monks alone that privilege of receiving bequests which was permitted to the "lowest of mankind, Heathen priests, actors, charioteers and harlots."

Large parts of the ecclesiastical revenues, however, arose from more honourable sources. Some of the estates of the Heathen temples, though in general confiscated to the imperial treasury, were alienated to the Christian churches. The Church of Alexandria obtained the revenue of the Temple of Serapis.[l]

These various estates and properties belonged to the Church in its corporate capacity, not to the clergy. They were charged with the maintenance of the fabric of the church, and the various charitable purposes, including the sustenance of their own dependent poor. Strong enactments were made to prevent their alienation from those hallowed purposes,[m] the clergy were even restrained from bequeathing by will what they had obtained from the property of the Church. The estates of the Church were liable to the ordinary taxes, the land and capitation tax, but exempt from what were called sordid and extraordinary charges, and from the quartering of troops.[n]

Application of the wealth of the Church.

---

[l] Sozomen, v. 7. The Church of Antioch possessed lands, houses, rents, carriages, mules, and other kinds of property. It undertook the daily sustenance of 3000 widows and virgins, besides prisoners, the sick in the hospitals, the maimed, and the diseased, who sat down, as it were before the Christian altar, and received food and raiment, besides many other accidental claims on their benevolence. Chrysostom, Oper. Montfaucon in his dissertation, gives the references.

[m] Canc. Carth. iii. 40; Antioch, 24. Constit. Apost. 40. Cod. Theodos. de Episc. et Clericis, t. 38.

[n] Planck, P. iii. c. vi. 3.

The bishops gradually obtained almost the exclusive management of this property. In some churches, a steward (œconomus) presided over this department, but he would, in general, be virtually under the control of the bishop. In most churches, the triple division began to be observed; one-third of the revenue to the bishop, one to the clergy, the other to the fabric and the poor; the Church of Rome added a fourth, a separate portion for the fabric.[o]

The clergy had become a separate community; they had their own laws of internal government, their own special regulations, or recognised proprieties of life and conduct. Their social delinquencies were not as yet withdrawn from the civil jurisdiction; but besides this, they were amenable to the severe judgments of ecclesiastical censure;[p] the lowest were liable to corporal chastisement. Flagellation, which was administered in the synagogue, and was so common in Roman society, was by no means so disgraceful as to exempt the persons at least of the inferior clergy from its infliction.[q]

---

[o] By a law of Theodosius and Valent. A.D. 434, the property of any bishop, presbyter, deacon, deaconess, sub-deacon, &c., or of any monk, who died intestate, and without legal heirs, fell, not to the treasury, as in ordinary cases, but to the church or monastery to which he belonged. The same privilege was granted to the Corporation of Decurions. Codex Theodos. v. lii. 1.

[p] Sozomen states that Constantine gave his clergy the privilege of rejecting the jurisdiction of the civil tribunal, and bringing their causes to the bishop. H. E. i. 9. But these were probably disputes between clergyman and clergyman. All others were cases of arbitration, by mutual agreement; but the civil power was to ratify their decree. In a Novella of Valentinian II., A.D. 452, it is expressly said,—"Quoniam constat episcopos et presbyteros forum legibus non habere * * nec de aliis causis præter religiosem posse cognoscere." Compare Planck, p. 300. The clericus was bound to appear, if summoned by a layman, before the ordinary judge. Justinian made the change, and that only in a limited manner.

[q] Bishops were accustomed to order flagellations. "Qui modus coercitionis, a magistris artium liberalium, et ab

But the more serious punishment was degradation into the vulgar class of worshippers. To them it was the most fearful condemnation to be ejected from the inner sanctuary and thrust down from their elevated station.[r]

As yet the clergy were not entirely estranged from society, they had not become a caste by the legal enforcement or general practice of celibacy. Clement of Alexandria asserts and vindicates the marriage of some of the Apostles.[s] The discreet remonstrance of the old Egyptian bishop perhaps prevented the Council of Nicæa from imposing that heavy burden on the reluctant clergy. The aged Paphnutius, himself unmarried, boldly asserted that the conjugal union was chastity.[t] But that, which, in the third century is asserted to be free to all mankind, clergy as well as laity, in Egypt;[u] in the fourth, according to Jerome, was prohibited or limited by vows of continence. It has been asserted,[x] and without refutation, that there was no ecclesiastical law or regulation which compelled the celibacy of the clergy for the first three centuries.

Celibacy of the clergy.

---

ipsis parentibus, et sæpe in judiciis solet ab Episcopis adhiberi." Augustin. Epist. cxxxiii.—High authority for the antiquity of flogging in public schools.

[s] The decrees of the fourth council of Carthage show the strict morals and humble subordination demanded of the clergy at the close of the fourth century.

[t] *Ἢ καὶ τοὺς Ἀποστόλους ἀποδοκιμάζουσι; Πέτρος μὲν γὰρ καὶ Φίλιππος ἐπαιδοποιήσαντο. Φίλιππος δὲ καὶ τὰς θυγατέρας ἀνδράσιν ἐξέδωκεν, καὶ ὅγε Παῦλος οὐκ ὀκνεῖ ἔν τινι ἐπιστολῇ τὴν αὐτοῦ προσαγορεύειν σύζυγον, ἣν οὐ περιεκόμιζεν διὰ τὸ* τῆς ὑπηρεσίας εὐσταλές.—Strom. l. iii. c. 6. On the question of the marriage of the Apostles and their immediate followers, almost everything is collected in a note of Coteierius, Patres Apostolici, ii. 241.

[t] Gelasii Hister. Conc. Nic. c. xxxii. Socrat. i. 11. Sozomen, l. 23. Barnnius insists upon this being *Greek* fable.

[u] *Ναὶ μὴν καὶ τὸν τῆς μιᾶς γυναικὸς ἄνδρα τανὸ ἀποδέχεται ἐὰν πρεσβύτερος ᾖ, κἂν διάκονος, κἂν λαϊκός, ἀνεπιλήπτως γάμῳ χρωμένος. Σωθήσεται δὲ διὰ τῆς τεκνογονίας*, Strom, iii. 12, 9.

[x] By Bingham, book iv.

Clement of Alexandria, as we see, argues against enforced celibacy from the example of the Apostles. Married bishops and presbyters frequently occur in the history of Eusebius. The martyrdom of Numidicus was shared and not dishonoured by the companionship of his wife.[7] It was a sight of joy and consolation to the husband to see her perishing in the same flames. The wives of the clergy are recognised, not merely in the older writings, but also in the public documents of the Church.[a] Council after council, in the East, introduced regulations, which, though intended to restrict, recognise the legality of these ties.[a] Highly as they exalt the angelic state of celibacy, neither Basil in the East, nor Augustine in the West, positively prohibits the marriage of the clergy.[b]

But in the fourth century, particularly in the latter half, the concurrent influence of the higher honours attributed to virginity by all the great Christian writers; of the hierarchical spirit, which, even at that time, saw how much of its corporate strength depended on this entire detachment from worldly ties; of the monastic system, which worked into the clerical, partly by the frequent selection of monks for ordination and for consecration to ecclesiastical dignities, partly by the emulation of the clergy, who could not safely allow themselves

---

[7] "Numidicus presbyter uxorem adhærentem lateri suo, concrematam cum cæteris, vel conservatam potius dixerim, lætus aspexit." Cyprian, p. 525. See in Bassage, Dissertatio Septima, a list of married prelates.

[a] Conc. Gang. c. 4. Conc. Ancyr. c. 10. This law allows any deacon to marry.

[a] In the West, the Council of Elvira commands the clergy to abstain from connubial intercourse and the procreation of children. Can. xxxiii. This was frequently re-enacted. Among others, Conc. Carthag. v. 2. Labbe, ii. 1246.

[b] Basil speaks of a presbyter who had contumaciously contracted an unlawful marriage. Can. ii. c. 27. On Augustine, compare Theiner, p. 154.

to be outdone in austerity by these rivals for popular estimation; all these various influences introduced restrictions and regulations on the marriage of the clergy, which darkened at length into the solemn ecclesiastical interdict. First, the general sentiment repudiated a second marriage as a monstrous act of incontinence, an infirmity or a sin which ought to prevent the Christian from ever aspiring to any ecclesiastical office.* The next offence against the general feeling was marriage with a widow; then followed the restriction of marriage after entering into holy orders; the married priest retained his wife, but to condescend to such carnal ties after ordination, was revolting to the general sentiment, and was considered to imply a total want of feeling for the dignity of their high calling. Then was generally introduced a demand of abstinence from sexual connexion from those who retained their wives: this was imperatively required from the higher orders of the clergy. It was considered to render unclean, and to disqualify even from prayer for the people, as the priest's life was to be a perpetual prayer.⁴ Not that there was as yet any uniform practice. The bishops assembled at the Council of Gangra ° condemned the

---

* Athenagoras laid down the general principle, ὁ γὰρ δεύτερος (γάμος) εὐπρεπής ἐστι μοιχεία. De Resurr. Carn. Compare Orig. contr. Cels. vii., and Hom. vi., in Num. xviii., in Luc. xvii., in Matt. Tertull. ad Uxor. 1-5. This was almost an universal moral axiom. Epiphanius said, that since the coming of Christ no digamous clergyman had ever been ordained. Barbeyrac has collected the passages of the Fathers expressive of their abhorrence of second marriages. Morale des Pères, p. 1. 29, 34, 37, &c. The Council of Neo-Cæsarea forbade clergymen to be present at a feast for a second marriage — πρεσβύτερον εἰς γάμους δυγαμοῦντων μὴ ἑστιᾶσθαι. Can. vii.

⁴ Such is the distinct language of Jerome. "Si laicus et quicunque fidelis uxore non potest nisi carent officio conjugali, sacerdoti, cui semper pro populo offerenda sunt sacrificia semper orandum est. Si semper orandum est, semper carendum matrimonio." Adv. Jovin, p. 175.

° In the Council of Gangra (about

followers of Eustathius, who refused to receive the sacraments from any but unmarried priests. The heresy of Jovinian, on the other hand, probably called forth the severe regulations of Pope Siricius.[f] This sort of encyclical letter positively prohibited all clergy of the higher orders from any intercourse with their wives. A man who lived to the age of thirty, the husband of one wife, that wife, when married, a virgin, might be an acolyth or subdeacon; after five years of strict continence, he might be promoted to a priest; after ten years more of the same severe ordeal, a bishop. A clerk, any one in holy orders, even of the lowest degree, who married a widow, or a second wife, was instantly deprived: no woman was to live in the house of a clerk.

The Council of Carthage, reciting the canon of a former council, commands the clergy to abstain from all connexion with their wives. The enactment is perpetually repeated, and in one extended to subdeacons.[g] The Council of Toledo prohibited the promotion of ecclesiastics who had children. The Council of Arles prohibited the ordination of a married priest,[h] unless he made a promise of divorce from the married state. Jerome distinctly asserts that it was the universal regulation of the East, of Egypt, and of Rome[i] to ordain

---

350) the preamble and the first canon do not appear to refer necessarily to the wives of the clergy. They anathematise certain teachers (the Eustathians) who had blamed marriage, and said that a faithful and pious woman who slept with her husband could not enter into the kingdom of heaven. A sacred virgin is prohibited from vaunting over a married woman, canon x. Women are forbidden to abandon their husbands and children.

[f] The letter of Siricius in Mansi Concil. fil. 6:33, A.D. 385.

[g] These councils of Carthage are dated A.D. 390, 418, and 419.

[h] "Assumi aliquem ad sacerdotium non posse in vinculo sacerdotii constitutum, nisi primum fuerit promissa conversio." A.D. 452.

[i] "Quid facient Orientis Ecclesiae? quid Ægypti, et sedis Apostolicae, quae aut virgines clericos accipiunt aut continentes; aut si uxores habuerint,

only those who were unmarried, or who ceased to be husbands. But even in the fourth, and the beginning of the fifth centuries, the practice rebelled against this severe theory. Married clergymen, even married bishops, and with children, occur in the ecclesiastical annals. Athanasius, in his letter to Dracontius, admits and allows the full right of the bishop to marriage.[k] Gregory of Nazianzum was born after his father was bishop, and had a younger brother named Cæsarius.[m] Gregory of Nyssa, and Hilary of Poictiers, were married. Less distinguished names frequently occur: those of Spyridon[n] and Eustathius.[o] Synesius, whose character enabled him to accept episcopacy on his own terms, positively repudiated these unnatural restrictions on the freedom and holiness of the conjugal state. "God and the law, and the holy hand of Theophilus bestowed on me my wife. I declare, therefore, solemnly, and call you to witness, that I will not be plucked from her, nor lie with her in secret, like an adulterer. But I hope and pray that we may have many and virtuous children."[p]

The Council in Trullo only demanded this high test of spirituality, absolute celibacy, from bishops, and left the inferior clergy to their freedom. But the earlier Western Council of Toledo only admitted the deacon,

---

mariti esse desistunt." Adv. Vigilantium, p. 281. Jerome appeals to Jovinian himself:—"Certè confiteris non posse esse episcopum qui in episcopatu filios faciat, alioqui si deprehensus fuerit, non quasi vir tenebitur, sed quasi adulter damnabitur." Adv. Jovin. 175. Compare Epiphanius, Hæres. liv. 4.

[k] Athanasii Epistola ad Dracontium.

[m] Gregory makes his father thus address him:—
Οὗτος τοσοῦτον ἱερεὺς ἱερέως βίον
'Οὔτοι ἀκμῆς θεοτόκου ἔχει χάριτι.
In Vita Sua, v. 512.

[n] Sozom. i. 11. Socrat. i. 12.
[o] Socrat. ii. 43.
[p] Synesii Epist. 105.

and that under restrictions, to connubial intercourse; the presbyter who had children after his ordination could not be a bishop.[q]

This overstrained demand on the virtue, not of individuals in a high state of enthusiasm, but of a whole class of men; this strife with nature, in that which, in its irregular and lawless indulgence, is the source of so many evils and of so much misery, in its more moderate and legal form is the parent of the purest affections, and the holiest charities; this isolation from those social ties which, if at times they might withdraw them from total dedication to their sacred duties, in general, would, by their tending to soften and humanise, be the best school for the gentle and affectionate discharge of those duties—the enforcement of the celibacy of the clergy, though not yet by law, by dominant opinion, was not slow in producing its inevitable evils. Simultaneously with the sterner condemnation of marriage, or at least the exaggerated praises of chastity, we hear the solemn denunciations of the law, and the deepening remonstrances of the more influential writers, against those secret evasions by which the clergy endeavoured to obtain the same without the practice of celibacy, to enjoy some of the pleasures and advantages without the crime of marriage. From the middle of the third century, in which the growing aversion to the marriage of the clergy begins to appear, we find the "sub-introduced" females constantly proscribed.[r] The intimate union of the priest

---

[q] Conc. Tolet. A.D. 400, can. i.
[r] They are mentioned in the letter of the bishops of Antioch, against Paul of Samosata. The Council of Illiberis (incautiously) allowed a sister, or a virgin, dedicated to God, to reside with a bishop or presbyter, not a stranger.

with a young, often a beautiful female, who still passed to the world under the name of a virgin, and was called by the priest by the unsuspected name of sister, seems from the strong and reiterated language of Jerome,¹ Gregory Nazianzen, Chrysostom, and others, to have been almost general. It was interdicted by an imperial law.²

Thus, in every city, in almost every town and every village of the Roman empire, had established itself a new permanent magistracy, in a certain sense independent of the government, with considerable inalienable endowments, and filled by men of a peculiar and sacred character, and recognised by the state. Their authority extended far beyond their jurisdiction; their influence

---

¹ "Unde sine nuptiis aliud nomen uxorum? Imo unde novum concubinarum genus? Plus inferam, Unde meretrices univiræ? Eadem domo, uno cubiculo, sæpe uno tenentur et lectulo. Et suspiciosos nos vocant, si aliquid existimamus. Frater sororem virginem deserit: cælibem spernit virgo germanum; fratrem quærit extraneum, et cum in eodem proposito esse se simulent quærunt alienorum spiritale solatium, ut domi habeant carnale commercium." Hieronym. Epist. xxii. ad Eustochium. If the vehemence of Jerome's language betrays his own ardent character and his monkish hostility to the clergy, the general charge is amply borne out by other writers. Many quotations may be found in Gothofred's Note on the Law of Honorius. Gregory of Nazianzum says,— Ἀρσενα παντ' ἐλέγχω, συνείσακτον τε μάλιστα. The language of Cyprian, however, even in the third century, is the strongest:—"Certè ipse concubitus, ipse amplexus, ipsa confabulatio, et inosculatio, et conjacentium duorum turpis et fœda dormitio quantum dedecoris et criminis confitetur." Cyprian justly observes, that such intimacy would induce a jealous husband to take to his sword. Epist. lxii. ad Pomponium.

But the canon of the Council of Nicæa, which prohibits the usage, and forbids the priest to have a subintroducta mulier, unless a mother, sister, or aunt, the only relationships beyond suspicion, and the still stronger tone of the law, show the frequency, as well as the evil, of the practice. Unhappily they were blind to its real cause.

² "Eam qui probabilem sæculo disciplinam agit decolorari consortio sororiæ appellationis non decet." But this law of Honorius, A.D. 420, allowed the clergy to retain their wives, if they had been married before entering into orders. See, too, the third and fourth canons of the Council of Carthage, A.D. 348.

far beyond their authority. The internal organisation was complete. The three great patriarchs in the East, throughout the West the Bishop of Rome, exercised a supreme, and, in some points, an appellant jurisdiction. Great ecclesiastical causes could be removed to their tribunal. Under them, the metropolitans, and in the next rank the bishops, governed their dioceses, and ruled the subordinate clergy, who now began to form parishes, separate districts to which their labours were to be confined. In the superior clergy had gradually become vested, not the ordination only, but the appointment, of the inferior; these could not quit the diocese without letters from the bishop, or be received or exercise their functions in another, without permission.

On the incorporation of the Church with the State, the co-ordinate civil and religious magistracy maintained each its separate powers. On one side, as far as the actual celebration of the ecclesiastical ceremonial, and in their own internal affairs in general; on the other, in the administration of the military, judicial, and fiscal affairs of the state, the bounds of their respective authority were clear and distinct. As a citizen and subject, the Christian, the priest, and the bishop, were alike amenable to the laws of the empire and to the imperial decrees, and liable to taxation, unless specially exempted, for the service of the state.[x] The

Union of Church and State.

---

[x] The law of Constantius which appears to withdraw the bishops entirely from the civil jurisdiction, and to give the privilege of being tried upon all charges by a tribunal of bishops, is justly considered by Gothofred as a local or temporary act, probably connected with the feuds concerning Arianism. Cod. Theod. xvi. 2, 12, with Gothofred's note. Valens admitted the ecclesiastical courts to settle religious difficulties and slight offences, xvi. 2, 23. The same is the scope of the more explicit law of Honorius. xvi. 2, 201. The immunity of the clergy from the civil courts was of very much later date.

Christian statesman, on the other hand, of the highest rank, was amenable to the ecclesiastical censures, and was bound to submit to the canons of the Church in matters of faith and discipline, and was entirely dependent on their judgement for his admission or rejection from the privileges or hopes of the Christian.

So far the theory was distinct and perfect; each had his separate and exclusive sphere; yet there could not but appear a debateable ground on which the two authorities came into collision, and neither could altogether refrain from invading the territory of his ally or antagonist.

The treaty between the contracting parties was, in fact, formed with such haste and precipitancy, that the rights of naither party could be defined or secured. Eager for immediate union, and impatient of delay, they framed no deed of settlement, by which, when their mutual interests should be less identified, and jealousy and estrangement should arise, they might assert their respective rights, and enforce their several duties. *Union of the Church and the State.*

In ecclesiastical affairs, strictly so called, the supremacy of the Christian magistracy, it has been said, was admitted. They were the legislators of discipline, order, and doctrine. The festivals, the fasts, the usages and canons of the Church, the government of the clergy, were in their exclusive power. The decrees of particular synods and councils possessed undisputed authority, as far as their sphere extended. General councils were held binding on the whole Church. But it was far more easy to define that which did belong to the province of the Church than that which did not. Religion asserts its authority, and endeavours to extend its influence over the whole sphere of moral action, which is, in fact, over the whole of human life, its habits, manners, conduct. Christianity, as the most profound moral religion, exacted the most complete and universal obedience; and as the acknowledged teachers and guardians of Christianity, the clergy continued to draw within their sphere every part of human life in which man is actuated by moral or religious motives. The moral authority, therefore, of the religion, and consequently of the clergy, might appear legitimately to extend over every transaction of life, from the legislature of the sovereign, which ought, in a Christian king, to be guided by Christian motive, to the domestic duties of the peasant, which ought to be fulfilled on the principle of Christian love.

But, on the other hand, the State was supreme over all its subjects, even over the clergy, in their character of citizens. The whole tenure of property, to what use soever dedicated (except in such cases as the State itself might legalise on its first principles, and guarantee, when bestowed, as by gift or bequest), was under its absolute control; the immunities which it conferred it might revoke; and it would assert the equal authority of the constitutional laws over every one who enjoyed the protection of those laws. Thus, though in extreme cases, these separate bounds of jurisdiction were clear, the tribunals of ecclesiastical and civil law could not but, in process of time, interfere with and obstruct each other.

But there was another prolific source of difference. The clergy, in one sense, from being the representative body, had begun to consider themselves the Church; but in another and more legitimate sense, the State, when Christian, as comprehending all the Christians of the empire, became the Church. Which was the legislative body,—the whole community of Christians? or the Christian aristocracy, who were in one sense the admitted rulers? And who was to appoint these rulers? It is quite clear that, from the first, though the consecration to the religious office was in the bishop and clergy, the laity had a voice in the ratification if not in the appointment. Did not the State fairly succeed to all the rights of the laity, more particularly when privileges and endowments, attached to the ecclesiastical offices, were conferred or guaranteed by the State, and therefore might appear in justice revocable, or liable to be regulated by the civil power?

This vital question at this time was still farther embarrassed by the rash eagerness with which the dominant Church called upon the State to rid it of its internal adversaries. When once the civil power was recognised as cognisant of ecclesiastical offences, where was that power to end? The Emperor, who commanded his subjects to be of one religion, might command them, by the same title, to adopt another. The despotic head of the State might assert his despotism as head of the Church. It must be acknowledged that no theory, which has satisfactorily harmonised the relations of these two, at once, in one sense separate, in another identical, communities, has satisfied the reasoning and dispassionate mind; while the separation of the two communities, the total dissociation, as it were, of the Christian and the citizen, is an experiment apparently not likely to advance or perpetuate the influence of Christianity.

At all events, the hasty and unsettled compact of this period left room for constant jealousy and strife. As each was the stronger, it encroached upon and extended its dominion into the territory of the other. In general, though with very various fortunes, in different parts of the world, and at different periods, the Church was in the ascendant, and for many centuries confronted the State, at least on equal terms.

<small>Marriage brought under ecclesiastical discipline.</small> The first aggression, as it were, which the Church made on the State, was in assuming the cognisance over all questions and causes relating to marriage. In sanctifying this solemn contract, it could scarcely be considered as transgressing its proper limits as guardian of this primary element of social virtue and happiness. In the early Church, the benediction of the bishop or presbyter seems to have been previously sought by the Christian at the time of marriage. The Heathen rite of marriage was so manifestly religious, that the Christian, while he sought to avoid that idolatrous ceremony, would wish to substitute some more simple and congenial form. In the general sentiment that this contract should be public and sacred, he would seek the sanction of his own community as its witnesses. Marriage not performed in the face of his Christian brethren was little better than an illicit union.[x]

It was an object likewise of the early Christian community to restrict the marriage of Christians to Christ-

---

[x] "Ideo penes nos occultæ conjunctiones, id est, non prius apud ecclesiam professæ, juxta mœchiam et fornicationem judicari periclitantur." Tertull. de Pudic. c. 4.

Though the rite was solemnised in the presence of the Christian priest, and the Church attempted to impose a graver and more serious dignity, it was not so easy to throw off the gay and festive character which had prevailed in the Heathen times. Paganism, or rather, perhaps, human nature, was too strong to submit. The austere preacher of Constantinople reproved the loose hymns to Venus, which were heard even at Christian weddings. The bride, he says, was borne by drunken men to her husband's house, among choirs of dancing harlots, with pipes and flutes, and songs, full, to her chaste ear, of offensive license.

ians—to discountenance, if not prohibit, those with unbelievers.⁷ This was gradually extended to marriages with heretics, or members of another Christian sect. When, therefore, the Church began to recognise five legal impediments to marriage, this was the Ist—difference of religion as between Christians and infidels, Jews, or heretics. The IInd was, the impediment of crime. Persons guilty of adultery were not allowed to marry according to the Roman law: this was recognised by the Church. A law of Constantius had made rape, or forcible abduction of a virgin, a capital offence; so, even with the consent of the injured female, marriage could not take place. III. Impediments from relationship. Here also the Church was content to follow the Roman law, which was as severe and precise as the Mosaic Institutes.⁸ IV. The civil impediment. Children adopted by the same father could not marry. A freeman could not marry a slave; the connection was only concubinage. It does not appear that the Church yet ventured to correct this vice of Roman society. V. Spiritual relationship, between godfathers and their spiritual children: this was afterwards carried much farther. To these regulations for the repression of im-

---

⁷ A law of Valentinian II., Theodosius and Arcadius (A. D. 389), prohibited the intermarriage of Jews and Christians. Codex Theodos. lll. 7, 2. It was to be considered adultery.— "Care, Christiane, Gentili aut Judæo filiam tradere; cave, inquam, Gentilem aut Judæum atque alienigenam, hoc est, hereticam, et omnem alienam à fide tuâ uxorem acceperis tibi." Ambros. de Abraham, c. 9. "Cum certissimè noveris tradi à nobis Christianam nisi Christiano non posse." Augustin. Ep. 234, ad Rusticum.

The Council of Illiberis had prohibited Christians from giving their daughters in marriage to Gentiles (propter copiam puellarum), also to Jews, heretics, and especially to Heathen priests. Can. xv. xvi. xvii.

⁸ See the various laws in the Cod. Theod., lib. iii. tit. 12, De Incestis Nuptiis.

290   DIVORCE.   Book IV.

proper connections were added some other ecclesiastical impediments. There were holy periods in the year, in which it was forbidden to contract marriage. No one might marry while under ecclesiastical interdict, nor one who had made a vow of chastity.

Divorce. The facility of divorce was the primary principle of corruption in Roman social life. Augustus had attempted to enforce some restrictions on this unlimited power of dissolving the matrimonial contract from caprice or the lightest motive. Probably, the severity of Christian morals had obtained that law of Constantine which was so much too rigid for the state of society, as to be entirely ineffective from the impossibility of carrying it into execution.[a] It was relaxed by Constantius, and almost abrogated by Honorius.[b] The inveterate evil remained. A Christian writer, at the beginning of the fifth century, complains that men changed their wives as quickly as their clothes, and that marriage chambers were set up as easily as booths in a market.[c] At a later period than that to which our

---

[a] Codex Theodos. iii. 16, 1. See vol. ii. p. 397.

[b] By the law of Honorius,—1. The woman who demanded a divorce without sufficient proof forfeited her dowry, was condemned to banishment, could not contract a second marriage, and was without hope of restoration to civil rights. 2. If she made out only a tolerable case (convicted her husband only of mediocris culpa), she only forfeited her dowry, and could not contract a second marriage, but was liable to be prosecuted by her husband for adultery. 3. If she made a strong case (gravis causa), she retained her dowry, and might marry again after five years. The husband, in the first case, forfeited the gifts and dowry, and was condemned to perpetual celibacy, not having liberty to marry again after a certain number of years. In the second, he forfeited the dowry but not the donation, and could marry again after two years. In the third, he was bound to prosecute his guilty wife. On her conviction, he retained the dowry, and might marry again immediately. Cod. Theodos. iii. xvi. 2.

[c] "Mulieres à maritis tanquam vestes subinde mutari, et thalamos tam sæpe et facile strui quam nundinarum tabernas." Asterius Amasenus apud Combefis. Auct. t. I.

The story has been often quoted

history extends, when Justinian attempted to prohibit all divorces except those on account of chastity, that is when the parties embraced the monastic life, he was obliged to relax the law on account of the fearful crimes, the plots and poisonings, and other evils, which it introduced into domestic life.

But though it could not correct or scarcely mitigate this evil by public law in the general body of society, Christianity, in its proper and more peculiar sphere, had invested marriage in a religious sanctity, which at least, to a limited extent, repressed this social evil. By degrees, separation from bed and board, even in the case of adultery, the only cause which could dissolve the tie, was substituted and enforced by the clergy instead of legal divorce. Over all the ceremonial forms, and all expressions which related to marriage, the Church threw the utmost solemnity; it was said to resemble the mystic union of Christ and the Church; till at length marriage grew up into a sacrament, indissoluble until the final separation of death, except by the highest ecclesiastical authority.[4] It is impossible to calculate the effect of this canonisation, as it were, of marriage, the only remedy which could be applied, first to the corrupt manners of Roman society, and afterwards to the consequences of the barbarian invasions, in which, notwithstanding the strong moral element in the Teutonic character, and the respect for women (which, no doubt, was one of the

---

from St. Jerome, of the man (of the lowest class) in Rome, who had had twenty wives, not divorced (he had buried them all); his wife had had twenty-two husbands. There was a great anxiety to know which would outlive the other. The man carried the day, and bore his wife to the grave in a kind of triumphal procession. Hieronym. Epist. xci, p. 745.

[4] The Eastern churches had a horror of second marriage; a presbyter was forbidden to be present at the wedding-feast of a digamist. Can. vii. See above.

original principles of chivalry), yet the dominance of brute force, and the unlimited rights of conquest, could not but lead to the perpetual, lawless, and violent dissolution of the marriage tie.*

Wills.
The cognisance of wills, another department in which the Church assumed a power not strictly ecclesiastical, seems to have arisen partly from an accidental cause. It was the custom among the Heathen to deposit wills in the temples, as a place of security; the Christians followed their practice, and chose their churches as the depositaries of these important documents. They thus came under the custody of the clergy, who, from guardians, became, in their courts, the judges of their authenticity or legality, and at length a general tribunal for all matters relating to testaments.

Thus religion laid its sacred control on all the material incidents of human life, and around the ministers of religion gathered all the influence thus acquired over the sentiments of mankind. The font of baptism usually received the Christian infant, and the form of baptism was uttered by the priest or bishop; the marriage was unhallowed without the priestly benediction; and at the close of life, the minister of religion was at hand to absolve and to reassure the departing spirit; at the funeral, he ratified, as it were, the solemn promises of immortality. But the great, permanent, and perpetual source of sacerdotal authority was the penitential discipline of the Church, which was universally recognised

---

* It is curious to trace the rapid fall of Roman pride. Valentinian made the intermarriage of a Roman provincial with a barbarian a capital crime (A. D. 370). Codex Theodos. iii. 14, 1. Under Theodosius, Fravitta, the Goth, married a Roman woman with the consent of the Emperor. Eunap. Excerpt. Legat. In another century, the daughters of emperors were the willing or the enforced brides of barbarian kings.

as belonging exclusively to the jurisdiction of the clergy. Christianity had sufficient power, in a certain degree, to engross the mind and heart, but not to keep under perpetual restraint the unruly passions or the inquisitive mind. The best were most conscious of human infirmity, and most jealous of their own slight aberrations from the catholic belief; the bad had not merely their own conscience, but public fame and the condemnatory voice of the community, to prostrate them before the visible arbiters of the All-seeing Power. Sin, from the most heinous delinquency, or the darkest heresy, to the most trivial fault or the slightest deviation from the established belief, could only be reconciled by the advice, the guidance, at length by the direct authority, of the priest. He judged of its magnitude, he prescribed the appointed penance. The hierarchy were supposed to be invested with the keys of heaven and of hell; they undoubtedly held those which unlock the human heart—fear and hope. And when once the mind was profoundly affected by Christianity—when hope had failed to excite to more generous obedience—they applied the baser and more servile instrument without scruple and without remorse.

Penitential discipline.

The penitential discipline of the Church, no doubt, grew up, like other usages, by slow degrees: its regulations were framed into a system to meet the exigencies of the times; but we discern, at a very early period, the awful power of condemning to the most profound humiliation, to the most agonising contrition, to the shame of public confession, to the abasing supplication before the priest, to long seclusion from the privileges and the society of the Christian community. Even then public confession was the first process in the fearful yet inevitable ceremonial. "Confession of sin," says Tertullian,[f] "is the proper discipline for the abasement and humiliation of man; it enforces that mode of life which can alone find mercy with God; it prescribes the fitting dress and food of the penitent to be in sackcloth and ashes, to darken the body with filth, to depress the soul with anguish; it allows only the simplest food, enough and no more than will maintain life. Constantly to fast and pray, to groan, to weep, to howl day and night before the Lord our God, to grovel at the feet of the presbyter, to kneel at the altar of God, to implore from all the brethren their deprecatory supplications." Subsequently, the more complete penitential system rigidly regulated the most minute particulars; the attitude, the garb, the language, or the more expressive silence. The place in which the believer stood, showed to the whole Church how far the candidate for salvation through Christ had been thrown back in his spiritual course, what progress he was making to pardon and peace. The penitent was clothed in sackcloth, his head was strewn with ashes; men shaved their heads, women left their dishevelled hair flung over their bosoms; they wore a peculiar veil. The severest attendance on every religious service was exacted, all diversions were proscribed, marriage was not permitted during the time of penance, the lawful indulgence of the marriage bed was forbidden. Although a regular formulary, which gradually grew into use,[g] imposed canonical penances of a certain period for certain offences, yet that period might be rigidly required or shortened by the authority of the bishop. For some offences the penitent, who it was believed

[f] De Pœnitentiâ, c. 9.
[g] On the Penitentiaries compare Latin Christianity, Book III. c. 5.

was abandoned to the power of Satan, was excluded from all enjoyment, all honour, and all society, to the close of life; and the doors of reconciliation were hardly opened to the departing spirit—wonderful proof how profoundly the doctrines of Christianity had sunk into the human heart, and of the enormous power (and what enormous power is not liable to abuse) in which the willing reverence of the people had invested the priesthood.

But something more fearful still remained. Over all the community hung the tremendous sentence of excommunication, tantamount to a sentence of spiritual death.[h] This sentence, though not as yet dependent on his will, was pronounced and executed by the religious magistrate. The clergy adhered to certain regular forms of process, but the ultimate decree rested with them.

Excommunication was of two kinds: first, that which excluded from the communion, and threw back the initiate Christian into the ranks of the uninitiate. Excommunicatio called. This separation or suspension allowed the person under ban to enter the church, to hear the psalms and sermon, and, in short, all that was permitted to the catechumen.

But the more terrible excommunication by anathema altogether banished the delinquent from the church and the society of Christians: it annulled for ever his hopes of immortality through Christ; it drove him out as an

---

[h] "Interfici Deus jussit sacerdotibus non obtemperantes, judicibus h æ ad tempus constitutis non obedientes; sed tunc quidem gladio occidebantur, quando adhæc et circumcisio carnis manebat. Nunc autem quia circumcisio spiritalis esse apud fideles Dei servos cœpit, spiritali gladio superbi et contumaces necantur, dum de ecclesiâ ejiciuntur." Cyprian. Epist. lxi.

"Nunc agit in ecclesiâ excommunicatio, quod agebat tunc in interfectis." Augustin. Q. 39, in Deuteron.

outcast to the dominion of the Evil Spirit. The Christian might not communicate with him in the ordinary intercourse of life: he was a moral leper, whom it was the solemn duty of all to avoid, lest they should partake in his contagion. The sentence of one church was rapidly promulgated throughout Christendom; and the excommunicated in Egypt or Syria found the churches in Gaul or Spain closed against him: he was an exile without a resting place. As long as Heathenism survived, at least in equal temporal power and distinction, and another society received with welcome, or at least with undiminished respect, the exile from Christianity, the excommunicated might lull his remaining terrors to rest, and forget, in the business or dissipation of the world, his forfeited hopes of immortality. But when there was but one society, that of the Christians, throughout the world, or at best but a feeble and despised minority, he stood a marked and branded man. Those who were, perhaps, not better Christians, but who had escaped the fatal censures of the Church, would perhaps seize the opportunity of showing their zeal by avoiding the outcast: if he did not lose civil privileges, he lost civil estimation; he was altogether excluded from human respect and human sympathies; he was a legitimate, almost a designated, object of scorn, distrust, and aversion.

The nature, the extent, and some of the moral and even political advantages of excommunication, are illustrated in the act of the celebrated Synesius.

Synesius. The power of the Christian bishop, in his hands, appears under its noblest and most beneficial form. Synesius became a Christian bishop without renouncing the habits, the language, and, in a great degree, the opinions, of a philosopher. His writings, more especially his Odes, blend, with a very scanty Christianity, the mystic theology of the later Platonism; but it is rather philosophy adopting Christian language, than Christianity moulding philosophy to its own uses. Yet so high was the character of Synesius, that even the worldly prelate of Alexandria, Theophilus, approved of his elevation to the episcopate in the obscure town of Ptolemais, near Cyrene. Synesius felt the power with which he was invested, and employed it with a wise vigour and daring philanthropy, which commanded the admiration both of philosophy and of religion. The lowborn Andronicus was the prefect or rather the scourge and tyrant of Libya; his exactions were unprecedented, and enforced by tortures of unusual cruelty even in that age and country. The province groaned and bled, without hope of relief, under the hateful and sanguinary oppression. Synesius had tried in vain the milder language of persuasion upon the intractable tyrant. At length he put forth the terrors of the Church to shield the people; and for his rapacity, which had amounted to sacrilege, and for his inhumanity, the president of the whole province was openly condemned, by a sentence of excommunication, to the public abhorrence, excluded from the society and denied the common rights of men. He was expelled from the church, as the Devil from Paradise; every Christian temple, every sanctuary, was closed against the man of blood; the priest was not even to permit him the rites of Christian burial; every private man and every magistrate was to exclude him from their houses and from their tables. If the rest of Christendom refused to ratify and execute the sentence of the obscure Church of Ptolemais, they were guilty of the sin of schism. The Church of Ptolemais would not communicate or partake of the divine mysteries with those who thus violated ecclesiastical discipline. The excommunication included the accomplices of the President's guilt, and by a less justifiable extension of power, their families. Andronicus quailed before the interdict, which he feared might find countenance in the court of Constantinople; bowed before the protector of the people, and acknowledged the justice of his sentence.[1]

The salutary thunder of sacerdotal excommunication might here and there strike some eminent delinquent;[k] but ecclesiastical discipline, which in the earlier and more fervent period of the religion, had watched with holy jealousy the whole life of the individual, was baffled by the increase of votaries, which it could no longer submit to this severe and constant superintendence. The clergy could not command, nor the laity require, the sacred duty of secession and outward penance from the multitude of sinners, when they were the *Ecclesiastical censures chiefly confined to heresy.* larger part of the community. But heresy of opinion was more easily detected than heresy of conduct. Gradually, from a moral as well as a religious power, the discipline became almost exclusively religious, or rather confined itself to the speculative, while it almost abandoned in despair the practical effects of religion. Heresy became the one great crime for which excommunication was pronounced in its most awful form; the heretic was the one being with whom it was criminal to associate, who forfeited all the privileges of religion, and all the charities of life.

---

[1] Synesii Epistolæ, lvii. lviii.
[k] There is a canon of the Council of Toledo (A.D. 408), that if any man in power shall have robbed one in holy orders, or a poor man (quemlibet pauperiorem), or a monk, and the bishop shall send to demand a hearing for the cause, should the man in power treat his message with contempt, letters shall be sent to all the bishops of the province, declaring him excommunicated till he has heard the cause or made restitution. Can. xi. Labbe, ii. 1225.

Nor was this all; in pursuit of the heretic, the Church was not content to rest within her own sphere, to wield her own arms of moral temperament, and to exclude from her own territory. She formed a fatal alliance with the State, and raised that which was strictly an ecclesiastical, an offence against the religious community, into a civil crime, amenable to temporal penalties. The Church, when she ruled the mind of a religious or superstitious emperor, could not forego the immediate advantage of his authority to further her own cause, and hailed his welcome intrusion on her own internal legislation. In fact, the autocracy of the Emperor over the Church, as well as over the State, was asserted in all those edicts which the Church, in its blind zeal, hailed with transport as the marks of his allegiance, but which confounded in inextricable, and to the present time, in deplorable confusion, the limits of the religious and the civil power. The imperial rescripts, which made heresy a civil offence, by affixing penalties which were not purely religious, trespassed as much upon the real principles of the original religious republic, as against the immutable laws of conscience and Christian charity. The tremendous laws of Theodosius,[m] constituting heresy a capital offence, punishable by the civil power, are said to have been enacted only as a terror to evil-believers, but they betrayed too clearly the darkening spirit of the times; the next generation would execute what the laws of the last would enact. The most distinguished bishops of the time raised a cry of horror at the first executions for religion; but it was their humanity which was startled; they did not perceive that they

---

[m] See ch. viii.

had sanctioned, by the smallest civil penalty, a false and fatal principle; that though, by the legal establishment, the Church and the State had become, in one sense, the same body, yet the associating principle of each remained entirely distinct, and demanded an entirely different and independent system of legislation and administration of the law. The Christian hierarchy bought the privilege of persecution at the price of Christian independence.

It is difficult to decide whether the language of the book in the Theodosian code, entitled "On Heretics," contrasts more strongly with the comprehensive, equitable, and parental tone of the Roman jurisprudence, or with the gentle and benevolent spirit of the Gospel, or even with the primary principles of the ecclesiastical community.[a] The Emperor, of his sole and supreme authority, without any recognition of ecclesiastical advice or sanction; the Emperor, who himself might be an Arian or Eunomian, or Manichean—who had so recently been an Arian—defines heresy to be the very slightest deviation from Catholic verity; and in a succession of statutes inflicts civil penalties, and excludes from the common rights of men, the maintainers of certain opinions. Nothing treasonable, immoral, dangerous to the peace of society, is alleged; the crime, the civil crime, as it now becomes, consists solely in opinions. The law of Constantine, which granted special immunities to certain of his subjects, might perhaps, with some show of equity, confine those immunities to a particular class.[b] But the gradually darkening statutes

---

[a] "Hæreticorum vocabule continentur, et latis adversus eos sanctionibus debent succumbere, qui vel levi argumento à judicio Catholicæ religionis et tramite detecti fuerint deviare." This is a law of Arcadius. The practice was more lenient than the law.

[b] The first law of Constantine restricts the immunities which he grants to Catholics. Cod. Theodos. xvi.

proceed from the withholding of privileges to the prohibition of meetings,[p] then through confiscation,[q] the refusal of the common right of bequeathing property, fine,[r] exile,[s] to capital punishment.[t] The latter, indeed, was enacted only against some of the more obscure sects, and some of the Donatists, whose turbulent and seditious conduct might demand the interference of the civil power; but still they are condemned not as rebels and insurgents but as heretics.[u]

In building up this vast and majestic fabric of the hierarchy, though individuals might be actuated by personal ambition or interest, and the narrow corporate spirit might rival loftier motives in the consolidation of ecclesiastical power, yet the great object, which was steadily, if dimly seen, was the advancement of mankind in religion, and through religion to temporal and eternal happiness. Dazzled by the glorious spectacle of provinces, of nations, gradually brought within the pale of Christianity, the great men of the fourth century of Christianity were not and could not be endowed with prophetic sagacity to discern the abuses of sacerdotal domination, and the tyranny which, long centuries after, might be exercised over the human mind in the name of religion. We may trace the

Objects of the great defenders of the hierarchical power.

---

[p] The law of Gratian (IV.) confiscates the houses or even fields in which heretical conventicles are held. See also law of Theodosius, viii.

[q] Leges vi. xii.

[r] Ibid. xxi.

[s] Ibid. xviii. liii. lviii.

[t] The law of Theodosius enacts this not against the general body, but some small sections of Manicheans, "Summo supplicio et inexpiabili poenâ jubemus affligi," ix. This law sanctions the ill-omened name of inquisitors. Compare law xxv. The "interminata poena" of law lx. is against Eunomians, Arians, and Macedonians.

[u] Ad Heraclianum, lvi. The imperial laws against second baptisms are still more singular invasions of the civil upon the ecclesiastical authority. xvi. tit. vi.

hierarchical principles of Cyprian or of Ambrose to what may seem their natural consequences, religious crusades and the fires of the inquisition; *we* may observe the tendency of unsocial monasticism to quench the charities of life, to harden into cruelty, grovel into licentiousness, and brood over its own ignorance; *we* may trace the predestinarian doctrines of Augustine darkening into narrow bigotry, or maddening to uncharitable fanaticism; *they* only contemplated, *they* only could contemplate, a great moral and religious power opposing civil tyranny, or at least affording a refuge from it; purifying domestic morals, elevating and softening the human heart;[x] a wholesome and benevolent force compelling men by legitimate means to seek wisdom, virtue, and salvation; the better part of mankind withdrawing, in holy prudence and wise timidity, from the corruptions of a foul and cruel age, and devoting itself to its own self-

---

[x] The laws bear some pleasing testimonies to the activity of Christian benevolence in many of the obscurer scenes of human wretchedness. See the humane law regarding prisoners, that they might have proper food, and the use of the bath. "Nec deerit antistitum Christianæ religionis cura laudabilis, quæ ad observationem constituti judicis hanc ingerat monitionem." The Christian bishop was to take care that the judge did his duty. Cod. Theodos. ix. 3. 7.

As early as the reign of Valentinian and Valens, prisoners were released at Easter (ob diem paschæ, quem intimo corde celebramus), excepting those committed for the crimes of treason, poisoning, magic, adultery, rape, or homicide, ix. 36. 3. 4. These statutes were constantly renewed, with the addition of some more excepted crimes —sacrilege, robbery of tombs, and coining.

There is a very singular law of Arcadius prohibiting the clergy and the monks from interfering with the execution of the laws, and forcibly taking away condemned criminals from the hands of justice. They were allowed, at the same time, the amplest privilege of merciful intercession. This was connected with the privilege of asylum. Codex Theodos. ix. 40. 16.

There is another singular law by which corporal punishments were not to be administered in Lent, except against the Isaurian robbers, who were to be dealt with without delay. ix. 35. 5, 6, 7.

advancement to the highest spiritual perfection; and the general pious assertion of the universal and unlimited providence and supremacy of God. None but the hopeful achieve great revolutions; and what hopes could equal those which the loftier Christian minds might justly entertain of the beneficent influences of Christianity?

We cannot wonder at the growth of the ecclesiastical power, if the Church were merely considered as a new sphere in which human genius, virtue, and benevolence, might develope their unimpeded energies, and rise above the general debasement. *Dignity and advantage of the clerical station.* This was almost the only way in which any man could devote great abilities or generous activity to a useful purpose with reasonable hopes of success. The civil offices were occupied by favour and intrigue, often acquired most easily and held most permanently by the worst men for the worst purposes. The utter extinction of freedom had left no course of honourable distinction, as an honest advocate or an independent jurist. Literature was worn out; rhetoric had degenerated into technical subtlety; philosophy had lost its hold upon the mind. Even the great military commands were filled by fierce and active barbarians, on whose energy Rome relied for the protection of her frontiers. In the Church alone was security, influence, independence, fame, even wealth, and the opportunity of serving mankind. The pulpit was the only rostrum from which the orator would be heard; feeble as was the voice of Christian poetry, it found an echo in the human heart. The episcopate was the only office of dignity which could be obtained without meanness, or exercised without fear. Whether he sought the peace of a contemplative, or the usefulness of an active life, this was the only sphere for the man of conscious mental strength; and if he felt the inward satisfaction that he was either securing his own, or advancing the salvation of others, the lofty mind would not hesitate what path to choose through the darkening and degraded world.

The just way to consider the influence of the Christian hierarchy (without which, in its complete and vigorous organisation, it is clear that the religion could not have subsisted throughout these ages of disaster and confusion) is to imagine, if possible, the state of things without that influence. Consider a tyranny the most oppressive and debasing, without any principles of free or hopeful resistance, or resistance only attainable by the complete dismemberment of the Roman empire and its severance into a number of hostile states; the general morals at the lowest state of depravation, with nothing but a religion totally without influence, and a philosophy without authority, to correct its growing cruelty and licentiousness; a very large portion of mankind in hopeless slavery, with nothing to mitigate it but the insufficient control of fear in the master, or occasional gleams of humanity or political foresight in the government, with no inward consolation or feeling of independence whatever. In the midst of this, contemplate the invasion of hostile barbarians in every quarter, and the complete wreck of civilisation; with no commanding influence to assimilate the adverse races, without the protection or conservative tendency of any religious feeling to soften them, and at length to re-organise and re-create, literature, the arts of building, painting, and music; the Latin language itself breaking up into as many countless dialects as there were settlements of barbarous tribes, without a guardian or sacred depositary. It is difficult adequately to darken the picture of ignorance, violence, confusion, and wretchedness; but without this adequate conception of the probable state of the world without it, it is impossible to judge with fairness or candour the obligations of Europe and of civilisation to the Christian hierarchy.

CHAPTER II.

Public Spectacles.

THE Greek and Roman inhabitants of the empire were
<small>Public spectacles.</small> attached with equal intensity to their favourite
spectacles, whether of more solemn religious
origin, or of lighter and more festive kind. These
amusements are perhaps more congenial to the southern
character, from the greater excitability of temperament,
the less variable climate, which rarely interferes with
enjoyment in the open air; and throughout the Roman
world, they had long been fostered by those republican
institutions which gave to every citizen a place and an
interest in all public ceremonials, privileges which, in this
respect, long outlived the institutions themselves. The
population of the great capitals had preserved only the
dangerous and pernicious part of freedom, the power of
subsisting either without regular industry or with but
moderate exertion. The perpetual distribution of corn,
and the various largesses at other times, emancipated
them in a great degree from the wholesome control of
their own necessities; and a vast and uneducated multitude was maintained in idle and dissolute inactivity. It
was absolutely necessary to occupy much of this vacant
time with public diversions; and the invention, the
wealth, and the personal exertions of the higher orders,
were taxed to gratify this insatiable appetite. Policy
demanded that which ambition and the love of popularity had freely supplied in the days of the republic,

and which personal vanity continued to offer, though with less prodigal and willing munificence. The more retired and domestic habits of Christianity might in some degree seclude a sect from the public diversions, but it could not change the nature or the inveterate habits of a people: it was either swept along by, or contented itself with giving a new direction to, the impetuous and irresistible current; it was obliged to substitute some new excitement for that which it peremptorily prohibited, and reluctantly to acquiesce in that which it was unable to suppress.

Christianity had cut off that part of the public spectacles which belonged exclusively to Paganism. Even if all the temples at Rome were not, as Jerome asserts, covered with dust and cobwebs,[a] yet, notwithstanding the desperate efforts of the old aristocracy, the tide of popular interest, no doubt, set away from the deserted and mouldering fanes of the Heathen deities, and towards the churches of the Christians. And if this was the case in Rome, at Constantinople and throughout the empire, the Pagan ceremonial was either extinct, or gradually expiring, or lingering on in unimpressive regularity. On the other hand, the modest and unimposing ritual of Christianity naturally, and almost necessarily, expanded into pomp and dignity. To the deep devotion of the early Christians the place and circumstances of worship were indifferent: piety finds everywhere its own temple. In the low and unfurnished chamber, in the forest, in the desert, in the catacomb, the Christian adored his Redeemer, prayed, chanted his hymn, and partook of the sacred elements. Devotion

---

[a] " Fuligine et aranearum telis omnia Romæ templa cooperta sunt: incundans populus ante delubra seminuta, currit ad martyrum tumulos." Epist. lvii. p. 590.

wanted no accessories; faith needed no subsidiary excitement; or if it did, it found them in the peril, the novelty, the adventurous and stirring character of the scene, or in the very meanness and poverty, contrasted with the gorgeous worship which it had abandoned; in the mutual attachment, and in the fervent emulation, which spreads throughout a small community.

But among the more numerous and hereditary Christians of this period, the temple and the solemn service were indispensable to enforce and maintain the devotion. Religion was not strong enough to disdain, and far too earnest to decline, any legitimate means of advancing her cause. The whole ceremonial was framed with the art which arises out of the intuitive perception of that which is effective towards its end. That which was felt to be awful was adopted to enforce awe; that which drew the people to the church, and affected their minds when there, became sanctified to the use of the Church. The edifice itself arose more lofty with the triumph of the faith, and enlarged itself to receive the multiplying votaries. Christianity disdained that its God and its Redeemer should be less magnificently honoured than the dæmons of Paganism. In the service it delighted to transfer and to breathe, as it were, a sublimer sense into the common appellations of the Pagan worship, whether from the ordinary ceremonial, or the more secret mysteries. The church became a temple;[b] the table of the communion an altar; the celebration of the Eucharist the appalling or the unbloody sacrifice.[c] The ministering functionaries multi-

---

[b] Ambrose and Lactantius, and even Irenæus, use this term. See Bingham, b. viii. 1, 4.

[c] The φρίκτη, or the ἀναίμακτος θυσία.

plied with the variety of the ceremonial; each was consecrated to his office by a lower kind of ordination; but a host of subordinate attendants by degrees swelled the officiating train. The incense, the garlands, the lamps, all were gradually adopted by zealous rivalry, or seized as the lawful spoils of vanquished Paganism and consecrated to the service of Christ.

The Church rivalled the old Heathen mysteries in expanding by slow degrees its higher privileges. Christianity was itself the great Mystery, unfolded gradually and in general after a long and searching probation. It still reserved the power of opening at once its gates to the more distinguished proselytes, and of jealously and tardily unclosing them to more doubtful neophytes. It permitted its sanctuary, as it were, to be stormed at once by eminent virtue and unquestioned zeal; but the common mass of mankind were never allowed to consider it less than a hard-won privilege to be received into the Church; and this boon was not to be dispensed with lavish or careless hands.[d] Its preparatory ceremonial of abstinence, personal purity, ablution, secrecy, closely resembled that of the Pagan mysteries (perhaps each may have contributed to the other); so the theologic dialect of Christianity spoke the same language. Yet Christianity substituted for the feverish enthusiasm of some of these rites, and the phantasmagoric terrors of others, with their vague admonitions to purity, a searching but gently administered moral discipline, and more sober religious excitement. It retained, indeed,

---

[d] It is one of the bitterest charges of Tertullian against the heretics, that they did not keep up this distinction between the catechumens and the faithful. "Imprimis quis catechumenus, quis fidelis, incertum est: pariter adeunt, pariter orant." Even the Heathen were admitted; thus "pearls were cast before swine." De Præscript. Hæret. c. 41.

much of the dramatic power, though under another form.

The divisions between the different orders of worshippers enforced by the sacerdotal authority, and observed with humble submission by the people, could not but impress the mind with astonishment and awe. The stranger, on entering the spacious open court, which was laid out before the more splendid churches, with porticos or cloisters on each side, beheld first the fountain or tank, where the worshippers were expected to wash their hands, and purify themselves, as it were, for the divine presence. Lingering in these porticos, or approaching timidly the threshold which they dared not pass, or, at the farthest, entering only into the first porch, or vestibule,* and pressing around the disciples to solicit their prayers, he would observe men, pale, dejected, clad in sackcloth, oppressed with the profound consciousness of their guilt, acquiescing in the justice of the ecclesiastical censure which

---

* There is much difficulty and confusion respecting these divisions of the church. The fact probably is, that, according to the period or the local circumstances, the structure and the arrangement were more or less complicated. Tertullian says distinctly, "non modò limine verum omni ecclesiæ tecto submoveretur." Where the churches were of a simpler form, and had no roofed narthex or vestibule, these penitents stood in the open court before the church; even later, the "flentes" and the "hiemantes" formed a particular class.

A canon of St. Gregory Thaumaturgus gives the clearest view of these arrangements: Ἡ πρόσκλαυσις ἔξω τῆς πύλης τοῦ εὐκτηρίου ἐστίν, ἔνθα ἑστῶτα τὸν ἁμαρτάνοντα χρὴ τῶν εἰσιόντων δεῖσθαι πιστῶν ὑπὲρ αὐτοῦ εὔχεσθαι· ἡ ἀκρόασις ἔνδοθι τῆς πύλης ἐν τῷ νάρθηκι, ἔνθα ἑστάναι χρὴ τὸν ἡμαρτηκότα, ἕως τῶν κατηχουμένων, καὶ ἐντεῦθεν ἐξέρχεσθαι· ἀκούων γάρ φησὶ τῶν γραφῶν καὶ τῆς διδασκαλίας, ἐκβαλλέσθω, καὶ μὴ ἀξιούσθω προσευχῆς· ἡ δὲ ὑπόπτωσις, ἵνα ἔσωθεν τῆς πύλης τοῦ ναοῦ ἱστάμενος, μετὰ τῶν κατηχουμένων ἐξέρχηται· ἡ σύστασις, ἵνα συνίσταται τοῖς πιστοῖς καὶ μὴ ἐξέρχηται μετὰ τῶν κατηχουμένων· τελευταῖον ἡ μέθεξις τῶν ἁγιασμάτων. Apud Labbe, Conc. l. p 842.

altogether excluded them from the christian community. These were the first class of penitents, men of notorious guilt, whom only a long period of this humiliating probation could admit even within the hearing of the sacred service. As he advanced to the gates, he must pass the scrutiny of the doorkeepers, who guarded the admission into the church, and distributed each class of worshippers into their proper place. The stranger, whether Heathen or Jew, might enter into the part assigned to the catechumens or novices and the penitents of the second order (the hearers), that he might profit by the religious instruction.[f] He found himself in the first division of the main body of the church, of which the walls were lined by various marbles, the roof often ceiled with mosaic, and supported by lofty columns with gilded capitals; the doors were inlaid with ivory or silver; the distant altar glittered with precious stones.[r] In the midst of the nave stood the pulpit, or reading-desk (the ambo), around which were arranged the singers, who chanted to the most solemn music, poetry, much of it

The penitents.

The narthex.

---

[f] This part of the church was usually called the narthex. But this term, I believe, of the sixth century, was not used with great precision, or rather, perhaps, was applied to different parts of the church, according to their greater or less complexity of structure. It is sometimes used for the porch or vestibule: in this sense there were several narthexes (St. Sophia had four). Mamachi (vol. l. p. 216), insists that it was divided from the nave by a wall. But this cannot mean the narthex into which the ἀκροώμενοι were admitted, as the object of their admission was that they might hear the service. "Episcopus nullum prohibeat intrare ecclesiam, et audire verbum Dei, sive haereticum, sive Judaeum usque ad missam catechumenorum." Concil. Carthag. iv. c. 84.

[r] "Alii aedificent ecclesias, vestiant parietes marmorum crustis, columnarum moles advehant, earumque deaurent capita, pretiosum ornatum non sentientis, ebore argentoque valvas, et gemmis distinguant altaria. Non reprehendo, non abnuo." Hieronym. Epist. viii. ad Demetriad.

familiar to the Jew, as belonging to his own sacred writings, to the Heathen full of the noblest images, expressive of the divine power and goodness; adapting itself with the most exquisite versatility to every devout emotion, melting into the most pathetic tenderness, or swelling out into the most appalling grandeur. The pulpit was then ascended by one of the inferior order, the reader of certain portions or extracts from the sacred volumes, in which God himself spoke to the awe-struck auditory. He was succeeded by an orator of a higher dignity, a presbyter or a bishop, who sometimes addressed the people from the steps which led up to the chancel, sometimes chose the more convenient and elevated position of the ambo.[b] He was a man usually of the highest attainments and eloquence, and instead of the frivolous and subtile questions which the Pagan was accustomed to hear in the schools of rhetoric or philosophy, he fearlessly agitated and peremptorily decided on such eternally and universally awakening topics as the responsibility of man before God, the immortality and future destination of the soul; topics of which use could not deaden the interest to the believer, but which, to an unaccustomed ear, were as startling as important. The mute attention of the whole assembly was broken only by uncontrollable acclamations, which frequently interrupted the more moving preachers. Around the pulpit was the last order of penitents, who prostrated themselves in humble homage during the prayers and the benediction of the bishop.

The preacher.

---

[b] Chrysostom generally preached from the ambo. Socr. vi. 5. Sozomen, viii. 5. Both usages prevailed in the West.

"Sew is conspicuis gradibus venerabilis arm Concionantorum plebs sedula circumstetat."
Sid. Apollon. can. xvi.
"Fronte sub adversâ gradibus sublime tribunal
Tollitur, antistes prædicat ende Deum."
Prudent. Hymn. ad Hippolyt.

Here the steps of the profane stranger must pause; an insuperable barrier, which he could not pass without violence, secluded the initiate from the society of the less perfect. Yet, till the more secret ceremonial began, he might behold, at dim and respectful distance, the striking scene, first of the baptized worshippers in their order, the females in general in galleries above (the virgins separate from the matrons). Beyond, in still further secluded sanctity, on an elevated semicircle, around the bishop, sat the clergy, attended by the subdeacons, acolyths, and those of inferior order. Even the gorgeous throne of the Emperor was below this platform. Before them was the mystic and awful table, the altar, as it began to be called in the fourth century, over which was sometimes suspended a richly-wrought canopy (the ciborium): the altar was covered with fine linen. In the third century, the simpler vessels of glass or other cheap material had given place to silver and gold. In the later persecutions, the cruelty of the Heathen was stimulated by their avarice; and some of the sufferers, while they bore their own agonies with patience, were grieved to the heart to see the sacred vessels pillaged, and turned to profane or indecent uses. In the Eastern churches, richly embroidered curtains overshadowed the approach to the altar, or light doors secluded altogether the Holy of Holies from the profane gaze of the multitude.

Such was the ordinary Christian ceremonial as it addressed the mass of mankind. But at a certain time, the uninitiate were dismissed, the veil was dropped which shrouded the hidden rites, the doors were closed, profane steps might not cross the threshold of the baptistery, or linger in the church, when the Liturgy of the faithful, the office of the Eucharist, began. The veil of concealment was first spread over the peculiar rites of Christianity from caution. The religious assemblies were, strictly speaking, unlawful, and they were shrouded in secrecy lest they should be disturbed by the intrusion of their watchful enemies;[1] and it was this unavoidable secrecy which gave rise to the frightful fables of the Heathen concerning the nature of these murderous or incestuous banquets. As they could not be public, of necessity they took the form of mysteries, and as mysteries became objects of jealousy and of awe. As the assemblies became more public, that seclusion of the more solemn rites was retained from dread and reverence, which was commenced from fear. Though profane curiosity no longer dared to take a hostile character, it was repelled from the sacred ceremony. Of the mingled multitude, Jews and Heathens, the incipient believers, the hesitating converts, who must be permitted to hear the Gospel of Christ, or the address of the preacher, none could be admitted to the sacraments. It was natural to exclude them, not merely by regulation and by the artificial division of the church into separate parts, but by the majesty which invested the last solemn rites. That which had concealed itself from fear, became itself fearful: it was no longer a timid mystery which fled the light, but an unapproachable communion with the Deity, which would not brook profane intrusion. It is an extraordinary indication of the power of Christianity, that rites in themselves so simple, and of which the nature, after all the concealment, could not but be known, should assume such unquestioned majesty; that, however significant, the

[1] "Tot hostes ejus, quot extranei ... quotidiè obsidemur, quotidiè prodimur, in ipsis plurimùm cœtibus et congregationibus opprimimur." Tertull. Apologet. 7.

simple lustration by water, and the partaking of bread and wine, should so affect the awe-struck imagination, as to make men suppose themselves ignorant of what these sacraments really were, and even when the high-wrought expectations were at length gratified, to experience no dissatisfaction at their plain, and in themselves, unappalling ceremonies. The mysteriousness was no doubt fed and heightened by the regulations of the clergy, and by the impressiveness of the service,[k] but it grew of itself out of the profound and general religious sentiment. The baptistery and the altar were closed against the uninitiate, but if they had been open, men would scarcely have ventured to approach them. The knowledge of the nature of the sacraments was reserved for the baptized; but it was because the minds of the unbaptized were sealed by trembling reverence, and shuddered to anticipate the forbidden knowledge. The hearers had a vague knowledge of these mysteries floating around them, the initiate heard it within.[m] To add to the impressiveness, night was sometimes spread over the Christian as over the Pagan mysteries.[n]

[k] This was the avowed object of the clergy. "Catechumenis sacramenta fidelium non produntur, non ideb fit, quod ea ferre non possunt, sed ut ab eis tanto ardentius concupiscantur, quanto honorabilius occultantur." Augustin. in Johan. 96. "Mortalium generi natura datum est, ut abstrusa fortius quaerat, ut negata magis ambiat, ut tardius adepta plus diligat, et eo flagrantius ametur veritas, quo vel diutius desideratur, vel laboriosius quaeritur, vel tardius invenitur." Claudius Mamert., quoted by Casaubon in Baron. p. 497.

[m] The inimitable pregnancy of the Greek language expresses this by two verbs differently compounded. Cyril of Jerusalem, in his Procatechesis, states the Catechumena περιηχεῖσθαι, the Faithful ἐνηχεῖσθαι, by the meaning of the mysteries.

[n] "Nocte ritus multi in mysteriis pergebantur; noctu etiam initiatio Christianorum inchoabatur." Casaubon, p. 490, with the quotations subjoined. This might have originated in the vigil of Easter being thus prolonged to midnight. It was an old Jewish tradition that the Messiah would come at the Passover at midnight. "Dicamus aliquid, quod forsitan lectori

316   BAPTISM.   Book IV.

At Easter, and at Pentecost,[a] and in some places at the Epiphany, the rite of Baptism was administered publicly (that is, in the presence of the Faithful) to all the converts of the year, excepting those few instances in which it had been expedient to perform the ceremony without delay, or where the timid Christian put it off till the close of life;[b] a practice for a long time condemned in vain by the clergy. But the fact of the delay shows how deeply the importance and efficacy of the rite were rooted in the Christian mind. It was a complete lustration of the soul. The Neophyte emerged from the waters of Baptism in a state of perfect innocence. The Dove (the Holy Spirit) was constantly hovering over the font, and sanctifying the waters to the mysterious ablution of all the sins of the passed life. If the soul suffered no subsequent taint, it passed at once to the realms of purity and bliss; the heart was purified; the understanding illuminated; the spirit was clothed with immortality.[c] Robed in

---

utile sit. Traditio Judæorum est Christum media nocte venturum in similitudinem Ægyptii temporis, quando Pascha celebratum est, et exterminator venit et Dominus super tabernacula transiit et sanguine agni postes nostrarum frontium consecrati sunt. Unde reor tradit:onem apostolicam permansisse ut in die vigiliarum paschæ ante noctis dimidium populos dimittere non licet expectantes adventum Christi, et postquam illud tempus transierit, securitate præsumta festum cunctis agentibus diem." Hieron. in Matt. 24.

[a] At Constantinople, it appears from Chrysostom, baptism did not take place at Pentecost. Montfaucon, Diatribe, p. 179.

[b] The memorable example of Constantine may for a time not only have illustrated but likewise confirmed the practice. See Gibbon's note (vol. III. p. 266) and the author's observations.

[c] Gregory of Nazianzum almost exhausts the copiousness of the Greek language in speaking of Baptism,— δῶρον καλοῦμεν, χάρισμα, βάπτισμα, χρίσμα, φώτισμα, ἀφθαρσίας ἔνδυμα, λουτρόν παλιγγενεσίας, σφραγίδα, πᾶν ὅτι τίμιον. Orat. xl. de Baptism. Almost all the Fathers of this age, Basil, the two Gregories, Ambrose (de Sacram) Augustine, have treatises on baptism, and vie, as it were, with each other, in their praises of its importance and efficacy.

white, emblematic of spotless purity,' the candidate approached the baptistery, in the larger churches a separate building. There he uttered the solemn vows which pledged him to his religion.² The symbolising genius of the East added some significant ceremonies. The Catechumen turned to the West, the realm of Satan, and thrice renounced his power; he turned to the East to adore the Sun of Righteousness,³ and to proclaim his compact with the Lord of Life. The mystic trinal number prevailed throughout; the vow was threefold, and thrice pronounced. The baptism was usually by immersion; the stripping off the clothes was emblematic of "putting off the old man;" but baptism by sprinkling was allowed, according to the exigency of the case. The water itself became, in the vivid language of the Church, the blood of Christ: it was compared, by a fanciful analogy, to the Red Sea: the daring metaphors of some of the Fathers might seem to assert a transmutation of its colour.⁴

The Sacrament of the Lord's Supper imperceptibly acquired the solemnity, the appellation, of a sacrifice. The poetry of devotional language kindled into the most vivid and realising expressions of awe and adoration. No imagery could be too bold, no words too glowing, to impress the soul more profoundly with the sufferings, the divinity, the intimate union of the Redeemer with his disciples. The invisible presence of the Lord, which the devout felt within the whole church, but more particularly in its more holy and secluded part, was gradually concentrated as it were upon the altar. The mysterious identification of the Redeemer with the consecrated elements was first felt by the mind, till, at a later period, a material and corporeal transmutation began to be asserted; that which the earlier Fathers, in their boldest figure, called a bloodless sacrifice, became an actual oblation of the body and blood of Christ. But all these fine and subtile distinctions belong to a later theology. In the dim vagueness, in the ineffable and inexplicable mystery, consisted much of its impressiveness on the believer, the awe and dread of the uninitiate.

These Sacraments were the sole real Mysteries; their nature and effects were the hidden knowledge which was revealed to the perfect alone.[x] In Alexandria, where the imitation or rivalry of the ancient mysteries, in that seat of the Platonic learning, was most likely to prevail, the catechetical school of Origen attempted to form the simpler truths of the Gospel into a regular and progressive system of development.[y] The works of

---

[x] "Quid est quod occultum est et non publicum in Ecclesiâ, Sacramentum Baptismi, Sacramentum Eucharistiæ. Opera nostra bona vident et Pagani, Sacramenta vero occultantur illis." Augustin., in Psalm, 103. Ordination appears to have been a sacral rite. Casaubon, p. 495. Compare this treatise of Casaubon, the xivth of his Exercitationes Anti-Baronianæ, which in general is profound and judicious.

[y] Upon this ground rests the famous Disciplina Arcani, that esoteric doctrine, within which lurked every thing which later ages thought proper to dignify by the name of the traditions of the church. This theory was first fully developed by Schelstrate, "De Disciplinâ Arcani," and is very clearly stated in Pagi, sub Ann. 118. It rests chiefly on a passage of Origen (contra Cels. L. 7.) who, after asserting the publicity of the main doctrines of Christianity, the incarnation, passion, and resurrection of Christ, and the general resurrection to judgement, admits that Christianity, like Philosophy, had some secret and esoteric doctrines. Pagi argues that, as the

Clement of Alexandria were progressive, addressed to the Heathen, the Catechumen, the perfect Christian. But the doctrine which was there reserved for the initiate had a strange tinge of Platonic mysticism. In the church in general the only esoteric doctrine, as I have said, related to the Sacraments. After the agitation of the Trinitarian question, there seems to have been some desire to withdraw that holy mystery likewise from the gaze of the profane, which the popular tumults, the conflicts between the Arians and Athanasians of the lowest orders, in the streets of Constantinople and Alexandria, show to have been by no means successful. The apocalyptic hymn, the Trisagion, makes a part indeed of all the older liturgies, which belong to the end of the third or beginning of the fourth century. Even the simple prayer of our Lord, which might seem appropriate to universal man, and so intended by the Saviour himself, was considered too holy to be uttered by unbaptised lips. It was said that none but the baptised could properly address the Almighty as his Father.*

That care which Christianity had assumed over the whole life of man, it did not abandon after death. In that solemn season it took in charge the body, which, though mouldering into dust, was to be revived for the resurrection. The respect and honour which human nature pays to the remains of the dead, and which, among the Greeks especially, had a strong religious hold upon the feelings, was still more profoundly sanctified by the doctrines and usages of Christianity. The practice of inhumation which prevailed in Egypt and Syria, and in other parts of the

Christian funerals.

Trinity was not among the public, it must have been among the esoteric tenets. There is no real ground for it. * Bingham, l. 4. 7. and x. 5. 9.

East, was gradually extended over the whole western world by Christianity.[b] The funeral pyre went out of use, and the cemeteries, which from the earliest period belonged to the Christians, were gradually enlarged for the general reception, not of the ashes only in their urns, but for the entire remains of the dead. The Eastern practice of embalming was so general,[b] that Tertullian boasts that the Christians consumed more of the merchandise of Sabæa in their interments than the Heathens in their fumigations before the altars of their Gods.[c] The general tone of the simple inscriptions spoke of death but as a sleep; "he sleeps in peace" was the common epitaph: the very name of the inclosure, the *cemetery*, implied the same trust in its temporary occupancy; those who were committed to the earth only awaited the summons to a new life.[d] Gradually the cemetery was, in some places, closely connected with the church. Where

---

[a] "Nec, ut creditis, ullum damnum sepulturæ timemus, sed veterem et meliorem consuetudinem humandi frequentamus." The speaker goes on, in very elegant language, to adduce the analogy of the death and revival of nature,—"Expectandum etiam nobis corporis ver est." Minuc. Fel. edit. Ouzel, p. 327.
During the time of the plague in Alexandria and Carthage, the Christians not only buried their own dead, but likewise those of the Pagans. Dion. Alex. apud Euseb. Hist. vii. 22. Pontius, in Vitâ Cypriani. Compare a curious Essay in the Vermischte Schriften of Böttiger, III. 14. Verbrennen oder Beerdigen.

[b] "Tinniumque et frigida massa
Liquido spargemus odore."
Prudent. Hym. de Exeq.

[c] "Martyris bi tumulum studeant perfundere nardo;
Et medicata pie referant unguenta sepulcra."
Paul. Nol. in Nat. S. Fel.

[c] Apologet. c. 42. Boldetti affirms that these odours were plainly perceptible on opening some of the Christian cemeteries at Rome. See Mamachi, Costumi dei Christiani, iii. p. 83. The judge in the acts of Tarachus (Ruinart, p. 385) says, "you expect that your women will bury your body with ointments and spices."

[d] "Hinc maxima cura sepulchris Impenditur, hinc resolutos Honor ultimus accipit artus Et funeris ambitus ornat.
. . . . . .
Quid tam flebile cavata,
Quid pulchra volunt monumenta?
Res quod nisi creditur illis
Non mortuus, sed data somno."
Prudent. in Exeq. Defunct.

the rigid interdict against burying within the walls of cities was either inapplicable or not enforced, the open court before the church became the place of burial.*

Christian funerals began early in their period of security and opulence to be celebrated with great magnificence. Jerome compares the funeral procession of Fabiola to the triumphs of Camillus, Scipio, or Pompey. The character of this female, who founded the first hospital in Rome, and lavished a splendid fortune in alms-giving, may have mainly contributed to the strong interest excited by her interment. All Rome was poured forth. The streets, the windows, the tops of houses, were crowded with spectators. Processions of youths and of old men preceded the bier, chaunting the praises of the deceased. As it passed, the churches were crowded, and psalms were sung, and their golden roofs rang with the sublime Alleluia.

The doctrine of the Resurrection of the body deepened the common and natural feeling of respect for the remains of the dead: † the

Worship of the Martyrs.

---

* There is a law of Gratian, Valentinian and Theodosius, forbidding burial, or the deposition of urns (which shows that cremation was still common), within the walls of Constantinople, even within the cemeteries of the apostles or martyrs. Cod. Theod. ix. 17. 6.

† In one of the very curious essays of M. Raoul Rochette, Mémoires de l'Académie, he has illustrated the extraordinary care with which the heathen buried along with the remains of the dead, every kind of utensil, implement of trade, down to the dolls of children; even food and knives and forks. This appears from all the tombs which are opened, from the most ancient Etruscan to the most modern heathen sepulchres. "Il y avait là une notion confuse et grossière sans doute de l'immortalité de l'âme, mais il s'y trouvait aussi la preuve sensible et palpable de cet instinct de l'homme, qui répugne à l'idée de la destruction de son être, et qui y résiste de toutes les forces de son intelligence et de toutes les erreurs même de la raison." p. 689. But it is a more remarkable fact that the Christians long adhered

worship of the relics of saints and martyrs still further contributed to the same effect. If the splendid but occasional ceremony of the apotheosis of the deceased emperor was exploded, a ceremony which, lavished as it frequently had been on the worst and basest of mankind, however it might amuse and excite the populace, could not but provoke the contempt of the virtuous; in the Christian world a continual, and in some respects more rational, certainly more modest, apotheosis was constantly celebrated. The more distinguished Christians were dismissed, if not to absolute deification, to immortality, to a state, in which they retained profound interest in, and some influence over, the condition of men. During the perilous and gloomy

to the same usage, notwithstanding the purer and loftier notions of another life bestowed by their religion. "La première observation qui s'offre à Boldetti lui-même et qui devra frapper tous les esprits, c'est qu'en décorant les tombeaux de leurs frères de tant d'objets de par ornement, ou d'usage réel, les Chrétiens n'avaient pu être dirigés que par ce motif d'espérance qui leur faisait considérer le tombeau comme un lieu de passage, d'où ils devaient sortir avec toutes les conditions de l'immortalité, et la mort, comme un sommeil paisible, au sein duquel il ne pouvait leur être indifférent de se trouver environnés des objets qui leur avaient été chers durant la vie ou de l'image de ces objets." Tom. iii. p. 692.

The heathen practice of burying money, sometimes large sums, with the dead, was the cause of the very severe laws against the violations of the tombs. In fact, these treasures were so great, as to be a source of revenue, which the Government was unwilling to share with unlicensed plunderers. "Et si aurum, ut dicitur, vel argentum fuerit tuâ indagatione detectum, compendio publico fideliter vindicabis, ita tamen ut abstinentia a cineribus mortuorum. Ædificis legant cineres, columnæ vel marmora ornent sepulcra: talenta non teneant, qui commercia vivorum reliquerunt. Aurum enim jussà sepulcro detrahitur, ubi dominus non habetur; imò culpæ genus est inutiliter abdita relinquere mortuorum, unde se vita potest sustentare viventium." Such are the instructions of the minister of Theodoric. Cassiod. Var. iv. 34.

But it is still more strange, that the Christians continued this practice, particularly of the piece of money in the mouth, which the Heathen intended for the payment of Charon. It continued to the time of Thomas Aquinas, who, according to M. R. Rochette, wrote against it.

days of persecution, the reverence for those who endured martyrdom for the religion of Christ had grown up out of the best feelings of man's improved nature. Reverence gradually grew into veneration, worship, adoration. Although the more rigid theology maintained a marked distinction between the honours shown to the martyrs and that addressed to the Redeemer and the Supreme Being, the line was too fine and invisible not to be transgressed by excited popular feeling. The Heathen writers constantly taunt the Christians with the substitution of the new idolatry for the old. The charge of worshipping dead men's bones and the remains of malefactors, constantly recurs. A Pagan philosopher, as late as the fourth century, contemptuously selects some barbarous names of African martyrs, and inquires whether they are more worthy objects of worship than Minerva or Jove.[f]

The festivals in honour of the martyrs were avowedly instituted, or at least conducted on a sumptuous scale, in rivalry of the banquets which formed so important and attractive a part of the Pagan ceremonial.[b] Besides the earliest Agapæ, which gave place to the more solemn Eucharist, there were other

Festivals

---

[f] " Quis enim ferat Jovi fulmina vibranti præferri Mygdonem ; Junoni, Minervæ, Veneri, Vestæque Sanxem, et cunctis (pro nefas) Diis immortalibus archimartyrem Nymphanionem, inter quos Lucitas haud minore cultu suscipitur atque alii interminato numero ; Diisque hominibusque odiosa nomina." See Augustin. Epist. xvi. p. 20.

[b] "Cum facta pace, turbæ Gentilium in Christianum nomen venire cupientes, hoc impediretur, quod dies festos cum idolis suis solerent in abundantiâ epularum et ebrietate consumere, nec facilè ab his perniciosissimis et tam vetustissimis voluptatibus se possent abstinere, visum fuisse majoribus nostris, ut huic infirmitati parti interim parceretur, diesque festos, post eos, quos relinquebant, alios in honorem sanctorum martyrum vel eos similli sacrilegio, quamvis simili luxu celebrarent." Augustin. Epist. xlix. p. 52.

kinds of banquets, at marriages and funerals, called likewise Agapæ;[1] but those of the martyrs were the most costly and magnificent. The former were of a more private nature; the poor were entertained at the cost of the married couple or the relatives of the deceased. The relationship of the martyrs extended to the whole Christian community, and united all in one bond of piety. They belonged, by a new tie of spiritual kindred, to the whole Church.

By a noble metaphor, the day of the martyrs' death was considered that of their birth to immortality; and their birthdays became the most sacred and popular festivals of the Church.[k] At their sepulchres,[m] or more frequently, as the public worship became more costly, in stately churches erected either over their sepulchres, or in some more convenient situation but dedicated to their honour, these holy days commenced with the most impressive religious service. Hymns were sung in their praise (much of the early Christian poetry was composed for these occasions); the history of their lives and martyrdoms was read[n] (the legends which

---

[1] Gregory Nazianzen mentions the three kinds. Οὐδ᾽ ἱερὴν ἐπὶ δαῖτα γενέθλιον, ἠδὲ θανόντων, Ἢ τινα νυμφιδίην σὺν πλεονέσσι θέων. Carm. 1.

[k] Γενέθλια, natalitia. This custom was as early as the time of Polycarp. The day of his martyrdom was celebrated by the Church of Antioch, Euseb. lib. iv. 15. Compare Suicer, in voce γενέθλιον. Tertullian instances the offerings for the dead, and the annual celebration of the birthdays of the martyrs as of Apostolic tradition. "Oblationes pro defunctis, in natalibus annuâ die facimus." De Coron. Mil. c. 2. Compare Exhortat. ad Cast. c. 11. In the treatise de Monogamiâ, he considers it among the sacred duties of a faithful widow, "offert annuis diebus dormitionis ejus."

[m] At Antioch, the remains of St. Juventinus and St. Maximinus were placed in a sumptuous tomb, and honoured with an annual festival. Theodoret, E. H. iii. 15.

[n] The author of the Acts of Ignatius wrote them, in part that the day of his martyrdom might be duly honoured. Act. Martyr. Ign. apud Cotelerium, vol. II. p. 161. Compare Acta St. Polycarpi.

FESTIVALS.

grew up into so fertile a subject for Christian mythic fable); panegyrical orations were delivered by the best preachers.º The day closed with an open banquet, in which all the worshippers were invited to partake. The wealthy Heathens had been accustomed to propitiate the Manes of their departed friends by these costly festivals; the banquet was almost an integral part of the Heathen religious ceremony. The custom passed into the Church; and with the Pagan feeling, the festival assumed a Pagan character of gaiety and joyous excitement, and even of luxury.ᵖ In some places, the confluence of worshippers was so great that, as in the earlier, and indeed the more modern religions of Asia, the neighbourhood of the more celebrated churches of the martyrs became marts for commerce, and fairs were established on those holidays.ᑫ

As the evening drew in, the solemn and religious

º There is a law of Theodosius the Great against selling the bodies of martyrs. Cod. Theod. ix. 17. 7.

ᵖ Lipsius considered these Agapæ derived from the Silicernium of the ancients. Ad Tac. Ann. vi. 5. "Quod illa parentalis superstitioni Gentilium essent similia." Such is the observation of Ambrose apud Augustin. Conf. vi. 2. Boldetti, a good Roman Catholic and most learned antiquarian, observes on this and other usages adopted from Paganism,—"Fu anche sentimento de' prelati di chiesa di condescendere con ciò alla debolezza de' convertiti dal Gentilesimo, per istaccarli più soavemente dall' antichi superstizioni, non levando loro affetto ma benzì convertendolo in buoni i loro divertimenti." Osservazioni, p. 46. Compare Marangoni's work "dei Cosa Gentilesche."

ᑫ Already had the Montanist asceticism of Tertullian taken alarm at the abuse of the earlier festival, which had likewise degenerated from its pious use, and with his accustomed vehemence denounced the abuse of the Agapæ among the Catholics. "Apud te Agape in sæculis fervet, fides in cullulis calet, spes in ferculis jacet. Sed major his est Agape, quia per hanc adolescentes tui cum sororibus dormiunt, appendices scilicet gulæ lascivia atque luxuria est." De Jejun. c. xvii.

There are many paintings in the catacombs representing Agapæ. Raoul Rochette, Mém. des Inscrip. p. 141. The author attributes to the Agapæ held in the cemeteries, many of the cups, glasses, &c. found in the catacombs.

thoughts gave way to other emotions; the wine flowed freely, and the healths of the martyrs were pledged, not unfrequently, to complete inebriety. All the luxuries of the Roman banquet were imperceptibly introduced. Dances were admitted, pantomimic spectacles were exhibited,[r] the festivals were prolonged till late in the evening, or to midnight, so that other criminal irregularities profaned, if not the sacred edifice, its immediate neighbourhood.

The bishops had for some time sanctioned these pious hilarities with their presence; they had freely partaken of the banquets, and their attendants were accused of plundering the remains of the feast, which ought to have been preserved for the use of the poor.[s]

But the scandals which inevitably arose out of these paganised solemnities awoke the slumbering vigilance of the more serious prelates. The meetings were gradually suppressed: they are denounced, with the strongest condemnation of the luxury and license with which they were celebrated in the church of Antioch, by Gregory of Nazianzum[t] and by Chrysostom. They were autho-

---

[r] Böttiger, in his prolusion on the four ages of the drama (Opera Lat. p. 326), supposed, from a passage of St. Augustine, that there were scenic representations of the deaths of martyrs. Müller justly observes that the passage does not bear out this inference; and Augustine would scarcely have used such expressions unless of dances or mimes of less decent kind. "Sanctum locum invaserat pestilentia et petulantia saltationis; per totam noctem cantabantur nefaria, et cantantibus saltabatur." Augustin. in Natal. Cyprian. p. 311.

[s] See the poem of Greg. Naz. de Div. Vit. Gener. Jerome admits the gross evils which took place during these feasts, but ascribes them to the irregularities of a youthful people, which ought not to raise a prejudice against the religion, or even against the usage. The bishops were sometimes called ρεμβόδμοι, feastlers on the dead.

[t] Carm. cxxviii., cxxix., and Oratio vi. Chrysostom, Hom. in. S. M. Julian.

ritatively condemned by a canon of the Council of Laodicea. In the West, they were generally held in Rome, and in other Italian cities, to a later period. The authority of Ambrose had discountenanced, if not entirely abolished them, in his diocese of Milan. They prevailed to the latest time in the churches of Africa, where they were vigorously assailed by the eloquence of Augustine. The Bishop of Hippo appeals to the example of Italy and other parts of the West, in which they had never prevailed, and in which, wherever they had been known, they had been suppressed by common consent. But Africa did not surrender them without a struggle. The Manichean Faustus, in the ascetic spirit of his sect, taunts the orthodox with their idolatrous festivals. "You have but substituted your Agapæ for the sacrifices of the Heathen; in the place of their idols you have set up your martyrs, whom you worship with the same ceremonies as the Pagans their gods. You appease the Manes of the dead with wine and with meat-offerings." The answer of Augustine indignantly repels the charge of idolatry, and takes refuge in the subtile distinction in the nature of the worship offered to the martyrs. "The reverence paid to martyrs is the same with that offered to holy men in this life, only offered more freely, because they have finally triumphed in their conflict. We adore God alone, we offer sacrifice to no martyr, or to the soul of any saint, or to any angel. * * Those who intoxicate themselves by the sepulchres of the martyrs are condemned by sound doctrine. It is a different thing to approve, and to tolerate till we can amend. The discipline of Christians is one thing, the sensuality of those who thus indulge in drunkenness and the infirmity of the weak is another."

So completely, however, had they grown into the habits of the Christian community, that in many places they lingered on in obstinate resistance to the eloquence of the great teachers of Christianity. Even the Councils pronounced with hesitating and tardy severity the sentence of condemnation against these inveterate usages, to which the people adhered with such strong attachment. That of Carthage prohibited the attendance of the clergy, and exhorted them to persuade the people, as far as possible, to abstain from these festivals; that of Orleans condemns the singing, dancing, or dissolute behaviour, in churches; that of Agde (Sens) condemns secular music, the singing of women, and banquets, in that place of which "it is written that it is a house of prayer;" finally, that in Trullo, held at Constantinople, as late as the beginning of the eighth century, prohibits the decking of tables in churches (the prohibition indicates the practice): and at length it provoked a formal sentence of excommunication.

---

⁷ Cont. Faust. lib. xx. c. xxi. One of the poems of St. Paulinus of Nola describes the general concourse to these festivals, and the riots which arose out of them.

"En nase esse frequentes
Per totum et vigiles extendunt gaudia
noctem.
Lætitia numeros, tenebras funalibus arcent.
Verum utinam sanis agerent hæc gaudia
votis,
Nec sua limitibus miscerent gaudia sanctis.
. . . ignoscenda tamen puto talia parens
Gaudia quæ ducant epulis, quia ancutibus
errur
Irrepit radibus, imo tanta muscula culpæ

Simplicitas pietate indit, male credula sanctus
Perfuncta halente mero gaudere sepulcris."
Carmen ix. in St. Felicem Martyrem.

⁸ It is high time that the catacombs should be withdrawn from the domain of Polemics and, if not of Poetry, of Romance, to that of sober History. According to the language of many modern writers, it would be supposed that for the first three centuries the Catacombs were the ordinary dwellings, the only places of divine worship for the Christians of

PROFANE SPECTACLES.

But notwithstanding all its efforts to divert and pre-occupy the mind by these graver or at least primarily religious spectacles, the passion for theatrical amusements was too strong to be repressed by

Profane spectacles.

Rome. A noble author, never to be mentioned without respect, writes about a whole population living in these dens and caves of the earth (Lord Lindsay, 'Christian Art,' i. pp. 4, 5). Even M. de Pressensé writes of the Church 'of the Catacombs, (i. 367). Cardinal Wiseman, though he has prudently laid the scene of his romance in the time of Diocletian, leads to the inference that those days represent the ordinary life of the Roman Christians of the first three centuries. It is assumed, or insinuated, that the whole period was a continuous persecution, that the Christians were (lucifugæ) obliged to shroud themselves from the eye of day; to conceal their ordinary worship and their mysteries alike under the earth. It might be supposed that Dodwell's unanswered and unanswerable Treatise de Paucitate Martyrum had never been written. In truth there was no general persecution of the Christians in Rome, from the reign of Nero, A.C. 65, to that of Decius, 249-251. During that period the Christians were in general as free and secure as other inhabitants of Rome. Their assemblies were no more disturbed than the synagogues of the Jews, or the rites of other foreign religions. How much earlier we know not, but we know that they had churches in the reign of Alexander Severus. The first Martyr-Pope, after apostolic times, was Fabianus in the reign of Decius. From this first terrible but brief onslaught under Decius, in which Cornelius, the successor of Fabianus also perished, to the general, and more merciless persecution under Diocletian and Galerius (A.C. 303) there were periods of local and very barbarous trial in many parts of the empire; the Roman Christians may not have escaped in the times of Claudius and Aurelian: but of any Roman persecution there is no trustworthy record; nor of any martyr-pope. Though it may have been occasionally interrupted, the public worship of Christ disdained concealment, lurked not in secret places, but confronted authority, and asserted its privilege of Roman citizenship.

No doubt from the profound reverence for the dead (deepened by the belief in perhaps the speedy resurrection of the body) there were in all the catacombs, what we may call mortuary chapels (one has been found in one of the Jewish catacombs) in which some funeral ceremony was performed; and to which the bereaved Christian would resort to mourn over the remains of the parent, the wife, or husband, or the child prematurely laid to rest. Sorrow would find its consolation in prayer. Natural grief, the quiet assurance of the peace in which the departed slept, the hope, the confidence in their immortality, all which the submissive, or rather rejoicing faith expresses so simply and so beautifully in all the earlier epitaphs, would lead to the more devout worship of God in these holy places. Nor would that be the natural and spontaneous offering of

Christianity. It succeeded in some humane improvements, but, in some parts, it was obliged to yield to the ungovernable torrent. The populace of an empire threatened on all sides by dangerous enemies, oppressed by a remorseless tyranny, notwithstanding the remonstrances of a new and dominant religion, imperiously demanded, and recklessly enjoyed, their accustomed diversions.* In some places, that which had been a delight became a madness; and it was a Christian city which first broke out in sedition and insurrection, whose streets ran with blood, from the rivalry of two factions in the circus. The Heathen World was degenerate even in its diversions. It was not the nobler drama of Greece, or even that of Rome; neither the stately tragedy, nor even the fine comedy of manners, for which the mass of the people endured the stern remonstrances of the Christian orator; but spectacles of far less intellectual pretensions, and far more likely to be injurious to Christian morals. The higher drama, indeed, was not,

---

private sorrow alone. The sepulchres of distinguished Christians, distinguished for Christian virtues of holiness and charity, would assemble the sad but at the same time triumphant Christians to celebrate the departure of such men from the sinful world—their departure to their Redeemer, Christ. Out of this reverent sorrow would grow, in times like the Decian persecution, over the graves of martyred bishops, like Fabianus and Cornelius, or in the more terrible persecution under Diocletian, that which in later times became the worship of the martyrs themselves. By the time of Jerome, this worship had become more common. To visit the tombs of the martyrs became a kind of pilgrimage. It is but in the course of things that martyr-worship multiplied the martyrs; till, after centuries, the whole line of Popes which are now deduced from St. Peter, become, according to some not very scrupulous or authentic lists, excepting one unfortunate Greek, honoured by this holy title.

* In the fifth century, Treves, four times desolated by the barbarians, no sooner recovered its freedom, than it petitioned for the games of the circus. "Ubique facies captæ urbis, ubique terror captivitatis, ubique imago mortis, jacent reliquiæ infelicissimæ plebis super tumulos mortuorum suorum, et in circenses rogas." Compare the whole passage, Salvian, de Gub. Del, vi.

as I shall show hereafter, entirely obsolete, but comparatively rare and unattractive.

The Heathen calendar still regulated the amusements of the people.[b] Nearly 100 days in the year were set apart as festivals; the commencement of every month was dedicated to the public diversions. Besides these, there were extraordinary days of rejoicing, a victory, the birthday of the reigning Emperor, or the dedication of his statue by the prefect or the provincials of any city or district. On the accession of a new Emperor, processions always took place, which ended in the exhibition of games.[c] The dedication of statues to the Emperors by different cities, great victories, and other important events, were always celebrated with games. The Christians obtained a law from Theodosius, that games should be prohibited on the Lord's day. The African bishops, in the fifth Council of Carthage, petitioned that this prohibition might be extended to all Christian holidays. They urged that many members of the corporate bodies were obliged

Heathen calendar.

---

[b] The ordinary calendar of holidays, on which the courts of law did not sit, at the close of the fourth century, is given by Godefroy (note on the Cod. Theodos. lib. ii. viii. 11.).

Feriæ æstivæ (harvest)	-	-	xxx
Feriæ autumnales (vintage)	-	-	xxx
Kalendæ Januarii	-	-	iii
Natalitia urbis Romæ	-	-	i
urbis Constantin.	-	-	i
Paschæ	-	-	xv
Dies Solis,[1] circiter	-	-	xlii
Natalitia Imperatorum	-	-	iv
			cxiv

Christmas-day, Epiphany, and Pentecost, were not as yet general holidays.

[c] The Constantinian Calendar (Græ-vii Thesaur. viii.) reckons ninety-six days for the games, of which but few were peculiar to Rome. Müller, ii. p. 49.

[1] The other Sundays were comprised in the summer, autumnal, and Easter holidays.

officially to attend on these occasions, and prevented from fulfilling their religious duties. The law of Theodosius the Elder had inhibited the celebration of games on Sundays,[4] one of the Younger Theodosius added, at Christmas, the Epiphany, Easter, and Pentecost, and directed that on those days the theatres should be closed, not only to the Christians, but to the impious Jews and superstitious Pagans.[e] But, notwithstanding this law, which must have been imperfectly carried into execution, the indignant preachers still denounce the rivalry of the games, which withdrew so many of their audience.[f] The Theoretica

The Theoretica. or fund for the expenses of public shows and amusements, which existed not only in the two capitals, but in all the larger cities of the Empire, was first confiscated to the imperial treasury by Justinian. Up to that time, the imperial policy had sanctioned and enforced this expenditure; and it is remarkable that this charge, which had been so long voluntarily borne by the ambition or the vanity of the higher orders, was first imposed as a direct tax on individuals by a Christian Emperor. By a law of Constantine, the Senate of Rome and of Constantinople were empowered to designate any person of a certain rank and fortune for the costly function of exhibiting games in these two great cities.[g] These were in addition to the spectacles exhibited by the consuls. In the other cities decemvirs were nominated to this office.[h] The only exemptions were

---

[4] Cod. Theod. xv. v. 2.
[e] Cod. Theod. xv. t. 5. L 5. A.D. 425. Müller, p. 50.
[f] See, for the earlier period, Apostolic Constit. ii. 60, 61, 62; Theophyl. ad Autolyc. iii. p. 396; for the later, Chrysostom, passe passim, Hom. contra Ant.; Hom. in princip. Act. L 58;

Hom. in Johann.
[g] Zosim. lib. ii. c. 38.
[h] See various laws of Constantius, regulating the office, the expenses, the fines imposed on the prætors, Cod. Theodos. vi. 3; Laws L 1-33. This shows the importance attached to the office. These munerarii, as well as

nonage, military or civil service, or a special indulgence from the Emperor. Men fled from their native cities to escape this onerous distinction. But if the charge was thrown on the treasury, the treasury could recover from the prætor or decemvir, besides assessing heavy fines for the neglect of the duty; and they were liable to be condemned to serve two years instead of one. In the Eastern provinces, this office had been joined with a kind of high-priesthood, such were the Asiarchs, the Syriarchs,[l] the Bithyniarchs. The most distinguished men of the province had been proud of accepting the station of chief minister of the gods, at the expense of these sumptuous festivities. The office remained under the Christian Emperors,[k] but had degenerated into a kind of purveyorship for the public pleasures. A law of Theodosius enacted that this office should not be imposed on any one who refused to undertake it.[m] Another law, from which, however, the Asiarchs were excluded,

---

the actors, were to do penance all their lives. Act. Conc. Illeb. can. 3. Compare Bingham, xvi. 4. 8. This same council condemned all who took the office of decemvir to a year's exclusion from the communion. Bingham, ubi supra.

[l] Malala, Chronograph. lib. xii. in art. Codex Theodos. vi. 3. 1.

[k] The "tribunus voluptatum" appears as a title on a Christian tomb. Bosio, Roma Sotterranea, p. 106. Compare the observations of Bosio.

[m] Cod. Theodos. xil. 1. 103. Compare the quotations from Libanius, in Godefroy's Commentary. There is a sumptuary law of Theodosius II. limiting the expenses: "Nec incondita plausorum insania curialium vires, fortunas civium, principalium domus,

possessorum opes, reipublicæ robur evellant." The Alytarchs, Syriarchs, Asiarchs, and some others, are exempted from this Law. C. T. xv. 9. 2. In Italy, at a later period, the reign of Theoderic, the public games were provided by the liberality of the Gothic sovereign: "Beatitudo alit temporum lætitia populorum." Cassiodorus, epist. i. 20. The Epistles of Theoderic's minister are full of provisions and regulations for the celebration of the various kinds of games. Lib. l. epist. 20, 27, 30, 31, 32, 33, lii. 51, iv. 37. Theoderic espoused the green faction; he supported the pantomime. There were still tribuni voluptatum at Rome, vi. 6. Stipends were allowed to scenici, ix. 21.

attempted to regulate the expenditure between the
mean parsimony of some, and the prodigality of others."
Those who voluntarily undertook the office of exhibiting
games were likewise exempted from this sumptuary law,
for there were still some, ambitious of this kind of
popularity. They were proud of purchasing at this
enormous price, the honour of seeing their names displayed on tablets to the wondering multitude,° and of
being drawn in their chariots through the applauding
city on the morning of the festival.

Throughout the empire, this passion prevailed in every
city,ᵖ and in all classes. From early morning to late
in the evening, the theatres were crowded in every
part.ᵠ The artisan deserted his work, the merchant
his shop, the slaves followed their masters, and were
admitted into the vast circuit. Sometimes, when the
precincts of the circus or amphitheatre were insufficient
to contain the thronging multitudes, the adjacent hills
were crowded with spectators, anxious to obtain a glimpse
of the distant combatants, or to ascertain the colour of
the victorious charioteer. The usages of the East and
of the West differed as to the admission of women to
these spectacles. In the East, they were excluded by
the general sentiment from the theatre.ʳ Nature itself,

ⁿ Symmachus, lib. x. epist. 28, 43.
Compare Heyne, Opuscula, vi. p. 14.

° Basil, in Psal. 61. Prudent.
Hamartigenia.

ᵖ Müller names the following cities,
besides the four great capitals, Rome,
Constantinople, Antioch, and Alexandria, in which the games are alluded
to by ancient authors, Gortyna, Nicomedia, Laodicea, Tyre, Berytus, Cæsarea, Heliopolis, Gaza, Ascalon,
Jerusalem, Berea, Corinth, Cirta,

Carthage, Syracuse, Catania, Milan,
Aquileia, Ravenna, Mentz, Cologne,
Treves, Arles. p. 53.

ᵠ Augustine, indeed, asserts, " per
omnes ferè civitates cadunt theatra
cavea turpitudinum, et publicæ pro-
fessiones flagitiorum." De Cons. Evangelist. c. 51.

ʳ There are one or two passages of
the Fathers opposed to this opinion.
Tatian says, τοὺς θεοὺς δεῖ μοιχεύων
ἐπὶ τῆς σκηνῆς σοφιστεύοντας αἱ

observes St. Chrysostom, enforces this prohibition.* It arose, not out of Christianity, but out of the manners of the East; it is alluded to not as a distinction, but as a general usage.‘ Chrysostom laments that women, though they did not attend the games, were agitated by the factions of the circus." In the West, the greater freedom of the Roman women had long asserted and still maintained this privilege.* It is well known that the vestal virgins had their seats of honour in the Roman spectacles, even those which might have been supposed most repulsive to feminine gentleness and delicacy; and the Christian preachers of the West remonstrate as strongly against the females as against the men, on account of their inextinguishable attachment to the public spectacles.

The more austere and ascetic Christian teachers condemned alike all these popular spectacles. From the avowed connection with Paganism, as to the time of their celebration,' their connection with the worship of Pagan deities, according to the accredited notion that all these deities were dæmons permitted to delude mankind, the theatre was considered a kind of temple of the Evil Spirit.[a] There were some, however, who openly vindicated these public exhibitions, and alleged the chariot of Elijah, the dancing of David, and the quotations of St. Paul from dramatic writers, as cases in point.

These public spectacles were of four kinds, independent of the common and more vulgar exhibitions, juggling, rope-dancing, and tumbling.[a]

Four kinds of spectacles.

I. The old gymnastic games. The Olympic games survived in Greece till the invasion of Alaric.[b] Antioch likewise celebrated this quinquennial festivity; youths of station and rank exhibited themselves as boxers and wrestlers. These games were also retained at Rome and in parts of Africa:[c] it is uncertain whether they were introduced into Constantinople. The various passages of Chrysostom which allude to them probably were delivered in Antioch. Something of the old honour adhered to the wrestlers and performers in these games: they either were, or were supposed to be, of respectable station and unblemished character. The herald advanced into the midst of the arena and made his proclamation, "that any man should

Gymnastic games.

---

[a] See the book de Spect., attributed to St. Cyprian. The author calls Idolatry, "Ludorum omnium mater." "Quod etim spectaculum sine idolo, quis ludus sine sacrificio (De spectaculis). Ludorum celebrationes deorum festa sunt." Lactant. Inst. Div. vi. 20.

[c] Compare the references to Chrysostom's works on the rope dancers, jugglers, &c. in Montfaucon, Diatribe, p. 194.

[b] Liban. de Vocat. ad Festa Olympiæ.

"Cuncta Palæsmnilis manus explorata cœnobis
Adsit, et Eleo pubes landata Tonanti."
Claudian, de Ft. Mal. Cons. 288.
This, however, may be poetic reminiscence. These exhibitions are described as conducted with greater decency and order (probably because they awoke less passionate interest) than those of the circus or theatre.

[c] They were restored in Africa, by a law of Gratian, A.D. 376. Cod. Theod. xv. 7. 3.

come forward who had any charge against any one of the men about to appear before them, as a thief, a slave, or of bad reputation."[d]

II. Theatrical exhibitions, properly so called. The higher tragedy and comedy were still repre- Tragedy and sented on the inauguration of the consuls at comedy. Rome. Claudian names actors of the sock and buskin, the performers of genuine comedy and tragedy, as exhibiting on the occasion of the consulship of Mallius.[e] During the triumph of the Christian Emperors Theodosius and Arcadius, the theatre of Pompey was filled by chosen actors from all parts of the world. Two actors in tragedy and comedy[f] are named as standing in the same relation to each other as the famous Æsopus and the comic Roscius. Prudentius speaks of the tragic mask as still in use; and it appears that females acted those parts in Terence which were formerly represented by men.[g] The youthful mind of Augustine took delight in being agitated by the fictitious sorrows of the stage.[h] Nor was this higher branch of the art extinct in the East: tragic and comic actors are named, with other histrionic performers, in the orations of Chrysostom,[i] and there are allusions in Libanius to mythological tragic fables and to the comedies of Menander.[k] But as these representations, after they had ceased to be integral parts of the Pagan worship, were less eagerly denounced by the Christian teachers,[m] the comparatively slight and

---

[d] Compare Montfaucon's Diatribe, p. 194.
[e] "Qui pulpita socco Personat, aut alto graditur majore cothurno." In Cons. Mall. 313.
"Pompeiana proscenia delectis actoribus personarent." Symmach. lib. x. ep. 29.
[f] Publius Pollio and Ambivius. Symmach. epist. x. 2.

[g] Donatus in Andriam, act. iv. sc. 3.
[h] Confess. iii. 2.
[i] Chrysostom, Hom. 10 in Coloss. v. ii. p. 403; Hom. 6 in Terræ mot. i. 780. i. p. 38. i. 731.
[k] Liban. vol. ii. p. 375.
[m] Lactantius inveighs with all the

scanty notices in their writings, almost our only records of the manners of the time, by no means prove the infrequency of these representations; though it is probable, for other reasons, that the barbarous and degraded taste was more gratified by the mimes and pantomimes, the chariot races of the circus, and the wild-beasts in the amphitheatre.[a] But tragedy and comedy, at this period, were probably maintained rather to display the magnificence of the consul or prætor, who prided himself on the variety of his entertainments, and were applauded, perhaps,[o] by professors of rhetoric, and a few faithful admirers of antiquity, rather than by the people at large. Some have supposed that the tragedies written on religious subjects in the time of Julian were represented on the stage; but there is no ground for this notion; these were intended as school books, to supply the place of Sophocles and Menander.

In its degeneracy, the higher Drama had long been supplanted by,—1st, the Mimes. Even this kind of drama, perhaps of Roman, or even of earlier Italian origin, had degenerated into the coarsest scurrility, and, it should seem, the most repulsive indecency. Formerly it had been the representation of some incident in common life, extemporaneously dramatised by the mime, ludicrous in its general character,

Mimes.

---

energy of the first ages against tragedy and comedy:—"Tragicæ historiæ subjiciunt oculis patricidia et incesta regum malorum, et cothurnata scelera demonstrant. Comicæ de stupris virginum et amiciliis meretricum; et quo magis suni eloquentes, eo magis persuadent, facilius inhærent memoriæ versus numeroni et ornati." Instit. vi. 20.

[a] Augustine, however, draws a distinction between these two classes of theatric representations and the lower kind:—"Scenicorum tolerabiliora ludorum, comœdiæ scilicet et tragœdiæ, hoc est fabulæ poëtarum, agendæ in spectaculo multâ rerum turpitudine, sed nullâ saltem, sicut aliæ multæ, verborum obscœnitate compositæ, quas etiam inter studia, quæ liberalia vocantur, pueri legere et discere coguntur a senibus." De Civ. Dei, lib. ii. c. 8.

[o] Müller, p. 139.

mingled at times with sharp or even grave and sententious satire. Such were the mimes of Laberius, to which republican Rome had listened with delight. It was now the lowest kind of buffoonery. The mime, or several mimes, both male and female, appeared in ridiculous dresses, with shaven crowns, and, pretending still to represent some kind of story, poured forth their witless obscenity, and indulged in all kinds of practical jokes and manual wit, blows on the face and broken heads. The music was probably the great charm, but that had become soft, effeminate, and lascivious. The female performers were of the most abandoned character,[p] and scenes were sometimes exhibited of the most abominable indecency, even if we do not give implicit credit to the malignant tales of Procopius concerning the exhibitions of the Empress Theodora, when she performed as a dancing girl in these disgusting mimes.[q]

2nd. The Pantomime was a kind of ballet in action.[r] It was the mimic representation of all the old tragic and mythological fables, without words,[s]

Pantomimes.

[p] Many passages of Chrysostom might be quoted, in which he speaks of the naked courtesans, meaning probably with the most transparent clothing (though women were exhibited at Antioch swimming in an actual state of nudity), who performed in these mimes. The more severe Christian preacher is confirmed by the language of the Heathen Zosimus, whose bitter hatred to Christianity induces him to attribute their most monstrous excesses to the reign of the Christian Emperor. Μῖμοί τε γὰρ γελοίων, καὶ οἱ κακῶς ἀπολούμενοι ὀρχησταί, καὶ πᾶν δ' τι πρὸς αἰσχρότητα καὶ τὴν ἄτοπον ταύτην καὶ ἐκμελῆ συντελεῖ μουσικῆν, ηὐξήθη τε ἐπὶ τούτου. Lib. iv. c. 33.

[q] Müller, 92, 103.

[r] Libanius is indignant that man should attempt to confound the orchestæ or pantomimes with these degraded and infamous mimes. Vol. iii. p. 350. The pantomimes wore masks, the mimes had their faces uncovered, and usually had shaven crowns.

[s] The pantomimi or dancers represented their parts,—

"Clausis faucibus et loquente manu,
Nutu, crure, genu, manu, rotato."
Sid. Apol.

or intermingled with chants or songs.[1] These exhibitions were got up at times with great splendour of scenery, which was usually painted on hanging curtains, and with musical accompaniments of the greatest variety. The whole cycle of mythology,[a] both of the gods and heroes, was represented by the dress and mimic gestures of the performer. The deities, both male and female,—Jupiter, Pluto, and Mars; Juno, Proserpine, Venus; Theseus and Hercules; Achilles, with all the heroes of the Trojan war; Phædra, Briseis, Atalanta; the race of Œdipus; these are but a few of the dramatic personages which, on the authority of Libanius,[x] were personated by the pantomimes of the East. Sidonius Apollinaris[y] fills twenty-five lines with those represented in the West by the celebrated dancers Caramalus and Phabaton.[z] These included the old fables of Medea and Jason, of the house of Thyestes, of Tereus and Philomela, Jupiter and Europa, and Danae, and Leda, and Ganymede, Mars and Venus, Perseus and Andromeda. In the West, the female parts thus exhibited were likewise represented by women[a] of whom there were no less than 3000 in Rome:[b] and so important were these females considered to the public amusement, that, on the expulsion of all strangers from the city during a famine, an excep-

---

[1] There was sometimes a regular chorus, with instrumental music. Sid. Apoll. xxiii. 268, and probably poetry composed for the occasion. Müller, p. 122.

[a] Greg. Nyssen. in Galland. Bibliothec. Patrum, vi. p. 610. Ambrose, in Hexaem. iii. 1. 5. Synes. de Prov. 9. p. 128, ed. Petav. Symmach. i. ep. 89.

[x] Liban. pro Salt. v. iii. 391.

[y] Sidon. Apoll. carm. xxiii. v. 267, 299.

[z] Claudian mentions a youth, who, before the pit, which thundered with applause,—

"Aut rigidam Nioben aut Sontem Tronda fingit."

[a] Even in Constantinople, women acted in the pantomimes. Chrysostom, Hom. 6 in Thessalon., denounces the performance of Phædra and Hippolytus, by women: 'Ἀσνὴρ σώματος τόσῳ φαινομένοις.

[b] Ammian. Marcell., xiv. 6.

tion was made by the prætor, in deference to the popular wishes, in favour of this class alone. The profession, however, was considered infamous, and the indecency of their attire upon the public stage justified the low estimate of their moral character. Their attractions were so dangerous to the Roman youth, that a special law prohibited the abduction of these females from their public occupation, whether the enamoured lover withdrew one of them from the stage as his mistress, or, as not unfrequently happened, with the more honourable title of wife.^c The East, though it sometimes endured the appearance of women in those parts, often left them to be performed by boys, with any thing but advantage to general morality. The aversion of Christianity to the subjects exhibited by the pantomimes, almost invariably moulded up as they were with Paganism, as well as its high moral sense (united, perhaps, with something of the disdain of ancient Rome for the histrionic art, which it patronised nevertheless with inexhaustible ardour), branded the performers with the deepest mark of public contempt. They were, as it were, public slaves, and could not abandon their profession.^d They were considered unfit to mingle with respectable society; might not appear in the forum or basilica, or use the public baths; they were excluded even from the theatre as spectators, and might not be attended by a slave, with a folding-stool for their use. Even Christianity appeared to extend its mercies and its hopes to this devoted race with some degree of rigour and jealousy. The actor baptized in the apparent agony of death, if he should recover, could not be forced

---

^c Cod. Theodos. xv. 7. 5.
^d Cod. Theodos. xv. 13. Compare Chastel, p. 211, concerning the laws which inflicted dishonour and incapacity on actors.

back upon the stage; but the guardian of the public amusements was to take care, lest, by pretended sickness, the actor should obtain this precious privilege of baptism, and thus exemption from his servitude. Even the daughters of actresses partook of their mothers' infamy, and could only escape being doomed to their course of life by the profession of Christianity, ratified by a certain term of probationary virtue. If the actress relapsed from Christianity, she was invariably condemned to her impure servitude.[e]

Such was the general state of the theatrical exhibitions in the Roman empire at that period. The higher drama, like every other intellectual and inventive art, had to undergo the influence of Christianity before it could revive in its splendid and prolific energy. In all European countries, the Christian mystery, as it was called, has been the parent of tragedy, perhaps of comedy. It reappeared as a purely religious representation, having retained no remembrance whatever of Paganism; and was at one period, perhaps, the most effective teacher, in times of general ignorance and total scarcity of books, both among priests and people, of Christian history as well as of Christian legend.[f]

But at a later period, the old hereditary hostility of Christianity to the theatre has constantly revived. The passages of the Fathers have perpetually been repeated by the more severe preachers, whether fairly applicable or not to the dramatic entertainments of different periods; and in general it has had the effect of keeping the actor in a lower caste of society; a prejudice often productive of the evil which it professed to correct; for men whom the general sentiment considers of

[e] Cod. Theodos. de Scenicis, xv. 7. 2. 4. 6. 9.
[f] The subject is reviewed in Latin Christianity, Book xiv. c. 4.

a low moral order will rarely make the vain attempt at raising themselves above it: if they cannot avoid contempt, they will care little whether they deserve it.

III. The Amphitheatre, with its shows of gladiators and wild-beasts. The suppression of those bloody spectacles, in which human beings slaughtered each other by hundreds for the diversion of their fellow men, is one of the most unquestionable and proudest triumphs of Christianity. The gladiatorial shows, strictly speaking, that is, the mortal combats of men, were never introduced into the less warlike East, though the combats of men with wild-beasts were exhibited in Syria and other parts. The former were Roman in their origin, and to their termination. It might seem that the pride of Roman conquest was not satisfied with the execution of her desolating mandates, unless the whole city witnessed the bloodshed of her foreign captives; and in her decline she seemed to console herself with these sanguinary proofs of her still extensive empire: the ferocity survived the valour of her martial spirit. Barbarian life seemed, indeed, to be of no account, but to contribute to the sports of the Roman. The humane Symmachus, even at this late period,[g] reproves the *impiety* of some Saxon captives, who, by strangling themselves in prison, escaped the ignominy of this public exhibition.[h] It is an humiliating consideration to find how little Roman civilisation had tended to

---

[g] "Quando prohibuisset privatâ custodiâ desperatæ gentis impios manus, cum viginti novem fractis sine laqueo fauces primus ludi gladiatorii dies viderit." Symmach. lib. II. epist. 46.

[h] It is curious that at one time the exposure to wild beasts was considered a more ignominious punishment than fighting as a gladiator. The slave was condemned to the former for kidnapping; the freeman to the latter. Codex Theod. iv. 18. 1.

mitigate the ferocity of manners and of temperament. Not merely did women crowd the amphitheatre during the combats of these fierce and almost naked savages or criminals, but it was the especial privilege of the vestal virgin, even at this late period, to give the signal for the mortal blow, to watch the sword driven deeper into the palpitating entrails.[i] The state of uncontrolled frenzy worked up even the most sober spectators. The manner in which this contagious passion for bloodshed engrossed the whole soul is described with singular power and truth by St. Augustine. A Christian student of the law was compelled by the importunity of his friends to enter the amphitheatre. He sat with his eyes closed, and his mind totally abstracted from the scene. He was suddenly startled from his trance by a tremendous shout from the whole audience. He opened his eyes, he could not but gaze on the spectacle. Directly he beheld the blood, his heart imbibed the common ferocity; he could not turn away; his eyes were riveted on the arena; and the interest, the excitement, the pleasure, grew into complete intoxication. He looked on, he shouted, he was inflamed; he carried away from the amphitheatre an irresistible propensity to return to its cruel enjoyments.[k]

Christianity began to assail this deep-rooted passion of the Roman world with caution, almost with timidity. Christian Constantinople was never defiled with the blood of gladiators. In the same year as that of the Council of Nicæa, a local edict was issued, declaring

---

[i] " Virgo—consurgit ad ictus, | Ni latest pars ulla animæ vitalibus imis,
Et quoties victor ferrum jugulo inserit, illa | Alitha impresso dum palpitat ense secutor."
Delicias ait esse suas, pectusque jacentis | Prudent. adv. Sym. ii. 1096.
Virgo modesta jubet, converso pollice, |
rumpi ; | [k] August. Conf. vi. 8.

the Emperor's disapprobation of these sanguinary exhibitions in time of peace, and prohibiting the volunteering of men as gladiators.[m] This was a considerable step, if we call to mind the careless apathy with which Constantine, before his conversion, had exhibited all his barbarian captives in the amphitheatre at Treves.[n] This edict, however, addressed to the prefect of Phœnicia, had no permanent effect, for Libanius, several years after, boasts that he had not been a spectator of the gladiatorial shows still regularly celebrated in Syria. Constantius prohibited soldiers, and those in the imperial service (Palatini), from hiring themselves out to the Lanistæ, the keepers of gladiators.[o] Valentinian decreed that no Christian or Palatine should be condemned for any crime whatsoever to the arena.[p] An early edict of Honorius prohibited any slave who had been a gladiator[q] from being admitted into the service of a man of senatorial dignity. But Christianity now began to speak in a more courageous and commanding tone.[r] The Christian poet urges on the Christian Emperor the direct prohibition of these inhuman and disgraceful exhibitions.[s] But a single act often affects the public mind much more strongly than even the most eloquent and reiterated exhortation. An Eastern monk, named Telemachus, travelled all the way to Rome, in order to protest against these disgraceful barbarities. In his noble

---

[m] Codex Theodos. xv. 12. 1.
[n] See vol. ii. p. 320.
[o] Codex Theodos. xv. 12. 2.
[p] Ibid. ix. 40. 8.
[q] Codex Theodos. ix. 40. 8.
[r] Ibid. xv. 12. 3.
[s] "Arripe dilatam tua, dux, in tempora famam,

Quodque patri superest, successor laudis habeto.
Ille urbem vetuit taurorum sanguine tingi,
Tu mortes miserorum hominum prohibeto uti:
Nullus in urbe cadat, cujus sit pœna voluptas,
Nec sua virginitas obiciet cædibus ora.
Jam solis contenta feris infamis arena,
Nulla cruentatis homicidia ludat in armis."
Prudent. adv. Sym. ii. 1121.

enthusiasm, he leaped into the arena to separate the combatants; either with the sanction of the prefect, or that of the infuriated assembly, he was torn to pieces, the martyr of Christian humanity.[t] The impression of this awful scene, of a Christian, a monk, thus murdered in the arena, was so profound, that Honorius issued a prohibitory edict, putting an end to these bloody shows. This edict, however, only suppressed the mortal combats of men;[u] the less inhuman, though still brutalising, conflicts of men with wild-beasts seems scarcely to have been abolished[x] till the diminution of wealth, and the gradual contraction of the limits of the empire, cut off both the supply and the means of purchasing these costly luxuries.[y] The revolted or conquered provinces of the South, the East, and the North, no longer rendered up their accustomed tribute of lions from Libya, leopards from the East, dogs of remarkable ferocity from Scotland, of crocodiles and bears, and every kind of wild and rare animal. The Emperor Anthemius prohibited the lamentable spectacles of wild-beasts on the Sunday; and Salvian still inveighs against those bloody exhibitions. And this

---

[t] Theodoret, v. 26.

[u] The law of Honorius is not extant in the Theodosian code, which only retains those of Constantine and Constantius. For this reason, doubts have been thrown on the authority of Theodoret; but there is no recorded instance of gladiatorial combats between man and man since this period. The passage of Salvian, sometimes alleged, refers to combats with wild-beasts,—"Ubi summum deliciarum genus est mori homines, aut quod est mori gravius acerbiusque, lacerari, expleri ferarum alvos humanis carnibus, comedi

homines cum circumstantium lætitiâ, conspicientium voluptate." De Gub. Dei, lib, vi. p. 51.

[x] "Quidquid monstriferis nutrit Gætulia campis, Alpinâ quidquid tegitur nive, Gallicis quiloquid Silva timet, jaceat. Largo ditescat arvum Sanguine, consuman toies spectacula monies."

Claud. in Cons. Mall. 306.

[y] A law of Honorius provides for the supply of wild beasts for the amphitheatre at Constantinople. It is a very curious provision. Cod. Theodos. xv. xi., 2.

amusement gradually degenerated, if the word may be used, not so much from the improving humanity, as from the pusillanimity of the people. Arts were introduced to irritate the fury of the beast, without endangering the person of the combatant. Such arts would have been contemptuously exploded in the more warlike days of the Empire. It became a mere exhibition of skill and agility. The beasts were sometimes tamed before they were exhibited. In the West, those games seem to have sunk with the Western empire;[1] in the East, they lingered on so as to require a special prohibition by the Council in Trullo at Constantinople, at the close of the seventh century.

IV. The chariot race of the circus. If these former exhibitions were prejudicial to the modesty and humanity of the Roman people, the chariot races were no less fatal to their peace. This frenzy did not, indeed, reach its height till the middle of the fifth century, when the animosities of political and religious difference were outdone by factions enlisted in favour of the rival charioteers in the circus. As complete a separation took place in society; adverse parties were banded against each other in as fierce opposition; an insurrection as destructive and sanguinary took place; the throne of the Emperor was as fearfully shaken in the collision of the Blue and Green factions, as ever it had been in defence of the sacred rights of liberty or of faith. Constantinople seemed to concentre on the circus all that absorbing interest, which at Rome was divided by many spectacles. The

The circus. Chariot races

---

[1] Agincourt, Histoire de l'Art, is of opinion that Theodoric substituted military games for theatrical shows, and that these military games were the origin of the tournaments. The wild beast shows were still celebrated at Rome. Cassiod. Epist. v. 42.

Christian city seemed to compensate to itself for the excitement of those games which were prohibited by the religion, by the fury with which it embraced those which were allowed, or rather against which Christianity remonstrated in vain. Her milder tone of persuasiveness, and her more authoritative interdiction, were equally disregarded, where the sovereign and the whole people yielded to the common frenzy. But this consolation remained to Christianity, that when it was accused of distracting the imperial city with religious dissension, it might allege, that this at least was a nobler subject of difference; or rather, that the passions of men seized upon religious distinctions with no greater eagerness than they did on these competitions for the success of a chariot driver in a blue or a green jacket, in order to gratify their inextinguishable love of strife and animosity.

CHAPTER III.

Christian Literature.

CHRISTIANITY was extensively propagated in an age in which Greek and Latin literature had fallen into hopeless degeneracy; nor could even its spirit awaken the dead. Both these languages had already attained and passed their complete developement; they had fulfilled their part in the imaginative and intellectual advancement of mankind; and it seems, in general, as much beyond the power of the genius of a country, as of an individual, to renew its youth. It was not till it had created new languages, or rather till languages had been formed in which the religious notions of Christianity were an elementary and constituent part, that Christian literature assumed its free and natural dignity.

The genius of the new religion never coalesced in perfect and amicable harmony with either the Greek or the Latin tongue. In each case it was a foreign dialect introduced into a fully-formed and completely organised language. The Greek, notwithstanding its exquisite pliancy, with difficulty accommodated itself to the new sentiments and opinions. It had either to endure the naturalisation of new words, or to deflect its own terms to new significations. In the latter case, the doctrines were endangered, in the former, the purity of the language; more especially since the Oriental writers were in general alien to the Grecian mind. The Greek language had indeed long before yielded to the conta-

minating influences of Barbarism. From Homer to
Demosthenes, it had varied in its style and
character, but had maintained its admirable
perfection, as the finest, the clearest, and
most versatile instrument of poetry, oratory,
or philosophy. But the conquests of Greece were as
fatal to her language as to her liberties. The Macedonian, the language of the conquerors, was not the
purest Greek,* and in general, by the extension over a
wider surface, the stream contracted a taint from every
soil over which it flowed. Alexandria was probably
the best school of foreign Grecian style, at least in
literature; in Syria it had always been infected in some
degree by the admixture of Oriental terms. The
Hellenistic style, as it has been called, of the New
Testament, may be considered a fair example of the
language, as it was spoken in the provinces among
persons of no high degree of intellectual culture.

The Latin seemed no less to have fulfilled its
mission and to have passed its culminating
point, in the verse of Virgil and the prose of
Cicero. Its stern and masculine majesty, its plain and
practical vigour, seemed as if it could not outlive the
republican institutions, in the intellectual conflicts of
which it had been formed. The impulse of the old
freedom carried it through the reign of Augustus, but
no further; and it had undergone rapid and progressive
deterioration before it was called upon to discharge its
second office of disseminating and preserving the
Christianity of the West; and the Latin, like the
Greek, had suffered by its own triumphs. Among
the more distinguished Heathen writers, subsequent to

---

* Compare the dissertation of Sturz on the Macedonian dialect, reprinted in | the prolegomena to Valpy's edition of Stephens' Thesaurus.

Augustus, the largest number were of provincial origin; and something of their foreign tone still adhered to their style. Of the best Latin Christian writers, it is remarkable that not one was a Roman, not one, except Ambrose, an Italian. Tertullian, Cyprian, Arnobius (perhaps Lactantius), and Augustine were Africans; the Roman education, and superior understanding of the last, could not altogether refine away that rude provincialism which darkened the whole language of the others. The writings of Hilary are obscured by another dialect of Barbarism. Even at so late a period, whatever exceptions may be made to the taste of his conceptions and of his imagery, with some limitation, the *Roman* style of Claudian, and the structure of his verse, carries us back to the time of Virgil; in Prudentius, it is not merely the inferiority of the poet, but something foreign and uncongenial refuses to harmonise with the adopted poetic language.[b]

Yet it was impossible that such an enthusiasm could be disseminated through the empire without in some degree awakening the torpid languages. The mind could not be so deeply stirred without expressing itself with life and vigour, even if with diminished elegance and dignity. No one can compare the energetic sentences of Chrysostom with the prolix and elaborate, if more correct, periods of Libanius, without acknowledging that a new principle of vitality has been infused into the language.

Christian literature.

But in fact the ecclesiastical Greek and Latin are new dialects of the ancient tongue. Their literature

---

[b] Among the most remarkable productions as to Latinity are the Ecclesiastical History and Life of St. Martin of Tours, by Sulpicius Severus; the legendary matter of which contrasts singularly with the perspicuous and almost classical elegance of the style. See post, on Minucius Felix.

stands entirely apart from that of Greece or Rome. The Greek already possessed the foundation of this literature in the Septuagint version of the Old, and in the original of the New Testament. The Vulgate of Jerome, which almost immediately superseded the older imperfect or inaccurate versions from the Greek, supplied the same groundwork to Latin Christendom. There is something singularly rich and, if I may so speak, picturesque in the Latin of the Vulgate; the Orientalism of the Scripture is blended up with such curious felicity with the idiom of the Latin, that, although far removed either from the colloquial ease of the comic poets, or the purity of Cicero, it both delights the ear and fills the mind. It is an original and somewhat foreign, but nevertheless an expressive and harmonious dialect.ᵃ It has no doubt powerfully influenced the religious style, not merely of the later Latin writers, but those of the modern languages of which Latin is the parent. Constantly quoted, either in its express words, or in terms approaching closely to its own, it contributed to form the dialect of ecclesiastical Latin, which became the religious language of Europe; and as soon as religion condescended to employ the modern languages in its service, was transfused as a necessary and integral part of that which related to religion. Christian literature was as yet purely religious in its scope; though it ranged over

---

ᵃ There appears to me more of the Oriental character in the Old Testament of the Vulgate than in the LXX. That translation having been made by Greeks, or by Jews domiciled in a Greek city, the Hebrew style seems subdued, as far as possible, to the Greek. Jerome seems to have endeavoured to Hebraise or Orientalise his Latin.

The story of Jerome's nocturnal flagellation for his attachment to profane literature rests (as we have seen) on his own authority; but his later works show that the offending spirit was not effectively scourged out of him.

the whole field of ancient poetry, philosophy, and history, its sole object was the illustration or confirmation of Christian opinion.

For many ages, and indeed as long as it spoke the ancient languages, the new religion was barren of poetry in all its loftier departments, at least of that which was poetry in form as well as in spirit. *Poetry.*

The religion itself was the *poetry* of Christianity. The sacred books were to the Christians what the national epic and the sacred lyric had been to the other races of antiquity. They occupied the place, and proscribed in their superior sanctity, or defied by their unattainable excellence, all rivalry. The Church succeeded to the splendid inheritance of the Hebrew temple and synagogue. The Psalms and the Prophets, if they departed somewhat from their original simple energy and grandeur in the uncongenial and too polished languages of the Greeks and Romans, still, in their imagery, their bold impersonations, the power and majesty of their manner, as well as in the sublimity of the notions of divine power and wisdom with which they were instinct, stood alone in the religious poetry of mankind.

The religious books of Christianity, though of a gentler cast, and only in a few short passages (and in the grand poetic drama of the Revelation) poetical in their form, had much, especially in their narratives, of the essence of poetry; the power of awakening kindred emotions; the pure simplicity of truth, blended with imagery and with language which kindled the fancy. Faith itself was constantly summoning the imagination to its aid, to realise, to impersonate those scenes which were described in the sacred volume, *Sacred writings.*

and which it was thus enabled to embrace with greater fervour and sincerity. All the other early Christian poetry was pale and lifeless in comparison with that of the sacred writers. Some few hymns, as the noble Te Deum ascribed to Ambrose, were admitted, with the Psalms, and the short lyric passages in the New Testament, the Magnificat, the Nunc Dimittis, and the Alleluia, into the services of the Church. But the sacred volume commanded exclusive adoration not merely by its sanctity, but by its unrivalled imagery and sweetness. Each sect had its hymns; and those of the Gnostics, with the rival strains of the orthodox churches of Syria, attained great popularity. But in general these compositions were only a feebler echo of the strong and vivid sounds of the Hebrew psalms. The epic and tragic form into which, in the time of Julian, the scripture narratives were cast, in order to provide a Christian Homer and Euripides for those schools in which the originals were interdicted, were probably but cold paraphrases, the Hebrew poetry expressed in an incongruous cento of the Homeric or tragic phraseology. The garrulous feebleness of Gregory's own poem does not awaken any regret for the loss of those writings either of his own composition or of his age.[4] Even in the martyrdoms, the noblest unoccupied subjects for Christian verse, the poetry seems to have forced its way into the legend, rather than animated the writer of verse. Prudentius—whose

---

[4] The Greek poetry after Nazianzen was almost silent; some perhaps, of the hymns are ancient (one particularly in Routh's Reliquiæ'. See likewise Smith's account of the Greek church. The hymns of Synesius are very interesting as illustrative of the state of religious sentiment, and by no means without beauty. But may we call these dreamy Platonic raptures Christian poetry?

finest lines (and they are sometimes of a very spirited, sententious, and eloquent, if not poetic cast) occur in his other poems, on these which would appear at first far more promising subjects is sometimes pretty and fanciful, but scarcely more.*

---

* One of the best, or rather perhaps prettiest, passages, is that which has been selected as a hymn for the Innocents' day:—

> "Salvete flores martyrum
> Quos lucis ipso in limine,
> Christi insecutor sustulit
> Ceu turbo nascentes rosas.
> Vos, prima Christi victima,
> Grex immolatorum tener,
> Aram ante ipsam simplices
> Palma et coronis luditis."

But these are only a few stanzas out of a long hymn on the Epiphany. The best verses in Prudentius are to be found in the books against Symmachus; but their highest praise is that, in their force and energy, they approach to Claudian. With regard to Claudian, I cannot refrain from repeating what I have stated in another place, as it is so closely connected with the subject of Christian poetry. M. Beugnot has pointed out one remarkable characteristic of Claudian's poetry and of the times—his extraordinary religious indifference. Here is a poet writing at the actual crisis of the complete triumph of the new religion, and the visible extinction of the old; if we may so speak, a strictly historical poet, whose works, excepting his mythological poem on the rape of Proserpine, are confined to temporary subjects, and to the politics of his own eventful times; yet, excepting in one or two small and indifferent pieces, manifestly written by a Christian and interpolated among Claudian's poems, there is no allusion whatever to the great religious strife. No one would know the existence of Christianity at that period of the world by reading the works of Claudian. His panegyric and his satire preserve the same religious impartiality; award their most lavish praise or their bitterest invective on Christian or Pagan: he insults the fall of Eugenius, and glories in the victories of Theodosius. Under the child of Theodosius,—and Honorius never became more than a child,—Christianity continued to inflict wounds more and more deadly on expiring Paganism. Are the gods of Olympus agitated with apprehension at the birth of their new enemy? They are introduced as rejoicing at his appearance, and promising long years of glory. The whole prophetic choir of Paganism, all the oracles throughout the world, are summoned to predict the felicity of the reign of Honorius. His birth is compared to that of Apollo, but the narrow limits of an island must not confine the new deity—

> "Non littora nostro
> Sufficerent angusta Deo."

Augury, and divination, the shrines of Ammon and of Delphi, the Persian magi, the Etruscan seers, the Chaldean astrologers, the Sibyl herself, are described as still discharging their poetic functions, and celebrating the natal day of this Christian prince. They are noble lines, as well as curious illustrations of the times:—

356 POETRY — SACRED WRITINGS. Book IV.

There is more of the essence of poetry in the simpler and unadorned Acts of the Martyrs, more pathos, oc-

> "Quæ tunc documenta futuri?
> Quæ voces avium? quando per inane volarus?
> Quis vatum discursus erat? Tibi corniger Ammon,
> Et dudum taciti superèr silentia Delphi.
> Te Perseu cecinêre Magi, te sensit Etruscus
> Augur, et irrupit Babylonius horruit auris:
> Chaldæi stupuere senes, Cumanaque rursus
> Intonuit rupes, rabidæ delubra Sibyllæ."
> Note on Gibbon, v. 248.

But Roman poetry expired with Claudian. In the vast mass of the Christian Latin poetry of this period, independent of the perpetual faults against metre and taste, it is impossible not to acknowledge that the subject matter appears foreign, and irreconcilable with the style of the verse. Christian images and sentiments, the frequent biblical phrases and expressions, are not yet naturalised; and it is almost impossible to select any passage of considerable length from the whole cycle, which can be offered as poetry. I except a few of the hymns, and even, as to the hymns (setting aside the Te Deum), paradoxical as it may sound, I cannot but think the later and more barbarous the best. There is nothing in my judgement to be compared with the monkish "Dies iræ, Dies illa," or even the "Stabat Mater."

I am inclined to select, as a favourable specimen of Latin poetry, the following almost unknown lines (they are not in the earlier editions of Dracontius). I have three reasons for my selection: 1. The real merit of the verses compared to most of the Christian poetry; 2. Their opposition to the prevailing tenet of celibacy, for which cause they are quoted by Theiner; 3. The interest which early poetry on this subject (Adam in Paradise) must possess to the countrymen of Milton.

> "Tunc oculos per cuncta jacit, mirator amœnum
> Sic florere loerum, sic puros fontibus amnes,
> Qualiter undantes stringerent gurgite ripas,
> Ire per arboreos saltus, campusque virentes
> Miratur; sed quid sit homo, quæ factus ad usum
> Scire cupit simplex, et non habet, unde requirat;
> Quo merito sibimet data sit præsentis mundi,
> Et domus alma nemus per flores regna paratum:
> Ac procul aspectat virides jumenta per agros;
> Et de se tacitus, quæ sint hæc cuncta, requirit,
> Et quare secum non sint hæc ipsa, volutat:
> Nam memorie carens, casu quo conferret, egebat.
> Viderat Omnipotens, hæc illum corde moventem,
> Et intervenies ait: Demus adjutoria facto:
> Participem generis: tanquam si discret auctor,
> Non solum decet esse virum, consortia blanda
> Noverit, unor erit, quam sit tamen ille maritus,
> Conjugium se quisque vocet, dolendo recurret
> Cordibus innocuis, et sit sibi pignus uterque
> Velle pares, et nolle pares, stans una voluntas,
> Par animi amorum, paribus concurrere votis.
> Ambo sibi requies cordis sint, ambo fideles,
> Et quicunque dolor caussa, sit causa duorum.
> Nox morti, jam veniet alma quies, oculosque supinat
> Hominis, et in dulcem solvuntur membra soporem.

&c.

casionally more grandeur, more touching incident and expression, and even, we may venture to say, happier invention than in the prolix and inanimate strains of the Christian poet. For the awakened imagination was not content with feasting in silence on its lawful nutriment, the poetry of the Bible; it demanded and received perpetual stimulants, which increased, instead of satisfying, the appetite. That peculiar state of the human mind had now commenced, in which the imagination so far

---

Sed quam jure Deus, nullo prohibente valeret
Demere particulam, de quo plus ipse pararat,
Ne vi oblata daret juveni sua costa dolorem,
Redderet et tristem subitò, quem lædere nollet,
Fur opifex vult esse suus; nam posset et illam
Pulvere de simili princeps formare puellam.
Sed quo plenus amor toto de corde veniret,
Noscere in uxore voluit sua membra maritum,
Dividitur contexta cutis, subducitur una
Ossibus costa viro, sed mox reditura marito.
Nam juvenis de parte brevi formatur adulta
Virgo, decora, rudis, matura tumentibus annis,
Conjugii, sobolisque capax, quibus apta probatur,
Et sine lacte pio crescit infantia pubes.
Excutitur somno juvenis, videt ipse puellam
Ante oculos astare suos, pater, inde maritus,
Non tamen ex costâ genitor, sed conjugis auctor.
Somnus erat partus, conceptus semine nullo,
Materiem sopita quies produxit amoris,
Affectusque novos blandi genuêre sopores.
Constitit ante oculos nullo velamine tecta,
Corpore nuda simul niveo, quasi nympha profundi,
Cæsaries intonsa comis, gena pulchra rubore,
Omnia pulchra gerens, oculos, os, colla, manusque,
Vel qualem possent digiti formare Tonantis.
Nescia mens illis, fieri quæ causa fuisset;
Tunc Deus et princeps ambos conjunxit in unum,
Et remeat sua costa viro; sua membra recepit;
Accipit et fœmina, quum non sit debitor ullus,
His datur omnis humus, et quicquid juncta creavit,
Aëris et pelagi fœtus, elementa duorum,
Arbitrio commissa manent. His, crescite, dixit
Omnipotens, replete solum de semine vestro,
Sanguinis ingenui nati nutrite nepotes,
Et de prole novos iterum copulate jugales.
Et dum terra fretum, dum cœlum sublevat aër,
Dum solis micat axe jubar, dum luna tenebras
Dissipat, et puro lucent mea sidera cœlo;
Sumere, quicquid habent pomaria nostra licebit;
Nam totum quod terra creat, quod pontus et aër
Protulit, addictum vestro sub jure manebit,
Deliciæque fluent vobis, et honesta voluptas;
Arboris unius tantum nescite saporem."

Dracontii Presbyt. Hispani Christ. sæcul. v. sub Theodos. M. Carmina, à F. Arevalo. Romæ, 1791. Carmen de Deo, lib. i. v. 348. 415.

predominates over the other faculties, that truth cannot help arraying itself in the garb of fiction; credulity courts fiction, and fiction believes its own fables. That some of the Christian legends were deliberate forgeries can scarcely be questioned; the principle of pious fraud appeared to justify this mode of working on the popular mind; it was admitted and avowed. To deceive into Christianity was so valuable a service, as to hallow deceit itself. But the largest portion was probably the natural birth of that imaginative excitement which quickens its day-dreams and nightly visions into reality. The Christian lived in a supernatural world; the notion of the divine power, the perpetual interference of the Deity, the agency of the countless invisible beings which hovered over mankind, was so strongly impressed upon the belief, that every extraordinary, and almost every ordinary incident became a miracle, every inward emotion a suggestion either of a good or an evil spirit. A mythic period was thus gradually formed, in which reality melted into fable, and invention unconsciously trespassed on the province of history. This invention had very early let itself loose, in the spurious gospels, or accounts of the lives of the Saviour and his Apostles, which were chiefly, I conceive, composed among, or rather against, the sects which were less scrupulous in their veneration for the sacred books. Unless Antidocetic, it is difficult to imagine any serious object in fictions, in general so fantastic and puerile.[f] This example had been set by some, probably, of the foreign Jews, whose apocryphal books were as numerous and

[f] Compare what has been said on the Gospel of the Infancy, vol. I. page 127; though I would now observe that the antiquity of this gospel is very dubious.

Legends.

Spurious Gospels.

as wild as those of the Christian sectaries. The Jews had likewise anticipated them in the interpolation or fabrication of the Sibylline verses. The fourth book of Esdras, the Shepherd of Hermas,[f] and other prophetic works, grew out of the Prophets and the book of Revelation, as the Gospels of Nicodemus, and that of the Infancy, and the various spurious acts of the different Apostles,[h] out of the Gospels and Acts. The Recognitions and other tracts which are called the Clementina, partake more of the nature of religious romance. Many of the former were obviously intended to pass for genuine records, and must be proscribed as unwarrantable fictions; the latter may rather have been designed to trace, and so to awaken religious feelings, than as altogether real history. The Lives of St. Anthony by Athanasius and of Hilarion by Jerome are the prototypes of the countless biographies of saints; and with a strong outline of truth, became impersonations of the feeling, the opinions, the belief of the time. We

Lives of Saints.

---

[f] The Shepherd of Hermas, as Bunsen has well shown, is a kind of ancient Pilgrim's Progress.—Christianity and Mankind, i. 182.

[h] Compare the Codex Apocryphus Novi Testamenti, by J. A. Fabricius, and Jones on the Canon. A more elaborate collection of these curious documents has been commenced (I trust not abandoned) by Dr. Thilo, Lipsiæ, 1832. Of these, by far the most remarkable in its composition and its influence, was the Gospel of Nicodemus. The author of this work was a poet, and of no mean invention. The latter part, which describes the descent of the Saviour to hell, to deliver "the spirits in prison," according to the hint in the epistle of St. Peter, (1 Peter iii. 19), is extremely striking and dramatic. This "harrowing of hell," as it is called in the old mysteries, became a favourite topic of Christian legend, founded on, and tending greatly to establish the popular belief in, a purgatory, and to open, as it were, to the fears of man, the terrors of the penal state. With regard to these spurious gospels in general, it is a curious question in what manner, so little noticed as they are in the higher Christian literature, they should have reached down, and so completely incorporated themselves, in the dark ages, with the superstitions of the vulgar. They would never have furnished so many subjects to painting, if they had not been objects of popular belief.

have no reason to doubt that the authors implicitly believed whatever of fiction embellishes their own unpremeditated fables; the colouring, though fanciful and inconceivable to our eyes, was fresh and living to theirs.

History itself could only reflect the proceedings of the Christian world, as they appeared to that world. We may lament that the annals of Christianity found in the earliest times no historian more judicious and trustworthy than Eusebius; the heretical sects no less prejudiced and more philosophical chronicler than Epiphanius: but in them, if not scrupulously veracious reporters of the events and characters of the times, we possess almost all that we could reasonably hope; faithful reporters of the opinions entertained, and the feelings excited by both. Few Christians of that day would not have considered it the sacred duty of a Christian to adopt that principle, avowed and gloried in by Eusebius, but now made a bitter reproach, that he would relate all that was to the credit, and pass lightly over all which was to the dishonour of the faith.[1]

[1] " In addition to these things (the appointment of rude and unfit persons to episcopal offices, and other delinquencies), the ambition of many; the precipitate and illegitimate ordinations; the dissensions among the confessors; whatever the younger and more seditious so pertinaciously attempted against the remains of the Church, introducing innovation after innovation, and unsparingly, in the midst of the calamities of the persecution, adding new afflictions, and heaping evil upon evil; all these things I think it right to pass over, as unbefitting my history, which, as I stated in the beginning, declines and avoids the relation of such things. But whatsoever things, according to the sacred Scripture, are ' honest and of good report:' if there be any virtue, and if there be any praise, these things I have thought it most befitting the history of those wonderful martyrs, to speak and to write and to address to the ears of the faithful." On this passage, de Martyr. Palæst., exil., and that to which it alludes, E. H. viii. 2, the honesty and impartiality of Eusebius, which were not above suspicion in his own day (Tillemont, M. E. tom. l. part i. p. 67), have been severely questioned.

The historians of Christianity were credulous, but of that which it would have been considered impiety to disbelieve, even if they had the inclination.

The larger part of Christian literature consists in controversial writings, valuable to posterity as records of the progress of the human mind, and of the gradual developement of Christian opinions; at times worthy of admiration for the force, the copiousness, and the subtlety of argument; but too often repulsive from their solemn prolixity on insignificant subjects, and above all, the fierce, the unjust, and the acrimonious spirit with which they treat their adversaries. The Christian literature in prose (excluding the history and hagiography), may be distributed under five heads :—I. Apologies, or defences of the Faith, against Jewish, or more frequently Heathen adversaries. II. Hermeneutics, or commentaries on the sacred writings. III. Expositions of the principles and doctrines of the Faith. IV. Polemical works against the different sects and heresies. V. Orations.

I. I have already traced the manner in which the apology for Christianity, from humbly defensive, became vigorously aggressive. The calm appeal to justice and humanity, the earnest deprecation

Apologies.

Gibbon's observations on the subject gave rise to many dissertations. Müller, de Fide Euseb. Cæs. Harolæ, 1813. Danzius, de Euseb. Cæs. H. E. Scriptore, ejusque Fide Historicâ rectê æstimandâ. Jenæ, 1815. Kestner, Comment. de Euseb. H. E. Conditoris Auctoritate et Fide. See also Reuterdahl, de Fontibus H. E. Eusebianæ, Lond. Goth. 1826, and various passages in the Excursus of Heinichen. In many passages it is clear that Eusebius did not adhere to his own rule of partiality. His Ecclesiastical History, though probably highly coloured in many parts, is by no means an uniform panegyric on the early Christians. Strict impartiality could not be expected from a Christian writer of that day; and probably Eusebius erred more often from credulity than from dishonesty. Yet the unbelief produced, in later times, by the fictitious character of early Christian History, may show how dangerous, how fatal, may be the least departure from truth. On pious fraud read Mosheim, Diss. i. 206, et seqq.

of the odious calumnies with which the Christians were
charged, the plea for toleration, gradually rise to the
vehement and uncompromising proscription of the folly
and guilt of idolatry. Tertullian marks, as it were,
the period of transition, though his fiery temper may
perhaps have anticipated the time when Christianity, in
the consciousness of strength, instead of endeavouring
to appease or avert the wrath of hostile Paganism,
might defy it to deadly strife. The earliest extant
apology, that of Justin Martyr, is by no means severe
in argument or vigorous in style, and though not
altogether abstaining from recrimination, is still rather
humble and deprecatory in its tone. The short apologetic orations—as the Christians had to encounter not
merely the general hostility of the Government or the
people, but direct and argumentative treatises, written
against them by the philosophic party—gradually swelled
into books. The first of these is perhaps the best, that
of Origen against Celsus. The intellect of Origen, notwithstanding its occasional fantastic aberrations, appears
to me more suited to grapple with this lofty argument
than the diffuse and excursive Eusebius, whose Evangelic
Preparation and Demonstration heaped together vast
masses of curious but by no means convincing learning,
and the feebler, more violent, and less candid Cyril
of Alexandria, in his Books against Julian. I have
already noticed the great work which perhaps might
be best arranged under this head, the "City of God"
of St. Augustine; but there was one short treatise
which may vindicate the Christian Latin literature
from the charge of barbarism: perhaps no late work,
either Pagan or Christian, reminds us of the golden days
of Latin prose so much as the Octavius of Minucius
Felix.

II. The Hermeneutics, or the interpretation of the sacred writers, might be expected to have more real value and authority than can be awarded them by sober and dispassionate judgement. But it cannot be denied that almost all these writers, including those of highest name, are fanciful in their inferences, discover mysteries in the plainest sentences, wander away from the clear historical, moral, or religious meaning, into a long train of corollaries, at which we arrive we know not how. Piety, in fact, read in the Scripture whatever it chose to read, and the devotional feeling it excited was at once the end and the test of the biblical commentary. But the character of the age and the school in which the Christian teachers were trained, must here, as in other cases, be taken into account. The most sober Jewish system of interpretation (setting aside the wild cabalistic notions of the significance of letters, the frequency of their recurrence, their collocation, and all those strange theories which were engendered by a servile veneration of the very form and language of the sacred writings) allowed itself at least an equal latitude of authoritative inference. The Platonists spun out the thoughts or axioms of their master into as fine and subtle a web of mystic speculation. The general principle of an esoteric or recondite meaning in all works which commanded veneration, was universally received; it was this principle upon which the Gnostic sects formed all their vague and mystic theories; and if in this respect the Christian teachers did not bind themselves by much severer rules of reasoning than prevailed around them on all sides, they may have been actuated partly by some jealousy, lest their own plainer and simpler sacred writings should appear dry and barren, in comparison with the rich and imaginative freedom of their adversaries.

III. The expositions of faith and practice may comprehend all the smaller treatises on particular duties; prayer, almsgiving, marriage, and celibacy. They depend, of course, for their merit and authority on the character of the writer.

Expositions of Faith.

IV. Christianity might appear, if we judge by the proportion which the controversial writings bear to the rest of Christian literature, to have introduced an element of violent and implacable discord. Nor does the tone of these polemical writings, by which alone we can judge of the ancient heresies, of which the heretics' own accounts have almost entirely perished, impress us very favourably with their fairness or candour. But it must be remembered that, after all, the field of literature was not the arena in which the great contest between Christianity and the world was waged; it was in the private circle of each separate congregation, which was constantly but silently enlarging its boundaries: it was the immediate contact of mind with mind, the direct influence of the Christian clergy and even the more pious of the laity, which were tranquilly and noiselessly pursuing their course of conversion.[h]

Polemical writings.

---

[h] I might perhaps have made another and a very interesting branch of the prose Christian literature, the epistolary. The letters of the great writers form one of the most valuable parts of their works. The Latin Fathers, however, maintain that superiority over the Greek, which in classical times is asserted by Cicero and Pliny. The letters of Cyprian and Ambrose are of the highest interest as historical documents; those of Jerome, for manners; those of Augustine, perhaps, for style. They far surpass those of Chrysostom, which we must, however, recollect were written from his dreary and monotonous place of exile. Yet Chrysostom's are superior to that dullest of all collections, the huge folio of the letters of Libanius.

These treatises, however, were principally addressed to the clergy, and through them worked downward into the mass of the Christian people: even with the more rapid and frequent communication which took place in the Christian world, they were but partially and imperfectly disseminated; but that which became another considerable and important part of their literature, their oratory, had in the first instance been directly addressed to the popular mind, and formed the chief part of the popular instruction. Christian preaching had opened a new field for eloquence.

V. Oratory, that oratory at least which communicates its own impulses and passions to the heart, which not merely persuades the reason, but sways the whole soul of man, had suffered a long and total silence. It had everywhere expired with the republican institutions. The discussions in the senate had been controlled by the imperial presence; and even if the Roman senators had asserted the fullest freedom of speech, and allowed themselves the most exciting fervour of language, this was but one assembly in a single city, formed out of a confined aristocracy. The municipal assemblies were alike rebuked by the awe of a presiding master, the provincial governor, and of course afforded a less open field for stirring and general eloquence. The perfection of jurisprudence had probably been equally fatal to judicial oratory; we hear of great lawyers, but not of distinguished advocates. The highest flight of Pagan oratory which remains is in the adulatory panegyrics of the Emperors, pronounced by rival candidates for favour. Rhetoric was taught, indeed, and practised as a liberal, but it had sunk into a mere, art; it was taught by salaried professors in all the great towns to the higher youth; but they were mere exer-

Christian oratory.

cises of fluent diction, on trite or obsolete subjects, the characters of the heroes of the Iliad, or some subtle question of morality.[m]

It is impossible to conceive a more sudden and total change than from the school of the rhetorician to a crowded Christian church. The orator suddenly emerged from a listless audience of brother scholars, before whom he had discussed some one of those trivial questions according to formal rules, and whose ear could require no more than terseness or elegance of diction, and a just distribution of the argument: emotion was neither expected nor could be excited. He found himself among a breathless and anxious multitude, whose eternal destiny might seem to hang on his lips, catching up and treasuring his words as those of divine inspiration, and interrupting his more eloquent passages by almost involuntary acclamations.[n] The orator, in the best days of Athens, the tribune, in the most turbulent periods of Rome, had not such complete hold upon the minds of his hearers; and—but that the sublime nature of his subject usually lay above the sphere of immediate action, but that, the purer and loftier its tone, if it found instantaneous sympathy, yet it also met the constant inert resistance of prejudice, and ignorance, and vice to its authority,—the power with which this privilege of oratory would have invested the clergy would have been far greater than that of any of the former political or sacerdotal dominations. Wherever the

---

[m] The declamations of Quintilian are no doubt favourable specimens both of the subjects and the style of these orators.

[n] These acclamations sometimes rewarded the more eloquent and successful teachers of rhetoric. Themistius speaks of the ἰαβοήσεις τε καὶ κρότους, οἴων θαμὰ ἀπολαύουσι παρ' ὑμῶν οἱ δαιμόνιοι σοφισταί. Banisius, p. 236, edit. Dindorf. Compare the note. Chrysostom's works are full of allusions to these acclamations.

oratory of the pulpit coincided with human passion, it
was irresistible, and sometimes when it resolutely encountered
it, it might extort an unwilling triumph:
when it appealed to faction, to ferocity, to sectarian
animosity, it swept away its audience like a torrent,
to any violence or madness at which it aimed; when
to virtue, to piety, to peace, it at times subdued the
most refractory, and received the homage of devout
obedience.

The bishop in general, at least when the hierarchical
power became more dominant, reserved for himself
an office so productive of influence and so liable to
abuse.[c] But men like Athanasius or Augustine were
not compelled to wait for that qualification of rank.
They received the ready permission of the bishop to
exercise at once this important function. In general, a
promising orator would rarely want opportunity of distinction;
and he who had obtained celebrity would

---

[c] The laity were long permitted to address the people in the absence of the clergy. It was objected to the Bishop Demetrius, that he had permitted an unprecedented innovation in the case of Origen: he had allowed a layman to teach when *the bishop was present*. Euseb. E. H. vi. 19. Ὁ δὲ δόγμων, εἰ καὶ λαϊκὸς ᾖ, ἔμπειρος δὲ τοῦ λόγου, καὶ τὸν τρόπον σεμνὸς, διδασκέτω. Constit. Apost. viii. 32. 23. "Laicus, praesentibus clericis, nisi illis jubentibus, docere non audeat." Conc. Carth. can. 98. Jerome might be supposed, in his indignant remonstrance against the right which almost all assumed of interpreting the Scriptures, to be writing of later days.

"Quod medicorum est, promittunt medici, tractant fabrilia fabri. Sola Scripturarum ars est, quam sibi omnes passim vindicant. Scribimus, indocti doctique poëmata passim. *Hanc garrula anus, hanc delirus senex, hanc sophista verbosus, hanc universi praesumunt, lacerant, docent antequam discant.* Alii addicto supercilio, grandia verba trutinantes, inter mulierculas de sacris literis philosophantur. Alii discunt, proh pudor! a feminis, quod viros doceant: et ne parum hoc sit quadam facilitate verborum, imò audaciâ, edisserunt aliis quod ipsi non intelligunt." Epist. l. ad Paulinum, vol. iv. p. 571.

frequently be raised by general acclamation, or by a just appreciation of his usefulness by the higher clergy, to an episcopal throne.*

But it is difficult to conceive the general effect produced by this devotion of oratory to its new office. From this time, instead of seizing casual opportunities of working on the mind and heart of man, it was constantly, regularly, in every part of the empire, with more or less energy, with greater or less commanding authority, urging the doctrines of Christianity on awe-struck and submissive hearers. It had, of course, as it always has had, its periods of more than usual excitement, its sudden paroxysms of power, by which it convulsed some part of society. The constancy and regularity with which, in the ordinary course of things, it discharged its function, may in some degree have deadened its influence; and in the period of ignorance and barbarism, the instruction was chiefly through the ceremonial, the symbolic worship, the painting, and even the dramatic representation.

Still, this new moral power, though intermitted at times, and even suspended, was almost continually operating, in its great and sustained energy, throughout the Christian world; though of course strongly tempered with the dominant spirit of Christianity, and, excepting in those periods either ripe for or preparing some great change in religious sentiment or opinion, the living and general expression of the prevalent Christianity, it was always in greater or less activity, instilling the broader principles of Christian faith and morals; if superstitious, rarely altogether silent; if appealing to passions which

---

* But compare Latin Christianity. Pope Leo I., vol. I. p. 168.

ought to have been rebuked before its voice, and exciting those feelings of hostility between conflicting sects which it should have allayed,—yet even then in some hearts its gentler and more Christian tones made a profound and salutary impression, while its more violent language fell off without mingling with the uncongenial feelings. The great principles of the religion,—the providence of God, the redemption by Christ, the immortality of the soul, future retribution,—gleamed through all the fantastic and legendary lore with which the faith was encumbered and obscured in the darker ages. Christianity first imposed it as a duty on one class of men to be constantly enforcing moral and religious truths on all mankind. Though that duty, of course, was discharged with very different energy, judgement, and success, at different periods, it was always a strong counteracting power, an authorised, and in general respected, remonstrance against the vices and misery of mankind. Man was perpetually reminded that he was an immortal being under the protection of a wise and all-ruling Providence, and destined for a higher state of existence.

Nor was this influence only immediate and temporary: Christian oratory did not cease to speak when its echoes had died away upon the ear, and its expressions faded from the hearts of those to whom it was addressed. The orations of the Basils and Chrysostoms, the Ambroses and Augustines, became one of the most important parts of Christian literature. That eloquence which, in Rome and Greece, had been confined to civil and judicial affairs, was now inseparably connected with religion. The oratory of the pulpit took its place with that of the bar, the comitia, or the senate, as the historical record of that which once had powerfully moved the minds of multitudes. No part of Christian literature so vividly reflects the times, the tone of religious doctrine or sentiment, in many cases the manners, habits, and character of the period, as the sermons of the leading teachers.

CHAPTER IV.

Christianity and the Fine Arts.

As in literature, so in the fine arts, Christianity had to await that period in which it should become completely interwoven with the feelings and moral being of mankind, before it could put forth all its creative energies, and kindle into active productiveness those new principles of the noble and the beautiful, which it infused into the human imagination. The dawn of a new civilisation must be the first epoch for the full developement of Christian art. The total disorganisation of society, which was about to take place, implied the total suspension of the arts which embellish social life. The objects of admiration were swept away by the destructive ravages of Barbarian warfare; or, where they were left in contemptuous indifference, the mind had neither leisure to indulge, nor refinement enough to feel, that admiration, which belongs to a more secure state of society, and of repose from the more pressing toils and anxieties of life.

Fine arts.

This suspended animation of the fine arts was of course different in degree in the various parts of Europe, in proportion as they were exposed to the ravages of war, the comparative barbarism of the tribes by which they were overrun, the station held by the clergy, the security which they could command by the sanctity of their character, and their disposable wealth. At every period, from Theodoric, who dwelt with vain fondness on the last struggles of decaying art, to Charlemagne, who seemed to hail, with prophetic taste, the hope of its revival, there is no period in which the tradition of art was not preserved in some part of Europe, though obscured by ignorance, barbarism, and that still worse enemy, if possible, false and meretricious taste. Christianity, in every branch of the arts, preserved something from the general wreck, and brooded in silence over the imperfect rudiments of each, of which it was the sole conservator. The mere mechanical skill of working stone, of delineating the human face, and of laying on colours so as to produce something like illusion, was constantly exercised in the works which religion required to awaken the torpid emotions of an ignorant and superstitious people.*

In all the arts, Christianity was at first, of course, purely imitative, and imitative of the prevalent degenerate style. It had not yet felt its strength, and dared not develope, or dreamed not of those latent principles which lay beneath its religion, and which hereafter were to produce works, in its own style, and its own department, rivalling all the wonders of antiquity; when the extraordinary creations of its proper architecture were to arise, far surpassing in the skill of their construction, in their magnitude more than equalling those wonders, and in their opposite indeed, but not less majestic, style, vindicating the genius of Christianity: when Italy was to transcend ancient Greece in painting as much as the whole modern world is inferior to Greece in the rival art of sculpture.

---

* The Iconoclasts had probably more influence in barbarising the East than the Barbarians themselves in the West.

I. Architecture was the first of these arts which was summoned to the service of Christianity. The devotion of the earlier ages did not need, and could not command, this subsidiary to pious emotion,—it imparted sanctity to the meanest building; now it would not be content without enshrining its triumphant worship in a loftier edifice. Religion at once offered this proof of its sincerity by the sacrifice of wealth to this hallowed purpose; and the increasing splendour of the religious edifices reacted upon the general devotion, by the feelings of awe and veneration which they inspired. Splendour, however, did not disdain to be subservient to use; and the arrangements of the new buildings, which arose in all quarters, or were diverted to this new object, accommodated themselves to the Christian ceremonial. In the East, I have already shown, in the church of Tyre, described by Eusebius, the ancient temple lending its model to the Christian church; and the basilica, in the West, adapted with still greater ease and propriety for Christian worship.[b] There were many distinctive points which materially affected the style of Christian architecture. The simplicity of the Grecian temple, as it has been shown,[c] harmonised perfectly only with its own form of worship; it was more of a public place, sometimes, indeed, hypæthral, or open to the air. The Christian worship demanded more complete enclosure; the church was more of a chamber, in which the voice of an individual could be distinctly heard; and the whole assembly of worshippers, sheltered from the change or inclemency of the weather, or the intrusion of unauthorised persons, might listen in undisturbed devotion to the prayer, the reading of the scripture, or the preacher.

[b] Vol. ii. pp. 239, 240.   [c] Vol. ii. pp. 340, 344.

One consequence of this was the necessity of regular apertures for the admission of light;[d] and these imperatively demanded a departure from the plan of temple architecture.

Windows had been equally necessary in the basilicæ for the public legal proceedings; the reading legal documents required a bright and full light; and in the basilicæ the windows were numerous and large. The nave, probably from the earliest period, was lighted by clerestory windows, which were above the roof of the lower aisles.[e]

Throughout the West, the practice of converting the basilica into the church continued to a late period; the very name seemed appropriate: the royal hall was changed into a dwelling for the GREAT KING.[f]

---

[d] In the fanciful comparison (in H. E. x. 4) which Eusebius draws between the different parts of the church and the different gradations of catechumens, he speaks of the most perfect as "shone on by the light through the windows:"—τοὺς δὲ πρὸς τὸ φῶς ἀνοίγμασι καταυγάζει. He seems to describe the temple as full of light, emblematical of the heavenly light diffused by Christ, — λαμπρὸν καὶ φωτὸς ἔμπλεω τά τε ἔνδοθεν καὶ τὰ ἐκτὸς: but it is not easy to discover where his metaphor ends and his fact begins. See Ciampini, vol. i. p. 74.

[e] The size of the windows has been disputed by Christian antiquaries: some asserted that the early Christians, accustomed to the obscurity of their crypts and catacombs, preferred narrow apertures for light; others that the services, especially reading the Scriptures, required it to be both bright and equally diffused. Ciampini, as an Italian, prefers the latter, and sarcastically alludes to the narrow windows of Gothic architecture, introduced by the "Vandals," whose first object being to exclude the cold of their northern climate, they contracted the windows to the narrowest dimensions possible. In the monastic churches, the light was excluded, "quia monachis meditantibus fortasse officielat, quo minus possent intento animo soli Deo vacare." Ciampini, Vetera Monumenta. This author considers that the parochial or cathedral churches may, in general, be distinguished from the monastic by this test.

[f] "Basilicæ priùs vocabantur regum habitacula, nunc autem ideo basilicæ divina templa nominantur, quia ibi Regi omnium Deo cultus et sacrificia offeruntur." Isidor, Orig. lib. v. "Basilicæ olim negotiis parae, nunc votis pro tuâ salute susceptis." Auson. Grat. Act. pro Consul.

The more minute subdivision of the internal arrangement contributed to form the peculiar character <small>Subdivision of the building.</small> of Christian architecture. The different orders of Christians were distributed according to their respective degrees of proficiency. But besides this, the church had inherited from the synagogue, and from the general feeling of the East, the principle of secluding the female part of the worshippers. Enclosed galleries, on a higher level, were probably common in the synagogues; and this arrangement appears to have been generally adopted in the earlier Christian churches.[f]

This great internal complexity necessarily led to still farther departure from the simplicity of design in the exterior plan and elevation. The single or the double row of columns, reaching from the top to the bottom of the building, with the long and unbroken horizontal line of the roof reposing upon it, would give place to rows of unequal heights, or to the division into separate stories.

The same process had probably taken place in the palatial architecture of Rome. Instead of one order of columns, which reached from the top to the bottom of the buildings, rows of columns, one above the other, marked the different stories into which the building was divided.

Christianity thus, from the first, either at once assumed, or betrayed its tendency to, its peculiar character. Its harmony was not that of the Greek, arising from the breadth and simplicity of one design, which, if at times too vast for the eye to contemplate at a single glance, was comprehended and felt at once by the mind; of which the lines were all horizontal and regular, and the

---

[f] " Populi confluunt ad ecclesias cæ- | discretione." Augustin. de Civ. Dei, ii. tâ celebritate, honestâ utriusque sexûs | 28. Compare Bingham, viii. 5, 5.

general impression a majestic or graceful uniformity, either awful from its massiveness or solidity, or pleasing from its lightness and delicate proportion.

The harmony of the Christian building (if in' fact it attained, before its perfection in the mediæval Gothic, to that first principle of architecture) consisted in the combination of many separate parts, duly balanced into one whole; the subordination of the accessories to the principal object; the multiplication of distinct objects coalescing into one rich and effective mass, and pervaded and reduced to a kind of symmetry by one general character in the various lines and in the style of ornament.

This predominance of complexity over simplicity, of variety over symmetry, was no doubt greatly increased by the buildings which, from an early period, arose around the central church, especially in all the monastic institutions. The baptistery was often a separate building, and frequently, in the ordinary structures for worship, dwellings for the officiating priesthood were attached to, or adjacent to, the church. The Grecian temple appears often to have stood alone, on the brow of a hill, in a grove, or in some other commanding or secluded situation. In Rome, many of the pontifical offices were held by patricians, who occupied their own palaces; but the Eastern temples were in general surrounded by spacious courts, and with buildings for the residence of the sacerdotal colleges. If these were not the models of the Christian establishments, the same ecclesiastical arrangements, the institution of a numerous and wealthy priestly order attached to the churches, demanded the same accommodation. Thus a multitude of subordinate buildings would crowd around the central or more eminent house of God. At first, where mere convenience was considered, and where the mind had not awakened to the solemn impressions excited by vast and various architectural works, combined by a congenial style of building, and harmonised by skilful arrangement and subordination, they would be piled together irregularly and capriciously, obscuring that which was really grand, and displaying irreverent confusion rather than stately order. Gradually, as the sense of grandeur and solemnity dawned upon the mind, there would arise the desire of producing one general effect and impression; but this no doubt was the later developement of a principle which, if at first dimly perceived, was by no means rigidly or consistently followed out. We must wait many centuries before we reach the culminating period of genuine Christian architecture.

II. Sculpture alone, of the fine arts, has been faithful to its parent Paganism. It has never cordially imbibed the spirit of Christianity. The second creative epoch (how poor, comparatively, in fertility and originality!) was contemporary and closely connected with the revival of classical literature in Europe. It has lent itself to Christian sentiment chiefly in two forms; as necessary and subordinate to architecture, and as monumental sculpture.

Sculpture.

Christianity was by no means so intolerant, at least after its first period, of the remains of ancient sculpture, or so perseveringly hostile to the art, as might have been expected from its severe aversion to idolatry. The earlier fathers, indeed, condemn the arts of sculpture and of painting as inseparably connected with Paganism. Every art which frames an image is irreclaimably idolatrous;[b] and the stern Tertullian reproaches Hermogenes

---

[b] " Ubi artifices statuarum et imaginum et omnis generis simulachrorum | diabolus sæculo intulit—caput facta est idololatriæ ars omnis quæ idolum

with the two deadly sins of painting and marrying.¹ The Council of Elvira proscribed paintings on the walls of churches,ᵏ which nevertheless became a common usage during the two next centuries.

In all respects, this severer sentiment was mitigated by time. The civil uses of sculpture were generally recognised. The Christian emperors erected, or permitted the adulation of their subjects to erect, their statues in the different cities. That of Constantine on the great porphyry column, with its singular and unchristian confusion of attributes, has been already noticed. Philostorgius indeed asserts that this statue became an object of worship even to the Christians; that lights and frankincense were offered before it, and that the image was worshipped as that of a tutelary god.ᵐ The sedition in Antioch arose out of insults to the statues of the emperors,ⁿ and the erection of the statue of the empress before the great church in Constantinople gave rise to the last disturbance, which ended in the exile of Chrysostom.ᵒ The statue of the emperor was long the representative of the imperial presence; it was reverenced in the capital and in the provincial cities with honours approaching to adoration.ᵖ The modest law of

---

quoque modo edit." Tertull. de Idol. c. iii. He has no language to express his horror that makers of images should be admitted into the clerical order.

¹ "Pingit illicitâ, nubit assiduè, legem Dei in libidinem defendit, in artem contemnit; bis falsarius et cauterio et stylo." In Hermog. cap. I. "Cauterio" refers to encaustic painting. The Apostolic Constitutions reckon a maker of idols with persons of infamous character and profession. viii. 32.

ᵏ "Placuit picturas in ecclesiâ esse non debere, ne quod colitur et adoratur, in parietibus depingatur." Can. xxxvi.
ᵐ Vol. ii. p. 337. Philostorg. ii. 17.
ⁿ Vol. iii. p. 123.
ᵒ Vol. iii. p. 144.
ᵖ Εἰ γὰρ βασιλέως ἀπόντος εἰκὼν ἀναπληροῖ χώραν βασιλέως, καὶ προσκυνοῦσιν ἄρχοντες καὶ ἱερομυρίαι ἐπιτελοῦνται, καὶ ἄρχοντες ὑπαντῶσι, καὶ δῆμοι προσκυνοῦσιν οὐ πρὸς τὴν σανίδα βλέποντες ἀλλὰ

Theodosius, by which he attempted to regulate these ceremonies, of which the adulation bordered at times on impiety, expressly reserved the excessive honours, sometimes lavished on these statues at the public games, for the supreme Deity.[q]

The statues even of the gods were condemned with some reluctance and remorse. No doubt iconoclasm, under the first edicts of the emperors, raged in the provinces with relentless violence. Yet Constantine, we have seen, did not scruple to adorn his capital with images both of gods and men, plundered indiscriminately from the temples of Greece. The Christians, indeed, asserted that they were set up for scorn and contempt.

Even Theodosius exempts such statues as were admirable as works of art from the common sentence of destruction.[r] This doubtful toleration of profane art gradually gave place to the admission of Art into the service of Christianity.

Sculpture, and, still more, Painting, were after no long time received as the ministers of Christian piety, and allowed to lay their offerings at the feet of the new religion.

But the commencement of Christian art was slow, timid, and rude. It long preferred allegory to repre-

---

πρὸς τὸν χαρακτῆρα τοῦ βασιλέως, οὐκ ἐν τῇ φύσει θεωρούμενον ἀλλ' ἐν γραφῇ παραδεικνυμένου. Joann. Damascen. de Imagin. orat. θ. Jerome, however (on Daniel), compared it to the worship demanded by Nebuchadnezzar. "Ergo judices et principes sæculi, qui imperatorum statuas adorant et imagines, hoc se facere intelligent quod tres pueri facere nolentes placuère Deo."

[q] They were to prove their loyalty by the respect which they felt for the statue in their secret hearts:—"excedens ultra hominum dignitatum supernonimial reservetur." Cod. Theod. xv. 4, 1.

[r] A particular temple was to remain open, "in quâ simulachra ferantur posita, artis pretio quam divinitate metienda." Cod. Theod. xvi. 10, 8.

sentation, the true and legitimate object of art.[a] It expanded but tardily during the first centuries, from the significant symbol to the human form in colour or in marble.

The Cross was long the primal, and even the sole, symbol of Christianity—the cross in its rudest and its most artless form; for many centuries elapsed before the image of the Saviour was wrought upon it. It was the copy of the common instrument of ignominious execution in all its nakedness; and nothing, indeed, so powerfully attests the triumph of Christianity as the elevation of this, which to the Jew and the Heathen was the basest, the most degrading, punishment of the lowest criminal,[b] the proverbial terror of the wretched slave, into an object for the adoration of ages, the reverence of

---

[a] Rumohr. Italienische Forschungen, i. p. 158. We want the German words *andeutung* (allusion or suggestion, but neither conveys the same forcible sense), and *darstellung*, actual representation or placing before the sight. The artists who employ the first can only address minds already furnished with the key to the symbolic or allegoric form. Imitation (the genuine object of art) speaks to all mankind.

[b] The author has expressed in a former work his impression on this most remarkable fact in the history of Christianity.

"In one respect it is impossible now to conceive the extent to which the Apostles of the *crucified* Jesus shocked all the feelings of mankind. The public establishment of Christianity, the adoration of ages, the reverence of nations, has thrown around the Cross of Christ an indelible and inalienable sanctity. No effort of the imagination can dissipate the illusion of dignity which has gathered round it; it has been so long dissevered from all its coarse and humiliating associations, that it cannot be cast back and desecrated into its state of opprobrium and contempt. To the most daring unbeliever among ourselves it is the symbol—the absurd and irrational, he may conceive, but still the ancient and venerable symbol—of a powerful and influential religion. What was it to the Jew and the Heathen?—the basest, the most degrading, punishment of the lowest criminal, the proverbial terror of the wretched slave! It was to them what the most despicable and revolting instrument of public execution is to us. Yet to the Cross of Christ men turned from deities, in which were embodied every attribute of strength, power, and dignity," &c. Milman's Bampton Lectures, p. 279.

nations. The glowing language of Chrysostom expresses the universal sanctity of the Cross in the fourth century. "Nothing so highly adorns the imperial crown as the Cross, which is more precious than the whole world: its form, at which, of old, men shuddered with horror, is now so eagerly and emulously sought for, that it is found among princes and subjects, men and women, virgins and matrons, slaves and freemen; for all bear it about, perpetually impressed on the most honourable part of the body, or on the forehead as on a pillar. This appears in the sacred temple, in the ordination of priests; it shines again on the body of the Lord, and in the mystic supper. It is to be seen everywhere in honour, in the private house and the public marketplace, in the desert, in the highway, on mountains, in forests, on hills, on the sea, in ships, on islands, on our beds, and on our clothes, on our arms, in our chambers, in our banquets, on gold and silver vessels, on gems, in the paintings of our walls, on the bodies of diseased beasts, on human bodies possessed by devils, in war and peace, by day, by night, in the dances of the feasting, and the meetings of the fasting and praying." In the time of Chrysostom the legend of the Discovery of the True Cross was generally received. "Why do all men vie with each other to approach that true Cross, on which the sacred body was crucified? Why do many, women as well as men, bear fragments of it set in gold as ornaments round their necks, though it was the sign of condemnation. Even emperors have laid aside the diadem to take up the Cross." [a]

---

[a] Chrysost. Oper. vol. i. p. 57. 569. cerning it. See in Munter's work (p. 68, et seq.) "Ipsa species crucis quid est nisi the various forms which the Cross as- forma quadrata mundi? Oriens de sumed, and the fanciful notions con- vertice fulgens; Arcton dextra tenet;

A more various symbolism gradually grew up, and extended to what approached nearer to works of art. Its rude designs were executed in engravings on seals, or on lamps, or glass vessels, and before long in relief on marble, or in paintings on the walls of the cemeteries. The earliest of these were the seal rings, of which many now exist, with Gnostic symbols and inscriptions. These seals were considered indispensable in ancient housekeeping. The Christian was permitted, according to Clement of Alexandria, to bestow on his wife one ring of gold, in order that, being entrusted with the care of his domestic concerns, she might seal up that which might be insecure. But these rings must not have any idolatrous engraving, only such as might suggest Christian or gentle thoughts, the dove, the fish,* the ship, the anchor, or the Apostolic fisherman fishing for men, which would remind them of children drawn out of the waters of baptism.ʸ Tertullian mentions a communion cup with the image of the Good Shepherd embossed upon it. But Christian symbolism soon disdained these narrow limits, extended itself into the whole domain of the Old Testament as well as of the Gospel, and even ventured at times

---

Auster in lævâ consistit; Occidens sub plantis formātur. Unde Apostolus dicit: ut sciamus, quæ sit altitudo, et latitudo, et longitudo, et profundum. Aves quando volant ad æthera, formam crucis assumunt; homo natans per aquas, vel orans, formâ crucis vehitur. Navis per maria antennâ cruci similatâ sufflatur. Thau literæ signum salutis et crucis describitur." Hieronym. in Marc. xv.

* The 'ΙΧΘΥΣ, according to the rule of the ancient anagram, meant Ἰησοῦς Χριστὸς Θεοῦ Υἱὸς Σωτήρ.

It is remarkable, according to the high authority of the Cavalier de Rossi, that after Constantine the ΙΧΘΥΣ as an anagram and as a symbol almost entirely disappears. It was a secret symbol used for the purpose of what we may venture to call Christian Freemasonry in early and dangerous times.—See the long and very curious letter addressed to Dom Pitra, Editor of the Spicilegium Solesmense, t. iii.; especially p. 498.

ʸ Clem. Alex. Pædagog. iii, 2.

over the unhallowed borders of Paganism. The persons and incidents of the Old Testament had all a typical or allegorical reference to the doctrines of Christianity.[a] Adam asleep, while Eve was taken from his side, represented the death of Christ; Eve, the mother of all who are born to new life; Adam and Eve with the serpent had a latent allusion to the new Adam and the Cross. Cain and Abel, Noah and the ark with the dove and the olive branch, the sacrifice of Isaac, Joseph sold by his brethren as a bondslave, Moses by the burning bush, breaking the tables of the law, striking water from the rock, with Pharaoh perishing in the Red Sea, the ark of God, Samson bearing the gates of Gaza, Job on the dung-heap, David and Goliah, Elijah in the car of fire, Tobias with the fish, Daniel in the lion's den, Jonah issuing from the whale's belly or under the gourd, the three children in the fiery furnace, Ezekiel by the valley of dead bones, were favourite subjects, and had all their mystic significance. They reminded the devout worshipper of the Sacrifice, Resurrection, and Redemption of Christ. The direct illustrations of the New Testament showed the Lord of the Church on a high mountain, with four rivers, the Gospels, flowing from it; the Good Shepherd bearing the lamb,[a] and sometimes the Apostles and Saints of a later time appeared in the symbols. Paganism lent some of her spoils to the conqueror.[b] The Saviour was represented under the

---

[a] See Mamachi, Dei Costumi de' primitivi Christiani, lib. l. c. iv.

[a] There is a Heathen prototype (see R. Rochette) even for this good shepherd, and one of the earliest images is encircled with the "Four Seasons" represented by Genii with Pagan attributes. Compare Munter, p. 61.

Tombstones, and even Inscriptions, were freely borrowed. One Christian tomb has been published by P. Lupi, inscribed "Diis Manibus."

[b] In three very curious dissertations in the last volume of the Memoirs of the Academy of Inscriptions on works of art in the catacombs of Rome, M.

person and with the lyre of Orpheus, either as the civiliser of men, or in allusion to the Orphic poetry, which had already been interpolated with Christian images. Hence also the lyre was the emblem of truth. Other images, particularly those of animals, were not uncommon.* The Church was represented by a ship, the anchor denoted the pure ground of faith; the stag implied the hart which thirsted after the water-brooks; the horse the rapidity with which men ought to run and embrace the doctrine of salvation; the hare the timid Christian hunted by persecutors; the lion prefigured strength, or appeared as the emblem of the tribe of Judah; the fish was an anagram of the Saviour's name; the dove indicated the simplicity, the cock the vigilance, of the Christian; the peacock and the phœnix the Resurrection.

But these were simple and artless memorials to which devotion gave all their value and significance; in them-

---

Raoul Rochette has shown how much, either through the employment of Heathen artists, or their yet imperfectly unheathenised Christianity, the Christians borrowed from the monumental decorations, the symbolic figures, and even the inscriptions, of Heathenism. M. Rochette says, "La physionomie presque payenne qu'offre la décoration des catacombes de Rome," p. 99. The Protestant travellers, Burnet and Misson, from the singular mixture of the sacred and the profane in these monuments, inferred that these catacombs were common places of burial for Heathens and Christians. The Roman antiquarians, however, have clearly proved the contrary. M. Raoul Rochette, as well as M. Rostelli (in an Essay in the Roms Beschreibung), consider this point conclusively made out in favour of the Roman writers. M. R. Rochette has adduced monuments in which the symbolic images and the language of Heathenism and Christianity are strangely mingled together. Munter had observed the Jordan represented as a river god.

* The catacombs at Rome are the chief authorities for this symbolic school of Christian art. They are represented in the works of Bosio, Roma Sotteranea, Aringhi, Bottari, and Boldetti. But perhaps the best view of them, being in fact a very judicious and well-arranged selection of the most curious works of early Christian art, may be found in the Sinnbilder und Kunstvorstellungen der alten Christen, by Bishop Munter.

The

selves they neither had, nor aimed at grandeur or beauty. They touched the soul by the reminiscences which they awakened, or the thoughts which they suggested; they had nothing of that inherent power over the emotions of the soul which belongs to the higher works of art.[d]

Art must draw nearer to human nature and to the

The recent discoveries in the Catacombs add some curious facts to the history of the symbolism of Christian art. In the catacomb of Callistus discovered and explored by the Cav. de Rossi, which contains according to his statement the remains of eleven Roman Pontiffs, from Pontianus to Melchiades, as well as those of St. Cæcilia, appear, in I fear fading colours, symbolic representations of the Rite of Baptism and of the Holy Eucharist. There is a man with a cloak or pallium over a tunic, laying hands on a naked child, just emerged from a stream of running water; on the other side is a seated figure, with a pallium, like the dress of a philosopher, apparently in the act of preaching.

The symbolism of the Eucharist is more various, in more than one picture, and therefore more obscure. In one is a table with loaves of bread, and a fish in a platter. On one wall is a man stretching out his naked arm over the bread, as if, according to De Rossi, in the act of consecrating it; on the other is a woman in the act of prayer—it is conjectured that she symbolises the Church. The fish (the Ἰχθύς), according to De Rossi, symbolises the Saviour; the real presence (or if I understand Cav. de Rossi, more than the real presence); but

how a symbol can be more than symbolic, I am at a loss to comprehend. C. de Rossi's connection of the remarkable representation of the scene in John xxi. 9 and 10, with the Eucharist seems to me a very perilous interpretation, especially to a devout Roman Catholic. Letter to Dom Pitra, quoted above. Note, p. 328.

[d] All these works in their different forms are in general of coarse and inferior execution. The funereal vases found in the Christian cemeteries are of the lowest style of workmanship. The senator Buonarotti, in his work, "De' Vetri Cemeteriali," thus accounts for this:—"Stettero sempre lontane da quelle arti, colle quali avessero potuto correr pericolo di contaminarsi colla idolatria, e da ciò avvenne, che pochi, o niuno di essi si diede alla pittura e alla scultura, le quali avranno per oggetto principale di rappresentare le deità, o le favole de' gentili. Niuhe, volendo i fedeli adornar con simboli devoti i loro vasi, erano forzati per lo più a valersi di artefici inesperti, e che professavano altri mestieri." See Maachi, vol. i. p. 275. Compare Rumohr, who suggests other reasons for the rudeness of the earliest Christian relief, in my opinion, though by no means irreconcilable with this, neither so simple nor satisfactory. Page 170.

truth of life, before it can accomplish its object. The elements of this feeling, even the first sense of external grandeur and beauty, had yet to be infused into the Christian mind. The pure and holy and majestic inward thoughts and sentiments had to work into form, and associate themselves with appropriate visible images. This want and this desire were long unfelt.

The person of the Saviour was a subject of grave dispute among the older fathers. Some took the expressions of the sacred writings in a literal sense, and insisted that his outward form was mean and unseemly. Justin Martyr speaks of his want of form and comeliness.[e] Tertullian, who could not but be in extremes, expresses the same sentiment with his accustomed vehemence. The person of Christ wanted not merely divine majesty, but even human beauty.[f] Clement of Alexandria maintains the same opinion.[g] But the most curious illustration of this notion occurs in the work of Origen against Celsus. In the true spirit of Grecian art and philosophy, Celsus denies that the Deity could dwell in a mean form or low stature. Origen is embarrassed with the argument; he fears to recede from the literal interpretation of Isaiah, but endeavours to soften it off, and denies that it refers to lowliness of stature, or means more than the absence of noble form or pre-eminent beauty. He then triumphantly adduces the verse of the forty-fourth Psalm, "Ride on in thy loveliness and in thy beauty."[h]

[Marginal note: Person of the Saviour.]

---

[e] Τὸν δειλὴ καὶ ἄτιμον φαίνοντα. Dial. cum Tryph. 85 and 88, 100.

[f] " Quodcumque illud corpusculum sit, quoniam habitum, et quoniam conspectum sit, si inglorius, si ignobilis, si inhonorabilis ; meus erit Christus. . . — Sed species ejus inhonorata, deficiens ultra omnes homines." Contr.

Marc. iii. 17. " Ne aspectu quidem honestus." Adv. Judæos, c. 14. " Etiam despicientium formam ejus hæc erat vox. Adeo nec humanæ honestatis corpus fuit, nedum cœlestis claritatis." De Carn. Christi, c. 9.

[g] Pædagog. iii. 1.

[h] 'Αμηχανὸν γὰρ ὅτῳ θεῖον τι

But as the poetry of Christianity obtained more full possession of the human mind, these debasing and inglorious conceptions were repudiated by the more vivid imagination of the great writers in the fourth century. The great principle of Christian art began to awaken; the outworking as it were, of the inward purity, beauty, and harmony, upon the symmetry of the external form, and the lovely expression of the countenance. Jerome, Chrysostom, Ambrose, Augustine, with one voice, assert the majestic and engaging appearance of the Saviour. The language of Jerome first shows the sublime conception which was brooding, as it were, in the Christian mind, and was at length slowly to develope itself up to the gradual perfection of Christian art. "Assuredly that splendour and majesty of the hidden divinity, which shone even in his human countenance, could not but attract at first sight all beholders." "Unless he had something celestial in his countenance and in his look, the Apostles would not immediately have followed him."[1] "The Heavenly Father poured upon him in full streams that corporeal grace, which is distilled drop by drop upon mortal man." Such are the glowing expressions of Chrysostom.[k] Gregory of Nyssa applies all the vivid imagery of the Song of Solomon to the person as well as to the doctrine of Christ; and Augustine declares that "He

πλέον τῶν ἄλλων προσῆν, μηδὲν ἄλλου διαφέρειν τοῦτο δὲ οὐδὲν ἄλλου διέφερεν, ἀλλ' ὅς φασί, μικρὸν, καὶ δυσειδὶς, καὶ ἀγενὲς ἦν. Celsus, apud Origen. vl. 75. Origen quotes the text of the LXX., in which it is the forty-fourth, and thus translated: Τῇ ὡραιότητί σου, καὶ τῷ κάλλει σου καὶ ἔντεινον, καὶ κατευοδοῦ, καὶ βασίλευε.

[1] "Certe fulgor ipse et majestas divinitatis occultæ, quæ etiam in humanâ facie relucebat, ex primo ad se recipientes trahere poterat aspectu." Hieronym. in Matth. c. ix. 9.

"Nisi enim habuisset et in vultu quiddam et in oculis sidereum, nunquam eum statim secuti fuissent Apostoli." Epist. ad Princip. Virginem.

[k] In Psalm xliv.

was beautiful on his mother's bosom, beautiful in the arms of his parents, beautiful upon the Cross, beautiful in the sepulchre."

There were some, however, who even at this, and to a much later period, chiefly among those addicted to monkish austerity, adhered to the older opinion, as though human beauty were something carnal and material. St. Basil interprets even the forty-fourth Psalm in the more austere sense. Many of the painters among the Greeks, even in the eighth century, who were monks of the rule of St. Basil, are said to have been too faithful to the judgement of their master, or perhaps their rude art was better qualified to represent a mean figure, with harsh outline and stiff attitude and a blackened countenance, rather than majesty of form or beautiful expression. Such are the Byzantine pictures of this school. The harsh Cyril of Alexandria repeats the assertion of the Saviour's mean appearance, even beyond the ordinary race of men, in the strongest language.[m] This controversy proves decisively that there was no traditional type, which was admitted to represent the human form of the Saviour. The distinct assertion of Augustine, that the form and countenance of Christ were entirely unknown, and painted with every possible variety of expression, is conclusive as to the West.[n] In the East we may dismiss at once as a

---

[m] 'Ἀλλὰ τὸ εἶδος αὐτοῦ ἄτιμον, ἐκλεῖπον παρὰ πάντας τοὺς υἱοὺς τῶν ἀνθρώπων. De Nad. Nos, lib. ii. t. i. p. 43.

[n] "Qua fuerit ille facie nos penitus ignoramus: nam et ipsius Dominicæ facies carnis innumerabilium cogitationum diversitate variatur et fingitur, quæ tamen una erat, quæcunque erat." De Trin. lib. vii. c. 4, 5.

The Christian apologists uniformly acknowledge the charge, that they have no altars or images. Minuc. Fel. Octavius, x. p. 61. Arnob. vi. post init. Origen, contrà Celsum, viii. p. 389. Compare Jablonski (Dissertatio de Origine Imaginum Christi, opuscul. vol. iii. p. 377) who well argues that, consistently with Jewish manners, there could not have been any likeness of the Lord. Compare Pearson on the Creed, vol. ii. p. 101.

manifest fable, probably of local superstition, the statue of Christ at Cæsarea Philippi, representing him in the act of healing the woman with the issue of blood.[o] But there can be no doubt that paintings, purporting to be actual resemblances of Jesus, of Peter, and of Paul, were current in the time of Eusebius in the East,[p] though I am disinclined to receive the authority of a later writer, that Constantine adorned his new city with likenesses of Christ and his Apostles.

The earliest images emanated, no doubt, from the Gnostic sects, who not merely blended the Christian and Pagan, or Oriental notions on their gems and seals, engraved with the mysterious Abraxas; but likewise, according to their eclectic system, consecrated small golden or silver images of all those ancient sages whose doctrines they had adopted, or had fused together in their wild and various theories. The image of Christ appeared with those of Pythagoras, Plato, Aristotle, and probably some of the eastern philosophers.[q] The Carpocratians had painted portraits of Christ; and Marcellina,[r] a celebrated female heresiarch, exposed to the view of the Gnostic church in Rome, the portraits of Jesus and St. Paul, of Homer,

Earliest Gnostic Images.

---

[o] Euseb. H. E. vii. 18, with the Excursus of Heinichen. These were, probably, two bronze figures, one of a kneeling woman in the act of supplication; the other, the upright figure of a man, probably of a Cæsar, which the Christian inhabitants of Cæsarea Philippi transformed into the Saviour and the woman in the Gospels: Τούτον δὲ τὸν ἀνδριάντα εἰκόνα τοῦ Ἰησοῦ φέρειν ἔλεγον. Eusebius seems desirous of believing the story. Compare Munter.

[p] Ὅτε καὶ τῶν Ἀποστόλων τῶν αὐτοῦ τὰς εἰκόνας Παύλου καὶ Πέτρου καὶ αὐτοῦ δὴ τοῦ Χριστοῦ διὰ χρωμάτων ἐν γραφαῖς σωζομένας ἱστορήσαμεν. Ibid. loc. cit.

[q] Irenæus de Hær. l. c. 84 (edit. Grabe). Epiphan. Hæres. xxvii. 6. Augustin. de Hæresib. c. vii. These images of Christ were said to have been derived from the collection of Pontius Pilate. Compare Jablonski's Dissertation.

[r] Marcellina lived about the middle of the second century, or a little later.

and of Pythagoras. Of this nature, no doubt, were the images of Abraham, Orpheus, Pythagoras, Apollonius, and Christ, set up in his private chapel by the Emperor Alexander Severus. These small images,[*] which varied very much, it should seem, in form and feature, could contribute but little, if in the least, to form that type of superhuman beauty, which might mingle the sentiment of human sympathy with reverence for the divinity of Christ. Christian art long brooded over such feelings as those expressed by Jerome and Augustine, before it could even attempt to embody them in marble or colour.[t]

---

[*] Of these Gnostic Images of Christ there are only two extant which seem to have some claim to authenticity and antiquity. Those from the collection of Chifflet are now considered to represent Serapis. One is mentioned by M. Raoul Rochette (Types Imitatifs de l'Art du Christianisme, p. 21); it is a stone, a kind of tessera with a head of Christ, young and beardless, in profile, with the word ΧΡΙΣΤΟΣ in Greek characters, with the symbolic fish below. This is in the collection of M. Fortin d'Urban, and is engraved as a vignette to M. R. Rochette's essay. The other is adduced in an "Essay on Ancient Coins, Medals and Gems, as illustrating the Progress of Christianity in the Early Ages, by the Rev. R. Walsh." This is a kind of medal or tessera of metal, representing Christ as he is described in the apocryphal letter of Lentulus to the Roman senate. (Fabric. Cod. Apoc. Nov. Test. p. 301, 302.) It has a head of Christ, the hair parted over the forehead, covering the ears, and falling over the shoulders; the shape is long, the beard short and thin. It has the name of Jesus in Hebrew, and has not the nimbus, or glory. On the reverse is an inscription in a kind of cabalistic character, of which the sense seems to be, "The Messiah reigns in peace; God is made man." This may possibly be a tessera of the Jewish Christians; or modelled after a Gnostic type of the first age of Christianity. See Discours sur les Types Imitatifs de l'Art du Christianisme, par M. Raoul Rochette.

[t] I must not omit the description of the person of our Saviour in the spurious Epistle of Lentulus to the Roman Senate (see Fabric. Cod. Apoc. N. T. i. p. 301). since it is referred to constantly by writers on early Christian art. But what proof is there of the existence of this epistle previous to the great era of Christian painting? "He was a man of tall and well-proportioned form; the countenance severe and impressive, so as to move the beholders at once to love and awe. His hair was of the colour of wine (vinei coloris), reaching to his ears,

The earliest pictures of the Saviour seem formed on one type or model. They all represent the oval countenance, slightly lengthened; the grave, soft, and melancholy expression; the short thin beard; the hair parted on the forehead into two long masses, which fall upon the shoulders.[u] Such are the features which characterise the earliest extant painting, that on the vault of the cemetery of St. Callistus, in which the Saviour is represented as far as his bust, like the images on bucklers in use among the Romans.[x] A later painting, in the chapel of the cemetery of St. Pontianus, resembles this;[y] and a third was discovered in the catacomb then called that of St. Callistus by Boldetti, but unfortunately perished while he was looking at it, in the attempt to remove it from the wall. The same countenance appears on some, but not the earliest, reliefs on the sarcophagi, five of which may be referred, according to M. Rochette, to the time of Julian. Of one, that of Olybrius, the date appears certain—the close of the fourth century. These, the paintings at least, are no doubt the work of Greek artists; and this head may be considered the archetype,

The earliest portraits of the Saviour.

with no radiation (sine radiatione, without the nimbus), and standing up, from his ears, clustering and bright, and flowing down over his shoulders, parted on the top according to the fashion of the Nazarenes. The brow high and open; the complexion clear, with a delicate tinge of red; the aspect frank and pleasing; the nose and mouth finely formed; the beard thick, parted, and the colour of the hair; the eyes blue, and exceedingly bright. . . His countenance was of wonderful sweetness and gravity; no one ever saw him laugh, though he was seen to weep; his stature was tall; the hands and arms finely formed. . . . He was the most beautiful of the sons of men." Compare Latin Christianity. The unanswerable proof that this description is of late date is that it was not produced at the second Council of Nicæa, at which time Christendom was ransacked to find proofs, good or bad, of early image worship.

[u] Raoul Rochette, p. 26.
[x] Bottari, Pitture e Sculture Sacre, vol. ii. tav. lxx. p. 42.
[y] This, however, was probably repainted in the time of Hadrian I.

the Hieratic model, of the Christian conception of the Saviour, imagined in the East, and generally adopted in the West.[a]

Reverential awe, diffidence in their own skill, the still dominant sense of the purely spiritual nature of the Parental Deity,[a] or perhaps the exclusive habit of dwelling upon the Son as the direct object of religious worship, restrained early Christian art from those attempts to which we are scarcely reconciled by the sublimity and originality of Michael Angelo and Raffaelle. Even the symbolic representation of the Father was rare. Where it does appear, it is under the symbol of an immense hand issuing from a cloud, or a ray of light streaming from heaven, to imply, it may be presumed, the creative and all-enlightening power of the Universal Father.[b]

---

[a] Rumohr considers a statue of the Good Shepherd in the Vatican collection, from its style, to be a very early work; the oldest monument of Christian sculpture, prior to the urn of Junius Bassus, which is of the middle of the fourth century. Italienische Forschungen, vol. I. p. 168. In that usually thought the earliest, that of Junius Bassus, Jesus Christ is represented between the Apostles, beardless, seated in a curule chair, with a roll half unfolded in his hand, and under his feet a singular representation of the upper part of a man holding an inflated veil with his two hands, a common symbol or personification of heaven. See R. Rochette, p. 43, who considers these sarcophagi anterior to the formation of the ordinary type.

[a] Compare Munter, ii. p. 49: "Ne- fas habent docti ejus (ecclesiæ Catholicæ) credere Deum figurâ humani corporis terminatam." August, Conf. vi. 11.

[b] M. Emeric David (in his Discours sur les Anciens Monumens, to which I am indebted for much information), says that the French artists had first the *heureuse hardiesse* of representing the Eternal Father under the human form. The instance to which he alludes is contained in a Latin Bible (in the Cabinet Impérial) cited by Montfaucon, but not fully described. It was presented to Charles the Bald by the canons of the church of Tours, in the year 850. This period is far beyond the bounds of our present history. See therefore E. David, pp. 43. 46.

The Virgin Mother could not but offer herself to the imagination, and be accepted at once as the subject of Christian art. As respect for the mother of Christ deepened into reverence, reverence bowed down to adoration; as she became the mother of God, and herself a deity in popular worship, this worship was the parent, and, in some sense, the offspring of art. Augustine, indeed, admits that the real features of the Virgin, as of the Saviour, were unknown.[a] But the fervent language of Jerome shows that art had already attempted to shadow out the conception of mingling virgin purity and maternal tenderness, which as yet probably was content to dwell within the verge of human nature, and aspired not to mingle a divine idealism with these more mortal feelings. The outward form and countenance could not but be the image of the purity and gentleness of the soul within: and this primary object of Christian art could not but give rise to one of its characteristic distinctions from that of the ancients, the substitution of mental expression for purely corporeal beauty. As reverential modesty precluded all exposure of the form, the countenance was the whole picture. This reverence, indeed, in the very earliest specimens of the art, goes still further, and confines itself to the expression of composed and dignified attitude. The artists did not even venture to expose the face. With one exception, the Virgin appears veiled on the reliefs on the sarcophagi, and in the earliest paintings. The oldest known picture of the Virgin is in the catacomb, once so called, of St. Callistus,

---

[a] "Neque enim novimus faciem Virginis Mariæ." Augustin. de Trin. c. vii. "Ut ipsa corporis facies simulacrum fuerit mentis, figura probitatis." Ambros. de Virgin. lib. li. c. 2.

in which also appears seated in the calm majesty, and in the dress, of a Roman matron. It is the transition, as it were, from ancient to modern art, which still timidly adheres to its conventional type of dignity.[d] But in the sarcophagi, art has already more nearly approximated to its most exquisite subject—the Virgin Mother is seated, with the divine child in her lap, receiving the homage of the Wise Men. She is still veiled,[e] but with the rounded form and grace of youth, and a kind of sedate chastity of expression in her form, which seems designed to convey the feeling of gentleness and holiness. Two of these sarcophagi, one in the Vatican collection, and one at Milan, appear to disprove the common notion that the representation of the Virgin was unknown before the Council of Ephesus.[f] That council, in its zeal against the doctrines of Nestorius, established, as it has been called, a Hieratic type of the Virgin, which is traced throughout Byzantine art, and on the coins of the Eastern empire. This type, however, gradually degenerates with the darkness of the age, and the decline of art. The countenance, sweetly smiling on the child, becomes sad and severe. The head is bowed with a gloomy and almost sinister expression, and the countenance gradually darkens, till it assumes a black colour, and seems to adapt itself in this respect to an ancient tradition. At length even the sentiment of maternal affection is effaced, both the mother and child become stiff and lifeless, the child is

---

[d] Bottari, Pitture e Sculture Sacre, t. iii. p. 111, tav. 216. See Mémoire de M. Raoul Rochette, Académ. Inscript.

[e] In Bottari there is one picture of the Virgin with the head naked, t. ii. tav. cxxvi. The only one known to M. Raoul Rochette.

[f] A.D. 431. This opinion is maintained by Basnage and most Protestant writers.

swathed in tight bands, and has an expression of pain rather than of gentleness or placid infancy.[g]

The apostles, particularly St. Peter and St. Paul, were among the earlier objects of Christian art. Though in one place, St. Augustine asserts that the persons of the Apostles were equally unknown with that of the Saviour, in another he acknowledges that their pictures were exhibited on the walls of many churches for the edification of the faithful.[h] In a vision ascribed to Constantine, but of very doubtful authority, the Emperor is said to have recognised the apostles by their likeness to their portraits.[i] A picture known to St. Ambrose pretended to have come down by regular tradition from their time: and Chrysostom, when he studied the writings, gazed with reverence on what he supposed an authentic likeness of the apostle.[k] Paul and Peter appear on many of the oldest monuments, on the glass vessels, fragments of which have been discovered, and on which Jerome informs us that they were frequently painted. They are found, as we have seen, on the sarcophagus of Junius Bassus, and on many others. In one of these, in which the costume is Roman, St. Paul is represented bald, and with the high nose, as

---

[g] Compare Raoul Rochette, page 35. M. R. Rochette observes much similarity between the pictures of the Virgin ascribed to St. Luke, the tradition of whose painting ascends to the sixth century, and the Egyptian works which represent Isis nursing Horus. I have not thought it necessary to notice further these palpable forgeries, though the object, in so many places, of popular worship.

[h] St. Augustin in Genesin, cap. xiii. "Quod pluribus locis simul eos (apostolos) cum illo (Christo) pictos viderint * * * in pictis parietibus." Augustin, de Cons. Evang. i. 16.

[i] Hadrian I. Epist. ad Imp. Constantin. et Iren, Concil. Nic. ii. art. 2.

[k] These two assertions rest on the authority of Joannes Damascenus, de Imagin.

he is described in the Philopatris,ᵐ which, whatever its age, has evidently taken these personal peculiarities of the Apostle from the popular Christian representations. St. Peter has usually a single tuft of hair on his bald forehead.ⁿ Each has a book, the only symbol of his apostleship. St. Peter has neither the sword nor the keys. In the same relief, St. John and St. James are distinguished from the rest by their youth; already, therefore, this peculiarity was established which prevails throughout Christian art. The majesty of age, and a kind of dignity of precedence, are attributed to Peter and Paul, while all the grace of youth, and the most exquisite gentleness, are centered in John. They seem to have assumed this peculiar character of expression, even before their distinctive symbols.

It may excite surprise that the acts of martyrdom did not become the subjects of Christian art, till far down in the dark ages. That of St. Sebastian, a relief in terra-cotta, which formerly existed in the cemetery of St. Priscilla, and that of Peter and Paul in the Basilica Siciniana, assigned by Ciampini to the fifth century, are rare exceptions, and both of doubtful date and authenticity. The martyrdom of St. Felicitas and her seven children, discovered in 1812, in a small oratory within the baths of Titus, cannot be earlier, according to M. R. Rochette, than the seventh century.º

The absence of all gloomy or distressing subjects is the remarkable and characteristic feature in the

---

ᵐ Γαλιλαῖος ἀναφαλαντίας ἐπίρρινος. Philop. c. xii.
ⁿ Munter says the arrest of St. Peter (Acts xii. 1, 3) is the only subject from the Acts of the Apostles among the monuments in the catacombs. ii. p. 104.
º Raoul Rochette, in Mém. de l'Académie, tom. xiii p. 165.

catacombs of Rome and in all the earliest Christian art. A modern writer, who has studied the subject with profound attention, has expressed himself in the following language:[p]—"The catacombs destined for the sepulture of the primitive Christians, for a long time peopled with martyrs, ornamented during times of persecution, and under the dominion of melancholy thoughts and painful duties, nevertheless everywhere represent in all the historic parts of these paintings only what is noble and exalted,[q] and in that which constitutes the purely decorative part only pleasing and graceful subjects, the images of the good shepherd, representations of the vintage, of the agape, with pastoral scenes: the symbols are fruits, flowers, palms, crowns, lambs, doves, in a word nothing but what excites emotions of joy, innocence, and charity. Entirely occupied with the celestial recompense which awaited them after the trials of their troubled life, and often of so dreadful a death, the Christians saw in death, and even in execution, only a way by which they arrived at this everlasting happiness; and far from associating with this image that of the tortures or privations which opened heaven before them, they took pleasure in enlivening it with smiling colours, or presented it under agreeable symbols, adorning it with flowers and vine leaves; for it is thus that the asylum of death appears to us in the Christian catacombs. There is no sign of mourning, no token of resentment, no expression of vengeance; all breathes softness, benevolence, charity."[r]

[p] M. D'Agincourt says, "Il n'a rencontré lui-même dans ces souterrains aucune trace de nul autre tableau (one of barbarian and late design had before been noticed) représentant une martyre." Hist. de l'Art.

[q] Des traits héroïques.

[r] Gregory of Nyssa, however, de-

308   THE CRUCIFIX.   BOOK IV.

It may seem even more singular, that the passion of our Lord himself remained a subject interdicted, as it were, by awful reverence. The cross, it has been said, was the symbol of Christianity many centuries before the crucifix.[a] It was rather a cheerful and consolatory than a depressing and melancholy sign; it was adorned with flowers, with crowns and precious stones, a pledge of the resurrection, rather than a memorial of the passion. The catacombs of Rome, faithful to their general character, offer no instance of a crucifixion, nor does any allusion to such a subject of art occur in any early writer.[b] Cardinal Bona gives the following as the progress of the gradual change. I. The simple cross.[c] II. The cross with the lamb at the foot of it.[d] III. Christ clothed, on the cross, with hands uplifted in prayer, but not nailed to it. IV. Christ fastened to the cross with four nails,

---

scribes the heroic acts of St. Theodorus as painted on the walls of a church dedicated to that saint. "The painter had represented his sufferings, the forms of the tyrants like wild beasts. The fiery furnace, the death of the athlete of Christ—all this had the painter expressed by colours, as in a book, and adorned the temple like a pleasant and blooming meadow. The dumb walls speak and edify."

[b] See, among other authorities, Munter, page 77. "Es ist unmöglich das alter der Crucifixe genau zu bestimmen. Von dem Ende des siebenten Jahrhunderts kannte die Kirche sie nicht."

[c] The decree of the Quinisextan Council, in 695, is the clearest proof

that up to that period the Passion had been usually represented under a symbolic or allegoric form.

[d] There is an interesting description by the Cav. de Rossi in the Spicilegium Solesmense, iv. p. 505, et seqq., on the form of the cross, as usually found in the catacombs. Before the beginning of the fourth century the simple cross + occurs rarely if at all. It is "dissembled," according to de Rossi's phrase, in various ways, as X, so as to be confounded with the initial letter of Christ, and takes other monogrammatic forms. Under Constantine and after Constantine it is generally the monogram with the Labarum. See pp. 329, 331 at the bottom, and 322.

[a] "Stab cruce sanguineis nivea stat Christus in agno, Agnus ut innocua injusto datur bestia letho." Pauli. Nolan, Epist. 32.

still living, and with open eyes. He was not represented as dead till the tenth or eleventh century.ʸ There is some reason to believe that the bust of the Saviour first appeared on the cross, and afterwards the whole person; the head was at first erect, with some expression of divinity; by degrees it drooped with the agony of pain, the face was wan and furrowed, and death, with all its anguish, was imitated by the utmost power of coarse art—mere corporeal suffering without sublimity, all that was painful in truth, with nothing that was tender and affecting. This change took place among the monkish artists of the Lower Empire. Those of the order of St. Basil introduced it into the West; and from that time these painful images, with those of martyrdom, and every scene of suffering which could be imagined by the gloomy fancy of anchorites, who could not be moved by less violent excitement, spread throughout Christendom. It required all the wonderful magic of Italian art to elevate them into sublimity.

But early Christian art, at least that of painting, was not content with these simpler subjects; it endeavoured to represent designs of far bolder and more intricate character. Among the earliest descriptions of Christian painting is that in the Church of St. Felix, by Paulinus of Nola.ᶻ In the colonnades

Paintings at Nola.

ʸ De cruce Vaticana. | ᶻ The lines are not without merit:

"Quo dure Jordanes suspenso gurgite fluit
Fluctibus, a facie divinæ restitit arcæ,
Vis nova divisit flumen; pars amne reclusa
Constitit, et fluvii pars in mare lapsa cucurrit,
Desilitque vadum: et validus qui forte ruebat
Impetus, adstrictus alia cumulaverat undas,
Et tremula compage minax pendebat aqua; mons
Inspectans trementes pedes arcule profundo;
Et medio pedibus siccis in flumine ferri
Pulverulenta hominum duro vestigia limo."

If this description is drawn from the picture, not from the book, the painter must have possessed some talent for composition and for landscape, as well as for the drawing of figures.

of that church were painted scenes from the Old Testament: among them were the Passage of the Red Sea, Joshua and the Ark of God, Ruth and her Sister-in-law, one deserting, the other following her parent in fond fidelity;[a] an emblem, the poet suggests, of mankind, part deserting, part adhering to the true faith. The object of this embellishment of the churches was to beguile the rude minds of the illiterate peasants who thronged with no very exalted motives to the altar of St. Felix—to preoccupy their minds with sacred subjects, so that they might be less eager for the festival banquets, held with such munificence and with such a concourse of strangers, at the tomb of the martyr.[b] These gross and irreligious desires led them to the church; yet, gazing on these pictures, they would not merely be awakened by these holy examples to purer thoughts and holier emotions; they would

---

[a] "Quum geminae exindunt sese in diversa sorores;
Hath sequitur sanctam, quam deserit Orpa, parentem:
Perfidiam nurus una, fide is nurus altera monstrat.
Præfert viam Deum patriæ, patriam altera vitæ."

[b] "Forte requiratur, quanam ratione gerendi
Sederit hæc nobis sententia, pingere sanctas
Raro more domos animantibus adsimulatis.
   *   *   *   turba frequentior hic est
Rusticitas non casta fide, neque ducta legendi.
Hæc adsueta sibi sacris servire profanis,
Ventre live, tandem convertitur adversa Christo,
Dum sanctorum opera in Christo miratur aperta.
Propterea visum nobis opus utile, totis
Feleis domibus picturâ ludere sanctâ:
Si forte attonitas hæc per spectacula mentes
Agrestum caperet fucata coloribus umbra,
Quæ super exprimitur litera—si litera monstret
Quod manus expleolit: dumque omnes picta vicissim
Ostendunt relegantque sibi, vel tardius escæ
Sunt memores, dum grata oculis jejunia pascunt:
Atque ita se meliori stupefactis insinuat usu,
Dum fallit pictura famem; sanctasque legenti
Historiae castorum operum subrepit honestas
Exemplis inducta piis; potatur hianti
Sobrietas, nimii subrepti oblivia vini:
Inumque diem ducunt spatio majore tenentes,
Pocula rarescunt, quia per miracula tracta
Tempore, jam paucis superant epulantibus horæ."

In Natal. Felic., Poema xxiv.

feast their eyes instead of their baser appetites; an involuntary sobriety and forgetfulness of the wine flagon would steal over their souls; at all events, they would have less time to waste in the indulgence of their looser festivity.

Christianity has been the parent of music, probably as far surpassing in skill and magnificence the compositions of earlier times, as the cathedral organ the simpler instruments of the Jewish or Pagan religious worship. But this perfection of the art belongs to a much later period in Christian history. Like the rest of its service, the music of the Church no doubt grew up from a rude and simple, to a more splendid and artificial form. The practice of singing hymns is coeval with Christianity; the hearers of the Apostles sang the praises of God; and the first sound which reached the Pagan ear from the secluded sanctuaries of Christianity was the hymn to Christ as God.[c] The Church succeeded to an inheritance of religious lyrics as unrivalled in the history of poetry as of religion.[d] The Psalms were introduced early into the public service; but at first, apparently, though some psalms may have been sung on appropriate occasions — the 73rd, called the morning, and the 141st, the evening psalm — the whole Psalter was introduced only as part of the Old Testament, and read in the course of the service.[e] With the poetry did they borrow the music of the Synagogue? Was this music the same which had filled the spacious courts of

Music.

---

[c] See the famous Epistle of Pliny.

[d] The Temple Service, in Lightfoot's works, gives the Psalms which were appropriate to each day. The author has given a slight outline of this hymnology of the Temple in the Quarterly Review, xxxviii, page 20.

[e] Bingham's Antiquities, vol. xiv. 1, 5.

the Temple, perhaps answered to those sad strains which had been heard beside the waters of the Euphrates, or even descended from still earlier times of glory, when Deborah or when Miriam struck their timbrels to the praise of God? This question it must be impossible to answer; and no tradition, as far as I am aware, indicates the source from which the Church borrowed her primitive harmonies, though the probability is certainly in favour of their Jewish parentage.

The Christian hymns of the primitive churches seem to have been eucharistic and confined to the glorification of their God and Saviour.[f] Prayer was considered the language of supplication and humiliation; the soul awoke, as it were, in the hymn to more ardent expressions of gratitude and love. Probably, the music was nothing more at first than a very simple accompaniment, or no more than the accordance of the harmonious voices; it was the humble subsidiary of the hymn of praise, not itself the soul-engrossing art.[g] Nothing could be more simple than the earliest recorded hymns; they were fragments from the Scripture—the doxology, "Glory be to the Father, and to the Son, and to the Holy Ghost;" the angelic hymn, "Glory be to God on high;" the cherubic hymn from Revel. iv. 12.—"Holy, holy, holy;" the hymn of victory, Revel. xv. 3., "Great and marvellous are thy works." It was not improbably the cherubic hymn, to which Pliny alludes, as forming part of the Christian

---

[f] Gregory of Nyssa defines a hymn —ὕμνος ἐστὶν ἡ ἐπὶ τοῖς ὑπάρχουσιν ἡμῖν ἀγαθοῖς ἀνατιθεμένη τῷ Θεῷ εὐφημία. See Psalm II.

[g] Private individuals wrote hymns to Christ, which were generally sung. Euseb. H. E. v. 28; vii. 24.

worship. The "Magnificat" and the "Nunc dimittis" were likewise sung from the earliest ages; the Halleluia was the constant prelude or burden of the hymn.[b] Of the character of the music few and imperfect traces are found. In Egypt the simplest form long prevailed. In the monastic establishments one person arose and repeated the psalm, the others sate around in silence on their lowly seats, and responded, as it were, to the psalm within their hearts.[f] In Alexandria, by the order of Athanasius, the psalms were repeated with the slightest possible inflection of voice; it could hardly be called singing.[k] Yet, though the severe mind of Athanasius might disdain such subsidiaries, the power of music was felt to be a dangerous antagonist in the great religious contest. Already the soft and effeminate singing, begun by Paul of Samosata, had estranged the hearts of many worshippers, and his peculiar doctrines had stolen into the soul, which had been melted by the artificial melodies, introduced by him into the service. The Gnostic hymns of Bardesanes and Valentinus,[m] no doubt, had their musical accompaniment. Arius himself had composed hymns which were sung to popular airs; and the streets of Constantinople, even to the time of Chrysostom, echoed at night to those seductive strains which denied or imperfectly expressed the Trinitarian doctrines.

Chrysostom arrayed a band of orthodox choristers, who hymned the coequal Father, Son, and Holy Ghost. The Donatists in Africa adapted their enthusiastic hymns to wild and passionate melodies, which tended to keep up and inflame, as it were, with the sound of the trumpet, the fanaticism of their followers.[a]

The first change in the manner of singing was the substitution of singers,[b] who became a separate order in the Church, for the mingled voices of all ranks, ages, and sexes, which was compared by the great reformer of church music to the glad sound of many waters.[c]

The antiphonal singing, in which the different sides of the choir answered to each other in responsive verses, was first introduced at Antioch by Flavianus and Diodorus. Though, from the form of some of the psalms, it is not improbable that this system of alternate chanting may have prevailed in the Temple service, yet the place and the period of its appearance in the Christian Church seems to indicate a different source. The strong resemblance which it bears to the chorus of the Greek tragedy, might induce a suspicion, that as it borrowed its simple primitive music from Judaism, it may, in turn, have despoiled Paganism of some of its lofty religious harmonies.

This antiphonal chanting was introduced into the West[d] by Ambrose, and if it inspired, or even fully

---

[a] "Donatistæ nos reprehendunt, quod sobriè psallimus in ecclesiâ divina cantica Prophetarum, cum ipsi ebrietates suas ad canticum psalmorum humano ingenio compositorum quasi tubas exhortationis inflammant." Augustin. Confess.

[b] Compare Bingham. The leaders were called ὑποβολεῖς.

[c] "Responsoriis psalmorum, cantu mulierum, virginum, parvularum consonans undarum fragor resultat." Ambros. Hexam. l. iii. c. 5.

[d] Augustin. Confess. ix. 7. 1. How indeed could it be rejected, when it had received the authority of a vision of the blessed Ignatius, who was said to have heard the angels singing in the antiphonal manner the praises of the Holy Trinity. Socr. H. E. vi. 8.

accompanied the Te Deum, usually ascribed to that prelate, we cannot calculate too highly its effect upon the Christian mind. So beautiful was the music in the Ambrosian service, that the sensitive conscience of the young Augustine took alarm, lest, when he wept at the solemn music, he should be yielding to the luxury of sweet sounds, rather than imbibing the devotional spirit of the hymn.¹ Though alive to the perilous pleasure, yet he inclined to the wisdom of awakening weaker minds to piety by this enchantment of their hearing. The Ambrosian chant, with its more simple and masculine tones, is still preserved in the Church of Milan; in the rest of Italy it was superseded by the richer Roman chant, which was introduced by the Pope, Gregory the Great.²

---

¹ "Cum reminiscor lachrymas meas quas fudi ad cantus ecclesiæ tuæ, in primordiis recuperatæ fidei meæ, et nunc ipsum cum moveor, non cantu sed rebus quæ cantantur, cum liquidâ voce et convenientissimâ modulatione cantantor: magnam instituti hujus utilitatem rursus agnosco. Ita fluctuo inter periculum voluptatis et experimentum salubritatis; magisque adducor, non quidem irretractabilem sententiam proferens cantandi consuetudinem approbare in ecclesia: ut per oblectamenta aurium, infirmior animus in affectum pietatis assurgat." Augustin. Confess. x. 33, 3. Compare ix. 7, 2.

² The cathedral chanting of England has probably almost alone preserved the ancient antiphonal system, which has been discarded for a greater variety of instruments, and a more complicated system of music, in the Roman Catholic service. This, if I may presume to offer a judgement, has lost as much in solemnity and majesty as it has gained in richness and variety. "Ce chant (le Plain Chant) tel qu'il subsiste encore aujourd'hui est un reste bien defiguré, mais bien precieux de l'ancienne musique, qui après avoir passé par la main des barbares n'a pas perdu encore toutes ses premières beantés." Millin, Dictionnaire des Beaux Arts.

CHAPTER V.

Conclusion.

THUS, then, Christianity had become the religion of the Roman world: it had not, indeed, confined its adventurous spirit of moral conquest within these limits; yet it is in the Roman world that its more extensive and permanent influence, as well as its peculiar vicissitudes, can alone be followed out with distinctness and accuracy.

Paganism was slowly expiring; the hostile edicts of the emperors, down to the final legislation of Justinian, did but accelerate its inevitable destiny. Its temples, where not destroyed, were perishing by neglect and peaceful decay, or, where their solid structures defied these less violent assailants, stood deserted and overgrown with weeds; the unpaid priests ceased to offer, not only sacrifice, but prayer, and were gradually dying out as a separate order of men. Its philosophy lingered in a few cities of Greece, till the economy or the religion of the Eastern Emperor finally closed its schools.

The doom of the Roman empire was likewise sealed: the horizon on all sides was dark with overwhelming clouds; and the internal energies of the empire, the military spirit, the wealth, the imperial power, had crumbled away. The external unity was dissolved; the provinces were gradually severed from the main body; the Western empire was rapidly sinking, and the

Eastern falling into hopeless decrepitude. Yet though her external polity was dissolved, though her visible throne was prostrate upon the earth, Rome still ruled the mind of man, and her secret domination maintained its influence, until it assumed a new outward form. Rome survived in her laws, in her municipal institutions, and in that which lent a new sanctity and reverence to her laws, and gave strength by their alliance with its own peculiar polity to the municipal institutions—in her adopted religion. The empire of Christ succeeded to the empire of the Cæsars.

When it ascended the throne, assumed a supreme and universal dominion over mankind, became the legislator, not merely through public statutes, but in all the minute details of life, discharged, in fact, almost all the functions of civil as well as of religious government, Christianity could not but appear under a new form, and wear a far different appearance than when it was the humble and private faith of a few scattered individuals, or of only spiritually connected communities. As it was about to enter into its next period of conflict with barbarism, and to undergo the temptation of unlimited power, however it might depart from its primitive simplicity, and indeed recede from its genuine spirit, it is impossible not to observe how wonderfully (those who contemplate human affairs with religious minds may assert how providentially) it adapted itself to its altered position, and the new part which it was to fulfil in the history of man. We have already traced this gradual change in the formation of the powerful Hierarchy, in the development of Monasticism, the establishment of the splendid and imposing Ritual; we must turn our attention, before we close, to the new modification of the religion itself.

Its theology now appears wrought out into a regular, multifarious, and, as it were, legally established system.

Christian theology of this period. It was the consummate excellence of Christianity, that it blended in apparently indissoluble union religious and moral perfection. Its essential doctrine was, in its pure theory, inseparable from humane, virtuous, and charitable disposition. Piety to God, as he was impersonated in Christ, worked out, as it seemed, by spontaneous energy, into Christian beneficence.

But there has always been a strong propensity to disturb this nice balance: the dogmatic part of religion, the province of faith, is constantly endeavouring to set itself apart, and to maintain a separate existence. Faith, in this limited sense, aspires to be religion. This, in general, takes place soon after the first outburst, the strong impulse of new and absorbing religious emotions. At a later period morality attempts to stand alone, without the sanction or support of religious faith. One half of Christianity is thus perpetually striving to pass for the whole, and to absorb all the attention, to the neglect, to the disparagement of, at length to a total separation from, its heaven-appointed consort. The multiplication and subtle refinement of theologic dogmas, the engrossing interest excited by some dominant tenet, especially if associated with, or embodied in, a minute and rigorous ceremonial, tend to satisfy and lull the mind into complacent acquiescence in its own religious completeness. But directly religion began to *Separation of Christian faith and Christian morals* consider itself something apart, something exclusively dogmatic or exclusively ceremonial, an acceptance of certain truths by the belief, or the discharge of certain ritual observances, then the transition from separation to hostility was rapid and unimpeded. No sooner had Christianity divorced morality as its inseparable companion through life, than it formed an unlawful connection with any dominant passion; and the strange and unnatural union of Christian faith with ambition, avarice, cruelty, fraud, and even licence, appeared in strong contrast with its primitive harmony of doctrine and inward disposition. Thus in a great degree, while the Roman world became Christian in outward worship and in faith, it remained Heathen, or even at some periods worse than Heathenism in its better times, as to beneficence, gentleness, purity, social virtue, humanity, and peace. This extreme view may appear to be justified by the general survey of Christian society. Yet, in fact, religion did not, except never at the darkest periods, so completely insulate complete. itself, or so entirely recede from its natural alliance with morality, though it admitted, at each of its periods, much which was irreconcileable with its pure and original spirit. Hence the mingled character of its social and political, as well as of its personal influences. The union of Christianity with monachism, with sacerdotal domination, with the military spirit, with the spiritual autocracy of the papacy, with the advancement at one time, at another with the repression, of the human mind, had each their darker and brighter side; and were in succession (however they departed from the primal and ideal perfection of Christianity) to a certain extent beneficial, because apparently almost necessary to the social and intellectual developement of mankind at each particular juncture. So, for instance, military Christianity, which grew out of the inevitable incorporation of the force and energy of the barbarian conquerors with the sentiments and feelings of that age, and which finally produced chivalry, was, in fact, the substitution of inhumanity for Christian gentleness, of the love of glory for the love of peace. Yet was this indispensable to the preservation of Christianity in its contest with its new eastern antagonist. Unwarlike Christianity would have been trampled under foot, and have been in danger of total extermination, by triumphant Mohammedanism.

Yet even when its prevailing character thus stood in the most direct contrast with the spirit of the Gospel, it was not merely that the creed of Christianity in its primary articles was universally accepted, and a profound devotion filled the Christian mind, there was likewise a constant undergrowth, as it were, of Christian feelings, and even of Christian virtues. Nothing could contrast more strangely, for instance, than St. Louis slaughtering Saracens and heretics with his remorseless sword, and the Saviour of mankind by the Lake of Galilee; yet, when this dominant spirit of the age did not preoccupy the whole soul, the self-denial, the justice, the purity, even the gentleness of such a man as St. Louis bore still unanswerable testimony to the genuine influence of Christianity. Our illustration has carried us far beyond the boundaries of our history, but already the great characteristic distinction of later Christian history had begun to be developed, the severance of Christian faith from Christian love, the passionate attachment, the stern and remorseless maintenance of the Christian creed without or with only a partial practice of Christian virtue, or even the predominance of a tone of mind, in some respects absolutely inconsistent with genuine Christianity. While the human mind, in general, became more rigid in exacting, and more timid in departing from, the admitted doctrines of the church, the moral sense became more dull and obtuse to the purer and more evanescent beauty of Christian holiness. In truth it was so much more easy, in a dark and unreasoning age, to subscribe, or at least to render passive submission to, certain defined doctrines, than to work out those doctrines in their proper influences upon the life, that we deplore, rather than wonder at, this substitution of one half of the Christian religion for the whole. Nor are we astonished to find those, who were constantly violating the primary principles of Christianity, fiercely resenting, and, if they had the power, relentlessly avenging, any violation of the integrity of Christian faith. Heresy of opinion, we have seen, became almost the only crime against which excommunication pointed its thunders. The darker and more baleful heresy of unchristian passions, which assumed the language of Christianity, was either too general to be detected, or at best encountered with feeble and impotent remonstrance. Thus Christianity became at the same time more peremptorily dogmatic, and less influential; it assumed the supreme dominion over the mind, while it held but an imperfect and partial control over the passions and affections. The theology of the Gospel was the religion of the world: the spirit of the Gospel very far from the ruling influence of mankind.

Yet even the theology maintained its dominion, by in some degree accommodating itself to the human mind. It became to a certain degree *mythic* in its character, and *polytheistic* in its form.

Now had commenced what may be called, neither unreasonably nor unwarrantably, the mythic age of Christianity. As Christianity worked downward into the lower classes of society, as it received the rude and ignorant barbarians within its pale, the general effect could not but be, that the age would drag down the religion to its level, rather than the religion elevate the age to its own lofty standard.

The connection between the world of man and a higher order of things had been re-established; the approximation of the Godhead to the human race, the actual presence of the Incarnate Deity upon earth, was universally recognised; transcendental truths, beyond the sphere of human reason, had become the primary and elemental principles of human belief. A strongly imaginative period was the necessary consequence of this extraordinary impulse. It was the reign of faith, of faith which saw or felt the divine, or at least supernatural, agency, in every occurrence of life, and in every impulse of the heart; which offered itself as the fearless and undoubting interpreter of every event; which comprehended in its domain the past, the present, and the future; and seized upon the whole range of human thought and knowledge, upon history, and even natural philosophy, as its own patrimony.

Faith.

This was not, it could not be, that more sublime theology of a rational and intellectual Christianity; that theology which expands itself as the system of the universe expands upon the mind; and from its wider acquaintance with the wonderful provisions, the more manifest and all-provident forethought of the Deity, acknowledges with more awestruck and admiring, yet not less fervent and grateful, homage the beneficence of the Creator; that Christian theology which reverentially traces the benignant providence of God over the affairs of men—the all-ruling Father—the Redeemer revealed at the appointed time, and publishing the code of reconciliation, holiness, peace, and everlasting life—

the Universal Spirit, with its mysterious and confessed but untraceable energy, pervading the kindred spiritual part of man. The Christian of those days lived in a supernatural world, or in a world under the constant and felt and discernible interference of supernatural power. God was not only present, but asserting his presence at every instant, not merely on signal occasions and for important purposes, but on the most insignificant acts and persons. The course of nature was beheld, not as one great uniform and majestic miracle, but as a succession of small, insulated, sometimes trivial, sometimes contradictory interpositions, often utterly inconsistent with the moral and Christian attributes of God. The divine power and goodness were not spreading abroad like a genial and equable sunlight, enlightening, cheering, vivifying, but breaking out in partial and visible flashes of influence. Each incident was a special miracle, the ordinary emotion of the heart was divine inspiration. Every individual had not merely his portion in the common diffusion of religious and moral knowledge or feeling, but looked for his peculiar and especial share in the divine blessing. His dreams came direct from heaven, a new system of Christian omens succeeded the old; witchcraft merely invoked Beelzebub or Satan instead of Hecate; hallowed places only changed their tutelary nymph or genius for a saint or martyr.

It is not less unjust to stigmatise in the mass as fraud, or to condemn as the weakness of superstition, than it is to enforce as an essential part of Christianity, that which was the necessary developement of this state of the human mind. The case was this,— the mind of man had before it a recent and wonderful revelation, in which it could not but acknow-

Imaginative state of the human mind.

ledge the divine interposition. God had been brought down, or had condescended to mingle himself with the affairs of men. But where should that faith, which could not but receive these high, and consolatory, and reasonable truths, set limits to the agency of this beneficent power? How should it discriminate between that which in its apparent discrepancy with the laws of nature (and of those laws how little was known!) was miraculous; and that which, to more accurate observation, was only strange or wonderful, or perhaps the result of ordinary but dimly seen causes? how still more in the mysterious world of the human mind, of which the laws are still, we will not say in their primitive, but in comparison with those of external nature, in profound obscurity? If the understanding of man was too much dazzled to see clearly even material objects; if just awakening from a deep trance, it beheld everything floating before it in a mist of wonder, how much more was the mind disqualified to judge of its own emotions, of the origin, suggestion, and powers, of those thoughts and emotions, which still perplex and baffle our deepest metaphysics.

The irresistible current of man's thoughts and feelings ran all one way. It is difficult to calculate the effect of that extraordinary power or propensity of the mind to see what it expects to see, to colour with the preconceived hue of its own opinions and sentiments whatever presents itself before it. The contagion of emotions or of passions, which in vast assemblies may be resolved, perhaps, into a physical effect, acts, it should seem, in a more extensive manner; opinions and feelings appear to be propagated with a kind of epidemic force and rapidity. There were some, no doubt, who saw farther, but who either dared not, or did not care, to stand across the torrent of general feeling. But the mass, even of the strongest minded, were influenced, no doubt, by the profound religious dread of assuming that for an ordinary effect of nature, which *might be* a divine interposition. They were far more inclined to suspect reason of presumption than faith of credulity. Where faith is the height of virtue, and infidelity the depth of sin, tranquil investigation becomes criminal indifference, doubt guilty scepticism. Of all charges men shrink most sensitively, especially in a religious age, from that of irreligion, however made by the most ignorant or the most presumptuous. The clergy, the great agents in the maintenance and communication of this <small>The clergy.</small> imaginative religious bias, the asserters of constant miracle in all its various forms, were themselves, no doubt, irresistibly carried away by the same tendency. It was treason against their order and their sacred duty, to arrest, or to deaden, whatever might tend to religious impression. Pledged by obligation, by feeling, we may add by interest, to advance religion, most were blind to, all closed their eyes against, the remote consequences of folly and superstition. A clergyman who, in a credulous or enthusiastic age, dares to be rationally pious, is a phenomenon of moral courage. From this time, either the charge of irreligion, or the not less dreadful and fatal suspicion of heresy or magic, was the penalty to be paid for the glorious privilege of superiority to the age in which the man lived, or of the attainment to a higher and more reasonable theology.

The desire of producing religious impression was in a great degree the fertile parent of all the wild <small>Religious inventions which already began to be grafted impressions.</small> on the simple creed of Christianity. That which was employed avowedly with this end in one generation, be-

came the popular belief of the next. The full growth of
all this religious poetry (for, though not in form, it was
poetical in its essence) belongs to, and must be reserved
for, a later period. Christian history would be incomplete without that of Christian popular superstition.

But though religion, and religion in this peculiar
form, had thus swallowed up all other pursuits and sentiments, it cannot indeed be said, that this new mythic
or imaginative period of the world suppressed the
developement of any strong intellectual energy, or
arrested the progress of real knowledge and improvement. This, even if commenced, must have yielded
to the devastating inroads of barbarism. But in truth,
however high in some respects the civilisation of the
Roman empire under the Antonines; however the useful, more especially the mechanical, arts must have
attained, as their gigantic remains still prove, a high
perfection, (though degenerate in point of taste, by
the colossal solidity of their structure, the vast buildings, the roads, the aqueducts, the bridges, in every
quarter of the world, bear testimony to the science as
well as to the public spirit of the age,) still there is a
remarkable dearth, at this flourishing period, of great
names in science and philosophy, as well as in literature.[b]

Effect on natural philosophy. Principles may have been admitted, and may have
begun to take firm root, through the authoritative writings of the Christian fathers, which,
after a long period, would prove adverse to the free
developement of natural, moral, and intellectual philosophy; and, having been enshrined for centuries as a
part of religious doctrine, would not easily surrender
their claims to divine authority, or be deposed from

---

[b] Galen, as a writer on physic, may be quoted as an exception.

their established supremacy. The church condemned Galileo on the authority of the fathers as much as of the sacred writings, at least on their irrefragable interpretation of the scriptures; and the denial of the antipodes by St. Augustine was alleged against the magnificent, but as it appeared to many no less impious than frantic, theory of Columbus.[c] The wild cosmogonical theories of the Gnostics and Manichæans, with the no less unsatisfactory hypotheses of the Greeks, tended, no doubt, to throw discredit on all kinds of physical study,[d] and to establish the strictly literal exposition of the Mosaic history of the creation. The orthodox fathers, when they enlarge on the works of the six days, though they allow themselves largely in allegorical inference, have in general in view these strange theories, and refuse to depart from the strict letter of the history;[e] and the popular language, which

[c] It has been said, that the best mathematical science which the age could command was employed in the settlement of the question about Easter, decided at the Council of Nicæa. See on the astronomy and geography of the fathers, Voss, Kritische Blätter, ii. 155 et seq.; also Whewell, Hist. of Inductive Sciences, i.*158, &c.

[d] Brucker's observations on the physical knowledge, or rather on the professed contempt of physical knowledge, of the fathers, are characterised with his usual plain good sense. Their general language was that of Lactantius:— "Quanto fuerit sapientius ac verius si exceptione factâ diceret caussas rationesque duntaxat rerum cœlestium rea naturalium, quia sunt abditæ, nec sciri posse, quia nollus doceat, nec quæri oportere, quia inveniri quærendo non possunt. Quâ exceptione interposita et physices admonuisset ne quærerent ex, quæ modum excederent cogitationis humanæ; et se ipsum calumniæ invidiâ liberasset, et nobis certe deliisset aliquid, quod sequeremur," Div. Instit. iii. 6. See other quotations to the same effect: Brucker, Hist. Phil. iii. p. 357. The work of Cosmas Indicopleustes, edited by Montfaucon, is a curious example of the prevailing notions of physical science.

[e] Compare the Hexaemeron of Ambrose, and Brucker's sensible remarks on the pardonable errors of that great prelate. The evil was, not that the fathers fell into extraordinary errors on subjects of which they were ignorant, but that their errors were canonised by the blind veneration of later ages, which might have been better informed.

was necessarily employed with regard to the earth and the movements of the heavenly bodies, became established as literal and immutable truth. The Bible, and the Bible interpreted by the fathers, became the code not of religion only, but of every branch of knowledge. If religion demanded the assent to a heaven-revealed, or heaven-sanctioned, theory of the physical creation, the whole history of man, from its commencement to its close, seemed to be established in still more distinct and explicit terms. Nothing was allowed for figurative or Oriental phraseology, nothing for that condescension to the dominant sentiments and state of knowledge, which may have been necessary to render each part of the sacred writings intelligible to that age in which it was composed. And if the origin of man was thus clearly revealed, the close of his history was still supposed, however each generation passed away undisturbed, to be imminent and immediate. The Day of Judgement was before the eyes of the Christian, either instant, or at a very brief interval; it was not unusual, on a general view, to discern the signs of the old age and decrepitude of the world; and every great calamity was either the sign or the commencement of the awful consummation. Gregory I. beheld in the horrors of the Lombard invasion the visible approach of the last day; and it is not impossible that the doctrine of a purgatorial state was strengthened by this prevalent notion, which interposed only a limited space between the death of the individual and the final judgement.[f]

---

[f] "Depopulatæ urbes, eversa castra, concremataæ ecclesiæ, destructa sunt monasteria virorum et fœminarum, desolata ab hominibus prædia, atque ab omni cultore destituta; in solitudine remansit terra, occupaverunt bestiæ locum, quæ prius multitudo hominum tenebat. Nam in hâc terrâ, in quâ nos vivimus, finem suum mundus jam non nuntiat sed ostendit." Greg. Mag. Dial. iii. 38.

But the popular belief was not merely a theology in its higher sense.

Christianity began to approach to a polytheistic form, or at least to permit, what it is difficult to call by any other name than polytheistic, habits and feelings of devotion. It attributed, however vaguely, to subordinate beings some of the inalienable powers and attributes of divinity. Under the whole of this form lay the sum of Christian doctrine; but that which was constantly presented to the minds of men was the host of subordinate, indeed, but still active and influential, mediators between the Deity and the world of man. Throughout (as has already been and will presently be indicated again) existed the vital and essential difference between Christianity and Paganism. It is possible that the controversies about the Trinity and the divine nature of Christ, tended indirectly to the promotion of this worship, of the Virgin, of angels, of saints and martyrs. The great object of the victorious, to a certain extent, of both parties, was the closest approximation, in one sense, the identification, of the Saviour with the unseen and incomprehensible Deity. Though the human nature of Christ was as strenuously asserted in theory, it was not dwelt upon with the same earnestness and constancy as his divine. To magnify, to purify this from all earthly leaven was the object of all eloquence: theologic disputes on this point withdrew or diverted the attention from the life of Christ as simply related in the Gospels. Christ became the object of a remoter, a more awful, adoration. The mind began therefore to seek out, or eagerly to seize, some other more material beings, in closer alliance with human sympathies. The constant propensity of man to humanise his Deity, checked, as it were, by the receding majesty of the Saviour, readily clung with its devotion to humbler objects.ᵉ The weak wing of the common and unenlightened mind could not soar to the unapproachable light in which Christ dwelt with the Father; it dropped to the earth, and bowed itself down before some less mysterious and infinite object of veneration. In theory it was always a different and inferior kind of worship; but the feelings, especially impassioned devotion, know no logic: they pause not; it would chill them to death if they were to pause for these fine and subtle distinctions. The gentle ascent by which admiration, reverence, gratitude, and love, swelled up to awe, to veneration, to worship, both as regards the feelings of the individual and the general sentiment, was imperceptible. Men passed from rational respect for the remains of the dead,ʰ the communion of holy thought and emotion, which might connect the departed saint with his brethren in the flesh, to the superstitious veneration of

Worship of saints and angels.

ᵉ The progress of the worship of saints and angels has been fairly and impartially traced by Shröck, Christliche Kirchengeschichte, viii. 161, *et seq.* In the account of the martyrdom of Polycarp, it is said, "we love the martyrs as disciples and followers of the Lord." The fathers of the next period leave the saints and martyrs in a kind of intermediate state, the bosom of Abraham or Paradise, as explained by Tertullian, contr. Marc. iv. 34. Apolog. tt. 47. Compare Irenæus adv. Hær. v. o. 31. Justin, Dial. cum Tryph. Origen, Hom. vii. in Levit.

ʰ The growth of the worship of relics is best shown by the prohibitory law of Theodosius (A.D. 386) against the removal and sale of saints' bodies. "Nemo martyres distrahat, nemo mercetur." Cod. Theodos. ix. 17. Augustine denies that worship was ever offered to apostles or saints. "Quis autem audivit aliquando fidelium stantem sacerdotem ad altare etiam super sanctum corpus martyris ad Dei honorem cultumque constructum, dicere in precibus, offero tibi sacrificium, Petre, vel Paule, vel Cypriane, cum apud eorum memorias offeratur Deo qui eos et homines et martyres fecit, et sanctis suis angelis cælesti honore sociavit." De Civ. Dei, viii. 27. Compare xvii. 10, where he asserts miracles to be performed at their tombs.

relics, and the deification of mortal men, by so easy a transition, that they never discovered the precise point at which they transgressed the unmarked and unwatched boundary.

This new polytheising Christianity therefore was still subordinate and subsidiary in the theologic creed to the true Christian worship, but it usurped its place in the heart, and rivalled it in the daily language and practices of devotion. The worshipper felt and acknowledged his dependency, and looked for protection, or support, to these new intermediate beings, the intercessors with the great Intercessor. They were arrayed by the general belief in some of the attributes of the Deity,—ubiquity[1] and the perpetual cognisance of the affairs of earth; they could hear the prayer;[k] they could read the heart; they could control nature; they had a power, derivative indeed from a higher source, but still exercised according to their volition, over all the events of the world. Thus each city, and almost each individual, began to have his tutelar saint; the presence of some beatified being hovered over and hallowed particular spots; and thus the strong influence of local and

---

[1] Massuet, in his preface to Irenæus, s. cxxxvi., has adduced some texts from the fathers of the fourth and fifth centuries on the ubiquity of the saints and the Virgin.

[k] Perhaps the earliest instances of these are in the eulogies of the eastern martyrs, by Basil, Greg. Naz. and Greg. Nyssen. See especially the former on the forty Martyrs. Ὁ θλιβόμενος, ἐπὶ τοὺς τεσσαράκοντα καταφεύγει, ὁ εὐφραινόμενος, ἐπ' αὐτοὺς ἀποτρέχει, ὁ μὲν ἵνα λύσιν ὄρρῃ τῶν δυσχερῶν, ὁ δὲ ἵνα φυλαχθῇ αὐτῷ τὰ χρηστότερα· ἐνταῦθα γυνὴ εὐσεβὴς ὑπὲρ τέκνων εὐχομένη καταλαμβάνεται, ἀποδημοῦντι ἀνδρὶ τὸν ἐπάνοδον αἰτουμένη, ἀρρωστοῦντι τὴν σωτηρίαν. Oper. vol. II, p. 155. These and similar passages in Greg. Nazianzen (Orat. in Basil.) and Gregory of Nyssa (in Theodor. Martyr.) may be rhetorical ornaments, but their ignorant and enthusiastic hearers would not make much allowance for the fervour of eloquence. Compare Prudent. in Hippolytum Martyrem. See also Van Dale, p. 230

particular worships combined again with that great universal faith, of which the supreme Father was the sole object, and the Universe the temple.[1] Still, how-

---

[1] An illustration of the new form assumed by Christian worship may be collected from the works of Paulinus, who, in eighteen poems, celebrates the nativity of St. Felix the tutelary saint of Nola. St. Felix is at least invested in the powers ascribed to the intermediate deities of antiquity. Pilgrims crowded from the whole of the south of Italy to the festival of St. Felix, Rome herself, though she possessed the altars of St. Peter and St. Paul, poured forth her myriads; the Capenian gate was choked, the Appian way was covered with the devout worshippers.[2] Multitudes came from beyond the sea. St. Felix is implored by his servants to remove the impediments to their pilgrimages from the hostility of men or adverse weather; to smooth the seas, and send propitious winds.[3] There is constant reference, indeed, to Christ[4] as the source of this power, yet the power is fully and explicitly assigned to the saint. He is the prevailing intercessor between the worshipper and Christ. But the vital distinction between this paganising form of Christianity and Paganism itself is no less manifest in these poems. It is not merely as a tutelary deity in this life, that the saint is invoked; the future state of existence and the final judgement are constantly present to the thoughts of the worshipper. St. Felix is entreated after death to bear the souls of his worshippers into the bosom of the Redeemer, and to intercede for them at the last day.[4]

These poems furnish altogether a curious picture of the times, and show how early Christian Italy began to

---

[1] "Sitpatam multis unam juvat arbitros urbem
Carnera, totque una composita examina vota.
Lucani cornui populi, colit Appula pubes;
Et Calabri, et cuncti, quos aluit æstus aternus,
Qui læva, et dextra Latium circumsonat unda.
 *   *   *   *
Et qua bis ternas Campania tota per urbes, &c.
Iamque cœlestium sacris procerum monumentis
Roma Petro Pauloque potens, ravescere gaudet
Hujus honore diei, partesque ex ore Capenæ
Millia profundens ad amicæ mœnia Nolæ
Dimittit duodena decem per millia denso
Agmine, confertis longe lateque Appia turbis."—Carm. iii.

[2] "De currere mollibus undis,
Et famulis famulum a puppi suggere ventos."—Carm. i.

[3] "Sic bonus o felixque tuis, Dominoque potentem Exorn,——
Liceat placati munere Christi
Post palagi finctus," &c.

[4] "Postlæque inormi
Ante tuos vultus, animas vectare paterno
Ne renovæ gremio l'omini fulgentis ad ora.
Posce ovium greges nos statui, si sequentia summa
Judicis, hoc quoque nos iterum tibi munere donet."—Carm. iri.

ever, this new polytheism differed in its influence, as well as in its nature, from that of Paganism. It bore a constant reference to another state of existence. Though the office of the tutelary being was to avert and mitigate temporal suffering, yet it was still more so to awaken and keep alive the sentiments of the religious being. They were not merely the agents of the divine providential government on earth, but indissolubly connected with the hopes and fears of the future state of existence.

The most natural, most beautiful, and most universal, though perhaps the latest developed, of these new forms of Christianity, that which tended to the poetry of the religion, and acted as the conservator

<small>Worship of the Virgin.</small>

become what it is. The pilgrims brought their votive offerings, curtains, and hangings, embroidered with figures of animals, silver plates with inscriptions, candles of painted wax, pendent lamps, precious ointments, and dishes of venison and other meats for the banquet. The following characteristic circumstance must not be omitted. The magnificent plans of Paulinus for building the church of St. Felix were interfered with by two wooden cottages, which stood in a field before the front of the building. At midnight a fire broke out in these tenements. The affrighted bishop woke up in trembling apprehension lest the splendid "palace" of the saint should be enveloped in the flames. He entered the church, armed with a piece of the wood of the true cross, and advanced towards the fire. The flames which had resisted all the water thrown upon them, retreated before the sacred wood; and in the morning every thing was found uninjured except these two devoted buildings. The bishop, without scruple, ascribes the fire to St. Felix :—

"Sed et hoc Felicis gratis nobis
Mupere contulit, quod præveniendo laborem
Utilibus flammis, operum compendia nobis
Præstitit."—Carm. x.

The peasant, who had dared to prefer his hovel, though the beloved dwelling of his youth, to the house of God or of his saint, seeing one of the buildings thus miraculously in flames, sets fire to the other.

"Et celeri peragit sua damna furore
Dilectasque domos, et insanus plangit amores."

Some of the other miracles at the shrine of St. Felix border close on the comic.

of art, particularly of painting, till at length it became the parent of that refined sense of the beautiful, that which was the inspiration of modern Italy, was the worship of the Virgin. Directly that Christian devotion expanded itself beyond its legitimate objects; as soon as prayers or hymns were addressed to any of those beings who had acquired sanctity from their connection or co-operation with the introduction of Christianity into the world; as soon as the apostles and martyrs had become hallowed in the general sentiment, as more especially the objects of the divine favour and of human gratitude, the virgin mother of the Saviour appeared to possess peculiar claims to the veneration of the Christian world. The worship of the Virgin, like most of the other tenets which grew out of Christianity, originated in the lively fancy and fervent temperament of the East, but was embraced with equal ardour, and retained with passionate constancy, in the West.[m]

The higher importance assigned to the female sex by Christianity, than by any other form at least of Oriental

---

[m] Irenæus, in whose works are found the earliest of those ardent expressions with regard to the Virgin, which afterwards kindled into adoration, may, in this respect, be considered as Oriental. I allude to his parallel between Eve and the Virgin, in which he seems to assign a mediatorial character to the latter. Iren. iii. 33, v. 19.

The earlier fathers use expressions with regard to the Virgin altogether inconsistent with the reverence of later ages. Tertullian compares her unfavourably with Martha and Mary, and insinuates that she partook of the incredulity of the rest of her own family. "Mater æquè non demonstratur adhæsisse illi, cum Martha et Maria aliæ in commercio ejus frequententur. Hoc denique in loco (St. Luc. viii. 20) apparet incredulitas eorum cum is doceret viam vitæ," &c. De Carne Christi, c. 7. There is a collection of quotations on this subject in Field on the Church, p. 264, et seqq. See this subject pursued in Latin Christianity.

The Collyridians, who offered cakes to the Virgin, were rejected as heretics. Epiph. Hær. lxxviii. lxxix.

The perpetual virginity of Mary was an object of controversy: as might be expected, it was maintained with unshaken confidence by Epiphanius, Ambrose, and Jerome.

religion, powerfully tended to the general adoption of the worship of the Virgin, while that worship reacted on the general estimation of the female sex. Women willingly deified (we cannot use another adequate expression) this perfect representative of their own sex, while the sex was elevated in general sentiment by the influence ascribed to their all-powerful patroness. The ideal of this sacred being was the blending of maternal tenderness with perfect purity—the two attributes of the female character which man, by his nature, seems to hold in the highest admiration and love; and this image constantly presented to the Christian mind, calling forth the gentler emotions, appealing to, and giving, as it were, the divine sanction to, domestic affections, could not be without its influence. It operated equally on the manners, the feelings, and in some respect on the inventive powers of Christianity. The gentleness of the Redeemer's character, the impersonation of the divine mercy in his whole beneficent life, had been in some degree darkened by the fierceness of polemic animosity. The religion had assumed a sternness and severity arising from the mutual and recriminatory condemnations. The opposite parties denounced eternal punishments against each other with such indiscriminate energy, that hell had become almost the leading and predominant image in the Christian dispensation. This advancing gloom was perpetually softened; this severity allayed by the impulse of gentleness and purity, suggested by this new form of worship. It kept in motion the genial under-current of more humane feeling; it diverted and estranged the thought from this harassing strife to calmer and less exciting objects. The dismal and the terrible, which so constantly haunted the imagination, found no place during the contemplation of the Mother and the Child, which, when once it became enshrined in the heart, began to take a visible and external form.[a] The image arose out of, and derived its sanctity from, the general feeling, which in its turn, especially when, at a later period, real art breathed life into it, strengthened the general feeling to an incalculable degree.

The wider and more general dissemination of the worship of the Virgin belongs to a later period in Christian history.

Thus under her new form was Christianity prepared to enter into the darkening period of European history —to fulfil her high office as the great conservative principle of religion, knowledge, humanity, and of the highest degree of civilisation of which the age was capable, during centuries of violence, of ignorance, and of barbarism.

---

[a] At a later period, indeed, even the Virgin became the goddess of war:—

Ἀεὶ γὰρ οἶδε τὴν φύσιν νικᾶν μάχη,
Τάξιν τὸ πρῶτον, καὶ μάχῃ τὸ δεύτερον.

Such are the verses of George of Pisidia, relating a victory over the Avars. On the whole subject of this Conclusion, I would venture to refer to the Hist. of Latin Christianity, especially to the chapters on Iconoclasm, and those in the Survey, relating to the popular Worship, the Literature, and the Fine Arts of Christianity.

(427)

INDEX.

The Roman numerals refer to the volumes; the Arabic figures denote the pages.

ABDUCTION.
ABDUCTION, over-rigour of Constantine's laws against, ii, 395, 396.
ABEL, principle in Valentinus's system represented by, ii, 73. In Marcion's Gospel, 79.
ABGAR, King of Edessa, ii, 74. An alleged correspondent with Jesus, ii, 58, 255.
ABLUTIONS, see *Baptism.*
ABRAHAM enshrined as a Deity by Alexander Severus, ii, 177. Probable origin of the Abrahamic religion, 178. Spot where the angels appeared to him, 349.
ABRAXAS, legend of, ii, 66, 67. Variety of attempts to interpret same, 66 *note.* Engraved on seals, iii, 189.
ABYSS, Valentinus's typification of the, ii, 69. Its place in the Ophitic system, 81.
ABYSSINIAN Christianity, character of, i, 48 *note.*
ACADEMICS, the, i, 35.
ACELDAMA, or the Field of Blood, purchase of, i, 318. Kuinoel's suggestion, *ibid note.*
ACHAIA, result of a trial between the Jews and Christians at, i, 397.
ACOLYTH, office and duties of the, iii, 266.
ACROPOLIS, Constantinople, ii, 332.
ACTS of the Apostles, why rejected by Mani, ii, 261. Lardner's suggestion, *ibid note.* See *Apostles.*
ACTS of the Martyrs, literary merit of the, iii, 356, 357.
ADAM CADMON, Mani's primal man, whence derived, ii, 260. His office

AFGHANS.
and attributes, 265. Man formed in his image, 266.
A-DEO-DATUS, Augustine's natural son, iii, 180. His baptism and death, 182.
ADERBIJAN, i, 63.
ADIABENI. See *Helen, Queen.*
ADRIANOPLE in Alexandria, cruelty of the Arians at, ii, 418, 419. See *Hadrianople.*
ADRIATIC, the, ii, 208, 223.
ADULIS, commerce through the port of, ii, 400.
ADULTERY, Constantine's law against, ii, 396, 397. See *Divorce.*
ÆDESIUS, Julian's interview with, ii, 437. See *Edesius.*
ÆLIA, new city founded by Hadrian on the site of Jerusalem, i, 421; iii, 191.
ÆLIUS, result of commission issued to, ii, 305.
ÆONS, ii, 53. Simon Magus as Æon, 47. The Æon Christ, 59. Æons of Gnosticism, 65. Valentinus's Æons, 69-73. Æons of Bardesanes, 75, 76. Rejected by Carpocrates, 80.
ÆSCULAPIUS, proscription of the worship of, ii, 345. See iii, 69.
AETIUS, heresy of, ii, 443. His origin and proselytising career, 443, 444. His attachment to the Aristotelian philosophy, 443 *note.* His follower Eudorus, 445. His banishment, 446. One of the heroes of Philostorgius, 446 *note.*
AFGHANS, country of the, ii, 250.

AFRICA.

AFRICA, Christian congregations in, ii, 111, 208, 276. Persecutions under Severus, 157. Priestly hatred excited by the progress of Christianity there, 158, 159. Character of African Christianity: type of same represented by Tertullian, 160-164. African martyrs: Felicitas, Perpetua, and others, 165-172. The Lapsi and Libellatici, 189. Rebellion under Maxentius, 287. College founded by the Africans in return for their oppressor's head, 290. Constantine's gifts to, and efforts to allay the contests in, their churches, 294, 295. Disorganising effects of persecution, 297. Episcopal power among them, 298. Oppressive conduct of the Prefect Abulinus, and fatal dissensions excited by it, 299. Devastation and distraction of its cities by the Donatists, 106-109. Source of its commercial prosperity, 307. Constantine's munificence to its churches, 311. See ii, 104. 110. 127.

AGABUS, famine predicted by, i, 375. His prophetic denunciation of Paul's imprisonment, 198.

AGAPÆ, iii, 123. The Agapæ of the Martyrs, 174. Denounced by Tertullian, 335 note. Paintings and remains, ibid.

AGATHO-DÆMON of Egyptian mythology, ii, 81, 82 note.

AGDE, council of, secular music condemned by the, iii, 128.

AGENARIO, occasion of change of name by, i, 40 note.

AGERATOS, the Æon, and his consort, ii, 70.

AGINCOURT, see D'Agincourt.

AGRIPPA, son of Herod Agrippa, sent to Rome, i, 181. Impression made upon him by Paul's defence, 405, 406. His edict in favour of the Jews, 445. See i, 42; ii, 9.

AGRIPPINA put to death, i, 404 note.

AHRIMAN, ii, 61. 252.

ALEXANDER SEVERUS.

AKINETOS, the Æon, and his consort, ii, 70.

ALARIC, alleged appearance of Minerva to, iii, 78 note. His assault on Rome: impartial in his fury, 96. See 316.

ALBINUS, Prefect of Judæa, i, 399-406. Oppression of Judæa under him, 459.

ALBINUS of Rome, vengeance of Severus on the friends of, ii, 155. His parallel of Constantine with Nero, 123, 123 note, 129.

ALCIBIADES, a Christian, reproved for his asceticism, ii, 161 note.

ALEMANNI, Julian's exclamation concerning the, iii, 5.

ALETHEIA, position assigned by Valentinus to, ii, 70.

ALEXANDER, Bishop of Constantinople, opposes the reception of Arius, ii, 181. Event ascribed to his prayers, 182.

ALEXANDER, Bishop of Rome, pretended discovery of a chapel dedicated to, ii, 103 note. His opposition to Arianism, 181. Ills comparison of Arius to Judas, 182.

ALEXANDER the Coppersmith, informer against St. Paul, i, 465.

ALEXANDER the Great, result of the monarchy established by, i, 1. His policy towards the religion of conquered nations, 5. Persian traditions regarding him, ibid note.

ALEXANDER the Jew of Ephesus, silenced by the mob, i, 450.

ALEXANDER, Patriarch of Alexandria, ii, 160. Conflicts between himself and Arius, 161. Rebuked by Constantine, 163. His secretary and successor, 175.

ALEXANDER, Saint, alleged discovery of the remains of, ii, 103 note.

ALEXANDER Severus, parentage and training of, ii, 177. Founders of systems deified by him, 177, 178; iii, 170. Encouragement afforded by him to Christianity and its fol-

ALEXANDRIA.

lowers, 179. His observation on making a grant of land to them, 180. Contrast between him and his successor, 185. Existence of Christian churches in his reign, iii, 129 *note*. See ii, 111.

ALEXANDRIA, its countless religious and philosophical factions, ii, 58. Centre of speculative and intellectual activity, 64. Notion in which the God of the Jews was looked upon, 67. Religious tone of its higher classes, 108. Chief scene of Christian suffering, 157. Soil of religious feuds, 158. Consequences thereof, 159. Sanguinary zeal of its populace, 188. Christian disputes satirised on its stage, 339. Its seven hundred Virgins, 362 *note*. Never at peace on religious matters, iii, 16. Imperial claim made to the fee simple of the city's site, 16, 17. Tumults under Julian, 17-19. Its bishops. See *Alexander the Patriarch; Athanasius, Saint; George of Cappadocia; Gregory of Cappadocia; Peter; Theophilus*. See also ii, 41, 55, 68, 351, 361, 370, 377 *note*. iii, 102.

ALEXANDRIAN school of Jews, i, 35. Their notion of a mediator, 71, 77. Combination of their system with Indian mysticism, ii, 41. Consequence of their presence at the Roman theatres, 97. Their prophetic books ascribed to the Sibyls, 119-121. See ii, 17 *note*, 68, 76, 285.

ALITURUS, the Jewish actor at Rome, i, 458 *note*. ii, 96. His influence with the Emperor, 97.

ALLEGORY, religious, transmutation of poetry into, ii, 184.

ALLELUIA, effect upon the philosopher Olympus of the, iii, 72. See also, iii, 154, 401.

ALPS, progress of Christianity after passing the, ii, 278. See 331.

ALTAR in the church, position and furniture of the, iii, 313.

AMBROSE.

ALYTARCHS, the, iii, 311 *note*.

AMANTIUS the Soothsayer, torture and execution of, 18, 19.

AMBO, position and use of the, 311, 313.

AMBROSE, St, influence over Gratian of, iii, 82. His sarcasm on rewards for virginity, 84. Character of his writings, 86. His reply to the apology of Symmachus, 87, 88. His flight from Milan, 89. His letter to Eugenius, 89 *note*. His influence and its causes, 102, 103. Practical character of his oratory and conduct, 150, 151. His parentage: Probus's prophetic monition to him, 151. Elected Bishop of Milan, 152. His advocacy of celibacy, and its effect on the Roman mothers, 152, 153. His efforts against slavery, 153, 154. His success as a negociator, 155. His conduct on the attempted seizure of a church by Justina's orders, 155-158. His reply to a courtier's threat, 158 *note*. His further conquests over Arianism and Paganism, 158, 159. Contrast between his practical statesmanship and his subtle theology, 159 *note*. Popular belief in his possession of miraculous power, 159, 160. Miracle accredited to him, 161. A man denial of same, *ibid note*. His magnificence in the conduct of the Church ceremonials, 162, 271. Result of his second embassy to Maximus, 162, 163. Destructive acts of distant Christians vindicated by him: his reproof of the Emperor on the occasion, 163-165. Penance imposed by him on the emperor for a sanguinary massacre, 166, 167. His protest against the murder of the Priscillianists, 169. His last hours and death, 169, 170. Hymn ascribed to him, 154. Value of his letters, 364 *note*. His Hexaemeron, 417 *note*. An advocate for the perpetual virginity of Mary, 424 *note*.

430 INDEX.

AMBROSIAN CHANT. See ii, 190; iii, 63 note, 116, 117, 214 note, 273 note, 274 note, 289 note, 308 note, 316 note, 325 note, 327 note, 351, 364 note, 387. 391 note, 394.

AMBROSIAN chant, the, iii, 404, 405.

AMERIUS, epistle to, ii, 466 note.

AMMIANUS Marcellinus, illustrative citations from, ii, 467 note; iii, 8 note, 18 note, 21, 36 note, 37 note, 41 note, 56 note, 68 note, 247 note.

AMMON, iii, 115 note.

AMMONIUS, fall of Paganism deplored by, iii, 73.

AMPHIPOLIS visited by Paul, i, 435.

AMPHITHEATRE, gladiatorial shows in the, iii, 143.

AMPHITRITE of Rhodes, the, ii, 335.

AMSCHASPANDS of the Zendavesta and Jewish Archangels, i, 68. Their number, ibid note. Introduced into Gnostic systems, ii, 62, 63.

AMULETS. See Talismans.

AMUSEMENTS. See Spectacles, public.

ANAN, murderer of Khosrov, his crime and his fate, ii, 255, 256.

ANAITIS, or Anahid, Babylonian Deity, principle personified by, ii, 257.

ANANAS. See Annas.

ANANIAS, the high priest, why sent prisoner to Rome, i, 385. 401, 402. Resumes the pontificate, 385. His character, 402.

ANANIAS and Sapphira, death of, i, 160.

ANASTASIA, sectarian attack on the, iii, 114.

ANASTASIS, description of the church of the, ii, 348, 349.

ANCHORITES, eastern localities peopled by, iii, 300. Their numbers, 309.

ANCYRA, council of, iii, 268 note, 278 note.

ANDEOLE, Saint, a doubtful martyr, ii, 156 note.

ANDREAS the Eunuch put to death, ii, 220.

ANTINOUS.

ANDREW the Apostle, i, 178. 210. 387.

ANDRONICUS of Caria, his unpardonable offence, iii, 41.

ANDRONICUS, Prefect of Libya, cruelties and exactions of, iii, 297. Sentence of the church upon him, 297, 398.

ANGEL of the Synagogue, ii, 18, 18 note.

ANGEL, or Bishop, ii, 16. See Bishops.

ANGELS, original Jewish notions of, i, 67. Elaboration of the system in Babylonia, 68. Archangels and guardian angels, ibid. Angelic image used by the Saviour, 69.

ANICII and Anuii, embracement of Christianity by the, iii, 92.

ANNA endowed with a prophetic knowledge of Christ's birth, i, 104.

ANNAS, or Ananas, the high priest, his influence in Jerusalem, i, 308. Grade of office held by him, 359 note.

ANNAS, or Ananus, son of the above, assumes the high-priesthood, i, 406. Question as to class of persons put to death by him, 407 note. Proof of his unpopularity, 408.

ANNONA, the, iii, 85 note.

ANNUNCIATION, the, i, 90.

ANOMEANS, doctrine of the, ii, 444, 445, 446.

ANTHEMIUS, Sunday wild beast spectacles prohibited by, iii, 146.

ANTHIMUS, Bishop of Nicomedia, beheaded, ii, 220, 221.

ANTHROPOMORPHISM of the Greeks, i, 16, 17 (See Greece). Its opponent and advocates in Alexandria, iii 103, 212, 213.

ANTHROPOS as a Gnostic manifestation, ii, 70.

ANTICHRIST, Nero expected to return as, i, 458 note; ii, 123, 124, notes. The name bestowed on Constantius, 425, 431.

ANTINOUS deified by Hadrian, ii, 106, 131.

ANTIOCH.

ANTIOCH in Pisidia, expulsion of Paul from, i, 190, 431.
ANTIOCH in Syria, commencement of a predicted famine in, i, 175, Paul summoned thither, 385. Head quarters of foreign Christian operations, 386. First Christian " church " formed there, 191, ii, 57. Persecution under Trajan, and destruction of the Pagan temple, ii, 101-103. Lament for Bishop Babylas, 188. Advancement and degradation of Paul of Samosata, 200-202. Anti-Christian placards in the streets, 231. Bishop Lucianus, 233. Martyrdom of one of its presbyters, 276. Arian struggles for supremacy, 373. Danger of an outbreak, 374. Incongruous passions of its populace, iii, 12. Reception of Julian by them, 13, 14. Re-edification and sudden destruction of the Pagan temple, 15, 16. Joy of its people at Julian's death, 31. Retort of a grammarian, ibid. Episcopal election feuds, 117. Insurrection under Theodosius, and spoliation of the imperial statues, 121. Same ascribed to diabolic agency, ibid note. Subsequent terrors of the inhabitants; result of appeals to the emperor's clemency, 124-128. Its council, 263 note, 267 note. Possessions and benevolences of its church, 275 note. Gymnastic games, 336. Its bishops, see Eustathius; Flavianus; Lucianus; Meletius; Paul of Samosata; Stephen. See also ii, 17 note, 62, 84, 115, 210, 222, 237, iii, 11, 26, 51, 65, 364, 378.
ANTIOCHUS the Great, i, 58 note.
ANTIOCHUS Epiphanes, persecution of the Jews by, i, 4 note. Construction put by them upon his death, 160.
ANTIPATER, Herod's eldest son, intrigues and death of, i, 52, 82.
ANTITHESES of Marcion, ii, 77, 79 note. See Marcion.
ANTONIA, the Temple fortress i, 117.
ANTONINES, the, ii, 98. Prevailing

APOLLONIUS.

spirit of their reign, 89. Their encouragement of education, iii, 6, 7 See Antoninus Pius, Marcus Aurelius.

ANTONINUS Pius, system of Hadrian pursued by, ii, 91, 109. Rescript in favour of the Christians ascribed to him, 110, 111. Some spurious, 110 note. His peaceful death, 111.
ANTONY, Saint, the representative of monastic life, iii, 201. His parentage and training, ibid. Invests himself of his possessions and becomes an anchorite, 201, 202. Character of his asceticism, 202. Favorability of the juncture at which he appeared and influence of his example, 202, 203.
ANUBIS, iii, 115 note.
ANULINUS, the spoiler of and afterwards the instrument of patronage to Christian churches, ii, 299. His interference sought by contending Christians, 302.
APE of Christianity, ii, 471.
APHRODITE, ii, 332. Her temple destroyed by Constantine, 345. Sacred site of one of her temples, 346.
APOCALYPSE, see Revelations.
APOCRYPHA, illustrative citation from the, i, 76 note q, 79 note a.
APOLLINE Christians and Apollinarians, ii, 31, iii, 4.
APOLLO, votaries of, ii, 91. Imperial consulters of his oracle, 212, 216, 227. Temples mentioned by Eumenius, 278 note. Expected rebuilding of his temple under Constantine, 284. Julian's rage at the state of his temple at Antioch, iii, 14. The gal abashed in the presence of a mind, 15. Re-edification and sudden burning of his temple, 15, 16. Destruction of his worship on Mount Casino, 98. See ii, 337.
APOLLONIA visited by Paul, i, 435.
APOLLONIUS of Tyana, nature of the legends of, i, 114. His parallel, ii, 47. Reply of Bardesanes to him, 74.

432 INDEX.

APOLLOS.

Enshrined by Alexander Severus as a deity, 177. Systems identified with him, 178. Character of his life, 184.
APOLLOS, espousal of Christianity by; lead taken by him, i, 446.
APOLOGISTS for Christianity, ii, 105 note, 106. Growing influence of the Apology, 109. Various Apologies and their authors, iii, 361, 362.
APOSTATES, laws against and penalties on, iii, 84 note, 101, 251 note.
APOSTLES, organization of the, i, 209. Their names, origin, &c., 210-212. Powers conferred on and dangers threatening them, 222. Jewish prejudices occasionally exhibited by them, 234. Their hopes and fears concerning Jesus, 237-240. Cause of their incredulity on His appearance after His Resurrection, 349, 350. Course taken by them after the Ascension, 351. Election of a new apostle, 352. Descent of the Holy Ghost among them, 353. Use made by them of the Gift of Tongues, and immediate fruits of their labours, 355-357. Their seizure and imprisonment, attitude before their persecutors, miraculous liberation, and re-imprisonment, 358-361. Punishment ultimately inflicted on them, 362. Chronological difficulties connected with their Acts and writings, 362, 363, notes. Occasion of their institution of the office of deacon, 363-364. Enrolment of Paul and Barnabas among them, 381, 386. Subsequent career and fate of the chosen twelve as far as known, 386. Spurious character of later writings concerning them, 387. Last Jewish illusion from which their minds were disenchanted, 418. Introduction of legendary accounts of their missions, ii, 11. How regarded by Simon Magus and his successors, 45, 47. Church dedicated to them, 133 note. Pillars commemorative of them,

ARCHELAUS.

349. Their portraits among the earliest efforts of Christian art, iii, 395. Constantine's alleged recognition of them in a vision, ibid. See also the names of the several Apostles.
APOSTLES and their substitutes, as rulers of the Church, ii, 15, 16 note, 18. 20-23.
APOSTOLIC Constitutions, iii, 258 note, 261 note, 275 note, 332 note, 367 note, 378 note, 423 note.
APOSTOLIC Creed, iii, 176.
APOSTOLIC succession and authority, claims of, ii, 105, iii, 356, 357 and notes.
APHETIUS, a self-styled god, and his parrots, legend of, ii, 50.
AQUILA AND PRISCILLA, St. Paul's hosts and friends, i, 397. 416, 417 note, 446.
ARABIAN tribes, fame of Abraham preserved by, ii, 349.
ARADION, castle of, bestowed on Mani, ii, 272.
ARAMAIC dialect, i, 183. Spoken in Galilee, 210 note. The vernacular of Palestine, 354.
ARAMAZD (Ormuzd), chief deity of the Armenians, ii, 257. See Oromasd.
ARBOGASTES confers the empire on Eugenius, iii, 89. His influence over Eugenius, 90.
ARCADIUS, Roman emperor, iii, 133. Splendour of his public appearances, 243, 244. His laws: against marriage of Jew and Christian, 289 note; against heretics, 300 note; against clerical interference with civil laws, 302 note; the theatre during his sway, 317.
ARCHANGELS, see Angels.
ARCHBISHOPS, rank and authority assigned to, iii, 264. See Bishops. Episcopacy.
ARCHELAUS (Herod), state of Judæa at the accession of, i, 83, 108. Character of his reign: his banishment,

INDEX.   433

ARCHELAUS.

130. His place of banishment, ii, 144.

ARCHELAUS, bishop of Cæsarea, alleged conference of Mani with, ii, 272. Question as to place and probability, 264 note, 272 note.

ARCHIMAGE, the, ii, 551.

ARCHITECTURE summoned to the service of Christianity, iii, 373. See *Church*.

ARCHON of the Jews, ii, 17 note.

ARDESCHIR Babhegan (Artaxerxes of the Greeks) restores the Persian monarchy and Zoroastrian religion, ii, 249–251. His edict against rival religions, 252. His testamentary injunction to his descendants, 253. Instigator of the murder of Khosrov, 255, 256.

AREOPAGUS, Paul's speech at the, i, 417.

AREOPOLIS, Pagan worship at, iii, 66.

ARETAS, seizure of Damascus by, i, 372.

ARIANS and Arianism. See *Arius*.

ARIANZA and Gregory of Nazianzum, iii, 110, 117.

ARISTIDES the Christian apologist, ii, 105 note, 107.

ARISTIDES the philosopher, occasion of an oration by, ii, 140 note. See ill, 69 note.

ARISTOBULUS, object contemplated by, i, 25 note.

ARISTOCRACY of Rome, iii, 244. Their manners, 246. See *Rome*.

ARISTOMENES, Julian's challenge to, ii, 473 note.

ARISTOPHANES, times unproductive of an, ii, 159.

ARISTOTLE, Simon Magus well read in, ii, 50 note. Deified by the Carpocratians, 80. His "sword," 252 note. Commencement of the strife between Aristotelianism and Platonism, 441 note.

ARIUS and Arianism, ii, 361. Consequences of divisions with the Atha-

VOL. III.

ARIUS.

nasians, 351. Principle of union among his opponents, 359. His personal appearance, character, and manners, 360. His conflict with the Patriarch Alexander and expulsion from Alexandria, 361. Composition and style of his *Thalia*, 361 note n. Character and object of his popular hymns, 362 note; iii, 401. Espousal of his tenets by the two Eusebii, 362. Tone of Constantine's reproof to him, ii, 362. Himself and adherents banished, 370. Terms of the sentence, *ibid note*. His party again in favour, 371. His recall from banishment, *ibid*. Ascendancy of his supporters over the emperor, 373. Their unjustifiable conduct in Antioch, 374. Determined refusal of his admission to communion, 375, 376, 381. His sudden death paralleled with that of Judas, 382. Violence of his followers in their attempts to regain authority, 414. Their quarrels with the Athanasians in Constantinople, 415. Their temporary predominance in Italy, 416. Their imperial champion, 425. An increase to their triumph, 426. Vengeance wreaked by them on the Athanasians, 429, 430. Superiority obtained by them, 442. Sources of disrepute brought upon their tenets, 444. Repudiation and subsequent adoption of their doctrines, 445, 446. Fatality of the triumph, 446. Constantius's error in enforcing the predominance of their tenets, 447. Emperor Julian's high-handed way of dealing with them, iii, 4, 5. Their reunion with the Church, 19. Ascendancy of Arianism under the influence of Valens, 44. Refusal of St Basil to admit Arians to communion, 45–47. Prevalence of Arianism among the Goths, 56–58. 59. Arian churches prohibited by Theodosius, 101. Arianism exhausted, 102. Suppressed by Theophilus, 103. Period of its dominance at Constantinople, 114. Eu-

2 F

434 INDEX.

ARLES.

press Justina's futile efforts in its behalf, 158, 159. Arian Council of Antioch, 168 note. See ii, 406. 413. 419 note, 420. 421-421. 435. 436 note, 438. 441. 442 note, 443.

ARLES, bishop of, ii, 301. 304. Its Council, 421; iii, 268 note. Its ordinance relative to priests' marriages, 380.

ARMENIA, number of Jews (A.D. 367) in, i, 59 note. Edicts resisted and worship rejected by its church, ii, 31. War made upon it by Maximin, 233. Magianism forced upon it, 253. 354. The first Christian kingdom, 254. Persecution suffered by ii, 354, 355. Authors of its histories, 255. Murder of its king, 255, 256. Its subjugation and reëstablishment as a kingdom, 256. Occasion of its erection into a Christian kingdom, 257, 258. Monumental inscription commemorative of its struggles, 258 note. Its apostle, see Gregory the Illuminator. See also ii, 222, 235. 235 note, iii, 60.

ARNOBIUS, iii, 351. 388 note.

ARNUPHIS, elemental manifestation superstitiously attributed to, ii, 241.

ARSACES, vestiges of the deification of kings of the line of, ii, 248.

ARSENIUS, machinations of the accusers of Athanasius defeated by, ii, 378, 379. Modes of self-torture adopted by him, iii, 205, 206.

ART, effect of Christianity on, iii, 247. Portraits of the Father, Saviour, Virgin, Apostles, &c, 389-396.

ARTACES, self-immolations at the funeral of, ii, 257.

ARTAXERXES. See Ardeschir.

ARTEMIUS, Duke of Egypt, condemnation and death of, iii, 17.

ARTICLES of Belief, period of the introduction of, ii, 152. See Church.

ASCENSIO Isaiæ, an apocryphal book, portions of the Gospel narrative confirmed by the, i, 91 note.

ATHANASIUS.

ASCENSION, the, i, 351.

ASCETICISM, source of, ii, 35, 36. Christianity outbidden by Eastern asceticism, 41. Asceticism in Saturninus's system, 63. See Essenes.

ASELLA, self-denying devotion of, iii, 231.

ASIA, cause of the rapid rise and fall of the empires in, i, 1. Earthquakes temp. Antoninus, ii, 131. Last of the Asiatic martyrs, 140. Marital jealousy of its tribes, 196. Religions of Asia, see Orientalism.

ASIATIC hours of the day, Dr. Townson's suggestion relative to the, i, 169 note.

ASIA Minor, rescript of Antoninus to the cities of, ii, 110. Its cities the source of poetico-prophetic forgeries, 120, 121. Violence of the persecutions there, 135. See ii, 32. 92. 103. 144. Progress of Maximus through its cities, iii, 2. Results of Chrysostom's visit, 137. See i, 444, 445. 448. 460. ii, 32. 92. 103. 144. 145. iii, 77. 110. 209.

ASIARCHS, functions of the, i, 449, 450, notes. Attempt of one to avert the martyrdom of Polycarp, ii, 138. Law from which they were exempted, iii, 133.

ASSOS, Paul takes ship at, i, 451.

ASTARTE, Queen of Heaven, and her attributes, i, 61; ii, 175. See Dea cælestis.

ASTERIUS Amasenus, illustrative citation from, iii, 290 note c.

ASTROLOGERS, their influence among the Romans, i, 42, 43.

ASYLUM, right of, restricted by Eutropius, iii, 133. Its original object and gradual abuse, 133-135.

ATHANASIUS, St, controversial point admitted by, ii, 368 note. His accusation against Arians and semi-Arians, 370 note. His antecedents, 375. Elevated to the Patriarchate of Alexandria, ibid. Braves all dangers to establish the

INDEX. 435

ATHANASIUS.

supremacy of his own opinions, 176. Ruse by which a charge against him was disproved, ibid note q. Multiplicity of charges against him, 177. His refutation of a "dead hand" accusation, 179. 180. Charge on which he was deposed from his see, 179. Confronts and demands justice of Constantine, ibid. New charge against him and sentence thereon, 379-381. His argument from the death of Arius, 181 note. Opposition and ultimate consent of the Emperor to his recall from banishment, 182, 383. His imperial and local partisans and opponents, 406, 410. His inflexible pursuit of his object and triumphant entry into Alexandria, 410-412. Result of the councils held at Tyre and Antioch, 412, 413. Again an exile and in Rome; his influence there, 413, 414. Effect of the controversy initiated by him, 416. His accusers summoned to Rome, 416, 417 His case submitted to a council at Sardica; result of same, 417-419. His triumphal re-entry into Alexandria in company with Constantius, 419, 420. Constantius again his enemy and accuser, 423-425. Orders issued for his removal, 427. Scene in his church on his attempted arrest: his escape, 428, 429. Treatment of his followers by the Arians, 430, 431. His asceticism in his forced solitude, 432. His admiration for Lucifer of Cagliari, 434. Contempt for the emperor shown in his Epistle to the Solitaries, 434, 435. His inflexible orthodoxy, 436. Style and character of his writings, 438, 439. His return from exile under and re-banishment by Julian, iii, 19. Received with favour by Jovian, 32. His fifth exile and death, 44. His pause in polemic warfare, 201 note. Not an advocate for church music, 401. See ii, 351. 426. 440. 441-3. iii, i, 150. 157. 181. 367.

AUGUSTINE.

ATHANASIUS, Arian bishop of Anazarba, ii, 444.
ATHEISM, Christians charged with, ii, 12. 145. 180.
ATHENAGORAS, principle regarding clerical marriages laid down by, ii, 279 note.
ATHENS, i, 433. Character of its Paganism, 435. Paul's harangue to its citizens, 436-441. Impulse given to its Paganism by Julian, iii, 11. Preserved from Alaric by Minerva, 78 note. See ii, 106. 110. 185. 351. iii, 78.
ATLAS of the Greeks, the Homophorus of Mani, ii, 260. 267. 268 note.
ATTALUS, a Phrygian convert, martyred, ii, 146. 148. His vision in prison, 161 note.
ATTALUS, the pagan emperor, iii, 96.
ATTICI of Rome, the, ii, 40.
AUGCRS, their "occupation gone," i, 28.
AUGUSTEUM, the, Constantinople, ii, 111.
AUGUSTI, the, sharers of Roman power, ii, 207. 221. 279. Impolicy of the system, 242.
AUGUSTINE, Saint, i, 28. Main argument of his *De Civitate Dei*, ibid note. Its occasion and contents, iii, 182-187. Inference from his quotation from Seneca, i, 430 note. On Nero's expected reappearance as Antichrist, ii, 123 note. Influence of African Christianity upon him, ii, 161; iii, 103. His escape from Manicheanism, ii, 271. 274; iii, 180. 181. His own words on the subject, ii, 174 note. Pagan rites at which he was present, iii, 79 note. His question to the Donatists, 91 note. Against the forcible demolition of heathen temples, 94 note. At issue with himself on the subject of miracles, 160 note. Most influential of all Christian writers since the apostles, 170. 177. Modern religious systems based

2 F 2

436 INDEX.

AUGUSTUS,
upon his writings, 171. Characteristics of his theology, 171-176; 176, 177, notes. His mental energy and extent of his learning, 177, 178. His life the type of his theology, 178. Popularity of his confessions, ii, 179. His parentage and youthful excesses, 179, 180. Influence of St Paul's writings and Ambrose's eloquence upon him, 181. Baptism of himself and his natural son, 182. Uneventfulness of his life, 187, 188, His end, 189. His notion of celibacy, 197. Subject of his dispute with Jerome, 232. His admiration for baptism, 316, 317, notes. His reply to a Manichean taunt, 327. His youthful delight in theatrical exhibitions, 337, 338 note. On the effect of gladiatorial shows, 344. On the personal appearance of Christ and the Virgin, 387, 388, 391. His opinion on church music, 405. Geographical dogma of his alleged against Columbus, 417. His allegation relative to saint-worship, 420 note. See ii, 110. Citations from or references to his writings, i, 35 note, 38 note, iii, 174 note, 278 note, 289 note, 295 note, 315 note, 323 note, 327 note, 334 note, 335 note, 351, 361, 364 note, 367, 375 note, 389 note, 392 note, 393 note, 395 note, 403 note, 404 note.

AUGUSTUS Cæsar's reign, why remarkable, i, 1. His deification, 39 note. Astrologers banished by him, 42. His decree for a census of Palestine and controversy concerning it, 99, 100. His rescript for the protection of the Jews, 445. His attempt to limit the right of divorce, iii, 290. See i, 416. ii, 5. 137.

AURELIAN, human sacrifices under, i, 36 note. His name among those of the persecuting emperors, ii, 138 note. Hostilities against the Christians under him, 199-203, 204.

BACCHUS.
AURELIUS, Marcus. See *Marcus Aurelius*.
AURELIUS Victor's character of Julian, iii, 28 note.
AUTOPHYES the Æon and his consort, ii, 70.
AUXENTIUS, contest for the bishopric vacated by the death of, iii, 152.
AVARS, Greek verses on the victory over the, iii, 426 note.
AVIDIUS Cassius a competitor for the empire, ii, 111. Period of his rebellion, 143 note.
AXUM, Mr. Salt's discovery in the ruins of, ii, 400 note.
AZIZ, king of Emesa, his reason for submitting to circumcision, i, 193 note.

BAAL, worship of, i, 61.
BAALBEC, style of the temple at, ii, 141, 146.
BAALPEOR, introduction into Rome of the rites of, ii, 173.
BABYLAS, Bishop of Antioch, worship of the relics of, ii, 188. Probable period of his martyrdom, and triumphant removal of his remains, iii, 15. See ii, 189 note.
BABYLON, efforts to identify Rome with, i, 60 note. The Babylon of the West, 456. Apocalyptic reference to its fall, ii, 117.
BABYLONIA, i, 57. History a blank relative to the settlement of the Jews there, 58. Influence exercised by them on its kings, people, and religion, 59, 60. Communications between it and Judæa, 105 note. Pestilence ascribed to the plunder of one of its temples, ii, 132. Early progress of Christianity, and residence of St Peter there, 248, 249. Zoroastrian persecutions, 251. Martyrdom of its Christian bishops, 254. See i, 63 note. ii, 92, 99, 263, 272.
BACCHUS, ii, 96.

INDEX. 437

BACCHUS.

BACCHUS Omestes, human sacrifices to, i, 26 note.
BACTRIA, i, 63, ii, 251.
BAGNIA, battle of, ii, 310.
BAGOAS, the eunuch, why put to death, 106, 107.
BAHARAM, Mani slain by, ii, 272.
BAIÆ, Bay of, a place of retirement for wealthy Romans, ii, 208.
BALK, country of the modern Afghans, ii, 250.
BAMPTON Lectures. See Conybeare; Milman.
BAPTISM and similar rites, i, 135. Antiquity of its use among the Jews, 135, 136. Charge against Chrysostom in reference to it, 139 note. Re-baptism of heretics, ii, 189 note. Manichæan baptism, 279. Constantine's tardy submission to it, 363, 364. Privileges of the baptized, iii, 315. Times and mode of its administration, 316, 317. Baptism of actors, 341, 342. Symbolic representations of the rite, 385 note.
BAPTISTERY, the, iii, 317.
BARABBAS, probable history of, i, 325. His release demanded, 336.
BARBARIAN captive chiefs, exposure in the gladiatorial arena of, ii, 289, 321; iii, 345. Crispus's campaign against them, ii, 322.
BARBARIANS, term applied by the Jews to the Greeks, i, 283.
BARBEYRAC, passages on clerical marriages collected by, iii, 279 note.
BARCHOCHAB, Jewish chief, successes of, i, 139 note. His defeat, 421.
BARDESANES, the poet of Gnosticism, ii, 58, 73. Long popularity and character of his hymns, 74. Identity of their number with the Psalms of David, 74 note. His system of Æons or Emanations, 75, 76. The disenchanter of the popular ear from his heretical strains, iii, 105. His hymns probably furnished with musical accompaniments, 403.

BASILIDES.

BAR-JESUS. See Elymas.
BARNAPH, prophecies of, ii, 64.
BARNABAS, character and influence of, i, 171. Espouses the cause of Paul, ibid. Arrival of himself and Paul at Jerusalem, 175. His enrolment among the apostles, 181. His association with Paul in missionary labours [see Paul]. Separates himself from Paul, 195.
BARONIUS, illustrative citations from, iii, 101 note. 277 note.
BARROW, Dr. i. 463 note.
BARTHOLOMEW, Saint, the Apostle, i, 151. 211. 387. See Nathanael.
BASIL, Saint, points in the character of, iii, 45. His dignified replies to the emissary of Valens, 46. His reception of Valens himself, ibid. Result attributed to his prayers, 47. Vein of Orientalism in his writings, 102. Estimate put on his writings by his contemporaries, 107. Effect of his influence on cænobitic institutions, ibid. His parentage and student life: injurious effect of his ascetic fervour, 108. Rules and practices of his monasteries, 109. His conduct in his archbishopric, 110. His death: style of his compositions, ibid. His views on clerical marriage, 278, 278 note. An admirer of baptism, 316 note. On an incident connected with the martyrdom of Gordius, 335 note. His opinion of human beauty, 388. Change in the Saviour's portraiture introduced by the monks of his order, 399. His eulogy on the forty martyrs, 421 note. See it, 461.
BASILICAS, or halls of justice, their adaptability for Christian worship, ii, 342-344; iii, 171. Appropriateness of the name for the purpose, 174. See II. 366. 366 note.
BASILEUS, disputed question as to the martyrdom of, ii, 117 note.
BASILIDES the Gnostic, ii, 58. His teachers: sources of his doctrines,

BASILIUS.

64. His Deity and Æons, and their attributes, 65-67. His curious theory of Christ and his sacrificed substitute, 68. See 64 notes, 69.

BASILIUS, deceived into a bishopric, iii, 121.

BASNAGE, references to the writings of, ii, 8 note; iii, 278, 394 notes.

BASSI, embracement of Christianity by the, iii, 92.

BATH-KOL, or voice from heaven, i, 284 note.

BATNE, reception of Julian at, iii, 26.

BATTLE in the night, a theological, ii, 369.

BATTLES: Bagola, ii, 310. Cibalæ, ii, 315. Hadrianople, ii, 319. Mardia, ii, 315. Milvian Bridge, ii, 289. Murca, ii, 421. Pollentia, iii, 94. Thapsus, ii, 159. Verona, ii, 281.

BEAUSOBRE's estimate of Simon Magus, ii, 46. 48.

BELGIUM ravaged by the Catti, ii, 112.

BENEDICT, Saint, Apollo-worship destroyed by, iii, 98. Founder of monastic communities in Italy, 209.

BENTLEY's reading of χοιρεία, flaw in, i, 194 note.

BEREA, separation of Paul from Timotheus and Silas at, i, 436.

BERNICE, Agrippa's sister, how obtained by Polemo, i, 192 note. Her entry with her brother, 405.

BERTHOLDT, character of the writings of, i, 55 note.

BETHABARA, John the Baptist's station on the Jordan, i, 114.

BETHANY (Beth-hana), derivation of the name, i, 106 note.

BETHESDA, healing of the sick at the pool of, i, 201.

BETHLEHEM, sanctity attached to, i, 99. Desecration of its gate by the Romans, 422. Pilgrimage of the whole world thither, iii, 191 note. Jerome's cell there, 332.

BETHPHAGE, etymology of, i, 306 note.

BLOOD.

BETHSAIDA, i, 178. 210. 211. 258. Retirement of Jesus into its adjacent desert, 224.

BEUGNOT's work on the Destruction of Paganism in the West, character of, iii, 67 note. Illustrative references to, or citations from, him, 79. 82. 97. 98. 355, notes.

BIGOTRY, cruel instance of, iii, 210 note. Classes furnishing its sternest executioners, 211.

BINGHAM, Joseph, Illustrative references to the writings of, iii, 97. 262. 264. 277. 308. 317. 319. 331. 375. 401. 404, notes.

BISHOPS, Institution of, ii, 15. 16. Nature of their authority, 22. Their ordination, 27. When first called pontiffs, 28. Arbiters of disputes, 114. Apostolic representation and something more claimed for them, ii, 16 note, 298; iii, 256. Their synods under Constantine, ii, 295. Regular attendants upon the court, 312. Licinius's conduct towards them, 316. Bishops, metropolitan and rural, their respective rank and functions, iii, 262-264. See Archbishops. Clergy. Episcopacy.

BITHYNIA, the scene of the first inroads of Christianity on Polytheism, ii, 92. Early success of Christianity there, 98.

BITHYNIARCHA, iii, 333.

BLANDINA, social status of, ii, 147. Her heroism under martyrdom, 147. 148.

BLASPHEMY charged on Jesus, i, 204. 249. 311. 327. On Stephen, 364. Its legal punishment, 374 note.

BLESILLA, St Jerome's beautific promise to, iii, 310.

BLIND, restoration by Jesus of the, and injunctions laid by Him on the cured, i, 222. 236. 250-252. Sublimth relief to the affliction specially prohibited, 252 note.

BLOOD, Judæo-Christian tenet of abstinence from, ii, 145. Prevalence

INDEX. 439

BOANERGES.

of the tenet among the early Christians, *ibid note.*
BOANERGES, Sons of Thunder, two disciples so named, i, 210.
BOHLEN, commendatory reference to a work of, ii, 31 *note*, 41 *note*.
BOLDETTI on Pagan burials and usages, 320. 322. 325, *notes.* Painting of the Saviour discovered by him, 391.
BONA, Cardinal, on the progressive changes in the representations of the Cross and the Saviour, iii, 398.
BONA DEA, orgies of the, i, 28.
BONIFACE IV, dedication of the Pantheon to the Virgin by, iii, 97.
BOSIO'S *Roma Sotteranea*, iii, 333. 384, *notes.*
BOSPHORUS, a rival Rome on the shores of the, ii, 329. 332. See *Constantinople.*
BOTHERIC, imperial representative, insulted, iii, 166.
BOTTARI *Pitture e Sculture Sacre*, iii, 391 *note.* Picture of the Virgin figured by, 394 *note.*
BÖTTIGER on representations of the deaths of martyrs, iii, 326 *note.*
BOURNOUF, value of works by, i, 66 *note.*
BRAHMA and Brahminism; excuse for teaching idolatry to the common people, i, 15 *note.* Point of resemblance between Platonism and Brahminism, 34. The great primal spirit of the system, 70 *note.* Its Divine word, 71. Active power of Brahma, 72 *note.* Sanscrit signification of Brahmin, 163 *note.* Elementary principle of higher Brahminism, ii, 34. Portion of the Divinity from which the Brahmen sprang, 35 *note.* See ii, 85. 115. 164.
BRIGHT'S 'History of the Church,' ii, 306 *note.*
BRITAIN, civilising influence of the Romans in, i, 2. As to St. Paul's alleged visit, 458 *note* q. Visited by Hadrian, ii, 104. Disturbances,

CABALA.

112. Settled by Severus, 154. Its representative in the Nicene Council, 365. See ii, 33. 343. 378. 381.
BROGLIE, De, on Origen and Tertullian, 164 *note.*
BRUMBES, De, theory of the Egyptian religion by, i, 16 *note.*
BRUCKER on the physical knowledge of the Fathers, iii, 417 *notes* d, e.
BUDDHISM, characteristics of, i, 93 *note.* Tradition of the birth of Buddh, 94 *note.* ii, 161 *note.* Elementary principle of the system, ii, 34 *note.* Primary theory of the Buddhist, 35. Female contact unlawful, 37 *note.* See ii, 248. 259, 269 *note.* 270.
BUNSEN, important fact established by, ii, 44 *note.* See also 51 *note.* 61 *note.* 79 *note*; iii, 80 *note.* 257 *note.* 359 *note.*
BUONAROTTI on vases found in Christian cemeteries, iii, 385 *note.*
BURGUNDIANS, form of Christianity embraced by the, iii, 57.
BURIAL customs and symbols among the ancient heathens and early Christians, iii, 319-331. 321, 322 *notes.* 383-385 *notes.*
BURNET and Mimon, Protestant travellers, erroneous inference of, iii, 384 *note.*
BURTON, Dr, on the chronology of Christ's life, i, 103 *note.* His ingenious suggestion relative to the Samaritans, ii, 108 *note.*
BUTTHOS, the Valentinian Æon, ii, 70.
BYTHOS, a name of the Father in Valentinus's system, ii, 69. 69 *note.* Produce of the Sons, 69 *note.*
BYZANTIUM razed to the ground by Severus, ii, 311, 312. Oracular prediction, 335 *note.* See *Constantinople.*

CAABA of Mecca, the, ii, 349.
CABALA, source of the, i, 60. Its early origin and contents, 61. Practisers

CÆDMON.

of the cabalistic art among the Jews, 417, 418. The cabalistic Sephiroth, ii, 11. 65. Cabalism a modifying element in Gnosticism, 61. 260.

CÆDMON. See *Adam Cædmon*.

CÆCILIA, St. burial place of the remains of, iii, 185 *note*.

CÆCILIAN raised to the see of Carthage, ii, 300. Opposed by the Donatists; charges against him, 301. Recriminations of the two parties, 303. Decision of the Council, 304. His ordination still denied, 310. Tenor of Constantine's letter to him, 314.

CÆLESTIUS, colleague of Pelagius, iii, 176.

CÆSAR, false prophecies of astrologers to, i, 42. "Render unto Cæsar," &c. 289 *note*. See *Cæsars*.

CÆSAREA, conflict of Jews and Greeks at, i, 183 *note*. Paul's imprisonment, 452, 453. ii, 256. Pagan cruelties, iii, 10. Julian's visit to, and proceedings in, the city, 45, 46. Basil's connexion with it, 108. Its archiepiscopate conferred on him, 110. Marriage ordinance of the Council of Neo-Cæsarea, 379 *note*. Its bishop, see *Eusebius*.

CÆSARIUS, brother of Gregory of Nazianzum, iii, 261.

CÆSARIUS, delegate of Theodosius, see *Hellabichus*.

CÆSARS, the first, period occupied by the line of, ii, 2. Apocryphal reference to the twelve Cæsars, 117. Sibylline prophecy, 122. A mournful birthday pleasantry, 171. Diocletian's two Cæsars, 207, 212, 223. 249. 279. See ii, 143. 219. 278. 196. See *Augustus*, *Julius Cæsar*.

"CÆSARS," the; character of Julian's work so called, iii, 3.

CAIAPHAS, motives of, for urging the sacrifice of Jesus, i, 265, 277. Jesus arraigned before him, 308-310. His conduct on the occasion, 311.

CAPPADOCIA.

CAIN, Gnostic symbolizations of, ii, 71. 81.

CALENDAR, heathen, festival regulations of the, iii, 111.

CALIGULA, i, 59. His persecution of the Jews, 173, 174. 418.

CALLIMACHUS the model of Propertius, i, 43.

CALLINICUM, burning of the Jewish synagogue at, iii, 163.

CALLISTUS, real cemetery of, ii, 188 *note*. Early Christian symbols found in the catacomb of, iii, 185 *note*. Representations of the Saviour and the Virgin on its walls, 191. 193.

CALVARY, erroneous notion regarding, i, 331 *note*. See 347.

CALVIN'S obligations to St Augustine, iii, 171.

CAMBYSES, conduct in Egypt of, i, 4 *note*.

CAMPUS Martius, strange scene in the, ii, 133 *note*.

CANA, anti-Kœrnian nature of the miracle at the marriage feast at, i, 152.

CANAANITES, Marcion's use of the massacre of the, ii, 78.

CANDACE, queen of Ethiopia, conversion of the officer of, i, 367.

CANIDIA, or Erictho, practices of, still surviving, iii, 98.

CANOPUS, destruction of the idolatrous worship, and end of the revels of, iii, 77. Why called "conqueror of the gods," 77 *note*.

CAPERNAUM, site and recommendations of, i, 154. 177. See ii, 78.

CAPITATION tax on the Jews, altered circumstances of the levy of the, ii, 2. 8.

CAPITOL, reproduction, at Constantinople, of the, ii, 333.

CAPITOLINE Jupiter, see *Jupiter Capitolinus*.

CAPITOLINUS, strange story of an impostor told by, ii, 132, 133, *note*.

CAPPADOCIA, dialect of, i, 412. See

CARACALLA.

II, 157, 209. Celebrated natives, see Basil; *George of Cappadocia; Gregory of Nazianzum; Gregory of Nyssa; Ulphilas.*
CARACALLA, II, 149. Contrast between his youthful disposition and later conduct, 155. Effect of extension of civic rights by him, 207 *note*, 241. See ii, 175.
CARAMALL'S the dancer, III, 140.
CARDWELL, Dr, on the visit of St Paul to Britain, I, 459 *note*.
CARPOCRATES, system and objects of worship of the followers of, ii, 80. Odiousness of their heresy, 81, 86. Community of women among them, 81 *note*. A charitable commentator on their practices, 86 *note*.
CARRIÆ, reception of Julian at, III, 26.
CARTHAGE, extinction of the older religion of, ii, 160. Character of the city under its Roman conquerors, *ibid.* Tertullian's prophetic threat, 164. Active charity of the Christians during a plague, 195. Uncharitable return of the heathen party, 196. Occasion of its devastation by Maxentius, 281. Dispute for its bishopric, and schism thereby generated, 197, 300-305. St Augustine's revelry in its pleasures, iii, 180. See II, 160 *note*, 185 *note*, 175. 190. 207. 283. References to decisions and ordinances of its councils, II, 190. 194. 308 *note*, iii, 221 *note*. 175 *note*. 277 *note*. 278 *note*, 280, 283 *note*, 311 *note*, 328. 311. 367 *note*. Its bishops, *see Cæcilian; Cyprian; Donatus; Mensurius.*
CASAUBON, passage misunderstood by, ii, 108, *note*. Other references to, iii, 115; 318, *notes*.
CASCAR, or CASHGAR, scene of an alleged conference between Archelaus and Maul, ii, 264 *note*, 272. 272 *note*.
CASÆ NIGRÆ, see *Donatus*.

CELIBACY.

CASINO, Mount, MS. account of a martyrdom found at, ii, 165 *note*. Destruction of idolatrous worship there, iii, 98.
CASIUS, Mount, ii, 105 *note*. Julian's idol-worship on, iii, 14.
CASSIAN, story of unnatural mysticism told by, iii, 210 *note*. Citations from his 'Institutes,' 199, 208, 209, 225, 403, *notes*.
CASSIODORUS, i, 102 *note*, iii, 333, 347, *notes*.
CASSIUS, competitor of Severus, ii, 116, See *Avidius Cassius*.
CASTOR and POLLUX, temple of, and their statues, ii, 332.
CATACOMBS, paintings in, 125 *note*. 184, 185, *notes*. 197, 198, 198 *note*. Alleged residence of early Christians, 128, 329 *note*. Mortuary chapels, 329 *note*, column 2. See *Burials*.
CATECHUMENS in the Manichean system, ii, 271. Their position in the Church, 342. In Christian Baptism, iii, 317.
CATHEDRAL chant of England, system preserved in the, iii, 405 *note*.
CATHOLIC Faith promulgated by Theodosius, iii, 100.
CATHOLICS, collision of the Donatists with the, II, 103-106. 308 *note*. 311 *note*. Charges of the latter against them, 306 *note*. 310. Their exultation on the death of Arius, 382. Alleged murder of a party of them, iii, 45.
CATONISM more obnoxious to Vespasian than Christianity, ii, 7.
CATTI, Belgium ravaged by the, ii, 112.
CELIBACY, element confirmatory of the sanctity of, i, 96. Its parent, ii, 36. The line of demarcation between Christian and Heathen, 17. Period of its exaltation by the church, 28. Condemned by Clement of Alexandria, 28 *note*; iii, 277, 278.

CELSUS.

Relaxation of laws unfavourable to it, ii, 398. Advocated by Ambrose, iii 152. Point passed over by controversialists, 196 note. How regarded by the fathers of the church, 197. Cause of its continuance and final recognition, 221. Not compulsory on the clergy during the first three centuries, 277, 278. Commencement of its enforcement on them, 278. Regulation of the Council in Trullo, 281. Evils generated by its enforcement, 282.

CELSUS, his mode of reconciling Paganism with Christianity, ii, 181, 181. See i, 108 *note*.

CELTS. See *Kelts*.

CEMETERIES of the early Christians, sanctity of the, ii, 142. See *Burials. Catacombs*.

CENTURION'S servant healed by Jesus, i, 212.

CEREMONIAL, religious. See *Church: Religion*.

CERES, fable of, i, 81. See ii, 172.

CERINTHUS, legend of St. John and, ii, 14. His descent and education, 55. Peculiarities of the system concocted by him, 56, 57. Ascription of the authorship of the 'Apocalypse' to him, 57 *note*. Modifying influence on his opinions, 59.

CHALCEDON, council of, laws promulgated by, iii, 101. 261 *note*. Its bishop, see *Maris*.

CHALDEANS, doctrine taken by the Greeks from the, i, 39. Their influence as astrologers, 43. Consulted by Marcus Aurelius, 139. An admission of his concerning them, 143 *note*. Mani's borrowings from them, 160. See ii, 33, 74, 76.

CHAM, prophecies of, ii, 64.

CHAMPAGNY, M. de, on the alleged correspondence between St. Paul and Seneca, i, 444 *note*.

CHANTS of the Italian and Roman churches, iii, 405. Cathedral chant of England, 405 *note*.

CHRISTIANITY.

CHAOS in the Ophitic system, ii, 81.

CHARIOT races, massacre arising out of, iii, 166. See *Circus*.

CHARLEMAGNE and art, iii, 373.

CHASTEL, Etienne, commendatory notice of a work by, iii, 67 *note*. See also 78, 146, 141, *notes*.

CHATEAUBRIAND, theory of Christianity sketched by, i, 48 *note*.

CHIFFLET, Gnostic images in the collection of, iii, 190 *note*.

CHILDREN. See *Infants*.

CHILON, charge of sorcery made by, iii, 16.

CHINA, higher classes less idolatrous than the common people in, i, 15 *note*. Dogma of the Creation under their system, 70 *notes*. Its Christian communities, ii, 11. Its ascetics, 16. See 248, 261.

CHIOS visited by Paul, i, 451.

CHOREPISCOPI, or rural bishops, establishment of, iii, 262, 263. See ii, 202.

CHRIST. See *Jesus Christ*.

CHRISTIANITY, epoch of the appearance of, i, 1. Its universality; favourableness of the times for its propagation, 7. Social element peculiar to it, 8. New era announced by the appearance of its Divine Author, *ibid*. Curious charge of the Chinese *élite* against its missionaries, 15 *note*. Revolution effected by it, 41. Characteristic distinction of this revolution, 44. Admixture of heathen rites and usages, 45. Design of this work, 46, 47. Phases of Christianity at different epochs, 47. Its aspect among barbarian believers, 48. Among the Abyssinians, *ibid note*. Not a self-developed system, nor to be accounted for on any ordinary principles, 48, 49. Emotions natural to so great an event, 49. Life of Christ necessary to its history, 50. Its religion essentially historic, 118 *note*. Elements of early evangelic history

CHRISTIANITY.
influencing its propagation and maintenance, 121-126. Commencing point of its history, 119. Resurrection of Jesus its basis, 140. Effect of its introduction upon all the arrangements of human society, 141, 142. Primary blessing too often lost sight of, 143 note. Descent of the Holy Ghost and Gift of Tongues, 151. Various explanations of the miracle, ibid notes. Scene of its enactment, 154. Classes from whom its first converts were taken, 163. Its first martyr, and influence of his martyrdom on its progress, 164-167 (see *Stephen*). Expulsion of its followers from Jerusalem and good seed thereby sown, 167. Sufferings of its apostles under Herod Agrippa, 174-176. Its progress in Judæa and Syria: first application of the term *Christians* to its followers, 177. Exclusive notions yet entertained by them, 177, 178. Gradual enlargement of the views of its apostles: systems opposed to and which ultimately became modified exponents of it, 378, 379. Its double conflict with external Judaism, and with the Judaism of its own church, and dying struggles of the latter, 179, 180. New phase in its development indicated by the secession of Paul and Barnabas, 381, 414. Its first "church," 389. Object of the compromise agreed to in the Council of Jerusalem, 392-394. Tradition of the divine warning sent to its followers before the siege of Jerusalem, 409. Probable effect on it of the fall of Jerusalem, 410, 411. Obstacles interposed to its progress by regard for the *Law*, and efforts of Paul to overcome them, 414-418. Hostility and final separation between it and Judaism, 419, 421. Distinguishing features of its conflicts with Judaism and with Paganism, 424, 425, 428. Important element of their own faith rendering its adoption more

CHRISTIANITY.
easy to the Jews, 426. Character of its first collision with Paganism, 430. Favorable action of Judaism upon its progress, 430, 431. Scene of its first public conflict with Paganism, 436. Its reception and establishment at Corinth, 441, 442. Persecution and slaughter of its followers under Nero, 454-457. Proofs of the reality of such persecution, 458 note. Occasion of the Neronian persecution, ii, 4. Its effect on the progress of Christianity, 5, 6. Truth illustrated by the contemptuous notice bestowed on Christianity during its first century, ii, 1, 2. External circumstances calculated to advance its growth, 3. How regarded during its first period, and incentives to popular delight in the sufferings of its followers, 4, 5. Vespasian's probable view of its chances of enduring, 6. Juxtaposition of the Christians and the Jews in relation to the Roman governors, 7-11. Charge of Atheism brought against its followers, 12. 145, 180. Influence of Orientalism on its progress, 10, 11. 43. Form in which ascetism became grafted on it, 12. Conservative influence of monasticism upon it, 44. Its contact and conflicts with Simon Magus and the Gnostics (see *Gnosticism; Simon Magus*). Its position, prospects, and progress under Trajan, Hadrian, and the Antonines, 88-91. 108. Element in its system which would be last understood, 91. First discovery by Polytheism of its aggressive power, 92. Value of Trajan and Pliny's correspondence as a record of its early history, and facts thereby elicited, 92-96. 98, 99. Probable cause of the persecution under Trajan, 99-101. Occasion of the cry "The Christians to the Lions," 102. 107. 127. Its advance under Antoninus Pius, 109-111. Its altered position under Marcus Aurelius, and

CHRISTIANITY.

causes thereof, 112-114. 128-130. Tertullian's plea for toleration, 115. Apprehended connexion of its progress with the fall of Rome, and confirmatory warrant for such apprehension, 116, 117. Christian interpolations in the Sibylline books, 118. 120, 124, 125. Martyrdom and persecutions under Marcus Aurelius, 134-140. 144-148 (see *Attalus*; *Blandina*; *Justin*; *Maturus*; *Polycarp*; *Ponticus*; *Pothinus*; *Sanctus*). Insecurity of the imperial throne, and vices of its persecutors favorable elements in the progress of Christianity, 150, 151. 153. Its condition under Commodus, 154. Its infant pupil Caracalla, 155. Loyalty of, and encouragement afforded to, its followers under Severus, 155, 156. Its progress and martyrs in Africa (see *Africa*). Change in its relation to society under Alexander Severus, 179. Grant of land for its worship by him, 180. Its silent progress and modifying influences on Heathenism, 180-183. 185, 211. Its fortunes under the Emperors Maximin I., Gordian, and Philip, 185-187. Martyrdoms and persecutions under Decius and Valerian, 187, 188. 190-198. Miserable deaths of its persecutors, 198, 199, 280. Its last collision under Aurelian, 199, 200, 203. Its condition at the accession of Diocletian, 204. 205. Relaxing effects of prosperity upon it, 205, 206. Improvement in its prospects on Diocletian's neglect of Rome, 208-210. Ambiguous position of Christian soldiers in the Roman army, 214. 215. Imperial deliberations as to course to be taken with the Christians, and issue thereof, 215-217. Wholesale persecutions inflicted by Diocletian and his co-ordinate sovereigns, 217-224. Vitality of Christianity under the same, 225, 227. Its triumph over Galerius: his repentant edict, 227, 228. Evidences of the extent of the persecution, 229,

CHRISTIANITY.

230. Repressive edicts of, and revival of persecution by Maximin II, 230-233. 235. Christian requital of Pagan cruelties, 336. Retractation of hostile edicts, and retaliation on Pagan persecutors, 237-239. Reconstruction and magnificence of the church of Tyre, 239, 240. Conversion of Constantine: diversity of motives prompting same, 245, 246. State of Christianity at the time, 247, 279. Its early successes in Parthia and Babylonia, 248, 249. Exterminating processes adopted against it in Persia, 252, 253. Its first kingdom and varying results of struggles with Paganism there, 254, 255, 256-258. Scheme of Mani for blending it with the Oriental systems, 259-274 (see *Mani*). Its triumphs in the east: complaints as to the numbers professing it, 275, 276. Considerations on this latter point, 276 *note*. Different circumstances affecting its propagation in the east and west, 276-279. Its state under Maxentius, 281, 282. Character given to it in connexion with Constantine's vision, 285-289. Great charter of its liberties, 290, 291. Tenor and spirit of Constantine's earlier laws in its favour, 291-293. 312. Proofs of the position accorded to it, 295. Popular passions called into action by questions concerning it, and first civil wars arising thereout, 296, 297. Growth of the sacerdotal power a necessary consequence of its development, 297, 298. Donatists and traditors: rival bishops: result of appeals to the civil power, 299-302. Action of the council thereon and persecution of the Donatists, 302-306. The Circumcellions, their ravages and subjugation, 306-310. Licinius's active enmity toward Christianity and its worshippers, and repeal of his edicts by Constantine, 316-319. Effect of the foundation of Constantinople upon its progress, 331. 338. Pagan

INDEX. 445

CHRISTIANITY.
temples, why unsuitable for its worship, 340. Adaptability of the basilica thereto, 342-344. Reinstated in the place of its birth, and erection of memorial churches on the holy sites there, 346-349. The Trinitarian controversy, 350-382 (see *Athanasius*; *Arius*; *Nicæa*; *Nicene Creed*; *Sabellianism*; *Trinitarianism*). Its legal establishment and effects thereof on itself, on the civil power, and on society, 389-392. Its humanizing influence upon legislation, 393-397. Its success in Æthiopia and Iberia, 400-404. Its position and dissensions under the sons of Constantine, 405, 406. The moral revolution worked by it less rapid than the theological, 407-409. The Athanasian controversy and its offshoots, 410-448. Character of the Christian dæmonology, 453. Its internal animosities and their consequences, 454. Conduct of the Emperor Julian towards its worshippers, iii, 4, 5, 7-9. Cruelties perpetrated upon them, 11. Character of Julian's writings against, and conflicts with it, 24, 25, 28, 29. Its position under Valentinian and Valens, and theological disputes under the latter, 32, 35, 36, 38, 44. Valens and Basil, 45, 46. Its effects in mitigating the evils of barbaric invasion, and blending rival races, 47-49. Its influence at distinct periods on literature, language, municipal institutions, and general habits, 51-54, 240-243, 245, 247, 248, 249. Its reception and influence among the Goths, 54-58. Its advance under Theodosius, 59-61. Belief of Christians in the existence of the heathen deities, 62, 63. Effect upon its peasant converts of their Pagan remembrances, 64, 65. Its war against the Pagan Temples, 66-72, 74-78. Rescripts and edicts of Theodosius in its favour, 72, 73, 90, 91, 100. A crisis testing its power,

CHRISTODORUS.
125. Labour of Chrysostom in its cause (see *Chrysostom*). Its position at the period of his fall, 149. Tone assumed by it under Ambrose's teachings, 153. How championed by him, 164-167. Point in which its divine mission was accomplished, 171. Nature of Jerome's influence over it, 190. Effect of monachism upon it and upon its preachers, 214, 218-220, 221-224. Dominance obtained by it in the Roman world, 238. Growth of its hierarchy and priesthood, and arrangements of its church (see *Baptism*; *Bishops*; *Church*; *Clergy*; *Councils*; *Deacons*; *Festivals*; *Hierarchy*; *Sacraments*). Its uses of wealth: a triumphant question, 272, 273. Its influence upon marriage, 291. Its penitential discipline, 293. Public spectacles cut off by it, 307. Seclusion and obscurity of its early worshipping places, *ibid*. Public amusements condemned by it, 341. Its way of dealing with actors and actresses, and with the drama, 341, 342. Sanguinary exhibitions suppressed by its influence: its martyr in the good work, 343-346. Character of its literature, sacred and secular, 349, 365 (see *Literature*). Its oratory, 365-370. Its connection with and influence on the fine arts, 371-405 (see *Architecture*; *Music*, *Paintings*; *Sculpture*; *Symbolism*). Form assumed by it as the religion of the Roman world, 406, 407. Its faith and morals never thoroughly separated, 408, 409. Its military phase, 409, 410. Its mystic age: faith: religious impressions, 411-416. Its effect on natural philosophy, 416-417. Its polytheistic forms: worship of saints, angels, and the Virgin, 419-426.

CHRISTMAS carols, early traditions surviving in, I, 127 *note*.

CHRISTODORUS on the statues in

CHRISTON.

Zeuxippus's gymnasium, ii, 166 note.
CHRISTOS, confusion of Christos with, i, 396 note. In the Gnostic systems, ii, 57. 61. 71.
CHRYSANTHIUS the sophist, recommended to Julian as a teacher, II, 457, 458. Doubtful honour declined by him, iii, 1.
CHRYSOSTOM, Dio, see Dio Chrysostom.
CHRYSOSTOM, Saint, act of Constantine approval by, ii. 400. Sarcasms of Julian confirmed by him, iii, 12. Character and influence of his writings and preachings, 102. 118. 122. 123. 151. 164 note. Meaning of his name, 119. His parentage, training, and adoption of a religious life, ibid. His mother's appeal to his affection, 120. His pious fraud on his friend, and monastic career, 121. His notion of the sacerdotal character, 122, 127. His description of the agonies of an Antiochian persecution, and consolatory ministrations to the sufferers, 122-127. Made Bishop of Constantinople, 129. His asceticism in his episcopate, 130, 131. His political difficulties, 131. Succours and pleads for Eutropius, 133. 135. Weak points in his character: governed by his deacon, 136. Occasion of clerical hostilities against him, 137. 138. His condemnations by councils, 139. 140, 141. Causes of Empress Eudoxia's enmities towards him, 140, 141. 144. 178. Catastrophes following each of his banishments, 142. 146. Infelicities of his exile, and harshnesses hastening his death, 146, 147. After-worship paid to his remains, 147. 148. Causes and object of the persecutions inflicted on him, 148. An obstinate enemy of his, 248. His view of the conduct of a prelate, 270. His profession of faith, 117 note. On the presence and participation of women

CIAMPINI.

in public spectacles, 135. 139 note, 140 note. Character of his epistles, 164 note. His eulogium on the sanctity of the Cross, 181. On the Saviour's personal appearance, 187. His band of choristers, 404. See ii, 189; iii, 13 note, 15 note, 104. 242 note, 243 note, 246. 264 note, 275 note, 281. 312. 316 note, 326. 317. 366 note, 395.
CHURCH, first Christian, i, 391; ii, 57. Period of the formation of churches, ii, 14. Origin of orders in it, 15. How originally formed, 16, 17. Difference between it and the synagogue, 18, 19. Model whereon formed, 19, 20. Its centre, 20, 21. Its elders, bishops, and other officers, 21-29. Founder of churches in Rome, 294. Churches in Constantinople, 311 note, 391. Adaptation of Basilicas, 343-344. 366 note. Memorial churches in Palestine, 348, 349. Relations of Church and State, 371; iii, 284-287. Effect of its power to receive bequests, ii, 315; iii, 273, 274. Permitted to accept gifts of land, ii, 319. Church unity, iii, 267. Application of its wealth, 275. Its cognizance of marriages and wills, 291, 292. Its alliance with the civil power for punishing heretics, 299. Arrangements for separation of its various orders of worshippers, 110-113; and for administration of its sacraments, 114-118. Peculiarities of its architecture, 373-376. Music in its services, 401-405. See Baptism; Bishops; Clergy; Festivals.
CHURCH disputes, see Arius; Athanasius; Donatists; Trinitarian Controversy.
CHURCH of England, as abandoned Article of the, i, 76 note.
CHUZA, Herod's steward, see Joanna.
CIAMPINI on church architecture, iii, 374 note. On ancient church art, 395.

CIBALÆ.

CIBALÆ, battle of, ii, 315.

CIBORIUM, the, or altar canopy, iii, 111.

CICERO on the religious policy of the Romans, i, 6. His theory of the religion of Egypt, 16 *note*. On human sacrifices, 27 *note*. Why he took refuge in philosophy, 30 *note*. On the hypocrisy of the soothsayers, 36. A question propounded by him, 38. See 35 *note e*, 437.

CICOGNARA, Count, on clerical dress, iii, 271 *note*.

CILICIA visited by Paul and Silas, i, 195.

CIRCUMCELLIONS, consequences of the barbarous fanaticism of the, ii, 306. Their insurrection and defeat of the Imperial troops, 308. Their equality proclamations, atrocities, and passion for martyrdom, 308, 309. Their defeat, 310.

CIRCUMCISION performed on Jesus, i, 101. Difficulties of Jewish Christians with regard to its abandonment, 182, 183. 192, 426. Inducements to kings for submitting to it, 192 *note*.

CIRCUS and chariot-races, ii, 194. Massacres and party disputes, iii, 166. 347.

CITY of GOD—*de Civitate Dei*. See *Augustine*.

CIVILIZATION under the Romans, i, 2. Its effects on the old religions, 25 ; ii, 278.

CLAUDIAN, Latin poetry revived by, i, 60. His satire on Eutropius, iii, 133. 245 *note*. His style, 351. Remarkable characteristic of his poetry, 355 *note*. See 336 *note*, 337. 337 *note e*, 140 *note*, 146 *note e*.

CLAUDIUS, satire aimed by Seneca, at, i, 29 *note*. Astrologers banished by him, 42. Alleged cause of his expulsion of the Jews from Rome, 396. Christian progress during his reign, 416. Re'axation of his edict,

CLERGY.

451. Severe alike to Christian and Jew, ii, 4.

CLEARCHUS befriends Maximus, iii, 42.

CLEMENT of Alexandria, allusion to the Λαϊκος by, ii, 26 *note*. Asserts St Paul to have been married, 37 *note*. His condemnation of celibacy, 38 *note*. On the community of women in the Carpocratian system, 81 *note*. His denunciation of luxuries, 209 *note*. Passage interpolated in his epistle, iii, 259 *note*. Further on the marriage of the apostles, 277. Passage thereon verbatim, 277 *note e*. Progressive nature of his works, 119. On the wife's signet ring, 182. On Christ's personal appearance, 386. See ii, 125. iii, 69. 197. 241, 242. 315. 441, *notes*.

CLEMENT of Rome, i, 471.

CLEMENT, St, question as to authenticity of the works of, ii, 45 *note*.

CLEMENTINA, the, nature of the writings so called, iii, 259.

CLEOPHAS and Mary, parents of James, one of the Apostles, i, 211.

CLERGY, first aristocratic, then despotic, i, 47. Their order legally recognised, ii, 113. Exemptions granted to them, 113, 114. Prohibition of their synods by Licinius, iii, 116. Influence acquired and authority claimed and exercised by them, iii, 49, 50, 304. Their interference in secular affairs, 131-133. Basis of their claim to supernatural power, 160. Their vices painted by Jerome, 228. Their relation to and influence over females, 229. Widening of the separation between them and the laity, and consequences thereof, 257, 258. One of their last triumphs, 261. Consequences of the increase of their power, 269 ; and contrast of same with Apostolic periods, 269-271. Their dress, 271 *note*. Their acquisition and uses of wealth, 272. How maintained, 271. Become a separate

CLINTON.

community, 276. Their liability to flagellation and other penalties, 276, 277. Institution of celibacy: effect of their debarment from conjugal rights, 277-282. Their *mulieres subintroductæ*, 282, 281-283 *note*. Advantages of their station, 303. Their dread of the charge of irreligion, 415. See *Bishops*; *Church*; *Episcopacy*.

CLINTON'S Fasti, ii, 92 *note*. 103 *note*.

CODEX Argenteus, contents and magnificence of the, iii, 55 *note*.

CŒNOBITISM, effects on the establishment of Christianity of, iii, 196, 197. Asceticism, practices, and numbers of its votaries, 208, 209. Its dangers, 210. See *Monachism*.

COINS of Rome, Christian symbols on, ii, 112.

COLLYRIDIANS rejected as heretics, iii, 424 *note*.

COLOSSÆ visited by Paul, i, 460.

COLUMBUS, clerical opposition to the theory of, iii, 417.

COMANA, Chrysostom's death-place, iii, 147.

COMEDY, see *Drama*.

COMITS, Roman auguries from, i, 4 *note*.

COMMANDMENTS uttered by Christ, effect of the, i, 180.

COMMODUS, human sacrifices offered by, i, 26 *note*. His brutal character and gladiatorial feats, ii, 151, 152. Usurps the attributes of Hercules, 152, 153 *note*. His attitude towards Christianity, 154. See ii, 149.

COMMUNITY of goods not an apostolic institution, i, 357. Mosheim's argument, *ibid note*.

COMMUNITY of women among the Carpocratians, ii, 81 *note*.

CONFESSION, Tertullian on, iii, 294.

CONSTANS, successor to Constantine, ii, 408, 410. Adheres to the cause

CONSTANTINE,

of Athanasius, 146, 411, 414. His law against Pagan sacrifices, 384. Council proposed by him, 417. His murder avenged, 420, 421. See ii, 416, 423; iii, 10.

CONSTANT'S work 'Sur la Religion,' its character, i, 10 *note*. Value of his 'Polythéisme Romain,' 19 *note*. His view of human sacrifices under the Romans, 26 *note*. On the causes of indecent rites, 70 *note s*.

CONSTANTIA'S dying plea for Arius, ii, 372.

CONSTANTINE the Great: his conversion a politic act, ii, 150. Motives for same, 246, 279. His charge against Diocletian, 311 *note*. Effect of his schemes on Maxentius, 124. Hopes of the Christians regarding him, 225. His dexterous escape from Galerius, 225, 281. His remonstrances against Maximin's cruelties, 233. Issuit of his victory over Maxentius, 237. Epoch marked by his reign, 241. The man for the epoch, 243. Consequence of his dissolution of the Prætorian bands, 244. Begins hostilities against Maxentius, 281, 283. Oscillating between two religions: his famous Vision and its results, 284-287, 286, 287, *notes*, 288. His life a Christian Cyropædia, 285 *note*. His religious views as interpreted by his conduct after his conquest of Maxentius, 289, 290. 321. Importance to Christianity of his Milan edict, 290, 291. 312. Recognises the Sabbath: Pagan rites suppressed by him, 292, 293. Christian churches founded, and synods assembled by him in Rome, 294, 295, 311. His conduct with regard to controversial questions referred to him, 302, 303 *note*, 303, 304, 306, 310, 359, 362, 363. His view of the position of the priesthood, 314. His war with and victory over Licinius, 315-319. His conduct to his ene-

INDEX.

CONSTANTINOPLE.

rules on the field and afterwards, 319, 320, 321. Occasion of his putting to death his son, nephew, and wife, 321-324. Pagan account of the transaction, 325, 326. His subsequent remorse, 327, 328. His resolution to remove the seat of empire; effect of same, 329-331. 370, 371. Ruling principle observed, and course taken by him in building and adorning Constantinople, 332-337; iii, 379 (on Constantinople). His edict relative to gladiatorial shows, ii, 339 note. Destroys a temple of Aphrodite, 345. His unotticial bit for his wardrobe, 348. His re-edification of holy places in Palestine, 347-349. His presidency of the Council of Nicæa, and banquet to the bishops, 166-368. His disposal of the libels of the bishops against each other, 367 note. Incentive to his recal of Arius, 372. Ascendancy of Eusebius of Nicomedia over him, 371. His decrees opposed, and himself confronted, by Athanasius, 376, 379. Occasion of his condemnation of Sopater, 380, 381. His banishment and deathbed recall of Athanasius, 381, 382, 383. His probable motives for deferring his baptism, 383, 384, iii, 116 note. Extent of his efforts towards the establishment of Christianity and suppression of Paganism, ii, 385-389, 391. His laws for the protection of children and women, and with regard to single and childless persons, 391-397, 399. Conduct of Pagans and Christians at his burial, 399, 400. His law regarding public festivals, iii, 332. His exhibition of captives at Treves, 345. See ii, 2, 149, 210, 230, 240, 254, 275, 299, 332, 344, 347; iii, 5, 65, 290, 300.

CONSTANTINOPLE, veneration of the Labarum at, ii, 287. Epoch marked by its foundation, and influence thereof on Christianity, 330, 331. Scheme contemplated in building

VOL. III.

CONSTANTIUS.

and ornamenting it, 332, 333. Ceremonials of its foundation and dedication, 332, 336. Its Christian churches, 333 note, 344; iii, 141. Principles embodied in the founder's statue, ii, 337. Christian and Pagan aspects of the new city, 338-340. Sources of its corn supplies, 360. Sanguinary tumults on account of church disputes, 414, 415; iii, 145. Attachment of its inhabitants to Christianity, iii, 11, 12, 51. Dominance of Arianism, 114. Visited by an earthquake, 142. Burning of St Sophia's Church, 146. Enthusiasm and party disputes kindled by its chariot races, 147, 348. See ii, 275, 290; iii, 65, 102, 111, 379. Its bishops, see *Alexander, Bishop of Constantinople*; *Chrysostom*; *Eudoxus*; *Gregory of Nazianzum*; *Ilenius*; *Maximus the Cynic*; *Nectarius*.

CONSTANTIUS Cæsar's humane conduct towards the Christians, ii, 221, 225. His peaceful end, 279.

CONSTANTIUS, son of Constantine, a supporter of Arianism, ii, 371. First prohibitor of sacrifices, 387 note. Honour rendered by him to his father's remains, 400. Not free from the stain of fratricide, 405. His reconciliation with and subsequent hostilities against Athanasius, 411. 419, 421, 424, 425, 427. His conduct on hearing of the murder of Hermogenes, 415. Abandons and again espouses the cause of the Arians, 420, 421, 422, 425, 442. Avenges the murder of Constans, 420, 421. Effect upon him of Bishop Valens' prophecy, 421. His claim to direct inspiration and squabbles with the Council of Milan, 425, 426. Rejection of his proposals by the women of Rome, 427, 442. Ferocious conduct of his troops and Arian adherents in Alexandria, 428-430. Character of invectives launched against him, 431-436.

2 G

CONSUBSTANTIALISM.

His reception of the deputies from the disputing sects, 445. 446. Consequences of his attempt to the dominance of Arianism, 447. Shape taken by his jealousy of Julian, 456. 460. 462. Julian's charge against him, 459. Character of his personal religion, 460. Contingency prevented by his death, 462. His removal of the statue of victory, iii, 81. Some of his laws: as to bishops, 284 note; for protecting women, 289; as to the prætors, 332 note; relative to soldier-gladiators, 345. See iii, 2. 10. 17. 30.

CONSUBSTANTIALISM, or doctrine of the *Homoousion*. See *Homoousios*.

CONYBEARE'S 'Bampton Lectures,' ii, 209 note.

COOS visited by Paul, i, 451.

COPONICH, defilement of the temples during the administration of, i, 167.

CORINTH, cause of the settlement of the Jews at, i, 396. Colony established by Julius Cæsar, 396, 441, notes. Disputes between Christians and Jews and result thereof, 396, 397. 443, 444. Settlement of the Christians, 417. 417 note, 433. The Venice of the old world, 441. Description of one of its fairs, 412 note. Nero's anticipated visit, 461. St Paul's residence in and connection with it, 416. 450. 451. 460. 462. ii, 21 note. State of its church, 25, 26. 26 note.

CORNELIUS, supernatural manifestation at the conversion of, i, 382. Class represented by him, and discussion raised on the question, *ibid* and note. Period of his conversion, 383. Its effect on the extension of Christianity, 385. Views probably held by him before his conversion, 410.

CORNELIUS, Bishop of Rome, on the ministerial establishment of Rome, ii, 210 note. Cyprian's epistle to him, iii, 259. 259 note. Onslaught in which he perished, 329 note.

COUNCILS.

CORPORAL punishment. See *Punishment*.

COSMAS Indicopleustes, ii, 400 note. His work a curious example of ancient physical science, iii, 417 note.

COSMOS, or seed of the universe, ii, 65 note.

COTELERIUS, information on clerical marriages collected by, iii, 277 note. See ii, 25 note; iii, 324 note.

COUNCILS and synods of the Church incompetent to the reconciliation of religious differences, ii, 305. References to some of their deliberations and ordinances, ii, 444; iii, 267, 268. 278. 285. 328. The earliest synod, iii, 261.

COUNCILS:
Alexandria, ii, 412.
Ancyra, iii, 268, 278, notes.
Antioch, ii, 412; iii, 268 note.
Arles, ii, 304. 423; iii, 268 note. 280.
Carthage, ii, 190. 194. 301. 308 note; iii, 271, 275, 277, 278, notes, 280. 283 note. 311 note, 328. 331. 367 note.
Chalcedon, iii, 101. 261 note, 264.
Constantinople, ii, 446; iii, 117, 268 note.
Elvira. See *Illiberis*, below.
Gangra, iii, 279. 279 note.
Illiberis, or Elvira, iii, 78, 250, 253, 268, 282, 289, notes, 378.
Jerusalem, i, 392.
Laodicea, iii, 261, 268, notes, 382 note.
Milan, ii, 417. 419. 423. 434; iii, 268 note.
Neo-Cæsarea, iii, 279 note.
Nicæa, ii, 320. 337. 364-370. 375; iii, 277. 283 note, 417 note.
Oak at Chalcedon, iii, 139.
Œcumenic, iii, 268 note.
Orleans, iii, 128.
Philippopolis, ii, 418.
Quinisextan, iii, 398 note.
Rimini, ii, 432. 445; iii, 268 note.

CRASSES.

Rome, ii, 302, 417; iii, 268 *note*.
Sardica, ii, 417; iii, 368 *note*.
Seleucia, ii, 432, 445, 446.
Sirmium Synod, ii, 445.
Toledo, iii, 280, 281, 298 *note*.
Tyre, ii, 413; iii, 368 *note*.

CRASSUS, a dupe to the Chaldeans, i, 42. Construction put by the Jews upon his death, 160. See ii, 451.

CREATION, Chinese dogma of the, i, 70 *note*.

CREATOR. See *Deity; God*.

CREEDS, necessity for and philosophy of, ii, 409, 440. The Nicene creed, ii, 268, 445. The Apostolic creed, iii, 176.

CRESCENS, the cynic, Justin's death attributed to the jealousy of, ii, 134.

CRETE, establishment of Christianity in, i, 459, 460; ii, 15.

CREUZER'S 'Symbolik,' value of De Guigniaut's rendering of, i, 10 *note*.

CRIMES against humanity, Constantine's laws relative to, ii, 393-398.

CRISHNA, Christ-like parallel in the traditions of, i, 94 *note*.

CRISPUS, ruler of the synagogue, conversion of, i, 397.

CRISPUS, son of Constantine, Christian tutor of, ii, 315, 322, 394. Naval victory achieved by him, 319, 322. Put to death by his father, 323. Crime charged upon him, 324. Memorial of his father's remorse, *ibid*. Presumed instigator and object of his murder, 324, 325.

CROSS, treatment of sufferers on the, i, 332. Represented on the walls of the Temple of Serapis, iii, 75 *note*. Long the sole symbol of Christianity, 180. Gradual change in art-representations of it, 198, 199.

CROSS of Christ, Constantine's vision of the, ii, 287. Alleged use of its nails, 337, 348. Imperial suppliants at its foot, 189. Legend of its discovery and effect thereof on Christian worship, 347, 348.

CYPRUS.

General acceptation of the legend, iii, 181.

CRUCIFIX, late adoption of as a Christian symbol, iii, 398. Munter's opinion, *ibid note*.

CRUCIFIXION of Jesus, thoughts on the, i, 331-335. See *Jesus*.

CTESIPHON, ii, 349.

CUCUSUS, Chrysostom's place of exile, iii, 146, 147.

CUMANUS, tumults and massacre during the prefecture of, i, 184, 201.

CURETON, Dr, Syriac Epistles published by, ii, 102; iii, 257 *note*.

CUSPIUS Fadus, no friend to the Sanhedrin, i, 184.

CYAXARES I. identified with Gushtasp, i, 64.

CYBELE, confusion of Christian worship with the worship of, ii, 83 *note*, 294. Her priests, 162. Mutilation and re-erection of her statue by Constantine, 335. Julian's assertion, 469 *note*. See ii, 185, 216, iii, 93.

CYNIC, position assumed in Greece by the, ii, 39. See *Crescens; Diogenes*.

CYPRIAN, Bishop of Carthage, montanist leanings of, ii, 161. On the re-baptism of heretics, 189 *note*. His story of a precociously orthodox infant, 190 *note*. His motive for accepting his bishopric, 192. His high notions of episcopal authority, 192, 193, 298; iii, 257 *note*, 258 *note*, 259, 259 *note*. Pagan animosity towards him, ii, 194, 197. Heroism of himself and Christian associates during a plague, 195. His exile, return, trial, and martyrdom, 196-198. Dogma repudiated by him, 441. Value of his letters, iii, 164 *note*.

CYPRUS, possessions of Barnabas in, i, 373. Conversions and Christian communities there, 377, 388, 389, 395, 430. Massacre of its inhabitants under Hadrian, i, 388 *note*; ii, 68, 69. Reception of Paul and Barnabas there, i, 389. Insurrec-

2 G 2

INDEX.

CYRENE,
tion under Trajan, II, 99. Its bishop, see *Epiphanius.*
CYRENE, Jews of, i, 354. Insurrection in, ii, 99.
CYRENIUS, Governor of Syria, and the census of Palestine at Christ's birth, chronological difficulties connected with, i, 99 note. Solution suggested by Zumpt, 100 note.
CYRIL of Alexandria and his books against Julian, iii, 35. 162. On the Saviour's personal appearance, 388. His words verbatim, ibid note.
CYRIL of Jerusalem, iii, 315. 317, notes.
CYROPÆDIA of Xenophon, i, 49. A Christian one, ii, 285.

DÆMONOLOGY and diabolical possession, belief of the Jews in, i, 68. 85. Relief of possessed ones by Jesus, 208. 217. 221. 214. Nature of the possession, 217 note. Pagan and Christian Dæmonology, ii, 451. A part of the Christian creed, iii, 203.
DÆMONS of the eastern and pagan systems, i, 69. 218 note; ii, 211. 265. 116. The Agatho-dæmon, II, 81. 82 note. See *Demiurge.*
D'AGINCOURT on Roman games, iii, 347 note. On paintings in catacombs, 197 note.
DAMARIS converted by St Paul, i, 440.
DAMASCUS, object and Divine frustration of Paul's mission to, i, 169. 170. Seized by Aretas, 372. Persecution of women there, ii, 211. Its temple consecrated to Christian worship, iii, 67.
DAMASUS, Bishop and Pontiff of Rome, supports the protest of the Christians against Idolatry, iii, 87. Takes Jerome into his confidence, 228. Scene on his contest for the Roman bishopric, 261. 274. See iii, 100.
DANIEL, Messianic belief grounded on the prophecy of, i, 54 note. 277. Probable intercourse between him

DECIUS,
and Zoroaster, 63. 64. Representation of Michael in his vision, 69.
DANTE's reference to Trajan's redemption from purgatory, ii, 103. 104. His 'Hell,' 265 note.
DAPHNE of Antioch, grove and voluptuous rites of, i, 396 note. Occasion of Christian devotions on its site, ii, 189. iii, 15. Same deserted, iii, 14. See iii, 11 note, 12.
DARA, persecution by the Christians at, ii, 358.
DARIUS, ii, 249. Saying of a Greek Philosopher to him, 446.
DARKNESS, the realm of, in Mani's system, ii, 265 note. Offerings to the powers of, 388. See *Demiurge.*
DARWIN'S theory of development, i, 9. note.
DAVID, prophecy of a Messiah from the line of, i, 54 note, 56. 76. 97. 150 note, 271. 292. Social state of his descendants at Christ's birth, 90. Domitian's order for their discovery, 90 note. ii, 9. His position in Marcion's Gospel, ii, 78. 79.
DAVID, M. Emeric, on the pictorial representation of the Eternal Father, iii, 192.
DEA cœlestis, Queen of Heaven, worship of, ii, 160 note. See *Astarte.*
DEACONS, institution of, i, 161. 364; ii, 15; iii, 350. Reverence to them enjoined, iii, 256 note. The archdeacon and subdeacon, 266.
DEAD Sea, why unfit for baptism, i, 133.
DEAF and dumb man cured, i, 216.
DECANI, the, of Bardesanes, ii, 75.
DECAPOLIS, reception of Jesus by the people of, i, 185. His restoration of the deaf and dumb man there, 236.
DECIUS, Emperor, ii, 104. 171. His persecution of the Christians, 187. 188. 193. 194. His choice of Valerian as censor, 190. Pagan and Christian accounts of his death, 198. 199.

INDEX. 453

DECURION.

DECURION, office of, ii, 313. Cause of its falling into disrepute, 313, 314. Exemptions, 314. Prohibitions, iii, 350 note. Privileges, 276 note.
DEDICATION, Jewish feast of the, i, 250 note. 256, 257 note. Attended by Jesus, 259.
DE GUIGNIAUT, M, references to the 'Religions de l'Antiquité' of, i, 10 note, ii, 35 note. iii, 69 note. His notion relative to Oriental parallels to Christian incidents, i, 94.
DEITY, predominant Jewish notion of the, i, 22. Cessation of His symbolical presence, 23. Pliny's notion, 19. Epicurean notions, 14. 439, 440. Virgil's notion, 41. Effect of Greek sculptural art upon popular notions, 437. Consequences of a superiority to vulgar notions on the subject, ii, 12. Union with the soul, 54. Deity of Gnosticism, 11. 58. 65-71. Tenet of Origen's odious to the monks, iii, 104. Conceptions of polytheistic Christianity, 419-421. Controversies on the subject, see Arius; Trinitarianism. See also God; Incarnation.
DELPHIC tripod, the, ii, 335. Its python pedestal, 337.
DEMAS, Paul deserted by, i, 461.
DEMETRIUS, anti-Christian tumult excited by, i, 449.
DEMETRIUS, bishop, ecclesiastical offence of, iii, 167 note.
DEMIURGE, or DEMIURGOS, creator or spirit of the material world, ii, 66 note, 67. 72. 73. 75. 77. 102 note. His angels, 67. The seven patriarchs his adherents, 79. The evil Demiurge prince of darkness, 81 note, 82.
DEMOCRITUS, iii, 3.
DEMOPHILUS, Arian bishop, iii, 45. Refuses to conform to the Nicene doctrine, 116.
DEMOSTHENES, iii, 7.
DE QUINCY, Quatremère, on the di-

DIOCLETIAN.

mensions of ancient temples, ii, 341 note.
DERBE, preaching of Paul and Barnabas at, i, 391.
DERVISHES, motives of, for secluding themselves, ii, 36.
DESERT, supposed scene of the Temptation, i, 148. Its suitability as a retreat for mystics and ascetics, ii, 41, 42.
DESTERS of Magianism, ii, 251.
DEVELOPMENT, theory of, i, 9 note.
DIAGORAS the Melian, i, 441.
DIANA of Ephesus, the multimamma, attributes symbolised by, i, 17. ii, 53 note. Wonders of her temple; the famous cry, 449, 450.
DIANA of Tauris, site of the altar of, i, 26 note.
DICÆARCHUS, irreligious sacrifices by, i, 6 note.
DIDYMUS the Blind, controversial abilities of, iii, 103 note.
DINOCRATES, story of the appearance of, ii, 169.
DIOCESE, origin of the, iii, 262.
DIO CHRYSOSTOM, description of a Corinth fair by, i, 442 note.
DIOCLETIAN, ii, 104. 149. 186. 199. 241. 256. 273. 276. 279. 295. 302. Point reached by Christianity at his accession, 150. 204-206. His origin and assumption of oriental majesty, 206, 207. His Augusti and Cæsars, and oppressive taxes, 207. 223. 242. His disregard of Rome, 208. 210. 242. His choice of a site for his retreat, 208, 233. Edict of his recently discovered, 208 note. Form of Paganism organised by him, 211, 212. His position and consultations in regard to Christianity, 213-216. Result of his appeal to the Oracle, 216, 217. Persecution of the Christians under himself and Galerius, 217-222. 297. iii, 329 note. His illness and abdication, 213 note. 222, 223. 224. 279.

454   INDEX.

DIODORUS.

280. Divination interdicted by him,
293. Effect of his financial system
on the Decurions, 111, 114. Right
of the clergy annulled by him, 115.
DIODORUS, Count, why assassinated,
iii, 18.
DIODORUS, antiphonal choral singing
introduced by, iii, 404.
DIOGENES, the cynic, on the fair doings
of the Corinthians, i, 442 note.
DION Cassius on the cruelties of
Nero's locum tenens, i, 462, 463.
A lost book of his, ii, 110 note.
Fragment relating to Commodus
recently recovered, 153 note. See
ii, 7, 9, 11, 13, notes.
DIONYSIAC rites prohibited, i, 6.
DIONYSIUS of the Areopagus, conversion of, i, 442.
DIONYSIUS, bishop of Milan, banished,
ii, 476 note.
DIONYSIUS of Halicarnassus, quotation
by Lord Macaulay from, i, 27 note.
Test applied to religion by him, 19.
DIOSCURI, the, ii, 135.
DISCIPLES of Jesus, i, 151, 158. Baptism administered by them, 165.
The two at Emmaus, 148.
DISCIPLINA Arcani, basis of the, iii,
118 note.
DISEASES, incurable, acquisition of, a
Christian merit, iii, 147 note.
DIVINATIONS interdicted, ii, 293; iii,
34. To what extent tolerated by
Valentinian, iii, 13. As practised
in Greece, 35. Details of the ceremony, 40, 41. Still extant in Italy,
98. See Magic.
DIVINE Word, see Logos.
DIVORCE among the Jews, peculiarities of, i, 99 note. Effect of the
severity of Constantine's Law, ii,
197, 198; iii, 290. Law of Honorius, 290, 291, notes.
DOCETÆ, theory of the, ii, 61. Doctrine of Docetism, 260, 354.
DODWELL'S view of the Neronian
persecution, i, 464 note. Date assigned by him to the Lyons martyrdoms, ii, 144 note. His treatise 'De
Paucitate Martyrum' unanswered
and unanswerable, iii, 329 note.
DOMITIAN'S order relative to David's
descendants and its result, i, 90
note, ii, 9, 10. His laws against
the Christians, i, 464 note. His
treatment of his own Christian
relatives, 11, 12. Alleged trial of
St. John before him, 14. See ii, 6,
11, 127.
DOMITILLA, niece of Domitian, ii, 11.
Banished by him, 12.
DONATISM, origin of, ii, 296, 297.
Opposition of the Donatists to decisions against them, 304. Exile
of their bishops and spoliation of
their churches, 305. Their virulent reprisals, 305, 306. Conduct
of their Circumcellion allies, 306-
309. Their defeat and obstinate
adherence to their tenets, 310, 311.
Difference between the Donatist
schism and the Trinitarian controversy, 350, 351. Revocation of
their banishment, iii, 4. See iii,
268 note, 301. 404.
DONATUS, Bishop of Casæ Nigræ,
offence charged on Bishop Mensurius by, ii, 300. Heads his party,
301. Called before the Council of
Rome, 303. His appeal to Constantine, 304.
DONATUS II, Anti-bishop of Carthage,
assumes the lead of the Donatists,
ii, 304.
DOROTHEUS the Eunuch put to death,
ii, 220.
DRACONTIUS, put to death, and his
remains insulted, iii, 18.
DRACONTIUS, samples of Christian
poetry from the collection of, iii,
356 note.
DRAMA, the, among the Romans, iii,
130, 137.
DRUIDISM driven out by Roman civilization, ii, 278.
DRUSILLA, how obtained to wife by

DRYDEN.

Asia, i, 392 note. Felix's agent in detaching her from her husband, ii, 46.

DRYDEN, Rousseau's theory anticipated by, i, 8 note.

DUALISM of Persia, creative theory of the, ii, 33. Incorporated in Mani's system, 259, 264.

DU BOIS GUICHAN'S 'Tacite et son Siècle,' i, 444 note.

DU PERRON, Anquetil, i, 62 note. His alleged forgery of the Zendavesta, 65 note. See 66 note, 68 note. ii, 247 note.

EARTH and Son, mythic marriage of the, i, 11, 13.

EARTHQUAKES in the East, ii, 102. 131. Smyrna, 140. Constantinople, iii, 142.

EAST, religions of the, see Orientalism.

EASTER, controversy relative to, ii, 164. iii, 263. 417 note.

'EATEN of Worms,' ii, 164. Rulers dying of the disease so called, 227.

EBAL and Gerizim, mountains on which the Law was read, i, 168. See Gerizim.

EBIONITES the last representatives of Judæo-Christianity, i, 379. ii, 355. Their social status, ii, 53 note.

ECCLESIA and Ecclesiasticos, personifications in the system of Valentinian, ii, 70.

ECCLESIASTICAL offences, first temporal punishment for, ii, 370. Ecclesiastical Greek and Latin, iii, 351. See Church. Clergy.

ECTHOLUS, restriction laid on Julian by, ii, 456.

ECLECTIC system, result of efforts to form an, ii, 159. Eclecticism of the Roman emperors, 186. Of Mani, 259. The Carpocratians eclectics, ii, 80.

ECLIPSE, a preternatural, ii, 164.

EDEN, Garden of, ii, 60.

EDESIUS taken into favour by the

EGYPT.

King of Ethiopia, ii, 401. See Ædesius.

EDESSA, rise of Gnosticism in, ii, 84. Julian's treatment of its Christian disputants, iii, 5. Its famous Temple, 67. Its king, see Abgar. See also ii, 113. iii, 104.

EDUCATION, public, denied by Julian to Christians, iii, 6. Vespasian's provisions for it in Rome, ibid.

EDESSA, object of communion with, ii, 40.

EGYPT, i, 1. Conduct of Cambyses in, 4 note. Grecian way of dealing with its deities, 5. Heeren's conjecture relative to its religious system, 16 note. Flight of Jesus and His parents thither, 107. Magic word at which its plagues were brought forth, 447. Expulsion of its religionists from Rome, ii, 3. Its religion incorporated into Gnosticism, 33, 65. Indian mysticism established in its deserts, 41. Lineal ancestors of its monks, 42. Indebtedness of the Basilidian system to its theology, 65, 66 note, 67. 67 note, 69. Marcion's application of an incident in its history, 78. Its Agatho-dæmon, 81, 82 note. Period of the insurrection under Trajan, 99. A city and temple founded and dedicated to Antinous, 106. Hadrian's description of the state of its religious society, 108 note. Its "mightiest ruin," 121. On Imperial proselytes of its religion, 153. 177. Monuments of its glory and superstition, 157. Moment deemed favorable by its priesthood for obtaining mastery over Christianity, 158. Assimilation of Platonism to its higher mythology, ibid. A parallel in number to its ten plagues, 187. Its magicians in the array against Constantine, 318. A Christian Egyptian at the court of the latter, 126. Theological controversies in its metropolis, Alexan-

456 INDEX.

EICHHORN.

dria (see *Alexandria*). Anti-Christian rescript sent to its court, iii, 62. Destruction of its temples and idols, 68-77. Rule of Theophilus, 102. See li, 12. 64. 76. 104. 113. 120. 133. 159. 228. 277. 360. 374. 378. iii, 105.

EICHHORN on the incidents connected with Stephen's martyrdom, i, 368 note. His conjecture relative to the altar "To the unknown God," 419 note.

EIRENE, church of, at Constantinople, ii, 111 note.

ELAGABALUS, worship imposed on the senate by, ii, 151. Etymology of his name, 173. Celebration of worship to him, 173. 174. His brutal licentiousness, 175. Religious system contemplated by him, ibid. His vagaries before his idol and human sacrifices on its altar, 176. Effect of his mother's training, 177.

ELAMITES, ii, 253 note.

ELDERS of the Jewish synagogue, ii, 17. Of the Christian church, 21.

ELECT, the, in Mani's system, ii, 273.

ELECTION, Augustine's theory of, iii, 175.

ELEUSIS and Eleusinian mysteries, i, 13 note. Their character, 33. 44 f. Hadrian a worshipper, ii, 105. The nave of the temple, 341 note. Its Hierophant, ii, 462. Re-edification of the temple, iii, 12. See iii, 78.

ELIJAH, or Elias, God's revelation to, i, 44. Expectation of his reappearance by the Jews, 88. 137. 149. Why held in reverence by them, 136. Prophetic references to him, 116. 117, notes, 138. 218. 219. 336. li, 106.

ELIZABETH, mother of John the Baptist, i, 89. The angel's declaration regarding her, 92. Incident connected with Mary's visit to her, 95. 97. Degrees of relationship be-

EPHRAEM.

tween them, 96 note. See *John the Baptist*.

EISLEY's 'Annotations on the Gospel,' value of, i, 100 note.

ELVIRA, or Illiberis, see, *under Councils, Illiberis*.

ELYMAS, or Bar-Jesus, Jewish wonder-worker, struck blind, i, 189. Consequences of his endeavour to outdo the apostles, 429 note. Effect of his influence on Sergius Paulus, 431.

EMANATION system of India, ii, 33. 14. 47. 56. Adopted by Mani, 260. See Æons.

EMBLEMS, see *Symbols*.

EMESA, the conical black stone of, ii, 173. Its triumphant conveyance into Rome, 174. Elagabalus consecrated to its service, 177. Massacre of its inhabitants, 223.

EMMAUS, appearance of Jesus to the disciples at, i, 148.

EMPEDOCLES, i, 55 note.

ENNIUS, irreligious system translated by, i, 41.

ENNOIA, principles represented in the Gnostic systems by the, ii, 69. 81.

ENOCH in Marcion's Gospel, ii, 79.

EPHESUS, Paul at, i, 198. 415 note. 444. Trade reasons for upholding its idolatrous worship, 429 note. Its famous temple and silver shrines, 445. Favour shown to the Jews, 445. Effect of Paul's preachings on its Jewish exorcists and Pagan image-mongers, 446-450. Coming over to the new faith, ii, 7. Its Christian church, 15. 16. The scene of the first recorded collision between Christianity and Orientalism, 53. Rise of Gnosticism, 84. See i, 460. ii. 13. 14. 21 note. 55. See *Diana of Ephesus*.

EPHRAEM, the Syrian, hymns of, ii, 74. A representative of Syrian mysticism, iii, 102. Sketch of his career, 104-106.

EPICTETUS.

EPICTETUS, i, 35.
EPICUREANISM, why congenial to the Greeks, i, 34. Anecdotes illustrative of the religious indifferentism of the Epicureans, 36. Lucretius a commender of their system, 41. Probable reception of St. Paul's orations by them, 438, 439, 440. The system in the shade, ii, 181. See ii. 126. 179. 470.
EPIPHANIES, character of, ii, 81.
EPIPHANIUS, Bishop of Cyprus, words of Mani given by, ii, 364 note. Visited by St. Jerome, iii, 225. On clerical marriages, 279 note. Character of his historical writings, 360. See iii, 281. 389. 424 note.
EPIRUS visited by Paul, i, 460.
EPISCOPACY, St. Jerome's account of the origin of, ii, 21 note. Its growth, iii, 249. The episcopate a necessity, 250-253. See *Bishops. Church. Clergy.*
EPISTOLARY Literature of Christianity, its character and value, iii, 364 note.
EQUINOXES, anciently set apart for religious solemnities, i, 12.
ERDIVRAPH, story of the origin and destiny of, ii, 250, 251. His seven days' sleep and vision, 251.
ERICTHO of Lucan, Gibbon's criticism on the, i, 43 note. Her descendants not extinct, iii, 98.
ERSKINE, Mr, on the authenticity of the Zendavesta, i, 65 note.
ERTANG, the Gospel of Mani, ii, 261, 262. 264. See *Mani.*
ESAU and his race, i, 411. His position in Marcion's Gospel, ii, 79.
ESDRAS, Book II, why valuable, i, 79. Epoch referred to in it, ii, 117. Source of the fourth book, iii, 359.
ESSENES, Messianic anticipation of the, i, 81. Peculiar knowledge claimed by them, 89. Their mode of life, 134-152. Their baptismal ceremonies, 135. Their aversion to

EUNOMIANS.

marriage: vital principle of their observances, 153. Opposition of Jesus to their system, 155 note, 197. Their position with regard to Him, 275. Character of their asceticism, ii, 41. See ii, 42. 61.
ETHIOPIA, ii, 13, 118. Preventive effect of a plague on Severus's operations, 157. Its conversion to Christianity, 400-403.
ETRUSCANS, Roman rites derived from the, i, 18. Their haruspices, iii, 26. Influences of their soothsayers in Rome, 35. 96.
EUCHARIST or Lord's Supper, origin of the, i, 104, 105. Its appointed administrators, ii, 24. 27. Adopted by the Manicheans, 370. Solemnized as a sacrifice, iii, 317, 318. Its symbolism, 385 note.
EUDOXIA, Empress, espouses the cause of Arianism, iii, 137, 138. Her hostility towards and triumph over Chrysostom, 140, 141. Occasion of her terror and remorse, 142. Her enmity again in the ascendant, 143. Scene on the erection of a statue to her, 144.
EUDOXUS of Antioch, Arian, ascendancy over Constantius of, ii, 445. Made Bishop of Constantinople, 446, 447. His influence over Valens, iii, 44.
EUGENIUS, Pagan joy at the accession of, iii, 89. His subservience to Arbogastes, 90. Defeated by Theodosius, 92. See 169. 208.
EUHEMERUS, character of the system of, i, 25 note. Same introduced into Rome, 41. His origin and pretended discovery, ibid note.
EUMENIUS on two temples of Apollo, ii, 278 note.
EUNAPIUS, charge against the black monks by, iii, 78 note. Other references to his writings, iii, 43, 75, 76, 293, notes.
EUNOMIANS, heresy of the, iii, 101 102. Law against them, 301 note.

458   INDEX.

EUNOMUS.

EUNOMIUS, one of the heroes of Philostorgius, ii, 446 note.
EUNUCH, primary meaning of the word, i, 167 note. Privileges of slaves mutilated for eunuchs, ii, 198. Government delegated to them, iii, 242.
EUPHRATES, natural boundary for Roman dominions, 88. See ii, 123 note, 132, 249.
EURIPIDES, iii, 354.
EUROPE, Christianity a new arbiter of the sovereignty of, ii, 151.
EUSEBIUS, Bishop of Cæsarea, on the James who presided at the Council of Jerusalem, i, 192 note. Tradition preserved by him, 409. Story of Nicolas and his wife, told by him, ii, 15 note. On Bardesanes, 74 note. Spurious rescript preserved by him, 110 note. Makes Constantius a Christian, 221 note. His inaugural discourse on the building of the church of Tyre, 239, 240. iii, 171, 174 note. On the object of Maximin's war against Tiridates. ii, 358. Question turning on a speech recorded by him, 276 note. A fact not ritiated by his silence, 313 note. On Constantine's Vision, on his clemency in battle, and on his motives for erecting Pagan statues, 285, 319, 336 note. Allies himself with the Arians, 162. His simile for the battling bishops, 164. His impression of, and share in, the meetings of the Council of Nicæa, 166, 167. His notion of Constantine's banquet to the bishops, 168. Point on which he was a recusant, and sense in which he subsequently accepted the same, 169, 170. Estimation in which he was held by Constantine, 171. Statements confirmed by his suspicious brevity, 173, 174. Numbered at the instance of Athanasius, 179. Concerning his statement that Constantine was a preacher, 181 note. On the extent of the emperor's suppression of, and toleration

EVAGRIUS.

to, Paganism, 185, 186. His character as a writer: principle gloried in by him, iii, 160, 162. See i, 90, 407, notes; ii, 9, 11, 13, 14, 105, 119, notes, 157, 279, 281, notes, 325, 327, 331, 335, 365, 369, 370, notes; iii, 273 note, 278, 330, 324, 367, notes, 389, 402, 401, notes.
EUSEBIUS, Bishop of Nicomedia and Constantinople, ii, 361, 362 note. Point on which he was a recusant, and for which he was banished, 369, 370. Suspicion attaching to him: grounds of his petition for reinstatement, 372. First denounced and then taken into favour by Constantine, 373. His charge against Eustathius, 374. Summoned to answer Athanasius, 379. His characterization of two candidates for his see, 408 note. Occasion of his enemies' taunts, 414. iii, 362.
EUSEBIUS, Bishop of Vercellæ, banished, ii, 426.
EUSEBIUS the eunuch, bold reply of Liberius to, ii, 426.
EUSTATHIUS, Bishop of Antioch, nature of the charge of heresy brought against, ii, 374. His mission to the Iberians, 404. Cause of the views of his followers regarding married priests, iii, 280, 281 note. See iii, 281.
EUSTOCHIUM, honour claimed by Jerome for, iii, 229 note. Character of his letter to her, 229, 230, notes.
EUTROPIUS, Proconsul, refusal of Pasiphilus to give evidence against, iii, 42.
EUTROPIUS, the eunuch, one of the few good deeds of, iii, 133. Result of Chrysostom's plea in his behalf, 135. His ultimate fate, ibid. See 248.
EUTYCHIANISM one of the products of the Athanasian controversy, ii, 416.
EVAGRIUS attempts to save the Christians from the Pagans, iii, 72. On the asceticism of Simeon Stylites, 205 note.

INDEX.   459

EVANGELISTS.

EVANGELISTS, discussions regarding the priority of the, i, 119. As to their sources of information, inspiration, style, &c, 120, 121, 259 note. 341. 345 note, 351 note. See Gospels.
EVE's seduction by the Serpent, in the Gnostic systems, ii, 83 note. Her position in Mani's system, 166.
EVIL, principle of, and ultimate identification of Satan therewith, i, 69. Its connexion with theories of the Temptation, 147. In the Gnostic systems, ii, 62, 63. Origin of evil, iii, 174. See Bardesanes; Basilides; Mani; Valentinus.
EVODUS, favourite of Severus, ii, 154.
EXCOMMUNICATION, origin of, iii, 252. By exclusion from communion, 295. By anathema, 295, 296.
EXODUS, illustrative references to the book of, i, 291, 302 note.
EXORCISM practised by the Pharisees, i, 218. Jewish exorcists and the name of Jesus, 198. 447. 448. Duties of the Christian exorcist, iii, 266.
EXPOSITIONS of Faith, iii, 161. What they comprehended, 364.
EZEKIEL's chariot, i, 162 note. His references to a future state, 73. His predictions and the Sibylline verses, ii, 19. Ezekiel Tragoedus, ibid note.
EZRA, re-migration of the Jews under, i, 58.

FABIANUS, Bishop of Rome, put to death, ii, 188. The first martyr pope, 188 note. 329 note. Cav. de Rossi's discovery regarding him, ii, 188 note.
FABIOLA, cause of the interest excited by the interment of, iii, 321.
FABIUS Maximus, conduct of, approved by the citizens, i, 6 note.
FABLE, religious, the supplanter of Nature-worship, i, 13. Vestiges of theogonic fables, 16. Class of Greek fables rejected by the Romans, 18

FELIX.

note. Strabo's reasoning on the need for fables, 17.
FABRICIUS, theory of Constantine's vision suggested by, ii, 286 note. See iii, 359 note.
FADUS. See Cuspius Fadus.
FAITH, object of the aspirations of, iii, 408. Establishment of its reign, 412. See Expositions.
FAMINES: Antioch, i, 375. Rome, ii, 112, 113.
FANATICISM, growth of, iii, 211.
FAQUIR, the, ii, 36.
FATALISM, Stoic doctrine of, i, 140.
FATHER, the. See Deity; God.
FATHERS, dependence of the Rabbins on the traditions of the, iii, 360.
FAUSTA, Constantine's second wife, put to death, ii, 324. Offences charged upon her, 324, 325. Gibbon's doubt regarding her, 325 note.
FAUSTA, Princess, and the Domus Faustæ, ii, 294 note.
FAUSTUS, the Manichæan, orthodox Christians taunted with idolatry by, iii, 327.
FEASTS. See Festivals.
FELICITAS, martyrdom of, ii, 165, 166. 172.
FELICITAS, Saint, and her seven children, ancient painting of the martyrdom of, iii, 396.
FELIX, commencement of the Judæan prefectship of, i, 384. A disturber of his rule, 400. Paul sent before him: his motive for leniency, 403; 404. Chronological difficulties relative to his administration, 404 note. His agent in his design on Drusilla, ii, 46.
FELIX, Bishop of Apthonga, consecrates Cæcilian, ii, 300. Crime charged on him, 303. Verdict thereon, 305.
FELIX, forced on Rome as its bishop, ii, 426. Refusal of Liberius to share the see with him, 427.

FELIX.

FELIX Minucius, see *Minucius Felix*.
FELIX, Saint, nature and extent of the adoration paid to, iii, 422 *note*.
FEMALES, laws of Constantine for the protection of, ii, 394-397. Extravagant toilettes of Roman Christian females, iii, 246, 247. The *Mulieres subintroductæ* of the clergy, 282. Actresses, see *Women Players*.
FESTIVALS of ancient Rome, their character, i, 18. Vitality of the Lupercalia, iii, 98. Church, festivals of the, iii, 121-128. Jewish, see *Dedication*. *Passover*. *Tabernacles*.
FESTUS, Prefect of Judæa, tyranny of, i, 399. His dealings with Paul, 405. His death and successor, 406.
FESTUS of Ephesus, cause of the removal and death of, iii, 41.
FETICHISM, nature of, i, 11. Origin of the word 'Fetiche,' *ibid note*. See 16 *note*.
FEUDAL system, groundwork of the, iii, 49.
FIELD's work on the Church, iii, 424 *note*.
FIG-TREE, the barren, cursed by Jesus, i, 284, 285. Fact symbolized by it, 285.
FINE Arts, see *Art*.
FIRE, why mortified among the Persians, ii, 35.
FIRE of London, 1666, classic parallel to the, i, 466 *note*.
FIRE-WORSHIPPERS spared by Ardeschir, ii, 252.
FIRMILIANUS on Apostolic authority, iii, 357 *note*.
FISHERMAN'S Porch, Church of the Apostles, ii, 400.
FISHES, the miraculous draught of, i, 178.
FLAGELLATION, amenability of the clergy to, iii, 276. Authority for its administration, *ibid note*.
FLAVIAN dynasty, ii, 2. 6. Occasion of foundation of a college in honour of the family, 290.

FULGENTIUS.

FLAVIANUS, subservience of Eugenius to, iii, 90.
FLAVIANUS, Bishop of Antioch, his welcome to Chrysostom, iii, 122. Mission of mercy undertaken by him, 125. Its result, 127. Antiphonal singing introduced by him, 404.
FLAVIUS Clemens, character and imperial kinship of, ii, 11. Why put to death; explanation of the idiosyncrasies of his character, 12. Peace-offering for his execution, 13.
FLAVIUS Sabinus, ii, 11.
FLECHIER, Vie de Theodose, iii, 106 *note*.
FLEURY, on Tyrolese martyrdom by, iii, 65 *note*. On consecrated vessels, 154 *note*. Miracle upheld by him, 160 *note*. Character of his writings, 111 *note*. See 106 *note*.
FLOGGING in schools, antique authority for, iii, 277 *note*.
FLORUS, Prefect of Judæa, effect of the tyranny of, i, 399. 384. 459. Date of his prefecture, 459 *note*.
FOWL, Chinese deity, tradition of the birth of, i, 94 *note*.
FORTUNE, statues and temples of, and their fate: Rome, ii, 282. Byzantium, 331. 336. Constantinople, iii, 5. 12.
FORUM at Rome, and temples surrounding it, ii, 341.
FRANKS, shape taken by the savage orthodoxy of the, ii, 155 *note*. See iii, 5. 60.
FRAVITTA, ancient Roman usage violated in the marriage of, iii, 292 *note*.
FREEMASONRY, early Christian parallel to, iii, 183 *note*.
FREE WILL and Necessity, iii, 173.
FRUMENTIUS, reception in Ethiopia of, ii, 401. Converted to Christianity and made Bishop of Axum, 402.
FULGENTIUS, Saint, unchristian axiom of, iii, 177 *note*.

FUNDANUS.

FUNDANUS. See *Minucius Fundanus*.
FUNERALS, Scythian custom of immolation at, ii, 357. Christian Funerals, iii, 319. Substitution of inhumation for cremation, 119, 120. Their magnificence, 121. Various burial customs of heathens and Christians, 120-122 notes. See 384 note.
FUTURE life and state, i, 25, 39, 205. See *Immortality of the Soul*.

GABELENTZ, Dr, edition of Ulphilas by, iii, 56 note.
GABRIEL, derivation of the name, i, 68 note. His appearance and promise to Zachariah, 88.
GAD, the prophet, loss of the books of, i, 51.
GAINAS the Goth, refusal of a church to, iii, 107.
GALATIA and the Galatians, and St Paul's Epistles, i, 415, 415 note. Nationality of the converts, 432. Re-visited by Paul, 444.
GALEN, an exception to the philosophic dearth of his time, iii, 416 note.
GALERIUS, emperor, suspicions regarding the wife of, ii, 205. His unsuccessful campaign, 215. Pagan fanaticism of his mother, 216. His inhuman persecution of the Christians, 217-221. Succeeds Diocletian, 224. Constantine's escape from him, 225, 281. His remorse, peculiar disease, repentant edict, and death, 227, 228, 275, 289. His unacquaintance with, and threat against, Rome, 242 note. Deified by Maxentius, 281. See ii, 229, 230, 279, 284.
GALERIUS Maximus, Proconsul of Carthage, ii, 196. His sentence on Cyprian, 197.
GALILEANS, Julian's epithet for the Christians, iii, 4, 5, 8, 37. See *Judas the Galilean*.
GALILEE, curious Talmudic passage relating to the people of, i, 182 note.

GELASIUS.

Density of its population according to Josephus, 183. Races inhabiting it, and their conflicts, *ibid* note. Their slaughter in the Temple, 232, 269. Suggested cause thereof, 312.
GALILEO, authorities relied on for the condemnation of, iii, 417.
GALLIENUS restores peace to the Christian church, ii, 199. Edict of his law, 204. Inroads of the Goths during his reign, iii, 54.
GALLIO, Roman proconsul in Judæa, result of an appeal against the Christians to, i, 397, 443, 444.
GALLUS, youthful imprisonment of, ii, 455. Chapel built by him and Julian, *ibid*. His death, 460. A suspected participator therein, iii, 17.
GAMALIEL, Paul's teacher, i, 361. His counsels to the Sanhedrin relative to the apostles, 361, 362.
GAMES, Gentile and idolatrous, ii, 96. Quinquennial, established by Hadrian, 106. Secular games under Philip, 240. Olympic games, iii, 336. See *Festivals*.
GANGES, purifying power ascribed to the, i, 135. The population on its shores, ii, 41.
GANGRA, council of, iii, 279. See *Councils*.
GAU, Nubia, inscription discovered at, ii, 400 note.
GAUDENTIUS, Bishop of Rimini, put to death, ii, 446.
GAUL civilised by Roman influences, i, 2. Ancient superstitions, 40. Its Christian congregations, ii, 113. Attack upon them, 145. Protected by Constantius, 225. Constitution of society, 278. Scene of Constantine's vision, 285. Dispute referred to its bishops, 302. Extirpator of its idolatry, iii, 78. See ii, 104, 123, 224, 281, 384, 385.
GAZA, Pagan cruelties in, iii, 10. Its temple closed, 66.
GELASIUS, pope, Roman games suppressed by, iii, 98. See 277 note.

GELON.

GELON, the tyrant, humane edict ascribed to, i, 27 note.
GENERIDES: cause of his throwing up his commission, iii, 95.
GENNESARET, lake or sea of, i, 151. 177, 210. Jesus crossing the lake, 225. Walking on its waters, 226. His interview with Peter, 350.
GENTILE proselytes, initiatory rites imposed upon, i, 136. 139. 213. Church formed by them, ii, 17, 19. Declaration of Jesus regarding them, i, 212. Paul's influence in their conversion, 381. Character of the first Gentile convert, 430. See ii, 96. 114.
GEORGE of Cappadocia, Arian bishop of Alexandria, character of, ii, 429, 431. iii, 16. A priest before he was a Christian, ii, 430. His machinations, persecutions, and trading speculations, 430, 431. His insults to Paganism, and murder by a mob, iii, 17. See iii, 18, 19.
GEORGE of Pisidia, verses on the Virgin by, iii, 426 note.
GEPIDÆ, Christianity embraced by the, iii, 57.
GERASA, Roman architecture at, ii, 146.
GERIZIM, the sacred mountain of the Samaritans, i, 167, 168. Legend of concealed sacred vessels, 172. See 170. 294.
GERMAN writers on Christianity, peculiarities of the speculations of, i, 259, 341, notes. German words lacking English equivalents, iii, 380 note.
GERMANICUS, the emperor, ii, 451.
GERMANICUS, the martyr, ii, 136.
GERMANY, confederacy against Rome of the nations of, ii, 131. 142. 145. 150. 225. 295; iii, 60. The "thundering legion," ii, 141. Transfer of the seat of government to its frontier, 313. Barbarities perpetrated upon its captive chieftains, 320.

GNOSTIC.

GERONTIUS, bishop of Nicomedia, deposed by Chrysostom, iii, 264 note.
GERVAISE, Ambrose's dream relative to the reliques of, 161.
GESENIUS on prophetic passages in Isaiah, i, 56, 60, notes. On a Samaritan poetic reference to the Messiah, 170 note.
GETA, martyrdom dated at the accession of, ii, 165.
GETHSEMANE, derivation of the word, i, 306 note.
GIBBON, Roman historian, on human sacrifices under the Romans, i, 27 note. His criticism on Lucan's 'Erictho,' i, 41. On a passage in Phlegon, 535 note. An improbable conjecture of his, 458 note. Anachronisms, ii, 251 note. A well-founded sarcasm, 313. Instance of his poetic taste, iii, 112 note. See i, 18 note. 61. 139 note. 337 note. ii, 10, 16, 31, notes. iii, 11, 23, 91, 116, 361, notes.
GLADIATORS, Jewish captives forced to exhibit as, ii, 97. Constantinople never disgraced by their presence, 119. iii, 144. Doom of criminals, ii, 394. System and practices in the Roman gladiatorial shows, iii. 143. 144. Effect of the spread of Christianity upon them, 145. Occasion of their abolition, 346. An imperial gladiator, see Commodus.
GLAUCIAS, alleged teacher of Basilides, ii, 64.
GNOSTIC systems and doctrines, chief parent of, i, 60. Scripture passages embarrassing to their ascetics, 153 note. Their contact with and influence on eastern Christianity, 179. ii, 37. 42. 44. 52. 297. Later Gnostics and Their Innovations, ii, 57. Their primal deity, 58, 60, 154. Cause of the unpopularity of Gnosticism, 84. Its attitude towards Paganism, 85. Its systems rejected by African Christianity, 160, 161. Its complication with

INDEX. 463

GOD.

Manicheism, 259, 260, 274. Birthplaces of its various sects, 277. Nature of its asceticism, 351. The Trinitarian controversy one of its growths, 352. Contempt of Gnostics for the Old Testament, iii, 258. Their hymns, 354. Their symbols and images, 181, 189. Their Æons, see Æons. Various exponents of Gnosticism and kindred systems, see Bardesanes; Basilides; Carpocrates; Cerinthus; Mani; Marcion; Ophites; Saturninus; Valentinus.

GOD, argument for the humanization of, i, 17 note. Early Jewish conceptions, 21, 22. Egyptian, Indian, and Grecian notions, 22, 23. Ultimate results of symbolizing Deity under the human form, 25. Elijah's description of God's revelation of Himself, 44. His position in the Christian system, 45. Modified notions of the one Supreme Deity, 70. Altar to the Unknown God, 439. Eichhorn's explanation, ibid note. See Deity.

GODS of Paganism, see Paganism.

GODEFROY, on intermarriage with a niece, ii, 107 note. See iii, 101, 111, 113, notes.

GOETIC sacrifices suppressed by Jovian, iii, 31 note. See 35.

GOLGOTHA, most probable derivation of, i, 331 note.

GOOD Friday tumult in Santa Sophia, iii, 145.

GOOD Shepherd, symbolic representation of the, iii, 181. Its heathen prototype, ibid note. An early statue, 192 note.

GORDIAN, reign of, ii, 186. See 171 note.

GORDIUS, circumstance connected with the martyrdom of, 335 note.

GORGONIUS martyred, ii, 220.

GOSPELS, scope and character of the, i, 49. Rousseau's testimony to their genuineness, ibid note. Apocryphal

GRATIAN.

corroboration of a portion of their narrative, 91 note. Distinguishing feature between the genuine and the apocryphal, ibid note u. Strauss's criticisms upon them, 110, 111, 228 note. Spurious gospels, their character and object, i, 114; iii, 358. Weisse's criticisms, 4, 115. Theories as to their origin, 117, 118. Chronological discrepancies, 119. Nature and extent of the inspiration of the Evangelists, 121. Objection common to all harmonies, 259 note. Gospel of the Judæo-Christians of Pella, 422. The last of the Gospels, ii, 53, 54. Gnostic attempts at reconciliation with the Gospel, 76. Its last ordeal, 204. Its progress arrested, 247. Crimes repressed by its influence, 198. See Evangelists; Jesus.

GOTHOFRED'S note on the law of Honorius, iii, 283 note, 284 note.

GOTHS, Christian deliverances and calamities due to the, ii, 117. Effect of their invasions on Roman greatness, ibid. Beneficial consequences to themselves of their capture of Christian slaves, iii, 54, 55. Their language and alphabet, 25. One cause of their possible loss of the art of writing, 55 note. Their energetic espousal of Arianism, 56-58, 59. Destructive effects of their invasions upon art, 178 note. See ii, 198, 218; iii, 60.

GRACCHI, the, iii, 92.

GRACE, Augustinian notion of, iii, 175.

GRANIANUS. See Serenus Granianus.

GRATIAN, emperor, iii, 57. 80. Influence of Ambrose over him, 82. Alarm of the Pagans at his refusal of the pontificate and degradation of the statue of Victory, 83-84. His murder, 85. His law against heresy, 100. 301 note. See 92. 116 note.

464   INDEX.

GREECE.

GREECE, political system derived from
    the monarchy of, i, 1. Its policy in
    religious matters, 5. Character of
    the anthropomorphism of the
    Greeks, 16, 17. Features in their
    religion rejected by the Romans, 18
    note. Influence fatal to their reli-
    gion, 25. Purification by washing,
    135. Jewish signification of the
    term "Greek," 183. Relative posi-
    tion of its magistracy and priest-
    hood, 428. Resort of women to its
    rivers, 433. Its social and religious
    system averse to Cœnobitism, ii, 38,
    39. Its deities carried to Constan-
    tinople, 335. Its temples, 341.
    Result of the distinctness and sub-
    tleness of its language, 152. Cha-
    racter of Notadic verses, 161, 162,
    notes. Its amusements in Constanti-
    nople, 194. Regard towards the dead,
    471. The hand of death upon its
    intellectual manifestations, iii, 1, 2.
    Public divination at an end, 35.
    Influence of persecution upon its
    literature, 41. Difference between
    Greek and Christian poetry, 111.
    No distinguished Christians among
    its natives, 106, 107. Its Olympic
    games, 336. Causes of the degene-
    racy of its language, 149, 150. See
    Athens ; Epicureanism ; Plato ;
    Pythagoras.
GREGORY of Cappadocia made Bishop
    of Alexandria, ii, 413.
GREGORY the Illuminator, apostle of
    Armenia, inauspicious parentage of,
    ii, 255. Alleged supernatural ac-
    companiment to his baptism, 256.
    His persecution and long imprison-
    ment, 257. Fruits of his prayers :
    made archbishop, 357, 358.
GREGORY of Nazianzum, miracle at-
    tested by, ii, 456 note. His inti-
    macy with Basil, 461, iii, 107. His
    birth and parentage, 110. His auto-
    biographic poems, iii, 110-112, 326
    note, 354. A bishopric forced upon
    him, 113. His labours as Bishop of
    Constantinople, 114. His disputes

HADRIAN.

    with Maximus the Cynic, 115, 116.
    His retirement and asceticism in his
    old age, 117. His views of baptism,
    316 note. See iii, 1, 8, 11, 47,
    notes. 102. 198, note. 281. 283.
    324 note, 421 note.
GREGORY of Nyssa, iii, 40 note. 47
    note. 102. Brother of Basil, 107.
    His remonstrance against pilgrim-
    ages, 192 note. On the heroic acts
    of Theodosius, 197, 198, notes.
    His definition of a hymn, 402 note.
    See 198 note, 281. 140 note, 387.
    421 note.
GREGORY I. (the Great), Pope, effect
    of a prayer of, ii, 103. Chant
    introduced by him, iii, 405. What
    he saw in the Lombard Invasion,
    418.
GRESWELL, Mr, on a passage in St
    Luke, i, 99 note. On facts in
    Christ's life, 103 note, 256 note.
    See i, 362, 403, notes. ii, 92 note.
GRIESBACH, on the Evangelists, i, 145
    note.
GROTIUS, views of, on some contro-
    verted points, i, 88, 128, 195, 247,
    311, 337, 362, notes.
GUIGNIAUT, see De Guigniaut.
GUIZOT, M, on passages in Gibbon, i,
    337 note, iii, 23 note.
GUNPOWDER Plot, classic parallel to
    the, i, 464 note.
GUSHTASP identified with Cyaxares, i,
    64 note.
GYMNASTIC games, iii, 336.
GYMNOSOPHISTS of India, ii, 74.

HAAG, Dr Martin, on the Zoroastrian
    writings, i, 63, 65, 66, notes. His
    notion of the Yathas, 67 note. On
    a separate evil spirit, 69 note.
HARET DEUM, Donatist bishop, on the
    persecutions of his party, ii, 306
    note. His name a Puritan anticipa-
    tion, 308 note.
HADRIAN, human sacrifices prohibited

INDEX.

HADRIANOPLE.

by, i, 26 *note.* Circumstances connected with the Jewish insurrection during his reign, 60, 139 *note,* 188 *note;* ii, 10, 53 *note,* 60. 99. 249. Christians permitted to reside in his new city, i, 421. 423. Jews prohibited, i, 423; ii, 346. His motive for limiting the boundaries of his empire, ii, 88. His attention to internal affairs and character as a statesman, 89. 91. 104-106. Extent of his travels, 104. 105, *notes.* His conduct towards Christianity, 106-108. Christianity beyond his comprehension, 108. His letter concerning, and curiosity on, religious matters, and his famous verses, 108 *notes.* 122, 123. See i, 421; ii, 62 *note,* 90. 109; iii, 70. 195 *note.*

HADRIANOPLE, battle of, ii, 319.

HÆREDIPETY, legacy hunting, a clerical vice, iii, 274.

HANNAH, parallel to the song of, i, 97.

HANNO, the Carthaginian, story told of, ii, 50 *note.*

HARMONIUS, long popularity of the hymns of, ii, 74. iii, 105.

HEATHENISM, ii, 97. Its sybils, 119. Sybilline denunciation of its fall, 120. Modifying influences of Christianity upon it, 181, 182. Julian's attempts connected with it, 185. 211. iii, 11. An aspect of Christianity astonishing to its followers, ii, 179. Adoption by Christian disputants of one of its evil practices, 174. Its late presence in Italy, iii. 98. Its calendar, 131. Its burial customs, 121 *note.* See *Paganism; Polytheism.* See also ii, 128. 349. 366. 376. 380. 384. 391. iii, 409.

HEAVEN, voices from, i, 88 *note.* 143. 144. Explanation of the phenomenon, 144 *note.* 284 *note.*

HEBREW, the original sacred, understood only by the learned, i, 354. Its first great Christian student, iii, 193.

HEBRON, originally a Levitical city, i,

VOL. III.

HELLANICHUS.

89. Scene of John's first teachings, 111. Site of the angels' visit to Abraham, ii, 349.

HECATE, wonders worked in the temple of, ii, 458.

HEDONE and Henosis, attributes personified by, ii, 70.

HEEREN on the religion of Egypt, i, 16 *note.*

HEGESIPPUS and the narrative of St. James's death, i, 407. Story related of Our Lord's family by him, ii, 9. Character of his stories, i, 407 *note.* ii, 10.

HEGEWISCH'S work on the happiest epoch of Roman history, ii, 7 *note.* Theory ably developed by him, 89 *note.* See 105 *note.*

HEINICHEN'S efforts relative to Hegesippus, i, 407 *note.* His characterization of the life of Constantine, ii, 285 *note.* His discussion of Constantine's vision, 286 *note.* On the Council of Nicæa, 366 *note.* See iii, 161. 189, *notes.*

HELEN of Troy, ii, 48.

HELENA, Queen of the Adiabeni, Jewish reverence for the memory of, i, 59.

HELENA, mother of Constantine, i, 59. Church built by her over Jacob's well, 168 *note.* Her religion, ii, 225. Crime detected by her, 324. Her restoration of the holy places at Jerusalem, 147.

HELENA of Tyre, companion of Simon Magus, ii, 47. Sublimed into an allegory, 48. Practice sanctified under her name, 86 *note.*

HELIOPOLIS, Pagan cannibalism at. iii. 11. One of its temples consecrated to Christian worship, 67.

HELIUS, Nero's freed slave and *locum tenens*, possibly Paul's murderer, i, 462.

HELLANICHUS and Cæsarius, delegates of Theodosius in Antioch, iii, 126. Their humanity, 127.

2 U

HELLADIUS.

HELLADIUS, murderous boast of, iii, 71.

HERCULES, ii, 130, 151. An imperial usurper of his attributes, 153. Greek epigram thereon, 153 *note*.

HERCULIUS, title assumed by Maximian, ii, 211, 224, 280.

HERESY and Heretics. Punishment for concealing works of, ii, 370 *note* 1. First heretics condemned to death, iii, 61, 167, 168. Edict of the three emperors against them, 100, 101. Ecclesiastical penalties for the offence, 298, 411. Severity of the laws of Theodosius, 299, 300. Law of Gratian, 301 *note*. Epiphanius's 'History of Heretical Sects,' 360. The 'Refuter of Heresies,' see *Hippolytus*. See iii, 424 *note*. See also *Jovinian; Manes; Vigilantius; Simon Magus*.

HERMENEUTICS, or commentaries on the sacred writers, iii, 361. Their character and contents, 361.

HERMES, or Terminus, i, 425.

HERMITS, ii, 42. Their retreats invaded by Valens, iii, 47 *note*. The alleged first hermit, 101 *note*.

HERMOGENES, Christ placed in the sun by, ii, 212. Sins laid to his charge by Tertullian, iii, 177, 178.

HERMOGENES, Roman commander, cause of his murder by the populace, ii, 415. See 423.

HEROD the Great, impolitic cruelty of, i, 52. His last popular exercise of authority, *ibid*. Causes of his unpopularity and hopes excited by his death, 51, 82. His testamentary cruelty and its motive, 83. Circumstances conducing to his edict for the slaughter of the innocents, 101, 102. Castle fortified by him, 105 *note*. Proof of the subtlety of his character, 107. His death, 108. Sublimated into an allegory, 116. Opposition to his introduction of games into Judæa, ii, 96. Peculiar disease

HIERAPOLIS.

of which he died, 117. See i, 90, 100, 104, 105, 166, 119.

HEROD Antipas, i, 108, 165. His incestuous marriage, and seizure of John the Baptist, 166. Provinces comprised in his tetrarchate, 183. His position with regard to Jesus, 184, 206. Attempts made to excite him against Jesus, 208. Tricked into consenting to the murder of John the Baptist, 223. Discomfiture of his army, 224. Jewish ascription of the cause thereof, *ibid note*. Growing jealous of Jesus, 230. His crafty designs regarding Him, 262. His practice with regard to the Sanhedrin, 315. His refusal to try and insulting treatment of Jesus, 324, 325. Intentions of Aretas against him, 372. His place of banishment, ii, 144.

HEROD Agrippa, accession of, i, 174. Ingratiates himself with the Jews and persecutes the Christians, 174, 175. His death, its nature, and how regarded by the Christians, 176. See 181, 186. His son, see *Agrippa*.

HEROD Archelaus, see *Archelaus*.

HEROD the Irenarch, treatment of Polycarp by, ii, 137.

HEROD Philip, i, 166.

HERODIANS, objects with regard to Jesus of the, 288, 289. Discomfited, 290.

HERODIAS, wife of Herod Philip, her incestuous marriage with her husband's brother, i, 166. Her animosity to John the Baptist, and trick by which she obtained his head, 223.

HERON the philosopher, iii, 115 *note*.

HESIOD and Julian's assertion regarding the writings of, iii, 2.

HERODOTUS

HEYNE on Zosimus, iii, 4) *note*. On Symmachus, 86 *note*, 114 *note*. On Orosius, 184 *note*.

HIERAPOLIS, Pagan cruelties and ceremonies under Julian in, iii, 10, 26.

HIERARCHICAL.

HIERARCHICAL power, objects and results of the establishment of, iii, 301, 302. See *Bishops; Church; Clergy; Episcopacy.*

HIEROCLES, persecution instigated by, ii, 212.

HIEROGLYPHICS, symbol for the world in, i, 72 *note.*

HIERONYMUS, see *Jerome.*

HIEROPHANTS, massacre of, iii, 78 *note.* See ii, 49. 58. 85 *note,* 185. 212. The Hierophant of Eleusis, ii, 462.

HILARIANUS, the procurator, and Perpetua the martyr, ii, 168, 169. 171.

HILARICS of Phrygia, offence charged against, iii, 41.

HILARY of Poictiers, his book against Constantius, ii, 433. Its style and character, 433. 434. *notes.* In exile, 442. Cause of Trinitarianism maintained by him, iii, 102. Not a celibatist, 281. His writings, 351.

HIPPO, Augustine made bishop of, iii, 188. A city of refuge, 189.

HIPPOCRATES' notion of dæmoniacal possession, i, 218 *note.*

HIPPODROME of Constantinople, ii, 332, 335. Its chariot games and factions, 336. 339.

HIPPOLYTUS, Bishop of Porto, the "Refuter of Heresies," work rightly assigned by Bunsen to, ii, 44 *note.* Story preserved by him, 50 *note.* On the doctrines of Basilides, 65 *note.* His book on the Ophites, 62, 81, *notes.* See 79 *note.*

HIRA, the cave of, Mohammed's retreat, ii, 263.

HISTORIANS, apology of Polybius for the fables of, i, 37.

HISTORY, as written by the early Christian historians, iii, 160.

HODGSON, Mr, reference to a tract by, ii, 35 *note.*

HOLIDAYS, heathen calendar of, iii, 111 *note.*

HOLY Ghost, descent upon Jesus of

HORMOUZ.

the, i, 143. Promised as the Comforter, 105. Its descent on the Day of Pentecost, 353. Interpretations of the latter miracle, 353, 354, *notes.* Poured out on the Gentiles, 382. "Received" in Ephesus, 446. In the system of Bardesanes, ii, 75. In Mani's system, 261. Controversies on the subject, 354-361.

HOLY Land, the first apostles limited to the, i, 222. Jesus on its borders, 234. Effect of Jerome's example on pilgrimages thither, iii, 191, 192. Female pilgrims, 229, 231. See *Palestine.*

HOMER's poetry and the anthropomorphism of the Greeks, i, 16. Fused with Plato by Julian, ii, 457. A Christian Homer, iii, 8. 354. See ii, 455. 471. iii, 7.

HOMERITES, country of the, ii, 400.

HOMOOUSIUS, or Homoousion (the doctrine of Consubstantialism), disputes concerning the, ii, 368, 369. 412. 438. Avoided by the Arian Goths, iii, 58 *note.*

HOMOPHORUS, the Atlas of Mani's system, 260. 262 *note,* 267, 368 *note,* 269. Office of his ally, Splendit-rœms, 267 *note.*

HONEY, wild, supply of, in the eastern regions, i, 155.

HONORIUS, laws of: for protecting the people's enjoyments, iii, 91; for the abolition of Paganism, 94. 95; relative to the clergy, 283, 284, *notes;* divorce, 290; gladiators, 346. Occasion of his entire prohibition of gladiatorial shows, 346. Never more than a child, 355 *note.*

HOOKER's quotation from Jerome, ii, 21 *note.*

HORACE, occasionally superstitious, i, 41. Touching Jewish synagogues, ii, 19 *note.* A characteristic of his poetry, iii, 111.

HORMOUZ, reception of Mani by, ii, 272.

448 INDEX.

HORUS.

HORUS and Sophia in the Valentinian system, ii, 71, 72.
HOSIUS, Bishop of Cordova, ii, 363. His disposition; mission confided to him, 364. His position in the Council of Nicæa, 365. Constantine's inspirer there, 367. Espouses the cause of Athanasius, 414, 416, 417, 418. His fall, 426. His death, 443. See 371.
HOUSEKEEPING, an ancient indispensable to, iii, 182.
HUG, Ge. man critic, i, 104, 118, 110, notes.
HUMAN mind, imaginative state of the, iii, 413.
HUMAN sacrifices under the Greeks and Romans, i, 26, 27, notes.
HUMANISM, Ephesian phasis of, ii, 55.
HUMANITY, laws tending to, ii, 391.
HUME's argument against a pure theism among barbarians, i, 11 note.
HUNS, the, iii, 60.
HUMBLY, Dr, on the Ignatian Epistles, reference to, iii, 257 note.
HYDE on the Persian religions, ii, 15 note.
HYMETTIUS, charge against, and principle involved in it, iii, 38, 39.
HYMNS; of Ephrem the Syrian, ii, 74, iii, 105; of the primitive churches, iii, 402. Gregory of Nyssa's definition, 402 note. Hymns of Arius, 403. Of the Gnostics, see Bardesanes; Harmonius.
HYRCANUS the High Priest, voice heard from heaven by, i, 88 note.

IALDABAOTH, prince of darkness, generation of, ii, 81.
IAMBLICHUS on the Mysteries, ii, 184. Fate of his scholar, Sopater, 180. His writings, iii, 2. Why held in awe by Julian, 3. Character of his metaphysics, 6. Escapes the vengeance of Valens, 41.
IBERIANS, converter of the, ii, 403.

IMMORTALITY.

ICONIUM, Paul and Barnabas driven from, i, 190.
ICONOCLASTS, barbarising influences of the, iii, 372 note.
IDACIUS, a persecutor of the Priscillians, iii, 160.
IDDO, the prophet, loss of the books of, i, 61.
IDELER's explanation of the luminous phenomenon which led the wise men to Jerusalem, i, 106 note.
IDOLS, address to the Emperor for the destruction of, iii, 10. Olympus's appeal for their preservation, 71. Ambrose's denunciation of idolatry, 87, 88. See Heathenism; Paganism.
IGNATIUS, Bishop of Antioch, theory of episcopal government of, ii, 25 note. Period of his martyrdom, 92 note. Tried before Trajan, 101. Inference from his epistles as to the extent of the persecution, 102, 103 note. Eager for martyrdom, 103. His claim of apostolic authority for the bishops, iii, 256. Object of the composition of his Acts, 124 note.
ILLIBERIS, or Elvira, council of, iii, 78, 240, 253, 268, 282, 289, 333, notes. 378.
ILLYRIAN shore of the Adriatic, Diocletian's palace on the, ii, 204, 231.
IMAGES of Christ, and of celebrated personages as objects of worship, source of the earliest, iii, 389, 390.
IMMOLATION, Scythian custom of, ii, 257. Prohibited by Theodosius, iii, 52.
IMMORTALITY of the soul, i, 35 note. Disbelief on the subject among Pagan authors, 39, 40. Shape taken by the doctrine under Christianity, 44, 45. Great event forming its groundwork as a Christian doctrine, 140. Views of German writers on the subject, 140, 141, notes. Its abiding influence over communities and individuals, 142, 143. Julian's view of the doctrine, ii, 465, 466.

IMPERIAL.

IMPERIAL history from the promulgation of Christianity to Constantine's accession, natural divisions of, ii, 2.
INCARNATION, Oriental and Christian doctrines of the, i, 92-94.
INDIA, great primal spirit of the theology of, i, 70 note. Universality of ablutions, 135. Vague geographical notions of the regions so called, ii, 13. 400. Work on the subject of its Christian communities, recommended, 11 note. Visited by Mani, 263. See *Emanation*; *Orientalism*.
INDIANS, most acceptable act of devotion among the, i, 447 note.
INFANCY, Gospel of the, object of its composition, i, 137 note. Its source, iii, 359.
INFANTS, Constantine's laws for protection of, ii, 191, 194. Doom of child-stealers, 194. When disinherited, 195. When bastardised, 197 note.
INNOCENTS, prelude to the slaughter of the, i, 102. Question as to number slain, 107 note.
INTESTATES' property, when to go to the Church, iii, 376 note.
IRAN, in the Magian system, principle personified by, ii, 252.
IRENÆUS, rabbinical notion given as a prophecy of Our Lord by, i, 419, 420 note. His assertion relative to St. Paul, 458. Fullest early authority on Simon Magus, ii, 47 note. His view of the Basilidean theory, 64 note. Controversy entered into by him, ii, 113. On the primacy of Peter, iii, 264 note. His enthusiasm in regard to the Virgin, 424 note. See i, 463 note. ii, 62 note. iii, 308, 389 notes.
ISAIAH, Messianic prophecies of, i, 56. 79. 88. 137 note, 175. 209. 225 note. His predictions and the Sibylline verses, ii, 119. See *Ascensio Isaiæ*.
ISCHYRAS, offence charged on Macarius by, ii, 377.

JAMES.

ISIDORE, persecution of, iii, 174.
ISIS and SERAPIS, i, 6 note, 40. Worship of Isis and Osiris, 12, 13. Vestiges of Isiac worship in England, 40 note. Temples of Isis, ii, 91. 177. A poetic lament for the goddess, 121, 121 note. An imperial votary to the Isiac mysteries, 151. See ii, 96. See *Serapis*.
ISLAMISM, ii, 31.
ISMAEL, high priest, parentage of, i, 402.
ISOCRATES and other Greek writers, Julian's notice of, iii, 7.
ISRAEL'S race and the Shiloh, i, 54.
ISRAELITES, place of the Ark of the, i, 19. See *Jews*.
ISTHMIAN Games, Corinth, i, 461.
ITALY, ancient rural gods of, i, 18. Festivals founded on its old legends, 20. Sibylline prophecy of its desolation, ii, 124. Ravages of pestilence, 133. Commanded to worship the sun, 175. Degraded into a province, 241. Its gods chiefly local, 278. Its representatives at the Council of Nicæa, 365. Prevalence of child-desertion and infanticide, 393. Its reception of Arianism, iii, 57. Divination and witchcraft still in existence, 98. See ii, 202. 277. 304-313.
ITHACIUS, a persecutor of the Priscillians, iii, 168.

JABLONSKI, character of an essay on Christmas Day by, i, 103 note. On Our Lord's likeness, iii, 188 note, 189 note. See i, 432 note.
JACOB, site and well consecrated to, i, 168. In Marcion's Gospel, ii, 79.
JAIRUS's daughter, raising of, i, 222.
JAMES, difficulty regarding the Apostles bearing the name of, i, 211.
JAMES, "the brother of the Lord," subsequently called the Just, i, 211. Office held by him, 386. 391 note. 406. Compromise effected by his

INDEX

JAMES.

influence, 191. His martyrdom and the mode of it, 405. See ii, 53 note.

JAMES, the son of Cleophas, i, 211.

JAMES and JOHN, the sons of Zebedee, i, 178. Singular names given to them, 210. Martyrdom of James, 174 and note. See John the Evangelist.

JANSENIUS, a remoulder of the Augustinian theology, iii, 171.

JAO, the mystic name, ii, 72.

JEHOVAH, of Jewish worship, i, 22, 62, ii, 59, 60. See Deity; God.

JEREMIAH, expected resurrection of, and its accompaniments, i, 149, 218, 219.

JERICHO, recognition of the Messiah by the blind man at, i, 268.

JEROME, Saint (*Hieronymus*), Buddhist tradition quoted by, i, 94 note. On St. John's long life, 210 note. On the origin of episcopacy, ii, 21 note. His works an evidence of the mystic enthusiasm of his times, iii, 18. His taunt against Basil, 45. His feelings regarding Prætextatus the Pagan, 81. Influences seen in his writings, 102. His testimony to Pelagius, 176. Two great services rendered by him to Christianity, 190, 191. Influence of his example on pilgrimages, 191, 192. Desire for monasticism inspired by him, 193, 194. Value of his Latin version of the Scriptures, and his qualifications for same, 190, 191, 193, 237. His contemptuous reference to marriage, 197 note. Makes Paul the first hermit, 201 note. On the retreat of St Anthony, 202. His self-torture and endurance in the desert, 204. On the use of the cilicium, 208 note. His career and trials, 224. Why obnoxious to the Roman clergy, 226, 232. His relationship towards females, 229, 230. His portraiture of two of them, 229 note. His Solomon's Song allusion to the Saviour, 230

JERUSALEM.

note. His celebration of Paula's charities and Christian heroism, 231, 232 note. His thirst for controversy, 232. His disputes with Augustine and Rufinus, 212, 231. His invectives against Jovinian and Vigilantius, 233-236. On clergy costume, 271 note. Vices charged and prohibitions laid by him upon the clergy, 274, 279 note, 280, 281, 283 note. His story of the husband of twenty wives and the wife of twenty-two husbands, 291 note. On the desertion of the heathen temples, 307. On church architecture, 311 note. Character of his Latin, 352. His nocturnal flagellation, 227 note. Feature of interest in his letters, 364 note. His denunciation of unauthorised interpretations of Scripture, 367 note. On the worship of the cross, 181, 182 note. On the portraiture of the Saviour, the Virgin, and the saints, 187, 193, 195. An asserter of the perpetual virginity of Mary, 434 note. See i, 263 note; iii, 25 note, 80 note, 209 note, 239, 247 note, 316 note.

JERUSALEM, City of, triumphal entry of Jesus into, i, 280-282. His prediction of its fall, and moral connexion between same and his murder, 296, 300. Its Apostolic Council, and compromise agreed to thereat, 192, 193. Probable effect of its fall on Christianity, 420. New city on its site, and interdiction thereof to the Jews, 421-423. See i, 113, ii, 343, 146, 148, 171, 174. See also Jews; Judea.

JERUSALEM, Temple of, transformed into a mart, i, 156, 157. Expulsion of the traders by Jesus, 158, 281. Historical events regarded as divine retribution for its profanation, 160. Lavish expenditure on its restoration, 160, 161. Its desecration by the Samaritans, 167. Slaughter of the Galileans, 231, 232, 269. Its

INDEX. 471

JESUITS.
destruction predicted by Jesus, 293.
The reading of its veil at the Crucifixion, 336. Its tribute, 426. Diversion of same by Vespasian, ii, 7.
Consequences of its destruction, ii, 6.
iii, 21. No sanctity beyond its bounds claimed by the Levites, ii, 18.
Julian's determination to rebuild it, iii, 21, 22. Prevention of the work by assumed preternatural agency, 22, 23. See i, 451. 452. 453. 459. ii, 121.

JESUITS in China, subject of surprise to, i, 94 note.

JESUS CHRIST, era announced by the appearance of, i, 8. His characterization of the Deity, 22. Himself and his age, 48, 49. Paul's language regarding him, 49. Account of his life necessary to a history of Christianity, 50. Difficulties in the way: scope of his life in this work, 51 (see *Messiah*). His proclamation of himself as the "Light of the world," 67. 94. Significant angelic simile used by him, 69. God's invisibility declared by him, 71. State of Judæa at his birth, 82, 83. Probable feelings of the people on the occurrence of that event, 84. Angelic annunciation thereof, 92.
Oriental parallel to incidents in his life, 94 note. His birth and birthplace, 102. Harmony of his mission with the mode of its first revelation, 103. Dispute as to the year and season of his birth, ibid note. His presentation in the temple, 104.
Simeon's benediction on and prediction regarding him, 105. Rabbinical accusation against him, 107 note.
Jewish fiction as to his parentage, and Origen's answer thereto, 108. note.
Commencement of his public life, 127.
Apocryphal Gospel of his infancy, 127 note. Surprise of the rabbis at his youthful questionings, 128. Unfavorable concomitants of his entry on his public career, 131. John the

JESUS CHRIST.
Baptist's avowal of inferiority to him, 142, 143). His baptism, 143.
Pointed out by John as the Expected One, 144. 149. His temptation and the various theories thereof, 144-148. His first disciples: commencement of his career, 151, 152. His first miracle: anti-sectarian principle enunciated in it, 152-154. His first appearance and reception at Jerusalem, 155, 156. His expulsion of the traders from the temple, and expectations raised thereby, 158, 159. Misapprehension by the Jews of his speech typifying his own death and resurrection as the destruction and restoration of the temple, 160. 198, 199. Pharisaic jealousy of him, 161. 162. 167. His interview with and declaration to Nicodemus, 162, 163. Caution observed by him in his first visit to Jerusalem, 164. His departure thence, 165. His apprehensions of the Pharisees and passage through Samaria, 166, 167. Effect produced by his example and precepts, 167, 168. His interview with the woman of Samaria, 169, 170. Ready acknowledgment of his Messiahship by the Samaritans, 171. His public assumption of his divine office and second miracle, ibid. Probable cause of his inhospitable reception by the Nazarenes, 174. Chronological point connected with his address to them in their synagogue, 175 note. Substance of same, and effect produced by it, 175, 176. Outrage committed by them upon him, 177.
Retires to Capernaum: its advantages as an abiding place, ibid. His choice of apostles: Peter's awe of him, 178. His reception in the Capernaum synagogue, 178, 179.
Radical differences between his teachings and the expoundings of the rabbis, and animosity of the latter towards him, 180-182. Miracles wrought by him at Capernaum, 182. Not regarded with hostility

172   INDEX.

JESUS CHRIST,

by Herod Antipas, 184, 206. Passes unmolested through Galilee, 185. Unique character of his ministrations as compared with those of other teachers, 185, 186. His open-air preachings and illustrative use of surrounding objects, 187, 188. His sermon on the Mount; chronological difficulties in relation to it, 188 and note. When same was delivered according to St. Luke, 212. Threefold view of the moral system propounded by him, 189-194. His conduct with regard to his countrymen, 195. Injunction laid by him on the healed lepar, ibid. Circumstances attending his second miracle, 195, 196. His intercourse with the publicans, 196, 197. His position at the close of the first year of his public life, 197.
Second Year of his public life.—Change of popular sentiment regarding him, 198, 199. Charge against him for healing on the Sabbath, 202. His defence; second charge against him grounded thereon, 203, 204. His answer thereto; effect upon the Sanhedrin of his assertion of his Messiahship, 204, 205. Retires again into Galilee; hostility of the Pharisees against him, 206. His declaration of his superiority to the Sabbath, 207. Pharisaic denunciation of his continued disregard of that day, 208. Secludes himself from public view, ibid. Organises his apostles; their names and social position, 209-212. Heals the centurion's servant, 212. Effect of his raising the widow's son, 213, 214. Question as to the design of the message sent to him by John the Baptist from prison, 214, 215. Signs appealed to by him as evidence of the commencement of the Messiah's kingdom, 215, 216. Contrast between himself and John, 216. His application of the incident of his anointment by a woman of ill-life, 217. Charged with work-

JESUS CHRIST,

ing by evil spirits; his disproval thereof, 217-219. Sign of Messiahship demanded of him by the Pharisees, 219. Declares the superiority of his spiritual ties to his family relationships, 220. Character and object of his parables, 220, 221. Question of the destruction of the possessed swine, 221. His raising of the daughter of Jairus, and other miracles and injunctions regarding them, 222. Sends out his apostles; effect of this step upon his position in public regard, 222, 223. His miracle of feeding the multitude and dangerous enthusiasm excited by it, 224, 225. His miraculous passage over the lake, 226. Disappointed hopes and desertion of the multitude, 226, 227. Continued adherence of the apostles; his prophecy of a traitor among them, 228. Fluctuations of feeling regarding him, and Strauss's inference therefrom, ibid note. His position at the close of the second year of his public life, 228, 229.
Third Year of his public life.—Probable cause of his absence from the third Passover; increased hostility of the Jews, 230, 231. Fatal result which his presence might have entailed, 232. His places of concealment, 232, 233. Fears excited at this time by his movements, 233, 234. Heals the daughter of the Canaanitish woman; prejudice of his apostles on the occasion, 234, 235. Further miracles and continued injunctions of secrecy in connection therewith, 236. Effect upon his apostles of his apparently contradictory conduct, 237, 238. His transfiguration and phenomena accompanying it, 239, 240. Incident of his payment of the tribute money, 240, 241. Occasion of his commendation of a child to the imitation of his apostles, 241, 242. His sudden appearance at the Feast of Tabernacles, and teachings and de-

INDEX.   473

JESUS CHRIST.
clarations there, 241-245. Perplexities of the Sanhedrin, 245, 246. His discomfiture of his opponents in the case of the woman taken in adultery, 246, 247. Fury excited by his references to Abraham and declaration of his own pre-existence, 247-250. Heals the blind man on the Sabbath, 250. Illegality of the act, 252 note. Abortive proceedings of the Sanhedrin thereon, 253-255. His rejection by the Samaritans, and reply to the demand of his disciples for summary vengeance on them, 256-258. His chosen seventy and their duties, 258, 259. At the Feast of the Dedication: interrogatories put to him by the Jews, 259, 260. Again charged with blasphemy; renewed attempt upon his life, 261. Threatened with the fate of John the Baptist: designs of Herod and the Pharisees, 262. His raising of Lazarus and its attendant circumstances, 263, 264. Final determination of the Sanhedrin concerning him, 264, 265.

His last Passover.—On his way to Jerusalem: recognised by two blind men whom he heals, 267, 268. Zaccheus's practical testimony to his belief in his Divinity, 268. State of feeling at this period: anticipated Messianic accompaniments disclaimed by him, 268, 269. Position towards him of the various sects, 270-272. Lesson inculcated by his recognition of the Samaritans, 272, 273. Obstacles to the appreciation by his countrymen of the unworldliness and comprehensiveness of his kingdom, 273, 274. How regarded by the Essenes, 275. Motives impelling the hostility of the rulers towards him, 276, 277. His demeanour anticipatory of his approaching end, 278. Abiding with Simon, late the Leper, 279. His anointment by Mary; Judas's economic protest, 279, 280. His enthusiastic reception at Jerusalem

JESUS CHRIST.
and in the Temple, and disposal of the remonstrances of the Pharisees and rulers, 281, 282. His discourse to the Greek proselytes, 283. Testimony from the heavens; effect of his mysterious allusions, 284. Truth symbolized by his curse upon the barren fig-tree, 284, 285, 286. Again expels the desecrators of The Temple and confounds his relentless interrogators, 285-287. Union of factions for his destruction, and efforts to entrap self-condemnatory replies from him, 288, 289. His confutation of the subtleties of the Sadducees, 290, 291. His conversion of the questioning scribe, 291. His renewed condemnation of the Pharisees, 292, 293. Approaching crisis in his fate, 293. His prediction of the destruction of the Temple, ibid. And of the future desolation of Jerusalem, 296, 300. Moral connexion between his death and the doom of the city, 296, 297. Immediate cause of his rejection by the Jews, 297-299. Evidence of his foreknowledge afforded by his prediction of the fall of Jerusalem, 300. Difficulties in the way of his seizure by the rulers, 300, 301. Motives of Judas to his betrayal, 301-303. The Last Supper and incidents connected with it, 304, 305. His agony in the garden of Gethsemane, 306. His rebuke to his betrayer and reproof to Peter, 307. Taken prisoner; dispersal of his followers, 308. Preliminary proceedings against him, 309. His arraignment before the Sanhedrin, 310. Declares himself the Messiah, 311. Result of his trial: insults of the soldiery, 312. Carried before Pilate, 317. Result of his examination before Pilate, and clamour of the Sanhedrin thereon, 321-323. Sent before Herod: insulting conduct of the latter towards him, 324, 325. Pilate's further efforts with the Jews in his behalf: the crown of thorns, 326-328.

474   INDEX.

JESUS CHRIST.
His condemnation by Pilate, 330.
Led forth to death: outrages of the
soldiers on him, ibid.
*Circumstances attendant on his Cru-
cifixion.*—Usages observed, 331-
333. The two malefactors, 333.
Conduct of the spectators, 334. His
words of comfort to the weepers and
prayer for his murderers, 334, 335.
The preternatural darkness; his
agony and death, 335, 336. The
rending of the veil of the temple and
opening of the sepulchres, 336, 337.
Burial of his body and apparent extinction of his religion, 338, 339.
Doctrine assumed by him as the basis
of his own doctrines, 340 note. Legend as to his substitute on the cross,
ii, 68.
The Resurrection.—Precautions of the
Sanhedrin to prevent the removal of
his remains, i, 344. Emotions of the
women on finding his sepulchre
empty, and vision seen by them,
346, 347. His appearance to Mary
Magdalene, and subsequently to the
other women and to the apostles,
348, 349. His ascension, 351.
Its necessity towards perfecting the
Divine scheme, *ibid note*. His glorious exaltation preached by the
apostles, 355, 356. Light in which
his death and resurrection were regarded by many Jewish believers,
418. Magic power ascribed to his
name, 447. His religion welcomed
by cruel ingenuities, 458.
Doubtful story of the search for
his kindred, ii, 9, 10. Estimate
formed of him by Simon Magus,
45, 51 *note*. His position and attributes in the various Gnostic and
cognate systems, 52, 54, 56, 57, 59-
61, 63, 71, 72 *note*, 73-75, 78, 80,
81, 82, 83, 84, *notes*, 162, 260.
261, 266, 268, 270, 308, 310, 311,
356. His throne in the Sibylline
writings, 118. Refusal of Polycarp to
blaspheme him, 137. Associated in
worship with the Queen of Heaven,
160 *note*. Alexander Severus's way

JEWS,
of showing homage to Him, 177, 178.
His alleged appearance in Constantine's vision, 285-287. How figured
as an image by Constantine, 117.
Heathen temple on the site of
his sepulchre, 346, 348 *note*.
Discovery of his cross (see *Cross,
Crucifix*). Controversies relative to
his identity in substance with the
Father (see *Homoousion*). Origen's
notion of the finiteness of his reign,
iii, 104. His personal appearance:
language of the fathers thereon,
386-388. Statues, images, and
paintings, 389-391. See ii, 7, 93,
94, 108 *note*, 137, 164, 167, 211,
285, 347. See also *Christianity;
Jews; Trinitarianism.*

JESUS Patibilis, the imprisoned light,
ii, 267.
JEWS, principle of Antiochus Epiphanes' persecution of the, i, 4 *note*.
Idea symbolised by their Shechinah,
21. Their earlier conception of the
Deity, 22. Cessation of their belief
in his symbolical presence, 23. Pompey's wonder at, and Tacitus's description of, their religious system,
23, 24. Forbidden initiation into
the Mysteries, 32 *note*. Footing
gained by their theism among the
Romans, 40. Their notions connected with the anticipated coming
of the Messiah, 54, 55, 147, 284.
349 (see *Messiah*). Results on their
religion of their mixture with other
races, 57. Their early adoption of
Greek manners, 58 *note*. Alleged
contempt of the Greeks and Romans
for them, *ibid note* q. Their settlement in Babylonia, royal proselytes
there, and influence over the religion
of its people, 58-60, 105. Their
Cabala and its origin, 61. Debasing
influence of the Syrian religions, 61.
Their notions as to communications
with the Deity, 71. Question of
their knowledge of a future state,
73. Their belief in preternatural
interpositions, and its influence over
them, 84, 85. Solemnities observed

JEWS.

by their priesthood in the Holy of Holies, 86, 87. Birth of the Messiah from a virgin not a notion originating with them, 94 *note*. Period of initiation of their sons into their religious ceremonies, 127. Law of parent and child among them, 129. Their struggle against Roman tyranny, 139 *note*. A French picture of their system, 140 *note*. Hostilities between them and the Samaritans: outrages of the latter on them, 167. Their notions of temporal prosperity or adversity as indicating divine favour or anger, 189, 190, 251, 252. Their treatment of lepers, 195. Unpopularity of publicans among them, 196. Their intense reverence for the Sabbath, and instances thereof, 199, 200. Bitter feeling roused in them by Jesus's anti-sabbatarianism, 204. Their determination to put him to death, 230. Occasion of their attempts to stone him, 240. Lesson taught them by the parable of the good Samaritan, 273. Obstacles to their recognition of Jesus as the Messiah, 273, 274. Policy formed on their rulers regarding him, 276, 277, 318. View taken of their character and institutions by their Roman masters, 118, 119. Their conduct towards Jesus antecedent to, and during his trial and crucifixion, 319 (see *Jesus*). Their disposal of executed criminals, 337 *note*. Diversity of languages among them in the Roman provinces, 354. Persecuted under Caligula, 173, 174. Their notion of the first Christian church, 391. Numbers of their persuasion at Thessalonika, 396 *note*. Period of the expiration of their hope of the Messiah, 410. Effect of the fall of Jerusalem upon most of their race, 411, 412. Their attachment to the *Law*, 413. Hostility between them and the Christians, and interdict put upon them by the Romans, 420-423. Usages

JOANNA.

among them harmonizing with the spirit of Christianity, 426. Result of their accusation of the Christians at Corinth, 443, 444. Imperial edict in favour of their race at Ephesus, 445. Practices and overthrow of the pretensions of their exorcists, 447, 448. Act deemed most inexpiable by them, 447 *note*. Ephesian anti-Christian insurrection in which they were implicated, 450. Their disclaimer and hatred of Christianity, 455, 456, 460. Their alleged hatred of the human race, 457. Their possible escape from proscription under Nero, 458. Claudius's dealing with them in Rome, ii, 4. Effects of their subjugation, 6, 8. Their last rally for independency, 10, 11. Their bond of union wherever settled, 17. Difference between their synagogues and Christian churches, 18, 19. Their later doctrine of angels and devils, 50. Not averse to popular amusements, 96. As captives forced to become gladiators, 97. Alexandrian Jews at the theatres, *ibid*. Their numbers in Babylon, and insurrection under Hadrian, 99. Their rebellion under Trajan, and its effects upon the Christians, 99-101. Alexandrian versification of their prophecies, 119. Their share in Polycarp's martyrdom, 138. Their erudition under Severus and Alexander Severus, 156, 179. Under Persian rule, 254. Their suburb in Rome, 294. Taken into favour by Julian, III, 21, 22. Interested in Chrysostom's cause, 143 *note*. Synagogue at Callinicum burned by the Christians, 163. Prohibitions put upon the Christians in Spain with regard to them, 268 *note*. See *Alexandrian School of Jews; Jerusalem, City of; Jerusalem, Temple of; Jesus; Judea; Law; Mesopotamia; Pharisees; Sanhedrin; Sadducees*.

JOANNA, wife of Chusa, Herod's steward, at Christ's sepulchre, i, 344.

476 INDEX.

JOANNES.

JOANNES Damascenus, statements on the authority of, iii, 193 note.
JOANNITÆ, followers of Chrysostom, laws against the, iii, 145 note.
JOB, attributes of Satan in the book of, i, 69.
JOHN the Baptist declares God's invisibility, i, 71. Phænomena connected with his birth, 85-89. Excitement consequent on that event, 97. Declaration of his mission, 98. His appearance as a public teacher, 112. Removes to the banks of the Jordan, 114. Asceticism of his habits: his costume and food, 134; 135. Interest excited by his preaching, 136. Intensity of his denunciations and adjurations, 137, 138. Proclaims the coming of the Messiah, 138, 139, 272. Feelings aroused by his mysterious language, 140. His pretensions tested by a deputation of the priesthood, 141, 148, 149. Question as to any early intimacy between himself and Jesus, 141, 142. Avows his inferiority to Jesus, and renders homage to him, 142, 143, 165. Talmudic illustration of his avowal, 143 note. His baptism of Jesus and announcement of his mission, 143, 144, 149, 150. His notice of the reserve maintained by Jesus, 164. Removes to a new station: his partisans jealous of Jesus, 165. His career drawing to a close, ibid. Why persecuted by Herod Antipas, 166, and note. Grotius's notion on this subject, 184 note. His testimony cited by Jesus, 204. Message sent by him from his prison to Jesus, and difficulties connected therewith, 214, 215. Contrast between himself and Jesus, 216. His murder, 217. Where perpetrated, ibid note. Popular rumour of his restoration to life in the person of Jesus, 224, 218. See 187, 124, 446.
JOHN, Saint, the evangelist and apostle, peculiarity of the Gospel of,

JOSEPHUS.

i, 154 note. Inapplicability of the appellation Boanerges to him, 210. Tradition relative to his long life, ibid note. Minute fact recorded by him only, 108 note. Procures admission for Peter to Jesus's trial, 309. View of his character afforded by internal evidence, 187, 188. His book of Revelations, 188, ii, 14. Legendary accounts of him: Cerinthus and the cauldron of oil, 13, 14, 14 note. Appearance and object of his Gospel, 53, 54. His Ephesian opponents, 55. Polycarp one of his hearers, 116. See ii, 7.
JOHN the Solitary, consulted by Theodosius, iii, 206.
JONAH, applicability of a passage from, ii, 445.
JONATHAN, the High Priest, assassinated, i, 385, 402.
JONES on the canon, iii, 159 note.
JONES, Sir William, on Du Perron's Zoroastrian discoveries, i, 65 note. References to his Menu, ii, 35 note, 37 note.
JORDAN, site of St John's baptismal station on the, i, 134.
JORNANDES on the Goths and Gepidæ, iii, 57 note.
JORTIN on the peculiarity of Christ's discourses, i, 187. References concerning Polycarp's martyrdom, ii, 139, 140, notes.
JOSEPH, son of Jacob, burial-place of, i, 168. Expectation of a Messiah descended from him, 171.
JOSEPH, husband of Mary, migration to Nazareth of, i, 91. His betrothal to Mary, ibid. His warning vision, 99. His position relative to the census ordered by Cæsar, 100, 101. Why he retired to Galilee, 108.
JOSEPH of Arimathea buries the body of Jesus, i, 338.
JOSEPHUS's assertions regarding the Messiah, i, 57 note, 81. On the oath to Cæsar taken by the Jews, 100. On the prodigies during the

INDEX. 477

JOVE.

siege of Jerusalem, 133. His precocity, 128. His account of Saint John the Baptist, 142 note. On John's influence and Herod's persecution of him, 166. His picture of a future life, 290 note. On the suspension of Vitellius's operations against Petra, 372. Discrepancies between him and Tacitus, 404 note. On the murder of St. James, 407, 407 note. His social position in Rome, ii, 9. On the Jewish Ethnarch, 17 note. See i, 58. 59 note, 100, 101 notes, 167. 406. 409.

JOVE, see *Jupiter*.

JOVIAN's refusal to serve in Julian's army, iii, 9. Christianity re-established in his reign, 31.

JOVINIAN, nature of the heresy of, iii, 233. His fourfold accusation, 233, 234. Fierceness of Jerome's invective against him, 235.

JOVIUS, title assumed by Diocletian, ii, 211.

JUDÆA, i, 52. 53. 106. 108. 130. Its state at Christ's birth, 82. Its state under Herod and his successor, 51. Reduced to a Roman province, 130. Oppressive conduct of its Roman governors and tax-farmers, 131. Conflicts of Pharisees and Sadducees, 132. Rebellion excited by Judas the Galilean, and excesses of his followers, 132. 133. Unfitness of its southern regions for baptismal rites, 111, 114. Its state under the prefects: Insurrections and predatory incursions, 183, 184. Powerlessness of its high priests, 185. Roman oppression at its height, 459. Kindled of Jesus summoned before its Roman procurator, ii, 10. Locality to which its rulers were banished, 144.

JUDAISM, ii, 5. 12. 84, 158. 163. 178. 260. 276. 355. Attempted alliance of Polytheism with it, iii, 21-24. See *Jerusalem. Jews. Judæa.*

JULIAN.

JUDAS the Galilean or Gaulonite, the Jewish insurrectionary leader, i, 132. 133. 191. 232. 315. 407 note. Hostility of his sect to Jesus, 270. His denunciation of the payment of tribute to the Romans, 289. Reappearance of his sons, 184. Gibbon's conjecture relative to his followers and the Christians, 458 note.

JUDAS, Thaddeus, or Lebbens, the apostle, brother of James, i, 211. Character of his epistle; his sphere of action, 387.

JUDAS Iscariot, derivation of the name, 272. His pretext for objecting to Mary's anointment of Jesus, 280. Motives assigned for his betrayal of Jesus, 301, 302. Amount of his reward, and service rendered for it, 302 note. His subsequent remorse and suicide, 303. Jesus's rebuke to him at the moment of his betrayal, 307. Scene enacted on his return of the price of his Master's blood, 317, 318. Arius's fate likened to his, ii, 182.

JUDE, "the brother of the Lord," cause and result of judicial proceedings relative to the grandsons of, ii, 10.

JUDGMENT, final, references to the, i, 456, ii, 161.

JULIAN's attempt to establish a Platonic Paganism, ii, 30, 182, 285, 311. His references to Constantine, 326 note, 387, 387 note. His saviour in his infancy, 405. Most remarkable part of his history: results of his short reign, 449-451. His religion and philosophy, 452. His education and Christian instructors, 454-456. Constantius' jealousy of and unchristian conduct towards him, 456, 459, 460. His intercourse with philosophers and communion with the invisible world, 457-459. His escape from his father's fate, 459. His residence at Athens: Gregory's por-

JULIANUS.
traitors of him, 461. Initiated at
Eleusis; declared Cæsar, 462. His
accession as emperor, 463. One
cause of his apostasy from Christianity, ibid. His public espousal
of paganism; form of that religion
adopted by him, 464, 465. His
view of the immortality of the
soul, 465, 466. His restoration of
Paganism, new priesthood and charitable institutions, 466-471. "The
Ape of Christianity," 471. His
ritual, religious instruction scheme,
revival of animal sacrifices, and personal devotions, 472-474. Character of the philosophers patronised
by him, iii, 1-3. His pretended
toleration of and sarcasms on Christianity, 3-6. His notion of the
vital principle of the Greek writers,
7. His trick upon the Christians
and consequences of their resentment of it, 9. His persecutions,
10. Result of his organising efforts
at Constantinople and Antioch, and
in Alexandria, 11-20. Ingratiates
himself with the Jews, 21. Miraculously foiled in his attempted rebuilding of their temple, 21-23.
His writings against Christianity,
24, 25. His apology for his filthy
beard, 25, 26. Manner of his
death; legend connected with it,
27. Result of his conflict with
Christianity, 28, 29. See i, 40
note. ii, 189, iii, 65, 81, 354.
JULIANUS, the centurion, his eques-
trian exploit in the Temple, i, 330
note.
JULIUS Antonius, edict of, i, 445.
JULIUS, bishop of Rome, ii. 443 note.
JULIUS Cæsar, a consulter of the
Chaldæans, i, 42. Colonised Corinth,
196 note. 441 note. See ii, 336
note.
JUNIUS Bassus, urn or sarcophagus
of, iii, 192 note, 395.
JUPITER, Jove, temples and adoration
of, ii, 91, 94, 120, 122, 213. De-
liverance ascribed to him, 141, 143

KHOSROVEDUGHT.
note. Outvoted in favour of Christ
by the Senate, iii, 92.
JUPITER Capitolinus, i, 5, ii, 7. Introduction of Oriental rites into his
temple, 171. See 190, 387.
JUPITER Laxlaris, description of the
rites of, i, 17 note.
JUPITER Olympius, ii, 105.
JUPITER Optimus Maximus, ii, 212.
JUPITER Philius, Maximin's image
to, ii, 232. His rites celebrated by
Julian, iii, 14.
JUPITER Stator, i, 19.
JUPITER the Thunderer, statue of,
iii, 89.
JUSTIN Martyr and the Sibylline
verses, ii, 135. His conversion and
martyrdom, ii, 134-135. His notion of the teaching of Socrates, 181
note. On converts, iii, 263 note.
Character of his Apology, 362. On
Christ's personal appearance, 386.
See ii, 110 note.
JUSTINA, empress, zealous in the
cause of the Arians, iii, 155. Her
quarrels with Ambrose; his pulpit
invectives against her, 155-158.
JUSTINIAN, confiscation of the Theoretica by, iii, 332.
JOTTA, suggestion regarding, i, 89
note.
JUVENAL'S lines on Chaldæans and
astrologers, i, 42 note. On the
treatment of Christian martyrs,
457 note.
JUVENTINUS, Saint, festivals in honour
of, iii, 324 note.

KAIOMERS in the Magian system, ii,
242.
KARAITES, religious ancestors of the,
i, 271. What they were, ibid.
KELTS in Constantine's army, ii, 281.
KESTNER'S commentaries on Euse-
bius, iii, 163 note.
KHOSROV, King of Armenia, and his
family murdered, ii, 255, 356.
KHOSROVEDUGHT, daughter of Khos-

INDEX. 479

KINGS

roy, saved from murder, ii, 256. Her conversion and alleged revelation to her, 257.
KINGS, book of, why omitted from his Bible by Ulphilas, iii, 56.
KLAPROTH'S eulogy on Buddhism, i, 93.
KLEUKER, i, 62 note, 64 note, 65 note, 68 note. His 'Anhang zum Zendavesta,' ii, 35 note. ii, 147 note.
KNITTEL, sacred manuscripts discovered by, iii, 55 note.
KNOWLEDGE, effect on Polytheism of the progress of, i, 25-29.
KORAN, source of some of the traditions of the, ii, 178. Story of the cave of Hira, 263. Criticisms thereon, ibid note.
KREUBER, amusing observations in a work by, i, 448 note.
KUINOEL on the reading of Jutta, i, 89. His theory of the possessed swine, 221 note.

LABARUM, Constantine's Christian standard, occasion of the, ii, 287. Its heathen element, 289. Victories ascribed to it, 318, 326. Christ's monogram removed, iii, 9. See 398 note u.
LA BASTIE, M. on laws against magic, ii, 188 note. His 'Mémoires des Inscriptions,' iii, 82 note x.
LABBE on Christian councils and canons, references to, 268, 278, 298, notes.
LABERIUS, the mimes of, iii, 139.
LABORDE on Roman architecture in the East, iii, 66 note.
LABYRINTH of Egypt, ii, 157.
LACTANTIUS, Christian tutor to Constantine's son, ii, 315. 322. Humane laws due to his advice, 394. Inveighs against tragedy and comedy, iii, 117 note. His contempt for physical knowledge, 417 note. See iii, 308, 335, 336, notes. 351.

LAW.

LÆLII of the Roman republic, ii, 40.
LÆTUS, the prefect, persecutor of the Christians, ii, 158, 159.
LAITY present at the Nicene Council, ii, 266. When permitted to officiate in the church, iii, 367. Lay elders, ii, 21 note.
LAMA, the, ii, 36.
LAMPADIUS, Tillemont's statement regarding, iii, 19 note.
LAMPRIDIUS, citations from, ii, 171, 176, 179, 180, notes.
LANGUAGE, iii, 51. 349. See Latin. Literature.
LANISTÆ, keepers of gladiators, iii, 145.
LAODICEA, a seat of portico-prophetic forgeries, ii, 120, 121. See Councils.
LAPSI, the fallen Christians of Africa, ii, 189.
LARDNER, Dr., on the date of Cyrenius's Judæan governorship, i, 91 note. On the Jewish census, 100 note. On dæmoniacs, 217 note. On persecutions under Antoninus and Aurelius, ii, 110 note. 144 note. On Manicheism, 361 note. 363 note. 368 note. See i, 407 note. iii, 91 note.
LATERAN basilica granted for a Christian church, ii, 294. 344.
LATIN Christianity, History of, see Milman.
LATIN language, kept alive by Christianity, iii, 51. 170. Never quite in harmony with the genius of the latter, 349.
LAW, tradition of the delivery of the, i, 71. Sons of the Law, 127. Place of its reading, 168. Given to Jesus, 175. Regulations for reading it, 175 note. Its conservators and interpreters, 179. ii, 19. Position of Jesus with regard to it, i, 180-182, 247. Its Sabbath-day ordinances, 200. Superstitious reverence paid to it, 413-415, 418. Same

LAZARUS.

decaying, 411. Scope of the Epistle to the Romans with regard to it, 417. Jaw and Gospel, 420. Embodied in the legislation of Christian Emperors, ii, 396.

LAZARUS, Jesus at the house of relatives of, i, 259. 263. 279. His death, 263. Raised from the sepulchre by Jesus, 264. His second death desired, 280. Why, 280 note.

LE BEAU, St. Martin's notes on, i, 69 note. iii, 14, 40, 55, 56, notes. See Saint Martin.

LE CLERC, i, 98 note, 407 note. Fearful sentence of St. Augustine quoted from his book, iii, 91.

LEGENDS, Christian, their character, iii, 158.

LEGION, the thundering, ii, 142.

LEMURIA (Remuria), object of the, i, 20 note.

LENTULUS, prohibition of human sacrifices by, i, 26 note.

LEONIDAS, father of Origen, martyrdom of, ii, 158 note.

LEPER healed by Jesus, i, 195, 279. The ten lepers, 278.

LESSING on Christ's promulgation of the Immortality of the soul, i, 340 note.

LIBANIUS on the employment of temple materials, ii, 467 note. On Julian's restoration of Paganism, 468. His writings and Julian's admiration for them, iii, 2, 3, 6. 351. 364 note. Retort of a grammarian to his sneer, 31. His insult to Christian worship, ibid note. His narrow escape from the charge of magic, 41. His oration for revenging Julian's death, 60, 71 note. His oration "For the Temples," 66. 79 note. His regret for his pupil's conversion, 119. On tragic fables, 337. On pantomimes, 339 note. 340. See ii, 387. iii. 4. 30, 31. 64, notes, 68, 68 note, 108, 123, 124, 241, 336, notes.

LOAVES.

LIBELLATICI, the, in the African church, ii, 189.

LIBRARIES and manuscripts, destruction of, iii, 41.

LIBERIUS, Bishop and Pope of Rome, compromise refused by, ii, 423. Stern against imperial offers, 426. Effect of his long exile upon his resolution, ibid. Female appeal for his liberation, 427. His return to his episcopate, 442. See 441.

LIBERTINES, sect of, i, 354.

LICINIUS, co-emperor, ii, 278. His war with and defeat of Maximin, 230, 238, 275. Joined in government with Constantine, 317, 290. Effect of his first war with Constantine, 315. Espouses the Pagan cause; persecutes the Christians, 316-318. His death, 319. 321. 321 note. Repeal of his anti-Christian edicts, ibid. His son put to death. 321. See ii, 330. 340. 350. 362. 363. 372. 387.

LIFE, future, see Immortality of the Soul.

LIGHT, great principle of, i, 105.

"LIGHT of the World," Christ's proclamation of Himself as the, i, 67.

LIGHTFOOT'S 'Harmony,' i, 54. 55, notes. On the Jewish notion of the Messiah. 74, 76 note. Sometimes misled by his rabbinism, 104 note. Temple service given by him, iii, 401 note.

LINDSAY, Lord, on the habitations of the early Christians, iii, 129 note.

LIPSIUS on the Agapæ, iii, 325 note.

LITERATURE of the ante-Christian era, character of the, i, 36-38. Influence of Christianity upon it, iii, 50, 51. Greek and Latin poetry, 111. Christian literature, 347-352.

LIVES of saints, iii, 359, 360.

LIVY, act of Numa admired by, i, 18.

LOAVES and fishes, miracle of the, i, 224. Its repetition, 236.

INDEX. 481

LOBE.

LOBE's edition of Ulphilas's Bible, iii, 56 note.

LOBECK's ' Aglaophamus,' i, 10 note. Points traced out by him, 16 note. Intenability of his views relative to mysteries, 31 note. Various theories stated by him, ibid.

LOCUSTS as an article of food, i, 115 note.

LOGOS, or Divine Word, place and office in oriental theology of the, i, 71, 72. Its definition in Revelation, 73. See ii, 54, 70, 71 note, 354, 355.

LOLLIANUS, why put to death, iii, 19. Occasion of the nicknames given to him, ibid.

LORD's Supper, see Eucharist.

LOMBARD invasion, event prefigured in Pope Gregory's imagination by the, iii, 418.

LUCAN and his witch Erictho, i, 41 note. Locality of his " Cumque superbis," &c. 60 note.

LUCIAN's treatise 'De Deâ Syriâ,' i, 194 note. An exponent of unbelief, ii, 181). His days past, 159. Not author of the ' Philopatris,' 159 note.

LUCIANUS, Bishop of Antioch, death in prison of, ii, 211. His assertion relative to Christianity, 276.

LUCIFER of Cagliari, representative of the Pope at the Milan Council, ii, 424. Admired by Athanasius, 433, 434. His banishment, and books against Constantius, 426, 434, 442.

LUCIUS, Arian bishop of Alexandria, iii, 44.

LUCRETIUS, a sponsor for Epicureanism, i, 41. Curious coincidence with his ' Nihil indiga nostri,' 418 note.

LUKE, Saint, and the census of the Jews, i, 100 note, 101. Probability inferred from his silence, 104. As to his account of the slaughter of the Galileans in the temple, 111, 231 note. His historical accuracy,

MACEDONICS.

189 note. Author of the Acts of the Apostles, 461. His reference to Simon Magus, ii, 47. His Gospel appropriated by Marcion, 79.

LUPERCALIA, long existence of the, iii, 98.

LUPI, ancient monumental inscription published by, iii, 381 note.

LUTHER, a reviver of Augustine's theology, iii, 171.

LYDIA of Thyatira, conversion of, and its attendant incidents, i, 433, 434.

LYDIA, a literary equivalent for all the gold of, iii, 1.

LYELL, Sir Charles, result of the late researches of, i, 9 note.

LYONS, settlement of Jews at, ii, 144. Its martyr, see Attalus. Its bishop, see Irenæus.

LYSIAS, Roman commander in Jerusalem, his first suspicion and later impression regarding St Paul, i, 400, 401.

LYSIAS, Greek author, iii, 7.

LYSTRA, Paul at, i, 388, 395. His illusage by its people, 391, 412. Its Jew residents, 431 note. Character of its Polytheism: view taken by its people of the Apostolic miracles, 411, 412, 435.

MACARIUS, offence charged against, ii, 377. Its recoil upon Athanasius, 379.

MACAULAY, Lord, on human sacrifices under the Romans, i, 27 note.

MACBETH, Lady, ancient parallel to an exclamation of, ii, 140 note.

MACEDONIA, i, 444. Paul's journey through, 450, 451. Dissertation on its dialect, iii, 150 note.

MACEDONIANS, the sect of, iii, 144. " Interminata poena " against them, 301 note.

MACEDONIUS the Arian: his qualifications for a bishop, ii, 408 note. Flaw in his election as Bishop of Constantinople, 415. His bloody

VOL. III.   2 I

INDEX.

MACEDONIUS,
passage to his episcopal throne, 427.
His heresies, 444; Depoted, 446.

MACEDONIUS the monk, bold remonstrance of, iii, 137.

MACHÆRUS, fortress of, John the Baptist's prison, i, 214.

MACKNIGHT on a Miracle of Jesus, i, 350 note.

MACRIANUS, anti-Christian edict suggested by, ii, 191.

MACRINUS, emperor, iii, 171 note.

MACROBIUS, statue of Serapis described by, iii, 69, 70, notes. On Prætextatus, 80 note.

MADAURA, place of Augustine's education, iii, 180.

MÆSO-GOTHIC alphabet, chief element of the, iii, 55.

MAGI or Magians: character of their theism, i, 15. Doctrine ascribed to them by Pausanias, 19. Nature of their system, 62. Its origin and promulgation, 63. Records containing its principles, 64. Points of similarity between it and the later prophetic writings, 67. Their visit to Bethlehem, 104 note. Suspicions excited thereby, 106, 107. Region from whence they came, 106 note. Revival of their system (Zoroastrianism), ii, 247. Number and wealth of its priesthood, 248. Its re-establishment and intolerance of its hierarchy, 249, 251, 252. Testamentary Injunctions of its Re-founder, 253. Murder of Christian bishops by its followers, 254. Antagonism of the system with Manicheism, 258, 259, 261. Mani one of Magian race, 263. Fate of Mani at their hands, 272. See *Zendavesta; Zoroaster*.

MAGIC, Athanasius charged with the practice of, ii, 178. Laws of Constantine and Constans against it, 188, 189 note. Prosecutions and persecutions, iii, 14-16, 17, 18. Execution for copying a magical book, 19. The last refuge of conscious weakness, 96.

MAGNENTIUS usurper of the western empire, ii, 420. His defeat at Mursa, 421. His inhuman sacrifices on that occasion, 421 note. Charge against Athanasius in connexion with him, 421.

MAGNIFICAT, the, iii, 354. Sung from the earliest ages, 401.

MAGUS, Simon, see *Simon Magus*.

MAHÁ Bhárata, reference to a tale in, ii, 17 note.

MAHOMET, see *Mohammed*.

MAI, Angelo, striking passage brought to light by, i, 15 note. Palimpsests of St. Paul published by him, iii, 56 note.

MAIMONIDES on the Cabala, i, 60 note.

MAIUMA, banquets so called, iii, 15.

MAJORINUS elected Bishop of Carthage, ii, 302. His successor, 304.

MALABAR, Christians settled on the coasts of, ii, 11.

MALACHI, the last of the prophets, i, 83, 117.

MALCHUS's ear struck off by Peter, and healed by Jesus, i, 308 and note.

MALLIUS, plays during the consulship of, iii, 137. Claudian's poem on the subject, 136 note, 137 note.

MAMACHI on architecture, art, &c. of the primitive Christians, iii, 311, 320, 335, 383, 385, notes.

MAMERTINUS on Julian's restoration of the Eleusinian temple, iii, 11 note u.

MAMMÆA, mother of Alexander Severus, character of, ii, 177.

MAMRE, celebrated tree of, ii, 349.

MAN not created, but found ready made by Satan, ii, 63 note.

MANES, festival of the, i, 20.

MANES, the heresiarch, system attempted by, i, 60, 61. See ii, 30.

MANI, attitude of Christians and Magians towards, ii, 254. Object aimed at, and sources drawn on, by him in the formation of his religious system, 259-261. His twelve apostles and his Erfang or Gospel, and his pictures in the latter, 261, 262. 264. His birth, race, and accomplishments, 263. Details of his system, 264-270. Artifice by which he was entrapped and murdered, 272. Propagation of his doctrines after his death, and persecution of his followers, 272-274. 274. 275; notes. Martyrs to his tenets, iii, 61. 168. Testamentary disability imposed on his followers, 101.

MANICHEISM, see ii, 297. 354. iii, 173. 457.

MANILIUS, verses from, i, 13 note.

MANNA, i, 225 note.

MANTINEA, games established in honour of Antinöus at, ii, 106.

MANUMISSION of slaves, ii, 395 note.

MANUSCRIPTS, destruction of, iii, 43.

MARANGONI 'dei cose Gentileschi,' iii, 135 note.

MARCELLA, Jerome's character of, iii, 229 note.

MARCELLINA, portraits placed in a Gnostic church by, iii, 389.

MARCELLINUS, see Ammianus Marcellinus.

MARCELLUS, charge founded on the plunder of the Sicilian temples by, i, 5 note.

MARCELLUS of Apamea, martyrdom of, iii, 67.

MARCELLUS, Christian soldier, occasion of the fame of, ii, 272.

MARCELLUS, Pope, degrading office forced by Maxentius on, ii, 383.

MARCIA, concubine of Commodus, humanizing influence of, ii, 154.

MARCION of Pontus, transformation and appropriation of the Gospels by, ii, 58. Opposed by Bardesanes, 74. Character and fundamental principle and details of his system, 77-79. His treatment of the Parable of the Prodigal Son, 80, note. In Rome: social rank of his followers, 84. Opposed by Tertullian, 161.

MARCOMANNIC war, aspect of Rome at the news of the, ii, 138. Compared with the second Punic war, 133.

MARCURIUS, defeat of the Circumcellions by, ii, 210.

MARCUS, Bishop of Jerusalem, settlement of the Christians under, i, 421.

MARCUS Aurelius Antoninus, i, 444. ii, 91. His character, 112. Causes of the hostility of his government to Christianity, 113, 125. Extent of his participation in the persecution of the Christians, 128. An alleged consulter of astrologers, 129. Surprised at the contempt of the Christians for death, 129, 130. His literary style, 129 note. An encourager of common informers, 130. His accession to empire, 131. Martyrdoms and persecutions under his rule, 134-140. 144-148. 154. Christians in his armies, 142. Providential storm (thundering legion) ascribed to his virtues, 143. Close of Rome's golden days with him, 149. Last effort of expiring Polytheism, 151.

MARCUS, see Mark.

MARDIA, battle of, ii, 315.

MARDONIUS, Julian's first instructor, character of the teachings of, ii, 455.

MAREOTIS, alleged profanation of a church in the, ii, 177. George of Cappadocia's trading speculation in the productions of the lake, 451.

MARIAMNE, Herod's wife, political consequences of the assassination of the sons of, i, 52. See 90. 166.

MARIS, Bishop of Chalcedon, a recusant at the Council of Nicæa, ii, 369. His retort to Julian's taunt upon his blindness, iii, 5.

MARK, Bishop of Arethusa, preserva-

MARK.

tion of the infant Julian by, ii, 405, 455; iii, 20. His murder and its cause, iii, 20.

MARK, Saint, Weisse's notion as to the composition of the Gospel of, i, 115. See 145 note.

MARK, see *Marcus*.

MARMARICA, see *Theonas*.

MARNAS, close of the temple of, iii, 66.

MARRIAGE, how regarded by the Jews, i, 94 note. The invention of Natan, ii, 61. Views of the Montanists, 161, 163. Disabilities imposed in certain cases by Constantine, 195, 197 note, 198. Contemptuous language of some of the fathers regarding it, iii, 196, 197, 198, notes. Restrictions and prohibitions as affecting the clergy and evil consequences thereof, 279-282, 283 note. Brought under ecclesiastical discipline, 288. Impediments recognised and insisted on by the church, 289. Made a sacrament, 291. View of the eastern church as to second marriages, 291 note. See ii, 17 note, iii, 113.

MARRIAGE-FEAST, miracle of Jesus, i, 153.

MARS, or GRADIVUS, divine ancestor of the Romans, i, 5, 18.

MARSH, bishop, his edition of Michaelis, i, 117.

MARTIN, Saint, of Tours, extirpator of idolatry in Gaul, iii, 78, 107. His protest against Priscillian's martyrdom, 168. Style and contents of his life by Sulpicius Severus, 151 note.

MARTIN, author, see *Saint Martin*.

MARTYRDOM, rage among the Circumcellions for, ii, 209. Of Christian soldiers under Julian, iii, 9. Of the missionaries in the Tyrol, 65 note. Martyr Festivals, 174. Not the subject of pictorial art till the dark ages, 196.

MARTYRS, law against selling the bodies of, iii, 135 note. Eminent Martyrs, see *Attalus*; *Babylas*;

MATTER.

Blandina; *Cyprian*; *Fabianus*; *Felicitas*; *Germanicus*; *James* "brother of the Lord;" *John the Baptist*; *Justin*; *Lucianus*; *Marcellus of Apamea*; *Maturus*; *Numidicus*; *Paul, Saint*; *Perpetua*; *Peter the Patriarch*; *Polycarp*; *Peter, Saint*; *Priscillian*; *Sebastian*; *Stephen, Saint*.

MARTYR-WORSHIP, iii, 122.

MARY, the Virgin, i, 92. Her betrothal to Joseph, 91. Gospel narrative of the Annunciation, 92. Incidents of her visit to Elisabeth, 96, 97. Wordsworth's sonnet to her, 96 note. Journey of herself and Joseph to Bethlehem, 98, 99. Their flight into Egypt and return to Galilee, 107, 108. Tutelary guardian of Constantinople, ii, 115 note. Early pictorial representations of her, iii, 193, 194. Tertullian's derogatory remark, 424 note.

MARY Magdalene, anointing Christ's feet, i, 117. At His sepulchre; vision seen by her, 145, 146, 147. His appearance to her, 148.

MARY the mother of James and Joses, at Christ's sepulchre, i, 145.

MARY and MARTHA, sisters of Lazarus, their devotion to Jesus, 263, 264, 279. Protest of Judas against Mary's anointment of Jesus, 280.

MASSACRE of Thessalonica, iii, 166.

MASSMANN'S edition of Ulphilas, iii, 56 note. Extract, 58 note.

MASSUET on the ubiquity of the saints, iii, 431 note.

MATHEMATICIANS expelled by Nero, ii, 4.

MATTER, Gnostic and oriental notions of, ii, 34, 56, 59, 64, 77, 80 note, 81 note, 360.

MATTER, M. on Menander's baptismal heresy, ii, 52 note. On Satan's relation to man, 63 note. On the interpretation of the mysterious word *Abraxas*, 66 note. On the notion of the beneficent serpent, 82 note.

INDEX.   485

MATTHEW.

MATTHEW, Saint, publican and afterwards Evangelist, called by Jesus, i, 197. 211. His Gospel, how formed, 115. Its language and character, 186, 187. Name the only Gospel received by the Judæo Christians of Pella, 422. And by the Carpocratians, ii, 80.
MATURUS, torture and martyrdom of, ii, 146, 148.
MAUNDRELL'S notice of Jacob's well, i, 168 *note.*
MAXENTIUS, human sacrifices by, i, 26 *note.* His assumption of the purple, ii, 224. His dissolute indulgences, 224. 281, 283. Why he identified himself with the cause of Polytheism, 225. 281. 283. Constantine's victory over him, 237. 244. 275. 289. 312. 322. 383 *add.* His deification of Galerius, 281. Devastates Carthage, 281. 297. Accusations against him relative to a Roman tumult, 282. His degradation of the pope, 283. Pagan enormities ascribed to him, 283. 284. African gratitude for the gift of his head, 290. See iii, 131.
MAXIMIA, result of a charge of magic by, iii, 16, 37.
MAXIMIAN (self-styled Herculius), ii, 211. His persecution of the Christians, 221. His reluctant abdication, 223, 224. Resumes the purple, 280. Anticipates the executioner's sentence, *ibid.* See 225. 276.
MAXIMILLA, apostle of Montanism, ii, 162.
MAXIMIN the Thracian, ii, 151. 173. 185. His treatment of the Christians, 186, 187.
MAXIMIN II.—Maximin Daia—disposition of, ii, 224. Why jealous of the edict in favour of the Christians, 328. Fruits of the humane zeal of his prefect, 229. His stratagem for overthrowing Christianity and reorganizing Paganism, 230-232. His persecution of the Christ-

MEDITERRANEAN.

ians and martyrdom of their bishops, 233, 276. His tyranny in gratifying his passions, 234, 235. His war with Armenia, 235, 236. Famine and pestilence in his dominions, 235-237. His apology for his persecutions, revenge on the Pagan priesthood, and pacificatory rescripts, 237, 238. 275. His miserable end, 278. 280. See 239. 279. 316. 340.
MAXIMIN, Valentinian's representative at Rome, antecedents of, iii, 16. His tortures of suspected persons, 17. His chief victims, 38.
MAXIMINIANS, an offshoot of the Donatists, doctrines asserted by the, ii, 310.
MAXIMINUS, Saint, annual festival in honour of, iii, 324 *note.*
MAXIMUS, Bishop of Turin, iii, 98 *note.*
MAXIMUS, the cynic, obtains and is driven from the bishopric of Constantinople, iii, 115, 116.
MAXIMUS the philosopher, commencement of Julian's acquaintance with, ii, 457. His alleged wonderful powers, 457, 458. Brings Julian into communication with the invisible world, 458, 459. His eminence in his own school, iii, 2. Summoned to Constantinople by Julian, *ibid.* His behaviour at court, 3. At Julian's death-bed, 27. Persecuted and tortured by Valentinian, 42. Tricks his wife into suicide, *ibid.* His fatal predictions and execution, 42, 43.
MAXIMUS, usurper in Gaul, result of Ambrose's missions to, iii, 155, 162. His reception of Ambrose's reproaches, 162, 163. Martyrdoms under him, 158.
MAXIMUS Tyrius, defence of Greek anthropomorphism by, i, 16 *note.*
MECCA, the Caaba of, ii, 149.
MEDITERRANEAN Sea, navigation, in Paul's time, of the, i, 45 z.

MEDIATOR.

MEDIATOR, universal notion of a, i, 70, 71.
MELETIUS, Bishop of Antioch, friend of Chrysostom, iii, 119.
MELETIUS, Bishop of Lyons, and his followers, ii, 160 *note*, 178.
MELITA, incident of Paul and the viper at, and its effect on the natives of, i, 452.
MEMNON, statue of, ii, 105 *note*.
MEMNONIUM, the, and the temples of Memphis, ii, 157.
MEMRA, or Divine Word, an appellation for the expected Messiah, i, 71, 80 *note*.
MENANDER, illustrative line from, i, 36. See i, 437, iii, 337.
MENANDER, doctrinal heir to Simon Magus, ii, 51, 52. His incongruous baptismal tenet, 52 *note*. His Gnostic scholars: Saturninus, 63; Basilides, 64.
MENSURIUS, Bishop of Carthage, accusations of the Donatists against, ii, 300. His death, *ibid*. His more rigorous successor, 301.
MENTAL derangement, a sign of Divine displeasure, ii, 280. Mosaical treatment of mental aberrations, 409.
MENU, see *Jonas*.
MERCURY extinguished in the Sibylline verses, ii, 130. Homage paid to him by Marcus Aurelius, 141, 143 *note*. His literary votaries, iii, 7.
MEROBAUDES, poet and general, statue raised to, iii, 95 *note*, 248. Style, and sample of his poem, 95 *note*.
MESOPOTAMIA, result of a rising of the Jews at, i, 60, ii, 99. Subject of conflicts between Rome and Persia, 249. Oppressions of the Jews, 254. Spread of monastic establishments, iii, 105.
MESSIAH, period of the general expectation of the, i, 54, 55. Calamities expected to herald his coming, *ibid note*, 139. Nature of the belief

MILAN.

regarding Him; Old Testament references to Him, 55, 56. Opinions of modern scholars, 56 *note*. Traditionary notions and their sources, 56, 57. Authorities, inspired and profane, 57 *note*. Application of the term "Light of the World" to Him, 67, 94. Identified with "the Word," 72. Association of His coming with the final resurrection, 74, 349. Expectations of the Palestinian Jews regarding Him, 75, 76, 284. Notions of the Alexandrian Jews: picture drawn by Philo, 77-79. Various ideas of the Messianic attributes, 80, 81. Illustrative citations, 80 *note*. Beliefs of the people and apprehensions of their rulers, 81, 82. Probable feelings excited by the birth of an infant Messiah, 84. Not expected by the Jews to be born of a virgin, 94 *note*. John the Baptist announces His coming and its purpose, 138-140. Notion of the double Messiah, 150 *note*. Samaritan notions and expectations regarding Him, 170-173. Blessings prophesied as his accompaniments, 215 *note*. Exclusive notions still entertained after the Resurrection, 377, 378. Merging of the term Messiah into that of Redeemer of the World, 380. Belief in His second coming, 418, 419. See *Jesus*.
MICHAEL, the archangel, signification of the name, i, 68 *note*. Daniel's visionary representation of him, 69.
MICHAELIS, Bishop Marsh's edition of, i, 117. On the phenomena accompanying the death of Jesus, 137 *note*. On the violence of the Jews in Stephen's case, 166 *note*. On the Nicolaitans, ii, 55 *note*.
MIHRAN, King of Iberia, occasion of the conversion of, ii, 401, 404.
MILAN, effect of the edict of, ii, 290 *note*, 312, 315. Ancient court-capital of the western empire, iii 1; iii, 102. Burial-place " ad Inno-

MILETUS.

antes," iii, 16 note. Ambrosian service in its church, 162. 405. See ii, 207. 244. See also Councils.

MILETUS, Paul at, i, 451. 460. Its oracle of Apollo, ii, 212. 216.

MILITARY Christianity, origin of, ii, 288. iii, 409.

MILL, James, point in Indian history slurred over by, i, 16 note.

MILLENNIUM, a fable "of Jewish dotage," i, 75 note. Periods of its expected coming, 419. Rabbinical expectations regarding it, 419 note. Allusions to it in apocryphal writings, ii, 118, 118 note. See i, 456. ii, 57 note.

MILLENNIUM of Rome, ii, 186.

HILLIN on the plain chant, iii, 405 note.

MILMAN's writings, quotations from, or references to: Bampton Lectures, i, 428-430 notes, 380 note. History of the Jews, i, 58, 60, 104, 388, notes. History of Latin Christianity, ii, 169 note: iii, 58, 96, 222, 237, 266, 294, 347, 368, 391, 424, 426, notes. Sanskrit translations, ii, 37 note.

MILTON, probable source of a paradisiacal picture of, i, 79. Belief embodied in his hymn on the Nativity, 103. His "limitary cherub," ii, 71.

MILVIAN Bridge, Battle of, ii, 289.

MIMES and PANTOMIMES of the Romans, iii, 118-142.

MIND, oriental and Gnostic notions of the, ii, 34. 65. 70, 71, 72. 260. Its imaginary state, iii, 413. See Mental derangement.

MINERVA and her Palladium, veneration for, ii, 174. The Lyndus statue carried to Constantinople, 335. Effect of her apparition on Alaric, iii, 78 note.

MINERVINA, Constantine's first wife, ii, 322.

MINUCIUS Felix, illustrative passages from, ii, 181. iii, 220 note. 388

MONACHISM.

note. High literary character of his "Octavius," 363 note.

MINUCIUS Fundanus, Hadrian's instructions to, concerning the Christians, ii, 107.

MIRACLES, considerations on, iii, 23. 24 notes. Augustine's argument on their continuance, 160 note.

MIRACLES of our Lord: Cana marriage feast, i, 152. The sick youth at Capernaum, 173. Healing of lepers and sick men, 195, 196. 201. The withered hand, 207. Centurion's servant, 212. Raising the widow's son, 213. Jairus's daughter, 222. Feeding the multitude, 224. Deaf and dumb restored, 236. Blind men healed, 250-252. 268. Raising of Lazarus, 263.

MISCHNA of the Jews, ii, 17.

MISOPOGON, the, Julian's apology for his beard, iii, 11, 13, 14, notes. Its style, 25.

MISSON, the traveller, erroneous inferences of, iii, 384 note.

MITHRA, human sacrifices offered to, i, 26 note. iii, 17. The mysteries carried into the Roman provinces, i, 40. His dwelling-place, ii, 260. See ii, 96. 165. 267. 278.

MIXES, consort of Buthios in the Valentinian system, ii, 70.

MOBEDS of Magianism, ii, 251.

MODESTUS's threats to, and surprise at the intrepid reply of Basil, ii, 45. 46.

MOHAMMED and Mohammedanism: notions borrowed from the Jews, i, 65 note. Sanctity of Abraham in the Koran, ii, 178. The cave of Hira, 263. Hatred for Manicheism, 271. Progress of Mohammedanism, 310. iii, 170. His coffin, iii, 75 note. See ii, 31. 36. 259. 349.

MOLOCH, worship of, i, 61. Brutal human sacrifices under Elagabalus, ii, 176.

MONACHISM and monastic institutions, ii, 44. Their growth under Basil,

MONAD.

iii, 108, 109. Upheld by Chrysostom, 131, 136. Jerome their great promoter, 190, 191. Their origin, 195, 196. Causes which tended to their promotion, 198-201. Inherent dangers of the system, 211. Its general effects on affairs religious and political, 214-216. Some of its advantages, 216-218. Its effects on the maintenance of Christianity, on the clergy, and in the promotion, 218-224. See *Cœnobitism, Monks*.

MONAD, the; the first father, and his various names and attributes in the Gnostic systems, ii, 69. 80, 81. 83 *note*.

MONARCHIANISM in the church, ii, 156 *note*.

MONICA, mother of St Augustine, iii, 179. Her distress at his heretical leanings, 181.

MONKS of Egypt, ancestry of the, ii, 43. Pressed into military service, iii, 47 *note*. Their activity in the destruction of pagan idols and temples, 61, 64. Edicts and popular outrages against them, 111. Their numbers, 209. See *Cœnobitium. Monachism*.

MONTANISM the last important modification of Christianity during the second century, ii, 86, 87. Point of union between it and African Christianity, 161. Its extra-Gnostic austerity and notions of marriage, 161, 162. Nature of Montanist enthusiasm, 162, 163. Heresy charged on Montanus, 163. Perpetua animated by its spirit, 167.

MONTFAUCON, Illustrative references to, ii, 400 *note*; iii, 243, 275. 316. 336. 317. 393, 417, *notes*.

MOON-WORSHIP, i, 61. ii, 112.

MOORS, Spain devastated by the, ii, 113. Their incursions, 159.

MORALITY, consequences of the divorce of Christianity from, iii, 409.

MORIAH, Mount, expected appearance of the Messiah in the temple on,

MYSTERIES.

i, 76. Its Samaritan rival, 168. Frustration of Julian's attempt to rebuild the temple, iii, 21-23.

MOSAIC institutes and laws: on marriage, i, 29 *note*. Platonism grafted thereon, ii, 41. Laws on the relations of the sexes adopted by the Christian church, ii, 196. iii, 289. See i, 415. 418. 420. 447. *See Law*.

MOSAIC theocracy, great principle of the, i, 189, 190, 339.

MOSES and the Messiah, i, 80 *note*. See ii, 17. 41. 178. 106.

MOSHEIM, quotations from, and references to, i, 67, 77. 101. 357, *notes*. ii, 4. 16, 55, 63. 81, *notes*. iii, 263. 361 *notes*.

MOUNT of Olives and Mount Olivet, i, 281. 351. 400. ii, 347.

MUCIUS the Abbot, inhuman sacrificers of, iii, 210, 211, *notes*.

MÜLLER, Max, views supported by the language-studies of, i, 9 *note*. 14 *note*.

MÜLLER 'De Genio, &c. Ævi Theodosiani,' and other works; citations from, and references to, iii, 243. 244, 247. 326, 331, 334, 338, 339, 340. 361, *notes*.

MUMMIUS, destroyer of Corinth, i, 396 *note*. 441 *note*.

MUNTER on the forms of the cross, and other topics connected with early Christian art, iii, 381, 383. 384. 389, 192. 196, 198, *notes*.

MURSA, battle of, consequences of the, ii, 431.

MUSES, the, ii, 115. iii, 7.

MUSIC in the church, Ambrose's care for, iii, 163. Its growth, 401-405.

MUSONICS silenced by Julian, iii, 9.

MYLITTA, Syrian deity, principle of the worship of, i, 61.

MYSTERIES, the last hope of the old religions, i, 31. Sources of their influence: their nature and objects, 31, 32. See *Eleusis. Magic*.

MYTHOLOGY.

MYTHOLOGY, growth of, i, 14. See *Polytheism.*

NAASSENES, worshippers of the Serpent, principle of their worship, ii, 11 *note.*

NAHARDEA, schools of learning in, ii, 249.

NAHASH, strange derivation of *vade* from, 83 *note.*

NAIN, raising of the widow's son at, i, 213.

NARTHEX, class of worshippers limited to the, ii, 144. iii, 311.

NATHANAEL, or Bartholomew, the Apostle, removal by Jesus of the doubts of, i, 151. His character and social position, 151. 211. His end unrecorded, 387.

NATIONS self-raised from savage life, theories regarding, i, 9 *note.*

NATURAL Philosophy, causes tending to the discouragement of, iii, 416, 417. Contempt of the fathers for its study, 417 *note.*

NATURE personified in the *Divna Multinamma*, ii, 51 *note.*

NATURE-WORSHIP, its character and exponents, i, 12, 13. Its form in Persia, 15. Its development in Greece, 16. Rites under which it had survived, 31. What it taught, 32. Phases of the doctrine of the immortality of the soul under it, 45. Form of it, set up by Elagabalus, ii, 173. Representative of it semi-deified by Alexander Severus, 178. Temples in the east, 248. Form adhered to by Tiridates, 256, 257.

NAUDET'S essay on Julian's educational system, iii, 6 *note.*

NAVE of the church, origin of the word, ii, 343.

NAZARENES, Neander's chapter on the, ii, 53 *note.*

NAZARETH, proverbial disrepute of, i, 91. 155. Reception and treatment of Jesus by its people, 174-177.

NEANDER, i, 11 *note.* 36 *notes.* On

NEUMAN.

Christ's birth, 103 *note.* Character of his great work, 114. Theory supported by him, ii, 16 *note.* On Gnosticism, 44 *note.* His low estimate of Simon Magus, 51 *note.* His chapter on the Ebionites, 53 *note.* His view of Marcion, 79 *note.* His Joannes Chrysostomus, iii, 18 *note.*

NEAPOLIS, Paul's first European landing-place, i, 395.

NEBUCHADNEZZAR, i, 63 *note* d. Holy things concealed on his destruction of the Temple, 149.

NECESSITY, Stoic doctrine of, i, 440.

NECROMANTIC arts, an imperial dabbler in, iii, 36. See *Divination. Magic.*

NECTARIUS, Bishop of Constantinople, sumptuous style of, iii, 110, 131.

NEHEMIAH, re-migration of the Jews under, i, 58.

NEPTUNE, temple of, at Corinth, i, 442 *note.*

NERGAL-SHAREZER, the archimagus, i, 63 *note.*

NERO degrades Pallas, and subsequently poisons him, i, 404 *note.* Burning of Rome and persecution of the Christians, 454- 458 *note.* 464 *note.* ii, 4, 8. His expected reappearance as antichrist, i, 458 *note.* ii, 123 *note,* 124. His visit to Corinth and representative at Rome, i, 461, 462. 465 (see *Rome*). State of Christianity during his reign, ii, 4, 5. Influence of a Jewish player over him, i, 458 *note.* ii, 96, 97. The matricide, 173. His theatrical exhibitions, 152. Altered destination of the materials of his circus, 295. See ii, 90. 104. 117. 323, 333 note d, 339.

NERVA, first act of the reign of, ii, 12. A supplementary Cæsar, 122.

NESTORIAN Christianity, i, 95 *note.* ii, 31. Effect of persecution, 353. See ii, 31 *note.* iii, 103.

NEUMAN'S Vartan, curious sentence in, i, 63 *note.*

490　　　　　　　INDEX.

NEW.

NEW Testament, peculiarity of, accepted by Marcion, ii, 77, 78. Its original Greek, ii, 152. See *Evangelists. Gospels.*

NICÆA, Council of, ii, 317 *note*. Occasion of its being called, 120, 127, 150. 164. The meeting, 165. Number of church dignitaries present, 166. Part taken by Constantine, 167. Duration and result of the sittings, 168. Its canon relative to *Mulieres subintroductæ*, iii, 283 *note*. The Easter question, 417 *note*. See iii, 55, 268 *note*, 277.

NICENE Creed, approach of Mani's system to the, ii, 251. 269. Word in the original which gave rise to centuries of hostility, 168, 169. Sense in which Eusebius of Cæsarea explained it, 170. Arius's contumacy and subsequent acceptance of it, 170, 181. Explanation and recall of the recusant bishops, 172, 173. See *Trinitarian Controversy.*

NICETAS, treatment of Polycarp by, ii, 137.

NICODEMUS'S visit to Jesus, and its result, i, 161-164. 199. His appeal to the Sanhedrin in His behalf, 246. Accusation against him, *ibid.*

NICODEMUS, Gospel of, its source, iii, 352.

NICOLAITANS, opponents of St John, ii, 55. Their origin, 55 *note.*

NICOLAS, story told of, and derivation of the name, ii, 55 *note.*

NICOMEDIA, ii, 207. Selected for his court by Diocletian, 208, 243. Importance of its bishops and its church, 210. First result of the edict of persecution, 217. Fate of the Christian who tore down the edict, 218, 219. Mysterious burning of the palace, and recriminations concerning it, 229. Wholesale cruelties and martyrdoms, 220, 221. Reception of Maximin, 333. Its metropolitan deposed, iii, 364. See ii, 222, 244. iii, 41.

ODIN.

NICOPOLIS visited by Saint Paul, i, 460.

NIEBUHR, theory of savage life controverted by, i, 9 *note*. His discovery of the poems of Merobaudes, iii, 95 *note*. See ii, 400 *note.*

NIGER, a competitor of Severus, refusal of the Christians to aid the cause of, ii, 146. 155, 156.

NILE, the, ii, 41, 121. 164. Identity of Serapis with the river, iii, 68, 75. Place of curiosity for the Nilometer, 75.

NINO, effect on the Iberians of the holy life of, ii, 403. Occasion of her conversion of their queen, *ibid*. Cross erected by her, and miracles attributed to her prayers, 404.

NITRIA, consequences of Chrysostom's protection of the fugitive monks of, iii, 209. Cœnobitic population of its desert, 209.

NORTES, heresy of, and epithet given to his followers, ii, 156.

NOLA, early paintings in the church of, iii, 399, 400.

NOVATIANUS and the Novatian heresy, ii, 289 *note*. iii, 267 *note*,

NUBIA, subject of a monumental inscription found in, ii, 400 *note*. Conversion of its tribes by Frumentius, 402.

NUMA, instance of wisdom in, i, 38. Numa the Second, ii, 126.

NUMERIAN'S murder, Diocletian's exculpatory appeal relative to, ii, 212.

NUMIDIA, influence of the Donatists in, ii, 310.

NUMIDICUS and his wife, martyrdom of, iii, 278.

NUNC DIMITTIS, early sung in the church, iii, 354, 403.

OCTAVIUS, human sacrifice ascribed to, i, 26 *note*. See *Minucius Felix.*

ODIN, character of the heaven of, i, 44 *note.*

INDEX. 491

ŒCUMENICAL.

ŒCUMENICAL council, the first, iii, 268 *note.*

ŒDIPODEAN weddings, ii, 146.

OGDOADS of Bardesanes, ii, 75.

OLD Testament, proscribed by the Gnostics, ii, 59, 78. The work of inferior angels, 80. Its God an evil spirit, 260. Its spirit beginning to dominate over the Gospel, 296. Its authority cited as a justification for massacre, 706.

OLIVES, see *Mount of Olives.*

OLYBII, Christianity embraced by the, iii, 92.

OLYBICS, Prefect of Rome, iii, 36.

OLYBRIUS, head of Christ on the sarcophagus of, iii, 391.

OLYMPIA, iii, 78.

OLYMPIAS praised for her incurable diseases, iii, 147 *note.*

OLYMPIC games, III, 336.

OLYMPUS concentrated into one supreme ruler, ii, 334.

OLYMPUS, the philosopher, excites an insurrection for the preservation of Paganism, iii, 71, 72. His prudent flight, 72.

ONAGER, the "wild ass," confession of, ii, 420.

ONESIPHORUS, Paul befriended by, i, 450.

OPHITES, or serpent-worshippers, religious system of the, ii, 81, 82. Object of Mosheim's dissertation, 81 *note.* Speculations on this and cognate systems, 82, 83 *notes.*

OPTATUS, bishop, why blamed with regard to some martyrs, ii, 170. Value of his works as a record of the Donatist controversy, 290 *note.* References to and citations from same, 301, 302, 306, 308, 309 *notes.*

OPTATUS, Pagan prefect, Chrysostom's enemy, iii, 137, 348.

ORACLES, human sacrifices commanded by, i, 26 *note.* Sibylline oracles, ii, 118, 120. Of Apollo, see *Apollo.* Answer to Maxentius, ii,

ORIGEN.

183. Touching Byzantium, 335 *note.* Delphi and Dodona, iii, 35.

ORATIONS of the Fathers, their place in Christian literature, iii, 369.

ORATORY, decay in Rome of, iii, 165. Its revival and power in the pulpit, 166-169.

ORO1ASTS of Phrygia, i, 453. Nature of the Orgiasm, ii, 167.

ORIENTALISM, influence on Christianity of, ii, 30, 31. Community of principles and tendency of ideas expressed by the term, 32. Its general character, 33. Its elementary principle and primary tenet, 34. Asceticism and celibacy, 35-37. Its progress in western Asia, and union with Christianity, 41-44. Scene of their first collision, 53, 54. Result of their combination and ultimate reaction, 57, 86. Mani's borrowings from it, 359. See *Corinthus, Gnosticism. Mani. Simon Magus.*

ORIGEN, illustrative passage from, i, 72 *note.* His answer to a Jewish invention, 108 *note.* Phlegonic passage discarded by him, 335 *note.* Writings wrongly ascribed to him, ii, 44 *note.* His sarcastic interpretation of 'Ebion,' 51 *note.* How prevented from sharing his father's martyrdom, 158 *note.* Sole labourer left in a persecuted region, 159. De Broglie's contrast between him and Tertullian, 164 *note.* An Imperial Roman lady exhorted by him, 177. His controversy with Celsus, 182. iii, 279 *note.* 362, 386. 387 *note.* 388 *note.* Torments inflicted on him, ii, 189. Opponent of his Platonic mode of arguing, 443 *note.* His notion of the Deity anathematised, iii, 104. Experiments of his followers upon the Gospels, 318. Charge against Bishop Demetrius relative to him, 367 *note.* On the Saviour's personal aspect, 386. See i, 423. iii, 420 *note.*

492 INDEX.

ORLEANS.

ORLEANS, amusements condemned by the Council of, iii, 328.
ORMUZD, Oromazd, or Auramazd, the good principle of the Persian system, i, 72 *note*. 75. 105. Enthraph's revelation from him, ii, 251. Antagonism between his followers and those of Ahriman, 251. Armenian form of worship at his altars, 257. His relationship to the primal man, 265. See *Aramazd*.
OROSIUS, citations from, iii, 74 *note*. 184 *note*.
ORPHEUS deified by Alexander Severus, ii, 177. See iii, 3.
OSIRIS and Isis—Sun and Earth—dualism of, i, 11, 13. See *Isis*.
OSIUS, Bishop of Cordova, complaint against, ii, 305. See *Hosius*.
OSTROGOTHS, iii, 57. See *Goths*.
OUM, the deity of the Indians, virtue of the name of, i, 447 *note*.
OVID'S Fasti, and the religion of the Romans, 18 *note*. His description of Majestas, 10 *note*. On the moral effect of ablutions, 135. Personal character of his poetry, iii, 111.

PACHOMIUS, founder of cœnobitic institutions in Egypt, iii, 208. Number of monks under him, *ibid note*.
PÆDERASTY, Christian dealing with the crime of, ii, 398.
PAGANISM, conciliatory attitude of the Gnostics towards, ii, 85. Call on the Pagans by the best Pagan emperor, 110, 111. Condemned by its own prophets, 120-124. A time of triumph, 159. Effect of Elagabalus's vagaries upon it, 176. Change in its tone, 183. New philosophic Paganism, 184-185, 211, 212, 291. Its approaching final combat with Christianity, 204. Maximin's measures for its reorganization, their failure, and his revenge, 231, 232. 238. Blessings ascribed to its gods, 244. Uniform conduct of Roman

PAGAN.

prefects with regard to it, 277. Maxentius's dealings with it, 281-284. Battle which decided its fate, 289. 312. View taken by its followers of a Christian emperor's crimes, 325, 326 *note*, 327, 328. Consideration shown to it and its deities in the founding of Constantinople, 333-337. 340. Extent of interference at that time with its worship, and of subsequent laws for its suppression, 345. 385-389. 391. Miscalculations of Pagans relative to Christian schisms, 359. Why they would hallow Sunday, 393. Their deification of the first Christian emperor, 399. Julian's declaration in its favour; scheme for its re-establishment, and persecutions towards that end, 449. 452. 453, 461. 464-474; iii, 5. 9-11. 12-16. 20. 22. 24. 26. Effect of Julian's premature death, 10, 11. Homage of its historian to Valentinian's toleration, 12. His cruel treatment of its practisers of divination and magic, 33-39. The like by Valens, 40-42. Dragging out its existence, 44. Result of Theodosius's determination to extirpate it, 61, 62. 66. 67. 70-77. 90-92. Rome its last refuge, 79. Its last deified follower, 81. Symmachus's appeal for its preservation, 86, 87. A gleam of hope, 89. Suppressive edict of Honorius, 94. Gothic consummation of its ruin, 96-98. See ii, 90, 93, 112, 114, 117, 143, 153, 163, 177, 182, 187, 201, 209, 220, 239, 247, 258, 260. 278, 285, 297, 310, 319; iii, 60, 338. 406. See also *Heathenism. Pagan temples. Polytheism*.

PAGAN sculpture, iii, 377-379. See *Greece*.

PAGAN temples in Byzantium, ii, 332. Why generally unsuitable for Christian worship, 340-342. Why suppressed in Syria, 345; iii, 66. Ruins at Gerasa, Petra, and

INDEX. 493

Baalbec, ii, 346. Shut up by Constantine, 185. Respect ordered to be paid to them, ii, 472. iii, 11. Alienation of their revenues, iii, 65, 84. Temples in Antioch, ibid. Libanius's oration "For the Temples," 66. Consecration of some to Christian worship, 66, 67. 97 note. Their destruction under Theodosius, 73-77. Number then in Rome, 79.

PAGI's chronology: his date of Ignatius's martyrdom, ii, 92 note. A probable conjecture of his, 98 note. On the 'Disciplina Arcani,' iii, 118 note.

PAINTING enlisted into Christian service, iii, 379. Gnostic paintings, 389, 390. Christian paintings: of the Saviour, 391. Of the Father, 392. Of the Virgin, 393, 394. Of the apostles, 395, 396. Late date of representations of martyrdoms, 396. The Nola paintings, 399, 400. Mani's paintings, ii, 262.

PALATINE Hill, Sun-temple erected by Elagabalus on the, ii, 174, 176.

PALATINI interdicted from exhibiting as gladiators, iii, 345.

PALESTINE, i, 57, 58. Apprehended march of the Babylonian Jews upon, 59. Controversy relative to Augustus's census of its people, 99. 100. Favourable site for a new religion, ii, 31, 32. Herodian innovation resisted by its people, 96. Permissive existence of Judaism under Hadrian, 249. Taken possession of by the Christians, 345, 346. Erection of churches on the holy sites, 347-349. Last abiding place of the Ebionites, 155. See ii, 30. 36. 37. 52. 100. See *Holy Land*.

PALEY'S explanation of a chronological difficulty, i, 99 note. See 217 note.

PALILIA, Italian rural rites, i, 18 note.

PALLADIUM, the, ii. 122, 174. Transported to Constantinople, 337.

PALLADIUS, pagan prefect, Christian office delegated to, iii, 44.

PALLADIUS, life of Chrysostom by, iii, 118 note.

PALLAS, Felix's brother, patronised and subsequently poisoned by Nero, i, 404 note.

PALMYRA, Paul of Samosata's religious project for, ii, 200. See iii, 66. Its Queen, see *Zenobia*.

PAMMACHIUS, why offended by Jerome, iii, 215.

PAN's statue transported to Constantinople, ii, 335.

PANTHEISM of India, i, 63; ii, 31. Pantheistic Deity. See *Serapis*.

PANTHEON of Rome, constituents of the, i, 6. Date of its dedication to the Virgin, iii, 27. Julian's Pantheon, ii, 465.

PANTOMIMES, Theodoric a supporter of, iii, 333 note. See *Mimes*.

PAPAL authority and pontifical dominion, growth at Rome of, ii, 330, 331, 390, 440, 441. See *Pontiff*.

PAPANOTICB, marriage eulogised in a single word by, iii, 277.

PAPHOS, i, 388. Rites for which it was renowned, 389, 394 note.

PAPIA Poppaean law against celibacy, ii, 199.

PARABLES of Jesus: the leaven and the grain of mustard, i, 181 note. The good Samaritan, 259 note, 273. The lord of the vineyard, and the marriage-feast, 287.

PARACLETE, Gnostic attributes of the, ii, 70. 77. In Montanism, 163. In Mani's system, 261.

PARADISE of Mohammed, i, 190.

PARTHENON, the; period up to which it was entire, iii, 78 note.

PARTHIA, ii, 31. 99. Pestilence brought thence by the imperial army, 128, 129. 132, 133. Religion of its natives: influence of the Magian priests, 247, 248. Apostolic labours of St Thomas and St Peter,

PASCHAL.

348. Tolerance of its kings, 253 *note*. See 252, 254.
PASCHAL, pope, legend of the removal of a saint's remains by, ii, 103 *note*.
PASIPHILUS, fortitude under torture of, iii, 42.
PASSOVER, the, and periodical assemblage of the Jews thereat, 154, 155, 198 *note*. Josephus's calculation of their numbers, 267. Customary hospitalities during the festival, 304 *note*. Custom relative to the release of criminals, 325. See 242.
PATMOS, sojourn and composition by St. John of the Revelations at, ii, 14.
PATRIARCHS of Holy Writ, beatitude of the, i, 297.
PATRIARCHS of the East, ecclesiastical powers claimed by the, iii, 264.
PATRICIUS of Lydia, unpardonable offence charged on, iii, 41.
PATRIPASSIANS, heresy of the, ii, 356.
PAUL, the fanatic chief, St. Paul confounded with, i, 400.
PAUL, Saint, the apostle, and his teacher, i, 361, 368. His origin, mental qualifications, and persecuting career as Saul of Tarsus, 368, 369. Revelation of his conversion to Ananias, 370. Reluctance of the Christians to admit him among them, 370, 371, 372. Obscurity of his early career as a Christian, 371. His sojourn in Arabia and escape from his Jewish persecutors there, 371, 372. Peculiar service for which he was qualified: new conspiracy against him, 373. Period of the arrival of himself and Barnabas at Jerusalem, 375. Fact in Christianity indicated by their enrolment, in the apostolic body, 381, 386. Occasion of his protection from the Jews by the Roman guards, 385. Summoned by Barnabas to Antioch, *ibid*. Point of time from which his apostolic predominance dates, 386. Reception of himself and Barnabas in Cyprus, 389, 472.

PAUL.

Their expulsion from Antioch in Pisidia, and ill treatment at Lystra, 390, 391, 431, 432. Himself and Barnabas at the Council of Jerusalem, 392. His Second Journey, 394. Separates from Barnabas and extends his journey into Europe, 395. His trade, 397 and *note* b. His proselytising labours at Corinth, 397, 441-444. Locality of the composition of his epistle to the Thessalonians, 397 *note* c. His Third Journey: circuit taken, 398. His motive in visiting Jerusalem: outrage inflicted on him there, 399. Error regarding him entertained by Lysias, 400. His harangue to the Jewish multitude: privilege which saved him from the scourge, 400, 401. Cited before the Sanhedrin, 401. Insult put upon him: his indignant retort upon the high priest, 402. Designs against his life, 403-405. His successful defence before Felix, and imprisonment in Cesarea, 403, 404. Before Festus and Agrippa: impression made by him upon the latter, 405. His departure for Rome, 406. Judaic exclusiveness against which his exertions were directed, 414. Scope of his epistles to the Galatians and to the Romans, 415-417. Inference deducible from his journey to Spain, 417 *note*. Judæo-Christian sect by whom his writings were rejected, 422. Himself and Barnabas regarded as heathen deities, 432. His reception in Phrygia, Galatia, and Macedonia, 432, 433. At Philippi; his imprisonment and its supernatural accompaniments, 433-435. His reception at Athens and oration to its citizens, 436-441. Forged correspondence between himself and Seneca, 444 *note*. His journey to Ephesus and length of stay there, 444-446. His miracles and Jewish ascription of their cause, 447. Effect of his teachings on the Jewish associates and Ephesian shrine-makers,

INDEX. 495

PAUL.

448-450. His subsequent course and last interview with his Ephesian brethren, 450, 451. Incident of the viper on his hand in Melita, 452. His arrival in Rome and proceedings there, 452, 483. Break-off of the Scripture record of his acts, 454 note. Probability of his having visited Spain, 458, 459. Question of his visit to Britain, ibid note. Evidences of the extent of his journeyings and grandeur of their results, 460, 461. Period assigned as that of his martyrdom, 461. His own presentiments of his approaching end, ibid. Coincidence of fact and tradition as to his martyrdom, 462. Site and manner of his death, 465. Embellishments of the story, 466. Disputed questions regarding his epistles, imprisonments in Rome, date of his death, &c., 467-472. Length of his residence at Corinth and Ephesus, II, 21 note. Extent of the recognition of his authority, 26. His alleged marriage, 37 note. Difference between his spirit and that of later martyrs, 103, 193 note. Disregard of his warning, 233. Maci's notion of his writings, 261. Early portraits of him, III, 395, 396.

PAUL of Samosata, Bishop of Antioch, character and religious project of, II, 200. His pride, magnificence, and church extravagances, 201. His defiance of the Synod and ultimate degradation, 202. Effect of his musical innovations, III, 403. See II, 368 note. III, 267, 282 note.

PAUL, a candidate for the see of Constantinople, Eusebius's death-bed recommendation of, II, 408. Bloody result of an attempt to force him from his church, 415. His expulsion and retirement, 415, 416. Acquitted of the charges against him, 417. Again expelled and ill-treated: suspicions as to his death, 422.

PAUL and Macurius, defeat of the Circumcellions by, II, 310.

PERATÆ.

PAULA, Jerome's favorite, sample of a letter of, III, 192 note. Her uncharitable charity, 231. Jerome's eulogium on her, 217 note.

PAULINUS, biographer of Ambrose, III, 151 note, 156 note.

PAULINUS, Bishop of Antioch, Aetius an attaché of, I, 443.

PAULINUS, the consul, II, 387 note.

PAULINUS, Saint, of Nola. Illustrative citations from poems of, III, 128 note, 198 note, 403 note. His verses on the paintings in his church, 399, 400, notes. His poetic celebration of the nativity of St Felix, 422 note. Incendiary miracle ascribed by him to St Felix, 423 note.

PAUSANIAS, points of belief disclaimed by, I, 38, 39.

PEARSON on St Paul's presence in Rome, I, 461 note. References to his work on the Creed, I, 150 note. III, 388 note.

PEDO, consul, killed by an earthquake, II, 102.

PEEL, late Sir Robert, on human sacrifices under the Romans, I, 27 note.

PELAGIANISM, III, 103, 173, 173 note, 176. Character and doctrines of Pelagius, 176, 177, notes.

PELLA, refuge of the forewarned Christians at, I, 409, 421.

PENANCE of Theodosius, Christian principle asserted in the, III, 167. Penitential discipline of the church, 292-295. Places in the church assigned to the various classes of penitents, 311, 312.

PENATES, guardians of the pagan's hearth, I, 426. II, 333.

PENITENTIAL discipline, see Penance.

PENTECOST, I, 236, 242, 350, 351. Miracle of fiery tongues, 353-355. Paul's appearance at the feast, 398.

PERATÆ, predominant feature of the doctrines of the, II, 83 note.

INDEX

PERDITION.

PERDITION, Augustinian notion of, iii, 175.

PERPETUA, Vivia, martyrdom of, ii, 165, 166-170, 171, 172.

PERSECUTION, its effect on the African Christians, ii, 399. Persecutions of the Christians under the Roman emperors, see *Aurelian. Decius. Diocletian. Domitian. Galerius. Julian. Marcus Aurelius. Maximian. Maximin. Nero. Trajan. Valerian.* See also *Christianity. Martyrdom.*

PERSIA, form of nature-worship in, i, 14. Analogy between its theism and that of the Jews, 21. Comparative purity thereof, 62. The good principle of its system, 73 *note.* Its idea of a Messiah, 75 *note.* Its dualistic system, ii, 33; 252. Sanctity of fire, 35. Treatment of Valerian by its rabble, 199. Revival of Zoroastrianism, 247. Object of Ardeschir's ambition, 251. Barrier presented by it to Christianity, 251. Priestly supporters of its kingly power, 253, 254. Emblematic feature of its religion, 262. Its "execrable usages and foolish laws," 273. Julian's expedition and its result, iii, 22, 26, 28. See ii, 279, 400. See *Magianism. Orientalism. Zoroastrianism.*

PESTILENCES and Plagues: Under Verus, ii, 132, 133. At Carthage, 195; iii, 120 *note.* Under Maximin, ii, 235, 236. In Armenia, 257.

PETER, Saint, or Simon Peter, the apostle: his epistle and the question of the identity of Babylon and Rome, i, 60 *note.* His origin, 178. His awe in the presence of Jesus, *ibid.* Why called Cephas, 210. Occasion of his declared pre-eminence among the Apostles, 238. His master's prediction of his denial of him, 304. Jesus's restraint of his indignation, 307. Admitted to the trial of Jesus, 309. His triple denial of his master and remorse therefor, 112, 113. Invested by Jesus with

PHARISEES.

the charge of his church, 330. His first proclamation of Christ crucified and exalted, 355, 356. Tone and substance of his second speech, 358. His language before the Sanhedrin, 361. Cast into prison and supernaturally liberated, 375. Effect of his vision annulling the distinction of meats, 381, 382. His later teachings and sphere of action, 387, 414. Question of his visit to, and foundation of the Church of Rome, 416 *note.* His alleged martyrdom, 457. Predominance accorded to him in Rome, 462. Sphere and share of Christianizing labours assigned to him, 462, 463. The pro and con of his alleged settlement at Rome, 463, 464 *notes.* Overtures of Simon Magus to him, and his refusal, ii, 45, 46, 47. Records of their orations, 45 *note,* 51 *note.* Secret traditions ascribed to him, 64. His residence in Babylonia, 248. Church dedicated to him at Rome, 291. Claim of apostolic descent from him, iii, 264. Assertions as to his primacy, 264 *note a,* 265 *note a.* Early portraits of him, 295, 296. See i, 386, 430. ii, 64, 308. iii, 100.

PETER, Patriarch of Alexandria, put to death, ii, 333. See iii, 100, 115.

PETRA, ruins of Pagan temples at, ii, 146. iii, 66.

PETRINE, or ultra-Judaic party, ii, 26.

PETRONIUS, the prefect, why apprehensive of a Jewish outbreak, i, 59. Effect of his humane delays, 174.

PHARISEES, oath of allegiance refused by, i, 100, 112. Their conflicts with the Sadducees, 132. Questions to John flamed by them, 148. Region in which they predominated, 182, 183. Conclusive argument with them against the claims of Jesus, 191. They commence hostilities against him, 206. Accuse him of working by evil spirits, 218. Demand signs of him, 219. Points

INDEX.   497

PHARATON,
of distinction between them and the
Sadducees, 246. Points of union
between them, 272. Their insidious
designs regarding Jesus, 162. Their
practices and doctrines the subject
of his denunciations and rebukes,
270, 292, 293; 359. Their confusion on his triumphal entry into
Jerusalem, 281. Their practice
with regard to capital punishment,
316 note. Tone of their administration of the law, 361. St. Stephen a victim to their vengeance,
365. Their phase of Christianity,
395. Influence of belief in the
resurrection upon them, 403. Sectarian distinction and symbols, 426.

PHARATON, the dancer, iii, 340.

PHÆDRA, a Roman parallel to, ii, 324, 325.

PHARAOH, i, 368. A word at which
he trembled, 447. A Persian Imitator, II, 255.

PHÆDRAS's wife, fine paid for the
Pharisees by, i, 100.

PHIDIAS, sculptures of, i, 25. 435;
ii, 115; 116.

PHILADELPHIA, see *Philomelium*.

PHILIP, the apostle, summoned by
Jesus, i, 157. His abiding-place, 211.

PHILIP, the deacon, conversion of the
eunuch by, i, 367. 367 note.

PHILIP, the emperor, ii, 173 note.
Refutation of his alleged conversion,
186. His magnificent celebration
of Rome's millennium, 186. 187.
Murdered, 187.

PHILIP, King of Macedon, treatment
of the religion of conquered nations
by, i, 6 note.

PHILIP, the prefect, cautious proceedings of, ii, 422. Suspicion attaching
to him relative to Bishop Paul's
death, *ibid.*

PHILIP II, of Spain, cause of the death
of, ii, 227.

PHILIP, Herod, see *Herod Philip*.

PHILIPPI, incidents of Paul's mission

VOL. III.

PHŒNICIA.
to and imprisonment at, i, 433-435.
Its itinerant traders in popular superstitions, 435. Its church, ii, 15.

PHILO, harmonization of Judaism and
Platonism attempted by, i, 25 note.
His argument against the Mysteries,
32 note. A valuable witness for
his own school, 57 note, 58. On
the influence of the Jews in Babylonia, 59, 60 note. On God's attributes, 71, 303 note. His notions
on the subject of a Messiah, 77-79.
Character of his rationalism, 114.
Modern parallel to him, 117. His
allegorical interpretations adopted by
Cerinthus, ii, 56. See ii, 42, 55 note.

PHILOMELIUM, or Philadelphia, epistle
from Smyrna to the church of, ii, 135.

PHILOPATRIS, the, iii, 395, 396.

PHILOSOPHERS of Julian's era, iii, 1-3.

PHILOSOPHUMENA of Hippolytus, discovery of its value to Gnostic
students, ii, 44 note. Story of a
pretended god, 50 note. On Basilides and his theory, 65 note. On
the Ophites, 82 note. See 55 note.

PHILOSOPHY, vanity of efforts to replace religion by, i, 30, 36. Why
insufficient for the purpose, 31. Accommodating to those whom it addressed, 34. Department in which
it nobly played its part, 35. When
almost extinct, iii, 43, 44. See
Natural Philosophy.

PHILOSTORGIUS, heroes of the history
of, ii, 446 note. On the worship of
a statue by Christians, iii, 378. Reference to his Fragments, ii, 442
note; iii, 40, 54, 56, notes.

PHINEAS cited as an authority for the
slaughter of unbelievers, ii, 306.

PHLEGON, disputed passage of, i, 335 note.

PHŒNICIA, ii, 32. Dualistic principle
of its cosmogony, 33. Elagabalus's
antics before its deity, 176.

2 K

PHOTINIANS.

PHOTINIANS, condemnation of the heresy of the, iii, 101.

PHOTIUS, writings preserved by the pious hostility of, ii, 446 note.

PHRYGIA, widespread propagation of the worship of, i, 40. Extravagances of its votaries, 412. Paul's journeys thither, 412, 444. Its Montanism a reaction on Gnosticism, 86, 161. Correspondence between its Christianity and its heathenism, 162. Its Christian colonists in Vienne and their disclaimer of Montanism, 144, 145, 162 note. See ii, 72, 92, 114, 117.

PILATE, Pontius, indignities offered to the Jews by, i, 131. His disregard for human life on occasions, 231, 232 note. Motives of the Sanhedrim in sending Jesus before him, 316, 317. His probable emotions at their conduct and at the nature of the charge, 318-320. His deference to their religious scruples, 321. His examination and declaration of the innocence of Jesus, 322, 323. Result of his efforts to induce the Jews to spare Him, 324-327. His wife's counsel, 327, 328. His motives for consenting to the sacrifice of Jesus, 328-330. Occasion of his disgrace, 365 note. His place of exile, ii, 144. False Acts ascribed to him, 231. Discovery of the inscription written by him for the Saviour's cross, 348. See i, 269, 276, 338, 339. ii, 61.

PILGRIM'S Progress, an ancient, iii, 359 note.

PILGRIMAGES to the Holy Land, iii, 191. Effect of Jerome's example, 192.

PINDAR, iii, 3. Composition of a Christian Pindar, 8.

PISTUS excluded from the see of Alexandria, ii. 413.

PLAGUES, see Pestilences.

PLANCK on the separation of the Jew

POETRY.

and Gentile converts, i, 414 note. On the potior principalitas, iii, 265.

PLATO'S Imaginary Republic, shortcomings of, i, 14. His belief in immortality, 19. Distinctive features of his 'Timæus' and his 'Republic,' ii, 39. Simon Magus well read in his works, 50 note. Worshipped by the Carpocratians, 80. Degeneracy of his disciples, iii, 2. His writings interdicted to the Christians by Julian, 8. See i, 418. ii, 80, i 79. 451.

PLATONIC Paganism, Julian's abortive attempt at, ii, 30, 452. Its great hierophant, 212. See ii, 76. 380.

PLATONISM, attempted harmonization of Judaism with, i, 25 note. ii, 158. Point of coincidence between it and Indian opinion, i, 13 note. Its doctrine of a Mediator, 70. Fate of a Christian Platonist, ii, 134. Platonic notion of dæmons, 211. Commencement of the strife between it and Aristotelianism in the church, 443 note. See ii, 41. 49. 50. 54. 61. 355.

PLEROMA, various Gnostic notions of the, ii, 58. 61. 69. 70. 72. 73. 76.

PLINY the elder, immortality of the soul contemned by, i, 19, 40. Illustrative passage, 40 note. See 106 note.

PLINY the younger; historical value of his correspondence with Trajan, ii, 92. Christians tortured and put to death by him, 93. 94. 94. 95. notes. Policy involved in his dealings with them, 98, 99. His reference to their sacred songs, 401 note, 402.

PLUTARCH'S suggestion as to the Egyptian religion, i, 16 note. On Epicurean hypocrisy, 76.

PLUTO, Serapian impersonation of, ii. 157.

POETRY, religion declining into, i, 35. Forswearing the old imaginative faith, 41. Its presence in the Gos-

INDEX. 499

POETS.

pel, 125. Transmutation into religious allegory, 184. Distinction between Grecian and Christian poetry, iii, 111. Attempt at a Christian Homer, 8, 354. Poetry of Christianity, 353-357. Specimen of a rare Latin poet, 356 *note.* Christian poets, see *Ephraem. Gregory of Nazianzum, Prudentius. Gnostic poets, see Bardesanes. Harmonius,* Pagan prophetic poetry, see *Sibylline verses.*

POETS, ancient, the priests of nature-worship, i, 13.

POLEMICAL works of the early Christians, their object and character, iii, 361, 364.

POLLENTIA, battle of, iii, 94.

POLYBIUS, i, 36. On the need of a religion for the common people, 17.

POLYCARP, ii, 135. Narrative of his martyrdom, 136-140. Shakespearian parallel to an incident in it, 140 *note.* The event made a celebration of the church, 124, 140, *notes.*

POLYTHEISM, Schlegel on the origin of, i, 13 *note.* Relaxing its hold, 23. Effect of the progress of knowledge, 25. Awaiting its death-blow, 41. Direct opposition of Christianity to it, 425. Sources of its hold upon the people and barriers interposed by it to a new order of things, 426, 427. In Rome, 426, 427. Its position in Greece, 428. Aspect it would present to a Christian teacher entering a heathen city, 428, 429, *notes.* Its phases in different localities, 435. Position of Christianity towards it, ii, 90, 96. Its outward splendour little affected by its internal decay, 96. Arraigned in Christian Apologies, 109. Its last effort, 151. Effect of Commodus's deification, 153. Satirized by Lucian, 183. Decaying beyond cure, 214, 338, 340, 345. Courting an union with Judaism, iii, 20. See ii, 99, 106, 204, 209, 211, 222, 225. See *Heathenism, Paganism.*

PORCH.

POMPEY, effect of the aspect of the Jewish Temple upon, i, 33. His reliance on astrologers, 41. Cause to which the Jews ascribed his death, 160. Wonder of his soldiers at the Sabbatarianism of the Jews, 300.

POMPONIUS, the deacon, ii, 169.

PONTIANUS, Saint, paintings in the chapel of, iii, 191.

PONTICUS martyred with Blandina, ii. 148.

PONTIFEX Maximus, Constantine hailed as, ii, 490.

PONTIFFS, discovery of the remains of, iii, 185 *note.*

PONTIFICATE of Pagan Rome, coveted and borne by emperors, i, 427; ii, 388; iii, 79. Refused by Gratian, 82. Its last act, 84. Gradual assumption of the Christian pontificate by bishops, ii, 28. Wealth and power of the pontiff of the west, iii, 265. See ii, 417 *note.* See also *Papal power. Pope.*

PONTICS, the demon, on the plague in Carthage, ii, 195, 195 *note;* iii, 320 *note.* On Cyprian's holiness in his retirement, ii, 196 *note.*

PONTIUS Pilate, see *Pilate.*

PONTUS, destruction of churches, and martyrdoms in, ii, 317. Disputes on the martyrdoms, 317 *note.*

POPES: the first martyr-pope, ii, 188, *note.* Growth of their power, 190. Establishment of their supremacy, iii, 50. Their difficulties with the nobles and the people, 130. Incentives to contests for the dignity, 274. See *Papal power. Pontificals.* See also *Bonifaces, Damasus, Gelasius, Gregory I. Liberius, Marcellus, Paschal, Siricius.*

POPPÆA, Agrippina discarded by Nero for, i, 404 *note.* Reasons for her alleged protection of the Jews, 458 *note.* 468, 469. ii, 97.

PORCH of the church, classes limited to the, iii, 310, 311.

2 K 2

INDEX.

PORCH.

PORCH, philosophy of the, ii, 114. See *Stoics*.
PORCIAN Basilica, result of Justina's demand for the, iii, 156.
PORPHYRY, or Porphyrius, his theory of the religion of Egypt, 16 *note*. On Buddhist asceticism, ii, 37 *note*. On the transmutation of poetry into religious allegory, 184.
PORSON, Professor, on the number of Christians in the east, ii, 376 *note*.
PORTRAITS, see *Painting*.
POST horses pressed and distressed in the service of disputing bishops, ii. 165, 445. See iii. 2.
POTHINUS, nonagenarian bishop of Lyons, killed by the rabble, ii, 146. His retort to his persecutors, 147.
PRÆTEXTATUS, proconsul of Achaia, privileges reclaimed for the Pagans by, iii, 33. His appeal for mercy to practisers of magic, 39. His high character, dignities, and honours, 80. Position of his wife: his apotheosis, 81. Their poetic addresses to each other, 81 *note*. His attempt to preserve Paganism, 83.
PRÆTORIAN guards, church destroyed by the, ii, 317.
PRAXITELES, i, 425. ii, 335.
PREACHER, office and qualifications of the, iii, 113.
PRELATES, see *Bishops*.
PREDESTINATION, see *Election*.
PRESBYTERS of the early church, ii, 14. Their original functions, 33. Their graduation into a sacerdotal order, 38. See iii, 112.
PRESSENSÉ, M. de, i, 457 *note*. On the church of the Catacombs, iii, 139 *note*.
PRICHARD, Dr, on Egyptian mythology, i, 12, 14, 16, *notes*.
PRIDEAUX, Dr, notions of, relative to Zoroaster, i, 61, 64 *note*.
PRIESTHOOD of the Christians, see *Clergy*.
PRIESTHOOD of the Jews their order

PROCOPIUS.

· of procedure in the Temple, i, 88. Jesus's tempter supposed to have been a high priest, 145. Position of the high priest in regard to the Roman governor, 185, 186. High priests, see *Ananias*. *Annas*. *Caiaphas*, *Ismael*, *Jonathan*.
PRIESTHOOD of the Pagans interdicted from public exhibitions, iii, 12. Confirmation of their privileges, 32. Abrogation of same, 84. See *Heathenism*, *Paganism*.
PRINCE of the Captivity, i, 90 *note*. ii, 249.
PRISCA, apostle of Montanism, ii, 162.
PRISCA and Valerian, wife and daughter of Diocletian, suspected of Christian leanings, ii, 205. Abomination forced upon them, 210.
PRISCILLA, see *Aquila*.
PRISCILLA, Saint, painting of a martyrdom in the cemetery of, iii, 196.
PRISCILLIAN and his followers the first heretics put to death, iii, 61. Circumstances of their martyrdom, 168. Ambrose's conduct relative to it, 169.
PRISCUS contemns philosophy as a fashion, iii, 3 *note*. At Julian's deathbed, 27. Result of his summons before Valentinian, 42.
PRISONERS, humane regulations regarding, iii, 302 *note*.
PROÆRESIUS, effect of Julian's edict on the teachings of, iii, 8.
PROBI, Christianity embraced by the, iii, 92.
PROBUS, Ambrose befriended and prophetically counselled by, iii, 151.
PROCONSUL and propraetor, difference between the two offices, i, 189, *note*.
PROCOPIUS lays the diadem at Jovian's feet, iii, 33. His rebellion, and hopes entertained of it, 39, 40. Astrological prediction of his elevation, 40.
PROCOPIUS on the public dancing of an empress, iii, 339.

INDEX. 501

PROCULUS.

PROCULUS, why taken into favour by Severus, ii, 154, 155.
PRODICIAN Gnostics, vicious tenets of the, ii, 81.
PRODIGAL son, parable of, rejected in Marcion's Gospel, ii, 80 note.
PROPERTIUS, lines from, i, 39 note. Character of his poetry, 43 note.
PROPHETS, source of a phrase relating to, i, 149 note. See 159 note.
PROSELYTES of the Gate, relation between the Jews and the, i, 182. Discussion regarding them, 381, 383, notes.
PROSTITUTION, notion of the Prodician Gnostics on, ii, 81 note.
PROTADIUS, Saint, legend of the discovery of the reliques of, iii, 161.
PROTESTANTS of Judaism, i, 271 note. Premature Protestants, iii, 333.
PROTOGENES of Orientalism, ii, 11.
PROVERBS, idea of Deity in the book of, i, 70 note.
PRUDENTIUS, eulogism on Julian by, iii, 28 note. On the vestal virgins, 84 note. On conversion to Christianity, 92 note. His poem on Theodosius's enactments and against Symmachus, 91, 93 note, 95 note. On the preacher, 112 note. Verses referring to sepulture, 130 note. On the Roman stage, 137. On gladiatorial shows, 144 note, 145 note. His style as a Latin poet, 353, 354, 355. His hymn for the Innocents' Day, 355 note. His verses against Symmachus, ibid. See 421 note, last line.
PSYCHIC principle of the Gnostics, ii, 67, 72, 73.
PTOLEMAIS, Bishop of, an adherent of Arius, ii, 363 note. See Synesius.
PTOLEMY, a name for the later Egyptian kings, i, 368. Temple ascribed to one of them, iii, 68, 69.
PTOLEMY, the philosopher, i, 106 note.
PUBLICANS or tax-farmers in Judæa,

RABBINS.

i, 131. Taken into favour by Jesus, 196, 197, 269, 270.
PUBLICUS Victor, the Descriptiones Urbis of, iii, 79 note.
PUNIC war, parallel to the, ii, 133.
PUNISHMENT, capital, for heresy, the first, iii, 167.
PUNISHMENTS, corporal, reason when not allowed, iii, 303 note.
PURIFICATION, Mosaic law relative to, i, 103.
PURITAN christian names, anticipation of, ii, 308 note.
PUTEOLI, Paul's sojourn at, i, 452.
PYE SMITH, Dr, on the Messiah, i, 80 note.
PYRRHONISTS, ii, 470.
PYTHAGORAS, system derived from the east by, i, 77. Anti-cœnobitic course taken by his followers, ii, 19. Simon Magus well read in his works, 50 note. Valentinianism traced to him, 69, note. Worshipped by the Carpocratians, 80. Information relative to mysticism to be found in his life, 184. His anonymous superior, iii, 7 note.
PYTHON, the mythic, ii, 137.

QUADRATUS: Occasion of the presentation of his Apology to Hadrian, ii, 105 note, 106.
QUINCY, Quatremère de, dimensions of ancient temples given by, ii, 141 note.
QUINISEXTAN council, and the symbolism of the Passion, iii, 398 note.
QUINTILIAN'S declamations, character of, iii, 166 note.
QUINTUS, a Phrygian braggadocio, cowardice, and apostacy of, ii, 136.

RABBI, Jesus saluted as, i, 162.
RABBINS and Rabbinical writers: On the coming of the Messiah, i, 44 note. Extent of credence to be given to their books, 57 note. One

502   INDEX.

RACES.

of their accusations against Jesus,
107 *note*. Character of their teachings and basis of their supremacy,
179. 411. On the waters of Siloah,
245. Period at which the Jews
surrendered themselves to their dominion, 411. Despotic authority
assumed by them, 426. The new
priesthood, ii, 17. See iii. 260.
RACES in the circus, party warfare
caused by, iii, 347. 348. See *Circus*.
RANKE's view of the object of em-
peror-worship, i, 29 *note*.
RAOUL-ROCHETTE, see *Rochette*.
RAPE and abduction, Constantine's
laws against, ii, 195. 396.
RAPHIA, in Palestine, Pagan worship
at, iii, 66.
RASK, Professor, on the antiquity of
the Zendavesta, i, 66 *note*.
RAVENNA, imperial court held at, ii,
111. iii, 96.
REDEEMER, see *Jesus Christ*; *Messiah*.
REDEMPTION, destruction of the Jewish hope of, i, 119. See *Schleiermacher*.
REGENERATION, see *Baptism*.
RELIGION: Peculiarities of the older
religions, i, 3. Treatment by vic-
tors of the religion of the vanquished, 3. 4. Ancient instances
of persecution, 4 *note*. Better system introduced by Alexander the
Great, 5. Policy of the Romans,
5. 6. Exhaustion of the old religions, 7. Their dissociating principle, 8. 9. Primary principles,
10. Best work on ancient religions,
ibid note. Effect of the progress
of knowledge, 25-29. Pagan notions
of the need of a religion for the
multitude, 16-18. True sources of
religious influence, 95. First blood
judicially shed for religious opinion,
iii, 61. 167. Results of attempts to
produce religious impressions, 415,
416. Religion and poetry, *see
Poetry*. Various religious systems,

ROMAN FEMALES.

see *Christianity*, *Gnosticism*, *Heathenism*, *Judaism*, *Mani*, *Orientalism*, *Paganism*, *Polytheism*, *Zoroastrianism*.
RELIQUES of saints installed as objects
of worship, iii, 160. See *Saints*.
REMISSION of sins, original Jewish
signification of, i, 98 *note*.
REMUSAT on the Chinese dogma of
the Creation, i, 70 *note*.
RESURRECTION, early Jewish doctrine
of the, i, 76. Classes and individuals excluded therefrom, *ibid note*.
See i, 440. See also *Immortality
of the Soul*.
RESURRECTION, church of the, built
on the site of the Holy Sepulchre,
ii, 348. Its magnificence, 349.
REUTERDAHL 'de Fontibus,' reference
to, iii, 363 *note*.
REVELATIONS, or Apocalypse, period
of the composition of the book of,
i, 388. Where written, ii, 14. Its
reference to the church of Ephesus,
16. Why Cerinthus was considered
its author, 17 *note*. Interpretations
of its reference to Babylon, 117.
RHINE, spread of the pestilence to the,
ii, 111. Its frontiers threatened,
225. Constantine's campaign, 289:
Julian's campaign, 449.
RIMINI, see *Councils*.
ROBINSON, Dr, on the site of the
transfiguration, i, 239 *note*.
ROCHETTE, M. Raoul, on heathen burials,
iii, 121, 122, *notes*. On the funereal
reliques of the Agapæ, 125 *note*.
On the heathen prototype for the
Good Shepherd, 181 *note*. On
Gnostic images of Christ, 190 *note*.
On portraits of the Saviour and
the Virgin, 191. 195 *note*. On a
painting of a martyrdom, 196. See
192. 194 *notes*.
ROMAN Catholics, classic parallel
to seventeenth century accusations
against the, i, 464 *note*.
ROMAN females, Pagan and Christian,

INDEX. 503

ROMAN LAWS.

iii, 230, 231. At gladiatorial shows, 344.

ROMAN laws adopted by the church, lii, 289.

ROMAN literature, culminating point of, iii, 350.

ROMANUS, endeavours to save the Christians at Edessa, iii, 72.

ROME, fundamental principle of the monarchy of, i, 1. Contrast between its systems of conquest and of government, 2 and *note*. Its civilizing influences, 2, 3. Its conduct with regard to the religions of conquered nations, 5, 6, 6 *note*. Nature of its own religious system, 18, 19. Points of distinction between the same and the religion of Greece, *ibid notes*. Deification of domestic virtues, 19, 20. Transmutation of its religion from a moral into a political power, 20. Influence fatal to its religion, 25. Human sacrifices, 26, 27, *notes*. Deification of the emperors and its consequences, 29. Instances, *ibid note*. Suitability of Stoicism to its people, 34, 35. Ready reception of foreign religions among them, 40. Irreligious belief and teachings of their poets, 41, 42. Fooling obtained by astrologers, 42, 43. Approach of Christianity, 44. Fable of their national origin an emblem of their spirit, 95. Baptismal lustrations among them, 135. Jewish apprehensions of destruction at their hands, 276, 277. Their law relative to the wives of provincial rulers, 327. Relationship between its Judæan prefects and the Jewish Sanhedrin, 385. Paul sent thither, 406. Jewish epithet for its people, 411. Paul's epistle to them, 416, 417, 467. Its religion a part of the state, 427. Burning of the city under Nero and persecution of the Christians, 454-457, 470; ii, 4, 5. Disputes as to Peter's visit, i, 452, 463, 463 *note*. Further as to

ROUSSEAU.

Paul's imprisonments and martyrdom, 465, 467-472. Commencement of barbarian encroachments on its borders, ii, 3. Sympathy for persecuted Christians, 5 *note*. Reception of Gnostic teachers by its higher classes, 84. Fears as to its fall with the fall of its old religion, 116, 117. Sibylline prophecies to that effect, 118, 120, 122-124. Visitations of physical calamities on the empire: earthquakes, inundations, famine, pestilence, 131-133, 195, 336. The capital deserted by the emperors, and lowered into the rank of a provincial city, 208, 210, 242-245, 310; iii, 80. Diocletian's triumph, ii, 122. Depreciation of its citizenship, 241. Consequences of the city's insults to Constantine, 328, 329. Its architectural features copied in Constantine's new city, 332, 333. Rifled of its venerated Palladium and statue of Victory, 337. iii, 83. Its forum, temples, basilicæ, and gods, ii, 343; 343 *note*; iii, 79. Source of its corn supplies, ii, 350. Its share in the Arian and Athanasian disputes, 423, 426, 427. Some at the apotheosis of Prætextatus, iii, 83. Fate of its vestals, 84. Cause of the consummation of its ruin, 96. Vicissitudes of its religion, *see Heathenism, Paganism, Polytheism*. Its rulers, see the names of the several *Emperors*.

ROME, council of, *see Councils*.

ROSENMÜLLER on Isaiah, i, 56 *note*. On the derivation of Nicolas, ii, 15 *note*. See i, 94, 150, 436, 445, 461, *notes*.

ROSSI on the first martyr-pope, ii, 188 *note*. On the anagram IXΘYΣ, iii, 182 *note*, 185 *note*. On the form of the cross, 198 *note*.

ROSTELLI on Christian symbolism, iii, 184 *note*.

ROTHE's arguments against lay-elders, ii, 25 *note*.

ROUSSEAU's theory anticipated, i, 8

504 INDEX.

ROUTH.

note. His testimony to the genuineness of the Gospels, 49 *note*.
ROUTH's 'Reliquiæ Sacræ,' references to and citations from, ii, 105 *note*, 276 *note*; iii, 354 *note*.
RUFINUS, iii, 69 *note*, 248. Jerome's controversy with him, 233.
RUMOHR's 'Italienische Forschungen,' iii, 380 *note*. His opinion on early Christian relievos, 385 *note*. On a statue of the Good Shepherd, 392 *note*.
RUSTAN, mythic Persian hero, expected reappearance of, ii, 252.
RUSTICUS, Justin Martyr summoned before, ii, 134.

SABAISM, see *Thabaism*.
SABBATH, rules for reading the Law on the, i, 175 *note*. Jesus in the synagogue thereon, 178. Jewish provisions for its rigid observance, 199, 200. Breaches thereof by Jesus, 199, 202-204, 206, 252. Charitable act expressly forbidden on that day, 252 *note*. Observed by the Manichæans, ii, 270. Constantine's rescript for its observance, 292, 392. Ground for Pagan acquiescence therein, 292, 393. Prohibition of games by Theodosius, iii, 331.
SABELLIANISM, propounder of, ii, 356. Its precise distinctions, 356, 357. Its supporters and opponents, 361, 369, 374. See *Le Beau*.
SABINUS, lenient edict issued by, ii, 339.
SACERDOTAL establishment of the Pagans, ii, 388, 389.
SACERDOTAL power, see *Bishops. Church. Clergy.*
SACRAMENTS of the church, secrecy of the, iii, 114. See *Baptism. Eucharist.*
SACRED writings of the early Christians, iii, 353. Poetry, 353-357. Legends and spurious gospels, 358. Lives of saints, 359. History, 360.

SAMARITAN.

Apologies, 361, 362. Hermeneutics, 363. Expositions of faith and polemical writings, 364. Orations, 365-370.
SACRIFICES, Pagan, suggested to Christians as the price of life, ii, 168, 169. Cyprian's refusal, 196. Results of refusal in other cases, 220, 221, 222. Constantine's prohibitory edicts, 385, 388, 388 *note*, 389, iii, 40 *note*. Theodosius's laws against them, 61, 62. See *Human Sacrifices.*
SACY, Silvestre de, on the Persian expectation of a Messiah, i, 75 *note*.
SADDER, of the Persians, Hyde's translation of the, i, 65 *note*.
SADDUCEES, the, i, 132, 190 *note*, 246. Nature of the doctrines held by them, 271. Point of union between them and the Pharisees, 272. Jesus's disposal of their subtleties, 290, 291. Sanguinary in their execution of public justice, 316 *note*. Predominance in the Sanhedrin attained by them, 359. Mani branded as a Sadducee, ii, 273.
SAINT CROIX, M, on the feeling of Greek and Latin authors towards the Jews, i, 58 *note*. On the extent of Hadrian's travels, ii, 104 *note*.
SAINT MARTIN, M, loss to the learned world by the death of, i, 59 *note*. See *Le Beau*.
SAINTS, lives of the, iii, 420. Worship of saints and angels, 419, 420. See *Reliques*.
SALAMIS, St Paul at, i, 188.
SALLUST, the prefect, effect of the remonstrance of, iii, 15. His rebuke to Julian, 20. The empire offered to him, 32.
SALLUST, Roman author, i, 35 *note*.
SAMARIA, Simon Magus in, ii, 45.
SAMARITAN Chronicle (Liber Josuæ), need for a critical edition of the, i,

SAMARITANS.

171 *note.* The Samaritan Letters, i, 170 *note.*

SAMARITANS, outrages on the Jews by the, i, 167. Site of their temple, 168. Interview of Jesus with one of their women, 169, 170, 170 *note.* Their expectation of a Messiah, 170, 171. Differences between their notions and those of the Jews, 172. Their mode of government and ready acknowledgment of Jesus, 172, 173. Their subsequent rejection of him, 256, 257. Parable of the Good Samaritan, 259 *note,* 273. Tumults between them and the Jews, 185. 401. II, 156. Dr. Burton's suggestion, II, 108 *note.*

SAMOS visited by Paul, i, 451.

SAMOTHRACE, sanctity of mysteries at, i, 433.

SANCHONIATHON, cosmogony of, ii, 33.

SANCTUS of Vienne, martyrdom of, ii, 146, 148.

SANDAUKE's sons sacrificed to Bacchus, i, 26 *note.*

SANHEDRIN, the rulers of the Jews; their functions, 130. Their character in popular estimation, 131. Alternate predominance of Sadducees and Pharisees among them, 132. Theory as to the tempter having been one of their body, 145, 146. Powers exclusively vested in them, 149 *note.* 159 *note.* Beginning to take account of Jesus, 161, 162. His Sabbath-breaking brought before them, 202. Their difficulty in the matter, 205. 244. 245. 250 *note.* Nicodemus's representation, 206. Their proceedings in reference to the healing of the man blind from birth, 253-255. Their determination on hearing of the raising of Lazarus, 264. On the watch, 267. Their dread of Pilate and of the Roman power, 269. Afraid of acting yet, 280. Jesus's apt replies to them, 283, 286, 287.

SATAN.

Their deep implication in his murder, and mainspring of the act, 297, 298. Their contempt for their instrument Judas, 303. Jesus in their toils: His condemnation, 309-312. Question as to their power to enforce their sentence, 313-315. Murderous act relative to a prior Sanhedrin ascribed to Herod, 315. Emotions of Pilate at their sending Jesus before him, and result of their interview with him, 316-323. Their precautions relative to his burial, 338. 349. Their probable impressions after consummating their purpose, 350. 352. 357. Their proceedings on the successful preachings of the apostles, 358, 359. Political revolution in their own body, 359. Their dismay at the miraculous release of their prisoners, 360. The apostles before them: effect of Gamaliel's counsels, 361. 362. Result of Stephen's arraignment before them, 364. 365. Their commission to Saul of Tarsus (Paul), 369. Their abortive efforts at revenge upon him, 401. 403. 405, 406. Victim sacrificed to their baffled hostility, 406. Refuge of their body on the destruction of Jerusalem, 409. See 251. 262. 272. 330. 333. 339.

SANHEDRIN of the Samaritans, constitution of the, 172. 173.

SAPOR, King of Persia, Constantine's letter to, ii, 281 *note.* His homage to a statue, iii, 76. Terms extorted from him after Julian's expedition, 28.

SARDICA, edict of the three emperors at, ii, 228. See *Councils.*

SARRAN, sacred trust fulfilled by the kings of, ii, 253.

SARRANIAN fire-worshippers, II, 31.

SATAN's earliest and latest attributes, i, 69, 69 *note.* The alleged creator of bad men, ii, 63. 63 *note.* Marriage his invention, 63. His slaves and associates, 73. See II, 82.

SATURNINUS.

SATURNINUS, the Gnostic, system of, ii, 57. 62-64. 75.
SATURNINUS the catechumen, ii, 165.
SATURUS, fellow-martyr with Perpetua and Felicitas, ii, 167. 170.
SAUL of Tarsus, see *Paul, Saint.*
SAVAGE life, theories regarding, i, 9 note.
SAVIGNY, opinion relative to Jesus supported by, i, 102 note.
SCALIGER, i, 407 note.
SCAPULA, prefect of Africa, Tertullian's letter and admonition to, ii, 116. 161. 164.
SCEVA, superstition of the sons of, i, 447. 448.
SCHELSTRATE, theory first developed by, i, 318 note.
SCHLEGEL, A. W., on the worship of civilized nations, i, 11 note.
SCHLEGEL, F, ii, 32 note. 63 note.
SCHLEIERMACHER'S essay on St Luke, i, 104 note. 118 note. His view of the doctrine of redemption, 141 note.
SCHLEUTNER on the principle of evil, i, 69 note.
SCHOOLMEN of Paganism, waste of ingenuity by the, iii, 1.
SCHRÖECK on saint and angel worship, iii, 420 note.
SCIPIO'S humane maxim, ii, 110.
SCRIBES, the, i, 180. Espousal of Christ's doctrines by one, 291. 292.
SCULPTURE less favoured by Christianity than by Paganism, iii, 377.
SCYTHOPOLIS, city of, its characteristic, i, 183 note.
SEASONS of mourning and rejoicing among the ancients, i, 12.
SEBASTIAN, Saint, representation of the martyrdom of, iii, 396.
SECUNDULUS, the catechumen, ii, 165.
SEDUCTION, laws against, ii, 395. 396.
SEJA and Segesta, site of the statues of, i, 18 note.

SERAPIS.

SELEUCIA, pestilence brought from, ii, 112. Its Christian communities, 249.
SELF-DENIAL, barbarous instance of, iii, 310 note.
SELF-TORTURE of the ascetics, iii, 205.
SEM-HAM-PHORASH, Jesus charged with working by the mysterious word, i, 318 note. Moses's wonderworking word, 447.
SENECA, object of the ΑποκολυτοκωσΙΣ of, i, 29 note. On Jewish proselytism, 430 note. Forged correspondence between him and St Paul, 444 note. Votary and victim of court intrigue, ii, 41. See i, 15-18 note.
SEPTUAGINT, interpolations in the: as to Pagan rites, i, 32 note. As to guardian angels, 68 note. The foundation of Greek ecclesiastical literature, iii, 352.
SEPULCHRE, holy, Pagan temple on the site of the, ii, 146. Sanctity of the spot, 147. Pagan temple replaced by a Christian church, 148. 149.
SEPULCHRES, violation of, a ground for divorce, ii, 397.
SERAPION, influence over Chrysostom of, iii, 136. Deprivation complained of by him, 213.
SERAPIS, treatment during the Republic of the temples of, i, 6 note. Hadrian's strange jumble of its worshippers with the Christians, ii, 108 note. Sibylline prophecy of its downfall, 122. Influence of the worship on Severus and his proceedings, 157. 158. How regarded by Alexander Severus, 177. Description of the temple and statue at Alexandria, iii, 67-70. Their destruction under Theodosius, 74. 75. Discovery of tricks practised by the priests, 74 note. Fears of the Christians after their triumph, 75. Object of the demolition, 76. 77. Transference of its revenues to

INDEX. 507

SERENUS.

the Christians, 275. See i, 40. 429 *note.* ii, 72. 165.
SERENUS Granianus, proconsul, ii, 107.
SERGIUS Paulus, favour shown to Paul and Barnabas by, i, 389. Incentive to his conversion, 431.
SERMON on the Mount, chronological perplexities concerning the, i, 188 *note.* When delivered, according to St Luke, 212. See 195 *note.*
SERPENT-WORSHIPPERS. See *Ophites.*
SERVIANUS, Hadrian's gossiping letter to, ii, 108 *note.*
SESOSTRIS, famous statue attributed to, iii, 69.
SEVENTY disciples, Jesus's choice of the, i, 258, 259.
SEVERUS, the blind butcher, alleged miraculous recovery of, iii, 161.
SEVERUS, ii, 116, 149. 151. Persecution of the Christians under him, 156. 163. Influence of the Serapian worship upon him, 157. 158. His end, 180. See *Alexander Severus, Sulpicius Severus.*
SEXTUS Rufus Festus, *Descriptiones Urbis* of, iii, 69 *note.*
SHAH-POOR, Mani repulsed by, ii, 263. Mani's reception by his son, 271.
SHAKSPEARE, ii, 112 *note.* Parallel in his Macbeth to an incident in a martyrdom, 140 *note.*
SHAMANISM, ii, 248.
SHECHINAH, idea symbolized by the, i, 21.
SHEPHERD of Hermas, source of the, iii, 359. Nature of the work, *ibid note.* See *Good Shepherd.*
SHEPHERDS, rebellion of, ii, 133.
SHEMHOLETH, i, 173. Mysterious words, see *Abraxas, Jao. Sem-hamphorash. Tetra-grammaton.*
SHILOH, expectation of the, i, 54.
SHRINES of Ephesus, fame of the, i, 445. 449.
SIBYLLINE books and verses, question

SIMON.

as to the origin of the, ii, 118. Interpolated by the Christians, *ibid.* Their allusions to the millennium, 118 *note.* Occasions of opening them, 119. 120. Pagan calamities foretold by them, 110-124. Use made of them by the Christians, 125. Consulted by Aurelian, 200. By Maxentius, 383. See 387.
SICHEM, Jewish perversion of the name of, i, 168. Site of the well, *ibid note.* See 172.
SICILY, dedication of temples to the Virgin in, iii, 97.
SIDONIUS Apollinaris, verses from, iii, 339 *note,* 340, 403 *note.*
SIGANFU, inscription of, iii, 71 *note.*
SIGE, or SILVGOS, of the Valentinians, ii, 69 *note.*
SILAS, or Sylvanus, Paul's companion, i, 395. 432.
SILCO, King of Nubia, discovery relating to, ii, 400 *note.*
SILOAM, fountain of, and Jewish rejoicings, i, 245.
SILOAM, pool of, i, 252.
SIMEON, the song of, i, 97 *note.* His knowledge of the future of the Child Jesus, 104. Remarkable point in his benediction on Him, 105.
SIMEON ben Hillel, why different from the above Simeon, i, 104, 105.
SIMEON, Bishop of Jerusalem, authenticity of the acts of, ii, 101. His martyrdom, 103 *note.*
SIMEON Stylites, iii, 205. Enthusiastic description of him, 205 *note.*
SIMON the Canaanite, why so called, i, 211, 212.
SIMON the Cyrenian, legend as to his substitution on the cross for Jesus, ii, 58.
SIMON the heresiarch, ii, 47 *note.*
SIMON the leper, host of, and probably cured by Jesus, i, 279.
SIMON Magus, i, 114. 171. His collision with St Peter, 381, ii, 45, 45 *note.* His view of the miracles

508   INDEX.

SIMON.

of Jesus, 41, 46. Query as to his identity with Felix's pander, 46. His real character and tenets, 47. His female confederate, 47-49, 51 note. 86 note. Source of his opinions; his avowed object, 49. Views of scholars as to himself and his system, 50, 51, notes. His successor, 62. Charge against his followers, 86 note. See 108 note.

SIMON Peter, see *Peter, Saint.*

SIMONIDES, barbarous death of, iii, 42.

SIN, confession of, and penance for, iii, 294.

SINGING and music in the church, iii, 401-405.

SION, the holy city, i, 78. Fortifications on the mount, 274.

STRICTUS, pope, marital interdiction laid on the clergy by, iii, 280.

SIRMIUM, temple of the Sun at, ii, 199. Its Arian formulary, 416. Result of its synod, 445. Contest for its bishopric, iii, 154.

SIXTOOS, ii, 69 note.

SLAVES and Slavery. Slaves inadmissible to the Scandinavian Valhalla, i, 44 note. Penalties for selling children into slavery, ii, 193, 194. Offence for which slaves were burned, 195. Ceremony of manumission, 195 note. iii, 141. Mutilation which entitled a slave to his freedom. ii, 198. Humanizing influence of Christianity, iii, 153, 240. Treatment of slaves under heathen rule, 241. Marital interdicts, 241, 289. See iii, 65 note.

SMINTHIAN Deity, the, ii, 117.

SMITH, Dr Pye, on the Messiah, i, 80 note.

SMITH'S account of the Greek church, iii, 354 note.

SMYRNA, church of, ii, 115. Its martyr-bishop (see *Polycarp*). Christian humanity there during an earthquake, 140.

SOCRATES, i, 418. ii, 179. Cause of

SOZOMEN.

his death, 441. Divine source of his instruction, ii, 181 note. See ii, 451.

SOCRATES, ecclesiastical historian, on the effect of national character on religion, ii, 163 note. Instance of his judgment and impartiality, 369 note. References, ii, 365 note. iii, 5, 9, 11, 17, 55, 56, 71, 104, 114, 371, 277, 281, 323, notes.

SOLOMON'S Song, Jerome's interpretation of, iii, 230 note.

SOLOMON'S Temple the starting point of a new era in Judaism, i, 23. Messianic notions in the "Wisdom of Solomon," 77. Part of the later Temple named after him, 260.

SOLVET on the happiest epoch of Roman history, ii, 2 note. On Hadrian's travels, 105 note.

SOOTHSAYERS, ii, 292. Laws against, 186. Their aid called for, iii, 96.

SOPATER, tenet denied by, ii, 326 note. His intimacy with Constantine, 380. Put to death, 389.

SOPHIA, Saint, church of, at Constantinople, ii, 333 note. Military assault therein on Chrysostom and his congregation, iii, 145.

SOPHIA (Wisdom) and Sophia Achamoth, in the Gnostic systems, ii, 70-73. 25, 81, 82.

SOPHISTS, a favourite resort of the, i, 442 note.

SOPHRONIA, occasion of the suicide of, ii, 282.

SOSTHENES, occasion of the maltreatment of, i, 443.

SOTADIC verse, character of the, ii, 161 note.

SOUL, see *Immortality of the Soul.*

SOUTH Sea Islanders, agents for the conversion of the, i, 48 note.

SOZOMEN on the Arian bishops, ii, 361 note. On penalties imposed on Arians, 370 note. iii, 101. His account of the murder of Bishop Mark, iii, 20, 29 note. On Saint

SPAIN.

Chrysostom, 136 note. 264 note. References, iii, 8, 11, 16, 56, 67, 71, 96, 104, 273-277, 281, 312, notes.

SPAIN, civilizing influences of Roman conquest in, i, 2. Paul's journey thither, 457 note. 458, 459, 461. Curious tradition among the Spanish Jews, *ibid*. Its Roman provinces wasted by the Moors, ii, 133. Constitution of society in later Roman times, 278. Its Donatist communities, 109. Its representative at the Council of Nice, 364, 365. Side taken by it in the Trinitarian controversy, iii, 61. See ii, 326, iii, 57.

SPECTACLES, public, see *Games*. *Gladiators*.

SPIRIT, the Holy, see *Holy Ghost*.

SPIRITS, evil, see *Dæmoniacs*.

SPLENDITENENS of Mani's system, ii, 260, 262 note.

SPYRIDON, a married ecclesiastic, iii, 281.

STANHOPE, earl, correspondence on human sacrifices, i, 27 note.

STANLEY, Dean, visit to Abraham's tomb by, ii, 349 note. See 366 note. 383 note.

STAR in the east at Christ's birth, astronomical considerations concerning the, i, 106 note.

STEPHEN, Saint, tradition alluded to by, i, 71. Animosity excited by his successful preachings, 364. His arraignment and martyrdom, 365, 366. Its most important result, 368. Dispersal of the Christians consequent thereon, 377.

STEPHEN, Bishop of Antioch, ignominiously deposed, ii, 420.

STILICHO, Ambrose's reply to the entreaty of, iii, 169.

STILPO, cause of the exile of, i, 441.

STOICS, system of the, why suitable to the Romans, i, 34, 35. Their portico in Athens, 436. Listeners

SUN-WORSHIP.

to St Paul, 438. Difference between their teachings and his, 440. Cause of their expulsion from Rome, ii, 7. Effect of Christian fortitude on an imperial Stoic, 119, 130.

STOLBERG, count, controversial point abandoned by, i, 416 note.

STONING, offence among the Jews legally punishable by, i, 374 note. 406.

STOWELL, lord, on the origin of nations, i, 9 note.

STRABO, coincidence pointed out by, i, 33 note. On the necessity for religious prodigies, 17. On the population of Galilee, 183 note. On the philosophers of Tarsus, 368 note. Jewish office named by him, ii, 17 note. See i, 416 note.

STRAUSS'S 'Life of Jesus,' references to, i, 89 note, 97 note. Critical remarks on his hypothesis, 109-115. Later reprobaters of his "timid orthodoxy," 117. His argument in reference to John the Baptist, 143 note. And against the genuineness of the Gospels, 228 note.

STURZ'S dissertation on the Macedonian dialect, iii, 350 note.

SUETONIUS on the Jewish expectation of a Messiah, i, 55. Source of the weakness ascribed by him to Flavius Clemens, ii, 12. See ii, 7, 8, 11, notes.

SULPICIUS Severus, iii, 78 note. Style and contents of his life of St Martin of Tours, 351 note.

SUN, preternaturally eclipsed, ii, 264. Christ's dwelling, 260, 268. Julius Firmicus Maternus's curious remonstrance on the luminary's behalf, iii, 465 note.

SUN-FESTIVALS noted by Bohlen, i, 12 note.

SUN-WORSHIP, forced on the Roman Senate, ii, 151. Sacrifices and extravagances of Elagabalus in regard to it, 173-175. Its temple at Sirmium, 199, 200. Diocletian a wor-

SUNDAY.

shipper, 212. Coincidence of the Christian sabbath with Sun-day, 292, 293. Its fane at Constantinople, 332, 337. Ardour of Julian's attachment, 465, 468. Its celebration at Antioch, iii, 13. See ii, 355, 400. Iii, 12, 19. See Commodus. Elagabalus.

SUNDAY, see Sabbath.

SUPERSTITIONS dominant in Rome, i, 42, 43. Awake and calling for vengeance on the Christians, ii, 126. See Divination. Heathenism. Magic. Paganism. Polytheism. Serapis. Sun-worship.

SUPPER of Our Lord, See Eucharist.

SWINE, demoniacally possessed, i, 221.

SYLVANUS, see Silas.

SYMBOLISM, Christian: the cross, iii, 380, 381. Enumeration of various early symbols, 382-385. Representations of the Father, 392.

SYMMACHUS'S oration to Theodosius, i, 28 note. His lament on the decadence of Paganism, iii, 95. Style and contents of his 'Apology,' 86, 87. 159. High offices held by him, 248. His reason for condemning the suicide of captives intended for gladiatorial murder, 141. See 80 note. 93. 334, 337, 340, notes.

SYMPHORIAN, Saint, Acts of, ii, 128 note.

SYMPLEGADES, parallel to the collision of the, ii, 164.

SYNAGOGUE of the Jews, teaching concerning the Messiah in the, i, 80. Synagogue of Nazareth, 175. Of Capernaum, 178, 226. Miracle in one, 207. Their multitude in Jerusalem, 391. No sanctity about them in the eyes of converts, 412. The Proseucha, 433. Augustus's law for their protection, 445. Difference between the synagogue and the church, ii, 18, 19. See i, 57 note. ii, 16. 16 note. 17.

SYNESIUS, clerical celibacy repudiated by, iii, 281. His character and

TACITUS.

opinions, 296, 297. His resolute dealing with Andronicus, 297. His hymns, 354 note.

SYNODS and councils of the Church, iii, 263, 285. See Councils.

SYRIA, debasing effect on the Jews of the religions of, i, 61. Migration of converts to its regions, 377. Christian colonies planted by St Paul, 195. 461. Its dissolute rites, 394. Hymns sung by its Christian population, ii, 74. Invaded, 132. Object of Severus's edict, 156. Destruction of and war against its temples, 243. iii, 66. 77. Effect of Arius's intercourse with its bishops, ii, 361, 362-369. 375. Law based on the laxity of its morals, 397 note. Poetic exponent of its dreamy mysticism, iii, 103, 105. Its gladiatorial shows, 345. Its national Paganism, see Sun Worship. See also ii, 104. 113. 144. 177. 228. 242.

SYRIAN historians of the early church, ii, 13.

SYRIANUS, duke, assault on Athanasius and his congregation by the troops of, ii, 428, 429.

STRIARCHS, the, iii, 333.

SYRO-PHŒNICIAN woman, consideration on Jesus's interview with the, i, 233-235.

TABERNACLES, Feast of, i, 240. 241. Appearance of Jesus thereat, 243-245.

TABOR, Mount, and the transfiguration, i, 239 note.

TACITUS, Roman historian, on the religion of the Jews, i, 24 note. His denunciation of astrologers, 42. 43 note. On the Jewish expectation of a Messiah, 55. On the influence of a belief in a future state, 73. On the influence of Pallas with Nero, 104 note. On the implication of the Christians in the burning of Rome, 456 note. ii, 5 and note. On an

TALISMANS.

amiable phase of tyranny, ii, 3 *note.*
See i, 455 *note* 1. 457 *note* o. ii, 7
note. iii, 69 *note.*
TALISMANS and amulets, fame of
Ephesus for, i, 445.
TALMUD, Babylonian, i, 60. ii, 249.
TALMUD, Jewish, references to the, i,
63 *note.* 68 *note.* Character of its
contents, 114. Figurative allusions
to the Messiah, 139 *note.* Harsh
conclusions deducible from passages
in it, 140 *note.* Parallel to John
the Baptist's shoe-latchet simile,
142 *note.* Its contrast of the Jews
and Galileans, 182 *note.* Talmudic
interpretation of a prophecy of
Daniel, 277. Effect of its acceptance as the national code, ii, 17, 18.
See i, 290 *note.* iii, 260.
TARGUMIN of the Rabbins, the, i, 67
note. Term applied by the Targu-
mists to the Messiah, 72.
TARSUS, Paul's birthplace, i, 368.
Philosophical and travelling habits
of its natives, *ibid note.*
TARTAR or Turkoman tribes, religion
of the, ii, 248.
TATIAN on public amusements, iii,
334 *note.*
TAXES in Jerusalem, how paid, i, 156
note. See Tribute.
TAYLOR, Jeremy, on the massacre of
the innocents, i. 107 *note.*
TE DEUM, reputed author of the, iii,
154.
TELEMACHUS the Monk, a martyr to
his heroic humanity, iii, 345, 346.
TEMPLE of the Jews, see *Jerusalem,
Temple of. Solomon's Temple.*
TEMPLES of the heathens,, see *Apollo.
Castor and Pollux. Baalbec. Pagan
temples. Serapis. Sirmium. Sun-
worship.*
TEMPLE-TAX, how levied in Jerusa-
lem, i, 156. 156 *note.* Vespasian's
idolatrous appropriation of it, ii, 7.
See i, 289 *note.*
TEMPTATION, the, i, 144. Theories

THALIA.

respecting it, 145-147. Site of its
occurrence, 148.
TERMINALIA, feast of, ii, 217.
TERMINUS, the Roman deity, attribute personified by, i, 19.
TERTULLIAN on Chrestos and Christos,
i, 196 *note.* His feelings relative to
the Jews, 423. 423 *note.* On St
John's cauldron of boiling oil, ii, 14.
Mosheim's reading of the passage,
14 *note.* On the adoption of celibacy, 17 *note.* His epithet for
Hadrian, 105 *note.* On the loyalty
of Christians to the ruling power,
116 *note.* His use of the word
"Sæculum," 118. On the miracle
of the thundering legion, 141.
Character of his writings, 161. iii.
177. 151. 362. Form of Christianity of which he was the type, ii,
161-163. Tone of his 'Apology': his
denunciation of Paganism, 163, 164.
Contrast between him and Origen,
164 *note.* And between him and
Cyprian, 192. Inference from his
passage relative to the Christians in
the east, 209 *note.* On the difference between clergy and laity, iii,
218 *note.* On confession and penance, 294. His charge against
heretics, 309 *note.* On martyr-
festivals, 324 *note.* 420. On the
abuse of the Agapæ, 325 *note.* Two
sins charged by him on Hermogenes,
177, 178. On an embossed communion cup, 382. On the Saviour's
personal aspect, 386. On the character of the Virgin, 424 *note.* See
ii, 113. iii, 197, 263, 288, 314.
403, *notes.*
TESTAMENT, New, see *Gospels. New
Testament.*
TESTAMENT, Old, see *Old Testament.*
TETRA-GRAMMATON, the wonderworking word, i, 219 *note.* 447.
THALES the Milesian, and his principle
of moisture, ii, 82 *note.*
THALIA, poem by Arius, its style and
contents, ii, 361, 363, *notes.*

THAPSUS.

TRAPSUS, Battle of, ii, 159.
THEATRE, the, in Polytheistic times, nature of its exhibitions, i, 429. Rome's burning made a theatrical show by Nero, 458 note. Jew players and Jew audiences, ii, 96, 97. The theatre in Constantinople, 194. The theatre deserted for the church, iii, 135. Various kinds of performances, 337-339. Character, privileges, and disabilities of female players, 340, 341. Baptismal privileges of actors, 341, 342. Penalty on actresses' daughters and on backsliding actresses, 342.
THEINER'S work on celibacy, its merits, iii, 197 note. 356 note. His list of monk-prelates, 337 note. See 278 note.
THEMISTIUS on Jovian's toleration, iii, 35 note. His address to and flatteries of Theodosius, 60, 95 note. Office conferred on him, 248. See 166 note.
THEODORA, the empress, exhibiting as a public dancer, iii, 339.
THEODORE of Mopsuestia, his theory of the Temptation, i, 145 note.
THEODORET on Constantine's suppression of Paganism, ii, 385. On the Christian rejoicings at Julian's death, iii, 19 note. On Valentinian's conduct, 33 note. 152 note. On Ephrem's learning. 105 note. On martyr festivals, 124 note. References, 8, 16, 20, 27, 31, 33, 56, 67, 143, 146, notes.
THEODORIC, interest taken in public games by, iii, 333 note. 147 note. His fondness for art, 372.
THEODORUS, saint, painting of the heroic acts of, iii, 198 note.
THEODOSIAN Code, ii, 398 note. Its contents and value, iii, 339. More important citations from it: concerning extravagance in costume, 247 note. Admission to orders, 250 note. Property of intestates, 276 note. Exemption of bishops from civil jurisdiction, 284 note.

THEOGONISM.

Intermarriage of Jews and Christians, 289 note. Marital rights and penalties, 290 note. 293 note. Against heresy, 300. 301 note. Treatment of prisoners, 302 note. Burials, 331 note. Against selling martyrs' bodies, 325 note. Penalties for kidnapping, 341 note. Preservation of statues, 379. 379 note. Prohibition of relique worship, 420 note.
THEODOSIUS the Great, Sibylline foresight of the iconoclasm of, ii, 121. Act adduced in justification of his severities against the Pagans, iii, 7 note. Causes of priestly influence over him, 59, 60. Pagan and Christian joy at his accession, 60. His origin: character of his Christianity, 60, 61. His edicts for the suppression of Pagan sacrifices, 61, 62. His agents in the demolition of Pagan temples, and their proceedings, 63, 64 (see Paganism. Scropis). His penalties on apostates, 84 note. 101. 253 note. Themistius's flatteries, 95 note. His laws against heretics, 100, 101. Trinitarian hopes on his accession, 114. His edict against the Arians, 116. Occasion of the revolt of, and insults offered to him by, the people of Antioch, 123, 124. Their subsequent panic and sufferings, 124, 125. Result of appeals to his mercy, 125-128. His accession to sole power, 163. Occasion of his rebuke by Ambrose, 163-165. His massacre of the Thessalonians and subsequent penance for the same, 166, 167. His victory over Eugenius and death, 92. 169. See ii. 190.
THEODOSIUS the younger, ii, 112.
THEODOSIS, Bishop of Nicæa, one of the five recusant bishops, ii, 369. Banished, 370. Anathema protested against by him, 372. Reinstated, 373. Charge against Eustathius joined in by him, 374.
THEOGONISM of the east, ii, 54-

THEOLOGY.

THEOLOGY, primary blessing lost sight of in, I, 343 *note*. Elements of rational and intellectual Christianity, III, 412. Augustinian theology, III, 171-175. See *Augustine*.

THEONAS of Marmarica, II, 363 *note*. One of the five recusant bishops, 369.

THEOPHILOSOPHIC systems of Rome; deification by Alexander Severus of their representatives, II, 177.

THEOPHILUS, Archbishop of Alexandria, III, 54, 70. Murderous result of his exposure of Pagan symbols, 71. His share in the destruction of the Serapeum, 73, 74. Bold and unprincipled, 102. His conduct in his see; character of his writings, 103. Anathema upon Origenism, 104. Intrigues against Chrysostom and presumed object thereof, 115 *note*. 138. His Council of the Oak and its decision, 139. 141. His flight from Constantinople, 142. Cause of his quarrel with the monks, 212.

THEORETICA, object of the, III, 213. Confiscated by Justinian, *ibid*.

THEOTECNUS, efforts to restore Paganism of, II, 232. His detected impostures and death, 239.

THERAPEUTÆ, or contemplatist monks of Egypt, I, 153. II, 36. Their Jewish ancestors, II, 42.

THESSALONICA, synagogue of the Jews at, I, 395. Occasion of their flight thither: proportion of Jews, Greeks, and Turks in its population, 395. 396, *notes*. Occasion of Paul's first epistle to its people, 397 *note*. Cause of the expulsion of Paul and his companions, 435. Antoninus Pius's edict, II, 110. Massacre under Theodosius, III, 166.

THEUDAS, insurrection of, I, 361. 384.

THEURGY of Appollonius, II, 178. 184. Sacrifices connected with it, 188. Theurgists of Julian's days, III, 14.

THISBET, alleged virgin birth of the

VOL. III.

TIMOTHEUS.

Shaka of, I, 94 *note*. Its ascetic devotees, II, 36.

THILO, Dr, collection of spurious gospels by, III, 359 *note*.

THIRLWALL, Dr. Connop, Bishop of St. David's, character of a work of, I, 118 *note*.

THOLUCK, M, views of, relative to the era of Christ's birth, I, 100, 102, *notes*.

THOMAS, Saint, the Apostle, I, 211. Region of his labours, 387, II, 248.

THRASEA, Roman patriot, II, 7. 41.

THUCYDIDES, vital principle in the writings of, iii, 7.

THYATIRA, Lydia's residence at, I, 431.

THYESTEAN feasts charged on the Christians, ii, 146.

TIBER, consequences of an inundation of the, ii, 132. See 281, 329.

TIBERIAS, Jewish Patriarch of, I, 423. II, 249.

TIBERIAS, sea of, I, 105 *note*. Its city and people, 154. 183 *note*. Removal of the Sanhedrin thither, 409.

TIBERIUS'S edict relative to human sacrifices, I, 36 *note*. Averse to his own deification, 29 *note*. Astrologers banished by him, 43. Elements in his character, 129. His death, 372. Cruelties of his time, 458. Divination interdicted by him, II, 293.

TIBERIUS Alexander, the apostate prefect, I, 384.

TILLEMONT, a defender of Hegesippus's narrative, I, 407 *note*. On the date of the earliest Christian churches, II, 179 *note*. His conjecture relative to Hosius, 364. On Lampadius's religion, III, 39 *note*. His perplexity about Gregory of Nazianzum, 110 *note*. Humiliating truth confessed by him, 137 *note*. See II. 7 *note*. III, 104, 108, 114, 118, 151, 178, 228. 360, *notes*.

TIMOTHEUS or Timothy, admitted to Jewish privileges, I, 395. His pa-

2 L

514 INDEX.

TIRIDATES.

rentage, 411 note. Mission on which he accompanied Paul, 197. 432.
461. Their separation, 436. Movements of Paul dependent on him, 459 note. Paul's Second Epistle to him, 461.
TIRIDATES, King of Armenia, oriental bigotry of, ii, 256. His cruel treatment of Gregory the Illuminator, 257. Occasion of his conversion, 257, 258.
TITUS, emperor, resistance of the Jews to, i, 119 note. See ii, 53 note.
TITUS, mission confided to, i, 460.
TOBIT, transition of belief traceable in the book of, i, 68 note.
TOLEDO, see Councils.
TONGUES, Gift of, i, 353-355.
TORTURE, Inquisitorial use of, ii, 93.
TOURNAMENTS, origin of, iii, 333 note.
TOWNSON, Dr, suggestion of, relative to Jesus and the woman of Samaria, i, 169 note.
TRACHONITES, robbers of the, i, 105 note.
TRADITION, Its influence on the Jewish notions of a Messiah, i, 56, 57. "The hedge of the law," 100.
TRADITORS and the crime of tradition, quarrels relating to, ii, 299-301, 303-306.
TRAGEDY and comedy on the Roman stage, iii, 337.
TRAJAN, emperor, condition of Rome and Christianity in the first years of, ii, 2. 6. The Jews, 10. Effect of his discipline and military successes, 88. His mental characteristics, 90. His politic regard for human life, 91. Value of his correspondence with Pliny, 92. His dealings with the Christians, 93. 94. 94 note. 99-101. Jewish rebellion under him, 99. 100. His probable ignorance of the differences between Jews and Christians, 101. Popish legend of his release from purgatory, 101. 104. Rescript against delation, 107. 107 note. See ii, 122. 451.

TURKESTAN.

TRANSFIGURATION, the, i, 219. Question as to its locality, 219 note.
TREVES, ii, 244. Exposure of captives in its arena, 289. 321. iii, 345. Seat of Constantine's councils, ii, 395. 111. Place of Athanasius's exile, 381. Barbarian desolations: Fondness for the circus, 330 note.
TRIBUTE, petition of Judæa and Syria for remission of the, i, 111 note. Its hatefulness, 269. Jesus's celebrated reply, 289 note.
TRINITARIANISM and the Trinitarian controversy, ii, 296. Period of the outbreak of the controversy, 350. Its origin, 352. Principle involved in it, 353. Notions of Noetus and Sabellius, 356. 357. General acceptance of the doctrine of a Trinity, 358. Arian conception, ibid. Principle of union among Arius's opponents, 359. 360. Usual imputation of Arians against Trinitarians, 374. Effect of the controversy in the west, 416. Triumph of Trinitarianism under Theodosius: formulary proclaimed by him and his co-rulers, iii, 100. First supporter of Nicene Trinitarianism, 110. Project with regard to the sacrament consequent on the controversy, 389. See Arius, Athanasius, Nicæa, Nicene creed.
TRISAGION, the, iii, 119.
TROAS, Paul's visits to, i, 451. 460.
TROJAN war, typical use of the, ii, 48 note.
TROPHIMUS, charge against Paul concerning, i, 399.
TRULLO, see Councils.
TSABAISM, character and followers of, i, 11, 12. Source of Information, 11 note. See ii, 75. 248.
TSCHIRNER's 'Fall des Heidenthums,' value of, ii, 117.
TURAN, principle represented in Magianism by, ii, 251.
TURKESTAN, inclusion of Mani ir,

INDEX. 515

TWELVE.

ii, 26]. Conference between him and Archelaus there, 264 *note*.
TWELVE Tables, penalty for divination by the laws of the, ii, 291.
TYRANNUS, cession to Paul of the school of, i, 446.
TYRE, Paul's voyage to, i, 451. Maximin's answer to its address, ii, 114. Magnificence of its rebuilt church, 239, 240, 144. iii, 173. Occasion and upshot of Athanasius's appearance before its synod, ii, 178, 179.

ULPHILAS, Bishop of the Goths, descent of, iii, 55. His translation of the Scriptures, and alleged reason for omitting the book of Kings, 55, 56. Fragments of his version now extant, 55 *note*. Modern editions of same, 56 *note*. Doctrinal result of his visit to the Constantinopolitan court, 56, 57. His Bible the Bible of all the Gothic races, 58 *note*.
UNITY of the Godhead, see *Deity. God. Trinitarian controversy.*
URBACIUS, Roman general, killed by the Circumcellions, ii, 308.
URSACIUS, Bishop of Singidunum, and Valens, Bishop of Mursa, espousal of Arianism by, ii, 418. Recant, 420. Relapse, 421. Head the Arians at Milan, 424.
URSICINUS, sanguinary episcopal combat between Damasus and, iii, 261, 274.
UTICA, preternatural eclipse of the sun at, ii, 164.

VALCKNÆR'S treatise, 'De Aristobulo Judæo,' ii, 119 *note*.
VALENS, Bishop of Mursa, revival of his influence over Constantius, 421. See *Ursacius, Bishop*.
VALENS, emperor of the east, condemnation of the Manichæans under, ii, 174 *note*. Refusal to serve in Julian's army, iii, 9 *note*. His accession: difference between him and

VALENTINIANISM.

Valentinian, 12. His dealing with Paganism, magic, and divination, 33, 34. Magical ceremonies having relation to himself, 40, 41. Number and eminence of the victims to his fears and vengeance, 41, 42. Ascendancy of Arianism under him, 44. His baptism and amenability to sacerdotal influence, 44, 45. Crime laid to his charge, 45. His interview with Basil and its effect upon him, 45-47. His approaching fate, 47. Compels the monks to become soldiers, 47 *note*. His defensors, 52. Power given by him to ecclesiastical courts, 384 *note*. See ii, 421. iii, 55. 59.
VALENTINIAN, emperor of the west, condemnation of the Manichæans under, ii, 174 *note*. Refused to serve in Julian's army, iii, 9 *note*, 12. View taken of his toleration by Pagans and Christians, 32. His revocation of Pagan endowments, 33. His cruelties in the suppression of magic: his two bears, 33, 34. Brutalities of his representative at Rome, 34-36. Occasion of his putting Amantius and Lollianus to death, 37. Escheats the revenues of Pagan temples, 65. His decree against condemnations to the arena, 145. See ii, 421. iii, 42, 83.
VALENTINIAN II, joint emperor of the west, iii, 57. Pagan associations from which his mind was free, 80. Sole emperor of the west, 85. Rival appeals of the Pagan and Christian champions to him, 85-88. Date of his murder, 89. Promulgation of faith of himself and coemperors, 100. Power asserted under, and protection afforded to, him by Ambrose, 153, 155. Anecdotes apropos thereto, 156, 156 *notes*. His throne secured by Theodosius, 161. His death, 169. References to his laws, 274, 276, 289, 292, *notes*.
VALENTINIANISM, the Gnostic system

2 L 2

516 INDEX.

VALENTINUS.

of Valentinus, ii, 69-73. Work containing a development of it, 69 *note*. 74 *note*. Consequences of an imperial order for restoration of a destroyed church of the sect, iii, 161.

VALENTINUS, the Gnostic hierophant, ii, 58. 64. His repeated excommunications from the Christian church and retirement to Cyprus, 68. Essential principle of his system, 69. Psalms written by him, 74 *note*; iii, 403. His reception at Rome, ii, 84. See *Valentinianism*.

VALERIA, wife of Galerius, suspected of Christianity, ii, 205. Forced to sacrifice to Pagan gods, 230. Maximin's insult: her forced wanderings and unjustifiable sentence, 235.

VALERIAN, emperor, promising commencement of the reign of, ii, 190. 191. His initiator into magic and instigator to acts of persecution, 191. Martyrdom of Cyprian under his rule, 194-198. His captivity and (alleged) fearful end, 199.

VALHALLA of Odin interdicted to slaves, i, 44.

VANDALS, effect on Africa of their invasions, ii, 159. Form of Christianity embraced by them, iii, 57.

VARTOBED, or Patriarch of Armenia, usual fate and glory of the, ii, 355.

VARUS, ii, 451.

VATICAN suburb in Rome, its usual occupants from earliest times, ii, 294.

VEDA, right associated by the Brahmins with the, ii, 35 *note*.

VENICE of the old world, the, i, 442.

VENUS, supernatural cause of the razing of a temple of, ii, 348.

VENUS Aphrodite, see *Aphrodite*. Venus (Cypris), ii, 336 *note*. Venus Urania, ii, 171. Venus Verticordia, her attributes, i, 19.

VERONA, battle of, important issue decided by the, ii, 281. 283.

VIRGINITY.

VERUS, emperor, reply of Bardesanes to the Pagan emissary of, ii, 71. Associated in empire with Marcus Aurelius, 131. Terrible accompaniment to his victory, 132.

VESPASIAN, emperor, a patron of astrologers, i, 43. Identified by Josephus with the Messiah, 57 *note*. 81. Objects aimed at by him, ii, 6. Anxious to curb far other enemies than the Christians, 7. His application of the Jewish Temple-tax, *ibid*. His provision in Rome for education, iii, 6.

VESTAL virgins of Rome, ii, 399. Re-eversion of their privileges under Valentinian, iii, 33. Falling into disrepute, 84. Ambrose's sarcasms upon them, 84. 88. Symmachus's appeal for them, 87. Their suppression urged by Prudentius, 94. Place assigned to them at public spectacles, 335. Christian virgins, see *Virginity*.

VETTIUS Epagathus, brave defence of the Christians of Vienne by, ii, 145.

VICTORY, statue of, doomed, and dragged from its pedestal, iii, 83. Restored by Eugenius, 89. Prudentius's allusion to the circumstance, 93.

VIENNE, narrative of martyrdoms at, ii, 144-148. Imputation shrunk from by its church, 162 *note*.

VIGILANTIUS, prematureness of the Protestantism of, iii, 233. Abused by Jerome, 235. 236.

VILLEMAIN, M, on the appeal of Chrysostom's mother, iii, 120 *note*.

VIRGIL'S theory of the universe, i, 41. Complexion of his philosophy, *ibid note*. His possible obligations to Alexandrian versifiers of the Hebrew Scriptures, ii, 119 *note*.

VIRGIN Mary, palatiation and worship of the, see *Mary the Virgin*.

VIRGIN, oriental traditions of supernatural birth from a, i, 94 *note*.

VIRGINITY, eloquence of the Fathers

INDEX.   517

VISIGOTHS,
on the subject of, ii, 197, 198.
Chief writers thereon, *ibid. notes.*
Vows to virginity compared with
the number of births in certain regions, 214 *note*. See *Vestal Virgins.*

VISIGOTHS, Frank pretext for a war
with the, ii, 351 *note.* See III, 57
note. See also *Goths.*

VITELLIUS, triumphant reception by
the Jews of, i, 366 *note.* Object
of his warlike preparations, and
cause of their suspension, 372.

VITRINGA on the functions of the
chief of the synagogue, ii, 16 *note.*

VIVIA Perpetua. See *Perpetua.*

VOICES from heaven: to Hyrcanus, i,
88 *note.* At the baptism of Jesus,
143. Explanatory remarks, 144
note. 284 *note.*

VOSS on the astronomy, &c, of the
fathers, iii, 417 *note.*

VOSSIUS, absurdity pointed out by, i,
107 *note.* Citations from his 'Historia Pelagiana,' iii, 173 *note.* 177
note.

VULGATE Bible the depository of the
Latin tongue, iii, 51. Character of
its Latin, 352.

WALLON on the slavery of antiquity,
iii, 241 *note.*

WALSH, Rev. R, on a medallic representation of the Saviour, III, 190
note.

WARBURTON'S theory of the mysteries, i, 11 *note.* ii, 105 *note.*

WEBER'S work on the Evangelical
writings, its character and object, i,
115, 116. Resemblance of his system to Philo's, 117. Distinction
drawn, but not always observed by
him, 121.

WESTERN empire, effect on Christianity
of its extinction, ii, 310.

WETSTEIN, i, 71 *note.* On the derivation of Nicolas, ii, 55 *note.*

WHATELY, Archbishop, theory of

WORSHIP.

savage life controverted by, i, 9
note. Passages in Milman's 'Bampton Lectures' quoted by him, 428
note.

WHELER'S travels, notices of Grecian
architecture in, iii, 78 *note.*

WHEWELL'S 'Inductive Sciences,' iii,
417 *note.*

WHITBY on remission of sins, i, 98
note.

WIDOW'S mite, the, i, 292.

WIDOW'S son, miracle of the raising
of the, i, 211.

WILLS, persons prohibited from making, iii, 101. Taken into ecclesiastical keeping, 292.

WILSON, Professor H. H. ii, 15 *note.*
His 'Hindu Theatre,' 17 *note.*

WINDISCHMAN'S 'Philosophie in fort-
gang der Weltgeschichte,' merit of,
ii, 12, 31, *notes.*

"WISDOM" of the Gnostics, see
Sophia.

"WISDOM of Solomon," Messianic
notions in the, i, 77. Notion traceable in it, 352 *note.*

"WISE men" in the synagogues, ii, 19.

WISEMAN, Cardinal, romance of, iii,
129 *note.*

WITCHCRAFT. See *Magic.*

WIVES, when unfit for the kingdom
of heaven, iii, 180 *note.*

WOMAN taken in adultery, conduct of
Jesus with regard to the, i, 246, 247.

WOMEN. See *Females.*

WOMEN-PLAYERS, under the Romans,
their number, character, and privileges, iii, 340, 341. Penalty on
apostate actresses, 343.

WORD, the, or Logos, i, 71. 78. In the
Gnostic system, ii, 70. See *Logos.*

WORDSWORTH'S sonnet to the Virgin
Mary, i, 96 *note.*

WORLD, belief, among the Jews, of the
approaching end of the, i, 418.

WORSHIP of the Virgin and the saints,
see *Mary the Virgin. Saints.*

XENOPHON.

XENOPHON's 'Cyropædia,' i, 49.
XERXES, destruction of Babylonian deities and priests by, i, 4 note. Revival of the old religion in his dominions, ii, 249.
YATHAS, Gathas, and Vendidads of Zaratushtra, i, 67 note.
YORE, discovery of vestiges of Isiac worship at, i, 40 note.

ZACCHEUS's practical testimony to his belief in Jesus, i, 268.
ZACHARIAH, father of John the Baptist, i, 86. His unusual stay in the Holy Place, and vision there, 87. Divine promise then made to him, and affliction accompanying it, 88. His return to his home, 89. Question raised as to its locality, ibid note. Birth of his son, and removal of his affliction, 97, 98.
ZAKENIM, or elders of the Jews, ii, 17.
ZARATUSHTRA Spitama, i, 67 note. Principle of evil in her theology, 69 note.
ZEALOTS, doctrinal descendants of Judas the Gaulonite, i, 111. Meaning of zealot, 112.
ZECHARIAH's prophecy fulfilled, i, 281.
ZEND, records of the Zoroastrian faith in the, ii, 250.
ZENDAVESTA, institutes of the, i, 65. Their discovery by Du Perron, ibid note. Inquiries of various authors regarding them, and result thereof, 65-67 notes. Dogma drawn by Basilides therefrom, ii, 64. See Amschaspands, Zoroaster.
ZENO, i, 418. ii, 179.
ZENOBIA, her politic indifference in religious matters, ii, 200. Favour

ZUMPT.

shown by her to Paul of Samosata, 200, 201. Result of the failure of her designs on Syria, 202.
ZEUXIPPUS, statues in the gymnasium of, ii, 336 note.
ZOE, or life, in the Gnostic system, ii, 70.
ZOROASTER and Zoroastrianism, notions of various writers on, i, 61. Symbol emblemed by his name, ibid note. Originality of the system, 64. His probable intercourse with Daniel, ibid. Rhode's theory regarding him, 64 note. Basis of Zoroastrianism, 70. Its idea of a resurrection and of a Messiah, 71-75. Effect of its revival on Christianity, ii, 30. 247. Embodiment of some of its tenets in Judaism, 41. 61. Its fusion with the various Gnostic and heretical systems, 64. 65, 71, 78 note. 80. 259, 264. 267. Region of its re-asserted supremacy, 249. Its antiquity and transitions, 250. Its remnants, 251 note. Effect of Ardeschir's edict in its favour, 252. Persecutions by its followers, 353.
ZOSIMUS, report relative to Constantine preserved by, ii, 335. The story not his invention, 336 note. On an oracle concerning Byzantium, 335 note. On the mutilation of Pagan statues, 336 note. On the Delphic tripod, 337. On the apparition of Minerva to Alaric, ii, 78 note. His ascription of female censors to Christianity, 319 note. See ii, 31. 357; iii, 41, 43, 52, 92, 96, 243, 332, notes.
ZUMPT on Cyrenius, Procurator of Syria, i, 100. On the effect of Christianity on population, iii, 214 note.

THE END.

www.ingramcontent.com/pod-product-compliance
Lightning Source LLC
Chambersburg PA
CBHW020857020526
44116CB00029B/334